HANDBOOK OF THE SOCIOLOGY OF RELIGION

Religion is a critical construct for understanding contemporary social life. It illuminates the everyday experiences and practices of many individuals; is a significant component of diverse institutional processes including politics, gender relations, and socioeconomic inequality; and plays a vital role in public culture and social change. This handbook showcases current research and thinking in the sociology of religion. The contributors, all active writers and researchers in the area, provide original chapters focusing on select aspects of their own engagement with the field. Aimed at students and scholars who want to know more about the sociology of religion, this handbook also provides a resource for sociologists in general by integrating broader questions of sociology (e.g., demography, ethnicity, life course, inequality, political sociology) into the analysis of religion. Broadly inclusive of traditional research topics (modernity, secularization, politics) as well as newer interests (feminism, spirituality, faith-based community action), this handbook illustrates the validity of diverse theoretical perspectives and research designs to understanding the multilayered nature of religion as a sociological phenomenon.

Michele Dillon is Associate Professor of Sociology at the University of New Hampshire. She chaired the American Sociological Association's Section on Religion, 2002–3, and is book review editor for the *Journal for the Scientific Study of Religion*. In addition to numerous journal articles, Dillon is the author of *Catholic Identity: Balancing Reason, Faith, and Power* (Cambridge, 1999) and *Debating Divorce: Moral Conflict in Ireland* (1993). She is currently writing on the life course patterns and implications of religiousness and spirituality.

Handbook of the Sociology of Religion

Edited by

Michele Dillon
University of New Hampshire

CAMBRIDGE
UNIVERSITY PRESS

PUBLISHED BY THE PRESS SYNDICATE OF THE UNIVERSITY OF CAMBRIDGE
The Pitt Building, Trumpington Street, Cambridge, United Kingdom

CAMBRIDGE UNIVERSITY PRESS
The Edinburgh Building, Cambridge CB2 2RU, UK
40 West 20th Street, New York, NY 10011-4211, USA
477 Williamstown Road, Port Melbourne, VIC 3207, Australia
Ruiz de Alarcón 13, 28014 Madrid, Spain
Dock House, The Waterfront, Cape Town 8001, South Africa

http://www.cambridge.org

First published 2003

Printed in the United States of America

Typefaces Stone Serif 9/12 pt. and Avenir   *System* LATEX 2ε [TB]

A catalog record for this book is available from the British Library.

Library of Congress Cataloging in Publication Data

Dillon, Michele, 1960–
Handbook of the sociology of religion / Michele Dillon.
    p.   cm.
Includes bibliographical references and index.
ISBN 0-521-80624-0 – ISBN 0-521-00078-5 (pbk.)
1. Religion and sociology.   I. Title.
BL60 .D54   2003
306.6–dc21   2002041240

ISBN 0 521 80624 0 hardback
ISBN 0 521 00078 5 paperback

Contents

List of Contributors

Nancy T. Ammerman
School of Theology and Department of
 Sociology
Boston University
Boston, MA 02215

Robert N. Bellah
Department of Sociology
University of California-Berkeley
Berkeley, CA 94720
E-mail: *yubin@socrates.berkeley.edu*

Peter Beyer
Department of Classics and Religious
 Studies
University of Ottawa
70 Laurier Avenue East
Ottawa
Canada K1N 6N5
E-mail: *pbeyer@uottawa.ca*

Patricia M. Y. Chang
Institute for the Study of Religion and
 American Life
Boston College
Chestnut Hill, MA 02467
E-mail: *changpc@bc.edu*

Mark Chaves
Department of Sociology
University of Arizona
P.O. Box 210027
Tucson, AZ 85721-0027
E-mail: *mchaves@u.arizona.edu*

Arnold Dashefsky
Department of Sociology
University of Connecticut
Storrs, CT 06269-2068
E-mail: *dashef@uconnvm.uconn.edu*

Lynn Davidman
Program in Judaic Studies
Brown University
Providence, RI 02904
E-mail: *lynn_davidman@brown.edu*

Grace Davie
Department of Sociology
University of Exeter
Exeter EX4 4RJ
England
E-mail: *g.r.c.davie@exeter.ac.uk*

N. J. Demerath III
Department of Sociology
University of Massachusetts
Amherst, MA 01003
E-mail: *demerath@soc.umass.edu*

Michele Dillon
Department of Sociology
University of New Hampshire
Durham, NH 03824
E-mail: *michele.dillon@unh.edu*

Helen Rose Ebaugh
Department of Sociology
University of Houston
Houston, TX 77204-3474
E-mail: *ebaugh@uh.edu*

Penny Edgell
Department of Sociology
University of Minnesota
Minneapolis, MN 55455
E-mail: *edgell@umn.edu*

Roger Finke
Department of Sociology
Pennsylvania State University
University Park, PA 16802-6207
E-mail: *rfinke@psu.edu*

Philip S. Gorski
Department of Sociology
University of Wisconsin
Madison, WI 53706
E-mail: *pgorski@ssc.wisc.edu*

John R. Hall
Department of Sociology
University of California-Davis
Davis, CA 95616
E-mail: *jrhall@ucdavis.edu*

Michael Hout
Department of Sociology
University of California-Berkeley
Berkeley, CA 94720-5100
E-mail: *mikehout@uclink4.berkeley.edu*

Fred Kniss
Department of Sociology and
    Anthropology
Loyola University
Chicago, IL 60626
E-mail: *fkniss@wpo.it.luc.edu*

Bernard Lazerwitz
Department of Sociology
Bar Ilan University
Ramat Gan
Israel

Jeff Manza
Department of Sociology
Northwestern University
Evanston, IL 60208
E-mail: *manza@northwestern.edu*

Michael McCullough
Department of Psychology
University of Miami
P.O. Box 248185
Coral Gables, FL 33124-2070
E-mail: *mikem@miami.edu*

Omar McRoberts
Department of Sociology
University of Chicago
Chicago, IL 60637
E-mail: *omcrober@uchicago.edu*

Mary Jo Neitz
Department of Sociology
University of Missouri
Columbia, MO 65201
E-mail: *neitzm@missouri.edu*

Milagros Peña
Department of Sociology
University of Florida
Gainesville, FL 32611-7330
E-mail: *mpena@soc.ufl.edu*

Wade Clark Roof
Department of Religion
University of California-Santa Barbara
Santa Barbara, CA 93106
E-mail: *wcroof@religion.ucsb.edu*

Darren Sherkat
Department of Sociology
Southern Illinois University
Carbondale, IL 62901-4524
E-mail: *sherkat@siu.edu*

Timothy Smith
Department of Psychology
Brigham Young University
Provo, UT 84602-5093
E-mail: *tim_smith@byu.edu*

Rodney Stark
Department of Sociology
University of Washington
Seattle, WA 98195
E-mail: *socstark@aol.com*

Laura Stephens
Department of Sociology
University of Arizona
P.O. Box 210027
Tucson, AZ 85721-0027
E-mail: *lstephens@u.arizona.edu*

Ephraim Tabory
Department of Sociology
Bar Ilan University
Ramat Gan 52900
Israel
E-mail: *tabore@mail.biu.ac.il*

Rhys H. Williams
Department of Sociology
University of Cincinnati
Cincinnati, OH 45221-0378
E-mail: *williary@ucemail.uc.edu*

Paul Wink
Department of Psychology
Wellesley College
Wellesley, MA 02481
E-mail: *pwink@wellesley.edu*

Richard Wood
Department of Sociology
University of New Mexico
Albuquerque, NM 87131-1166
E-mail: *rlwood@unm.edu*

Nathan Wright
Department of Sociology
Northwestern University
Evanston, IL 60208
E-mail: *n-wright@northwestern.edu*

Robert Wuthnow
Department of Sociology
Princeton University
Princeton, NJ 08544-1010
E-mail: *wuthnow@princeton.edu*

Acknowledgment

I extend my sincere thanks to all of the contributors to this volume, many of whom, in addition to working on their own chapter, read and commented on the contributions of others.

Acknowledgements

PART ONE

Religion as a Field of Sociological Knowledge

CHAPTER ONE

The Sociology of Religion in Late Modernity

Michele Dillon

If there had been any doubt about the sociological importance of religion, the terrorist events of Tuesday morning, September 11, 2001, and their aftermath renewed our awareness that religion matters in contemporary times. The terrorist actions crystallized how adherence to a religious fundamentalism can destroy lives and forever change the lives of many others. The public's response to the terrorist attacks pointed to a different side of religion: the positive cultural power of ritual to recall ties to those who have died and to reaffirm communal unity and solidarity in a time of trial. Who would have thought that at the beginning of the twenty-first century improvised public memorials mixing flowers, photographs, steel and styorofoam crosses, and candlelight vigils would illuminate downtown Manhattan, that most modern and urbane of metropolises?

Clearly, the dawning of a new century has not been accompanied by the eclipse of religion in individual lives and in public culture. Despite, and perhaps because of, disenchantment with our increasingly rationalized society, religion continues to provide meaning and to intertwine daily social, economic, and political activity. That the continuing significance of religion in late modern society was not anticipated by classical social theorists and is at odds with much of contemporary theory is due to many factors. From an intellectual perspective it largely reflects both the overemphasis on reason and the tendency to relegate religion to the realm of the nonrational that are characteristic of modern social thought. Starkly phrased, the former places a calculating, instrumental rationality as the overarching determinant of all forms of social action while the latter sees religion and reason as inherently incompatible.

The dominance of instrumental reason envisaged by Max Weber (1904–5/1958) has certainly come to pass. Few would challenge the view that an economic-technological rationality is the primary engine of our globalizing society. The logic of free trade, for example, gives legitimacy to companies to relocate to cities, regions, and countries where production costs are comparatively lower. Technological development allows corporations to have more cost-effective communication with their customers via the Internet, and consequently many companies have chosen to bypass the human distributors whom until very recently were a key component of their corporate relational network; travel agents and car dealers are two such visible groups of "techno-victims." When Boeing relocated from Seattle to Chicago and when Guinness relocated from Ireland to Brazil the means-end calculations did not quantify the costs of community

3

disruption or the emotional and cultural loss attendant on disrupting the homology of symbol and place. In today's world, as exemplified so well by professional sports, teams are moveable and fan loyalty is almost as commodified as the players' contracts.

The rationality codified in the professions as a whole means that specialization rather than renaissance breadth is the badge of honor. Thus in sociology, as Robert Wuthnow argues (Chapter 2), subspecialization rather than personal bias largely accounts for many sociologists' inattention to questions in subfields such as religion because they perceive them as falling outside their primary specialization. Even though sociology emphasizes the interrelatedness of social phenomena, institutional practices (e.g., publishing and promotion decisions) and the rational organization of the discipline require specialization (e.g., the separate sections within the American Sociological Association, each with its own membership, council, and newsletter).

Yet despite the dominance of a calculating rationality there also are many instances of nonstrategic action and of contexts in which both coexist. Ethics still have a place in individual and corporate behavior even in the most strategic of techno-economic domains. For example, Cantor Fitzgerald, the government bonds trader that lost over two-thirds of its employees during the terrorist destruction of the World Trade Center, was widely praised for its initial compassionate response to the victims' families (e.g., providing food and other facilities at a local hotel to cater to victims' families). Although within a week after the attack it cut its missing employees from the payroll stating that this would avoid bookkeeping distortions, subsequently Cantor Fitzgerald executives publicly committed to devote 25 percent of the partners' profits over the next ten years to the victims' families, a decision that seemed motivated more by ethical rather than economic considerations (notwithstanding the good public relations it garnered).[1] More generally, in advanced capitalist societies such as the United States, there is still some recognition that loyalty to family, community, and nation is a legitimate factor in economic decision making notwithstanding the constant evidence of the excesses of corporate greed and their tendency to obscure the hold of ethical behavior in the marketplace. In short, instrumental reason is not the sole engine of modern life; the moral, emotional, or what Durkheim (1893/1997) termed the noncontractual, elements of contract continue to shape social behavior even if frequently in ambiguous ways.

That reason and emotion are intertwined rather than anathema was the focus of Douglas Massey's 2001 presidential address to the American Sociological Association. Massey (2002: 2) emphasized that "humans are not *only* rational. What makes us human is the *addition* of a rational component to a pre-existing emotional base, and our focus should be on the interplay between rationality and emotionality, not theorizing the former while ignoring the latter, or posing one as the opposite of the other (emphasis in original)." The interplay between reason and sentiment is most clearly demonstrated by Robert Bellah's analysis of the "ritual roots of society and culture" (Chapter 3, this volume). Bellah draws on recent advances in neurophysiology, Paleolithic archaeology, ethnomusicology, and anthropology to elaborate the foundations of ritual in human society. He focuses on the centrality of symbolic exchange in human evolution and of the individual's deep-seated need to relate to other social beings. Bellah observes that

---

[1] See the full-page advertisement by Cantor Fitzgerald, *The New York Times*, October 31, 2001, p. C3. Subsequently, Cantor Fitzgerald reported a profitable fourth quarter for 2001.

the synchronizing rhythm of conversational speech and gesture and the affirmation of social solidarity that they imply recognize, however implicitly, the nonutilitarian dimension, or the sacredness, of social life. Drawing on the creative ambiguity inherent in Emile Durkheim's (1912/1976) conceptualization of ritual and the virtual interchangeability of religious and social behavior, Bellah points to the many expressions of ritual in everyday life – rituals of dinner, sports, military drill, academia, and of politics. He argues that such diverse rituals may "be seen as disclosing an element of the sacred, and thus of the religious, at the very basis of social action of any kind."

For Bellah as for other sociologists (e.g., Collins 1998; Goffman 1967), ritual is the most fundamental category for understanding social action because it expresses and affirms the emotional bonds of shared meaningful experience and individuals' social belongingness. Bellah is keenly aware that the utilitarian rationality of our market society may obscure and at times destroy bonds of solidarity. Yet, he is unequivocal that "we remain surrounded by ritual in a myriad of forms," and, "if we look in the right places" we may even see its disclosure in the economic realm.

As underscored by Bellah's analysis, the sacred, or the nonrational, pulsates in many sites and intertwines with formal rational processes. Reason matters but so, too, does the individual's need to connect with others and to experience a sense of social mutuality. Thus as Erik Erikson (1963) theorized, the development of interpersonal trust is critical to individual and societal well-being; social life requires us to have meaningful and purposeful relations with others. It is precisely the enduring need for human interconnectedness that makes the search for some form of communal solidarity a smoldering ember stoking much of social action. The power of religion lies, in part, in the resources it provides toward the creation and shaping of meaningfully connected individual and communal lives; the religious or the sacred thus endures notwithstanding the overarching presence of rationality in society.

REASON IN RELIGION

Having emphasized that the nonrational is constitutive of human society, it is important also to acknowledge that reason has a solid place in religion. Much of social theory leaves this unsaid. Consequently it is sometimes assumed that religion and practical reason are incompatible. This perspective is most clearly evident in the writings of Jurgen Habermas (1984, 1987). Habermas rejects a one-sided rationality that privileges strategic action and instead proposes a nonstrategic, communicative rationality grounded in a process of reasoned argumentation. In doing so, however, he negates the relevance of nonrational elements to communicative exchange. He dismisses arguments that he sees as tainted by their association with sentiment, faith, and tradition, and therefore omits a huge sweep of resources used in everyday practices. Although Habermas is right in being suspicious of the ways in which sentiment and tradition frequently obscure the power inequalities that allow some "truths" to dominate institutional practices, his strict boundary between religion and reasoned argumentation presents religion as a monolithic, dogmatic force. He thus ignores the openness of diverse religious traditions to reasoned self-criticism and debate and the centrality of doctrinal and practical reasoning in individual and collective interpretations of religious teachings (Dillon 1999b).

In the same way that strategic and nonstrategic action coexist, overlap, and can be compartmentalized in daily life, religion and reason, too, coexist and can be interspersed and segmented within religious traditions and in individual and institutional practices. For many individuals and groups, the continuing relevance of religion derives from the fact that religious institutions, doctrines, and practices are, at least partially, open to reasoned criticism and to change. Although the founding narratives of religious traditions may be seen as divinely inspired, their subsequent institutionalization is a social process. Because religious institutions are social institutions whose practices evolve over time and adapt to changing cultural and historical circumstances, the boundaries of religious identity are contestable and mutable.

For example, many practicing Catholics maintain their commitment to Catholicism while nonetheless challenging church teachings on gender and sexuality. Feminist Catholics invoke historical and doctrinal reasons, such as the presence of women in scriptural and historical accounts of early Christianity and church doctrines on equality, to argue against what they see as the theological arbitrariness of the church's ban on women priests. Similarly, gay and other Catholics question why official markers of Catholic identity give substantially greater weight to sexual morality than to the living out of everyday Christian ethics of justice. Many of these Catholics, therefore, stay Catholic but reflexively critique Catholicism and do so in ways that enable them to be not only Catholic but to meld their religious and other social identities. Indeed, in this regard, the negotiation of religious identity in contemporary America provides a good exemplar of the practical compatibility of what – in a pluralistic and multicultural society – may sometimes appear as anomalous identities (Dillon 1999a: 255–6).

The intertwining of religion and reason in everyday life also means, for example, that although many Americans express belief in God and the afterlife (e.g., Greeley and Hout 1999), this does not necessarily mean that they anticipate actually having an afterlife and, in any case, may go about their daily activities with a certain religious indifference. Religion matters in many lives and, in public culture but it is not the only or the most important thing and its relevance ebbs and flows relative to what else is going on. In short, across the diverse personal and institutional contexts of daily life reason and religion are sometimes coupled and sometimes decoupled (cf. Dillon 2001).

THE SOCIOLOGY OF RELIGION

The intellectual bias in social theory toward the incompatibility of rationality and religion has residues in sociology as a whole. Although sociology takes vocational pride in examining the unexpected and debunking stereotypical assumptions about human behavior (Portes 2000), it has been slow in moving beyond stereotyped views of religion. It is not surprising that sociology, itself a product of the Enlightenment, should have a long tradition of skepticism toward religion. Karl Marx's (Marx and Engels 1878/1964) popularized idea of religion as an alienating and suppressive force and Sigmund Freud's (1928/1985) emphasis on its illusionary power continue to flicker a dim shadow over the perceived social relevance of religion. Thus in a recent study on social responsibility, Alice Rossi (2001: 22) explicitly acknowledged her "special difficulty" and surprise "as a political liberal and religious skeptic" with the finding that religion emerged as having a major effect. Although a distinguished sociologist, survey researcher, and ex-president of the American Sociological Association, Rossi admitted that she "came close to not including even one measure of religiosity" in family of origin questions (2001: 305).

Notwithstanding the fact that highly regarded research organizations (e.g., the National Opinion Research Center's General Social Survey) provide cumulative data documenting the persistence of religion as an important dimension of Americans' lives, religion is frequently the forgotten or excluded variable in social scientific studies and literature reviews. It is tempting for sociologists to shy away from incorporating religion because of perceptions that religion detracts from reflexivity and social change and the very act of studying religion might be interpreted as legitimating religious belief. Yet sociologists study small firms, income inequality, and gang violence without any presumed implication that the empirical patterns observed are desirable or that the sociologist has a vested biographical interest in the topic. A research interest in religion is more likely to trigger a hermeneutic of suspicion (cf. Ricoeur 1981). But, as Robert Wuthnow shows (Chapter 2, this volume), the line in sociology as a whole between normative interests and empirical questions is quite blurred. As he points out, the respective theories of Marx, Weber, and Durkheim provide conceptual frameworks for incorporating normative concerns; thus for example, a sociologist can study poverty by using a Weberian analysis to study social class without having to acknowledge that one actually cares about inequality. All sociological topics have underlying normative implications and the sociology of religion is not necessarily more value-laden than other fields. One can be a religious skeptic or a religious believer and still be a good sociologist – that is, being able to recognize the significance of religion when it pertains to the social universe being investigated.

The sociology of religion treats religion as an empirically observable social fact. It thus applies a sociological perspective to the description, understanding, and explanation of the plurality of ways in which religion matters in society. Sociologists of religion are not concerned with inquiring into whether God exists or with demonstrating the intellectual compatibility of religion and science. The focus, rather, is on understanding religious beliefs and explaining how they relate to worldviews, practices, and identities, the diverse forms of expression religion takes, how religious practices and meanings change over time, and their implications for, and interrelations with, other domains of individual and social action. As a social fact, religion is similar to other social phenomena in that it can be studied across different levels and units of analysis and drawing on the plurality of theoretical concepts and research designs that characterize the discipline.

WHY STUDY RELIGION?

Religion is a key construct for understanding social life in contemporary America and in other parts of the world. Religion ought to be of interest to sociologists because (a) it helps shed light on understanding the everyday experiences of the majority of Americans; (b) it is an important predictor of a variety of social processes ranging from political action to health outcomes; and (c) it has the potential to play a vital emancipatory role in processes of social change.

Religion and social understanding. National representative surveys (e.g., Gallup and Lindsay 1999; Greeley and Hout 1999) document that the majority of American adults have a religious affiliation (59 percent), believe in God (95 percent) and the afterlife (80 percent), pray (90 percent), and read the Bible (69 percent), and a substantial number (40 percent) report regular attendance at a place of worship. Moreover, 87 percent of Americans say that religion is important in their lives. These numbers on their own mean that even if it did not have any explanatory power religion would still have a pivotal role in the process of understanding how modern Americans construe their lives and the social and physical world around them. In view of the salience of religion in America it is not surprising that socioreligious issues (e.g., abortion, the death penalty, welfare reform, stem cell research, prayer in school, public displays of religious symbols, government vouchers for religiously affiliated schools) are a marked feature of political debate and judicial case loads. Religious institutions also play an extensive role in American society with denominational organizations, churches, and religiously affiliated schools, colleges, hospitals, social service agencies, and religious publishing and media companies contributing substantially to the domestic and international economy.

Many of the *Handbook* chapters focus on understanding the role of religion in daily life, with several authors providing information about the rich diversity of practices comprising the contemporary religious landscape. For example, Helen Rose Ebaugh focuses on the religious practices of new immigrant groups in America (Chapter 17). Her comparative ethnographic study of congregations in Houston included, for example, a Greek Orthodox church, a Hindu temple, a Muslim mosque comprised primarily of Indo-Pakistani members, a Vietnamese and a Chinese Buddhist temple, and Mexican Catholic and Protestant churches. As Ebaugh documents, the ethnoreligious practices of these diverse groups significantly impact American religion as well as urban culture through the physical reproduction of home-country religious structures such as temples, pagodas, and golden domes and the use of native construction materials and artifacts. At the same time, Ebaugh shows that, as it was for nineteenth-century European immigrants, religion is a major factor shaping the ethnic adaptation and assimilation patterns of new immigrants. Religion provides a communal anchor enabling immigrants to maintain social ties to their home culture and traditions while simultaneously giving them access to social networks and structures that pave the way for their participation in mainstream society.

Religion as social explanation. Religion does not only help us understand social experiences and institutional practices; it also serves as a powerful source for explaining a wide range of social attitudes and behavior. For example, Manza and Wright (Chapter 21) demonstrate that religion exerts a significant influence on individual voting behavior and political party alignments in America and Western Europe. The religious cleavages they identify in American society include church attendance, doctrinal beliefs, denominational identities, and local congregational contexts. Importantly, as Manza and Wright show, religious involvement is not simply a proxy for other variables such as social class, ethnicity, or region but exerts an independent effect in shaping voters' choices. They observe, for example, that there has not been a significant realignment of Catholic voters since the 1950s and, although Catholics have become more economically conservative, their Republican shift on economic issues has been offset by their increasingly moderate positions on social issues.

Religion as an emancipatory resource. It is common for mass media portrayals to emphasize the negative and defensive aspects of religion. Clearly, this characterization fits to some extent with religion's role in conserving traditional practices in a time of social change, and its political use in defensive alignments against modern culture. Moreover, as John Hall (Chapter 25) elaborates, there is "an incontrovertibly real connection between religion and violence." The negative aspects and consequences of religion, however, should not obfuscate the potential emancipatory property of religion and the resources it provides in struggles against institutional and social inequality.

Today, diverse faith-based groups challenge inequality both within religious institutions and in other institutional and social locales. For example, Richard Wood (Chapter 26) uses his ethnographic research in California to show how doctrinal beliefs and religiously-based organizational resources are used in community justice projects focused on achieving greater equity in access to socioeconomic resources (e.g., better jobs and health care for poor, working families). He emphasizes the multi-issue, multifaith, and multiracial character of faith-based community organizing. When Latinos, Whites, African Americans, and Hmong gather together to lobby for health care and share personal experiences and inspirational scriptural invocations, such meetings help to build bonds of social trust both within and across communities. This is a process, as Wood argues, that revitalizes political culture while simultaneously working toward a more just society. In short, across many diverse sites and for many different groups (see also McRoberts, Chapter 28; Neitz, Chapter 20; Peña, Chapter 27; Williams, Chapter 22), religion can become a vibrant resource not solely in resisting domination but in collective activism aimed at eliminating inequality.

THE HANDBOOK

The intention behind this *Handbook* was to bring together current research and thinking in the sociology of religion. The authors were invited to write original chapters focusing on select aspects of their own engagement with the field. For some contributors this involved integrating ideas they have pondered and argued with over a number of years, whereas for other authors it involved discussion of their current research. In either case, the chapters are ambitious; rather than being reviews of the literature on specific topics they are comprehensive and coherent without necessarily attempting to impose closure on the ambiguities, subtleties, and controversies that characterize the sociological study of religion. The intent is not to settle intellectual debates but in some instances to propose new ways of seeing by reframing the questions that might be asked or shifting the frames – of time, space, methods, and constructs – used in researching specific questions.

The *Handbook* provides a compendium for students and scholars who want to know more about the sociology of religion and a resource for sociologists in general who will find that several of the chapters integrate questions in other areas of sociology (e.g., inequality, ethnicity, life course, identity, culture, organizations, political sociology, social movements, health). The collection provides ready access to vibrant areas of inquiry in the sociology of religion. Accordingly, the subject matter covered is broadly inclusive of traditional research topics (e.g., modernity, secularization, politics, life course) and newer interests (e.g., feminism, spirituality, violence, faith-based community action). Some subjects, for a variety of reasons, are not included but are nonetheless important. Questions addressing, for example, the direct and indirect effects of religion on local, national and international economies (cf. Smelser and Swedberg 1994), or the mutual links between religion and mass media (cf. Hoover 1997), are not discussed in this collection but clearly deserve sociological attention.

The *Handbook* aims to illustrate the validity of diverse theoretical perspectives and research designs and their applicability to understanding the multilayered nature of religion as a sociological phenomenon. The research findings reported draw on comparative historical (e.g., Finke and Stark; Gorski; Hall), survey (e.g., Chaves and Stephens; Dashefsky et al.; Hout; Manza and Wright; McCullough and Smith; Roof); longitudinal life course (e.g., Dillon and Wink; Sherkat); and ethnographic case study, interview, and observation (e.g., Davidman; Ebaugh; Edgell McRoberts; Kniss; Peña; Wood) data. Our ability to apprehend the multidimensionality of a social phenomenon is enriched when we have access to different kinds of data and research sites and are able playfully to entertain the explanatory value of diverse theoretical approaches.

This *Handbook* reflects the specific historical and cultural context from which it has emerged, namely late-twentieth-early-twenty-first-century American sociology. Most of the authors are American, most of the empirical research discussed derives from American samples, and the themes engaged reflect a largely American discourse. Nevertheless, some of the authors are non-American and work outside the United States (e.g., Beyer, Davie, Lazerwitz, Tabory), and several contributors include a comparative cross-national perspective (e.g., Beyer, Davie, Finke and Stark, Gorski, Dashefsky, Lazerwitz and Tabory, Manza and Wright, Hall, Wood). The North American/Western perspective articulated is not intended to suggest that religion is not important elsewhere or that the sociology of religion is not exciting in, for example, Asian or Latin American countries. Rather, the sociology of religion is an engaged field internationally (evident, for instance, in the number and range of foreign conferences pertinent to the field). But to give voice in a single handbook to the important religious trends, topics, and perspectives in a broader selection of countries would not be practical or intellectually coherent. It is my hope, nonetheless, that the substantive questions addressed in this volume will be of use to scholars working outside of American academia and that it will contribute to ferment in the sociology of religion in sites far beyond American borders.

The *Handbook* is divided into six parts. Part I focuses on religion as a field of sociological knowledge. Following this chapter, Robert Wuthnow (Chapter 2), sensitizes readers to some of the tensions in studying religion sociologically and how they can be legitimately circumvented from within the discipline and with an eye to interdisciplinary collaboration. Robert Bellah, as already indicated, provides a strong rationale in Chapter 3 for the enduring social relevance of religion crystallized in diverse everyday rituals. Chapters 4 and 5 focus on the societal evolution of religion and of religion as a field of inquiry. Peter Beyer traces the consequences of modernity and of wide-ranging global sociohistorical processes on the construction of world religions and religion's diverse social forms. Beyer focuses on the boundaries between religion and nonreligion, and between religions, and considers the process by which these distinctions get made and their social consequences (Chapter 4). Grace Davie (Chapter 5) examines the centrality of religion in classical sociological theory and elaborates on the different contextual reasons for the subsequent divergent paths that theorizing and research on religion have taken in North America (which emphasizes religious vitality) and Europe (where secularization prevails). She, too, emphasizes religion's global dimensions and points to the contemporary sociological challenge posed by global religious movements [e.g., Pentecostalism, Catholicism, fundamentalism(s)].

Part II is broadly concerned with the conceptualization and measurement of religion and social change. The first two chapters in this section focus specifically on measurement considerations. Michael Hout (Chapter 6) highlights the significance of demography as an explanation of religious stability and change. He shows how changing demographic patterns (e.g., marital, fertility, and immigration rates) alter the religious composition and levels of church attendance, and he emphasizes the importance of having large and detailed data sets so that the direct and counteracting effects of changing demographics on religion can be tracked. Mark Chaves and Laura Stephens (Chapter 7) focus on the problems associated with using self-report measures of church attendance as the standard indicator of American religiousness. They discuss, for example, how social desirability and the ambiguities between church membership, attendance, affiliation and religious sensibility may distort survey respondents' accounts of their church habits, thus complicating sociological assessments of the stability of religious activity over time.

Chapters 8 and 9 engage the ongoing secularization debate in sociology. Roger Finke and Rodney Stark, the two sociologists most closely identified with the religious economies model of religious behavior (i.e., that interreligious competition enhances religious participation) draw on their extensive historical and cross-national research to argue for the greater explanatory value of their perspective over a secularization paradigm (Chapter 8). They emphasize how the supply-side characteristics of a religious marketplace (e.g., deregulation, interreligious competition and conflict) account for variations in levels of religious commitment. Philip Gorski, by contrast (Chapter 9), draws attention to the interplay between sociocultural, political, and religious factors in a given historical context. Gorksi argues that credible empirical claims for either secularization or religious vitality must be grounded in a much longer historical and a much broader geographical frame (encompassing, for example, religious practices in Medieval and post-Medieval Europe) than is used in current debates. Moreover, because Christianity is rife with ebbs and flows, any observed decline, Gorski points out, may be cyclical and reversible.

The interrelated links between theoretical conceptualization and empirical data on our understanding of the changing dynamics of religion are illustrated in the final two chapters of this section. Patricia Chang (Chapter 10) discusses changing sociological approaches to the study of religious organizations and the ways in which they converge with, and diverge from, the sociological analysis of nonreligious organizations. She elaborates on the highly decentralized nature of the religious sphere and the significance of the diversity of its organizational forms and institutional practices. Wade Clark Roof (Chapter 11) focuses on new forms of spiritual engagement in American society and their increasing autonomy from traditional religious structures and conventional ways of thinking about religion. His analytical schema recognizes the distinctions but also the overlap between religious and spiritual identities, and he argues for new definitions of religion that explicitly integrate the more psychological aspects of a seeker spirituality with traditional sociological models of religion.

The second half of the *Handbook* is more explicitly concerned with the links between religion and other domains of social behavior. Part III focuses on religion and life course issues. Darren Sherkat's research investigates the life course dynamics of religious socialization (Chapter 12). He shows that, whereas parents are key agents of influence on their young children, adult children can influence the religious behavior of their aging parents whom in turn can impact their adult children especially as they themselves assume responsibility for children's socialization. Penny Edgell highlights the responsiveness of religious congregations to the varying life-stage needs of their members (Chapter 13). She finds that, while congregations embrace a traditional nuclear family model, they nonetheless make incremental adjustments in their rhetoric and routines in order to be more inclusive of the diversity of contemporary families (e.g., single-parent and dual-career families). Michele Dillon and Paul Wink (Chapter 14) use longitudinal life course data to examine religiousness and spirituality in the second half of adulthood. In their sample, religiousness and spirituality increase in older adulthood for both men and women, and although the two religious orientations have different emphases, both are positively associated with altruism, purposeful involvement in everyday activities, and successful negotiation of the aging process. In Chapter 15, Michael McCullough and Timothy Smith present a critical review of the rapidly expanding body of interdisciplinary research on religion and health. Focusing on depression and mortality, their meta-analyses indicate that, on average, individuals who are religiously involved "live slightly longer lives and experience slightly lower levels of depressive symptoms" than those who are less religious.

Part IV focuses on religion and identity. Religion has long played a major role in anchoring ethnic and national identities and current scholarship additionally recognizes the multiple, cross-cutting ways that religion intersects with gender, sexuality, race, and social class. Nancy Ammerman (Chapter 16) argues that while religious institutions are important sites for the construction of religious identities they are not the only suppliers of religious narratives. She elaborates, rather, that as identities intersect and are embodied in diverse institutional, relational and material contexts, religious and other identity signals are shaped from numerous religious and nonreligious locales (e.g., commodified evangelical body tattoos, clothing, and jewelry in pop culture). In Chapter 17, Helen Rose Ebaugh, as already noted, elaborates on the ethnoreligious practices of new immigrant congregations and shows how they mediate cultural assimilation while simultaneously highlighting the increased deEuropeanization of American religion and culture. Dashefsky, Lazerwitz, and Tabory focus on the sociohistorical and cross-cultural variations in the expression of Jewish identity (Chapter 18). They find, for example, that Israeli Jews are far more likely than American Jews to observe kosher food regulations, but within Israel, Jews of Middle Eastern descent are far more likely than Euro-Israeli Jews to do so. The specific religious practices of different Jewish subgroups is due in part as Dashefsky et al. show to their minority cultural status vis-à-vis the larger society.

The multiple pathways toward the realization of, or engagement with, a religious identity means that, as Lynn Davidman argues, one can be Jewish without being observant (Chapter 19). She discusses the routine ways individuals integrate a "religious" element into their lives independent of formal religious participation. For her respondents, being Jewish involves scripts and practices that are derived from familial, cultural, and historical connections to Judaism and that provide them with a coherent, but what they regard as a nonreligious, Jewish identity.

Mary Jo Neitz emphasizes the "embodiment" of religious identities (Chapter 20). Reviewing the influence of feminist inquiry on the sociology of religion, she discusses the importance of studying religion as found in the "location of women" and their experiences rather than from the standpoint of traditional institutional boundaries and theoretical categories. Neitz points to the diversity of women's experiences and observes that while in some women's lives (e.g., those who experience personal violence), religion can be a site of oppression it can also be used as a resource in resisting patriarchal structures and expectations.

The chapters in Part V examine the multilevel connections between religion, politics, and public culture. Jeff Manza and Nathan Wright, as already indicated, investigate the continuing influence of religion on individual voting behavior (Chapter 21). Sociologists interested in the dynamics of social movements necessarily encounter the organizational and cultural resources provided by religion. As shown by Rhys Williams (Chapter 22), religion and religious communities comprise a natural base for social movement activism. He discusses the multiple resources (e.g., rituals, rhetoric, clergy leaders) religion provides for collective mobilization and the dilemmas religious social movements confront in negotiating the external political and cultural environment (e.g., political compromise versus ideological purity).

The multidimensional relation between religious worldviews and moral-ideological conflict is the concern of Fred Kniss (Chapter 23). Arguing against the use of dichotomized categories (e.g., liberal versus conservative) in studying cultural conflict, Kniss's broader perspective facilitates greater recognition of peripheral groups (e.g., Mennonites, Buddhists), and shows how intragroup ideological nuances and ideologies that juxtapose values (e.g., scriptural authority and egalitarianism) may shape public discourse. Jay Demerath explores cross-national differences in the links between religion, nationhood, and civil society (Chapter 24). He elaborates on the diverse intellectual and practical ways in which civil religion is understood, and illustrating its differential sociopolitical implications points, for example, to the fractured social order that characterizes societies in which two or more competing civil religions dominate (e.g., Israel, Northern Ireland).

John Hall presents an extensive analysis of the relatively understudied theoretical and empirical links between religion and violence (Chapter 25). He proposes an exploratory typology to characterize the range of "cultural logics" that underpin the possibility of religious violence. Hall discusses the importance of such factors as nationalism, colonialism, the presence of religious regimens, interreligious competition, and establishment repression of countercultural religious movements. Arguing that "there is no firewall between religion and other social phenomena," Hall notes that while violence in many sociohistorical instances is independent of religion, religion, nonetheless, often becomes "the vehicle for" and "not merely the venue of" the violent expression of social aspirations.

The three chapters that comprise the final section, Part VI, focus on religion and socioeconomic inequality. As noted earlier, Richard Wood (Chapter 26) analyzes the history and character of faith-based community justice organizing. Milagros Peña focuses on the links between Latinas' everyday realities, faith-based community involvement, and political consciousness (Chapter 27). She shows that Latinas' pastoral and community activities empower them to be "active agents of social change" who stand against oppressive social practices. Focusing on "border realities" in El-Paso (Texas)-Juarez (Mexico), Pena's ethnographic research points to how Latinas' political consciousness comes from their everyday encounters with poverty, intimidation, and violence and is nurtured through their participation in faith-based community groups and centers that facilitate their mobilization against exploitation. Here, too, similar to Wood's findings, the social activism crosses religious, ethnic, and social class boundaries.

In the third chapter in this section, Omar McRoberts uses his study of a largely poor, African-American Boston neighborhood to challenge the validity of a worldy/ otherworldly dichotomy to describe the black church (Chapter 28). He shows, for example, that many theologically conservative ("otherworldly") Pentecostal-Apostolic churches engage in prophetic and socially transformative activism. McRoberts also discovers that, independent of theology, ideological constraints such as perceptions of racism and government malintention can hinder pastors' readiness to avail of public funds for church based social projects. This finding takes on added significance in view of current government attempts to extend the institutional role of churches and faith-based organizations in welfare provision.

A NOTE TOWARD THE FUTURE

Religion continues to be a significant dimension intertwining individual lives, collective identities, institutional practices, and public culture, and, although in some circumstances it has a negative impact (e.g., violence), in other situations it holds an emancipatory charge (e.g., faith-based organizations). Sociologists have made significant theoretical and empirical advances in understanding religion but much, of course, remains unknown. One of the challenges lies in apprehending the local and global diversity of religious worldviews and practices and their social and political implications. The cumulative body of research that is emerging on new immigrants' religious practices fills an important gap in this regard. But other gaps remain. We need, for example, to pay fuller attention to the breadth and depth of religion across diverse sociohistorical contexts. As Philip Gorski (Chapter 9) points out, "situating the present more firmly within the past" provides for a richer theoretical and empirical understanding of present trends and cross-national variations in religion. At the micro-level, the task is to achieve a better understanding of religion as lived in different sociobiographical contexts and to explore how macro structural and cultural changes shape the religious practices of individuals and of specific historical cohorts. Related to this, for example, is the "new" reality presented by the post-1960s increased differentiation of religiousness and spirituality. We are thus required to design studies that can capture the changing contemporary situation while simultaneously placing these patterns in their sociohistorical and geographical context.

Moreover, since religion has emerged as a powerful explanatory variable in analyses of behavior across a range of social domains (e.g., politics, health, social responsibility, violence) we need to be alert to the possible implications of religion and spirituality in other previously understudied spheres. Notwithstanding the institutional pressures toward specialization within sociology, it is evident that many sociologists of religion fruitfully engage ideas and topics that cut across other subfields (e.g., organizations, political sociology). Additional areas of intradisciplinary specialization that could be engaged more systematically by sociologists of religion include economic sociology, education, popular culture, and law and criminology. Although researchers have begun to write about pertinent themes within these respective areas, our knowledge of how religious practices shape and are shaped by activity in these domains is still quite preliminary.

Irrespective of what specific question is investigated, the inevitable challenge is to identify the various mechanisms underlying the implications of religion for other social phenomena. Under what conditions does, for example, the substance of specific doctrinal or spiritual beliefs matter and with what social consequences; and in what circumstances are the characteristics of the local or macro societal context in which religion is practiced more substantively interesting than the religious practices per se?

Before being able to address any such questions, however, sociologists must invariably wrestle with questions of measurement. Given that religion is such a multifaceted construct, its operationalization in any given study will necessarily omit some dimensions and emphasize others. With varying substantive purposes, some studies will want to focus on religious affiliation and belief, others on church attendance irrespective of affiliation, and still others on the importance of religion in the respondent's everyday life. Scholars new to the field will find a great resource in the well-validated and wide-ranging questions on religion that are asked in the General Social Survey. Finding comparable measures that can capture the more spiritual and less overt behavioral dimensions of religion is more difficult. But just as we treat religion as an observable social fact so, too, must we operationalize spirituality in order to be able to assess the expanding place of spiritual seeking and practices in individual lives and contemporary culture. All measures have imperfections but as a first step we can begin by testing the conceptual and empirical differences and overlap between religiousness and spirituality.

As a final thought, knowledge of social life as a whole would be enhanced if sociologists were to begin to think of religion as a variable somewhat akin to, for example, social class, race, or gender (cf. Wuthnow, Chapter 2, this volume). Most sociologists today recognize these variables in shaping and differentiating social experiences and practices. Consequently, irrespective of a theoretical interest in stratification many sociologists include measures of social class in their research designs. A similarly inclusive disposition toward the probable social relevance of religion may lead sociologists to serendipitous discoveries and fuller explanations of otherwise puzzling patterns and outcomes.

CHAPTER TWO

Studying Religion, Making It Sociological

Robert Wuthnow

Not long ago, a student stopped by with a problem. "I have this great topic on religion," she began, "but I don't know how to make it sociological." We chatted briefly about her topic (why siblings often have such different views about religion), and after I suggested some readings, she went away. But her question stayed with me. She was interested in studying religion, but puzzled about how to do it sociologically.

This student's quandary speaks volumes about religion as a field of sociological inquiry and the intellectual challenges facing it at the start of the twenty-first century. Her question stayed with me because it had been asked so often before. In my experience, the question often surfaces most forcefully when students contemplate topics for their senior thesis. They typically select a topic after weeks of anguishing to find something that will engage their attention longer than any project they have ever worked on before. They want it to be meaningful, perhaps helping them to sort out their own beliefs and values, or addressing some issue in the wider society. For one or both of these reasons, they settle on something having to do with religion (interfaith marriage, gender and religion, the religious experiences of a particular ethnic or immigrant community, how religion motivates altruism, why some people believe in God and others don't, whether religion influences how people vote, why people join cults, or religion and the family, to name a few). They are not untutored in sociology, either. By this time, they have generally taken one or two theory courses, one or two methods courses, and four or five other sociology courses. Yet they are puzzled how to approach their topic sociologically. Indeed, sociology and religion somehow strike them as strange bedfellows. And if seniors are plagued with this perception, students who encounter the discipline for the first time in a course on sociology of religion generally are, too. How a sociological perspective on religion differs from, say, a survey of American religion course in a religion department or American studies program will probably not be immediately apparent.

Undergraduates are not the only ones with such questions. Serving on editorial boards, one frequently hears comments such as, "It's an interesting book, but it isn't very sociological," or "This would be a good article for a religion journal, but not for a journal in sociology." And participating in tenure review committees, one hears questions being raised about the importance of work in sociology of religion to the discipline as a whole.

Such comments are frequent enough that graduate students lie awake at night, pondering their futures as sociologists of religion, and wonder if they've made a big mistake. Oh, well, they console themselves, maybe someday when I have tenure I can do what I really want to do. They temporarily overlook the fact that more than a few of their senior mentors have found the strain sufficiently great that they have abandoned the field entirely, fleeing to presumably greener pastures in religious studies departments, seminaries, or programs in American studies, Judaica, or the Middle East (cf. Wentz 1999).

But undergraduates' concerns, if not unique, are refreshingly candid. Graduate students, by the time they have passed their theory and methods requirements and attended a few faculty forums, are generally asking different questions, like "What kind of recommendation letters does Professor X write?" or "Has anybody else analyzed this data set yet?" In comparison, undergraduates (for all their labors in academe) still have one foot firmly planted in the real world. They sometimes pick topics because they are truly important and because they think these topics will make a difference to how they and others will relate to their work, their families, and their communities. Their questions about how to study religion and make it sociological have to be taken seriously.

In this chapter, I want to consider why the study of religion so often appears to exist in tension with the discipline of sociology. My argument suggests that the tension is less serious than is often imagined to be; indeed, that it arises largely because of misunderstandings about theory, misunderstandings about method, and misunderstandings about normative perspectives. Having considered each of these ways in which the sociological study of religion is frequently misunderstood, I turn in the last part of the chapter to a discussion of the basis for disciplinary integrity in sociology of religion and of the possibilities for fruitful interdisciplinary exchange. But first it is necessary to set aside two commonly expressed objections to the idea that the study of religion and sociology can be easily reconciled.

OBJECTION #1: SOCIOLOGISTS THINK RELIGION IS STUPID

A more elaborate formulation of this objection goes as follows: Sociology, like other social science disciplines, was born of the Enlightenment. Some of its founders, like August Comte, believed that religion would gradually be replaced by philosophy, which, in turn, would be replaced by science (include sociology). Other founders, such as Karl Marx, believed that religion was an oppressive system that enlightened thinkers (like himself) needed to debunk, while others found company in Emile Durkheim's atheism or in Max Weber's much-quoted lament about being religiously unmusical. As sociology developed, it largely accepted the proposition that the world would gradually become less and less religious. Religion, therefore, might remain as a kind of backwash among the unenlightened, but was not a subject to which any self-respecting academician would want to devote much time.

This characterization of the history of sociology is sometimes supported by complaints about the state of sociology of religion within the larger discipline. Undergraduates may notice that the professors in their other courses seldom include any reference to religion or seem embarrassed if the subject arises and they may observe that courses in organizations, stratification, family, and criminology are offered regularly, while sociology of religion may be taught infrequently or in another department. Graduate students may express fears about diminishing job prospects if they write a dissertation about religion, and faculty specializing in sociology of religion sometimes argue that their work receives no respect in their departments or among the discipline's leaders.

But several pieces of evidence run counter to the idea that it is hard to study religion sociologically (and get away with it) because sociologists think religion is stupid. For one, the historical argument can fairly easily be turned on its head. If Weber thought himself to be religiously unmusical, he nevertheless devoted a large chunk of his life to studying it (writing major treatises on the Protestant ethic, ancient Judaism, the religions of China and India, as well as important comparative essays). Durkheim's last great work, to which he devoted some fifteen years of his life, was his *Elementary Forms of the Religious Life* (1912/1976). Even Marx wrote more extensively (and more sympathetically) about religion than the casual reader typically recognizes. Indeed, political scientists (who may lament the paucity of reflection about religion in their classical texts) typically argue that sociology has been the natural place in which to take seriously the study of religion because it figured so prominently in the writings of all the discipline's founders.

A survey of the field at present also gives the lie to assertions about sociologists being disinterested in religion. More than five hundred sociologists hold membership in the Sociology of Religion Section of the American Sociological Association, putting it squarely in the middle in size among the nearly forty sections of which the Association is currently composed. Most of these members also belong to such organizations as the Association for the Sociology of Religion and the Society for the Scientific Study of Religion. At least two journals (*Sociology of Religion* and *Journal for the Scientific Study of Religion*) are devoted almost entirely to social scientific studies of religion, and scarcely a year goes by without articles about religion appearing in such nonspecialized journals as the *American Journal of Sociology, American Sociological Review, Social Forces,* and *Sociological Forum.* These articles, moreover, are not simply the work of a few specialists who focus entirely on religion, but are authored by sociologists working in such areas as stratification, family, demography, migration, and race relations.

One might object that sociologists of religion are a die-hard breed, stubbornly studying religion even though most of their peers believe it to be increasingly irrelevant to an enlightened world. This view appears to have been more prevalent a generation ago than it is today. By the early 1960s, the legacies of Marx, Weber, and Durkheim had been recast to form what was widely known as modernization theory. In its various versions, modernization theory suggested that industrialization, science and technology, education, and expanding economic markets were gradually forging a culture in which religion would no longer play much of a role. By the end of the 1970s, it was significantly harder to take such arguments seriously. The 1979 Iranian revolution, in which followers of Shi'ite Muslim Ayatollah Ruhollah Khomeini (many of whom were college educated professionals and business owners) overthrew the government of Mohammad Reza Shah Pahlavi (which had prided itself on its modernizing efforts), provided a wake-up call to Western social scientists: Religion was still a force to be reckoned with in world affairs. The 1978 mass suicide of some nine hundred followers (most of whom were Americans) of cult leader Jim Jones in Jonestown, Guyana, prompted questions about the lingering power of religion in affairs of the heart. Among sociologists themselves, the turmoil of the late 1960s and early 1970s surrounding the civil rights movement and the protests against the Vietnam War stimulated rethinking of the modernization paradigm along lines ranging from greater awareness of upheaval and social conflict, to interest in "postmodernist" literary perspectives and new thinking from feminist theory and women's studies, to recognition of the roles that religion often plays in countercultural movements and ethical behavior. The nation also had a self-proclaimed "born again" president in the person of Southern Baptist Jimmy Carter and would soon see fundamentalist leaders such as the Reverend Jerry Falwell and the television preacher Pat Robertson gaining a platform in partisan politics. Sociologists might still be mildly puzzled (or even put off) by many of these manifestations of religious vigor, but religion had clearly become difficult to ignore.

None of this resurgence of religious vitality necessarily ran counter to the assumption that religion was stupid (or at least retrograde). Indeed, surveys of faculty and graduate students conducted in the late 1970s demonstrated relatively high rates of religious unbelief among social scientists, compared to the public and even compared to faculty and graduate students in the natural and applied sciences (Wuthnow 1989: 142–57). But sympathy for one's subject matter has seldom been a prerequisite for research and teaching: Sociologists routinely study homicide without being sympathetic to murders; racial discrimination, without sympathy for racists; revolutions, without being revolutionaries; and so on. Just as Weber had done, sociologists at the end of the twentieth century included prominent figures who studied religion from the perspective of atheism or agnosticism, no less than ones drawn to it because of personal faith.

To suggest, then, that the tensions between religion and sociology can be understood in terms of sociologists taking a dim view of religion does not get us very far. To be sure, a sociologist specializing in formal organizations or criminology may not immediately express enthusiasm for the latest work in sociology of religion. But that response reveals more about the high degree of specialization within subfields that now characterizes the discipline than it does something peculiar to the study of religion.

OBJECTION #2: SOCIOLOGY HAS A QUIRKY VIEW OF THE WORLD

If the tensions between religion and sociology cannot be understood in terms of sociologists having a jaundiced view of religion, they also cannot be explained by ascribing a quirky view of the world in general to sociologists. Let us return momentarily to my student who wonders how to make her study of religion "sociological." Part of her difficulty may be that she thinks sociologists view the world through different eyes than everyone else. Why would she possibly think that? Perhaps because sociology is a language she has acquired later in her intellectual development than virtually every other subject: like most college students, her secondary education exposed her to history, literature, biology, chemistry, and physics, but not to sociology; she came to it only in college. Or perhaps her sociology professors have bent over backward to disabuse her of the suspicion that sociology is basically common sense: telling her that it requires special thinking, that it is difficult, and that she must learn a new vocabulary. Now that she has a big project ahead that must be "sociological," she realizes there must be an alien culture into which she must translate her interests to make them acceptable.

This concern may be particularly worrisome for a student tackling a topic about religion. Faith systems (not uniquely) have a way of resisting encroachment. This is how they survive (and why some critics call them closed systems). If, as our student has observed, one sibling is often more devout than another sibling, a faith system may explain this in terms of God's mysterious grace bringing light to some and darkness to others. Even for a student who does not fully believe this explanation, it may seem mischievous to look for explanations in birth-order patterns or family dynamics. Doing so somehow seems disrespectful of those who believe in grace. Making it sociological may be even less attractive if the student thinks there are odd sociological notions about family dynamics that even she would find difficult to accept.

The surprising thing, however, is that the student is already casting her topic largely in sociological terms. Her question may have been prompted by comparing her own religious views with those of a sibling, but she is not proposing to write an autobiography. Nor is she asking questions like: Does God really exist? Will siblings recognize each other in heaven? Or what does the Qu'ran say about siblings? The sociological perspective is already guiding her thinking. In large measure, this is because she knows she is writing a paper for sociology and has perhaps absorbed more of the sociological perspective in her courses than she realizes. But a sociological perspective has also become commonplace in contemporary culture. Newspapers and television programs frequently report the results of sociological studies. And, in a religiously diverse culture, we have all learned to separate ourselves at least to a small degree from our own religious beliefs and practices, making it possible to look with some detachment at these beliefs and practices. We can ask why some people are more religious than others or why people adhere to different religions. Thus, the idea that sociology has a quirky view of the world turns out to be less of a problem than at first might be imagined.

Beyond formulating the topic in sociological terms, though, the student probably does need to apply some specialized knowledge to it from sociology. Newspaper knowledge can scarcely stand in for the thousands of person-years that professional sociologists devote to probing the mysteries of human behavior. The same student would hardly assert, "I have an interesting topic about amino acids, but I'm not sure how to bring in molecular biology." She would recognize that certain skills, concepts, and previous studies would need to be mastered in the course of pursuing her research.

What is puzzling, therefore, is why the student thinks the specialized language of sociology will deaden, rather than enliven, her project. Sociologists take pride in having developed what they sometimes lovingly refer to as a sociological imagination. They mean that certain skills, concepts, and studies actually do help people see things that others would miss. These tools of the trade should be cumulative enough that a student having majored in sociology does not have to ask about sociology as if it were an alien language. Certainly they should be regarded as helpful (which, in the case of many students, they are), rather than as a meaningless series of hoops to jump through. Even if some anxiety is present about having to learn new ideas, the student should relish this opportunity to see further and more acutely than in the past.

But let us suppose that the student is not simply reacting with fear of the unknown, but with some intuitive discomfort about sociology. If we consider the possibility that there may be some basis for her concern about sociology not quite fitting what she wants to learn, then it becomes necessary to probe more deeply. What is it about sociology – or the ways in which it is often perceived – that makes it hard for some students (and professors) to see its value to the study of religion? Answering this question requires us to turn first to a consideration of the ways in which sociological theory is often misunderstood.

MISUNDERSTANDINGS ABOUT THEORY

When asked what makes their work distinctively sociological, sociologists sooner or later resort to the argument that their discipline is guided by theory. They eschew studies that are not theoretical enough. To be relevant, a work must be theoretical (or at least have obvious theoretical implications). What does this mean in the study of religion?

One meaning of theory in sociology is that the discipline is a theory-building enterprise. In this interpretation, the goal of sociological inquiry is to create a persuasive theory of human behavior based on axiomatic laws and scientific generalizations, a bit like achieving a unified theory of the universe. A generation ago (and periodically thereafter) sociological thinking about theory-building was preoccupied with the question of reductionism; that is, with whether or not a good theory of human behavior needed to be constructed within the social sciences at all, or whether everything could just as easily be reduced to biological or chemical explanations. That issue was largely resolved by arguing that human behavior *could* be reduced but that sociological explanations nevertheless remained interesting. It left open the question of what exactly a theory (let alone a theory of religion) might look like.

The closest candidate for a truly comprehensive theory of religion was the idea of secularization, which in turn was grounded in assumptions about modernization. Secularization theory drew on Marx, Weber, and Durkheim, among others, to suggest that the social influence of religion had diminished between roughly the fifteenth century and the twentieth century. Secularization was taken to be an instance of institutional differentiation, the process by which institutions in larger, more complex, economically developed societies become more autonomous from one another. The idea of secularization, therefore, placed the study of religion in a larger historical context, suggesting some of the important processes to be observed, and providing a central interpretation of these processes (Swatos and Christiano 1999; Gorski 2000).

As modernization came increasingly to be questioned during the 1970s and 1980s, so did secularization theory. Efforts to derive testable hypotheses from this theory often failed to take into account its emphasis on long-term processes, but these efforts also suggested its limitations in the short-run. Religious commitment in the United States, for instance, did not appear to be diminishing, despite the fact that industrialization, science and technology, and higher education were all increasing. Nor was it easy to explain the rise of new religious movements or the resurgence of evangelical and fundamentalist movements within this framework. If theory-building meant conducting studies of religion aimed at buttressing the ideas of modernization and secularization, then fewer and fewer sociologists of religion appeared to be interested in this endeavor.

Currently, a few sociologists of religion continue to search for a unified theory of human behavior that can make sense of religion. During the 1980s, for instance, there was a temporary flurry of interest in rational choice theory, an idea borrowed from economics that aimed to explain behavior in terms of the choices made by rational individuals trying to maximize their personal gratification (Young 1997). This perspective failed to have any significant impact on the larger discipline of sociology, other than to fuel the growth of a new subfield known as economic sociology, largely because it denied the very social embeddedness of individuals that is central to sociological understandings of human behavior and, as some critics observed, rested on assumptions that rendered it difficult to prove or disprove convincingly with empirical evidence (Smelser 1994, 1995). For those interested in studying religion, the insights it yielded also proved extremely limited. A student interested in sibling differences in religious behavior, for instance, might learn that one sibling had a stronger "preference" for religious gratifications, but remain curious about the reasons behind this preference, the extent to which upbringing played a role, and the ways in which siblings with different beliefs manage to negotiate their relationships with each other.

Most sociologists, however, do not in practice appear to be seeking a unified theory of human behavior (Martin 1999). In the discipline at large, theory-building now appears to be understood in practice as a *means* to an end, rather than as an end in itself. That is, textbook depictions of theory as a parsimonious set of deductive propositions that organize a large number of the regularities of social life seem to have virtually no counterpart in the ways in which empirical sociology is actually conducted. Instead, theory is better described as a set of *sensitizing concepts* that help one to make sense of some empirical findings. These concepts may be loosely translated from one study to another, but their role is mainly to generate empirical insights, rather than to be welded into a theory that explains all aspects of human behavior. Ideas about social class, gender, race, ethnicity, identity, self, movement, subculture, power, mobilization, social capital, community, and individualism all function largely in this manner as sensitizing concepts.

Understood this way, theory is seen more as a *tool* for the study of religion, rather than an endeavor that diverts attention from truly attempting to understand religious behavior. A student interested in siblings need not seek to cast her project as a contribution to secularization theory or rational choice theory, but can find her study enriched by considering such sensitizing concepts as birth order effects, sibling rivalry, gender differences, and styles of parenting.

If sensitizing concepts are selected almost entirely on the basis of how much they contribute to our understanding of one small aspect of the world, the question that then must be asked is how much does the study of religion contribute to our understanding of *other* aspects of social life? In other words, is the study of religion relatively isolated from work in the wider discipline, or is there fruitful exchange and, if so, is the study of religion a borrower that depends mostly on insights from other subfields or a contributor that generates theoretical insights of wider interest?

Much of the work that has been done by sociologists of religion over the past quarter century or so, it surely must be conceded, has had relatively little impact on the wider discipline of sociology. And, to the extent that this is the case, some tension is likely to be perceived between the study of religion (no matter how sociological) and the study of other aspects of social life. Yet this is understandable because religion itself is such a rich field of social inquiry. Describing the internal workings of an immigrant church or explaining why young people join esoteric religious movements are examples of important research topics in the sociology of religion – whether or not they happen to be of interest to students of criminology or economic sociology. Indeed, a proper understanding of theory as a set of sensitizing concepts helps to reinterpret the meaning of an accusation that someone's work is "not theoretical." What the critic is probably saying is that she or he has a certain set of concepts that happen to be of interest (organizations, power, crime) and that a study of some aspect of religion happens not to deal with those concepts.

Despite the relatively high degree of specialization that isolates all subfields from one another, there is nevertheless some interplay among the concepts that prevail in various subfields. Is sociology of religion mostly a borrower or a contributor? There is a good deal of evidence that research on religion has borrowed heavily from other areas of sociology in recent years. Research on evangelicalism, for instance, has borrowed from the literature on subcultures to explain why evangelicalism persists – indeed, flourishes – in a pluralistic cultural setting (Smith 1998). Understandings of markets and consumer behavior have been applied to the study of spirituality (Roof 1999a). Neoinstitutional perspectives on organizations have been imported to account for conflicts within congregations (Becker 1999). But sociology of religion also has exported a number of insights to other parts of the discipline. The idea of charisma has been widely used to understand leadership styles in organizations and social movements (Zablocki 1980). Understandings of ritual and religious symbolism have been applied to studies of secular organizations (Bell 1997). And ideas about theological conflicts have been extended to the study of cultural conflicts more generally (Hunter 1991).

Examples such as these, taken by themselves, prove little except that studies of religion are not quite as isolated from larger sociological discourse as skeptics sometimes suppose. But an important part of what makes the study of religion sociological is not just evidence of conceptual borrowing. It is, rather, the extent to which studies of religion actually help to illuminate the most critical issues in sociology. On this score, issues concerning race, gender, and social class – the issues that perhaps occupy more attention in sociology than any others at present – are especially worth considering.

Studies of religion have contributed to understandings of race in several significant ways, not least of which is the continuing racial separation that characterizes most American congregations and denominations. Any effort to make sense of racial segregation or the presence or absence of cross-racial ties in social networks sooner or later acknowledges that religion constitutes an important factor. In addition, the role of religious organizations as a resource in lower-income communities marked by racial identities is also increasingly recognized (Anderson 1992, 1999). African-American churches, for example, play an important role in mobilizing social and political activity in many urban neighborhoods (Patillo McCoy 1998; Harris 1999). Some research also documents the role of cross-racial religious alliances in generating social movements and as a base for community mobilization (Marsh 1997).

The relationships between gender and religion have been examined to an even greater extent in recent years than those involving race. Gender is an important consideration for studies of religion because women take a more active interest in nearly all forms of religious expression than do men and because many of the more interesting developments in religion in recent years have been spearheaded by women (Davidman 1991; Eller 1993). The gendered character of religious leadership and of religious arguments about clerical authority remain of special interest as well (Chaves 1997). Studies of gendered behavior in other contexts also increasingly pay attention to the role of religion. Research on attitudes toward abortion, for example, reveals the extent to which these attitudes are reinforced through interaction with like-minded persons in religious settings, while studies of the family, in which new questions are being raised about the roles of fathers and the consequences of divorce, show that parental behavior varies considerably depending on patterns of religious involvement (Luker 1984; Ginsburg 1998; Wall et al. 1999; Wilcox 1998).

Social class, perhaps curiously, has received less attention in studies of religion than one might have imagined, given the continuing importance of social class as a reality and as a topic of sociological inquiry. Although the relationships between social class and religion were emphasized in classical sociological work (especially that of Marx and Weber), relatively few empirical studies in recent years have examined these relationships. Yet some research on the ways in which people themselves make sense of their class position suggests that religious beliefs and religiously based assumptions about morality play an important role in these understandings (Lamont 1992). The relevance of religion to perpetuating or combating social class differences is also evident in a number of recent studies concerned with the relationships between religion and volunteering, philanthropic giving, community organizing, civic engagement, and understandings of social justice (Ronsvalle and Ronsvalle 1996; Verba et al. 1995; Wuthnow 1991, 1994, 1998).

These are but some of the ways in which sociology and the study of religion intersect theoretically. If theory is misunderstood as the search for a tightly constructed set of deductive principles around which to organize all aspects of human behavior, then there is indeed likely to be a sense of unease when students try to study religion and make it sociological. But if theory is understood as a set of sensitizing concepts, then these concepts are merely tools that can enrich the study of religion. Indeed, a great deal of what we now know about such important topics as congregational life, religious experience, the role of religion in politics, the religious underpinnings of self-development, and the place of religious organizations in communities, to name a few, stems from inquiries in which sociological concepts have been employed.

MISUNDERSTANDINGS ABOUT METHOD

For many students and those in the larger public who may be interested in religion, the characteristic most likely to be associated with a "sociological" study is its use of certain methods. These methods may be attractive to some and repugnant (or mysterious) to others. But here again, there is considerable misunderstanding.

One common misunderstanding, especially among students or scholars relatively unfamiliar with the discipline, is that sociology implies number-crunching. This impression, like most stereotypes, is partially rooted in fact: Many of the research articles dealing with religion, especially in the discipline's nonspecialized journals, utilize quantitative data, effectively analyzing it for patterns and trends in such behavior as attendance at religious services or beliefs about God. But sociology of religion, perhaps to a greater degree than many other subfields, has maintained a desirable balance between quantitative and qualitative approaches. Quantitative studies, often involving large-scale surveys, provide valuable descriptive evidence on the religious beliefs and practices of the U.S. population or the populations of other countries; indeed, a surprising amount of attention has been devoted in recent years to developing more refined estimates of basic facts as how many people actually attend religious services and whether or not rates of religious participation are holding steady or declining (Gallup and Lindsay 1999; Hadaway et al. 1993, 1998; Hout and Greeley 1998; Woodberry 1998; Putnam 2000). At the same time, ethnographic approaches involving extensive participation and firsthand observation are helpful for understanding the internal dynamics of congregations and religious movements, while in-depth interviews, speeches, published texts, and archival materials provide insights into the nature of religious discourse (Becker and Eiesland 1997).

Although these various methods all contribute valuable information, it is important to acknowledge another common misunderstanding: that quantitative data in itself is somehow inimical to the study of religion (perhaps because it simplifies a necessarily complex topic). Quite the contrary. Polls and surveys about religion have become so common in recent years that they are now intrinsic to our understanding of who we are religiously: Let one poll show a slight upward trend in church attendance and journalists announce a "religious awakening"; let another poll show a slight decrease, and religion suffers from a "collapse." The challenge is for all educated people, whatever their discipline, to gain at least a rudimentary understanding of surveys, sampling, and statistical analysis. Surprising at it may seem, especially with the amount of polling that accompanies national elections, it is still possible to find graduate and undergraduate students (often in the humanities) who do not understand how generalizations can be made from a small sample to a large population, when or when not to use the term "sample," and how one might possibly "control for" the effects of race, gender, or education level. Students who have not already done so, should consult one of the many readable introductions to sociological methods (e.g., Babbie 1997).

Just as quantitative data require skill to collect and interpret, qualitative studies also depend on specialized training. Here the difficulty arises from scholars not taking seriously enough the particular training to which sociologists of religion are typically exposed. Armed with an interesting topic and confidence that one is a good conversationalist, literary critics, theologians, and historians (perhaps with the encouragement of a small research grant) set off to do qualitative interviews not realizing that the craft of framing questions, asking them properly, and including the right follow-ups should be as foreign to them as that of a sociologist examining rare manuscripts in an archive. At minimum, scholars interested in utilizing qualitative methods should gain a rudimentary understanding of the skills required (Burawoy 1991; Strauss and Corbin 1998; Atkinson 1998).

Whether quantitative or qualitative data are used, an additional misunderstanding is that work is somehow more sociological if it employs explicit hypotheses than if it does not. Hypothesis formulation is a valuable exercise in sociology, but there is also a reason why it seems strange to the inquiring student: It frequently takes the form of pitting one naïve view of the world against an equally naive view, instead of recognizing that events typically have multiple causes and multiple explanations. Where hypotheses are most helpful is determining whether or not one has an argument at all. Sociological studies of religion, in this respect, are helped by having a clear, strong, and compelling argument, just as work in other disciplines is.

As the sociology of religion has matured, the single methodological characteristic that most often sets good work apart from mediocre work continues to be the strategic use of comparisons. Quantitative research necessarily involves comparisons; qualitative work should, too. Students of religion, too, often neglect this basic insight, either because they want to examine one case intensively or because they refuse to consider what an appropriate comparison might be. The intellectual challenge is to recognize the rich possibilities that are always present for comparisons, including temporal and spatial comparisons, as well as ones based on gender, religion, or ethnicity.

MISUNDERSTANDINGS ABOUT NORMATIVE CONCERNS

Besides theoretical and methodological questions, concerns about normative issues persistently emerge in the relationships between religion and sociology. My student who is interested in sibling differences is likely to think it strange that sociology requires bracketing her interests in healing conflicts between siblings or finding ways to combat authoritarian parenting styles that may be rooted in religious beliefs. To be told that she must approach her topic "scientifically" will seem odd when she knows that she selected it because of some deep concern from her personal experience. Adopting a "value-neutral" perspective will seem strained if she recognizes that much of what she reads in sociology is hardly free of normative concerns.

These concerns can be illustrated by a graduate student who, when asked by another member of a seminar if her work was going to include a normative focus, vehemently denied that she had any normative intentions. Her study – an interesting analysis of Jewish *kitsch* (Nike yarmulkes, Mickey Mouse dreidls, plastic Torahs) – was to focus purely on a description of the phenomenon under investigation and an explanation of why some people were attracted to it more than others. But why, I wondered, was she interested in the topic in the first place? And what difference would it make if she succeeded in producing a brilliant study of it?

This example suggests the difficulty of drawing a hard-and-fast line between normative concerns and empirical concerns (and of associating sociology exclusively with the latter). The student came to her topic because of an interest in material culture, which has recently attracted attention as a dimension of religious expression that may have deeper meaning and more staying power than theological arguments do, especially in a religiously diverse context (McDannell 1995; Joselit 1994; Wuthnow 1999). Yet the student also recognized that goods produced for mass consumption can trivialize the sacred, leaving it somehow inauthentic. In addition, one person's definition of *kitsch* may be another person's definition of fine art (often because of social class differences). In short, the project was thoroughly laced with normative issues, and to ignore them would be to diminish the importance of doing it. What the student meant to say was that she was not going to take a stand *at the start* as to whether *kitsch* was good or bad. Hopefully, by the end of her study, she would be in a position to make some evaluative claims.

To be sure, one of the fears on the part of scholars in the discipline at large that sometimes influences their perceptions of work in sociology of religion is that its authors are themselves so wedded to a particular religious orientation that their study (if not their entire career trajectory) will be guided by that commitment. This fear, however, fades in comparison to the greater concern that scholarship (in whatever field) is pursued simply as a kind of game, perhaps to promote one's career or because an oddity occurred to them that nobody else had examined. The intellectual challenge is identifying problems of sufficient gravity to make some difference to an audience beyond that of a few like-minded peers. If this challenge is not met, then adopting a "sociological" stance toward religion will seem peculiar indeed.

Concerns about normative issues require us to return briefly to the subject of theory. The works of Marx, Weber, Durkheim, and other classic figures remain of interest to contemporary sociologists of religion, not so much for specific testable hypotheses that may have been neglected by previous generations of scholars, but as a kind of common moral discourse. In part, this discourse is the glue that holds the field together, just as stories of founding figures provide cohesion to a nation: If nothing else, people who otherwise share little can sense an affinity for one another because they have read the same authors and know the same books. In larger measure, though, the classic works serve as a legitimate way of bringing *normative concerns* into a scholarly setting that often pretends not to honor such concerns. Studying the poor can be justified in terms of a Weberian analysis of social class, for instance, rather than having to acknowledge that one actually cares about the poor.

As the classic works fade farther into the past, one of the challenges facing sociologists of religion is finding a language in which to express their normative concerns. For many, concerns about racial oppression, gender inequality, and discrimination based on sexual preference provide such a language. But such languages always require close examination, extension, and reinvention. In the future, the greatest intellectual challenge posed by normative concerns is likely to be that of religious pluralism. Greater diversity and more extensive interaction among members of religious communities will necessitate confronting thorny questions about the correctness of particular religious teachings and the survival of particular religious communities.

A BASIS FOR DISCIPLINARY INTEGRITY

Thus far, I have argued that studies of religion blend more easily with the theoretical concerns of sociology as a discipline than is sometimes supposed, that there is considerable room for methodological diversity, and that students of religion need not leave their normative concerns at the door in order to do respectable sociology. But if all this is the case, then the question arises: Isn't the study of religion pretty easily turned into an interdisciplinary affair? The answer to this question, I think, is to a large extent, yes, and I will say more about that in a moment. But first it does seem to me that disciplines such as sociology still matter and we need to be clear about why they matter.

When I say that disciplines matter, I mean this in both an intellectual and a pragmatic sense. Intellectually, they matter (or should matter) because they embody a corpus of insights and understandings that cannot be readily found elsewhere; and pragmatically, they matter (or should matter) because they exercise certain enforceable standards of evaluation over the work of practitioners who identify with them. But what can the basis of this intellectual and pragmatic "matter-ing" be? It cannot be, I have suggested, that sociology is bending its efforts toward the construction of a distinctive theoretical edifice that matters more than any of the substantive topics it addresses, and it cannot be the deployment of a methodological apparatus that only its practitioners are skilled in using. Bringing distinctive normative concerns – or avoiding all such concerns – cannot be a basis for a disciplinary integrity, either.

The single defensible basis for a distinct approach to the study of religion that we would call sociological has to be an arbitrary one: That the academic enterprise at this stage in its development has become so vast and so complex that specialization is a necessity. It is a necessity both for the production of good scholarly work and for the evaluation of such work. The goal of scholarship, not only in research but also in teaching, is surely to nurture "A" quality work over "B" quality work and to encourage more "B" quality work than "C" quality work, and so on. But to do so requires focusing one's time and energy, learning a certain body of literature, and mastering an appropriate set of research skills. To evaluate such work also requires a similar focusing of time and energy.

Disciplinary boundaries are, for this reason, arbitrary but also necessary. They are arbitrary because many different clusters of specialization and expertise are conceivable. The ones that happened to take shape did so for historical and institutional (as well as intellectual) reasons, but others could have developed under other circumstances. They are necessary, however, because scholarship is always a social enterprise, rather than purely the work of isolated individuals. Scholars draw ideas from others with whom they interact intellectually, professionally, and socially, and these networks become the basis for evaluating one another's work.

For all its diversity, sociology of religion is a well-institutionalized subfield within the discipline of sociology (which is also well-institutionalized). Its practitioners conduct much of the best work available on such topics as the social correlates of religious belief and participation, religious movements, the social characteristics of congregations, and the emergence and functioning of diverse religious subcultures. Their interests frequently overlap with scholars in religious studies, anthropology, political science, psychology, history, and theology. Yet the work of sociologists of religion draws distinctively on its own intellectual traditions, mentoring relationships, and social networks.

Intradisciplinary interaction between sociologists of religion and sociologists with interests in other fields is also encouraged – and should be encouraged – by the existence of such institutional configurations as departments, disciplinary majors, and disciplinary graduate programs. Unlike religious studies programs, where research often concentrates entirely on the texts and practices of particular religious traditions, sociology of religion functions primarily at the intersection of religious factors and other aspects of social life (such as family, political behavior, communities, work, sexuality, the arts, and leisure). The best research often combines insights about religion with new developments in these other specialty areas. Indeed, one clear mark of the effectiveness of sociology of religion as a subfield is the fact that studies of other social phenomena increasingly include measures of religion as a factor to consider, just as they do measures of social class, gender, and race.

If this argument for disciplinary integrity emphasizes convenience more than some might like, its value lies in defending disciplinary boundaries without elevating them too high. Networks among peers, mentors, and students within sociology should be cultivated, as they currently are, but not to the point of discouraging interdisciplinary work. Furthermore, the networks that bind sociologists of religion to one another are likely to be stronger than those that develop between sociologists of religion and sociologists with other areas of specialization – a possibility that grows with the expansion of e-mail, the Internet, and other forms of electronic communication. Thus, students who come to professors seeking help in making their studies of religion more sociological are likely to find themselves referred to books, articles, and opportunities for direct contact with specialists at other universities as much as with faculty in other departments at their own university.

OPPORTUNITIES FOR MULTIDISCIPLINARY EXCHANGE

Although disciplinary boundaries need to be preserved, opportunities for sociologists of religion to interact with scholars in other fields have increased over the past few decades and appear likely to develop further in the foreseeable future. These opportunities come about through participation in multidisciplinary organizations (such as the Society for the Scientific Study of Religion and the American Academy of Religion), through specialized programs and new majors for undergraduates (such as American Studies, African-American Studies, or Women's Studies), and through various research centers and institutes (Roof 1999b).

One form of interaction across disciplines consists of research and teaching involving scholars from different disciplines, or work done by an individual scholar that intentionally spans disciplines. Examples include studies combining history and ethnography, historical data with new insights from gender studies or organizational analysis, or sociological studies of congregations that include theological interpretations (Orsi 1985; Griffith 1997; Hall 1999). Sociological concepts and methods are frequently evident in such studies, even when the primary author's training is in another discipline. A second form of interaction consists of organized research projects or centers. Interaction of this kind has increased in recent years as funding for research has become more readily available. Yet another form of multidisciplinary interaction occurs through programs and centers specifically designed to encourage exchanges across a variety of disciplines.

The principal advantage of multidisciplinary interaction is that it encourages scholarship to be clearer about its assumptions and the reasons for its existence. A further advantage of multidisciplinary interaction (perhaps as a by-product) is that it often generates greater appreciation of the strengths of a particular disciplinary approach. In addition, multidisciplinary research and teaching integrates the study of religion into various disciplines and departments, showing that religion is not an autonomous realm, populated only by believers and fellow travelers, but a feature of human life that has broad implications for the understanding of such diverse topics as politics, ethics, and literature.

CONCLUSION

Perhaps the most daunting aspect of studying any topic concerning religion and wanting to make it sociological is that the number of studies, faculty, and students interested in such topics has mushroomed during the past fifty – and even the past twenty – years. Part of this growth is attributable to the fact that higher education generally has expanded during this time, and the growth also has been fueled by resources from foundations for sponsored research and by greater inclusion of courses about religion in universities. Whereas the challenge in an earlier era was to find any relevant information on particular topics, now the challenge is sorting out the best studies and concentrating on topics that are truly worthy of one's time.

What makes this explosion of information manageable is the fact that electronic indexing and reference services now make it possible to search more easily for relevant studies. Texts, anthologies, and handbooks provide starting points, but are readily supplemented by online syllabi, discussion groups, abstracts, and full-text journals. A student interested in sibling differences in religion need only identify a few key words in order to locate dozens of relevant articles and books.

Electronic information nevertheless cannot fully address the lingering concern that there may be something awkward about studying religion from a sociological perspective. This awkwardness, I have suggested, stems largely from misunderstandings about sociological theory, methods, and normative concerns. Sociology, just as religion, adapts to its surroundings by creating an identity for itself and by developing arguments that justify its existence. Wading into the literature produced by earlier generations of sociologists, one often senses that they protested too much – producing studies and treatises that aimed mostly to demonstrate that it was beneficial to adopt a sociological perspective on the world. As the discipline has matured, there has been less need of such posturing. And, as sociology gains a firmer sense of its own identity, the study of religion will surely find even more room in which to flourish.

CHAPTER THREE

The Ritual Roots of Society and Culture

Robert N. Bellah

There is probably no better place to begin a discussion of the place of ritual in the sociology of religion than with a famous passage in Emile Durkheim's *The Elementary Forms of Religious Life*:

> Life in Australian [Aboriginal] societies alternates between two different phases. In one phase, the population is scattered in small groups that attend to their occupations independently. Each family lives by itself, hunting, fishing–in short, striving by all possible means to get the food it requires. In the other phase, by contrast, the population comes together, concentrating itself at specified places for a period that varies from several days to several months. This concentration takes place when a clan or a portion of the tribe . . . conducts a religious ceremony.
>
> These two phases stand in the sharpest possible contrast. The first phase, in which economic activity predominates, is generally of rather low intensity. Gathering seeds or plants necessary for food, hunting, and fishing are not occupations that can stir truly strong passions. The dispersed state in which the society finds itself makes life monotonous, slack, and humdrum. Everything changes when a [ceremony] takes place. . . . Once the individuals are gathered together a sort of electricity is generated from their closeness and quickly launches them into an extraordinary height of exaltation. . . . Probably because a collective emotion cannot be expressed collectively without some order that permits harmony and unison of movement, [their] gestures and cries tend to fall into rhythm and regularity, and from there into songs and dances (1912/1976: 214–16).

Thus Durkheim makes his critical distinction between profane time, which is "monotonous, slack and humdrum," and sacred time which he characterizes as "collective effervescence." Sacred time is devoted primarily to ritual. Further, the community that ritual creates is at the center of Durkheim's definition of religion: "A religion is a unified system of beliefs and practices relative to sacred things, that is to say, things set apart and forbidden – beliefs and practices which unite into one single moral community called a Church, all those who adhere to them" (ibid.: 47).[1]

Since ritual, for Durkheim, is primarily about the sacred in a sense in which the religious and the social are almost interchangeable, subsequent work on ritual under

---

[1] In the original, the entire definition is in italics.

his influence has not moved far beyond him by placing ritual at the core of any kind of social interaction whatsoever. While, on the one hand, this might be seen as broadening the idea of ritual to include "secular ritual," the same development, on the other, might be seen as disclosing an element of the sacred, and thus of the religious, at the very basis of social action of any kind. Recent work of Randall Collins represents this development most clearly. In *The Sociology of Philosophies* (1998), he combines Durkheim and Goffman (1967) to define the basic social event as, in Goffman's phrase, an interaction ritual. At the most fundamental level interaction rituals involve:

1. a group of at least two people physically assembled;
2. who focus attention on the same object or action, and each becomes aware that the other is maintaining this focus;
3. who share a common mood or emotion.

In this process of ritual interaction the members of the group, through their shared experience, feel a sense of membership, however fleeting, with a sense of boundary between those sharing the experience and all those outside it; they feel some sense of moral obligation to each other, which is symbolized by whatever they focused on during the interaction; and, finally, they are charged with what Collins calls emotional energy but which he identifies with what Durkheim called moral force. Since, according to Collins (1998: 22–4), all of social life consists of strings of such ritual interactions, then ritual becomes the most fundamental category for the understanding of social action. Collins then makes another move that has, I believe, the greatest significance:

> Language itself is the product of a pervasive natural ritual. The rudimentary act of speaking involves...group assembly, mutual focus, common sentiment; as a result, words are collective representations, loaded with moral significance. (ibid.: 47)

RITUAL AND THE ORIGIN OF LANGUAGE

This observation of Collins, in turn, suggests a digression into the present evolutionary understanding of the origin of language. The origin of language was for long a taboo subject because it opened the door to unrestrained speculation. The question remains and probably will always remain, speculative, but advances in neurophysiology on the one hand and Paleolithic archaeology on the other have opened the door to much more disciplined forms of speculation such as that of Terrence Deacon (1997) in his book *The Symbolic Species*. Deacon is a biological anthropologist and neuroscientist and his book is subtitled "the co-evolution of language and the brain." Deacon is trying to understand the emergence of language among our ancestral hominids whose brains were not organized for language use, although, as we know, our nearest primate relatives can, with the most enormous effort and external training, be taught at least a rudimentary use of words. But, as Deacon puts it, "The first hominids to use symbolic communication were entirely on their own, with very little in the way of external supports. How then, could they have succeeded with their chimpanzeelike brains in achieving this difficult result?...In a word, the answer is ritual."

Deacon (ibid.: 402–3) makes the case for the parallel between teaching symbolic communication to chimpanzees and the origin of language in ritual as follows:

> Indeed, ritual is still a central component of symbolic "education" in modern societies, though we are seldom aware of its modern role because of the subtle way it is woven into the fabric of society. The problem for symbolic discovery is to shift attention from the concrete to the abstract; from separate indexical links between signs and objects to an organized set of relations between signs. In order to bring the logic of [sign-sign] relations to the fore, a high degree of redundancy is important. This was demonstrated in the experiments with the chimpanzees.... It was found that getting them to repeat by rote a large number of errorless trials in combining lexigrams enabled them to make the transition from explicit and concrete sign-object associations to implicit sign-sign associations. Repetition of the same set of actions with the same set of objects over and over again in a ritual performance is often used for a similar purpose in modern human societies. Repetition can render the individual details of some performance automatic and minimally conscious, while at the same time the emotional intensity induced by group participation can help focus attention on other aspects of the object and actions involved. In a ritual frenzy, one can be induced to see everyday activities and objects in a very different light.[2]

But if repetition and redundancy are always, as we shall see, important in ritual, what was the evolutionary push that made the transition from indexical to symbolic signs essential, and therefore the ritual mechanism so indispensable? Deacon describes the situation at the period of this critical transition:

> The near synchrony in human prehistory of the first increase of brain size, the first appearance of stone tools for hunting and butchery, and a considerable reduction in sexual dimorphism is not a coincidence. These changes are interdependent. All are symptoms of a fundamental restructuring of the hominid adaptation, which resulted in a significant change in feeding ecology, a radical change in social structure, and an unprecedented (indeed, revolutionary) change in representational abilities. The very first symbols ever thought, or acted out, or uttered on the face of the earth grew out of this socio-ecological dilemma, and so they may not have been very much like speech. They also probably required considerable complexity of social organization to bring the unprepared brains of these apes to comprehend fully what they meant.... Symbolic culture was a response to a reproductive problem that only symbols could solve: the imperative of representing a social contract. (ibid.: 401)

Ritual is common in the animal world, including among the primates. But nonhuman ritual is always indexical, not symbolic; that is, it points to present realities, not to future contingencies. The primary focus of animal ritual is on issues of great importance and uncertainty: Sex and aggression. Through ritual actions animals represent to each other their readiness or unreadiness for sexual contact or for combat. Through the ritual "dance" an unwilling partner may be "persuaded" to engage in sexual intercourse,

---

[2] In spite of the Durkheimian echoes of this passage, Deacon makes no reference to Durkheim, nor to Goffman or Collins. The strength of disciplinary boundaries seems to have necessitated independent discovery, although we cannot rule out the influence of unconscious diffusion of ideas.

or an originally combative opponent may be persuaded to offer signs of submission. Such ritual behaviors help to make possible these inherently difficult transactions.

The "reproductive problem" to which Deacon suggests symbolism was the solution, however, required more than assuring a present response; it required assurance of future actions – it required promises. At the point where efficient adaptation to the environment made cross-gender pair bonding necessary, with its division of labor between the provision of meat and care of infants, the stability of what was now necessarily "marriage" required more than nonsymbolic ritual.

> Sexual or mating displays are incapable of referring to what might be, or should be. This information can only be given expression symbolically. The pair-bonding in the human lineage is essentially a promise, or rather a set of promises that must be made public. These not only determine what behaviors are probable in the future, but more important, they implicitly determine which future behaviors are allowed and not allowed; that is, which are defined as cheating and may result in retaliation. (ibid.: 399)

Another advantage of symbolic ritual as against purely nonhuman animal ritual is that it gives rise not to ad hoc relationships, but to a whole system of relationships:

> Ritualized support is also essential to ensure that all members of the group understand the newly established contract and will behave accordingly. As in peacemaking, demonstrating that these relationships exist and providing some way of marking them for future reference so that they can be invoked and enforced demand the explicit presentation of supportive indices, not just from reproductive partners but from all significant kin and group members.... Marriage and puberty rituals serve this function in most human societies.... The symbol construction that occurs in these ceremonies is not just a matter of demonstrating certain symbolic relationships, but actually involves the use of individuals and actions as symbol tokens. Social roles are redefined and individuals are explicitly assigned to them. A wife, a husband, a warrior, a father-in-law, an elder – all are symbolic roles, not reproductive roles, and as such are defined with respect to a complete system of alternative or complementary symbolic roles. Unlike social status in other species, which is a more-or-less relationship in potential flux, symbolic status is categorical. As with all symbolic relationships, social roles are defined in the context of a logically complete system of potential transformations; and because of this, all members of a social group (as well as any potential others from the outside) are assigned an implicit symbolic relationship when any one member changes status. (ibid.: 406)

And Deacon points out that, over the last million years, although language undoubtedly developed toward more self-sufficient vocal symbol systems, whose very power was the degree to which they could become context-free, nonetheless, "symbols are still extensively tied to ritual-like cultural practices and paraphernalia. Though speech is capable of conveying many forms of information independent of any objective supports, in practice there are often extensive physical and social contextual supports that affect what is communicated" (ibid.: 407).

Deacon's argument runs remarkably parallel to that of Goffman, Collins, and of course Durkheim. The point is that symbolism (including centrally language), social solidarity based on a moral order, and individual motivation to conform, all depend on ritual. But Deacon, as we have seen has indicated that the very first emergence of symbolism "may not have been very much like speech." There is reason to believe that full linguisticality, language as, with all its diversity, all known human cultures have had it, is relatively recent, perhaps no older than the species Homo Sapiens, that is 120,000 years old (Nichols 1998). But symbol using hominids have been around for at least a million years. Can we say anything about what kind of proto-language such hominids might have used? Perhaps we can in a way that will further illuminate the nature of ritual.

RITUAL AND THE ORIGIN OF MUSIC

While in the last decade or two a number of valuable books concerned with the origins of language have been published, it was not until the year 2000 that an important volume entitled *The Origins of Music* (Wallin, Merker, and Brown) appeared. A number of articles in this edited volume begin to indicate what the "ritual" that Deacon suggests provided the context for the origin of language might have been like: Namely, it involved music. The ethnomusicologist Bruno Nettl, in discussing features of music found in all cultures, writes: "It is important to consider also certain universals that do not involve musical sound or style. I mentioned the importance of music in ritual, and, as it were, in addressing the supernatural. This seems to me to be truly a universal, shared by all known societies, however different the sound" (2000: 468). He draws from this the conclusion that the "earliest human music was somehow associated with ritual" (ibid.: 472). But "music" in most cultures involves more than what can simply be heard, as our current usage of the word implies. As Walter Freeman (2000: 412) puts it, "Music involves not just the auditory system but the somatosensory and motor systems as well, reflecting its strong associations with dance, the rhythmic tapping, stepping, clapping, and chanting that accompany and indeed produce music." And Ellen Dissanayake (2000: 397) writes, "I suggest that in their origins, movement and music were inseparable, as they are today in premodern societies and in children.... I consider it essential that we incorporate movement (or kinesics) with song as integral to our thinking about the evolutionary origin of music."

While the contributors to *The Origins of Music* are not of one mind about the social function of music that gave it its evolutionary value, several of them emphasize the role of music in the creation of social solidarity. As Freeman (2000: 420) puts it, "Here [in music] in its purest form is a human technology for crossing the solipsistic gulf. It is wordless [not necessarily, R.B.] illogical, deeply emotional, and selfless in its actualization of transient and then lasting harmony between individuals.... It constructs the sense of trust and predictability in each member of the community on which social interactions are based." Dissanayake (2000: 401), who locates music fundamentally in the mother-infant relationship in the human species with its much longer period of infant dependence on adult care, compared to any other species, writes:

> I suggest that the biologically endowed sensitivities and competencies of mother-infant interaction were found by evolving human groups to be emotionally affecting and functionally effective when used and when further shaped and elaborated in culturally created ceremonial rituals where they served a similar purpose – to attune or synchronize, emotionally conjoin, and enculturate the participants. These unifying and pleasurable features (maintained in children's play) made up a sort of

behavioral reservoir from which human cultures could appropriate appealing and compelling components for communal ceremonial rituals that similarly promoted affiliation and congruence in adult social life.[3]

Finally, Freeman (2000: 419), unlike Deacon, brings us back to Durkheim when he quotes a passage from *The Elementary Forms*:

> Emile Durkheim described the socializing process as the use of "...totemic emblems by clans to express and communicate collective representations," which begins where the individual feels he *is* the totem and evolves beliefs that he will become the totem or that his ancestors are in the totem. Religious rites and ceremonies lead to "collective mental states of extreme emotional intensity, in which representation is still undifferentiated from the movements and actions which make the communion toward which it tends a reality to the group. Their participation in it is *so effectively lived* that it is not yet properly imagined."

Dissanayake emphasizes the socializing and enculturating aspects of the quasi-ritual interactions between mother and infant, interactions that actually create the psychological, social and cultural capacity of children to become full participants in society. While we might think of these "socializing" or even "normalizing" functions of ritual as Durkheimian, we should not forget that Durkheim believed that through experiences of collective effervescence, not only was society reaffirmed, but new, sometimes radically new, social innovations were made possible. Freeman (2000: 422) puts this insight into the language of contemporary neurobiology:

> I conclude that music and dance originated through biological evolution of brain chemistry, which interacted with the cultural evolution of behavior. This led to the development of chemical and behavioral technology for inducing altered states of consciousness. The role of trance states was particularly important for breaking down preexisting habits and beliefs. That meltdown appears to be necessary for personality changes leading to the formation of social groups by cooperative action leading to trust. Bonding is not simply a release of a neurochemical in an altered state. It is the social action of dancing and singing together that induces new forms of behavior, owing to the malleability that can come through the altered state. It is reasonable to suppose that musical skills played a major role early in the evolution of human intellect, because they made possible formation of human societies as a prerequisite for the transmission of acquired knowledge across generations.

Having seen how much light this new work on the origins of music has shed on questions of the place of ritual in human evolution, let us finally return to the question raised by Deacon about the fact that early symbol use "may not have been very much like speech," but was probably some kind of proto-language. Steven Brown (2000) starts from the point that, although language and music today are clearly different in that their primary locations in the brain are different, nonetheless, even in terms of brain physiology, there is a great deal of overlap between them. He then suggests that language and music form a continuum rather than an absolute dichotomy, with language

---

[3] Erik H. Erikson (1968) suggested that the "greeting ceremonial" between mother and child, marking the beginning of the infant's day, was the root of the ritualization process and traced stages of ritualization through later developmental phases.

in the sense of sound as referential meaning at one end, and music in the sense of sound as emotive meaning at the other. What is interesting is the range of things in between, with verbal song at the midpoint (verbal song is the commonest form of music worldwide). Moving toward language as referential meaning from the midpoint we have poetic discourse, *recitativo*, and heightened speech. Moving toward music as emotive meaning from the midpoint we have "word painting," *Leitmotifs*, and musical narration (ibid.: 275). From this existing continuum, from features of their overlapping location in brain physiology, and from parsimony in explanation, Brown argues that rather than music and language evolving separately, or emerging one from the other, the likeliest account is that both developed from something that was simultaneously proto-language and proto-music and that he calls "musilanguage" (ibid.: 277). If we postulate that musilanguage was also enacted, that is, involved meaningful gesture as well as sound, then we can see ritual as a primary evolutionary example of musilanguage and note that even today ritual is apt to be a kind of musilanguage: However sophisticated its verbal, musical, and gestural components have become, they are still deeply implicated with each other.

THE NATURE OF RITUAL

Having considered the roots of ritual and its most fundamental human functions, we will now consider somewhat more closely the basic features of ritual. The most important book on ritual in recent years is Roy Rappaport's (1999) *Ritual and Religion in the Making of Humanity*.[4] Rappaport's first, and highly condensed, definition of ritual is *"the performance of more or less invariant sequences of formal acts and utterances not entirely encoded by the performers"* (ibid.: 24). Rappaport's stress on "invariant sequences of formal acts and utterances" brings us back to features of musilanguage that may have been essential in the transformation of meaningless sound sequences into highly condensed, in the sense of undifferentiated, but still referentially/emotively meaningful, sound events. A key aspect of these transitional events is redundancy, essential in helping humans move from indexical to symbolic meaning. According to Bruce Richman (2000: 304), musical redundancy is communicated in three forms: (a) repetition; (b) formulaicness, that is, "the storehouse of preexisting formulas, riffs, themes, motifs and rhythms"; and (c) expectancy "of exactly what is going to come next and fill the upcoming temporal slot." In the redundancy created by expectancy, the most important element is tempo, the rhythm that may be created by drumming, the stamping of feet, or other means. It is noteworthy that humans are the only primates with the ability to keep time to an external timekeeper, such as the beating of a drum (Brown et al. 2000: 12). This ability to "keep together in time" is probably one of several biological developments that have evolved synchronously with the development of culture, but one of great importance for the ritual roots of society.[5] In any case, it is closely related to the "more or less invariant sequences of formal acts and utterances" that are central to Rappaport's definition of ritual.

---

[4] Keith Hart, in his preface to this posthumously published book, invokes Emile Durkheim's *Elementary Forms of the Religious Life* and holds that Rappaport's book is "comparable in scope to his great predecessor's work" (p. xiv) – a judgment with which I agree.

[5] On the coevolution of mind and culture, see Clifford Geertz (1973: 55–83).

From his very condensed original definition of ritual Rappaport draws implications which he spends the rest of a rather long book developing. For our purposes, the most important implications have to do with the creation of social conventions, a moral order, a sense of the sacred, and a relationship to the cosmos, including beliefs about what lies behind the empirical cosmos (Rappaport 1999: 27). Rappaport, like most other writers on ritual, is aware of the wide variety of actions that can be classified under this term. One defining feature of ritual for him is performance (ibid.: 37). In his usage of this potentially ambiguous term, performance carries the sense of what is called in the philosophy of language performative speech: Something is not simply described or symbolized, but done, enacted. This gets back to Deacon's point about promises or Freeman's emphasis on trust. The sheer act of participating in serious rituals entails a commitment with respect to future action, at the very least solidarity with one's fellow communicants. Thus, as Rappaport uses the term, it would explicitly not be the same as participating in a dramatic "performance," where the actor sheds the "role" as soon as the performance is over, and the audience, however moved, goes away knowing it was "only a play." On the contrary, serious ritual performance has the capacity to transform not only the role but the personality of the participant, as in rites of passage (Van Gennep 1908/1960). The fundamental relationship between saying and doing Rappaport (1999: 107) sees as establishing "convention in ritual" and the "social contract and morality that inhere in it." This is the ground, he argues, for "taking ritual to be humanity's basic social act."

Talal Asad (1993) in an important critique of anthropological theories of ritual as "symbolic action," that is, action whose meaning can simply be read off by the anthropological observer, emphasizes instead the older Christian meaning of ritual as discipline. In this he would seem, in part, to be paralleling Rappaport's distinction between dramatic performance, which is expressive of meaning but has no moral consequence, and ritual as performative in the sense of a fundamental change of disposition on the part of the participant. Asad (1993: 78) writes:

> [The] idea of the sacraments as metaphorical representations inhabits an entirely different world from the one that gives sense to Hugh of St. Victor's theology: "Sacraments," he stated, "are known to have been instituted for three reasons: On account of humiliation, on account of instruction, on account of exercise." According to this latter conception, the sacraments are not the representation of cultural metaphors; they are parts of a Christian program for creating in its performers, by means of regulated practice, the "mental and moral dispositions" appropriate to Christians.

It is precisely the element of discipline or external constraint that Radcliffe-Brown, as quoted by Rappaport, sees in the ritual dances of the Andaman Islanders:

> The Andaman dance, then, is a complete activity of the whole community in which every able-bodied adult takes part, and is also an activity to which, so far as the dancer is concerned, the whole personality is involved, by the intervention of all the muscles of the body, by the concentration of attention required, and by its action on the personal sentiments. In the dance the individual submits to the action upon him of the community; he is constrained by the immediate effect of rhythm, as well as by custom, to join in, and he is required to conform in his own actions and movements to the needs of the common activity. The surrender of the individual

to this constraint or obligation is not felt as painful, but on the contrary as highly pleasurable.[6]

Although ritual is deeply involved with what Marcel Mauss (1935/1973: 70–88) called "techniques of the body," it also at the same time involves a complex set of meanings, which cannot simply be read off from the ritual but must be understood in the context of the whole form of life of the ritual participants. One of Rappaport's (1999: 70–4) most interesting ideas is his typology of three levels of meaning that are normally involved in ritual. *Low-order meaning* is grounded in distinction (a dog is not a cat) and is virtually the same as what is meant by information in information theory. Low-order meaning answers the question "What is it?" but it doesn't have much to say about the question "What does it all mean?" *Middle-order meaning* does not so much distinguish as connect: its concern is with similarities, analogies, emotional resonances and its chief form is metaphor (the fog comes on little cat feet). Art and poetry operate primarily at this level and it is very important for ritual, in which the focus on techniques of the body in no way excludes symbolic meanings. Since ritual depends heavily on exact repetition, it cannot convey much information – it doesn't tell one anything new – but it does link realms of experience and feeling that have perhaps become disconnected in the routine affairs of daily life. *High-order meaning* "is grounded in identity or unity, the radical identification or unification of self with other" (Rappaport 1999: 71). Such meaning, the immediate experience of what has been called "unitive consciousness,"[7] can come in mystical experience, but, according to Rappaport, the most frequent context for such an experience is ritual. Here he links back to Durkheim's famous definition of ritual – it is in the effervescence of ritual that the individual concerns of daily life are transcended and society is born.

The world of daily life – economics, politics – is inevitably dependent on information, on making the right distinctions. Rational action theory assumes that all we need is information, in this technical sense of the term. But Rappaport, with Durkheim, argues that if rational action were all there is, there would be no solidarity, no morality, no society, and no humanity. The Hobbesian world of all against all is not a human world. Only ritual pulls us out of our egoistic pursuit of our own interests and creates the possibility of a social world. As this highly condensed resumé of Rappaport's argument suggests, there is reason to wonder about the future of ritual in our kind of society. Technological and economic progress is based on the enormous proliferation of information, but information is in a zero/sum relation to meaning. Undermining middle- and high-order meaning is not just a threat to ritual and religion, if Rappaport is right, but to society and humanity as well.

RITUAL IN VARIOUS SPHERES OF LIFE

Our society does not understand ritual very well, and for many of us even the term is pejorative; furthermore, the great religious rituals that in almost all earlier societies

---

[6] Rappaport (1999: 221), quoting A. R. Radcliffe-Brown, *The Andaman Islanders*, 1922/1964, pp. 251–2. Asad (1993: 83–134) emphasizes the painful aspect of ritual discipline, but he focuses particularly on the sacrament of penance.

[7] Abraham Maslow (1962) calls such experiences "peak experiences," which may or may not be explicitly religious.

carried what Rappaport calls high-order meaning have been privatized so that they act, not for society as a whole, but only for the particular groups of believers who celebrate them. The ambiguous term secularization might be used to describe not only the alleged decline of religion, but the decline of ritual as well. But, although some forms of ritual have become less evident, or have retreated from the public sphere, it is also true that even in contemporary society we remain surrounded by ritual in a myriad of forms. It might even be argued that ritual is to be found everywhere that humans live together if we look in the right places, although where those places are may be very different from one society to the next. I recognize that this assertion raises questions about the very concept of ritual, to which I will return briefly at the end of this chapter. First, I would like to pursue a bit further the idea of interaction ritual as developed by Goffman and Collins.

Like so much else in the study of ritual, the idea of interaction ritual can be found in germ in Durkheim's *Elementary Forms*:

> [The] stimulating action of society is not felt in exceptional circumstances alone. There is virtually no instant of our lives in which a certain rush of energy fails to come to us from outside ourselves. In all kinds of acts that express the understanding, esteem, and affection of his neighbor, there is a lift that the man who does his duty feels, usually without being aware of it. But that lift sustains him; the feeling society has for him uplifts the feeling he has for himself. Because he is in moral harmony with his neighbor, he gains new confidence, courage, and boldness in action – quite like the man of faith who believes he feels the eyes of his god turned benevolently toward him. Thus is produced what amounts to a perpetual uplift of our moral being. (1912/1976: 211)

Goffman (1967) made the point that any social interaction, even between two persons, inevitably has a ritual dimension involving stylized elements of both speech and gesture. Collins has built on Goffman's work to argue that the basic social fact is the local interaction ritual, and that individuals cannot be said to have a higher degree of reality than the interaction in which they engage since they are in fact constituted in and through the interaction. Goffman (1967) saw deference as one indispensable element in interaction ritual. In hierarchical societies, the ritual enactment of shared moral understandings expresses a sacred hierarchical order and the place of the interacting partners in it. In our society, in which the moral order emphasizes equality, even though hierarchy is inevitably present there is a special effort to protect the sacredness of the individual person, no matter how disparate the status of the individuals involved. Even in a relatively fleeting encounter, then, the basic elements of ritual can be discerned: The synchronizing rhythm of conversational speech and gesture and the affirmation of social solidarity that they imply, regardless of the content of the conversation, and, if only by implication, the recognition of the sacredness, either of the code governing the interaction, the individuals interacting, or both.

Even in mundane daily life, ritual is not only a matter of occasional meeting and parting; it is very much part of the periodicity of life. Eating together may well be one of our oldest rituals, since humans are the only primates who regularly share food.[8] Margaret Visser (1992: xii–xiii) has made the case for the centrality of what she calls

---

[8] The classic discussion of this issue is Glynn Isaac (1978).

"rituals of dinner," because eating together is just the sort of occasion that makes ritual necessary. She writes,

> Table manners are social agreements; they are devised precisely because violence could so easily erupt at dinner. Eating is aggressive by nature and the implements required for it could quickly become weapons; table manners are, most basically, a system of taboos designed to ensure that violence remains out of the question. But intimations of greed and rage keep breaking in: Many mealtime superstitions, for example, point to the imminent death of one of the guests. Eating is performed by the individual, in his or her most personal interest; eating in company, however, necessarily places the individual face to face with the group. It is the group that insists on table manners; "they" will not accept a refusal to conform. The individual's "personal interest" lies therefore not only in ensuring his or her bodily survival, but also in pleasing, placating, and not frightening or disgusting the other diners.

Although Visser underlines the elements of personal interest and group pressure, which are always involved in ritual, one would need to add that the "ritual of dinner," in the sense of "breaking bread together," implicitly, and often explicitly, has a religious dimension, as when there is a blessing before or after the meal, or, as in some Asian societies, a token offering to the ancestors precedes the meal.

Periodicity is characteristic of ritual of a wide variety of types ranging from the most secular, or even trivial, to the most solemn and religious. Academic life is highly ritualized and the school year is marked by numerous ritual events. Sporting events, both professional and collegiate have become highly ritualized in modern societies, and follow different seasonal patterns depending on the sport. A full discussion of the senses in which sporting events can be interpreted as rituals would exceed the bounds of this chapter. Suffice it to say that the absence or weakness of the performative dimension in Rappaport's sense makes sporting events, like concerts, operas, plays or movies seen in theaters, problematic as ritual events in the full sense of the word. If involvement with a team becomes a major life concern, or even gives rise to "fan cults" in some cases, this might move such sporting events more fully into the ritual category. Political life also gives rise to various periodicities, including national holidays, elections, inaugurations, and so forth (the nation-state as a sacred object will be considered later in this chapter). Religious ritual has a strong tendency toward periodicity – Judaism, Christianity, and Islam require weekly worship – and yearly liturgical calendars are widespread. Economic transactions, as Durkheim pointed out, are the least likely to be ritualized, being highly utilitarian in character. Nonetheless, economic exchange in premodern societies is often accompanied by ritual, and a full analysis of economic life in our own society would probably discover more than a few ritual elements.

William McNeill (1995), in his important book *Keeping Together in Time: Dance and Drill in Human History*, deals with many issues relevant to the concerns of this chapter, but he begins with military drill, not something students of ritual would usually start with. The two places where what McNeill (ibid.: 1–11) calls "muscular bonding" has been most central have been, in his analysis, religion and the military. Learning that from McNeill, I was not entirely surprised to discover, as I did in the recent spate of publicity about him, that not only was Colin Powell raised an Episcopalian, but that his service as an altar boy prepared him psychologically for a career in the army. The proximity of Episcopal liturgy and military life, while making a certain amount of sense, was not something I would spontaneously have imagined. McNeill does a great deal to clarify this otherwise somewhat disconcerting conjuncture. His starting point is frankly autobiographical: How did it happen that as a draftee in 1941, while enduring basic training in a camp on the barren plains of Texas, he actually enjoyed the hours spent in close-order drill? His answer in his admittedly somewhat speculative history of keeping together in time (after all who bothered much to write about such things) is that "moving our muscles rhythmically and giving voice consolidate group solidarity by altering human feelings" (ibid.: viii).

Virtually all small communities of which we have knowledge, whether tribal or peasant, have been united on significant occasions by community-wide singing and dancing, usually more or less explicitly religious in content. (McNeill [ibid.: 65] points out that what we today usually mean by "dancing," namely paired cross-gender performances with some degree of sexual intent, is, when viewed historically, aberrant to the point of being pathological.)

McNeill (ibid.: 86–90) notes that in complex societies divided by social class muscular bonding may be the medium through which discontented and oppressed groups can gain the solidarity necessary for challenging the existing social order, using early prophetism in Israel as an example. He puts in perspective something that has often been noticed, namely that the liturgical movements of the more advantaged members of society are apt to be relatively sedate, whereas those of the dispossessed can become energetic to the point of inducing trance.

Close-order drill, McNeill's starting point, turns out to have emerged in only a few rather special circumstances, although dancing in preparation for or celebration after military exploits is widespread in simple societies. Here again there are ambiguities. Intensive drill in the Greek phalanx or trireme provided the social cohesion and sense of self-respect that reinforced citizenship in the ancient *polis*, but in early modern Europe its meaning was more ambiguous, sometimes reinforcing citizenship, sometimes absolutism. McNeill gives the interesting example of the strongly bonded citizen armies of the French Revolution that then turned out to be manipulable elements in the establishment of Napoleon's autocracy (ibid.: 113–36). His comments on the use of rhythmic motion, derived in part from military drill but in part from calisthenics, in the creation of modern nationalism, culminating in Hitler's mass demonstrations (inspired in part by the mass socialist parades on May Day, which in turn were inspired in part by Corpus Christi celebrations), are very suggestive (ibid.: 147–8). But if such sinister uses of keeping together in time are always possible, all forms of nationalism have drawn on similar techniques.

Benedict Anderson, in his valuable analysis of modern nationalism, describes what he calls unisonance, which is another form of keeping together in time:

> [T]here is a special kind of contemporaneous community which language alone suggests – above all in the form of poetry and songs. Take national anthems, for example, sung on national holidays. No matter how banal the words and mediocre the tunes, there is in this singing an experience of simultaneity. At precisely such moments, people wholly unknown to each other utter the same verses to the same melody. The image: unisonance. Singing the Marseillaise, Waltzing Matilda, and Indonesia Raya provide occasions for unisonality, for the echoed physical realization of the imagined community. (So does listening to [and maybe silently chiming in with] the recitation of ceremonial poetry, such as sections of *The Book of Common*

Prayer.) How selfless this unisonance feels! If we are aware that others are singing these songs precisely when and as we are, we have no idea who they may be, or even where, out of earshot, they are singing. Nothing connects us all but imagined sound. (1991: 145)

I would like to point out how, through the prevalence of television, rituals today can be shared by millions within and even beyond the nation state. I think of two instances: One where ritual worked effectively and one where it collapsed. I am old enough to remember well the November afternoon in 1963 when John F. Kennedy was shot in Dallas, Texas. For the following three days, millions were glued to their television screens as a ritual drama of great complexity unfolded. The rituals were both national and religious. They involved the casket lying in state in the Rotunda of the United States Capitol, and then being taken by procession to the railway station, from which it was transported by train to Boston for a Catholic funeral mass presided over by the Cardinal Archbishop of Boston. The sudden loss of a head of state is apt to be traumatic in any society. The three days of ritual following Kennedy's death did seem to help make it possible to return to some kind of normal life after such a catastrophe.

In democratic societies, elections are ritual events, even if minimally religious ones. The very fact that millions of people go to the polls on one day and that there is great national attention to the outcome guarantees a high order of emotional intensity to such an event. Since television, elections have gathered very large audiences to await the outcome and the ritual concession and acceptance speeches that follow. But in the United States federal election of 2000, nothing seemed to go right. The television media made two wrong calls as to who won the election and then had to admit that the election in Florida, on which the electoral college vote hung, was too close to call. What followed was anything but effective ritual. Almost every key actor in the events after the election failed to follow the appropriate ritual script – indeed things reached the point where it wasn't clear what the script was. The resolution of the election by a partisan vote of the Supreme Court of the United States, which has no role to play in elections according to the American Constitution, was the final failure of ritual closure. A failed electoral ritual produced a winner with severely damaged legitimacy.[9]

In a society in which more and more human interactions are mediated by the market, and orientation to the market competes with traditional religion and nationalism for the loyalty of many citizens, one may wonder what form the ritual expression of solidarity will take, or whether it can really be diminished or eliminated, leaving theorists of ritual to wonder if their basic assumptions will be disconfirmed. At the moment, it seems far too early to draw so drastic a conclusion.

CONCLUSION

Finally, I would like to turn to some methodological issues which I have avoided so far in this chapter. Catherine Bell, in two very useful books, *Ritual Theory, Ritual Practice* (1992) and *Ritual: Perspectives and Dimensions* (1997), has summarized the present state of ritual studies and some of the difficulties and ambiguities which have arisen within the field. She intelligently reviews the history of theorizing about ritual in the social sciences and religious studies and points to the wide variety of views, but also to the lack of

---

[9] Clifford Geertz (1973: 142–69) brilliantly describes a failed ritual of much more modest scale.

progress toward reaching anything like a consensus. Reflecting the somewhat skeptical mood that is not uncommon in religious studies today, she raises the question as to whether the widespread belief that ritual is universally benign is an improvement over an older notion of ritual as regressive habit, suggesting instead that ritual, like all human action, is involved in contexts of power and subject to many forms of manipulation. She cites Vincent Crapanzano's (1981) study of Moroccan male initiation rites, which "cruelly traumatize a child in ways that benefit the conservatism of the social group," as a rare example of an anthropological study that shows ritual to be other than uniformly benign. She also suggests that ritual is very much in the eye of the beholder, each theorist finding what he or she is looking for. Bell stops short of complete nominalism and in fact develops several useful typologies for thinking about aspects of ritual, but in the welter of competing theories she is tempted, like many scholars today, to opt for a healthy skepticism. Yet also, like many contemporary critics, her work is subject to the same critique she makes of others. Starting as she does from a view that human action is fundamentally strategic (1992: 81), it is not surprising that the manipulative element, which is always present in ritual to be sure, will receive heightened attention.

As any reader of this chapter will know, I believe that we cannot do without general terms in the social sciences, even though many such terms are of recent and Western origin. Healthy skepticism about them is always in order, but that does not mean that they cannot refer to real features of the real world. I have argued that ritual is not only real, but, in agreement with Rappaport, that it is "humanity's basic social act," a position that, though contestable, has a great deal of evidence in its favor.

CHAPTER FOUR

Social Forms of Religion and Religions in Contemporary Global Society

Peter Beyer

CONCEIVING AND DEFINING RELIGION AND RELIGIONS

It may seem to many readers that *religion* is a fairly straightforward notion, easily bring-ing to mind clear and concrete pictures: A group of Muslims at daily prayer, a Christian priest saying mass, a Buddhist monk or nun meditating, a person lighting a votive or holiday candle, and myriad other possibilities. Yet, as in several other domains of social life, such as art, sport, and that ever elusive term, culture, what seems clear at a quick and first glance is anything but upon further reflection. If a Shakespearean play and neolithic cave paintings count as art, what about the arrangement of flowers on the dining room table, a television advertisement, or the rousing performance of a popu-lar politician on the hustings? If ice dancing is an Olympic sport, why isn't ballroom dancing even a sport? If dim-sum is part of Chinese culture, how many kung-fu centers do there have to be in Houston or San Francisco before they become an expression of American culture? Similarly, while most readers may agree that what happens in a Jewish synagogue or at a Shinto shrine qualifies as religion, many people in Western countries have just as serious doubts about what happens at a Scientology course as government officials in China have about Falun Gong. The Church of Jesus Christ of Latter-Day Saints and the Brahma Kumaris are clearly religious groups; are they also Christian and Hindu, respectively?

How important such questions are varies according to time, place, and circum-stance. If the Christian status of Mormons and the cultural status of kung-fu establish-ments are currently not all that critical in the United States, the Islamic status of Baha'is in Iran or the cultural implications of the magazine, *Sports Illustrated*,[1] in Canada have in recent years been hotly debated or highly consequential issues. Ambiguities and dis-agreement in these matters can often be of great practical importance; they interest more than detached intellectual observers. Moreover, it seems that the sorts of dispute that arise with regard to these concepts are basically of three kinds, two of them having

---

[1] *Sports Illustrated*, a large American-based sports magazine, publishes a Canadian issue, but sells advertisements at relatively low prices to Canadian companies, thus making it harder for Canadian-based magazines to survive only in the Canadian market. The argument against what *Sports Illustrated* does has been framed in Canada as a matter of defending "Canadian culture."

to do with boundaries, and one with the valuation of these concepts in their social contexts. Thus, we have disagreement about what does and does not belong in a category like religion or culture; we debate the boundaries between members of a category, such as where one religion ends and another begins; but we can also contest the status of the categories themselves. We do this, for instance, when we discuss the legitimacy of what can be claimed by appealing to categories like religion, culture, sport, art, or a number of other social forms.

In one sense, problems of this nature are as old as human history. Boundaries are the very stuff of social structures and human knowledge: We make distinctions and thereby create ordered worlds. Yet, although social order would be impossible without them, these social forms also always seem in one way or another to be problematic, to not quite "work" (e.g., Berger and Luckmann 1966; Douglas 1966). That said, however, the specific ways that this general feature works itself out in contemporary society has its particular and somewhat unique characteristics when compared to societies of the past. It is to the contemporary situation with respect to the idea of religion that this chapter addresses itself.

Sociological discussions about defining religion have almost always come to the conclusion that this is a difficult exercise about which there is little agreement. Generally, these debates hover around the central organizing distinction between substantive and functional definitions or restrictive and expansive ones (e.g., O'Toole 1984; Hervieu-Léger 2000). More often than not, substantive definitions, which focus on what religion *is*, tend to be restrictive; and functional definitions, which center on what religion *does*, lean toward being more expansive in what they include. Accordingly, the most typical criticism of substantive/restrictive definitions is that they include too little, perhaps on the basis of an implicit theological bias that wishes to exclude "false" religion. By contrast, a frequently cited weakness of functional/expansive definitions is that they exclude too little, thus rendering the term meaningless and perhaps even betraying an antireligious bias: What "religion" does can be done (better) by many other things, like the state, art, sport, medicine, or science. Thus, from the nature of the functional/substantive difference and the criticisms of either side, it becomes evident that all three of the axes of dispute I mentioned above are at work. Sociologists have disputed the boundary between religion and nonreligion, what counts and doesn't count. They have disagreed on how valuable or important religion is, whether it is necessary or not. And behind both issues is that of internal variety: They assume that there are many religions, irrespective of whether the favored approach is substantive or functional.

In both sociological and nonsociological realms, therefore, the term religion remains somewhat elusive. And this along similar lines of dispute. One reason for this parallelism is undoubtedly that the two domains exist in the same social and historical context. That fact leads to this hypothesis: The definitional or conceptual difficulties with respect to religion point to a social context that encourages and perhaps even requires "religion" to be multivalent. In other words, the problem is not in the ambiguous or variable nature of "religion itself," whatever that may be but, rather, in a social context that makes such ambiguity sensible. It is this variability of religions in that social context which is the specific focus of this chapter. The sections that follow explore various aspects of this overall question, and they do so by translating it into two interrelated matters: The social context of contemporary global society and the social forms that religion and religions typically seem to take in this context. The main argument is that the intensified globalization of society over the past few centuries has generated a situation that favors certain social forms of religion and religions yielding, among other things, the conceptual ambiguity just discussed.

DIFFERENTIATED RELIGION IN GLOBAL SOCIETY

If we accept that the social forms that religion takes in contemporary global society are to a large degree peculiar to that context, then it follows that assuming these forms to be historically universal would create even more confusion. This sort of projection does in fact take place quite frequently, in particular among academic and theological observers. Academics, in spite of protests to the contrary, regularly assume that so-called world religions such as Hinduism and Daoism have a long history and have existed as such at least since the first millennium B.C.E. They are not alone, however. Often theological observers from within these religions insist on similar observations: For instance, neo-Vedantic Hindu thinkers who style Hinduism as an ancient religion centered on the Vedic scriptures (e.g., Dalmia and von Stietencron 1995); or post-Meiji Restoration Shinto theologians who successfully asserted Shinto as a unified and ancient tradition[2] distinct from Buddhism and dating back at least to the eighth century C.E. While such projections can and do make analytic and theological (not to mention political) sense, they also tend to hide the degree to which this differentiation of religions as mutually distinguishable and historically self-identified entities is of comparatively recent origin, and would make little sense if we were not all observing from the same contemporary social context.

A number of contemporary critiques of the concept of religion point out the degree to which the current meaning of the word is in fact of Western and not at all of global provenance (e.g., W. Smith 1978; Fitzgerald 1997; Chidester 1996). Historically speaking, this is an accurate observation. The idea of religion as a distinct and differentiable social domain did originate in European-based society and one could argue that it refers more easily to religions like Christianity, Judaism, and Islam than it does to other religious traditions. It would, however, be entirely misleading to assume, in addition, that the word religion has always had this meaning among Europeans, or that other parts of the world have not now incorporated this meaning into their own languages and applied it to at least some of their indigenous religious traditions. In fact, this supposedly Western concept did not exist in the West before about the seventeenth century and did not really solidify until well thereafter (W. Smith 1978; Despland 1979). And words such as *dharma* in India, *agama* in Indonesia, *zongjiao* in China, and *shukyo* in Japan do today have very similar meanings to Western variants of *religio*; and refer explicitly to entities such as Hinduism, Buddhism, Jainism, and Daoism, not just the Abrahamic religions.

The question that emerges, therefore, is how did we arrive at this differentiation of religion as something distinct and as something that inherently manifests itself in, among other forms, a plurality of mutually distinguishable religions? The answer has much to do with the development of global society over the last few centuries.

---

[2] To be sure, these Shinto priests, scholars, and political leaders also claimed that Shinto was *not* a religion, but this also had more to do with the historical context and what the word religion implied for them, than it did with the characteristics of what they reinvented as Shinto. See Hardacre 1989: esp. 34f, 63f.

The fact that this modern understanding of religion as differentiated and plural developed first specifically in seventeenth-century Europe is of some significance. Already in the sixteenth century, the prolonged and violent conflict that came in the wake of the Protestant Reformation impressed on many elite Europeans the idea that religious *differences* are fundamental and intractable. By the beginning of the eighteenth century, we see crystallizing a double notion. First, people do not just have religion, they have *a* religion, implying both something distinct and more than one possibility. Second, therefore, there exist distinct religions, now in the plural. Initially, the religions thus recognized were few: Christianity, Judaism, and Islam, with a broad residual category of heathenism or paganism. In the context of their imperial expansion virtually all around the world over the next two centuries, however, European observers "found" an increasing number of other major religions, including what by the nineteenth century began to be called Buddhism, Hinduism, Daoism, and Confucianism.[3]

Although religious conflict in Europe and European imperial expansion were important for this discovery of religions, other factors were just as critical. Prime among these were the close association of religion and nation, the eventual collaboration of non-European elites in the construction of some of these religions, and the rise of increasingly powerful institutional domains more and more independent of religion.

The seventeenth-century solution to the prolonged religious conflict in Europe was the Treaty of Westphalia, which coordinated religious and political identity: Protestant rulers would have Protestant subjects; Catholic rulers would have Catholic subjects. After the French Revolution and especially in the nineteenth century, we see solidifying the further idea that states gain their primary legitimacy as agents and expressions, not of rulers, but of nations, cultural units that in most cases carried forth the Westphalian formula to include a particular religion as a central element in national identity. This overlapping of nation, state, and religion was by no means rigidly consistent or even always straightforward, but it did have the effect of institutionalizing a triple plurality: There are many states, which correspond to the many nations. And these nations are very frequently the carriers of different religions.

The European observers who carried forth the global expansion of European influence did not simply apply this formula to everyone else. Indeed, their dominant attitude, especially among the Christian missionaries, was that most of the others were heathens, targets for conversion, not carriers of yet other religions. In some cases, however, such observers did "discover" additional and distinct religions, notably other so-called world religions such as Buddhism, Daoism, and Hinduism. These efforts by themselves did not, however, lead to the differentiation of these entities as yet more self-identified, popularly, and officially recognized religions. For this additional step to happen, indigenous carrier elites had to take up this task of revisioning the complex and to some degree amorphous religious traditions of their civilizations as delimited and recognizable religions, formally on a par with and distinct from the others, in particular, given the religious identity of the Westerners, with Christianity. Where this additional vital step happened, we witness the construction, imagining, recognition, and to varying degrees organization of religions such as Hinduism, Sikhism, Jainism, Buddhism, and, perhaps less clearly, Daoism. Where we meet the failure of indigenous

---

[3] For a fuller discussion, see Beyer 1998, 1999. See also Almond 1988; Harrison 1990; Jensen 1997; W. Smith 1978; Despland 1979; Dalmia and von Stietencron 1995.

carriers to join sufficiently in the reconstructive enterprise, it is far more difficult to maintain that what observers see are anything more than labels of convenience for the sake of analysis. This has been the fate, thus far, of "Confucianism" and the religious traditions of most aboriginal cultures around the world: There is much behind these labels that may well be religious, but their carriers do not generally consider or practice them *as religions*.

A third key factor in the historical differentiation of religion and religions has to do with developments outside this domain, in "nonreligion." As with all socially significant categories, the identity of religion depends to some extent on the difference between what counts as religion and what does not. European society at the time of the Reformation had a double compatibility in this regard. On the one hand, the visibility, power, and clearly religious identity of the Roman Catholic church provided a concrete institutional model that could stand for religion positively. On the other hand, however, early modern Europe also was a time of the gradual development of other institutional domains that increasingly, over subsequent centuries, established themselves as independent of religious tutelage and eventually even of religious legitimation. These included above all the capitalist economy, the sovereign political state (together with its administrative and military arms), the related domain of positive law, modern science, and later also academic education, medicalized health, art, mass media, and sport. The rise of these nonreligious systems was critical for developing and treating religion as something distinct and different. Not only did religion appear in contrast to these nonreligious social spheres, the different spheres, including especially religion, modeled themselves to some extent on each other in the process of their institutional (re)construction. What religion and the religions have become, what social forms they now typically take in today's world society has occurred in the context of this modeling.

It was largely on the basis of the technical efficiency and power that these differentiated domains afforded them, that the Europeans were able to extend their influence around the world between the sixteenth and twentieth centuries. They had better and better weapons and means of transportation/communication. With increasing efficiency, they could mobilize human and nonhuman resources. And the logic of these systems drove them further and further in search of markets, resources, power, knowledge, and souls. Their imperialist drive constitutes half the reason for the intensified globalization of society over those same centuries, in particular the last two. The other half consists in the responses of those on whom the Europeans imposed themselves and their vision of the world.

In every part of the globe, local people were faced with the question of how to react to the increasing power to the Europeans. In many cases, their options were quite restricted, especially in those regions that the conquerors succeeded in colonizing, notably the Americas and Australasia. There, the indigenous people that survived the onslaught usually tried to carry on their religiocultural traditions to some extent, but over time the prevailing pattern was conversion to Christianity, albeit not infrequently a Christianity syncretized with an array of aboriginal religious elements and styles. The reconstruction of indigenous traditions as distinct religions did occur in some cases, such as the Longhouse religion founded by Handsome Lake in early-nineteenth-century North America. These, however, remained quite limited in their impact and size. Of significance in the Americas also were the religious traditions brought by Africans in the context of the slave trade. Especially in the later twentieth century, the descendants of these involuntary colonists have become the prime carriers of a number of increasingly distinct religions such as Vodoun, Candomblé/Santería/Yoruba, Umbanda, and Rastafarianism, all to a large extent based on a reconstruction and reinvention of African traditions. During this same period, the prevailing approach of aboriginal peoples in the Americas has been, as noted above, to refuse reconstruction of their religious traditions as religions, insisting instead that these are undifferentiable dimensions of aboriginal culture.

In other parts of the world, with the limited exception of parts of Southern Africa, European colonization was not an option. It is these areas that have been witness to the (re)construction of all the other so-called world religions, almost invariably as key aspects of the responses to European power. Whether we are dealing with the invention of State Shinto in post-Meiji Restoration Japan, the crystallization and solidification of Hindu and Sikh religion in South Asia, the increased orthodoxification of Islam from Northern Africa to the Indonesian archipelago, the reimagination of a unified Buddhism in East Asia, or its nationalization in Sri Lanka, the movements toward the clearer identification of these various traditions as religions have been an important dimension in the attempts of people in these regions to respond to European power by appropriating and adapting the latter's dominant instrumentalities, including that of "religion." Moreover, in most cases, this appropriation of distinct religious identity has occurred in tandem with the assertion of national identities as the basis of founding modern sovereign states. Even where indigenous elites expressly refused to imagine local traditions as a religion, such as in China with "Confucianism," this happened as part of strategies for constructing a strong nation and state that would allow China to become great again. That possibility, in turn, points to some rather important ambiguities in this entire historical development, ambiguities that concern the boundaries of religions, their relations to each other, but also critically the status of thus reconstructed religions with respect to the other, "secularized" domains or systems. It is to a discussion of these ambiguities that we now turn.

RELIGIONS, CONTESTED BOUNDARIES, AND MATTERS RELIGIOUS OUTSIDE RELIGIONS

Although the last few centuries have indeed witnessed the sort of revisioning of religions just outlined, this has not occurred without contestation, and even open opposition. Aside from direct clashes between religions, such disputes have followed the lines discussed at the beginning of this chapter: Struggles over the distinction between religions, contention about the relations between religion(s) and other domains of social life, and disagreement about the value of that which is meant by religion. Often enough, more than one of these have been at issue. Since here cannot be the place for a thorough discussion of the complex ways in which these conflicts have manifested themselves, a brief overview will suffice to give an idea.

Struggles over the distinction between religions are perhaps best exemplified in the case of Hinduism versus Sikhism. Sikh traditions had their origin in the sixteenth century, when Muslims ruled the subcontinent. In that context they from early on focused on the difference between Sikhs and Muslims. Only in the later nineteenth century, under British rule, did Sikhs begin to insist with increasing consistency that they also were not Hindus. The historical situation in which this occurred is of course quite complex, but critical for the development were aspects of British colonial policy that encouraged the identification of distinct religious communities and, in that context, the simultaneous elaboration, reconstruction, and imagining by Hindu elites of Hinduism as a unified and distinct religion that could *subsume* Sikhs. Given various Muslim movements that also sought to articulate Islamic identity, and in light of Christian, Muslim, and even Hindu efforts to convert Sikhs to *these* religions, a series of Sikh movements such as Singh Sabha and the Akali movement progressively consolidated the institutional, symbolic, and ritual bases of a clearly separate Sikhism (e.g., Jones 1976; Kapur 1986; McLeod 1989). Typical for such processes, the reconstruction of Sikhism as a distinct religion was not so much the invention of something new, as it was the selective recombination of long established elements with new items. Distinction from other religions in effect required the "orthodoxification" of Sikhism to an extent that had not occurred before. The upshot is that today the specifically Khalsa Sikh identity has become recognized almost universally among Sikhs as the standard of Sikh orthodoxy. And any efforts by others, such as more recently the Hindu nationalist Rashtriya Swayamsevak Sangh and Vishva Hindu Parishad, to publicly claim Sikhism as a variant on Hinduism, have been vigorously opposed by Sikhs. Other examples of problematic lines of demarcation between religions would be the above-mentioned cases of Baha'i and Islam in Iran, Hinduism and variants such as the Brahma Kumari or even the International Society for Krishna Consciousness (Hare Kirshna), and the status of groups such as Jehovah's Witnesses or the Unification Church with relation to Christianity. In each of these cases, the dispute is over questions of "orthodoxy" but, with the exception of the Iranian example, translated into distinctions between religions (that is, religion/religion) rather than that between religion and antireligion (that is, religion/heresy).

Without doubt, the most frequently contentious issues with respect to religion in contemporary society have had to do with the boundary between religion and nonreligion. Disputes of this kind generally follow one of two directions: Either they concern the restriction of religion to its "proper sphere," in other words, the secularization of putatively nonreligious spheres along with the privatization of religion; or they are about what social formations will count as religion. The clearest examples of the former are religious movements and orientations that not only advocate the relevance of religious precepts in all spheres of life, but go further to insist that religious norms and often also religious authorities should directly control the operation of all these domains. Religion from these perspectives cannot be only a private affair of individuals and groups; it also must be public and collectively obligatory. Much discussed examples of this possibility are various militantly Islamic movements in countries as diverse as Algeria, Nigeria, Iran, Afghanistan, and Indonesia; Christian rightism in the United States; some forms of Sikh separatism in India; and certain directions among religous Zionists and ultra-Orthodox Judaism in Israel (Beyer 1994; Kapur 1986). The degree to which such movements advocate the "de-differentiation" of religion and other spheres varies enormously, but one aspect that is strikingly consistent is that they almost always seek to define, deeply influence, and very often take over modern states or subunits of them.

As concerns what will count as religion, here again, the states and their legal systems are frequently involved in helping to determine these parameters. The vast majority of state constitutions guarantee "freedom of religion," thus lending religion a high degree of legitimacy and a certain autonomy. To count as a religion affords distinct rights and it can therefore become important to know and to decide which claimants to the category will be acknowledged. Thus, to mention briefly a few examples, in Canada, Wiccans have sought to have their beliefs and practices accorded recognition as a legitimate religion (even though, perhaps somewhat ironically, many of them also reject the category in other respects) in child custody and other legal cases. In China, the government has declared Falun Gong a "cult" (*xiejiao* = evil teaching),[4] expressly denying it the protection of a religion. In Indonesia, the religious traditions of various aboriginal peoples are not recognized as religion (*agama*) unless they affiliate and identify with one of the five officially recognized religions (Schiller 1997: 109ff). Otherwise, they can only claim the less-privileged category of culture (*adat*). And in South Africa, there are strong movements to have African indigenous religions recognized formally by the government as legitimate religions, equal in dignity to others, especially the "world religions." In reverse direction, various religious strands have wished to avoid the category, sometimes as in the case of State Shinto to avoid the limitations that freedom of religion and the differentiation of religion imply; at other times because of a relatively negative valuation of the category.

The positive and negative evaluations of religion in contemporary global society stem from some of the features already indicated, and others besides. On the positive side, a movement or set of beliefs and practices accorded the status of a religion can in most parts of the world claim a certain autonomy of operation and dignity of recognition; even more so now that the former Soviet bloc has disintegrated along with its expressly "atheistic" policies. The adherents of a recognized religion can in that light expect their faith not to be a basis of discrimination in other spheres of life, such as politics, economics, and education. On the negative side, the category of religion may in various circumstances appear as a foreign, especially Western, imposition. It may carry the hue of being considered "irrational," "ideological," or "illusionary." It may imply the unacceptable imposition of outside authority in a domain that is deemed to be highly personal. Or it may carry with it the kind of restriction in sphere of operation that the notions of secularization and privatization imply. The carriers of potential religion may reject the category and seek not to be included under it for any of these reasons. Thus, for example, many Muslims insist that Islam is not a religion, but "a way of life." Most Chinese reject that "Confucianism" and an array of other traditional "religious" practices are religion or a religion, asserting instead that these things are about ethics, philosophy, or more broadly that they are simply aspects of Chinese "culture." Followers of the Maharishi Maheshyogi's Transcendental Meditation and its successor organizations consistently present their beliefs and practices as more science than religion. And, especially in Western countries, a wide variety of seemingly religious practitioners ranging from New Age to human potential movements, from "spirituality in the workplace" to Wicca and neopaganism explicitly reject the term religion in favor of less authoritarian, more individualistic categories such as "spirituality" (cf. Heelas 1996). The latter, along with "culture," is also more favored by many representatives and practitioners of traditional North American aboriginal practices.

---

[4] I thank Dr. Wang Jiwu and Dr. Li Qiang for information regarding this case and the word usages.

Aside from these various forms of contestation around the category of religion, it is also quite clear that, throughout the world, an important array of beliefs and practices that might count as religion end up escaping inclusion under its umbrella for no other reason than that no movement has arisen to effect such incorporation. In other words, not everything potentially "religious" ends up being included within a religion or being deliberately denied that classification. Under this heading would fall many of the things that appear under the analytic category of "popular" or "folk" religious practices, ranging from the many local temples to various indigenous deities in China, to shamanistic traditions in many cultural regions of the world, to "witchcraft" beliefs and practices in various parts of Africa. If one adds these exclusions from the category to the contestations surrounding it outlined above, the question that inevitably poses itself is, how religion actually acquires social form in these circumstances. What forms give religion and religions concrete expression beyond that of an observer's category? To some degree, as noted, outside recognition as religion is of course critical. But this cannot be all. For religion to acquire a distinct social existence, there must be ways of giving it structured social form. The next section address itself directly to this question of the social forms of religion and religions.

SOCIAL FORMS OF RELIGION AND RELIGIONS IN GLOBAL SOCIETY

To a large degree, the question of social form is another way of asking how religion/nonreligion and religion/religion boundaries are created and reproduced. Observation and categorization as religion is an important part of that, but various other mechanisms make the category concretely visible in our social worlds. These strategies can be divided into three dimensions, namely spatial, temporal, and social. We can isolate particular places as manifesting what we call religion; we can delimit specific times as religious times; and we can attach religion to certain persons. Thus, throughout the history of human societies, we find the more or less clear identification of sacred places, sacred times, and sacred persons. These have by no means been absolute distinctions: Sacred places can be temporary, sacred times can be vague as to their beginning and end, and persons can acquire and lose sacred status. Moreover, the implicit distinction between sacred and profane that such identification implies may itself be rather fluid given that in many of these social contexts, differentiating the religious from the nonreligious in any consistent way is not that important. For historical reasons, as outlined above, it is precisely this distinction, however, that is at issue in contemporary society. The development of powerful nonreligious social systems such as economy, state, science, or education provides the context for a more visible distinction of religion as something different. The notion of a plurality of religions means that this construction of religion will happen to a large extent as their carriers identify different religions in comparison and in contrast to others. This double challenge of institutionalizing religion as both "something else" in comparison to the putatively nonreligious and as a "different something" in contrast to other religions calls for forms and mechanisms that make clear when, where, and for whom which set of religious rules applies. All three of these modes of demarcation are important, but the "for whom" question in contemporary global society seems to be the one that is most consistently critical and contentious.

The most widespread social forms of religion and religions in contemporary society can be divided into four types: (a) organization, (b) state religion, (c) social movements, and (d) communitarian/individual.[5] The last category is the limiting case that also includes the boundary between religion that is institutionalized as such and that which is at best only analytically distinct. None of the four is mutually exclusive.

1. Organized Religion

One of the more notable features of contemporary global society is the proliferation of organizations in virtually every sphere of social life. Although these are certainly not evenly distributed in this society, any more than is wealth or power, they effect social life in all parts of the world. The most powerful of these are economic and political organizations. Yet, both at the national and the international level, an ever increasing number of nonbusiness and nonstate organizations make their presence felt in our daily lives. Among these is a complex array of religious organizations of greatly varying power, size, internal structure, and degree of stability. More than any of the other forms, it is organizations that give religions the concrete presence that is at issue here. Although the Christian Roman Catholic church (along with its numerous subsidiary organizations such as religious orders) is no doubt the largest and most evident of these, every other recognizable and recognized religion has them. They range from Buddhist monasteries to Hindu temple organizations, from Muslim Sufi brotherhoods (*tariqat*) to Christian Pentecostal churches, from organizations that run major Muslim, Hindu, or Christian pilgrimage centers to international Daoist societies. Their span can be anything from extremely local to worldwide, from the storefront church in Brooklyn, New York, to the international Orthodox Jewish Agudat Israel. Moreover, organizations are perhaps the most important mechanism for giving form to a new religion, or for concretizing variations in already recognized ones. Some relatively new religions such as the Baha'i Faith or the Church of Scientology, as well as old ones such as the Roman Catholic church, locate organization at their theological core and have successfully established themselves or maintained their presence largely through their concerted organizational strategies.

The great advantage of organization in contemporary global society is that it offers a very effective way of generating social boundaries that need not be all-encompassing. Organizations define themselves by making a distinction between those who belong and those who do not, between social action that is part of the organization and that which is not. They structure that difference through rules that govern belonging or not belonging, inside and outside, especially through social roles such as member, client, office holder, and so forth. Organizations thus tend to be quite clear about who is subject to their rules, when they are so subject, and where their most typical activity takes place. Moreover, organizations almost always articulate a clear purpose to which

---

[5] The typology suggested here may seem to bear some relation to the more familiar sociological typology of religious collectivities that distinguishes denomination, church, sect, and cult. While there is certainly an overlap as concerns the organized and state religion forms, the sect and cult have little place in the present scheme. To the extent that they are represented at all, it is under the organized, and to some extent under the social movement and communitarian forms. A precise comparison is beyond the scope of the present chapter, as is a detailed elaboration of the suggested typology.

their activity is oriented. As such, they can give concrete and representative form to intrinsically partial and abstract functions, goals, ideas, and categories. In a complex and pluralistic social environment, organizations are social structures well suited to carrying out differentiations that would otherwise be unsustainable or simply not recognized by many or even most members of the society. They range in their strategies from including some members of society totally to including all members of society for certain purposes and at certain times or in certain places. Most are located somewhere in between. Their internal structure can be quite clear as in formal organizations like business corporations, state bureaucracies, or universities. They also can take more informal shape, shading off in the extreme case into mere social networks centred on some purpose or idea.[6] The modern category or idea of religion(s), ambiguous, contested, and relatively recently constructed as it has been, benefits greatly from the possibilities afforded by the organizational social form. Indeed, without it, religion, like virtually every other major functional sphere, would have little hope of operating as a differentiated social domain at all. That, of course, includes the state.

2. Politicized Religion

As noted above, the carriers of religion in the contemporary world sometimes resist the category because it implies acceptance of the secularization of nonreligious domains and thereby the restriction of religion to its own domain. A common direction for this resistance to take is the politicization of religion, which is to say making the state and its legislative, legal, administrative, and military structures instruments for collectively enforcing the precepts and practices of the religion in question. This direction can yield a distinct social form of religion in contemporary society to the extent that religious structures become an express aspect or arm of the state; or, what amounts to the same, the state becomes an expression of the religion. The capacity of the state to set collectively binding norms for the people within its territorial boundaries and thus its ability to make a particular religion an unavoidable part of these people's daily lives lends the religion a clear presence as a religion over and beyond what nonstate religious organizations can do in this regard (e.g., Beyer 1994). Today, this way of giving religion form is most radically evident in certain Muslim countries like Iran and Afghanistan, but varying degrees of it also can be found in a number of other countries where state identities or ideologies include a particular religion. Examples of the latter would be Israel, India, Pakistan, Bangladesh, Zambia, Sri Lanka, Thailand, Indonesia, Russia, and, to an increasingly less effective sense, European countries like Great Britain, Sweden, or Germany. One should note, however, that in none of these cases does the religion in question, whether it is Islam, Christianity, Judaism, Buddhism, or Hinduism, lack organizational expression as well. State religion, or the use of the state to give social form to a religion is in that sense a supplementary form. Only through the extreme use of this possibility, such as in the case of the Taliban in Afghanistan, can the politicized or state form of religion become the primary form. In other instances in which organized religion is weak or contested, for example Hinduism in contemporary India, the involvement of the state apparatus in a vague and general way does relatively little

---

[6] For a good overview of the ranges that the form of organization can cover, see McCann (1993).

for the differentiation of the religion beyond giving its name a certain public symbolic prominence.

There is, of course, another side to the state giving form to religions, and this involves the already mentioned efforts of states to regulate religions and control what counts as religion. In most countries around the world, religion and religions have become a political issue in this sense. Some states, such as Indonesia, China, and to a lesser extent Russia, currently expressly limit what may count as religion to a restricted list. In Indonesia, only Islam, Protestantism, Catholicism, Hinduism, and Buddhism are recognized religions. In China it is the same list, only Daoism substitutes for Hinduism. In Russia, under current law, only religious organizations that had established themselves in Russia by a certain date count as legitimate religions. In most other countries, what counts as one of the religions is not that clearly spelled out, but disputes over new and marginal religious movements in countries as varied as Japan, Argentina, and France point to at least an implicit model of religion in operation, one that favors heavily the "world religions" and those with a long history in the country in question.

3. Social Movement Religion

Turning to the social movement as another way of giving form to religion, analysis reveals this as another supplementary form which is nonetheless sufficiently independent to warrant separate treatment. Exactly what constitutes a social movement is a much debated issue. For the present purposes, the description of certain common features can serve to delimit what is at issue. As the word indicates, social movements "move": They consist in the mobilization of people, ideas, and material resources to bring about change in existing social arrangements or to generate new ones (e.g., Klandermans et al. 1988; Zald and McCarthy 1987; Williams, Chapter 22, this volume). As such, in the contemporary world, they typically have organizations closely associated with them, but they are not simply coterminous with them. One thinks, for instance, of post-1960s social movements in the West such as the women's or environmental movement. Although each has organizations identified with it, such as the American National Organization of Women or Greenpeace, it is movement events like protests, diverse publications and public discussions, lobbying efforts, and other symbolic gestures that also give these movements their concrete social presence, to such an extent that it is these more than the organizations that call for names by which they can be called. Unlike organizations, the action that typically constitutes them is not so much member action but action by anyone that furthers and reproduces the movement. Social movements are thereby comparatively amorphous, lacking clear form, but they are nonetheless real as concerns social importance and effect. Movements, by contrast with organizations, rely far more on the symbolic possibilities of space and time, or particular places and particular times, than they do on particular people.

Most of those things commonly called religious movements in the sociological literature, especially the new religious movements, are in fact not social movements in the sense just described, but rather organizations that are founded at a particular time and seek to spread in terms of membership. This is the case with new religious movements such as the Brahma Kumaris, the Church of Scientology, Falun Gong, the Unification Church, or Soka Gakkai, religious organizations originating in India, the United States, China, Korea, and Japan, respectively. There are, however, other religious movements that would fall under this type quite clearly. Examples are Transcendental Meditation, New Age, neopaganism (Wicca), Tai Chi, and Qi Gong.[7] In each of these cases, although there may exist organizations associated with them – or, what amounts to the same, there also exist organized forms of these movements – the dominant form of participation is episodic, occasional, largely uncontrolled by any sort of convergent authority, and to the extent that it is regular, quite often individual as opposed to collective. In certain cases, such as Transcendental Meditation, there has been a move toward the clearly organized form in recent decades as the movement itself faded. In others, such as notably the example of Western neopaganism, the movement ideology rejects organization as illegitimate concentration of what is for them a basically individual religious authority. Neopagans of this sort will therefore congregate for specific events like festivals and local circle meetings, but there are few if any "rules of membership," let alone well-defined offices of a stable organization. Indicative of the relative distinctiveness of this social form of religion is that even those that wish deliberately to avoid greater convergence, organization, recognition by the state and other social agencies as a "religion," seem to find themselves under a fair amount of pressure to go just in these directions. In some cases like the neopagans, the primary reason may be the "freedom of religion" that such congregation and recognition typically brings. In others, such as Transcendental Meditation, the difficulty of maintaining the dynamism and constant mobilization of a movement may make the concentration and regularization of organization seem an attractive strategy to follow.

4. Communitarian/Individualistic Religion

The final form, communitarian/individualistic can be dealt with briefly because, as noted, it represents the boundary "form" between religion that is institutionalized as such, and that which is religious but unformed as religion except perhaps analytically by observers. In much of the world today, as in times past in most societies, what we now call religion is practiced locally and even regionally, but without a strong sense of the system of practices and beliefs being part of a larger whole or of it being a clearly differentiated activity called religion. Contemporary examples may be the local religious practices in India, China, or different parts of Africa, the religious dimensions of life among various aboriginal peoples all over the world, the individual and often idiosyncratic practices of individuals made famous by Bellah and his collaborators (Bellah et al. 1985) under the heading of "Sheilaism," and perhaps a whole array of cultural practices that have escaped incorporation into one of the religions. Examples of the latter would be Western "secular" celebrations of holidays such as Halloween, Easter (bunnies and eggs, not Jesus on the cross), and Groundhog Day. All of these manifestations are religious in the sense that one could and occasionally does observe them as religion. But they do not belong to that category in any consistent fashion because insiders do not seek to have them recognized as religion or reject such categorization; or because no formed and recognized religion successfully claims them. In fact, these manifestations can appear as religion only by association with the other forms. It is

---

[7] These latter two can also fall under Daoism, just as Transcendental Meditation may under some circumstances be claimed by Hinduism. Since the text is dealing with social forms rather than again the question of the boundaries of specific religions, I leave that issue aside here.

the formed religions that act as implicit models for religion as such, and therefore any sort of social activity that bears resemblance to them may on occasion be observed and treated as religion. The category itself has acquired this expansive capacity. This, however, raises the question that so many sociologists and other observers have raised with regard to religion: Are there defining characteristics that all those things that end up counting as religion have in common?

At the core of the analysis presented in this chapter is that, ultimately, it is the religions that determine what counts as religion, not a set of defining characteristics in abstraction from them (e.g., Beyer 2001). Nonetheless, as a general observation, we can say that almost all those forms that make up religion in this way seem to be centrally concerned with one manner or another of supra-empirical or transcendent dimension, realm, or beings which contrasts expressly with the empirical, material, ordinary, or immanent domain of other spheres of life and is seen from the religious perspective to be determinative of them. Moreover, almost all those things that fall under the category of religion exhibit some range of, usually ritual, techniques and procedures that claim to render communicative access to that transcendent domain. That said, however, the ways of understanding transcendence and the ways of constructing access to it vary so greatly among religions and in many ways bear clear resemblance to forms that are not deemed to be religion, that this formal commonality is by itself not sufficient to determine the practical boundary between religion and nonreligion. For this extra and critical step, the contrasts and forms that have been the topic of discussion in this chapter are much more determinative.

CHALLENGES OF RELIGIONS IN GLOBAL SOCIETY

In light of the variety of forms that religion and religions take in today's world and the contestations that are an integral part of that formation, it should not be surprising that the observation and study of religions rarely yields any sort of unanimity or even general agreement over what precisely is at issue. The modern category of religion and the religions is historically speaking a comparatively recent social construction and therefore attempts to understand "religion as such" are bound to run into difficulty if they do not take into account the social and historical context in which this construction has come to make sense. Religion in contemporary global society is not a well-delimited and self-evident form that is simply waiting for critical observation. It is rather more an important and somewhat arbitrary field of contestation (Bourdieu and Wacquant 1992) or differentiated societal system (Luhmann 2000) that gains its form and meaning entirely within the larger social context in which it operates. In this light, a more important question to pose of contemporary religion than what religion is or what it does (the substantive versus functional debate) is the question of what religion and the religions are becoming. Given that not everything conceivably religious ends up counting as religion, what kind of religion and religions does our contemporary situation favor? It is with a consideration of this question that this chapter concludes.

To address this question, one can return to the fundamental distinctions between religion and nonreligion and between one religion and another. From this perspective, one of three logical possibilities will inform the directions in which we are headed in global society. On the extreme ends, religion as a category may lose the distinct form that it currently has, yielding a situation in which religion will be perhaps an analytical category, but otherwise, to use Thomas Luckmann's (1967) term, religion will be "invisible." Equally extreme, all religions may meld into one, generating a single global religion like there is currently a single global economy. Judging by empirical trends thus far, both these possibilities seem anywhere from extremely unlikely to impossible. Distinctly religious forms, such as the ones just discussed, are if anything on the increase and certainly not on the decline as some secularization perspectives of the 1960s may have implied (e.g., Wilson 1969; Berger 1967; Luckmann 1967). There is also no sign that the very diverse religious directions that we currently see in the world are in any way heading toward convergence as one global religion; nor does any of the currently formed religions seem to have the wherewithal to absorb all others within itself. That may be the pious hope of many ardent Christians, Buddhists, Muslims, or other missionizing religion, but little empirical evidence points in such a direction.

With the extreme possibilities set aside, there remains only the continuation of the mixed and ambiguous situation that we currently have: A plurality of formed and identified religions in a context where the boundaries around the category are frequently contested by insiders and outsiders; and in which a significant amount of social action that can and does count as religion escapes consistent inclusion in one of these religions. If we accept that this possibility represents the fate of religion for the foreseeable future, the question that then comes to the forefront asks which religions are favored by the situation and what sort of broader social influence they can expect.

Given the historically somewhat arbitrary and accidental way in which the current group of religions have formed and been identified, one answer to this question is probably that contemporary global society very much favors those religions that have the most widely recognized identity and the most elaborate forms: The so-called world religions, first Christianity, Islam, Buddhism, Hinduism; and then on a somewhat smaller scale, Sikhism, Judaism, and Jainism. These are certainly the ones that are most consistently formally recognized and represented in state constitutions, legislation, and government policy. They are the main players in interreligious events like the formal interreligious dialogues and the recent World Parliament of Religions. And most of them exhibit a high level of organization and self-identification on the part of religious leaders and adherents. Their high level of public recognition also makes them the most likely candidates for the state-religion form discussed above.

Beside this relatively small group, however, the late-twentieth-century world also has been witness to the rise or continued elaboration of a wide variety of other religions which benefit from varied degrees of internal formation and external recognition. This group is quite large, but here are a few examples: Zoroastrianism, Umbanda, Daoism, Vodoun, Shinto, Mormonism, Baha'i, Cao Dai, Yoruba/Santería/Candomblé, Rastafarianism. And, finally, no observer can help marveling at the constant variety of new religions that arise, sometimes to fade into oblivion, sometimes to grow and aspire to recognized religion status. With all this formation and consolidation of religions throughout the world, it seems safe to predict that religion and the religions will remain an effective social category. The remaining and concluding question, however, is just how powerful the religions are or can become.

The frequency of the politicization of religion, especially in the form of religiopolitical movements around the world, gives us an indicator of how one might answer this question. The dominant rationale of such movements, ranging from liberation theological movements in Latin America and the Christian Right in the United States to Soka Gakkai in Japan and Hindu Nationalism in India, is that they seek to have religious orientations and precepts made the basis of collectively binding decisions and norms in a given country or region, and even the entire world. Another way of putting this is that they seek to make religion, and specifically a particular religion, a *public* and obligatory affair, not something restricted to the relatively *private* proclivities of its voluntary adherents (e.g., Beyer 1994). Such efforts are commensurate with the typical claims of religions to be providing access to the most solid and true foundations of all human existence, in essence to an absolute and transcendent reality. What the high incidence of religiopolitical movements indicates, however, is that such broad collective influence for religions is problematic, that it does not occur very often through the straightforward reproduction of religion among adherents. And indeed, this trend is not surprising given the combination of the secularization of the most powerful nonreligious social domains and the institutionalized pluralization of religions.

In terms of the distinctions that have been central to the present analysis, the religion/nonreligion difference along with the religion/religion distinction push religion and religions in the direction of a restricted domain in which one can participate through a large variety of religions, or not at all. Globally speaking, the situation is somewhat similar with other major collective and globalized categories like nations and cultures. The former have typically been identified with states and usually stand for or constitute the particular identity of a state, that which renders it distinct from all the others. The latter is also a highly contested category that, along with nation, is often bound up with the sorts of religiopolitical movements that are at issue. In this light, the politicization of religions is an intermittent but frequent response to the tendency toward the privatization of religion. It does not seem unreasonable to conclude, therefore, that broad power for religions will remain a concrete possibility in particular regions where a high degree of politicization succeeds; but that, in the light of the continued reproduction of a plurality of religions and the constant rise of new ones, privatization is just as, if not more, likely to represent the dominant trend. Ambiguity, it seems, is the constant companion of the modern global category and social forms of religion.

CHAPTER FIVE

The Evolution of the Sociology of Religion

Theme and Variations

Grace Davie

The beginnings of the sociology of religion are barely distinguishable from the beginnings of sociology per se. This is hardly surprising, given that its earliest practitioners were the founding fathers of sociology itself, all of whom were committed to the serious study of religion as a crucial variable in the understanding of human societies. Of course, they did this from different perspectives – the outlining of which will form an important part of the paragraphs that follow – but in the early days of the discipline, the paramount significance of religion for human living was taken for granted, if not universally approved. In later decades this significance was seriously questioned, not least by sociologists of religion themselves – a fact exemplified in their prolonged preoccupation with the secularization thesis. In the last two decades, however, the tide of opinion has begun to turn in a different direction, driven – very largely – by the overwhelming (and at times somewhat frightening) presence of religion in the modern world. Given the undeniable relevance of the religious factor to the geopolitical configurations of the new century, the sociological study of religion has gained a new urgency. New tools of analysis and new conceptual understandings are becoming increasingly necessary if sociologists are to understand (a) what is going on and (b) how they might contribute to an evidently important debate.

This trajectory – from taken-for-granted significance, through assumed decline, to a reestablished place in the canon – forms the theme of this chapter. It will be exemplified in various ways, referring in turn to theoretical debate, methodological endeavor, and substantive issues. It will, however, be overlaid, by a number of significant variations. In the main, these relate to the different contexts in which sociologists work, contrasts that take into account *both* national or regional differences *and* the pressures that derive from professional obligations (research does not take place in a vacuum). It is unlikely, for example, that a European sociologist employed by a Catholic organization in the immediate postwar period would be preoccupied by the same questions as an American working for a secular organization in the same decade. The fact that these two parts of the world were, then as now, experiencing entirely different patterns of growth and/or decline simply reinforces the point already made.

With this double aim in mind – that is, to establish and exemplify the theme, but at the same time to take into account at least some of the major variations – this chapter is structured as follows. It begins with an account of the founding fathers

(Karl Marx, Max Weber, and Emile Durkheim), underlining their enduring legacy to the sociology of religion – noting, however, that this legacy resonates differently. Not only do fashions come and go, but crucially in this case, the availability of good translation is a necessary preliminary for the great majority of readers. The lack of uniformity becomes even more explicit as the sociology of religion moves forward: An entirely different agenda emerges in Europe from that in the United States. The evolution in continental (primarily Catholic) Europe concerns, very largely, the emergence of a fully fledged sociology of religion from what has been called *sociologie religieuse*, a metamorphosis that took place in a part of the world heavily influenced by decline at least in the formal indicators of religious activity. Unsurprisingly, such debates are less relevant in the Anglo-Saxon world, where a very different way of working has evolved. These contrasting evolutions form the substance of the second section of the chapter.

The third will continue the contrast, introducing the two competing theoretical paradigms in the subdiscipline: secularization theory and rational choice theory. Both are covered in some detail in later chapters (e.g., Chapters 8 and 9). The point to be made in this chapter concerns the emergence of two contrasting theories at different times, in different places, to answer different questions – their roots go back centuries rather than decades (Warner 1997). This is far from being a coincidence; sociological thinking, like the world that it tries to explain, is contingent. The fourth and final section will suggest, however, that the time has come to move beyond these two paradigms (with the implication that either one or the other is correct, but not both) to more sophisticated tools of analysis, if we are to understand an increasingly global phenomenon. It is unlikely that one conceptual frame will suffice to explain all cases. A series of substantive examples will be used to illustrate both commonality and difference in the subject matter of sociology – across a range of global regions and in a wide variety of contexts.

THE FOUNDING FATHERS

In their sociological writing, Marx, Weber, and Durkheim were reacting to the economic and social upheavals of the late nineteenth and early twentieth centuries, prompted more often than not by the devastating consequences that rapid industrialization had inflicted on the European populations of which they were part. The study of religion could hardly be avoided within this framework, for religion was seen as an integral part of the society that appeared to be mutating beyond recognition. Each writer, however, tackled the subject from a different perspective (Giddens 1971; Löwith 1982; O'Toole 1984).

Karl Marx (1818–83) predates the others by at least a generation. There are two essential elements in the Marxist perspective on religion: The first is descriptive, the second evaluative. Marx described religion as a dependent variable; in other words, its form and nature are dependent on social and above all economic relations, which form the bedrock of social analysis. Nothing can be understood apart from the economic order and the relationship of the capitalist/worker to the means of production. The second aspect follows from this but contains an evaluative element. Religion is a form of alienation; it is a symptom of social malformation which disguises the exploitative relationships of capitalist society. Religion persuades people that such relationships are natural and, therefore, acceptable. It follows that the real causes of social distress cannot be tackled until the religious element in society is stripped away to reveal the injustices of the capitalist system; everything else is a distraction.

Subsequent debates concerning Marx's approach to religion have to be approached with care. It has become increasingly difficult to distinguish between (a) Marx's own analysis of religious phenomena, (b) a subsequent school of Marxism as a form of sociological thinking, and (c) what has occurred in the twentieth century in the name of Marxism as a political ideology. The essential and enduring point to grasp from Marx himself is that religion cannot be understood apart from the world of which it is part; this is a crucial sociological insight and central to the evolution of the subdiscipline. It needs, however, to be distinguished from an overdeterministic interpretation of Marx that postulates the dependence of religion on economic forces in mechanical terms; this is unhelpful. The final point is more political. It may indeed be the case that one function of religion is to mitigate the very evident hardships of this world and so disguise them. Marx was correct to point this out. Nowhere, however, does Marx legitimate the destructive doctrines of those Marxist regimes that maintained that the only way to reveal the true injustices of society was to destroy – sometimes with hideous consequences – the religious element of society. Marx himself took a longer-term view, claiming that religion would disappear of its own accord given the advent of the classless society: Quite simply, it would no longer be necessary. The inevitable confusions between Marx, Marxism, and Marxist regimes have, however, had a profound effect on the reception of Marx's ideas in the twentieth century. The total, dramatic, and unforeseen collapse of Marxism as an effective political creed in 1989 is but the last twist in a considerably longer tale.

In many ways, Max Weber's (1864–1920) contribution to the sociology of religion should be seen in this light. Rather than simply refuting Marx, Weber's theorizing vindicates much of what Marx himself suggested, as opposed to the vulgarizations of later disciples. Weber stresses the multicausality of social phenomena, not least religion; in so doing he conclusively refutes the standpoint of 'reflective materialism' whereby the religious dimensions of social living simply reflect the material (Giddens 1971: 211). But the causal sequence is not simply reversed; indeed, the emergence of what Weber calls "elective affinities" between material and religious interests are entirely compatible with Marx's own understanding of ideology. The process by which such affinities come into being must, however, be determined empirically – they vary from case to case.

Weber's influence spread into every corner of sociology, never mind the sociology of religion, generating a huge secondary literature – the remarks that follow are inevitably skeletal. Absolutely central, however, to Weber's understanding of religion is the conviction that this aspect of human living can be constituted as something other than, or separate from society or "the world." Three points follow from this (Beckford 1989: 32). First, the relationship between religion and the world is contingent and variable; how a particular religion relates to the surrounding context will vary over time and in different places. Second, this relationship can only be examined in its historical and cultural specificity. Documenting the details of these relationships (of which elective affinities are but one example) becomes, therefore, the central task of the sociologist of religion. Third, the relationship tends to develop in a determinate direction; a statement which indicates that the distance between the two spheres, religion and society, is being steadily eroded in modern societies. This erosion, to the point where the religious factor ceases to be an effective force in society, lies at the heart of the process known as secularization – through which the world becomes progressively "disenchanted."

These three assumptions underpin Weber's *magnum opus* in the field, *The Sociology of Religion* (Weber 1922/1993), that is, his comparative study of the major world faiths and their impact on everyday behavior in different parts of the world. Everyday behavior, moreover, becomes cumulative as people adapt and change their lifestyles; hence, the social consequences of religious decisions. It is at this point that the question of definition begins to resonate, for it is clear that, *de facto* at least, Weber is working with a substantive definition of religion, despite his celebrated unwillingness to provide a definition as such. He is concerned with the way that the *content* (or substance) of a particular religion, or more precisely a religious ethic, influences the way that people behave. In other words, different types of belief have different outcomes. Weber goes on to elaborate this theme: The relationship between ethic and behavior not only exists, it is socially patterned and contextually varied. Central to Max Weber's understanding in this respect is, once again, the complex relationship between a set of religious beliefs and the particular social stratum that becomes the principal carrier of such beliefs in any given society. Not everyone has to be convinced by the content of religious teaching for the influence of the associated ethic to be widespread. The sociologist's task is to identify the crucial social stratum at the key moment in history; it requires careful comparative analysis.

Such questions, moreover, can be posed in ways that are pertinent to the twenty-first century rather than the early modern period, the focus of Weber's attentions. One such, for instance, might engage the issue of gender rather than class or social stratum: Why is it that women seem to be more preoccupied by religion than men at least in the Christian West (Walter and Davie 1998)? Will the disproportionate influence of women as the principal carriers of the religious tradition in modern Western societies have an effect on the content of the tradition itself, or will a male view continue to dominate despite the preponderance of women in the churches? What is the relationship between lifestyle and belief in such societies when the roles of men and women are evolving so rapidly?[1] Such questions are just a beginning, but indirectly at least they build on the work of Max Weber; the approach, once established, can be taken in any number of directions. Inquiries also could be made, for example, about minority groups, especially in societies that are both racially and religiously diverse; it is likely that minorities – and the key carriers within them – will sustain their traditions in ways rather different from the host society, a contrast that leads at times to painful misunderstandings.

Emile Durkheim (1858–1917), the exact contemporary of Weber, began from a very different position. Working outward from his study of totemic religion among Australian Aborigines, he became convinced above all of the binding qualities of religion: "Religion celebrates, and thereby reinforces, the fact that people can form societies" (Beckford 1989: 25). In other words, his perspective is a functional one. Durkheim is concerned above all with what religion does; it binds people together.

---

[1]   A recently published account of religion in Britain (Brown 2001) turns on precisely this point: That is, the crucial importance of women in the religious life of Britain up to and indeed after World War II. The 1960s and, more especially, the feminist revolution were the watershed in this respect – no longer were women prepared to be the carriers of familial piety. Not everyone would agree with this argument, but Brown is undoubtedly correct to highlight the significance of gender in the analysis of religious change (and not only in Britain).

What then will happen when time-honored forms of society begin to mutate so fast that traditional patterns of religion inevitably collapse? How will the essential functions of religion be fulfilled? This was the situation confronting Durkheim in France in the early part of the twentieth century (Lukes 1973; Pickering 1975). Durkheim responded as follows: The religious aspects of society should be allowed to evolve alongside everything else, in order that the symbols of solidarity appropriate to the developing social order (in this case incipient industrial society) may emerge. The theoretical position follows from this: Religion as such will always be present for it performs a necessary *function*. The precise nature of that religion will, however, differ between one society and another and between different periods of time in order to achieve an appropriate "fit" between religion and the prevailing social order. The systemic model, so dear to functionalists, is immediately apparent.

Of the early sociologists, Durkheim was the only one to provide his own definition of religion. It has two elements:

> A religion is a unified system of beliefs and practices relative to sacred things, that is to say, things which are set apart and forbidden – beliefs and practices which unite into one single moral community called a Church, all those who adhere to them. (Durkheim 1912/1976: 47)

First there is the celebrated distinction between the sacred (the set apart) and the profane (everything else); there is an element of substantive definition at this point. The sacred, however, possesses a *functional* quality not possessed by the profane; by its very nature it has the capacity to bind, for it unites the collectivity in a set of beliefs and practices which are focused on the sacred object. Acting collectively in a moral community, following Durkheim, is of greater sociological importance than the object of such actions. The uncompromisingly "social" aspects of Durkheim's thinking are both an advantage and disadvantage. The focus is clearly distinguishable from the psychological (a good thing), but the repeated emphasis on society as a reality *sui generis* brings with it the risk of a different sort of reductionism – taken to its logical conclusion religion is nothing more than the symbolic expression of social experience. Such a conclusion disturbed many of Durkheim's contemporaries; it is still to some extent problematic, and for sociologists as well as theologians (but see Bellah, Chapter 3, this volume).

The evolution of the sociology of religion cannot be understood without extensive knowledge of the founding fathers and their continuing influence (O'Toole 1984, 2000). A further point is, however, important. The availability of their writing should not simply be assumed; it depended (indeed it still depends) amongst other things on competent and available translations. Willaime (1999), for example, underlines the fact that the arrival of Weberian thinking in French sociology in the early postwar period offered significant alternatives to those who were trying to understand the changes in the religious life of France at this time. Weber's work (or to be more accurate parts of his work) became available in English almost a generation earlier (*General Economic History, The Protestant Ethic and the Spirit of Capitalism*).[2] It follows that a careful mapping of the dates of translations of key texts between German, French, and English would

---

[2] Swatos, Kivisto, and Gustafson (1998) stress an additional point. Quite apart from the question of translation, Weber's acceptance into English-speaking sociology was curiously delayed; he remained relatively unknown until his discovery by Talcott Parsons. The arrival of large

reveal interesting combinations of theoretical resources in different European societies (as indeed in the United States). What was available to whom in the development of theoretical thinking is not something that should be taken for granted; it could and should be subject to empirical investigation.

THE SECOND GENERATION: OLD WORLD AND NEW

In fact, almost half a century passed before a second wave of activity took place. It came, moreover, from a very different quarter – from within the churches themselves. Such activity took different forms on different sides of the Atlantic. In the United States, where religious institutions remained relatively buoyant and where religious practice continued to grow, sociologists of religion in the early twentieth century were, very largely, motivated by and concerned with the social gospel. A second, rather less positive, theme ran parallel; one in which religion became increasingly associated with the social divisions of American society. *The Social Sources of Denominationalism* (Niebuhr 1929) and rather later *Social Class in American Protestantism* (Demerath 1965) are titles that represent this trend.

By the 1950s and 1960s, however, the principal focus of American sociology lay in the normative functionalism of Talcott Parsons, who stressed above everything the integrative role of religion. Religion – a functional prerequisite – was central to the complex models of social systems and social action elaborated by Parsons. In bringing together these two elements (i.e., social systems and social action), Parsons was drawing on both Durkheim and Weber. Or, as Lechner puts this, "Durkheim came to provide the analytical tools for Parsons's ambivalent struggle with Weber" (Lechner 1998: 353). Ambivalent this struggle may have been, but Parsons's influence was lasting; it can be seen in subsequent generations of scholars, notably Robert Bellah and Niklas Luhmann. The relationship with American society is also important. The functionalism of Parsons emerged from a social order entirely different from either the turbulence that motivated the Founding Fathers or the long-term confrontations between church and state in the Catholic nations of Europe, most notably in France (see later); postwar America symbolized a settled period of industrialism in which consensus appeared not only desirable but possible. The assumption that the social order should be underpinned by religious values was widespread.

Such optimism did not last. As the 1960s gave way to a far less confident decade, the sociology of religion shifted once again. This time to the social construction of meaning systems epitomized by the work of Berger and Luckmann (1966). The Parsonian model is inverted; social order exists but it is constructed from below. So constructed, religion offers believers crucial explanations and meanings which they use to make sense of their lives, not least during times of personal or social crisis. Hence Berger's (1967) idea of religion as a form of "sacred canopy" that shields both individual and society from "the ultimately destructive consequences of a seemingly chaotic, purposeless existence" (Karlenzig 1998). The mood of the later 1970s, profoundly shaken by the oil crisis and its effects on economic growth, reflects the need for meaning and purpose (no longer could

---

numbers of German scholars in the United States as the result of Hitler's rise to power hastened a process that had already started in the 1930s. A second "renaissance" occurred in the West as a whole in the 1980s.

these simply be assumed). The 1970s merge, moreover, into the modern period, a world in which conflict – including religious conflict – rather than consensus dominates the agenda (Beckford 1989: 8–13). Religion has not only become increasingly prominent but also increasingly contentious.

In Western Europe, the sociology of religion was evolving along very different lines. Religious institutions on this side of the Atlantic were far from buoyant, a situation displayed in the titles published in France in the early years of the war. The most celebrated of these, *La France, pays de mission* (Godin and Daniel 1943), illustrates the mood of a growing group within French Catholicism who were increasingly worried by the weakening position of the Church in French society. Anxiety proved, however, a powerful motivator. In order that the situation might be remedied, accurate information was essential; hence, a whole series of enquiries under the direction of Gabriel Le Bras with the intention of discovering what exactly characterized the religion of the people, or lived religion (*la religion vécue*) as it became known?

Accurate information acquired, however, a momentum of its own, which led to certain tensions. There were those, in France and elsewhere, whose work remained motivated by pastoral concern; there were others who felt that knowledge was valuable for its own sake and resented the ties to the Catholic Church. What emerged in due course was an independent section within the Centre National de la Recherche Scientifique, the Groupe de Sociologie *des Religions*. The change in title was significant: "Religious sociology" became "the sociology of religions" in the plural. There was, however, continuity as well as change. The initial enthusiasm for mapping, for example, which began with Boulard and Le Bras on rural Catholicism (1947), and continued through the work of Boulard and Rémy on urban France (1968), culminated in the magnificent *Atlas de la pratique religieuse des catholiques en France* (Isambert et Terrenoire 1980). Alongside such cartographical successes developed explanations for the geographical differences that emerged. These explanations were primarily historical, their sources lay deep within regional cultures. There was nothing superficial about this analysis that could, quite clearly, be applied to religions other than Catholicism.

Willaime (1995: 37–57; 1999), Voyé and Billiet (1999), and Hervieu-Léger and Willaime (2001) tell this primarily French (or more accurately francophone) story in more detail: that is, the emergence of accurate and careful documentation motivated primarily by pastoral concerns, the establishment of the Groupe de Sociologie des Religions in Paris in 1954, the gradual extension of the subject matter beyond Catholicism, the development of a distinctive sociology of Protestantism, the methodological problems encountered along the way, and, finally, the emergence of an international organization and the "deconfessionalization" of the sociology of religion. The evolution of the Conférence internationale de sociologie religieuse, founded in Leuven in 1948, through the Conférence internationale de sociologie des religions (1981) to the present Société internationale de sociologie des religions (1989) epitomizes this story. It marks a shift from a group primarily motivated by religion to one that is motivated by science, an entirely positive feature. It is, however, a story that emerges – and could only emerge – from a particular intellectual context, Catholic Europe. Such initiatives have been crucial to the development of the sociology of religion; they lead, however, to preoccupations that are not always shared by scholars from other parts of the world.

The British case forms an interesting hybrid within this bifurcation: British sociologists of religion draw considerably on American (English-speaking) literature, but operate in a European context – that is, one of low levels of religious activity. In many ways, they face in two directions at once (Davie 2000). They are more influenced by pluralism than most of their continental colleagues (hence a long-term preoccupation with new religious movements rather than popular religion); this fits well with the American literature. The parameters of religious activity in Britain are, however, very different from those in the United States and here the work of American scholars has proved less helpful. What is evident, however, is the inability of most (if not quite all) British – and American – scholars to access the sociological literature in any language other than their own. The question of translation continues to resonate. Most continental scholars can do better, leading to a noticeable imbalance in sociological writing. Many of the latter, for example, make reference to the English-speaking literature in their work; the reverse, however, is seldom the case until the pressure to provide an English language edition becomes overwhelming.

THE TWO PARADIGMS: SECULARIZATION THEORY VERSUS RATIONAL CHOICE

These differences in emphasis between European and American sociology continue into the contemporary period, and with important theoretical consequences. Contrasting religious situations have led not only to very different conceptual formulations but also to a lively debate concerning the scope or range of each approach. In Europe, for example, what has become know as the secularization thesis remains the dominant paradigm (although markedly less so as time goes on); in North America, rational choice theory has offered a convincing alternative. The substance of both these theories, together with the polemics that surround them, will be considered in Part II of this volume; there is no need to embark on that enterprise here. What is important in terms of a chapter concerned with the different evolutions of the sociology of religion is (a) the genesis of each theoretical outlook and (b) the scope and range of their possible application. The two points are interrelated.

Warner's (1993) article on a new paradigm[3] for the sociological study of religion in the United States, for example, marks a watershed in American understandings of their own society. From this point on, the secularization thesis, already critiqued by increasing numbers of scholars on both sides of the Atlantic, has to justify its applicability to the American situation; no longer can its scope be taken for granted.[4] Obviously the process is a gradual one, and as Warner himself makes clear, his own article was part of the process that he was trying to describe; in retrospect, however, no scholar can afford to ignore this contribution to the literature, whether they agree with it or not. Decisions have to be made regarding the appropriateness of secularization theory to the American case (or indeed to any other), where once they were simply assumed.

Even more essential to a chapter concerned with sociological variations, however, is the point introduced by Warner in the 1993 article, but considerably expanded in 1997

---

[3] The terms "new paradigm" and "rational choice theory" are almost interchangeable. As Warner himself makes clear, their meanings are close if not quite identical.

[4] The continuing debates in the *Journal for the Scientific Study of Religion*, together with the collection of papers brought together by Young (1997), provide ample proof of the tenacity with which scholars, both European and American, adhere to either the secularization debate or the new paradigm as their preferred mode of theorizing.

(Warner 1997: 194–6): namely, the European origins of the secularization thesis as opposed to the American genesis of the new paradigm. The beginnings of the two models go back centuries rather than decades. To be more precise, the secularization thesis finds its roots in medieval Europe some eight hundred years ago. The key element is the existence of a monopoly church with authority over the whole society; both church and authority are kept in place by a series of formal and informal sanctions. It is, moreover, the monopoly itself that provides the plausibility structure – the authority is not only unquestioned, but unquestionable. Given the inseparability of monopoly and plausibility, the latter will inevitably be undermined by increasing ideological and cultural pluralism, a relentless process with multiple causes. Documenting this process, or gradual undermining, is a central task of sociologists, who quite correctly describe their subject matter (a metanarrative) as the process of secularization.

The alternative paradigm, or metanarrative, begins rather later – say, two hundred rather than eight hundred years ago and in the new world not the old, to be more precise in the early years of the United States as an independent nation. Here there was no monopoly embodied in a state church, simply a quasi-public social space that no single group could dominate. All kinds of different groups or denominations emerged to fill this space, each of them utilizing particular religious markers as badges of identity (religion was much more important in this respect than social class). Simply surviving required considerable investment of time, talent, and money, not least to attract sufficient others to one's cause in face of strong competition. The possibilities of choice were endless, and choice implies rejection as well as acceptance. The affinities with modern-day America are immediately apparent, a situation admirably described in Ammerman's *Congregations and Community* (Ammerman 1997a). Such a book could not have been written about Europe.

Interestingly, as Warner himself makes clear, the classics can be drawn on in both situations, although in rather different ways. Identities, for example, can be constructed in Durkheimian terms in relation to the whole society (in Europe) or to a particular community within this (in the United States). Likewise, Protestant sects can be seen as undermining a European monopoly or, rather more positively, as competitors in an American market – either way, Weber's insights are helpful. Conversely, attempts to impose either the secularization or the rational choice (religious economies) paradigm wholesale on to the alternative context really do cause trouble. Such attempts arise from a conviction that one paradigm, and only one, must be right in all circumstances. That, in my view, is mistaken. Which is not to say that elements of each approach cannot be used to enlighten certain aspects of the alternative situation – clearly, that can be done and to considerable effect. A useful illustration of positive application can be found, for instance, in Hamberg and Pettersson's (1994) testing of the rational choice hypothesis in different regions of Sweden. More precisely, the authors investigate the effect of pluralism on religious activity in Sweden. Their findings support the rational choice approach and in one of the most religiously homogeneous societies of Europe.

The crucial point to grasp, however, lies very much deeper and illustrates, once again, the essential difference between Europe and the United States in terms of religious understandings. More specifically, it lies in the fact that Europeans, as a consequence of the state church system (an historical fact whether you like it or not) regard their churches as public utilities rather than competing firms. That is the real legacy of the European past. With this in mind, it is hardly surprising that Europeans bring to their religious organizations an entirely different repertoire of responses from their American counterparts. Most Europeans, it is clear, look at their churches with benign benevolence – they are useful social institutions, which the great majority in the population are likely to need at one time or another in their lives (not least at the time of a death). It simply does not occur to most of them that the churches will or might cease to exist but for their active participation. It is this attitude of mind that is both central to the understanding of European religion and extremely difficult to eradicate. It, rather than the presence or absence of a market, accounts for a great deal of the data on the European side of the Atlantic. It is not that the market isn't there (it quite obviously is in most parts of Europe, if not quite in all); it is simply that the market doesn't work, given the prevailing attitudes of large numbers in the population.

What I am trying to say, using a geographical rather than sociological metaphor, is that a map of the Rockies (i.e., more rigorous versions of rational choice theory) has to be adapted for use in Europe – just like the map of the Alps (secularization theory) for those who venture in the reverse direction. The map of the Rockies can, however, open up new and pertinent questions if used judiciously and not only to test the significance of religious pluralism strictly speaking (see Hamberg and Pettersson 1994). Interesting possibilities emerge, for example, in the cultural as well as organizational applications of rational choice theory (RCT) – not least with respect to televangelism. Why is it that the European market fails to operate with respect to this particular form of religion? Or to put the point even more directly, why has it not been possible to *create* a market for this particular product? Is it simply the lack of a suitable audience or is something more subtle at stake?[5] It might, in addition, be useful to examine in more depth, and over a longish historical period, the relationship between capital and religion in Europe. In different historical periods, this has been extremely strong (hence, for example, the wealth of religious art and architecture, particularly in Southern Europe – Tuscan examples come particularly to mind). Currently, however, the relationship is weak, or at least much weaker, although it is interesting to discover how much Europeans are willing to invest in their religious buildings at the turn of the millennium, even among Nordic populations where churchgoing is notoriously low (Bäckström and Bromander 1995). Used imaginatively, RCT can open up new and interesting areas of enquiry on both sides of the Atlantic.

All too easily, however, the debate turns into a sociological fight to the death in which one paradigm has to emerge the winner. One form of this "fight" can be found in repeated attempts to identify the real "exceptionalism." Is this to be the United States, that is, a vibrant religious market in a highly developed country, but clearly without parallel in the modern (developed) world? Or is this to be Europe, the only part of the world in which secularization can be convincingly linked to modernization, but no longer – as was assumed for so long – a global prototype with universal applicability? Casanova (2001) is one author anxious to escape from this repetitive and circular argument; we need, he argues, to think increasingly in global terms.

---

[5] There is plenty of evidence that Europeans feared that televangelism would penetrate European culture given the increasing deregulation of the media; in Britain, for example, it became a major preoccupation in parliamentary debate (Quicke and Quicke 1992).

BEYOND THE PARADIGMS: A GLOBAL CHALLENGE

What, then, confronts the sociologist of religion who is willing to take the global challenge seriously? This question can be answered in two ways – first, by using a geographical frame, and then by considering a range of global social movements that are essentially religious in nature. Both approaches have implications for empirical as well as theoretical sociology and both can be found in the useful collection of essays edited by Berger (1999).

A Geographical Perspective

In the previous sections, a firm distinction was made between the old world and the new, contrasting both the empirical realities and the sociological thinking in Europe with their counterparts in the United States. Without, for the time being, venturing beyond Christianity, it is now necessary to take into account at least parts of the developing world: Latin America, sub-Saharan Africa and the Christianized parts of the Far East (for example South Korea and the Philippines). In none of these places are the indicators of secularization persuasive; quite the reverse, in fact, as traditional forms of Christianity compete with innovative expressions of the faith – notably widespread and popular Pentecostalism – for the attentions, in many cases, of growing populations. It is true that the traditional disciplines of the Christian churches may be breaking down, but not in favor of the secular. The movement, rather, is toward new (much less controllable) expressions of Christianity and emergent hybrids, notably in the Latin American case, where an individual may be one thing in the morning (a Christian denomination) and quite another (not least an Afro-Brazilian variant) in the afternoon. Add to this already extensive list the parts of the world dominated by other world faiths – the hugely varied Islamic nations, the competing religious traditions of the Middle East, the Sikhs and Hindus of the Indian subcontinent and the great diversity of Eastern religions – and Berger's claim that the developing world is "as furiously religious as ever" seems well justified (Berger 1992: 32).

In geographical terms, the only possible exceptions to a religious worldview are Japan and West Europe, together with West Europe's outposts in the form of the English-speaking Dominions – all of which, it is important to note, constitute developed global regions. (The great unknown remains, of course, the immense Chinese population, in which it is still difficult to predict what is likely to happen in religious terms both in the short and long term.) The fact that the two most secularized parts of the globe are two of the most developed does, however, give pause for thought regarding the possible connections of modernization and secularization – the core of both modernization and secularization theory (Inglehart 1990, 1997).[6] These cases, however, need to be balanced against the United States, which – it is abundantly clear – remains a very notable exception; the relationship is by no means proven.

The situation is, in fact, confused rather than clear-cut, a fact revealed in the rich selection of material brought together in Heelas and Woodhead (2000), and increasingly in the most recent textbooks concerned with the sociology of religion (Aldridge 2000).

---

[6] Interestingly, Inglehart's most recent account is rather more nuanced. Economic modernization is indeed associated with value change, but such change is path dependent. In other words, the broad cultural heritage of a society (not least the religious element) leaves an imprint that endures despite modernization (Inglehart and Baker 2000).

It becomes increasingly apparent, for example, that different trends may well coexist *within* the same society, quite apart from the contrasts between different global regions. We need tools of analysis that are able to cope with this complexity.

Thematic Approaches

A thematic approach to the same question tackles the material from a different perspective – looking in turn at three global social movements: (a) global Catholicism, (b) popular Pentecostalism, and (c) the possibly overlapping category of fundamentalism (encompassing a variety of world faiths).

Casanova (2001) points out the paradox in modern currents of Catholicism. At precisely the moment when European expressions of Catholicism begin to retreat almost to the point of no return – as the convergence between state and church through centuries of European history becomes increasingly difficult to sustain – Catholicism takes on new and global dimensions. It becomes a *trans*national religious movement, and as such has grown steadily since 1870 (the low point of the European Church). The Papal Encyclicals from this time on are concerned primarily with the dignity of the human person and with human (not only Catholic) rights, a movement that accelerates rapidly as a result of the Second Vatican Council. Transnational Catholic movements begin to grow (for example, Liberation Theology, the *Opus Dei* and *Communione e Liberazione*), centers of learning become equally international, so, too, does the Roman Curia emerging as it does from cross-cutting, transnational networks. One aspect of such links is the growing tendency toward movement, manifested among other things in the increasing popularity of pilgrimage. Most visible of all, however, is the person of the Pope himself, without doubt a figure of global media proportions. The Pope goes nowhere without planeloads of the world's media accompanying him, and his health is the subject of constant and minute speculation in the international press. Conversely the capacity of the Pope to draw huge crowds of Catholics (not least young people) to one place can be illustrated in the World Youth Days that took place as part of the millennium celebrations in Rome 2000: Two million young people came together in the final all-night vigil and Sunday morning mass at the Tor Vergata University (August 19–20). Few, if any, secular organizations could compete with these numbers.

It is hardly surprising that the different elements that make up this increasingly global movement attract negative as well as positive comments. That is not the point. The point is the existence of a transnational form of religion with, at the very least, considerable influence on a wide range of moral and ethical debates, crucial factors for the sociologist of religion at the beginning of the twenty-first century.

Global Pentecostalism is rather different in that its immediate impact is less visible. Its effect on huge and probably growing numbers of individuals is, however, undeniable, a phenomenon that is attracting the attention of increasing numbers of scholars and in a variety of disciplines. The literature, as a result, is growing fast (see, for example, Corten 1997).

Coleman (2001), Freston (2001), and Martin (2002) offer state-of-the-art accounts of this phenomenon, each concentrating on a different dimension. Coleman, for example, is primarily concerned with "Health and Wealth" Christians and how they establish effective global communications, not least by means of electronic technologies. Freston concentrates on the political dimensions of evangelical Christianity, an aspect that is particularly difficult to discern given the fragmented, fissiparous, and often apolitical (at least in a conventional sense) nature of the movement. Martin, in contrast, is concerned first and foremost with the cultural aspects of Pentecostalism, and more especially with cultural change. His book is wide ranging, covering the diaspora populations of the Far East in addition to North America, Latin America, and sub-Saharan Africa. The movement of Pentecostal Christians from one part of the world to another and the ways in which their churches enable such migrations (both culturally in terms of motive and organizationally in terms of welcome) provides an important cross-cutting theme.

As a postscript to this discussion, it is important to note that, in a developed theoretical chapter, Martin pays considerable attention to the absence of Pentecostalism as a widespread and popular movement in both Europe and the United States. Currents of Pentecostalism do, of course, exist in Europe – both within and outside the historical churches – but they are not large in numerical terms (nor in consequence all that influential). In terms of global Pentecostalism, the notion of European exceptionalism appears to gain a certain credibility.[7] The American case is rather different. Here it is the vigorous nature of the evangelical constituency that is resistant to newer forms of Pentecostalism. In other words, the movement exists, but is substantially contained within the existing denominations; there is no need to "walk out" (Martin's term) into new forms of religious organization to find salvation. It follows, however, that neither the European nor the American experience will be all that helpful in understanding popular Pentecostalism in other parts of the world; there is a need for more innovative sociological thinking.

Fundamentalism(s) – whether in the singular or in the plural – is one of the most controversial and debated terms in both academic and popular discussion. One focus of this debate concerns the largely unresolved issue of whether a term that was used initially to describe currents of conservative Protestantism popular in the early twentieth century in parts of the United States can be helpfully transposed to a series of trends visible in a variety of world faiths some sixty or seventy years later (a theme that picks up the central argument of this chapter). The fact that the terminology is difficult should not, however, detract from the evidence that these trends are indeed taking place – reversing in many ways the expectations of the Western (often European) observer, who assumed not only decreasing levels of global religiosity as the twentieth century drew to a close, but that such religion as continued to exist would manifest increasingly "reasonable" tendencies.

That did not happen, at least not universally. What has happened – in different places and in different world faiths – has been the emergence of a range of reactive, conservative religious movements, resisting, in some cases, the modernizing trends evident within the major faiths (modern biblical criticism, for example) or, in others, the incursions of modernization (very often associated with secularization) from the outside. Once again, the scholarly literature is immense. A huge, and – to some extent – representative set of volumes (although not everyone would agree with its findings) can be found in the *Fundamentalism Project*, published through the early 1990s by the University of Chicago Press (Marty and Appleby 1995). For our purposes, two aspects can be drawn from this vast accumulation of scholarship: First, the discussion of the

---

[7] Partial exceptions to the exception exist on the margins of Europe. See, for example, the gypsy population of parts of central Europe and the interesting case study taken from Southern Italy quoted in Martin (2002).

concept of fundamentalism itself and, second, the range and location of the case studies which form the heart of the empirical project.

The great variety of movements that are considered under the heading of "fundamentalism" display what the authors call "family resemblances" – leading to the creation of an "ideal-type" (in the Weberian sense) of fundamentalism, against which any particular case can be measured. Not all examples will meet all the criteria set out, but in order to be included they need to meet a minimum number. Several subtypes emerge within the overall concept. The important point to grasp, however, is the notion of fundamentalism as a "heuristic device," which enables us to examine – not, it is important to remember, always to approve – a wide variety of religious movements currently active in the modern world.

The associated case studies are taken from all the major world faiths and from almost all parts of the globe. What, however, is striking from the point of view of a chapter concerned with the different contexts of sociological development is, once again, the relative absence of examples from Europe, although not in this case from America. The three potential candidates for Europe are the following: Traditional "Lefebvre type" Catholicism, Ulster Protestantism, and the Italian-based youth movement – *Communione e Liberazione* (already mentioned in connection with global Catholicism). In terms of the ideal-type of fundamentalism, however, none of the three fit the criteria completely or convincingly. The first is closer to traditionalism than a reactive fundamentalist movement, the second is more of an ethnic nationalism than a social movement, and the last has been described by Italian commentators (Pace and Guolo 1998) as a "fondamentalismo ben temperato"; it is, in other words, a partial illustration of fundamentalism, displaying some of the "family resemblances" but lacking, in particular, any sustained reference to a sacred text.

The American case raises rather different issues, some of which connect very directly with the rational choice paradigm introduced in the previous section. Conservative forms of Protestantism (and perhaps of Catholicism, too), whether these are full-fledged fundamentalisms or not, quite clearly form an important part of the American religious market. One of the most successful applications of rational choice theory, moreover, has been to explain the relative popularity of conservative (high cost) as opposed to liberal (low cost) choices in the religious life of the United States (Iannaccone 1992a, 1994). Rather more problematic, however, are the attempts to apply the same type of theorizing to forms of fundamentalism found outside America – in places, for example, where the concept of the market has virtually no resonance. In such cases, additional factors have to be taken into account to understand the reactive, high cost, and, at times, violent nature of religious activity.

Bearing such complexities in mind, how should the sociologist of religion working at the beginning of the new century proceed? First, surely, by acknowledging the urgency of the task – we need to understand what is happening given the salience of the religious factor in geopolitics of the modern world. Then, perhaps, by returning to the essentially Weberian statement invoked in the introductory paragraphs of this chapter, namely that sociological thinking, like the world it tries to explain, is contingent. With this in mind, it is very unlikely that one theoretical frame – be it European or American or another – will fit all cases. This does not mean that either secularization theory or rational choice theory should be totally abandoned; they should however be used judiciously and are likely to make more sense in some parts of the world than in others.[8]

Whatever the theoretical difficulties, it is abundantly clear – given the nature of the religious phenomena described in this section – that a global frame of reference is increasingly necessary. And within such a framework, careful comparative analysis becomes the most obvious way to work if we are to reveal the specific features of particular cases, from which accumulations of data begin to emerge. Patterns and connections begin to form, which in turn suggest heuristic (and sometimes full-fledged theoretical) possibilities, for example the "ideal type" of fundamentalisms already outlined. Martin's work on global Pentecostalisms offers another example (Martin 2002). Building from encyclopedic reading in the field, largely of relatively small-scale anthropological studies, Martin constructs a framework through which to "make sense" of these very different situations. The framework is strong enough to guide the reader's thinking, but sufficiently flexible to allow the empirical material to speak for itself. Among many emergent themes, Martin makes it abundantly clear that circumstances alter cases, once again underlining the essential point: The world is indeed contingent and effective sociological thinking must take account of this fact, if it is to understand (or even begin to understand) the bewildering variety of ways in which religion and modernity interconnect.

---

[8] It is interesting, for example, that Finke and Stark's contribution to this volume makes reference to both the Latin American (Pentecostal) and the fundamentalist cases. RCT undoubtedly sheds light on these examples (especially the former), alongside other theoretical perspectives. Gill's work (1998, 1999) on Latin America is particularly helpful in this respect.

PART TWO

Religion and Social Change

CHAPTER SIX

Demographic Methods for the Sociology of Religion

Michael Hout

The sociology of religion may not overlap with demography in many people's minds, but two facts about the past one hundred years of American religion indicate how demography helps shape the religious landscape. Fact 1: Most people practice the religion their parents taught them. That means that the principal factor in the changing religious composition of any given society (and of the United States in particular) is the number of children each adult has to teach, that is, the relative fertility rates of different religions (Hout, Greeley, and Wilde 2001). Fact 2: Most people who have switched from one religion to another have switched from their parents' religion to their spouse's religion. That means that the prevalence, timing, and selectivity of marriage also affects the distribution of people across religions. In this chapter, I will lay out some of the demographer's concepts and methods that have the greatest utility for the sociologist of religion.

To motivate attending to the details, however, let us consider a "thought experiment" – not a flight of fancy, something close to the way societies are organized. Imagine a country that has two religions, one larger than the other. Imagine further that, over time, the minority religion grows faster than the majority one. To be realistic, it would be okay to imagine that the population as a whole grows and that both groups grow with it; the key condition is that the smaller one is growing faster than the larger one. Throw in one more (realistic) supposition: Suppose that in the imagined country most people practice their parents' religion at a rate comparable to the rate at which Americans do. If these three things are all true, then, as time goes on, the minority religion will come closer and closer to being the same size as the larger one. Given enough time and a constant difference in fertility, the minority religion would eventually become as large as the majority religion; they could even reverse rank, that is, the one that was originally smaller could become the majority religion and the one that was originally larger could become the minority religion.

Casual observers of the imagined society I was referring to would wonder why the minority faith was growing. Some might figure that members of the initially larger religion were switching to the smaller alternative. But we know it's demography, not switching that is changing the population. In fact, the country's religious distribution is changing without any individual actually changing religion. The combination of differing demography and stable intergenerational religious socialization would be sufficient to equalize or even reverse the relative sizes of the religions. It looks like the process that lies beneath the so-called decline of the mainline Protestant denominations in the United States (Hout et al. 2001). Imagine if their higher fertility made Catholics the dominant religion in Northern Ireland or Muslims the dominant religion in Israel (see Kennedy 1973 for a discussion of the Northern Irish case). Suddenly demography looks relevant for religion after all.

The power of demographic analysis comes from this ability to understand how society changes even when no member of society has changed. That makes it a quintessentially sociological form of explanation – at once powerful, complete, and free of reference to individual change. Arthur Stinchcombe considered this style of demographic explanation in his classic text, *Constructing Social Theories* (1968), but too few sociologists practice it.

Research has shown that demography plays a role in real life; it is far more than thought experiments. As religious researchers accumulate ever-longer time series and ever-more-sophisticated databases, the potential for evaluating demographic explanations of religious beliefs and practices will grow. And future sociologists of religion will see a demography chapter as a natural part of their handbook.

BASICS: POPULATION, EVENT, AND EXPOSURE

The most basic notion in demography is the "population," the pool of people being studied. The demographer's concept of population includes the everyday meaning, that is, the people inside some geographic or political boundary. But in principle, a population is any aggregation worth studying, for example, Protestant clergy, people raised Jewish, native-born children of immigrants. Make population as broad or narrow as your theory warrants. Populations do not even necessarily have to be composed of living beings, for example, Catholic parishes, utopian communes, and faith-based social welfare agencies might be populations (e.g., Carroll and Hannan 2000). The idea is so basic that it probably seems trite, but it is also so basic that it is completely indispensable.

The twin ideas of "event" and "exposure" are also essential ideas to demographers. They are less intuitive. A demographer's understanding of what counts as an event is a bit narrower than the everyday usage. Demographers are mostly interested in events that have consequences for the size of the population; births, deaths, and moves into or out of a population can be thought of as the main events. Marriages, divorces, enrollment in school, retirements, and other important transitions that are closely tied to the life cycle have gotten attention from demographers over the years. For religious researchers the list would be expanded to include baptisms, confessions of faith, and annulments for individuals as well as foundings, mergers, and schisms within populations of religious organizations (e.g., denominations, congregations, or monasteries). In principle, though, any event might be studied using demographic methods.

"Exposure" is the opportunity or risk of experiencing an event. Demographers characteristically use the phrase "exposure to risk" even when the event in question is more of an opportunity than a risk for what amounts to historical reasons: The ideas arose first in the study of mortality. Exposure is important because events cannot happen to people who are not exposed to the risk (or opportunity) of the event occurring. For the demographer, exposure is important because some women are too young to have children; some are too old; married people cannot get married again without first getting divorced, and so on. In religious research, this is likely to be more simple: A person cannot convert from religion A to B unless she is an A to begin with. The most basic activity in demographic research consists of measuring "rates" – the ratio of the number of events to the number of people at risk of having an event. Most people are familiar with the idea of a fertility rate, defined as the ratio of births to women of childbearing age. Similarly, the marriage rate is the ratio of the number of marriages to the number of unmarried people; the divorce rate is the ratio of the number of divorces to the number of married people. Rates are important because they estimate the probability that the event in question will happen to an individual much more accurately than do estimates that mix into the calculation people who are not at risk of having the event occur.

All of this linking people to the risk of events comes together in a simple equation that is true by definition: The number of events equals the probability that an event will occur to a person at risk of the event times the number of people at risk. This simple reexpression of the obvious becomes important when change occurs. The number of events may change over time if either the rate or the number of people at risk changes. So, for example, the number of births in the United States rose from 1980 to 1989 even though the birth rate did not because the number of women between fifteen and forty-nine years old increased. This is useful because while probabilities refer to behavior of individuals, the number of people at risk is the factor that refers only to the population and does not involve behavior per se. When a change can be attributed to a change in the probability of an event occurring, then the explanation lies in something that influences the behavior of interest. By contrast, if the number of events increases or decreases because the number of people at risk changed, then "demography" is the full explanation – as in nobody behaved any differently, there just happened to be more people to act in the usual way. When demography is the full explanation, theories about behavioral change are irrelevant.

The most obvious application in the sociology of religion would be to note that the number of church members in a given locale or denomination rose because the population increased. Trivial as it sounds, this was an important point to be made when the Archdiocese of San Francisco closed several parishes in commercial districts while opening new suburban parishes. The *San Francisco Examiner* asked in an editorial why the residents of the commercial districts were giving up religion. The newspaper missed the point that as the office buildings replaced apartments, the population in those districts declined. The people still there were as religious as ever – they used that fact about themselves to lobby the bishop to reverse his decision. But there were fewer of them in the old neighborhood and more in the suburbs. The reallocation of priests made demographic sense and told nothing about the relative piety of downtown and suburban Catholics.

HETEROGENEITY AND EXPLANATION

The idea of linking people at risk of events to the rate at which those events occur has even greater payoff when the rates in question vary systematically across important categories. Then the distribution of the population across those categories can come into the explanation of observed changes in either the number of events or in the overall rate at which those events occur. Most characteristically, the mortality rate varies a great deal with age: The mortality rate is much lower for people in their twenties than for people in their sixties. Then a change in the population that increases the number of twenty-somethings while the number of sixty-somethings stays the same or goes down will decrease the overall mortality rate. The number of deaths in Florida rose dramatically in the 1950s and 1960s despite improved overall longevity in the United States because so many people retired to Florida during those years, not because the environment in Florida suddenly became hazardous.

The religious connection here is in the relationship between age and religiosity. The currently aging American population will probably increase the church attendance rate because church attendance is also lower for twenty-somethings than it is for sixty-somethings. We may never see this change, however, because rising immigration and falling marriage and fertility counteract it. The analysis of the heterogeneity in all these rates is grist for the demographer interested in religious behavior.

DEMOGRAPHY AND RELIGIOUS RESEARCH

Religion has long been recognized by demographers as an important factor in fertility and migration. More recently, demographers have become aware of important religious differences in mortality. Hummer et al. (1999) published life tables for the religiously active and inactive that show the advantage that the religious enjoy. McCullough et al. (2000) compiled forty-two independent studies of religious involvement and mortality. Not only did researchers consistently find that involvement in religion prolongs life, but they also found that religion adds to the effects of things – like stable marriage – that often go with religious involvement.

An earlier line of research documented large differences between the fertility of Catholics and Protestants during the baby boom (e.g., Westoff and Jones 1979; Mosher and Bachrach 1996). At the point of peak difference (in the late 1950s), Catholic women were averaging one more birth than Protestant women were having. By 1970 – a span of just fifteen years – the difference was gone. Although most researchers gave scant attention to differences among Protestant women of different faiths, recent work shows that they were just as large as the Protestant-Catholic gap (Hout et al. 2001). Women from evangelical and fundamentalist denominations were averaging one birth more than women from mainline denominations were having. This gap, too, was gone by the early 1970s. Another way to summarize this pattern is to note that women from mainline Protestant denominations contributed what amounted to a baby blip; the baby boom was concentrated among Catholic, evangelical, and fundamentalist women.

These studies view religion as the cause of important demographic differences. The persistence of religion from one generation to another means that demographic differences based in religion in one generation show up as religious differences based in demography a generation later. I have already referred to the recent work my colleagues and I have done on the role of fertility differences in the decline of mainline Protestant denominations. In a companion paper we ask why Catholics' demographic advantages – higher fertility from 1920 to 1975 and greater immigration in both the first twenty and last twenty years of the last century – did not raise the Catholic share of the U.S. population above 25 percent. Without a demographer's sensibility, of course, the nearly constant share of the population that is Catholic is not problematic in the least. Who worries about nontrends? But this is an interesting puzzle. The Catholic advantage in fertility and migration should have resulted in between 32 and 35 percent of adults being Catholic in the late 1990s. The steady 25 percent that is observed over and over in national surveys implies that something is interfering with the growth of the Catholic population. In fact, 33 percent of American adults interviewed in the late 1990s were raised Catholic (according to the General Social Survey). Ten percent had left the Church – half to Protestant denominations, nearly half to no religion at all, and the small remainder to non-Christian religions. The demographic analysis does not explain the trend in this case. It points to the phenomenon to be explained. But without reference to demography we are not aware that there is anything to explain. Once we see the demographic advantages that the Catholic Church had for most of the twentieth century, its constant proportion in the population becomes a puzzle to be solved.

DATA NEEDS AND RESOURCES

Demographic research on religion has long been hampered by the lack of religion data in the census. Demographers thrive on fine-grained comparisons over long periods of time. The catalogue of religious data is very thin on both counts. Other countries' censuses routinely record the prevalence of religion in the population. In nations where religious divisions overlap with political conflict – I already mentioned Israel and Northern Ireland and it is true in Canada, Australia, and the Netherlands as well – census returns are anxiously monitored for signs of advantage or disadvantage. The U.S. census does not ask about religion, initially because census officials and congressional leaders in the late 1930s thought that it was a bad idea to have lists of Jews stored in one place and more recently because census items must now be tied to the evaluation of specific social and economic policies. The U.S. Bureau of the Census did conduct surveys of religious bodies in 1906, 1916, 1926, and 1936. But inconsistent definitions of membership across denominations and over time limit their usefulness.

The typical survey is sufficient to track the relative sizes of the Protestant and Catholic populations, the population with no religion, and some of the larger Protestant denominations (e.g., Baptists, Methodists, and Lutherans). But groups that are less than 5 percent of the adult population – interesting groups like Jews, Muslims, Mormons, and members of the traditionally African-American churches – are impossible to assess reliably in a single survey of eight hundred to two thousand adults, and few researchers have the resources to interview more than two thousand adults.

The General Social Survey, an ongoing project that used to interview about fifteen hundred adults every year and now interviews three thousand adults in even-numbered years, has become an invaluable resource for religious researchers interested in these churches that comprise less than 5 percent of adults (e.g., Smith 1990 and the GSS website: www.icpsr.umich.edu/gss). The GSS does not get any more Jews, Muslims, or Jehovah's Witnesses than any other survey of that size, of course, but because it has such high standards of keeping the design and questions the same year after year, data from several years can be combined to gain insight about these smaller religions and denominations. Since its inception, but especially since 1983, the GSS also has taken pains to distinguish precisely among denominations as similar-sounding (but doctrinally very different) as the United Church of Christ and the Church of Christ, the Church of God and the Church of God in Christ, and the Southern Baptist Convention, the American Baptist Convention, and the National Baptist Convention. In all, the GSS codes 177 Protestant denominations, the distinction between Roman Catholic and Orthodox Christianity, three Jewish denominations, five non-Christian faiths, and no religion.

Very few other surveys take religion that seriously. Researchers affiliated with the Gallup Polls, most notably George Gallup, Jr., have written extensively about religion. But the Gallup data are much harder to use because of design changes, wording changes, and few attempts to enumerate more finely than seven or eight Protestant categories. Just as an example, the ubiquitous question about Americans' belief in God at first appears to be an important time series stretching back to the 1930s. Two important wording changes break that trend line at crucial points; most recently the addition of the phrase "or a higher power" to the question in 1976 reversed a downward trend in response to the simpler question "Do you believe in God?" (see Bishop 1999).

CONCLUSION

Demography and religion have a fruitful past and a promising future. We can claim Durkheim's *Suicide* (1897/1951) as the first study in over a century of research linking demography and religion. Researchers have looked at the consequences of religion for demography – first in the fertility studies from the 1930s to the 1980s, more recently in studies of religion and longevity – and (less often) at the consequences of demography for religion. Both kinds of research have illuminated social change and helped us understand religion's role in American society.

The future is not guaranteed. The cutting edge of this kind of research depends on infusions of mass data. With no questions about religion in the census, the continuation of long-term studies such as the GSS are essential to our ability to keep doing this important work.

CHAPTER SEVEN

Church Attendance in the United States

Mark Chaves and Laura Stephens

Although there is more to religious belief and practice than participation in organized religion, and although media reports sometimes make it appear that new and unconventional forms of religiosity are swamping more traditional practice, the collective expression of religion in the United States still mainly means attendance at weekend religious services. When people who say they did *not* attend religious services in the past week are asked in surveys whether they participated in some other type of religious event or meeting, only 2 percent say yes. If other sorts of religious activity have increased, that increase is not much at the expense of traditional weekend attendance at religious services. For this reason, the level of participation in traditional worship services – church and synagogue attendance – and trends in those levels, remain valuable, if mundane, windows onto American religion and its collective expression.

For many years scholars of American religion agreed on two basic facts about church attendance: (a) on any given weekend approximately 40 percent of Americans attend religious services, and (b) this rate has been essentially stable at least since the 1950s. In this chapter, we review the evidence about the contemporary level of attendance at religious services, and we review the evidence about trends in that participation. Regarding the first, recent research has shown that weekly attendance in the United States is significantly lower than 40 percent. Regarding the second, recent research has unsettled the previous consensus about stability in attendance over time. Although recent research has not yet definitively established that there has been decline rather stability, several major studies point in that direction, and these studies are suggestive enough to throw into question what previously appeared to be a settled matter. In exploring the factual matters at issue here, we will see that assessing the level of religious participation in the United States, and interpreting its meaning, is a more complex matter than one might initially expect. In the conclusion, we discuss the meaning of religious participation levels and trends for larger questions about religion's social significance in the United States.

HOW MANY AMERICANS ATTEND RELIGIOUS SERVICES?

Very few findings within sociology become widely and firmly established as solid social facts. However, the claim that approximately 40 percent of the population of the

United States attends religious services on a weekly basis had, until recently, enjoyed this status. This fact had been freely reported by historians and journalists. For example, the religion column in a 1991 issue of *The New York Times* began by stating, "Nearly all surveys of American churchgoing habits show that roughly 40 percent of Americans attend church once a week" (Goldman 1991). Additional evidence of the wide acceptance of this statistic is found in introductory sociology and methods textbooks, which almost uniformly report the 40 percent figure in their chapters on religion or survey research (see, for example, Babbie 1992: 398; Johnson 1992: 548; Kornblum 1991: 514; Luhman 1992: 414; Thio 1992: 393). This example, from a 1992 textbook, is typical: "Forty-two percent [of Americans] state that they attended a church or synagogue during the preceding seven days. During the last half century, these figures have shown some consistency.... [T]here has been virtually no change in the percentage of Americans who attended services during the week before they were interviewed" (Luhman 1992: 414).

This claim – that 40 percent of Americans attend religious services in any given week – was based on remarkably stable results from surveys in which respondents are asked to report on their own church attendance practices. The Gallup Organization, for example, asks people: "Did you, yourself, happen to attend church or synagogue in the last seven days?" In 1998, 40 percent of Americans answered yes to this question, with Catholics showing higher rates of attendance (46 percent) than Protestants (42 percent) (Gallup and Lindsay 1999). Similarly, the General Social Survey asks respondents "How often do you attend religious services?," coding their responses into a set of categories ranging from "never" to "several times a week." In 1998, the weekly attendance rate implied by the distribution of responses to this question was 38 percent (Davis et al. 1998).

It now appears, however, that taking at face value the accuracy of individuals' reports of their own religious behavior gave us a misleading picture about levels of religious participation. Hadaway et al. (1993) opened debate on this question by comparing the rates of church attendance based on the self-reports of respondents with rates based on observing and counting the number of people actually present at religious services. They did two things.

First, they examined weekly attendance among Protestants in Ashtabula County, Ohio. In response to a telephone survey of 602 randomly selected county residents, 35.8 percent of self-identified Protestants said they had attended religious services in the past seven days, a number nearly identical to the weekly church attendance rate found in a 1991 sample of all Ohio residents (Bishop 1992), and very similar to rates obtained in national surveys. After using telephone books and newspapers, and driving every road in the county to identify churches appearing in neither of those sources, Hadaway et al. found 159 Protestant churches in Ashtabula county. Attendance rates from each of the churches were obtained through denominational yearbooks, telephone interviews, letters, and church visits. The result: Although 35.8 percent of Ashtabula Protestants claimed to have attended church in the past seven days, only about 20 percent of Protestants actually attend church on an average Sunday.

This pattern of substantial overreporting of church attendance is not peculiar either to Protestants or to Ashtabula county. The second piece of research in this article was an examination of weekly attendance rates among Catholics in eighteen dioceses around the country. In national polls, about 50 percent of Catholics say they attend church on any given Sunday. Hadaway et al. assessed the accuracy of this number by comparing it to mass attendance data collected in many Catholic dioceses. In these dioceses, parishes conduct a systematic count of attendees at every mass on a designated weekend. Sometimes counts are done several weekends in a row, in which case the numbers from each weekend are averaged to estimate the number attending on any given weekend. Hadaway et al. inflated the attendance numbers reported by dioceses in order to account for the very few parishes whose attendance numbers were not included in the diocese-wide counts. These adjusted counts became the numerator of a count-based attendance rate for each diocese.

The denominator was an estimate of the number of Catholics living in the geographical area covered by each diocese. Hadaway et al. used a nationally representative survey of religions affiliation that had a large enough sample to reliably estimate the proportion of self-identified Catholics within each diocese (Kosmin 1991). The total population of each diocese, drawn from the 1990 U.S. census, was multiplied by the proportion of Catholics in each location to produce an estimate of the number of self-identified Catholics in each diocese. At this point, a count-based church attendance rate was calculated by dividing the adjusted attendance figures by the number of Catholics in each diocese.

Again the results were clear. Catholic attendance at mass is substantially lower than the 50 percent figure suggested by research based on self-reported attendance rates. Although there was significant variation across dioceses, when the count data were aggregated only about 28 percent of Catholics attended church on a weekly basis, again leading to the conclusion that church attendance rates are only about half what previously existing data would lead one to believe. Chaves and Cavendish (1994) supplemented this study by gathering data on a total of forty-eight Catholic dioceses, representing approximately 38 percent of Catholics in the United States. The result was unchanged.

This conclusion – that weekly church attendance in the United States is about half what the conventional wisdom held it to be, about 20 percent for Protestants and about 25 percent for Catholics – was criticized in several ways, none of which, in our view, quite hit the target. Consider four of the criticisms, and the responses to them. All of the responses described below are drawn from Hadaway et al. (1998).

One line of criticism takes issue with the construction of the denominator in Hadaway et al.'s Catholic estimates (Caplow 1998). This criticism begins with the observation that more people identify as Catholics than are actively involved in parish life. As described above, Hadaway et al. used the number of people identifying as Catholics as the denominator in their calculation of the count-based church attendance rate within each Catholic diocese. Since the number of people who are active enough to be on the official rolls of Catholic parishes is smaller than the number of people who simply identify themselves as Catholic, dividing the number of attenders by the number of people actually registered at Catholic parishes rather than the number of people who self-identify as Catholic would produce a higher weekly attendance rate – and a smaller gap between self-reported and actual attendance rates.

However, this reduction in the gap between self-reported and actual attendance rates ignores the fact that the high attendance rates from conventional surveys also are based on the number of self-identified Catholics who respond to the survey. To use a different denominator in a count-based rate would lead to comparing apples and oranges. It is difficult to see what the point would be of using the number of registered Catholics as the denominator in a count-based attendance rate while simultaneously using the number of self-identifying Catholics as the denominator in a survey-based attendance rate. Using the number of registered Catholics as the denominator in calculating a count-based attendance rate would indeed generate a higher rate, but it would not reduce the gap between self-reported and actual attendance rates when both are based on the same denominator.

A second criticism accepts the fact that survey-based church attendance rates are inflated but argues that much of this inflation can be attributed to problems in survey techniques rather than to an overreporting of religious activities on the part of survey respondents (Woodberry 1998). Church attenders are oversampled by most surveys, this argument goes, because churchgoers are generally easier to contact and are more cooperative respondents, and they are particularly overrepresented in telephone surveys that do not make many repeat telephone calls in an effort to reach people who do not respond to the first few attempts at telephone contact. If this is true, survey-based attendance rates will be artificially high, but they will be high because churchgoers are overrepresented among respondents to surveys, not because people overreport their attendance.

The main problem with this criticism is that the count-based attendance rates observed by Hadaway et al. were well below rates generated by *all* conventional survey techniques, including surveys using face-to-face interviews and multiple callbacks. It is therefore not plausible to argue that sampling bias has produced a large portion of the gap between count-based and survey-based attendance estimates.

A third criticism comes from using checks internal to conventional surveys to assess the reliability of self-reported attendance (Hout and Greeley 1998). When, for example, wives' reports about their husbands' church attendance are compared to what husbands say about themselves, the numbers are nearly identical. This similarity, the argument goes, suggests that people accurately report the frequency of their own attendance at religious services. Another kind of reliability check offered by these critics is to examine the attendance rates of people thought to be unlikely to exaggerate their church attendance. According to Hout and Greeley (1998), two such groups of people are intellectuals and members of "skeptical" professions, such as scientists and artists. The logic here is that such people are unlikely to exaggerate their church attendance because frequently attending religious services would not be considered desirable within their occupational reference group. Since individuals in these two categories are not likely to overreport their attendance, the argument goes, their reports can be considered true measures of church attendance. And since the self-reported attendance of people in these categories is not much less than the self-reported attendance of everyone else, this comparison, like the first comparison, is taken to mean that there is very little overreporting of church attendance in surveys.

These comparisons are not persuasive checks on the reliability or validity of self-reported attendance. Regarding the first internal check, it is not at all surprising that wives' reports of their husbands behavior are consistent with husbands' reports of their own behaviors. The likely reason for this is that whatever dynamics govern self-reported attendance also govern how someone reports a spouse's attendance. It is not evidence that contradicts the presence of a large gap between self-reported and actual attendance rates. The second internal check is even less convincing. The assumption that intellectuals and skeptical professionals will be less likely than others to overreport church attendance is not tenable. It is, after all, the *more* highly educated who are most likely to overreport other behaviors, such as voting. Moreover, the operationalization of "skeptical professional" used by the critics includes athletes, artists, television announcers, and university professors, among others. This eclectic group holds no common disposition or training that would lead them to be less likely to exaggerate their church attendance. More generally, it is not credible to rely on comparisons of self-reports among subgroups of survey respondents rather than on comparisons between self-reports and an external criterion such as head counts.

A fourth criticism of the Hadaway et al. claim that weekly church attendance is substantially lower than 40 percent was that their results were based on aggregate rather than individual-level data (Hout and Greeley 1998). Hadaway et al., after all, based their conclusions on comparisons between survey data and head-count data that did not permit any direct examination about which specific individuals might be overreporting their own attendance. It would be more persuasive if one could compare the actual church attendance of the exact same individuals who claimed in a survey to have attended. In a different study, Marler and Hadaway did just this (1999). After conducting telephone interviews of adults belonging to a single large evangelical church, asking them if they had attended church services during the previous week, Marler and Hadaway matched each individual's response to attendance sheets from the previous week kept by the church. The result: Only 115 of the 181 people who claimed to have attended church actually had attended. Although approximately 60 percent of these people said that they had attended, only 38 percent actually had attended.

Evidence from other studies consistently supports the conclusion that religious service attendance is substantially overreported in conventional surveys. Marcum (1999) compares attendance reports based on head counts within Presbyterian congregations to self-reports obtained through conventional survey designs. He finds that the self-reports produce attendance levels almost double what they actually are: seventeen people report attending for every ten that actually are there. Hadaway and Marler (1997b) find substantial overreporting when they compare surveys to actual counts of attending Catholics in a Canadian county. As far as we know, no researcher who has compared self-reported to actual attendance has found something other than that the latter is much smaller than the former.

Other researchers have investigated this issue by using innovative survey techniques designed to minimize overreporting. Presser and Stinson (1998) examine data from studies in which people are asked to complete diaries concerning their daily activities. Although this method still relies on respondents' self-reports, it is likely to reduce overreporting for two reasons. First, the respondent is not engaged in face-to-face interaction with an interviewer, which ought to reduce respondents' propensity to engage in impression management. Second, the respondent is not made aware of the fact that religious participation is of particular interest to the researchers, making the issue of religion much less salient to informants and reducing the pressure to conform to perceived social norms regarding religious participation. Using this arguably more valid method of measuring church attendance, Presser and Stinson find that claimed rates of church attendance are approximately one-third lower than with the traditional survey approach. Similar results were found in a study of British respondents in which traditional surveys predicted a church attendance rate of about 21 percent and the time diary approach yielded a lower estimate of 14 percent (Hadaway and Marler 1997a).

The bottom line here is that recent research has overturned an earlier conventional wisdom about the level of weekly religious participation in the United States. To the best of our current knowledge, the weekly attendance rate in the United States is closer to 20 percent than to 40 percent.

From a broader perspective, it should not be surprising that individuals overreport their religious service attendance when they are directly asked. We know that other sorts of socially desirable behaviors are overreported, and we know that socially undesirable behaviors are underreported. For example, more people claim to have voted than actually did (Parry and Crossley 1950; Traugott and Katosh 1979; Silver, Anderson, and Abramson 1986, Presser and Traugott 1992). Presser and Traugott (1992) report that about 15 percent of voters report their voting activity inaccurately. Furthermore, since almost all of this error comes from people who have not voted claiming that they have, about 30 percent of nonvoters are misclassified as voters. Similarly, young people tend to underreport undesirable behaviors such as drug use (Mensch and Kendel 1988). In the light of this broader phenomenon, well-known in survey research, it would be surprising if religious service attendance was *not* overreported in conventional surveys.

Overreporting socially desirable activity probably is not the only mechanism leading people to exaggerate their religious service attendance. The fact that overreporting is reduced when religious service attendance is asked about indirectly (as in the time-use diaries) rather than directly suggests that something else might be going on. We speculate that survey respondents may perceive a question that is literally about religious service attendance to be a request for information about the person's identity as a religious or nonreligious person. On this scenario, respondents who inaccurately report their literal church attendance may be intending to *accurately* report their identities as religious individuals who attend services more or less regularly, even if not weekly. From this perspective, one plausible interpretation of the attendance rates generated by conventional surveys is that they are picking up the percentage of Americans who think of themselves as "church people," even if they attend less than weekly.

Although weekly attendance at religious services now appears to be less frequent than previously believed, it still is the case that Americans attend religious services at higher rates than people in most of the industrialized West. A recent study of sixty-five countries, for example, found that 55 percent of Americans said they attend religious services at least once a month, compared with 40 percent in Canada, 38 percent in Spain, 25 percent in Australia, Great Britain, and West Germany, and 17 percent in France (Inglehart and Baker 2000). Additionally, among advanced industrial democracies the United States still stands out for its relatively high level of religious belief. Fifty percent of Americans said "10" when asked to rate the importance of God in their lives on a scale of 1 to 10. That's compared with 28 percent in Canada, 26 percent in Spain, 21 percent in Australia, 16 percent in Great Britain and West Germany, and 10 percent in France. Among advanced industrial democracies only Ireland, at 40 percent, approaches the U.S. level of religious belief. As in other arenas, a kind of American exceptionalism holds when it comes to religion.

WHAT IS THE TREND IN ATTENDANCE AT RELIGIOUS SERVICES?

Some researchers have argued that religious participation has increased over the long haul of American history (Finke and Stark 1992). This claim is based on increasing rates

of church *membership*. In 1789 only 10 percent of Americans belonged to churches, rising to 22 percent in 1890, and reaching 50 to 60 percent in the 1950s. Today, about two
thirds of Americans say they are members of a church or synagogue. These rising church
membership numbers, however, are potentially misleading about underlying religious
participation rates because churches have become much less exclusive clubs than they
were at earlier points in our history. Today, fewer people attend religious services than
claim formal membership in religious congregations, but that situation was reversed
earlier in our history. Thus, a historic increase in formal church membership may not
be a valid indicator of historic increase in religious participation. The changing meaning and standards for official church (and synagogue) membership make it difficult to
know what long-term trends in membership imply about trends in religious participation. The historical record, at the moment, seems too spotty to say anything definitive
about long-term national trends in religious service attendance. Still, one prominent
historian of American religion who has reviewed the available historical evidence has
argued that "participation [as opposed to formal membership] in [U.S.] congregations
has probably remained relatively constant" since the seventeenth century (Holifield
1994: 24).

Rising church membership rates notwithstanding, self-reported church attendance
has appeared to be remarkably stable for as long as we have survey research on this
topic. The Protestant rate has hovered around 40 percent since the 1940s. Although self-
reported Catholic church attendance declined markedly during the 1960s and 1970s –
from about 70 percent reportedly attending weekly to about 50 percent – the Catholic
numbers, too, have been stable for about twenty years. These remarkably stable survey
numbers are the basis for the standard view that church attendance in the United
States – whatever the level of overreporting – has been essentially constant at least
throughout the second half of the twentieth century.

Several recent studies, however, have shaken the view that religious service attendance in the United States has been essentially stable in recent decades. We already
have discussed Presser and Stinson's (1998) contribution to knowledge about the contemporary weekly attendance rate. They also examine time-use diary evidence spread
over several decades, and they find evidence of decline in church attendance during the
last third of the twentieth century, from about 40 percent in 1965 to about 25 percent
in 1994. Hofferth and Sandberg (2001) find a similar decline – from 37 percent in 1981
to 26 percent in 1997 – in church attendance reported in children's time-use diaries.
Because there are reasons, discussed earlier, to believe that the indirect approach used
in time diary studies measures church attendance more accurately than the direct approach used in conventional surveys, these findings raise considerable doubts about
the meaning of the stability produced by decades of surveys that directly ask people
about their religious service attendance.

Additional evidence of decline comes from Robert Putnam's recent monumental
book on civic engagement in the United States. Putnam (2000) combines survey data
from five different sources and finds the same decline in religious participation as did
Presser and Stinson. This is important in itself. But perhaps even more compelling –
because of the context it provides – are Putnam's findings about a whole range of civic
and voluntary association activities that are close cousins to religious participation.
Virtually every indicator of civic engagement currently available shows decline in the
last third of the twentieth century. Here is a partial list of indicators that follow this

pattern: Voting, attending a political meeting, attending any public meeting, serving as an officer or committee member in any local club or organization, participating in a local meeting of any national organization, attending a club meeting, joining a union, participating in a picnic, playing sports, working on a community project.

The details vary for specific items, but the consistency – across many different indicators drawn from many different sources – is impressive. For item after item, trend line after trend line, decline starts sometime in the last third of the twentieth century and continues into the present. This casts new light on the religious participation trend. Religious participation, it seems, is a special case of something much more general: Civic engagement. The newly reported findings of decline in virtually all sorts of civic engagement since the 1960s, together with the direct evidence for decline in some of the best data on religious participation itself, add weight to the notion that religious participation in the United States has indeed declined in the last third of the twentieth century. Seen in this context, it would be a great surprise indeed to learn that religious participation, alone among all sorts of civic engagement, has failed to decline. Those still wishing to maintain that religious participation has been stable over the last three or four decades now must face the additional burden of explaining how it could be that religious trends are so different from trends affecting virtually every other type of voluntary association.

There is another important detail on which recent evidence is converging. Presser and Stinson, among others, found that more recent generations attend religious services at lower rates than did previous generations when they were the same age. Chaves (1989, 1991) found this same pattern, and Putnam finds it as well across a strikingly wide range of activities, including church attendance. Declining participation in all sorts of voluntary associations, including religious ones, is not occurring so much because individual people have become less involved over the last three or four decades. Rather, more recently born cohorts of individuals do less of this activity than older cohorts, and those born earlier are inexorably leaving the scene, being replaced by less civically engaged recent generations. Even if not a single individual changes his or her behavior over time, it still is possible for widespread social change to occur via generational turnover, and this seems to be largely what is happening with civic engagement in general, and with religious participation in particular.

So, have U.S. church attendance rates been stable over recent decades, or have they declined? The evidence is conflicting. Those wanting to argue in favor of stability can point to traditional surveys, but they then need to explain why surveys using an indirect approach, such as time-use studies, find decline. They also need to explain why church attendance trends are different than trends in most every other type of civic engagement. Those wanting to argue in favor of decline, by contrast, need to explain why that decline is not evident in traditional surveys.

We can offer a plausible account for why traditional surveys might show stability over time even if weekly attendance truly has declined Recall our suggestion that survey respondents may perceive a direct question that is literally about religious service attendance to be, instead, an inquiry about that person's identity as a religious or nonreligious person. It seems plausible to suggest further that the proportion of Americans who truly attend religious services weekly might have declined at the same time that the proportion who think of themselves as "church people" – and who may very well attend services more or less regularly, if not weekly – has remained stable. If the standard survey questions actually tap a person's religious identity more than their literal church attendance, and if the true trend has been for people to attend less often but still regularly enough to consider themselves religiously committed, then this would produce stability over time in the standard surveys even in the face of real decline in weekly attendance. The basic idea is that a real decline in attendance, if it takes the form of many people shifting from weekly to, say, monthly attendance, might not register in standard surveys.

This is, admittedly, speculation, but it is plausible speculation, and we find it difficult to develop a similarly plausible account in the other direction – one that would explain why time-diary evidence shows decline over time if stability is the true picture. All in all, although it is not yet possible to say that the new research has definitively established that religious participation in the United States has declined, our view is that the evidence and arguments for decline are, at this writing, more compelling than the evidence and arguments for stability.

The emerging picture, then, is of an American society in which, since the 1960s – but not before – people engage in less and less religious activity. This is occurring, it seems, without any decline in belief in the supernatural or concern about spirituality. Interestingly, this pattern is not limited to the United States. On the contrary, it characterizes many countries around the world. Although advanced industrial societies vary quite widely in their aggregate levels of religious participation and religious belief, they show basically similar trends over recent decades: Down on religious participation, stable on religious belief, and up on thinking about the meaning and purpose of life (Inglehart and Baker 2000). Some, although not all, ex-Communist societies show increases in both participation and belief, but that is a subject for another essay.

CONCLUSION

The current state of knowledge about religious service attendance in the United States should not comfort those who expected modernity to be fundamentally hostile to religion. It seems that religious participation was either stable or increasing for two centuries, including the late nineteenth and early twentieth century decades during which the United States changed from a predominantly rural to a predominantly urban society. Moreover, many conventional religious beliefs remain popular and show no sign of decline even now. At the same time, however, what we know about church attendance also should not comfort those who believe that there has been no important change, or that social changes associated with modernity do not have potentially negative consequences for religious belief and practice. It seems likely – although not yet definitively established – that religious participation has declined in the United States, as in many parts of the industrialized world, over the last three or four decades. Cross-national evidence also indicates that certain aspects of "modernity" – more industrial employment and higher overall standards of living – are indeed associated with less traditional religious belief among people (Inglehart and Baker 2000). Beware simple tales about secularization, but also beware wholesale rejections of secularization.

Although trends in church attendance are intrinsically interesting, we also know that focusing exclusively on religious practice – or even on the combination of religious practice and belief – misses something crucial about religion's social significance. Consider, for example, the difference between two charismatic worship services, complete with speaking in tongues, one occurring in an urban Pentecostal church on a Sunday morning in the contemporary United States, the other occurring outside a village in colonial central Africa at a time early in the twentieth century when, as Karen Fields (1985) has described, charismatic religion – simply by encouraging baptizing and speaking in tongues – challenged the traditional religious authority on which colonial rule was based. Or consider, to offer another example, the difference between two "new age" religious groups, both of which encourage certain kinds of physical exercise in order to achieve spiritual peace and growth, one meeting in a YMCA somewhere in New York City, the other meeting in a park somewhere in Beijing. In each example, the exact same religious action takes on a dramatically different meaning and can lead to very different consequences depending on the institutional and political context in which it occurs. In some times and places speaking in tongues, or seeking health by stretching one's limbs, or some other religious practice, shakes social institutions and provokes hostile reactions. In other times and places, such displays shake nothing at all beyond the bodies of the faithful, and they provoke little hostility or, indeed, any reaction at all. The social significance of religious practice – its capacity to mean something beyond itself – depends on the institutional and political arrangements in which it occurs.

From this perspective, it is reasonable to wonder about the relevance of continuing high levels of religious belief and practice to larger questions about religion's social significance in the United States. High levels of interest in things spiritual and supernatural probably means that both old religions and new religious movements continually will try to mobilize that interest, and some of them probably will achieve great success in bringing people into the fold, increasing their religious beliefs and activities, and gathering resources sufficient to build impressive religious organizations. Less clear, however, is the extent to which even a wildly successful religious movement should be taken to indicate much of a gain in religion's social significance if its success mainly means influencing what people do with some of their leisure time each week in a society where such activity only occasionally reverberates beyond the walls of a religious meeting place. Numerical increases within the United States in specific religious traditions or in specific types of religious practice are interesting to chart in their own right. But such increases within a society where religious institutions are not, in general, directly connected to other important social institutions lack the social consequences they would have in a society in which this or that religious tradition or practice constitutes a challenge to the authority of political leaders or social elites. Religion's place in the institutional system of most advanced industrial societies limits the capacity for religious belief and activity to be socially consequential. It limits a religious movement's capacity to be world-changing, even if it converts millions.

The social significance of religious belief and participation, however common they remain, depends fundamentally on the institutional settings in which they occur. This is why the religious movements of our day with the greatest potential for increasing religion's social significance may not be those movements that simply seek new converts or influence individuals' religious belief and practice, however successful they might be. The movements with the greatest potential for increasing religion's social significance may be those seeking to change a society's institutional arrangements by expanding religion's authority over decisions and actions currently outside its purview. Such movements, when they succeed, change, among other things, the social meaning and significance of religious participation. This is the essence of activist fundamentalist religious movements around the world, whatever the religious tradition in which they occur.

CHAPTER EIGHT

The Dynamics of Religious Economies

Roger Finke and Rodney Stark

An immense intellectual shift is taking place in the social scientific study of religion. During the past few years many of its most venerated theoretical positions – faithfully passed down from the famous founders of the field – have been overturned. The changes have become so dramatic and far-reaching that R. Stephen Warner identified them "as a paradigm shift in progress" (1993:1044), an assessment that since then "has been spectacularly fulfilled," according to Andrew Greeley (1996: 1).

This chapter reviews a small portion of this major paradigm shift: the dynamics of religious economies. Elsewhere (Stark and Finke 2000) we offer a more complete theoretical model, developing propositions explaining individual religious behavior, the dynamics of religious groups, and a more comprehensive examination of religious economies. Here our goals are far more modest. First, we will briefly contrast the new paradigm with the inherited model. Next, we offer a few of the foundational propositions for understanding religious economies. Finally, we use recent research to illustrate the dynamics of religious economies.

A PARADIGM SHIFT

The Old Paradigm

Since the founding of the social sciences, the study of religion has been dominated by a paradigm where religion is explained as an epiphenomenon, serving as a salve for social ills, and relying on the unchallenged religious authority of a monopoly to make religious beliefs plausible. As an epiphenomenon, Durkheim (1912/1976) and others viewed religion as an elaborate reflection of more basic realities. Marx and Engels (1878/1964: 16) explained, "All religion . . . is nothing but the fantastic reflection in men's minds of those external forces which control their daily lives." As a salve for social ills, religion was a painkiller for frustration, deprivation, and suffering. Proponents of this paradigm viewed religion as serving to appease the lower classes, legitimate existing political power, and impede effective rational thought. Finally, the plausibility of the religious beliefs, they argued, relied on the support of a religious monopoly. Using the memorable imagery of Peter Berger, a "sacred canopy" encompassing all social institutions and suffusing all social processes provides religion with unquestioned authority and plausibility. Berger (1967: 48) noted that "When an entire society serves as the plausibility structure for a religiously legitimated world, all the important social processes within it serve to confirm and reconfirm the reality of this world."

But if there is a single thesis that has united this paradigm, it is that the rise of modernity is the demise of religion. Social scientists and assorted Western intellectuals have been promising the end of religion for centuries. Auguste Comte (1830–42/1969), famous for coining the word sociology, announced that, as a result of modernization, human society was outgrowing the "theological stage" of social evolution and a new age was dawning in which the science of sociology would replace religion as the basis for moral judgments. Max Weber (1904–5/1958) later explained why modernization would cause the "disenchantment" of the world, and Sigmund Freud (1928/1985) reassured his disciples that this greatest of all neurotic illusions would die on the therapist's couch. More recently, the distinguished anthropologist Anthony F. C. Wallace (1966: 264–5) explained to tens of thousands of American undergraduates that "the evolutionary future of religion is extinction."

For proponents of this paradigm, the secularization thesis was nestled within the broader theoretical framework of modernization theories, proposing that as industrialization, urbanization, rationalization, and religious pluralism increase, religiousness *must* decline (Hadden 1987; Finke 1992). Keep in mind that modernization is a *long, gradual, relatively constant process*. In terms of time series trends, modernization is a long, linear, upward curve, and secularization is assumed to trace the reciprocal of this curve, to be a long, linear, downward curve. Each trend represents a semievolutionary process that is virtually inevitable. Since modernization is so advanced in many nations that "postmodernism" is the latest buzzword, it must be assumed that secularization is at least "ongoing" to the extent that a significant downward trend in religiousness can be seen.

This ongoing process of secularization was expected to occur at several levels, from individual consciousness and commitment to the vitality of the local church to the authority and power of religion in the larger institutions. One of the most well-respected proponents of the traditional model, Bryan Wilson (1982: 149) explained that, for individuals, secularization results in a "decline in the proportion of their time, energy, and resources which [individuals] devote to super-empirical concerns" and would lead to a "gradual replacement of a specifically religious consciousness . . . by an empirical, rational, instrumental orientation." Beyond the individual, he described secularization as including a "decay of religious institutions" and a "shift from religious to secular control of various of the erstwhile activities and functions of religion." Likewise, Peter Berger, long the most sophisticated modern proponent of the secularization thesis, was entirely candid about the effects of secularization on individuals. Having outlined the aspects of secularization for social institutions, Berger (1967: 107–8) went on to explain that the "process of secularization has a subjective side as well. As there is a secularization of society and culture, so there is a secularization of consciousness." Recently, Berger (1997) gracefully withdrew his support for the theory of secularization. We cite this passage from his earlier work not to emphasize our previous disagreement with Berger, whose work we always have much admired, but as a contrast to the recent tactic by other proponents of secularization, who seek to evade the growing mountain of contrary evidence by redefining the term of secularization.

In recent years, secularization has been defined and redefined in several ways (Hanson 1997; Tschannen 1991; Dobbelaere 1987; Shiner 1967), with one definition identifying secularization as *deinstitutionalization* (Dobbelaere 1987; Martin 1978). This definition, often referred to as the macro version (cf. Lechner 1996), refers to a decline in the social power of once-dominant religious institutions whereby other social institutions, especially political and educational institutions, have escaped from prior religious domination. If this were all that secularization means, and if we limited discussion to Europe, there would be nothing to argue about. Everyone must agree that, in contemporary Europe Catholic bishops have less political power than they once possessed and the same is true of Lutheran and Anglican bishops (although bishops probably never were nearly so powerful as they now are thought to have been). Nor are primary aspects of public life any longer suffused with religious symbols, rhetoric, or ritual. These changes have, of course, aroused scholarly interest, resulting in some distinguished studies (Casanova 1994; Martin 1978). But, the prophets of secularization theory were not and are not merely writing about something so obvious or limited. Karel Dobbelaere (1997: 9), a leading proponent of the macro secularization thesis, writes that the "the religiousness of individuals is *not* a valid indicator in evaluating the process of secularization." Yet, a couple years earlier he and Lilliane Voyé (1994: 95) explained that "the successful removal by science of all kinds of anthropomorphisms from our thinking have transformed the traditional concept of 'God as a person' into a belief in a life force, a power of spirit and this has also gradually promoted agnosticism and atheism – which explains the long-term decline of religious practices." Thus, predictions on the inevitable decline of individual consciousness and commitment remain.

An Emerging New Paradigm

The assault on the old paradigm has come on many fronts. The standard measures of modernity (e.g., urbanization, industrialization, rationalization, and religious pluralism) have failed to show a consistent secularizing effect on religion. Indeed, increasing urbanization and industrialization were associated with increasing levels of religious participation in late-nineteenth- and early-twentieth-century America (Finke and Stark 1988, 1992; Finke 1992) and throughout Christian history urban areas have often been the centers for religious revivals and more orthodox religious behavior (Stark 1996).

Even religious pluralism and rationality, long perceived to be the most corrosive elements of modernity, fail to garner research support. Beginning in the late 1980s a series of qualitative studies questioned the secularizing effects of religious pluralism and the incompatibility of religion and rationality. In her observational study of Catholic charismatics, Mary Jo Neitz (1987: 257–8) found that their full awareness of religious choices "did not undermine their own beliefs. Rather they felt they had 'tested' the belief system and had been convinced of its superiority." Lynn Davidman's (1991: 204) field study of upper-middle-class Jewish women who converted to Orthodoxy, stressed the benefits of intra-Jewish pluralism and the careful process of evaluation before joining the community – concluding that "pluralization and multiplicity of choices available in the contemporary United States can actually strengthen Jewish communities." After interviewing 178 evangelicals from 23 states, Christian Smith and his colleagues (1998: 104) concluded, "For evangelicals, it is precisely by making a choice for Christ that one's faith becomes valid and secure. There is little reason to believe, therefore, that the modern necessity of having to choose one's own religion makes that religion any less real, powerful, or meaningful to modern believers."

Numerous quantitative research projects have also questioned the secularizing effects of religious pluralism. Although mired in methodological controversies (see Olson 1998; Finke and Stark 1998), a couple of conclusions can be drawn.[1] First, the key distinction is between areas having no pluralism and those having some degree of religious choice and competition (Finke, Guest, and Stark 1996; Hamberg and Pettersson 1997; Pettersson and Hamberg 1997). Religious markets have a saturation point beyond which additional options do not raise levels of participation. Second, despite ardent criticism questioning the beneficial effects of high religious pluralism, few of the critics propose a return to the old paradigm explanation. Even the critics recognize that a monopoly church supported by the state will not increase religious plausibility and activity.

Perhaps the most critical blow to the secularization thesis, however, is that the trend line forecasted by the old paradigm isn't supported by the data. A mounting body of research has questioned the nostalgic views of past piety and contemporary accounts of depleted religious activity. This argument has been refuted most forcefully in the United States, where a rise in modernity was accompanied by a rise in religious activity (Finke and Stark 1992; Warner 1993). Yet, nostalgic myths of past piety and recent surges in religious activity extend far beyond the United States. The most prominent historians of medieval religion now agree that there never was an "Age of Faith" in Western Europe (Morris 1993; Duffy 1992; Sommerville 1992; Bossy 1985; Obelkevich 1979; Murray 1972; Thomas 1971; Coulton 1938). Even the strongest advocates of the old paradigm concede that, in terms of organized participation, the Golden Age of Faith never existed (Bruce 1997). And, when it comes to contemporary religion, the religious revivals around the globe have become too frequent and too sizeable to ignore. From Islam in the Middle East and Africa to Christianity in Latin America, Eastern Europe, and Korea, religion has proven compatible with increasing modernity.

This lack of support for the secularization thesis, however, does not suggest that religion is always increasing or that modernity is associated with an ever increasing level of religious involvement. Although research refuting the secularization thesis has frequently emphasized increasing religious involvement, the new paradigm does not replace the prediction on the inevitable demise of religion with an equally implausible prediction on the inevitable ascension of religion. Moreover, for the new paradigm, modernity is not the causal engine driving religious change. The reasons given for doubting (or believing) religious teachings are mostly unrelated to anything specific to modernity and have remained relatively unchanged throughout recorded history (Smith et al. 1998; Stark and Finke 2000). Instead, the new theoretical developments attempt to move beyond nebulous forces of modernity leading to an inevitable religious decline to specific propositions attempting to explain religious variation.

---

[1] Mark Chaves and Philip Gorski (2001) cited Dan Olson's work as "decisively" refuting the hypothesis. But Olson and coauthors David Voas and Alasdair Crockett recently concluded: "results from previous cross-sectional studies on pluralism and religious involvement must now be abandoned" because of a "mathematical relationship between measures of religious participation and the index of pluralism (Voas, Olson, and Crockett 2002).

When comparing the old and new paradigms, the contrasts are many. Rather than treating religion as an epiphenomenon, where the "real" causes of religious phenomena must be uncovered, the new paradigm accepts that religious doctrines per se can have consequences. Whereas the old paradigm was content to identify religion as the opium of the people, the new paradigm notes that religion is also often the "amphetamine" of the people, in that it was religion that animated many medieval peasant and artisan rebellions (Cohn 1961), generated repeated uprisings among the native peoples of Africa and North America against European encroachment (Wilson 1975), and recently served as a major center of mobilization against the tyrants of Eastern Europe (Echikson 1990). Instead of attributing religious decisions to unique or irrational cognitive processes, the new paradigm views religious decision making as compatible with rational, instrumental, and scientific thinking (Wuthnow 1985; Stark and Bainbridge 1987; Stark, Iannaccone, and Finke 1996). And, contrary to the old paradigm's confidence in the superiority of monopoly faiths supported by the state, the new paradigm argues that deregulating religion and increasing competition will spur religious activity. Finally, rather than attempting to explain how modernity causes an inevitable decline in the *demand* for religion, the new paradigm attempts to explain religious variation by looking at the *supply* of religion.

In the remainder of this chapter, we will review how a few propositions on religious economies can help to explain variation and change in religion. We then apply these propositions to three international settings.

RELIGIOUS ECONOMIES AND SUPPLY-SIDE CHANGES

Within all social systems there is a relatively distinct subsystem encompassing religious activity (Stark 1985). We identify this subsystem as a religious economy and define the religious economy as *consisting of all the religious activity going on in any society, including a "market" of current and potential adherents, a set of one or more organizations seeking to attract or maintain adherents, and the religious culture offered by the organization(s).* Just as a commercial economy can be distinguished into elements of supply and demand, so, too, can a religious economy. Indeed, it is the emphasis on the supply side that so distinguishes the new from the old paradigm, for the latter has stressed demand as the primary dynamic propelling religious change. Whereas the old paradigm argued that the forces of modernity reduced the demand for religion, the new paradigm argues that the structure of the religious market can alter the supply of religion.

Regulating Religion

The most significant feature of a religious economy is the degree to which it is deregulated and therefore market-driven as opposed to being regulated by the state in favor of monopoly. The most immediate impact of regulation is on the supply of religions available to people, and the peoples' freedom to choose any of the available religions. This leads to our first proposition on religious supply.

#1: To the degree that a religious economy is unregulated, it will tend to be very pluralistic. Because religious markets are composed of multiple segments or niches, with each sharing particular religious preferences (needs, tastes, and expectations), no single religious firm can satisfy all market niches (see Stark and Finke 2000). More specifically, pluralism arises in unregulated markets because of the inability of a single religious firm to be at once worldly and otherworldly, strict and permissive, exclusive and inclusive, expressive and reserved, or (as Adam Smith put it) austere and loose, while market niches will exist with strong preferences on each of these aspects of religion. Thus, no single religious organization can achieve monopoly through voluntary assent – religious monopolies rest on coercion.

By the same logic, it becomes clear that religious economies never can be fully monopolized, even when backed by the full coercive powers of the state. Indeed, even at the height of its temporal power, the medieval church was surrounded by heresy and dissent (Lambert 1992). Of course, when the repressive efforts of the state are sufficiently intense, religious firms competing with the state-sponsored monopoly will be forced to operate underground. But whenever and wherever repression eases, pluralism will begin to develop. And this pluralism will be sustained by specialized religious firms, each anchored in a specific niche or a complementary set of niches.

Regulation and Sacralization

Although we strongly disagree with Berger's earlier contentions that religious pluralism will erode the plausibility of all religions, we do agree that monopolies are far more effective in exerting power over other institutions.

#2: To the degree that a religious firm achieves a monopoly, it will seek to exert its influence over other institutions and thus the society will be sacralized. The term sacralized means *that there will be little differentiation between religious and secular institutions and that the primary aspects of life, from family to politics, will be suffused with religious symbols, rhetoric, and ritual.* This is precisely the social phenomenon that so often is mistaken for universal piety. The Age of Faith attributed to medieval Europe, for example, is based on the fact that religion was intertwined with other institutions, especially politics and education, and because the presence of religion was so impressively visible. Traveling across Europe today, one's attention constantly is drawn to the magnificent churches and cathedrals that dominate local landscapes. Because all these buildings were built many centuries ago, they seem to offer undeniable proof that once-upon-a-time faith was so universal and robust as to erect these marvelous structures. The truth is quite different. These structures were, in effect, extracted from an unwilling and sullen populace who seldom crossed their thresholds – at least, not for religious purposes. It was because of the piety (and interests) of the medieval ruling classes that religion was so omnipresent and visible on all public occasions. For example, all ceremonies were religious in character, especially political ceremonies such as coronations. Indeed, in sacralized societies political leadership per se typically has a vivid religious hue, as in the "divine right" of kings and emperors. Close ties between religious and political elites are inherent in religious monopolies since without such ties religious monopolies are impossible. Sacralization of the political sphere is the *quid pro quo* by which a religious firm enlists the coercive powers of the state against its competitors.

The inverse of the sacralization, which occurs with religious monopolies, is the desacralization that occurs when monopolies lose the capacity to regulate the religious economy.

#3: To the degree that deregulation of the religious economy occurs in a previously highly regulated economy, the society will be desacralized. When the state, for whatever reasons, no longer ensures claims of exclusive legitimacy by the monopoly faith, desacralization must ensue. Where there are a plurality of religious firms, no one of them is sufficiently potent to sustain sacralization.[2] Nor can sacralization be sustained by some coalition of competing religious firms, for any statements emitted by such a group must be limited to vague generalizations to which all can assent. Perhaps such is the stuff of "civil religion" (Bellah 1967), but it is not the stuff of sacralization. But then, neither is it necessarily a symptom of religious decline.

Desacralization, as we define it, is identical to what many scholars have referred to as the macro form of *secularization*. So long as this definition of secularization is limited to the differentiation of religious and other primary social institutions, we accept it. However, few who apply the term secularization to institutional differentiation are able to resist linking desacralization to a general decline in individual religious commitment (the micro version of secularization), because they are convinced that only religious monopolies can sustain belief. We take the entirely opposite position. Our model of religious economies holds that the demise of religious monopolies and the deregulation of religious economies will result in a general *increase* in individual religious commitment, as more firms (and more motivated firms) gain free access to the market.

As the examples on Latin America and the United States will illustrate, there is often a substantial lag between changes in regulation and changes in sacralization. A former religious monopoly supported by the state often retains cultural standing, as the legitimate and normal church, long after losing much of its temporal power. This cultural standing will initially prevent the acceptance of new religions, slowing the development of religious pluralism, and will allow the once monopoly religion to retain a strong foothold in education, politics, and other institutions. Moreover, before competing religions can challenge the dominant religion's close ties to such institutions, they first must capture a sizeable segment of the religious market. This organizational growth requires the gradual development of social ties and a cultural acceptance often involving several generations. Realize that if a group begins with one thousand members and grows at the astounding rate of 10 percent per year, it will need seventy-five years to reach one million members. Thus, following the deregulation of a religious economy, there are often lengthy delays before a new supply of religions flourish and the extensive process of desacralization ensues.

Religious Competition and Commitment

Yet, if monopolies are effective in infusing the public arena with religious symbolism and supporting majestic and well-funded religious buildings, they are ill-equipped for mobilizing the commitment and support of the people. Herein lies the key distinction between the old and new paradigm. We argue that the founders were entirely wrong about the harmful effects of religious competition. Rather than eroding the plausibility

---

[2] This may well be the reason that sociologists regard religious monopolies as the basis for strong faith and pluralism as inevitably eroding faith. If Peter Berger's notion of the "sacred canopy" is equated with the sacralization of societies, then it is true that a single canopy is necessary, and that multiple canopies don't suffice. But, when the sacred canopy line of thought is construed to mean that personal piety is more abundant under monopoly faith, that is clearly wrong.

of all faiths, competition results in eager and efficient suppliers of religion just as it does among suppliers of secular commodities, and with the same results: far higher levels of overall "consumption."

#4: To the degree that religious economies are unregulated and competitive, overall levels of religious commitment will be high. Conversely, lacking competition, the dominant firm(s) will be too inefficient to sustain vigorous marketing efforts and the result will be a low overall level of religious commitment as the average person minimizes and delays payment of religious costs. Notice our theoretical emphasis on *competition*. Religious pluralism (the presence of multiple suppliers) is important *only* insofar as it increases choices and competition, offering consumers a wider range of religious rewards and forcing suppliers to be more responsive and efficient. A society whose religious economy consists of a dozen rigid castes, each served by its own independent, distinctive religious firm, would be highly pluralistic, but utterly lacking in religious competition. Functionally, the situation of any given individual in such a society would be identical with the situation of an individual in a society having only one, monopoly religious firm. And our prediction would be the same: That within each caste there would be the same low levels of religious commitment as are expected in monopolized religious economies.

Pluralism and competition usually are linked, but when they are not, it is competition that is the energizing force. Misunderstanding of this point seems to have arisen because, lacking direct measures of competition, we often have used measures of pluralism as proxy measures of competition. As noted earlier, however, *above a certain level, pluralism becomes redundant*. In principle, maximum diversity is not reached until everyone in a given population belongs to her or his own individual congregation of one. Not surprisingly, we have discovered that there is a "ceiling effect" – that beyond a certain point the market is *saturated* and additional pluralism does not increase the overall level of religious participation.

This theoretical emphasis on competition also suggests that *individual religious groups will be more energetic and generate higher levels of commitment to the degree that they have a marginal market position – lack market share*. That is, other things being equal, small religious minorities will be more vigorous than will firms with a large local following. Thus, for example, Roman Catholics will be more active, the *less* Catholic their community.

Finally, we should acknowledge that sometimes *conflict can substitute for competition* as the basis for creating aggressive religious firms able to generate high overall levels of religious commitment.

#5: Even where competition is limited, religious firms can generate high levels of commitment to the extent that the firms serve as the primary organizational vehicles for social conflict. Conversely, if religious firms become significantly less important as vehicles for social conflict, they will be correspondingly less able to generate commitment. Consider the example of the society noted above in which a dozen rigid castes each has its own religious firm. Now suppose there is a high level of conflict among these castes and that the religious firms serve as the organizational basis for these conflicts. Perhaps the temples serve as the gathering place for planning all political action, protest demonstrations begin at the temples, and religious symbols are used to identify caste solidarity. In these situations, religious commitment would be inseparable from group loyalty, just as high levels of Catholic commitment in Ireland and Quebec both symbolized and sustained opposition to the English ruling elites in each society. The same principle applies to Islamic "fundamentalism." Opposition to political, economic, and cultural colonialism has found its firmest institutional basis in the mosque. In the following section, we illustrate this proposition with a more extensive discussion of the Catholic Church in Quebec.

ILLUSTRATING THE EFFECTS OF REGULATION

Rather than reviewing the extensive research literature addressing the above proposi-tions, the following section will illustrate how the propositions can be applied to three very different settings. First, we will turn to the United States, a nation in which the religious economy has been largely deregulated for over two centuries. Next, we will turn to Latin America. Here we will review nations where the Roman Catholic Church held a strong alliance with the state for over four centuries. Our final example will be Quebec, Canada, where we observe the changes in the Roman Catholic Church as it relinquishes its role as the mobilizing force against English ruling elites.

The Lively Experiment in America

The prominent historian Sidney Mead (1963: 52) once noted that the "Revolutionary Epoch is the hinge upon which the history of Christianity in America really turns" and explained that "religious freedom and separation of church and state" were at the cen-ter of these changes. Long before Mead made these observations, however, nineteenth-century European visitors were quick to comment on the sectarianism and religious vitality resulting from the "voluntary principle" (Powell 1967). Indeed, two of the ear-liest surveys of American religion, *America* by Philip Schaff (1855/1961) and *Religion in the United States of America* by Robert Baird (1844/1969), used the voluntary principle to explain the unusually high level of religious activity and the growing number of sects in the United States. Although both authors denounced the religious competition and sectarianism that splintered the unity of God's kingdom, they acknowledged that the religious freedoms have "brought gospel influences to bear in every direction" (Baird 1844/1969: 409).

Yet, the growth of organized religion, which captured the attention of Alexis de Tocqueville (1831/1969), Andrew Reed (1835), and other prominent European visitors, did not arise overnight. Despite increasing religious toleration and eroding support for the religious establishments throughout the colonial era, only 17 percent of the population (including children) were adherents of a church in 1776. This rate doubled to 34 percent by 1850, but it wasn't until the early twentieth century that the level of adherence began to approach contemporary rates – 56 percent in 1926 compared to 62 percent in 1980 (Finke and Stark 1992). Despite the aggressive evangelical outreach and rapid growth of the Protestant sects, and the effective outreach of the Roman Catholics and Lutherans to new immigrants, it was well over one hundred years (1906) after deregulating the American religious economy before churches enrolled 50 percent of the population.

Although all areas of the United States, including Mormon Utah, now offer a plethora of religious choices, this was not the case in early America. When looking at

Table 8.1. Competition and Church Attendance in New York Towns, 1865

	Number of denominations in a New York town			
	0	1–2	3–4	5+
Towns with >25% church attendance	0%	18%	55%	84%
N =	42	280	37	237

Table 8.2. Competition and Commitment in American Towns and Villages, 1923–1925

	Number of churches per one thousand population			
	One	Two	Three	Four or More
Percent who belong to a church	27.4	36.0	34.8	43.4
Percent enrolled in Sunday schools	15.8	22.3	25.2	37.4

Source: Adapted from Brunner (1927: 74).

New York cities in 1865 and 1875, we found that the greatest jump in church attendance came between cities having no religious choice and those having some (see Table 8.1). Even as late as the 1920s, when Edmund deS. Brunner (1927) conducted a series of exceptionally well-executed studies of religious life in 138 small towns and villages, religious choice was lacking in many rural communities (see Table 8.2). Once again, a sharp increase in involvement occurs between those communities having some choice as compared to those with none. The diffusion of religious movements throughout the nation, combined with increasing population density and improved transportation, has gradually led to a nation in which religious choice is ubiquitous.

Like religious choice and popular religious involvement, there also was a substantial lag between the deregulation of religion and the desacralization of related institutions (Moore 1986). Perhaps the easiest to document is the relationship between religion and the emerging public (common) schools in the nineteenth century. The Catholic historian Jay Dolan (1985: 266) explains that the public schools "became the established church of the American republic" intolerant of other religious ideologies. This intolerance led to the formation of an extensive Catholic school system, holding the firm backing of the American bishops and the Vatican. In 1875, the Vatican warned (Ellis 1962: 401, 404) that "evils of the gravest kind are likely to result" from the American public schools and that if Catholic parents sent their children to the public schools "without sufficient cause and without taking the necessary precautions... if obstinate, cannot be absolved." Even the nineteenth-century educational reformer Horace Mann, who often is credited with the gradual removal of religion from the public schools, took a stance of retaining religious instruction on Christian morals and continuing the use of the King James Bible in the classroom (Butts and Cremin 1958). Writing in 1848, he commented that the idea of removing religious instruction from the public schools was unthinkable to the entire population: "I do not suppose a man [sic] can be found in Massachusetts who would declare such a system to be his first choice" (Blau 1950: 188). When the Supreme Court ruled against school sponsored prayers in 1962 (*Engel v. Vitale*), the outcry was immediate, as the ruling represented one more step in the desacralizing of American institutions (Reichley 1985: 145).

Following the deregulation of the American religious economy in the late eighteenth century, the level of involvement increased steadily until reaching a plateau in approximately 1926. Religious pluralism continued to increase with all areas of the nation now having a wide range of religious options, and the process of desacralization has gradually differentiated religious and social institutions. For each of these areas, however, the changes began immediately following religious deregulation, but required several generations before the full impact could be seen. The next section turns to Latin American nations, where the deregulation, or separation of church and state, has occurred more recently and less completely.

Supply-Side Changes in Latin America

For over four centuries, the Roman Catholic Church was the established church of Latin America. The Church received generous financial and legislative support from the state and exerted extensive influence over other social institutions, including education, family, and politics. But the newly independent republics of the early nineteenth century began questioning this relationship, and by the late nineteenth and early twentieth century the governments sought formal disestablishment. Although new religions still faced strong resistance and stiff regulations, with Catholicism remaining the dominant cultural force and holding close ties with the political and social elites, the eroding authority of Catholicism opened the door for foreign missions. By the 1930s, a growing wave of evangelical Protestant missionaries began to arrive. Initially, the progress was extremely slow, requiring time for social networks and trust to develop between the missionaries and the locals. Following World War II, however, the primary missionary work was progressively taken over by local converts and a rapid growth ensued. Not only were the locals more effective in missionizing, they were more difficult for the Catholic church to regulate (Gill 1998, 1999). Whereas foreign missionaries can be evicted or denied entry, local citizens are more difficult to control.

The consequences of this gradual reduction in religious regulation were similar to those in the United States. First, the reduced regulations lowered the entry costs for new religions and resulted in a flowering of new sects. This new supply of religions included numerous Protestant sects, Mormons, Jehovah Witnesses, multiple indigenous religions, and movements combining religious traditions. Second, as the operating costs of the new religions were reduced, the rapid growth of the upstart sects resembled that of the early-nineteenth-century American upstarts (see Martin 1990: 36–42). As early as 1973, the Brazilian newspaper *Estado de Sao Paulo* argued that Brazil had more "real" Protestants than "real" Catholics, noting that there were now more ordained Protestant pastors than ordained Catholic priests (Stoll 1990: 6). David Martin (1990: 50) reports that, in the late 1960s, evangelical Protestants held fifteen million adherents and two decades later the number was "at least forty million." If current rates of Protestant growth hold for another twenty years, Protestants will be the majority in many Latin nations – they already make up the majority of those actually in church each Sunday. Third, the aggressive marketing of the new religions has forced the once established church to increase its appeal to the people. When Protestant competition first challenged Catholicism in the 1940s and 1950s, the Church turned to the state for protection (Gill 1999). By the late 1960s, after the state proved ineffective in eliminating the challengers, the Church increased its own evangelical efforts using techniques that were remarkably similar to their Protestant competitors, for example, "Bible reading, lay leadership, and close-knit fraternal groups" (Stoll 1990: 30). The Church's ability to increase seminary enrollment, and to generate other institutional resources from (and for) the people, has been positively related to the level of competition being faced (Stark 1992; Gill 1999). The higher the rate of evangelical Protestants in a nation, the more aggressively the Catholic Church markets the faith.

The process of desacralization also has accompanied the gradual deregulation of religion in Latin America. Initially, the state led the charge, seeking to reduce the influence of the church in the political, educational, and economic arenas. Throughout Latin American nations, the Church lost properties and landholdings, education became more secularized, religious toleration was granted, and the civil registry was not administered by the Church. But as religious competition increased and the people became the core of the Church's resources, the Church started to distance itself from the state. Based on quantitative data on Latin American nations, and cases studies of individual nations, Anthony Gill (1998:104) reports that "religious competition is the best predictor of episcopal opposition to authoritarian rule compared to a variety of other potential explanations." Now appealing to the people for favor, rather than the state, the church no longer offers a blind allegiance to political leaders and is frequently a potent force of opposition.

Conflict and Commitment in Quebec

The previous examples have illustrated how religious deregulation leads to an immediate increase in religious supply and to gradual increases in the level of religious involvement and desacralization. Yet the final proposition, that sometimes *conflict can substitute for competition*, has not been addressed. Here we turn to Quebec, Canada, to illustrate this proposition.

When Canada was seized from France by force of arms, those French residents not deported to Louisiana remained a subjugated ethnic minority. In this situation, mass attendance was inseparable from political and cultural resistance, with French Canadians long displaying remarkably high levels of religious commitment. According to national surveys reported by Barrett (1982), 83 percent of Catholics attended weekly in 1946 as did 65 percent in 1970. Why? Because the church was the only major organization under the control of French Canadians; all other institutions including political parties were dominated by English Canadians.

Writing in 1937, historian Elizabeth Armstrong explained that in the "175 years since the conquest [the Roman Catholic Church] has become more and more closely identified with the interests and aspirations of the French Canadian people until it almost seems that the Church is French Canada" (Armstrong 1937/1967: 36). For French Canadians, the Catholic Church protected their rights, guarded their institutions, and preserved the French culture and language. Armstrong recognized that the people's allegiance to the Church even surpassed their allegiance to the faith: "Doubtless there are many people who do not accept the teaching of the Church, but they are apt to go to mass and to keep their opinions to themselves" (Armstrong 1937/1967: 38). Beginning with the "quiet revolution" from 1960 to 1966, however, French Canadians began to acquire more rights over their own institutions and in 1974 the National Assembly adopted French as Quebec's official language (Moniére 1981). The Church was no longer the sole guardian of French Canadians' institutions and culture.

Stripped of its significance as the organizational basis for resisting outside domination, the Catholic Church in Quebec quickly began to display the typical inefficiencies of a monopoly faith. Indeed, based on the 1990 World Values Survey, Catholic mass attendance now is significantly lower in Quebec (29 percent weekly) than elsewhere in Canada (47 percent weekly), fully in accord with the thesis that the Catholic Church generates greater commitment in places where it is a minority faith. Given the Church's greatly reduced sociopolitical role, both the high level of Catholic practice in the past and its recent, rapid decline, are consistent with our theory. As stated in proposition 5, if religious firms become significantly less important as vehicles for social conflict, they will be correspondingly less able to generate commitment. No longer the guardian of French institutions and culture, the Church is generating less membership commitment.

CONCLUSION

Despite refuting the secularization thesis, and other long-held propositions of the old paradigm, the new paradigm does not replace predictions on the inevitable decline in the demand for religion with equally implausible predictions on an inevitable increase. Instead, the new paradigm attempts to explain variation in religious activity by placing attention on the changing religious supply.

This chapter reviewed a few propositions on religious economies to illustrate how the new paradigm explains religious change. We argued that the most significant feature of a religious economy is the degree to which it is deregulated and therefore market-driven. The effects of such regulation are many, with the most immediate impact being the supply of religions available to people, and the people's freedom to choose any of the available religions. But the long-term effects of changes in regulation are changes in the sacralization of the society and the religious commitment of the people. As illustrated by the United States and Latin America, religious deregulation leads to an increasingly desacralized society, where there is increasing differentiation between religious and secular institutions. This is a very gradual process, with the once privileged establishments holding cultural and political advantages long after the official ties between church and state were severed.

Religious deregulation also generates religious competition between a growing number of energetic and efficient religious firms; a competition that increases the overall level of religious commitment. In the case of the United States and Latin America, deregulation unleashed a host of new competing sects that displayed rapid organizational growth. Like desacralization, however, this growth required a substantial period of time. After approximately fifty years of rapid growth, Latin American sects are now enrolling a substantial portion of the population. For the United States, it was well over one hundred years before over one half of the population joined a church. In each case, the religious groups with a marginal market position generated the highest levels of member commitment.

The final proposition stressed that conflict can substitute for competition in generating religious commitment. When serving as the organizational basis for resisting oppression or outside threats, a monopoly firm can generate very high levels of commitment. Once the religious firm is no longer the vehicle for social conflict, however, the firms will display the typical inefficiencies of a monopoly faith. We offered the example of Quebec, but Ireland, Poland, and many Islamic nations also could illustrate how conflict can substitute for competition.

This chapter offers only a brief introduction to the dynamics of religious economies. Along with ignoring the micro (individual decision making) and the organizational foundations, we have lacked the space needed to review many other key propositions on religious economies (Stark and Finke 2000). For example, what explains the over- or undersupply of religious firms in various market niches? What factors determine the formation of new religious groups and the level of tension they hold with the sociocultural environment? How is a group's tension related to market niches and organizational growth? Yet, even with this brief introduction, we have tried to illustrate the power of the religious market structure, or supply-side changes, for explaining religious variation and change.

CHAPTER NINE

Historicizing the Secularization Debate

An Agenda for Research

Philip S. Gorski

The trends are quite clear: In most parts of the West, Christian belief and practice have declined significantly, at least since World War II, and probably for much longer (e.g., Ashford and Timms 1992; Davie 1999). The variations are also quite clear: In a few countries, such as Ireland and Poland, levels of belief and practice are still very high; in others, however, such as Sweden and Denmark, they are quite low.

But what do these trends and variations mean? And how might we explain them? Current thinking on these questions among sociologists of religion is dominated by two opposing positions. The first is classical secularization theory, which sees the recent decline of Christian religiosity as part of a general trend toward greater "secularity" and an inevitable consequence of "modernization." The second is the "religious economies model." It argues that transhistorical and cross-national variations in "religious vitality" are caused by differences in the structure of "religious markets," and, more specifically, that the freer religious markets are, the more vital religion will be.

Who is right? The diehard defenders of secularization theory? Or their upstart critics from the religious economies school? In my view, the answer is "probably neither." I say "neither" because there is now a great deal of evidence which speaks against both of these theories – against the view that modernization inevitably undermines religion and against the view that "free markets" (in religion) generally promote it – evidence, moreover, which seems better accounted for by other theoretical perspectives that have been forgotten or ignored in the recent debate. But I would add the qualification "probably," because the accumulated evidence is still too thin historically and too narrow geographically to allow for any credible judgements: as sociologists of religion, we know a great deal about the twentieth-century West, but relatively little about anything else.

For those interested in advancing the current debate, then, two tasks would seem to be of especial importance. One is to revive and/or elaborate alternative theories of religious change. In what follows, I will discuss two perspectives that I regard as particularly promising: (a) a *sociopolitical perspective*, which focuses on conflict and competition between religious and nonreligious elites and movements; and (b) *a religiocultural perspective*, which focuses on the relationship between religious and nonreligious values and worldviews, both within different religious traditions, and across different stages of religious development. The second task is to contextualize the postwar developments, both historically and sociologically. This means studying the ebbs and flows of secularity over the *longue duree*, and examining the interactions between religious and nonreligious actors and institutions.

THE RECEIVED ORTHODOXY: CLASSICAL SECULARIZATION THEORY

The roots of classical secularization theory can be traced back to the early nineteenth century and the writings of Henri Saint-Simon and Auguste Comte.[1] Although their analyses differed somewhat in the details, both argued that human history passes through a series of distinct stages, in which the power and plausibility of traditional religion are gradually and irreversibly undermined by the growing influence of the state and of science (Saint-Simon 1969; Comte 1830–42/1969). In their view, modernity and religion don't mix. This view was later echoed in the writings of sociology's "founding fathers" – Marx, Durkheim, and Weber. While each viewed Christianity somewhat differently, all agreed that its significance was definitely on the wane. This became the dominant view within Anglo-American sociology as well. With the notable exception of Parsons (1963), postwar sociologists of religion all agreed that the public influence of religion was shrinking, and many thought that private belief itself was bound to decline or even disappear (e.g., Berger 1967; Luckmann 1963). During the 1960s, the "secularization thesis" was integrated into "modernization theory" and became one of its central axioms. As societies modernized, they became more complex, more rationalized, more individualistic – and less religious. Or so the argument went. Today, of course, modernization theory has few adherents – except among sociologists of religion. While the rest of the discipline has moved on to other approaches, present-day defenders of secularization theory continue to use the old modernization-theoretic framework (e.g., Dobbelaere 1981; Wilson 1982; Bruce 1996), a framework that still bears strong resemblances to the classical theory of secularization propounded by Comte and Saint-Simon.

From the perspective of classical secularization theory (henceforth: CST), then, the decline in orthodox Christian beliefs and practices in most parts of the West is interpreted as a part of a more general decline in the power of religious institutions and ideas and explained with reference to various social processes (e.g., differentiation, rationalization, industrialization, and urbanization), which are loosely bundled together with the rubric of "modernization." As social institutions become more differentiated and social life becomes more rationalized, the argument goes, religious institutions and beliefs lose their power and plausibility.

In support of these claims, defenders of secularization theory usually point to two well-documented developments. The first is the establishment and expansion of secular institutions in the fields of social provision, education, moral counseling, and other fields of activity once dominated by the church, a development they characterize as a "loss of social functions." The second is the long-term decline in orthodox Christian practice and belief noticed by contemporary observers beginning in the late nineteenth century and subsequently confirmed in opinion polls throughout the postwar period. The fact that these declines have been especially pronounced among industrial workers

---

[1] For a more detailed discussion of the development of secularization theory, see especially Tschannen 1992.

and educated city-dwellers – by some standards, the most "modernized" sectors of society – seemed to underscore the connection between secularity and modernity.

There are two main sets of objections one might raise against CST. One regards evidence and interpretation. As we have seen, secularization theorists view the recent downtrend in orthodox Christianity as part of a long-term decline in religiosity *per se*. However, it is not at all clear that the twentieth-century downtrend is really part of a long-term decline, and proponents of CST have not produced much hard evidence to suggest that it is. The usual way of "proving" this claim is to assault the reader with a barrage of twentieth-century evidence, and then confront them with a romanticized portrait of the Middle Ages, in which Christendom is all-encompassing, and all are devout Christians – a portrait that is no longer credible.[2] Unless and until better evidence is forthcoming, the hypothesis of long-term decline must remain just that – a hypothesis. And even if such evidence were forthcoming, it still would not suffice to prove the broader claim that religion *per se* is in decline. After all, the simple fact that orthodox Christianity has lost ground does not necessarily imply that religion itself is on the wane. For example, it could be that Christianity is in a transitional phase, similar to the one that occurred during the Reformation era. Or, it could be that other religions will eventually take its place, in much the same way that Christianity supplanted "paganism" in late Antiquity. Or it could be that the very nature of religiosity is changing, as it did in the Axial Age transitions that occurred in many parts of the world roughly two millennia ago. And even if religion *per se* is really on the wane of late, there is no reason to assume that the decline is permanent or irreversible. The history of religion is rife with ebbs and flows, and Christianity is no exception to this rule. Maybe the recent decline is really just a cyclical downturn of sorts. To make a strong case for long-term decline, then, secularization theorists would need to extend their analysis back beyond the modern era, something they have not yet done.

This brings us to the second set of objections. They concern the theory itself and, more specifically, the claim that the recent downtrend in Christian devotion can be traced to the effects of "modernization." If this claim were correct, then we would expect to find a strong, inverse relationship between the various dimensions of modernization (e.g., industrialization, urbanization, differentiation, and rationalization) and various indicators of secularization (e.g., levels of religious belief and participation). In other words, we would expect to find strong correlations between modernization and secularization across both time and space. As we have seen, there is some evidence that seems to support this claim. When we begin to compare different countries, however, the picture becomes more complex – and less clear-cut (on the following, see especially Höllinger 1996). Take Scandinavia and the Benelux nations, for example. Despite their late industrialization and sparse population, and the existence of unified state churches, the Scandinavian countries, have long been, and still remain, the least devout and observant countries in Western Europe. In Belgium and the Netherlands, by contrast, where urbanization and industrialization began much earlier, and a higher degree of church-state separation prevails, orthodox Christianity is relatively stronger. Nor are these the only anomalies of this sort. Why, one might ask, are the Italians more observant than the Spanish? And why are Americans generally more observant than

---

[2] For a typical example of this rhetorical procedure, see Bruce 1996. The classic critiques of this romanticized view of the Middle Ages are Delumeau (1977) and Thomas (1971).

Europeans? It is not at all clear that these differences in religious observance can be traced to differences in modernization.

There is also another anomaly that is worth noting: the difference in Protestant and Catholic rates of observance. Based on the classical theory, we might expect "supernatural" forms of religious faith such as Catholicism and fundamentalist Protestantism, to decline more quickly than more "rational" types of religiosity, such as liberal Protestantism. But in fact the very opposite appears to be the case. Throughout the West, Catholics are more observant than Protestants, and fundamentalist and evangelical Protestants are more observant than their "liberal" and "mainline" coreligionists. Thus, there are important variations – cross-national and interdenominational variations – which do not readily conform to the expectations of secularization theory. It is precisely these variations that the next theory – the religious economies model – claims to explain, and it is to that theory that I now turn.

PRETENDERS TO THE THRONE: THE RELIGIOUS ECONOMIES MODEL

Why do levels of religious belief and practice vary so much from one country to the next? As we have just seen, classical secularization theory does not provide a complete or satisfying answer to this question. It is this deficit that the religious economies model (REM) seeks to address. Drawing on neoclassical economics, proponents of the REM argue that "religious vitality" is positively related to "religious competition" and negatively related to "religious regulation." More specifically, they argue that where "religious markets" are dominated by a small number of large "firms" (i.e., churches) or heavily "regulated" by the state, the result will be lethargic (religious) "firms," shoddy (religious) "products," and low levels of (religious) "consumption" – in a word: Religious stagnation. By contrast, where many firms compete in an open market without government interference, individual firms will have to behave entrepreneurially, the "quality" and "selection" of religious products will be higher, and individual consumers will be more likely to find a religion which is to their liking and standards. If there are variations in the level of "religious vitality," they conclude, these are due not to "secularization" but to changes in the "religious economy."

Since the late 1980s, proponents of the religious economies model have produced a steady stream of books and articles that appear to confirm the theory (e.g., Finke and Stark 1988; Stark and Iannaccone 1994; Finke, Guest, and Stark 1996; Finke and Stark, Chapter 8, this volume; for an exhaustive bibliography, see Chaves and Gorski 2001). Most of them have focused on the effects of religious competition, rather than religious regulation. The most pertinent of these studies examine the relationship between "religious pluralism" (operationalized in terms of the Herfindahl Index, a standard measure of market concentration) and "religious vitality" (operationalized in terms of religious belief, church membership, or church attendance) (e.g., Finke and Stark 1988, 1989; Finke 1992; Stark et al. 1995; Finke et al. 1996; Hamberg and Pettersson 1994, 1997; Johnson 1995; Pettersson and Hamberg 1997). These studies generally find a positive relationship between religious pluralism and religious vitality.[3] Based on these

---

[3] There is also a second and smaller group of studies that examines the relationship between the relative size of a particular religion – its "market share" – and its internal "vitality" (e.g., Stark and McCann 1993). These studies show that minority religions receive more support from their

findings, the leading proponents of the REM claim to have disproven the secularization thesis and argue that the term "secularization" should be "dropped from all theoretical discourse" (Stark and Iannaccone 1994: 231). Is their claim justified?

The work of the religious economies school has been challenged on a number of different fronts. Some scholars accepted the empirical findings, but questioned their theoretical significance (e.g., Lechner 1991; Yamane 1997; Gorski 2000). They pointed out that secularization theory is a theory, not only of individual behavior, but also, and indeed *primarily*, of social-structural change. In their view, secularization refers first and foremost to an increasing differentiation between the religious and nonreligious spheres of life, and only secondarily to its effects on individual behavior. Since the REM focuses exclusively on individual behavior, they argue, it does not really address the core claim of secularization theory and speaks only to those versions of the theory that postulate a direct connection between increasing (social-level) differentiation and decreasing (individual-level) religiosity.

Other scholars have challenged the reliability and validity of the findings themselves (e.g., Blau et al. 1992; Breault 1989a, 1989b; Olson 1998, 1999). Using new datasets of their own, or reanalyzing REM data, these scholars often obtained null or negative correlations between pluralism and vitality. Defenders of the REM then challenged these results on methodological grounds (Finke and Stark 1988; Finke et al. 1996). The ensuing debate was long and complex, but the key issue was Catholics. Many of the analyses that had yielded a positive correlation between religious pluralism and religious vitality also included a statistical control for "percent Catholic." Advocates of the REM defended this procedure on the grounds that the Catholic Church displayed a high degree of "internal pluralism," and that treating it as a single denomination would therefore distort the findings. Critics pointed out that the positive relationship between pluralism and vitality usually disappeared or became negative when the control was removed (see especially Olson 1999). More important, they showed that removing *any* group with the characteristics of the (American) Catholic population – large in overall size but varied in local presence – would *automatically* result in a positive finding, and for purely arithmetic reasons!

On the whole, then, the REM's claims to have disproven the secularization thesis and laid the foundations for a "new paradigm" in the sociology of religion are somewhat overblown. As we have seen, the central findings of the REM do not really address the core concerns of secularization theory, and are themselves open to dispute. Indeed, in a recent survey of the literature on "religious pluralism" and "religious participation," Chaves and Gorski (2001) found that the balance of evidence actually tips *against* the REM, once we exclude analyses that employ inappropriate measures of competition or statistical controls for percent Catholic.

Of course, it is possible that further research could tip the balance back the other way. But this seems unlikely to me. For even a cursory review of the comparative and historical evidence reveals two large and potentially troubling anomalies for the REM. The first regards Catholic-Protestant differences. As we saw earlier, overall levels of Christian practice in various Western countries are closely related to the proportion of the

members than majority religions, a finding that also has been replicated by scholars working outside the religious economies perspective (e.g., Zaleski and Zech 1995; Johnson 1995; Perl and Olson 2000; but see also Phillips 1998).

populace that is Catholic: The highest levels of religious participation are to be found in homogeneously Catholic countries (e.g., Ireland, Poland, Italy, Austria), while the lowest levels are in homogeneously Protestant countries (e.g., the Scandinavian lands), with confessionally mixed countries (e.g., Germany, the Netherlands and Britain) generally falling somewhere in between. This state of affairs is very much at odds with the competition thesis – the thesis that greater competition is always correlated with greater vitality – and, indeed, statistical analysis suggests that this thesis cannot be sustained for Western Europe as a whole (Chaves and McCann 1992).

Now, it could be that the relationship between Catholicism and vitality is actually spurious, and that the actual cause of the observed variations is religious regulation. In other words, one could argue that the differences between Catholic, mixed, and Protestant countries are really due to differences in the level of state control over the church. For it is true that the Catholic Church often has more institutional and financial autonomy than its Protestant rivals, and it is also true that the Protestant Churches in the confessionally mixed countries of North Atlantic Europe are more autonomous than their Protestant brethren in the Scandinavian countries. And, in fact, this hypothesis – that religious regulation is negatively related to religious vitality – has withstood statistical scrutiny (Chaves and McCann 1992). Unfortunately, it is not clear that the regulation hypothesis can withstand historical scrutiny. If the regulation hypothesis were correct, then one would expect that the historical declines in religious vitality that began during the late nineteenth century and accelerated during the 1960s would have been preceded by increases in religious regulation. But this does not appear to have been the case. In most countries, levels of religious regulation actually declined during this period. What is more, there is some evidence that suggests that these declines in regulation were actually preceded by declines in vitality. Thus, both the sign and the direction of the relationship between regulation and vitality appear to have been the opposite of those predicted by the REM (see Gorski and Wilson 1998; Bruce 1999). Why?

I now turn to a third approach that suggests some possible explanations for these anomalies.

A THIRD APPROACH: THE SOCIOPOLITICAL CONFLICT MODEL

Different as they may be in most other respects, there is at least one important similarity between classical secularization theory and the religious economies model: Neither pays much attention to politics. For classical secularization theorists, of course, politics plays no role whatsoever: "Religious decline" is the product of deep-rooted, socioeconomic changes, such as urbanization and industrialization. As for the supply-side model, politics do enter in to some degree, but only as an exogenous and secondary factor, that is, as state "regulation" of the "religious economy." There are other scholars, however, for whom politics has loomed larger and been more central, in both the *explanans* and the *explanandum*. They see sociopolitical conflict as the master variable in the secularization process, and changes in church-state relations as a key part of the outcome. But these scholars have played little role in the recent debate over secularization, perhaps because most of them are historians. This is unfortunate, since their work speaks directly to the problems at hand, and may help to resolve some of the anomalies generated by classical secularization theory and the religious economies model. I will refer to their approach as the sociopolitical conflict model (henceforth: SPCM).[4]

In the English-speaking world, the best known and most cogent proponents of the SPCM are probably David Martin (in sociology) and Hugh McLeod (in history) (Martin 1978; McLeod 1995, 1996; see also Höllinger 1996). On first reading, their views may seem very similar to those of Stark et al., insofar as they stress the effects of "competition" and "pluralism." And, in fact, members of the religious economies school often cite proponents of the sociopolitical conflict model in support of their own positions. On closer inspection, however, the resemblance between the two models proves to be superficial, for when Martin and McLeod speak of "competition," they mean competition not only between different churches, as in the REM, but also competition between different worldviews, both religious and secular. In particular, they argue that Protestant, Catholic, and Jewish religious communities were competing, not just with one another but also with "political religions," such as socialism, liberalism, nationalism, and, later, fascism. Similarly, when McLeod and Martin discuss the effects of "pluralism," they understand them in political rather than (quasi-)economic terms. Their central line of argument could be summarized as follows: In situations of religious monopoly, church and state will tend to become closely identified with one another, and social protest and partisan opposition will tend to evolve in an anticlerical or anti-Christian direction; a high level of religious disengagement is the result. In situations of religious pluralism, by contrast, in which some churches and church leaders are institutionally and politically independent of the state and the ruling elite, opposition to the existing regime did not automatically translate into opposition to the religion *per se*, and could even be expressed in religious terms; here, the degree of religious disengagement is likely to be lower.

The advantage of this approach can be seen in its ability to account for one of the major anomalies generated by the religious economies approach, namely, the paradoxical combination of decreasing "vitality" with increasing "pluralism" and decreasing "regulation," which can be observed in many parts of the West beginning in the late nineteenth century.[5] From the perspective of the SPCM, the decrease in "vitality" – in orthodox belief, belonging and participation – *was* the result of competition, but the competition came, not from other churches, but rather, from nonreligious movements, which offered many goods previously monopolized by the church: Comprehensive worldviews, a social safety net, and communal and associational life. One of the things that these movements often fought for was a loosening of ties between church and state – that is, a decrease in religious "regulation." In this, they were sometimes aided and abetted by "sectarian" religious movements, who bridled at the privileges of state churches. To the degree that they were successful, these campaigns against religious

---

[4] It should be emphasized at the outset that the "sociopolitical conflict model" is not a model in quite the same sense or the same degree as secularization theory or the religious economies approach, since it is not rooted in a general theory of social change (e.g., "modernization theory") or human behavior (e.g., "neoclassical economics") and is not associated with a particular "school" or discipline. Rather, it is an interpretive framework that has emerged out of the historical researches of a loose-knit group of scholars.

[5] Interestingly, there is now some research that suggests that the recent increase in religious nonaffiliation in the United States may be partly a reaction to the close ties between Christian fundamentalists and conservative Republicans. On this, see Hout and Fischer (2002).

regulation created a situation more conducive to the growth of religious pluralism, that is, to the emergence and growth of alternative religions, and thereby reinforced and expanded the constituency which supported decreased regulation. From the perspective of the SPCM, then, the combination of decreasing vitality, increasing pluralism, and decreasing regulation is not paradoxical, and the fact that decreasing vitality preceded decreased regulation and increased pluralism is no longer anomalous.

But what about the second anomaly facing the REM, namely, the greater religious vitality of contemporary Catholicism? To my knowledge, this problem has not been explicitly addressed by advocates of the SPCM. But the SPCM does suggest a possible answer: One might hypothesize that varying levels of religious vitality are bound up with varying responses to the secularist movement. In most places, Catholics responded to the socialist and liberal "threat" by building social milieux and political parties of their own. The result of these efforts was Christian Democracy, a movement that remains powerful even today in many parts of Europe (e.g., Hanley 1994; Becker et al. 1990). Similar responses can be seen in some Protestant countries, such as Norway and the Netherlands (Scholten 1969). But the resulting movements and parties may not have been as broad (socially and geographically) or as deep (organizationally and politically) as their Catholic counterparts, perhaps because the Protestant Churches lacked a centralized leadership structure capable of coordinating the various movements, or perhaps because the Protestant churches were more (financially) beholden to, and thus less (politically) autonomous from, the state. But these are no more than tentative hypotheses. Historians have only begun the task of identifying and explaining these cross-national differences, and have not yet brought quantitative data or comparative methods to bear in any systematic way. Clearly, this is one area in which historical sociology and the sociology of religion could contribute to the study of secularization.

One also might extend this general line of argument to explain intraconfessional variations in religious vitality, that is for the varying levels of religious vitality that we observe *within* the Catholic and Protestant blocs, between Italy (high) and France (low), for instance, or Norway (low) and Sweden (very low). One could hypothesize that these variations in religious vitality were because of variations in the relative success of the Christian Democratic movement and its various Protestant analogues, and one might attempt to explain these latter differences with the standard tools of social movement theory (i.e., "resources," "political opportunity," "frames"). Here is another area in which sociologists – especially political sociologists – might be able to add to the debate.

The SPCM is also superior to its rivals in another respect: It provides a concrete explanation for macro-societal secularization, that is, for the diminution of religious authority within particular institutions or sectors of society. Proponents of the REM have either ignored this second, macro-societal dimension, or defined it away, by insisting – quite wrongly! – that secularization refers only to a decline in individual religiosity. This cannot be said of the classical secularization theorists or their present-day defenders, of course, for whom the sharpening of boundaries between religious and nonreligious roles and institutions, and the declining scope of religious authority within various sectors of society has always been a – even *the* – key aspect of secularization. But they have tended to explain macro-societal secularization in a vague and often tautological fashion, as the result of other macro-societal trends, such as "modernization," "differentiation," and "rationalization," which are closely related to secularization. By contrast, the SPCM suggests a much more concrete and clear-cut explanation of macro-societal secularization, an approach that focuses on battles between religious and secularist movements for control of particular institutions and sectors, such as schools and education, or marriage and moral counseling. Indeed, scholars working within this tradition have already produced case studies of societal secularization for specific countries and contexts (for overviews and references, see Bauberot 1994). What they have not produced, at least not yet, are systematic typologies and comparisons, which would allow one to classify and explain the forms and degrees of macro-societal secularization across various countries and contexts. This, too, is an area in which sociologists might be able to contribute.

Unlike its rivals, then, the SPCM suggests clear and plausible answers for one of the key questions that confronts contemporary sociologists and historians of religion, namely: What explains the recent historical trends and cross-national variations in both Christian religious practice and macro-societal secularization? There are at least two other sets of questions, though, which the SPCM does *not* answer – or even begin to address. We have already encountered the first. It concerns the theoretical interpretation of the historical trends, whether they point to decline, downturn, transition, or transformation. These are not the kinds of questions that are susceptible to a definitive answer; the social sciences are often poor at predicting the future. But it would be possible to shed some light on them, by situating the present more firmly within the past. Thus, one of the key tasks for future research will be to put what we know about the modern trends into historical perspective. The first step in this process would be to trace out the ups and downs – for ups and downs – in Christian practice and ecclesiastical authority as far back as the historical literatures and sources allow. In the case of ecclesiastical authority, this should not be a difficult task. The institutional history of the Western Church and its involvement in politics, education, charity, art, the family and other fields are well documented and well studied. Tracking the level of Christian belief and practice across time would be a more difficult undertaking, but not an impossible one. Early modern and medieval historians have unearthed a great deal of evidence on the religious practices of the premodern populace, some of it quantitative in form. By mining local and regional studies, and combining them with modern sources, such as census data and survey research, it should be possible to piece together some sort of picture of religious participation for various parts of Europe perhaps as far back as the late Middle Ages.

The next step in the process would be to put the patterns themselves in context – to figure out what they tell us about changes in religiosity *per se*. In this regard, it is important to bear in mind that variations in religious participation are not necessarily the result of variations in individual religiosity. They also can be – and sometimes are – caused by social factors such as the geographical proximity of religious services (a serious problem during the Middle Ages) or laws requiring regular church attendance (a common provision in the Reformation era) or influenced by the presence (or absence) of nonreligious incentives, such as access to church schools or eligibility for religious charity. Variations in religious participation also may reflect changes in the *quality of collective religiosity* rather than the quantity of individual religiosity. *Caeterus paribus*, a religion that sees ritual life and priestly intervention as a *sine qua non* of individual salvation (e.g., Catholicism) is likely to generate higher levels of religious participation than one which sees individual salvation as the result of individual faith (e.g., Lutheranism) or predestination (e.g., Calvinism). Thus, it could be that the observed variations in religious participation are due less to changing levels of individual religiosity than to changes in the character and context of religious belief.

This brings us to the second and deeper problem which confronts the SPCM: the roots of the sociopolitical conflicts themselves. The SPCM treats these conflicts as a given and focuses on their dynamics and effects. But it says nothing about their underlying causes, about the social and cultural conditions of possibility for the emergence of political religions and secular ideologies. From the vantage point of the present, this development has a certain self-evidence. But it is important to bear in mind that in many and perhaps even most times and places, sociopolitical opposition was expressed *through* religion rather than against it. This was particularly true in late medieval and early modern Europe, where biblical doctrine was the *lingua franca* of upstarts and malcontents of all stripes from the Hussite Rebellion through the Revolution of 1525 to the English Civil War. In modern Europe, however, revolutionaries learned to speak other languages as well, languages such as nationalism and socialism, which were un- or even antireligious. What is more, large numbers of people were willing to listen to them. But where did these languages come from? And why did they resonate so widely? These are important questions for which the SPCM has no answers. To address these issues, we need another set of conceptual tools.

A FOURTH APPROACH: NOTES TOWARD A SOCIOCULTURAL TRANSFORMATION MODEL

Classical sociological theory suggests two possible approaches to the preceding questions. The first is inspired by Durkheim's writings on the division of labor (Durkheim 1893/1997) and the sociology of religion (Durkheim 1912/1976). For most of the last two millennia, one could argue, intellectual labor in Western societies has been monopolized by the priestly classes. Since the Renaissance, however, the number of nonpriestly intellectuals has grown steadily, and various groups of experts and professionals have taken shape (e.g., jurists, bureaucrats, scientists, and psychologists). In order to establish their jurisdiction over areas of knowledge and practice previously controlled by members of the priestly classes, they have had to draw sharp lines between religious and nonreligious domains and institutions. The result of this development has been the gradual removal of religious language and authority from an ever-expanding swath of social life, and the articulation of nonreligious sources of moral valuation (on this, see especially Taylor 1989).

The second approach derives directly from Weber's sociology of religion and, more specifically, from his essay on "Religious Rejections of the World" (cf. Weber 1919/1946). In traditional societies, argues Weber, religion and "the world" were of a piece. The divine, however conceived, resided within the world, and "salvation" consisted of worldly well-being (i.e., health, wealth, and progeny). With the emergence of "world-rejecting religions" in South Asia and the Middle East roughly two millennia ago, this original unity of religion and world was broken asunder, and individual salvation and the divine were catapulted into another realm, a transcendental beyond. The implications of this transformation are difficult to overstate. Wherever it took place – in India and China, Persia and Palestine, Rome and Mecca – religious and nonreligious values and activities now existed in a state of tension with one another. The demands of the divine were not easily reconciled with the realities of the world: blood-kin versus coreligionists, the Sermon on the Mount versus *raison d'etat*, brotherly love versus the profit motive, revelation versus reason – these are some of the stations along the westward branch of the road that Weber wishes to describe. It is not a straight path, but a spiralling one, in which the ongoing conflict between the religious and the nonreligious leads not only to ever sharper institutional boundaries between the various "life orders" but also to greater and greater theoretical consistency within the individual "value-spheres" (political, economic, aesthetic, erotic, scientific). The consequence, says Weber, is an ever growing differentiation between the religious and the nonreligious, both institutionally and intellectually, a tendency that, for various reasons, Weber believes has gone further (so far) in the West than in other parts of the world.

These two approaches are not necessarily at odds with one another. In fact, they might even be seen as complementary. For each addresses a question which the other leaves unanswered. The neo-Weberian approach explains why religious and nonreligious spheres of knowledge came to be separate, something that the neo-Durkheimian approach takes for granted. For its part, the neo-Durkheimian approach identifies the actors who drew the boundaries, something that Weber (uncharacteristically) omits from his analysis. Nor are these approaches at odds with the SPCM. On the contrary, they might deepen our understanding of the "secular revolution" of the late nineteenth century.

CONCLUSION: AN AGENDA FOR RESEARCH

I have pursued two aims in this chapter, one critical, the other constructive. On the critical side, I have tried to identify the empirical and theoretical shortcomings of the two perspectives that have dominated recent discussions of secularization: Classical secularization theory (CST) and the religious economies model (REM). One problem that is common to both, I have argued, is that they are insufficiently historical, albeit in somewhat different ways. The problem with CST, historically seen, is that it is premised on a truncated and romanticized version of Western religious development: Truncated, insofar as it tends to juxtapose the modern era to the Middle Ages and ignore the intervening centuries; and romanticized insofar as it adopts a rose-tinted picture of the Middle Ages as a period of universal belief and deep piety, a picture that is very much at odds with contemporary historiography. As I have argued elsewhere (Gorski 2000), once the Reformation era is inserted back into the narrative, and a more realistic view of the Middle Ages is adopted, the story line of Western religious development becomes more complicated, and the classical tale of an uninterrupted decline in religious life beginning in the Middle Ages becomes very difficult to sustain. For what we see is not simply (quantitative) decline, but (quantitative) revival (in ecclesiastical influence) and (qualitative) transformation (in individual religiosity) – a multidimensional ebb and flow.

The problem with the REM rests on a somewhat different but equally flawed picture of Western religious history, a picture that is at once foreshortened and anachronistic: foreshortened in that it focuses almost exclusively on the nineteenth and twentieth centuries, thereby ignoring the medieval as well as the early modern period, and anachronistic in that it tends to see earlier historical periods through a twentieth-century lens. This leads to some rather egregious errors of interpretation. Consider the claim that low levels of church membership in colonial New England indicate a low level of "religious vitality." This ignores the rigorous standards for church membership then in force, and the large numbers of "hearers" who filled colonial pews. Or consider the claim that widespread "superstition" among medieval parishioners indicates a state of religious stagnation. This emphasis on knowledge and belief ignores the ritual and communal dimension of religious life in the Middle Ages (Gorski 2000). Once we correct for errors of this sort, the antisecularization story that underlies the REM – a story of ever increasing religiosity since the Middle Ages – becomes just as hard to defend as its classical rival. In my view, then, both CST and the REM are based on implausible narratives of Western religious development.

This brings me to the constructive aspect of the chapter, which is the attempt to outline some possible alternatives to CST and the REM, which I have dubbed the sociopolitical conflict model (SPCM) and the sociocultural transformation model (SCTM), and to suggest some possible directions for future research. In their present forms, both of these models are open to some of the criticisms I have leveled against CST and the REM. For example, the SPCM in its current form might be accused of a foreshortened historical perspective. With the exception of David Martin (1978), researchers working within the framework of the SPCM have focused mainly on the late nineteenth and early twentieth centuries. This is unfortunate, because there is good reason to believe that a more generalized version of the SPCM could be used to analyze other episodes of secularization, such as the privatization of religion that occurred in the wake of the Thirty Years' War (Kosselleck 1988) or the process of disaffiliation (*Entkirchlichung*) that followed the upheavals of the 1960s (Hout and Fischer 2002). In both of these instances, religious ideas and institutions suddenly found themselves confronted with ir- or antireligious world pictures and social movements. And it seems likely that a more serious engagement with the historical record might turn up other episodes of structural or cultural secularization.

For its part, the SCTM (à la Weber) might be accused of a truncated historical perspective, insofar as it focuses mainly on the beginning (antiquity) and end (modernity) of the secularization story, with little attention to anything in between. This is also unfortunate, because Weber's analysis of the growing tensions between the religious and nonreligious "value-spheres" contains allusions to numerous episodes of conflict between priestly and nonpriestly intellectuals and their respective supporters (conflicts over religious mission and *raison d'état*, Christian charity and capitalist imperatives, sexual morality and erotic experience, and so on), which could be analyzed for their contribution to the secularization process, using the conceptual tools that have been developed for the study of "boundary-formation" in science studies and other subfields of sociology (Gieryn 1999; Lamont and Fournier 1992).

Despite these narrative gaps, the SPCM and the SCTM, in my view, are still more historicized, and indeed more sociological, than their predecessors and rivals, CST and the REM. For unlike CST, the SPCM treats secularization as a historically variable and contingent outcome, rather than as a universal and inevitable developmental trend, thereby leaving open the possibility that secularization is an episodic, uneven and perhaps even reversible process. CST, by contrast, is still framed by a high modernist meta-narrative that sees religion and tradition as inherently opposed to science and progress in a way that even many modern-day progressives and scientists would now find hard to swallow. And unlike the REM, the SCTM treats religion as something that varies not only in its quantity but also in its quality, thereby avoiding the anachronisms that often plague the REM (e.g., equating seventeenth- and twentieth-century church membership as operational equivalents that "mean" the same thing). Proper interpretation of quantitative variation requires greater sensitivity toward contextual – and sociological – nuance. And proper analysis of secularization processes requires greater attention toward macro-societal transformations.

In closing, let me sum up what I mean by "historicization" and, thus, what I think would be involved in "historicizing the secularization debate": (a) adopting a longer-range (and fully encompassing) historical perspective that extends well beyond the modern era; (b) engaging in a more serious and sustained way with the relevant historical sources and literatures, so as to develop a clear sense of the temporal and spatial contours of secularization in all its dimensions; (c) viewing secularization as a contingent outcome of particular events involving particular actors; and (d) being more sensitive to changes in the context and content of religious practice and belief.

I do not think historicization is a panacea, nor do I wish to denigrate nonhistorical strategies of research. But I do think that the literature on secularization could stand a dose of history, and that greater attention to the past might shed new light on the present. Only by contextualizing the recent episodes of secularization will we be able to assess their larger significance.

CHAPTER TEN

Escaping the Procrustean Bed

A Critical Analysis of the Study of Religious Organizations, 1930–2001

Patricia M. Y. Chang

INTRODUCTION

In reviewing the literature that has emerged around the study of American religious institutions over the past seventy years one is reminded of the story of Procrustes, the infamous robber of Attica who is said to have made his victims fit his bed by stretching them if they were too short, or cutting their legs if they were too long. Similarly, religious scholars have sought to fit institutional manifestations of American religion into theoretical beds that were poorly fitted to their inherent qualities and characteristics.

This chapter offers a critical review of the literature examining religious organizations in America. Beginning with Max Weber's (1925/1978) studies of church bureaucracy and ending with more recent excursions into neoinstitutional theory, it highlights some of the ways that our adoption of various theoretical lenses has obscured the view of the forest by continually pointing toward particularly interesting trees. In an attempt to get the forest in view again, it then points to the kinds of variation that often have been neglected, and suggests a refocusing on the social processes that give the religious landscape its contour.

In this sense, the chapter is a call for new approaches to the study of religious institutions. I seek to encourage perspectives that examine religion from a supraorganizational level of analysis, focusing on the cultural processes that shape American society and its religious institutions, and the boundary setting processes that define identity and meaning. Conversely, while reviewing these perspectives, I also make the case that what is unique about the religious sector is that organizational actors have strong identities that affect what these organizations absorb or reject in their institutional environments. Unlike some organizational theories that assume that organizational actors automatically conform to the cultural norms of their environments, this chapter argues that the strong cultural traditions of religious organizations cause them to exercise a high degree of agency, causing them to interact selectively with their environment.

Before beginning however, certain caveats are in order. Given the growing diversity of religion in America, it is important to state at the outset the limits of the observations put forward in these pages. This chapter limits its arguments to the American religious sector in the belief that the legal parameters established by the religion clause in the First Amendment have had such a unique influence in shaping the dynamics of religious institutionalism that it would be imprudent to generalize beyond this case. The arguments here also particularly reflect the conditions of Christian institutions within the United States. In part, this is because the theoretical perspectives discussed in this chapter implicitly rest on the assumption that religious individuals are empowered by a sense of individual efficacy that is directly shaped by Protestant Christian worldviews and therefore are most likely to be applicable in these subcultures. These biases are evident in the intellectual history that has shaped the problems that we see before us. The next section offers a schematic overview of the main themes that have influenced the study of religious organizations in America since the 1930s.

WEBER'S STUDIES OF THE CHURCH

Much of the inspiration for research on religious organizations comes from Max Weber's studies of the Catholic Church. It is through the study of this singular organization that Weber worked out many of his ideas about authority, legitimacy, and bureaucracy.

One of the central themes that occupied Weber's attention was the problem of the "routinization of charisma" (1925/1978: 246). Weber observed that many religious movements are founded by persons with strong personal charisma but lose strength after the original leader dies. The death of a leader creates an authority crisis in which followers face the problem of transferring legitimate authority from a single charismatic leader who has the emotional loyalty of followers, to a permanent structure that can facilitate the movement's continued survival.

As with most issues, Weber saw various solutions to this problem, but was most intrigued by the way the Catholic Church addressed this issue by institutionalizing the personal charisma of Christ within a hierarchical system of sacred offices. In this case, objective structures successfully replaced charismatic leadership, but not without cost. Weber realized that in the process of its institutionalization, the Church became deeply committed to the goal of worldly dominion, and was forced to compromise the purity of its Christian ideals to form the necessary alliance with secular authority that would help it achieve this goal. In reaction to these compromises, Weber observed that revolutionizing sects would frequently emerge, championing the pure idealism of Christ and calling on the Church to return to a more pure vision of Christian idealism. These sects were sometimes tolerated, sometimes persecuted, and often co-opted as monastic orders within the Church. Nonetheless, they represent an inherent tension posed by the routinization of charisma.

Weber's student, Ernst Troeltsch elaborated Weber's insights on this topic in *The Social Teachings of the Christian Churches* (Troeltsch 1981). In this text, Troeltsch works out the spiritual and institutional implications of the tension between the worldly and ideal goals of the Christian tradition in the historical context of the European Catholic Church. Troeltsch elaborates the church and sect as sociological ideal types that he describes as being on the opposite ends of a continuum. In this schema, the church is characterized by a number of qualities that are consequences of its goal of achieving world dominion. This goal leads it to be socially conservative, in alliance with the secular political order, and intent on dominating the masses through various political and institutional devices (Troeltsch 1981: 331). Weber felt that to accomplish universal dominion churches also tended to adopt specific organizational features such as a professional class of clergy to control the sacred, the objectification of religious teachings and principles into rationalized dogma and rites that could be culturally transmitted, and the formation of a hierocratic and compulsory authority structure (1925/1978: 1164).

The "sect-type," located at the opposite end of the continuum, is characterized by a stance that is explicitly in opposition to the worldly values of the established church. Sects are characterized by their goal of leading a pure, inner-directed life guided by the moral example of Christ and his apostles. Consequently, Weber and Troeltsch characterized the sect as a small voluntary community, living apart from society, and focusing on the achievement of inner perfection. Their community is characterized by a direct personal fellowship with other members in the sect, equality among members, and a special and personal relationship with God.

Within the Catholic Church, Troeltsch saw the compromises that the church made with secular values and authority as the price that it paid to perpetuate its dominance in the world. The sects, by contrast, because they tended to reject secular values and cultivated a worldview that was more inner-directed, sought to be independent of worldly ambitions. For Weber and Troeltsch, these two organizational forms were interdependent elements that existed in a dynamic tension with one another. The sect served as a source of moral idealism that periodically renewed the ideals and integrity of the church, while the church served as a vehicle through which these ideals could be spread universally (Troeltsch 1981: 337).

The Church-Sect Typology

The formalization of the "church-sect typology" based on the writings of Weber and Troeltsch inspired a large number of studies in the sociology of religion from about the 1930s to the late 1960s (Niebuhr 1929; Yinger 1946; Berger 1954; Johnson 1957; Wilson 1959; Goode 1967a; Goode 1967b). Scholars sought to use Weber and Troeltsch's descriptions about "church-types" and "sect-types" to classify the kinds of worshipping communities they observed in the United States. They pursued this intellectual strategy assuming that there was a limited number of forms that a worshipping community could take, and that these forms followed a natural life cycle that evolved between sect and church. Their goal was to discover the dynamics of this natural order, which would enable them to classify religious communities into different organizational types that they believed also would be associated with typical religious behaviors.

Unfortunately, the "church-sect typology" was formulated from various observations, insights, and analyses made by Weber and Troeltsch that were scattered among their various writings. These writings were sufficiently ambiguous that the appropriate interpretation of the crucial characteristics and dimensions of this typology were hotly contested. H. Richard Niebuhr (1929), for example, argued that the appropriate dimension should be based on the social and ethical characteristics of religious communities, while Becker (1932) sought to emphasize the kinds of social relationships different collectives had with society, and Berger (1954) proposed a dimension based on the "nearness of the religious spirit."

In addition to arguing over what conceptual dimensions and characteristics were appropriate, scholars attempted to repair gaps that Weber and Troeltsch failed to antici- pate in the American context by identifying additional organizational "types." Niebuhr (1929) introduced the concept of a "denomination" into wide usage, a phrase that he used to lament the fragmentation of the Christian Church into numerous sects. Becker (1932) introduced the concept of a "cult" to denote a more loosely organized form of sect in which members are more transient. Yinger (1946) introduced the concept of an "established sect" to identify those sects that had managed to convey the passion of their spiritual ideals to subsequent generations, and as an intermediary stage between the church and sect types. Wilson (1959) proposed classifying sects on the basis of their worldviews and proposed a four-part classification scheme.

The proliferation of new "types," the persistence of confounding empirical evi- dence, and the lack of agreement on appropriate conceptual dimensions eventually muddled the concept of a church sect typology entirely. Eventually there was general agreement among scholars to abandon use of the typology altogether (Demerath 1967; Eister 1967; Goode 1967a; Goode 1967b). One of the reasons the church-sect approach failed was because these scholars assumed that the church-sect dynamic that Weber identified *within* the Catholic Church could explain the variety of voluntary religious communities *across* America. They ignored the fact that the characteristics Weber and Troeltsch associated with each type were predicated on the particular situation in which the Catholic Church exerted a monopoly in the country in which it operated.

In abandoning the church-sect typology, scholars, unfortunately, also abandoned some of Weber's more useful insights. In particular, they failed to pursue Weber's in- sight that Christian idealism and Christian domination inherently led to conflicts over strategy and practice. In the Catholic Church, these conflicts led to the formation of monastic orders that remained under the nominal auspices of the Pope. However, in the United States, these conflicts lead to a variety of different organizational forms. American scholars despaired because these new forms did not conform to Weber's de- scription of a sect, and while they often linked this difference to the lack of a religious establishment in the United States, they failed to exploit that insight.

The dynamic that Weber and Troeltsch saw as generating monastic orders within the Catholic Church generates a greater pluralism through schisms within the American context. The conflict is the same, but the institutional trajectory differs because of the free market nature of the social context. In a study of Protestant denominations between 1890 and 1980, Liebman, Sutton, and Wuthnow (1988) observed fifty-five schisms among the 175 denominations they examined. In other words, within a hundred year span, over 30 percent of the population of denominations experienced internal conflicts that resulted in the formation of a new religious denomination. Schisms are perhaps the single strongest factor contributing to the growth and pluralism of religion in America, yet they remain fairly under examined as an organizational phenomenon. We do not know how schismatic groups organize their practices, the likelihood that they will retain the organizational structures of their founding church, or the probability that they will adopt the organizational practices that are fashionable at the time of schism. We also do not know if particular kinds of religious groups are more likely to schism, the probabilities associated with survival, or the likelihood of reabsorption or merger. Given that schism is such a powerful dynamic in the America religious landscape, it is unfortunate that it has attracted so little attention (Liebman et al. 1988).

Religious Organizations as Bureaucracies

After having abandoned the church-sect typology, religious scholars began to turn to the field of organizational studies for explanatory strategies. Research on the behavior of nonreligious organizations seemed to offer promising avenues of inquiry and these approaches were avidly pursued by religion scholars.

Inspired by the trends in organizational research, several studies in the 1960s and 1970s focused on the effects of bureaucratization in Protestant denominations (Harrison 1959; Winter 1967; Primer 1979; Takayama 1979). These studies suggested that Protestant denominations had grown in size, function, and administrative complexity over the past number of years. Scholars assumed that this growth in bureaucracy could also be associated with a concentration of decision-making authority (Harrison 1959; Winter 1967; Takayama 1974) and also a growing similarity or isomorphism in the organizational structures of religious institutions, which they ultimately argued was a sign of increasing secularization. Their arguments suggested that as denominations became more bureaucratic, decision makers would become more professional and their decisions would be more strongly influenced by the values of their professional functions, rather than their religious beliefs (Winter 1967). This, scholars argued, would produce bureaucratic structures that were oriented to their functional, as opposed to their theological purposes, and would in turn, erode the theological distinctiveness of each denomination. Peter Berger argued that "Internally, the religious institutions are not only administered bureaucratically, but their day to day operations are dominated by the typical problems and 'logic' of bureaucracy" (Berger 1967: 140). For Berger, this homogenization of structure contributed to the overall secularization of society.

Despite the relative absence of actual empirical evidence, the inevitability of secularization via bureaucratization was often taken for granted among social scientists during this time. The inherent assumption in this attitude is that bureaucratic rationales are inconsistent with religious idealism and that religion and rationality are antithetical to one another. This perspective is so pervasive in the literature and also so contrary to the historical record that it needs to be critically examined. This view makes a crucial assumption about what it means to be religious. It assumes that religious values are necessarily secularized if they involve decision makers who are concerned with making both moral choices and organizationally efficient choices. It implies that the influence of professional managers, rather than clergy or laypersons, undermines the operation of religious decision-making structures. It assumes that decisions made by experienced administrators are less "religious" than those made by clergy or laity.

Reflection on this topic still seems overshadowed by the implicit assumptions of the church-sect typology, that is, that the worldly church is inevitably corrupt, and the sect is invariably pure and idealistic. Yet neither of these scenarios is supported in the United States, where churches tend to pursue religious idealism with a shamelessly pragmatic worldliness as their God-given right. For Weber (1925/1978), the church was inevitably corrupted by its goal of world dominion because the strategies by which the Catholic Church pursued this imperative required it to ally with states that practiced secular abuse and tyranny. In the United States, no such alliance exists and world dominion is pursued through strategies of voluntary conversion thus avoiding the kind of political pollution that Weber envisioned. Consequently, religious groups have developed strategies that closely reflect religious ideals and priorities. At the same time, the competitive environment that voluntary conversion fosters also nurtures a worldliness and pragmatism that are often overlooked in theoretical schema.

The most successful religious groups have been those who have been most pragmatic and flexible, overcoming traditional constraints and adapting strategies to achieve their goals. At the turn of the nineteenth century, the fastest-growing groups were the Baptists and Methodists who abandoned the requirements of having a college-educated ministry and the practice of assigning ministers to a particular geographic parish (Finke and Stark 1992). Instead, they developed a system that utilized lay preachers who traveled continually across the frontier, and who spoke to their listeners in a simple common language, often improvising text and message to suit their audiences. These preachers created a wave of religious revivals that drew thousands to fields and camp meetings where these lay ministers baptized converts by the score. Successful meeting practices were refined and taught as strategic techniques to produce successful revivals. Charles Finney, one of the most well-known revivalists of his time, wrote explicit directions on how to plan, organize, and implement a camp meeting that would produce successful conversions (Finney 1979). The most successful religious evangelists were highly entrepreneurial and saw their efficiency as a way of serving God, rather than as evidence of secularization. As the historian Frank Lambert observes,

> by applying means from the world of commerce to publicize his meetings, Whitefield generated large, enthusiastic crowds. Like the rest of us, the evangelist constructed his social reality with the elements at hand, and in the mid-eighteenth century, commercial language, and techniques abounded, affording him a new way of organizing, promoting, and explaining his evangelical mission. (Lambert 1990)

More recently, evangelicals have made innovative use of television, radio, and publishing media to saturate the popular culture with Christ-centered messages. And even the Catholic Church has taken to marketing the Pope's image on everything from ballpoint pens to t-shirts (Moore 1994).

Less well known are the sophisticated national marketing strategies that religious entrepreneurs pioneered in their attempts to spread the influence of Bibles and religious tracts to people all over the nation in the early nineteenth century. The American Tract Society, whose goal was to influence the coming of the millennium by marketing religious tracts to everyone in the nation, reports publishing and distributing 32,179,250 copies of tracts in the first decade of its existence between 1825 and 1835. It did so through a complex distribution system that utilized professional managers, a network of regional sales managers, and an army of door-to-door salesmen and women who peddled tracts within their neighborhoods (Griffin 1960; Nord 1995; Schantz 1997). The models of mass marketing used by these religious entrepreneurs arguably influenced lay leaders to apply similar methods in their nonreligious enterprises. Sociologists who have been quick to fit narratives of such innovative behavior into secularization theory have failed to see that religious zeal was often the inspiration for developing creative models of greater organizational efficiency. The rationalization of efficiency in American religion, far from being a sign of secularization, has in fact been the hallmark of its successes. American religion has inspired waves of institutional civil reform by connecting the passion of individualist evangelical worldviews to national enterprises.

The dichotomy that scholars suggest exists between professional rationality and religious spiritualism has thus been woefully misleading. This kind of opposition implicitly creates a romantic image of religious communities and their members as being inner-directed, otherworldly, and removed from the realities of everyday life, which is not only patently at odds with the pragmatic kind of religion that most Americans practice but also is at odds with the primary social teachings of the Christian churches that direct members to engage the world (Bacon 1832; Hollenbach 1989; see also McRoberts, Chapter 28, this volume). If one accepts a religious worldview that seeks to engage and transform the world, then it seems to follow that pragmatism and entrepreneurialism are consequences of that religious spirit and cannot be categorized as inherently secular. The historical record in fact shows that the most influential proponents of religion in America were adept at employing both of these characteristics.

Neoinstitutional Theory

As growth in religious membership began to confront secularization theory with increasing evidence of its own demise, scholars began to turn away from "bureaucracy as secularization" arguments and move toward what are broadly called "open systems" approaches in organizational studies. Open systems approaches focus on how an organization's interchanges with the environment affect organizational behavior. Consequently, they tend to place greater attention on the kinds of relationships that an organization has with customers, suppliers, and regulators than it does on the internal politics or power struggles within an organization (Scott 1987).

Of the various open systems approaches available, religion scholars have been particularly attracted to a perspective called neoinstitutional theory (Meyer and Rowan 1977; Powell and DiMaggio 1991). This theory is attractive to religion scholars, because it emphasizes the role of cultural processes in shaping organizational behavior. It argues that the formal structures of organizations arise not from the functional demands of work activities but, rather, from a need to conform to the myths and rituals that define legitimate behavior within an institutional sector. Neoinstitutionalists argue that, when organizational practices become highly legitimated, they diffuse rapidly across an institutional sector. Conformity to these practices signals the legitimacy of the adopter and makes it easier for the organization to make important connections with other institutional actors in the field. A simple example of the way cultural signaling operates is illustrated in the typical advice one receives to dress well when applying for a bank loan. Dressing conservatively and respectably signals conformity to normative values that the lender correlates with one's reliability in repaying the loan. Similarly, neoinstitutionalists argue that organizational behavior is often guided by conscious and unconscious motivations to appear competent and successful in order to cultivate the kind of trust that encourages others in their environment to engage in risk-taking relationships (Powell and DiMaggio 1991). Neoinstitutionalists emphasize the degree to which organizations are constituted by this ritualistic behavior and how this behavior is often so deeply encoded within routines, scripted behaviors, and practices that are defined as "rational" that managers are unaware that they are enacting ritualistic behaviors (Meyer and Rowan 1977).

Religion scholars are attracted to a neoinstitutional schema in part because it is one of the few organizational perspectives that pay attention to the role of cultural and symbolic processes relative to organizations. Since the centrality of culture and symbol are precisely what makes religious organizations different from secular organizations, this approach has naturally elicited the attention of religious scholars but it has also frequently misled them.

Religious organizations are distinct in that they are usefully conceived as having an *internal* culture that intentionally sets them apart from other communities of religious believers. Indeed, their very identity rests on this distinctive culture. This culture guides the blueprint of their formal structure, flavors the meaning of their behaviors, and forms a reservoir of experience that they draw on when making difficult decisions. This culture manifests itself most directly in boundary setting behaviors that distinguish religious insiders from religious outsiders.

Neoinstitutionalists, by contrast, focus entirely on how *external* cultural processes affect organizational behavior. Neoinstitutionalists explicitly ignore the internal culture of organizations that religion scholars focus on as an important determinant of behaviors. Neoinstitutionalists treat organizational leaders as automatons who reflexively respond to environmental cues. They see cultural processes in the environment as exerting a homogenizing influence while cultural differences among organizations are virtually ignored (DiMaggio 1988).

This lack of fit between neoinstitutional and religious approaches is not merely one of a difference in the locus of analysis. Real empirical differences exist between the sectors neoinstitutionalists have tended to study, and the religious sector. Empirical investigations that have supported neoinstitutional theory have all been conducted in social sectors that are highly "institutionalized," that is, where social networks are already dense through the effects of federal regulation, technological standardization, or financial centralization. In comparison, the religious sector is very weakly institutionalized, showing little evidence of centralization, standardization, or regulation (Scott and Meyer 1991). In fact, no study using neoinstitutional theory has been able to show the effects of institutional isomorphism in the religious sector to the extent found in other organizational populations. The most rigorous empirical attempt to apply neoinstitutional theory to an organizational population in the religious sector found, in fact, that neoinstitutional hypotheses predicting the rapid and universal diffusion of organizational practices related to the ordination of women were not supported (Chaves 1997).

Rather than being an uncomfortable anomaly, however, the weakness of institutionalizing processes is a revealing insight that allows one to usefully compare the differences in the institutional patterns of strong and weak institutional sectors. Strongly institutionalized sectors tend to be highly integrated by institutional practices and norms brought about by technological standardization, centralization, or government regulation found in the health, education, technology, and the arts sectors (DiMaggio 1991; Meyer and Scott 1992; Scott 1995). Each of these sectors is distinguished by strong organizational rules that permit the easy identification of a population of organizational actors, the clear definition of many normative practices, and the easy measurement of organizational outcomes.

By contrast, the religious sector is highly decentralized, organizational practices vary broadly, and a number of differing organizational forms can be identified. The field is not regulated by federal or industry rules or standards and there is no centralized institution that controls access to resources.[1] The weakness of institutionalizing processes is so marked that even the labels associated with the basic activities of religious life are contested. This can be illustrated with a few examples.

The concept of "membership" is a case in point. All churches have members, but each faith tradition has a very different conceptualization of what constitutes membership in their tradition. In the Catholic Church, for example, membership is virtually a birthright. Infants are baptized into the church by their parents without any conscious election on their part. In most Protestant churches, baptism is prohibited until a person is of an age to make a personal witness to God. In Baptist churches, one is not considered a member until one is baptized. Some denominations require that baptism be performed by full immersion, others argue that sprinkling is appropriate, and each has their own belief about the appropriate age at which baptism can occur. Similarly, some denominations require members to attend religion classes before becoming a member, while others simply ask for a declaration of faith. The wide variations in practices and beliefs surrounding the concept of membership suggest that the organization, rather than the environment determines the meaning and exercise of membership. This in turn is evidence that institutionalizing processes in the religious environment are weak.

Variations in the understandings of what "clergy" symbolizes is another illustration of the weakness of a shared interorganizational culture. In the Episcopal Church, for example, ordination transmits the authority of Christ in a direct line from the apostle Peter to every priest. This apostolic succession is the way that the Church legitimates the authority of its teachings and structures. Other denominations, however, believe in the "priesthood of all believers," meaning that they believe no individual has a greater right to interpret God's authority, although some are "called" by God to preach. Yet even these denominations sometimes distinguish between different kinds of ordination. The Presbyterian Church and the Church of the Nazarene, for example, have different levels of ordination, that are associated with different levels of privilege and responsibility, while many recognize only one form of ordination.

The meaning of ministry, the definition of "clergy," and the symbolic significance of ordination tend to vary by denomination. Organizational authority also overrides occupational authority. Unlike most so-called professional occupations, there is no professional class of "clergy" whose authority transcends the authority of individual denominations. There is no professional equivalent of the American Bar Association or the American Medical Association that establishes professional norms or practices or standards of training. Clergy are ordained within their own denomination, and the rights and privileges of ordination are limited to that denomination. Training and educational requirements for clergy are determined by the denomination rather than the profession and these requirements vary widely. Some denominations have no educational requirements other than literacy in reading the Bible, while others require an advanced masters degree in divinity. Some denominations vest local churches with the

---

[1] An exception to this may be the recent formation of the Office for Faith Based Organizing started by President George W. Bush. Depending on how it is implemented, new federal regulations may influence the creation of new religious forms that will adopt standardized forms in response to state regulation.

authority to examine and ordain clergy, while others require approval by a regional body, and others require that clergy be approved by a national board. In some denominations, wages and benefits are supervised by the national denomination, and in others clergy wages and benefits are negotiated on a case-by-case basis between the pastor and the local church. Thus, one cannot speak of the occupational rights and privileges of clergy as a profession that transcends the rights and privileges granted by a particular organization. Some denominations contribute to a retirement plan and provide organizational health benefits, while in other denominations, clergy are expected to make their own arrangements.

Further reflecting this organizational autonomy, denominations in America do not even share a common set of labels for describing their religious workers. Although the generic term "clergy" is often used, each organization makes its own traditional distinctions resulting in a confusing proliferation of titles including minister, reverend, priest, deacon, rector, vicar, superintendent, bishop, pastor, presbyter, monsignor, brother, sister, father, curate, and so on. It is difficult to imagine any other occupation in which the definition of one's job is so dependent on the particular organization one works for (Chang 2001).

The authority of organizational labels, definitions, and understandings over interorganizational meaning systems and the lack of shared occupational, professional, or cultural understandings in key areas of religious activity illustrate the cultural decentralization of the religion sector and the weakness of so-called institutionalizing processes. In highly institutionalized sectors, occupational categories are standardized and, by extension, so are the skills, rights, and privileges that are associated with those categories. Skills are transferable from one organization to the next. Certain employee rights such as protection from sexual discrimination, unjust termination, and health benefits are widely recognized from organization to organization. A computer programmer's skills are recognized to be legitimate regardless of what company he or she works for. This is not the case for religious workers, whose relevance is limited within defined organizational boundaries.

Another reflection of the weakness of institutionalizing processes characterizing the religious sector is illustrated in the variety of labels used to designate local worshipping communities. Although the term congregation has become widespread in the general literature, many faith traditions resist the historical and cultural values associated with this term. Alternative terms include association, temple, synagogue, ashram, class, group, fellowship, or church. Supralocal terms include synod, presbytery, diocese, parish, district, church, denomination, or association. These terms have different meanings in each denominational tradition and like the other differences noted above, persist as a way of marking cultural boundaries and differentiating themselves from others within the diverse traditions of American religion.

Unsurprisingly, generalists in American religion have often found the semiotic and semantic schemas by which religious groups define such common properties as members, clergy, and worshipping units to be awkward impediments to the understanding of general trends, such as shifts in church growth. More often than not these anomalies are considered to be irksome and embarrassing. However, it is important to see that these differences are important boundary markers of group identity in an institutional field where organizations in fact are very similar in terms of their history, background, and theological authority. The authority of most American Protestant denominations traces its historical and theological identity back to Martin Luther, the Protestant Reformation, and European cultural roots. In these ways, variations of American Protestantism are very similar. Yet, when the denominational group is under external strain or conflict, they derive power and group solidarity from their differences and thus tend to celebrate their distinctiveness. In Bourdieu's terms, the religious sector is a site of continuous cultural struggle over the authority of symbols. These differences in turn broadly reflect the struggles that they have with society and the conflicts they have in reconciling religious and secular authority (Bourdieu 1990).

Baptists for example, strongly identify with being outsiders. They have tended to appeal to the poorer and more marginal elements of society as members and have cultivated an image that associates the purity of their belief with the more primitive and simple aspects of Christianity. They model themselves on the poor, small, democratic band of apostles who followed Christ, and rigorously reject the hierarchical and the authoritarian aspects of Christian institutionalism. However, over time, the Southern Baptists, for example, have become a denomination with millions of members, financial resources of several billion dollars, national seminaries, and national agencies that operate with multimillion-dollar budgets. Nonetheless, their identity as a "primitive" church remains the basis of their solidarity and their identity and they explicitly seek to counter the suggestion that they are a large, corporate, institutional church. They continue to distinguish themselves in their promotional literature and in their relationships with outsiders as an organization in which the local church remains autonomous, and in control of the denomination's resources.

Neoinstitutional theory is useful for religion scholars not because the religious environment conforms to standard notions of institutionalization but because it is the exception that proves the rule. It is a sector in which no single organization dominates, in which attempts at standardization fail, in which each organization is independent, autonomous, and guided by a strong internal culture. It is a sector in which organizational agency is strong, which makes organizations very selective in the way they adopt strategies from the environment. This in turn leads to the exercise of greater organizational innovation and creativity, leading to the formation of new organizational forms.

While neoinstitutional perspectives offer value in providing articulate ways of viewing highly institutionalized environments, they generally work less well in the religious sector because they do not provide a conceptual apparatus that is flexible enough to make sense of the kinds of continual change and innovation that characterizes institutional religious behavior. Neoinstitutionalist theories are weakest when called on to explain change or innovation, and this is precisely what conditions in the religious sector foster. Consequently, the religion sector may be a valuable site for neoinstitutionalists to study precisely because the religious sector contains many of the features that neoinstitutionalists have difficulty explaining, that is, a variety of strong organizational cultures, a high degree of agency, and organizational practices that display a profound amount of creativity and innovation.

New Directions for Studying the Religion Sector

This chapter began by telling the story of Procrustes who had an unusual way of fitting his guests into his available accommodations. The practice of theory driven research has often taken this approach, focusing selectively on the kinds of data that can best test particular hypotheses and truncating observations that do not fit (Lieberson 1985). The literature review above has suggested that when the facts have not fit the theory, scholars often have shifted their focus to a new set of issues. At risk of shifting the lens once again, I offer the following suggestions that attempt to guide the field in a new direction.

Proposition 1: Religion scholars need to distinguish between organizational studies that focus on a single organization and those that consider the organization as a product of broader environmental processes. Historically, the tendency has been to focus on the dynamics of one or two organizations and to generalize from this to the whole. This needs to be corrected by studies that look at a larger sample of organizations, and also take a more considered look at what can be called the religious sector, that is, the patterns of institutional relationships that affect religious membership organizations but may also include religious colleges, voluntary associations, paradenominational associations, charities, and so on. While there is ample room for the study of organizations at both the organizational unit of analysis and the sectoral level of analysis, the more important concern is for researchers in both camps to maintain an intellectual dialogue with one another.

Proposition 2: Our empirical definition of the religious sector should depend on our theoretical focus. For the study of denominational membership, for example, we may wish to define the religious sector as the population of denominations that compete for members. For a study of how religion affects political behavior, however, we may wish to define the religious sector as including local congregations, denominations, ecumenical groups, religious interest groups, and ideological interest groups participating within the political process. The religious sector is potentially vast, and definitions of the sector as a causal agent must rely on the theoretical conception of causal processes. At the same time, theoretical formulation requires more focused information about the kinds of networks and relationships that religious organizations build around their organizational goals. Some of this empirical work is already being pursued by researchers and the picture that emerges of religious organizations and their institutional partners will begin to provide valuable insights into how religious congregations engage their local communities while pursuing their mission.

Proposition 3: Religion scholars must think of the religious sector not as a separate part of American society but as a set of institutional actors that is influenced by, and interacts with, the other major social institutions in American society. Religious movements have played a role in all the major social reform movements of the past two centuries, and have provided models for our most enduring civil institutions including our civil government, poor relief, education, and our attitudes toward a collective morality. Sociologists need to reclaim this territory both in their intellectual studies, and in their approach to current social problems and issues.

Proposition 4: Following from the critique of neoinstitutional theory, we need to understand how institutionalizing processes guide organizational behavior in the religious sector, how these processes differ from other institutional sectors, and what this means.

How has the religious sector resisted pressures to centralize, standardize, and become more culturally comprehensible? What does this imply about the conditions of sectoral evolution? These kinds of questions depend on the collection of comparable empirical data, and a stronger historical understanding of the institutional development of religious organizations. The lack of standardization in the religious field makes the collection of this archival data enormously complex, but ways around these difficulties must be found.

Undertaking this enterprise will force scholars to move out of a parochial focus on religious organizations alone and underline the necessity of broadening their focus to other organizational populations. How are patterns of religious development different from the development of new industries? New political movements? The development of the arts sector? The development of the nonprofit sector? The computer industry? We can only gain an understanding of how the religious sector has developed by comparing it to the experiences of other institutional sectors.

Proposition 5: Attempts to classify static organizational types are problematic because the religious sector is inherently dynamic. New organizational forms are continually being formed through schism, merger, and the syncretic merger of ideas and organization. Traditional organizations also regenerate themselves constantly, adopting new organizational forms and structures from the social behaviors around them. Religious scholars need to reimagine the American religious landscape to include not only the mainline denominations that have been the focus of the majority of religious research, but the new religious movements, spiritual groups, and grassroots ideological movements as well.

Rather than focus on identifying typologies of organizations, sociologists need to focus on the kinds of social processes that delineate new social forms, what organizational scholars refer to as boundary setting and boundary spanning processes (Scott 1987). They need to focus not on organizations themselves but on the social processes that are likely to create new social and organizational forms that may in turn create new religious identities.

Focusing on social processes compels us to take a serious look at the forces that divide the religious landscape, as well as those that create common ground. Views on the tension between evangelicalism and progressive social justice, millennialism, political participation, homosexuality, and the ordination of women are examples of some of the social processes that have segregated people within their faith tradition. How have these cleavages affected religious organizations? Have they led to new forms of worship? New special interest groups? Schisms within churches?

By contrast, globalization, the Internet, ethnic assimilation, and missionary programs may act as boundary spanning processes that have helped to spur the merging of different communities of faith in new ways. Internal strife over biblical interpretation that has divided some denominations has created common cause among conservative groups across denominations. Issues such as abortion have caused the Southern Baptists and the Catholic hierarchy to come together in dialogue over other possible shared beliefs (Dillon 1995). Religion scholars need to find new ways to attend to the extra- and interinstitutional conversations that are occurring between new partners in the religious sector as a way of understanding where new capacities for religious development are occurring.

Proposition 6: Religion scholars have to begin to question the frameworks that they are most familiar with and ask how well the conceptual categories we use reflect the reality that is before us. Our persistence in studying religious denominations in spite of the fact that individuals may not construct their identity in denominational terms is one example of how we must question the adequacy of our causal assumptions.

We also must question the tendency to study the organizations that are able to provide the best organizational information, which tends to be the Protestant mainline denominations. We need to think more closely about why some denominations collect data about their members, churches, and clergy, while others do not, and how this may bias our investigations. Organizations tend to keep records on institutional features that the organization values, or needs to monitor. Our data collection strategies may thus partially be an artifact of the phenomena we are trying to explain.

Researchers need to question the social categories that they bring to religious research and push harder to collect data that are comprehensive. In particular, we need to broaden our understandings of how non-Protestant, non-Christian, and nondenominational churches fit into our schemas. We are more likely to gain an understanding of the directions in which we are headed by reaching out to the more marginalized religions than we are by continuing to focus on the declining mainline denominations.

These propositions offer some guidelines to keep in mind as we pursue the study of religious institutions in this millennium. Overall, it pushes toward the development of broader and more dynamic theoretical strategies that try to capture the mechanisms by which religion evolves, rather than the development of static categories that will be outdated by the time they reach publication. It is not an easy task, but it may be one that helps us to think more proactively about the role religious institutions play in shaping our society.

CHAPTER ELEVEN

Religion and Spirituality

Toward an Integrated Analysis

Wade Clark Roof

For religion in modern societies, the early-twenty-first century is a time of considerable and often subtle transformation. One such subtlety is the growing attention to personal spiritual well-being and the ferment surrounding whatever people take to be sacred. Voices to this effect are heard within congregations of many differing faith traditions and in many other, seemingly less likely places, such as in self-help groups and at retreat centers; in motivational training sessions within corporations and businesses; in hospitals and medical schools, where they attend to the power of prayer and meditation; in popular books, films, and on radio and television talk shows engaging people to talk about their lives; and on the ever-expanding number of pages on the Internet devoted to spiritual growth. Because interest in spirituality is so widespread and arises across many institutional sectors, both religious and nonreligious, and is sustained by the rise of what we might appropriately call a market-oriented "spirituality industry," the topic is properly deserving of attention in a systematic study of religious and spiritual change.

Some commentators view much of the talk about spirituality as shallow and flaky, and of little good consequence for religious conviction, others attach more significance to what they see, or believe to be happening, but very few serious observers take the position that we should shut our eyes to these developments. Spirituality is now less contained by traditional religious structures and Americans – whether we like it or not – are increasingly aware of alternatives for nurturing their souls. Social scientists thus face new challenges in understanding these popular-based spiritual currents and what they might mean for religious communities and institutions. Without some consideration of this broadened scope of experiential concerns, we cannot fully grasp how the American religious landscape is evolving as we move into the new century.

The purpose of this chapter is twofold: one, to describe recent trends in spirituality within the American context; and, two, to propose an analytic scheme helpful in understanding these trends and for relating them to the study of religion more generally. The latter builds on the former and is our chief aim. Proposing an analytic approach is made difficult because words such as "spirituality" and "spirit" have many meanings in popular parlance today. "Religion" and "religious" as well have various connotations in the contemporary context.

In the way I use the word in this chapter, "religion" refers to scripture, ritual, myths, beliefs, practices, moral codes, communities, social institutions, and so forth – that is, the outward and objectified elements of a tradition. The adjective "religious" implies some degree of grounding on the part of an individual or community within such a symbolic universe. Spirituality is more elusive and varying in its meaning, both historically and currently. In Christian usage the term derives from the Latin *spiritus*, breath, from *spirare*, to blow or breathe. By the twelfth century, Christian spirituality came to refer more to the subjective life of faith as opposed to a more visible corporeality or materiality (see Wulff 1997). Still more recently, the term has been broadened beyond its traditional usage involving faith grounded in a tradition and affirmation of a transcendent Deity to refer to the presence of the human spirit or soul, and the human quest for meaning and experiential wholeness. Hence, the word "spiritual" when used today may refer to the inner life that is bound up with, and embedded within, religious forms, or much more loosely in keeping with humanistic psychology as a search on the part of an individual for reaching, through some regimen of self-transformation, one's greatest potential. Anthropologically, it is assumed by many scholars that the spiritual quest is rooted in the biological, psychological, and linguistic conditions of human life and culture without which religion itself would be inconceivable (Torrance 1994). Given the history of the term and its current usage, we must proceed cautiously recognizing its many nuances. At the same time, we should strive for as much clarity and order as possible to assist sociologists in carrying out a more systematic analysis of religion and spirituality, and in particular, the intimate relations between these two realities.

I

In *After Heaven: Spirituality in America Since the 1950s*, Robert Wuthnow argues that religion over the past half-century has undergone a major transition. He writes that "a traditional spirituality of inhabiting sacred places has given way to a new spirituality of seeking" and that "people have been losing faith in a metaphysic that can make them feel at home in the universe and that they increasingly negotiate among competing glimpses of the sacred, seeking partial knowledge and practical wisdom" (1998: 3). He juxtaposes "dwelling" and "seeking" to emphasize the dramatic character of this transition. To dwell is to inhabit a sacred space, to feel at home and secure in its symbolic universe. In dwelling, one finds order and meaning in established rituals and everyday practices. To seek is to explore new spiritual vistas, to search for the sacred or for epiphanies that point us in its direction. By its very character, the seeking mode involves openness to a multiplicity of possibilities. Whereas the former is a model of habitation, of groundedness and clear boundaries locating the sacred, the latter implies process, movement, and expansiveness in a world that is anything but fixed. In one, spirituality is cultivated through customary teachings and practices that anchor and sustain one within an intact life-world; in the other, the search for new teachings and practices, including often eclectic combinations, promises to uncover fresh meaning and new moorings. The first conveys an image of settled life, the second that of a journey.

Wuthnow emphasizes that we should think of the two types of spirituality not in opposition to one another but in a dialectical relationship. Fixed worlds can become stifling, and thus generate a search for greater openness and freedom; and journeys and pilgrimages in search of something not yet attained may result in a reanchoring of religious life, even if ever so provisional. The great world religious traditions themselves offer rich symbolic imageries of both types. Commenting on biblical imageries, Wuthnow observes that:

> ...habitation spirituality is suggested in stories of the Garden of Eden and of the promised land; it consists of temple religion; and it occurs in the time of kings and of priests. A spirituality of seeking is tabernacle religion, the faith of pilgrims and sojourners; it clings to the Diaspora and to prophets and judges, rather than to priests and kings. The one inheres in the mighty fortress, the other in desert mystics and itinerant preachers. The one is symbolized by the secure life of the monastery, the cloister, the shtetl; the other by peregrination as a spiritual ideal. The difference is depicted lyrically in the story of the Shulamite woman who at first revels in the security of her spiritual home – "our bed is green/the beams of our houses are cedar/and the rafters of fir" – and who then wanders, seeking restlessly to find the warmth she has lost – "I will rise now...../and go about the city/in the streets and in the squares/I will seek the one I love." (1998: 4)

This example from the Song of Songs cautions against a simple dichotomy of the two spiritual styles, or our overlooking that the two may actually alternate in "lived" religion. Even in a highly seeker-oriented culture as we know it in contemporary America, religious dwelling and spiritual searching often blend in new and creative ways. As the lyrics illustrate, an individual's psychological frame can switch from one spiritual mode to the other rather abruptly. Rather than thinking of "dwellers" and "seekers" as character types, the two are better viewed as modes of apprehending the spiritual, either through existing ritual and symbolic systems or through more open-ended, exploratory ways.

In the United States, much attention over the past several decades was given to individual subjectivity in religion. "Religious individualism," as described by survey researchers, broke into the news in the late 1970s when the pollster George Gallup, Jr., reported that eight out of ten Americans agreed with the statement that "an individual should arrive at his or her own religious beliefs independent of any churches or synagogues" (Princeton Religion Research Center 1978). Whether such individualism was all that much higher than in previous years was less the point than the fact that Americans had become more aware of the role they themselves were playing in shaping their religious lives. Normative definitions of religious faith and behavior had themselves become highly recognized as subjective. Gallup, in this same news release, found that roughly the same proportion of Americans agreed that "a person can be a good Christian or Jew if he or she doesn't attend church or synagogue." The test of faith lay not simply in keeping with what tradition taught, but in how it was viewed and appropriated by the individual and made his or her own.

Not surprisingly, much debate ensued in the mid-to-late 1980s on "Sheilaism," the term that comes from Robert Bellah et al.'s *Habits of the Heart* describing a radically individualistic religion where, as these authors say, "God is simply the self magnified" (1985: 235). They pointed to a greater "expressive individualism," or concern with the cultivation of the self and its search for greater meaning and fulfillment. More than just a topic for academic discussion, this more expansive, self-focused style of individualism was very much a topic for church and civic leaders, politicians, and cultural commentators. More often than not, the discussion focused on the dire implications for religious institutions in their loss of membership loyalty and support, and far less on what this deeper inward turn might mean spiritually for the individuals themselves, or for the rise of a spiritual quest culture permeating not just the larger environment but the churches, synagogues, and temples that were a part of that environment.

Terms such as narcissism, privatism, and "Me-ism" surfaced as descriptions of the cultural mood at the time. Research documented relatively high levels of religious switching, or movement from one religious affiliation to another, and, likewise, much movement in and out of active participation within congregations of various traditions. Religion emerged as an important institutional arena in which to observe the expression of individual subjectivity and fluidity. Observed as well were high levels of biblical illiteracy and a growing lack of familiarity with religious denominations and traditions. Not surprisingly, this was the time when the impact of the large post–World War II boom generation was very much being felt on all the major social institutions. Having grown up on television, lived through the Vietnam War and Watergate, and caught up in the cultural revolutions with regard to race, sex, and gender and lifestyle, the baby boomers became well known for their distrust of institutional authority, for developing new styles of networking and decision making, and for turning inward on themselves. This triad of experiences – shifts in notions of authority, institutional realignments, and self-focused inwardness – came together making this generation a crucial carrier of cultural and religious changes. More than any other constituency, it is this generation, so argues Robert Putnam (2000), that became the vanguard for what he describes as a culture of "bowling alone," or the decline in civic and religious involvement following the 1950s.

But the religious changes were complex and subtle. The enhanced subjectivity and moral and cultural relativism of the period generated a fundamentalist religious resurgence, aimed at reclaiming an external authority – described variously as Scripture, tradition, or God. Yet we should be cautious not to exaggerate the strictness of this resurgence. For despite all the talk of "a return to stricter moral standards," almost half of the evangelical and fundamentalist respondents in our survey reported being uncomfortable with rigid moral rules and insisted, above all else, on following the dictates of their own conscience (Roof 1999a). The mood of the time favored moral accountability, but not at the expense of individual freedom and even flexible religious styles. Especially in the aftermath of the therapeutic culture of the 1960s and 1970s, the "new evangelicalism" would take on some features that distinguished it from the more conservative, fundamentalist-leaning Protestantism.

The appeal of popular evangelical faith that has emerged in the years since lies in no small part to its focus on personal needs, and not simply on dogma or strict morality. Psychological categories such as "self," "fulfillment," "individuality," "journey," "walk," and "growth" became prominent in its rhetoric reconciling a legitimate self with a deeply embedded American religious narrative emphasizing the benefits of faith (Hunter 1987: 50–75). Survey analysis shows in fact that "personal need" indicators better explain evangelical involvement than do the more customary socioeconomic variables that have long been used by social scientists (Shibley 1996). Put simply, evangelicals are well on their way toward being absorbed into an accommodating middle-class culture that encourages self-expression and creativity, acceptance of diversity, and, perhaps most revealing of all, a softening of traditional assumptions about human depravity. Religious appearances and rhetoric notwithstanding, the enormous social and cultural transformations for evangelicals have produced a moral and religious ambiguity not unlike that many Americans face wanting, as the psychologist Robert Jay Lifton (1993: 9) points out, to be "both fluid and grounded at the same time, however tenuous that possibility." Lifton's description flies into our face, but it is paradigmatic perhaps of life in the late modern, or postmodern world.

The actual changes in religious behavior for younger generations of Americans do not permit easy generalizations. Surveys suggest a slight decline in attendance at religious services, but the patterns are complex. For example, among the baby boomers who had "returned" to active participation in 1988–9 in our survey after having "dropped out" at an earlier time in their lives, only 43 percent in 1995–6 reported they attended religious services even as often as once a month or more. Having dropped out of a religious congregation once, if they returned to active participation they could also drop out again, and indeed they did. Yet there was an opposite movement as well calling into question any simple notion of secular drift. Among those who had dropped out of religious participation at the time of the first survey, one-third in 1995–6 said they attended religious services weekly or more, and one-half actually two or three times a month (Roof 1999a: 117–20). When asked for their reasons for either getting involved or dropping out, our respondents often mentioned subjective concerns such as "feeling comfortable with the congregation," "spiritual concerns," and "family and/or lifestyle." Inner realities took precedence over external explanations.

Older sociological models for explaining religious life seem less and less appropriate in a culture that emphasized so much personal choice and inner well-being. Moreover, our interviews following the surveys revealed that people often made cosmic leaps, at times affirming theistic faith, then later seriously questioning it; they switched from one ideological extreme to the other seemingly with ease, and often altered their views of God or the sacred, even when remaining outwardly loyal within the same faith tradition. While such fluidity is hardly new in the American context, our findings underscore just how unbounded and protean personal religion in the latter decades of the twentieth century had become. Clearly, too, the movement back and forth between a radically self-focused spirituality, on the one hand, and a more dweller-focused spirituality involving a transcendent conception of God, on the other, was not all that uncommon. Those who were long-time participants in church and synagogue often dropped out to see where the freedom of their inner quests would take them while their polar opposites – the metaphysically homeless – dropped in on congregations to see what was happening and it might be relevant to them. Unquestionably, Robert Bellah and his associates in *Habits of the Heart* were correct when they observed fifteen years earlier that the two – that is, an internal versus an external religious orientation – organize much of American religious life and, more directly to the point of this discussion, that "shifts from one pole to the other are not as rare as one might think" (1985: 235).

This observation of a protean religious style, consistent with what William McKinney and I called the "new voluntarism" (Roof and McKinney 1987), stands in stark contrast to the cultural-war model presuming rigid and strong boundaries separating liberals and conservatives. Correct in its description at the extremes, this latter model espoused in the 1980s overlooks a vast majority of Americans who are not so ideologically consistent but are more pragmatic in their moral and religious views.

Over against an alleged growing polarization between liberals and conservatives pulling Americans into one or another camp, or "cultural wars," the story of far greater consequence for religion in these years, it would seem, is what Philip Cushman (1995) describes as "the rise of a new sovereign self." An individualistic ethos, a therapeutic mentality, and a growing consumerism all conspired to bring about a cultural redefinition of the self. Any such redefinition holds enormous implications for spirituality both in inward realities and outward expressions – and in ways that cannot be contained institutionally or even within ideological camps. Cushman captures the far reaches of the psychological transformation now underway when he writes: "The new cultural terrain was now oriented to purchasing and consuming rather than to moral striving, to individual transcendence rather than to community salvation; to isolated relationships rather than to community activism; to an individual mysticism rather than to political change" (1999: 130).

Admittedly, Cushman captures the more extreme of current cultural trends, and minimizes the continuing, and often remarkably strong bonds within religious communities – be they Catholic, Jewish, Islamic, liberal, or conservative Protestant. Religious communities continue to exercise some degree of constraint on an excessive self-preoccupation, a point we ought not overlook. Amid all the cultural changes, for many Americans religious communities serve as centers of moral and theological interpretation, and thereby provide guidance for the everyday lives of their members. Churches, synagogues, temples, mosques, and other religious gatherings serve as subcultures that filter and shape spiritual expressions. Religious dwelling is of course possible within a dynamic psychological culture that privileges movement over stability, and journeys over destinations; it simply requires a degree of boundary maintenance that would not be as necessary in an environment defined more by tradition.

Furthermore, public responsibility and altruism have not disappeared as moral ideals, but instead have become reoriented within a highly subjective cultural context. While it might seem that in a self-absorbed culture acts of charity would readily diminish, or take on less significance to those committing them, research shows that a positive, albeit slight, relationship actually exists between the two (Wuthnow 1991: 22). Reaching out to help others need not be at odds with one's wanting to receive a sense of self-satisfaction for such action; indeed, the act and the motive easily co-vary. A self-focused culture might well inflate one's wish for internal rewards when helping others, and give rise to a distinctive rhetoric expressing those wishes, but it need not necessarily erode good deeds or the spiritual meaning people may obtain from engaging in them. Instrumentalism, or the tendency to view religion from the standpoint of its manifest personal benefits, is very much a driving force in our culture as many commentators would agree, but to dismiss religion as having become little more than psychology is to throw the baby out with the bath water. We grasp the situation better if we recognize that in contemporary America we have an expanding and richly textured set of religious discourses that draw heavily upon psychological and self-referential terms for describing the motives behind an individual's religious beliefs, practices, and charitable acts.

II

How might we reconceptualize spirituality in keeping with such trends? How are we to understand the transformations in religious dwelling and the increased significance of spiritual seeking? The need for new perspective arises in part because in an age of highly privatized religion and attention to the instrumental functions of faith, "spirituality" becomes distinguished from "religion" in popular thinking, but also, and more seriously, as sociologists of religion we do not have a well-developed interpretive paradigm for a proper analysis. Given the evolution of our discipline, the sociological study of religion concerns itself largely with congregations, social institutions, and religious movements, and generally proceeds with assumptions about individuals as religious actors with "demand" needs, that is, for meaning and belonging. Typically, it is presumed that people are socialized into a particular faith through their upbringing, or that individuals later on make rational choices as adults about the congregations they join – but in neither instance is religion itself as a category problematized. If the definition of religion is addressed at all, usually it has to do with the relative merits of substantive versus functional approaches. Little attention is given to the psychological frames people bring to historic beliefs and practices. What do people have in mind when they say they are religious? What do they mean when they use a word like spiritual? Or, to sharpen the problem further, what is meant when as some people now say "I'm spiritual but not religious," or that their spirituality is growing in importance but the impact of religion on their lives has declined? Only recently have such questions come to be dealt with in a more serious manner as scholars begin to recognize that "lived religion," as opposed to religion as an abstraction about normative belief or an institution, is extraordinarily complex and subtle, and even more so in the American setting in which religion is regarded as highly voluntary in character.

To begin with, we should note that such questions arise during a time of considerable personal autonomy for Americans generally. Over the past half-century, there has been, in Phillip E. Hammond's words, "both an enlarged arena of voluntary choice and an enhanced freedom from structural constraint" (1998: 11). As options in matters of lifestyle, sexuality, and the family sphere have increased, so likewise within the religious sphere. The prevailing culture of choice erodes the binding quality of religious reality and transforms it as an institutional presence in society into a more individually centered, subjective reality. With greater choice comes a fundamental shift in how the church and other religious bodies function within the larger society – away from collective-expressive functions to more individual-expressive ones, as Hammond puts it. In effect, churchgoing becomes less a "habit" or "custom" and more a personal "preference" related largely to one's tastes, recognized needs, and states of mind. Religion thus loses its traditional Durkheimian role of expressing collective unity in ceremony, symbol, and ritual. Not that religion loses all its public force within society, but to the extent it exerts influence it is mainly within the individual life-sphere. In keeping with Peter Berger's (1967) widely accepted argument about privatization in the modern context, the religious world shrinks becoming less and less an overarching canopy of meaning for the society as a whole and is reduced to smaller realms, namely personal and family life. Counter trends toward deprivatization are identifiable currently, but the dominant thrust is still in the opposite direction at present.

Even within the family sphere, this privatizing trend is apparent. Greater attention to personal life comes at a time when shared religious unity has become problematic for many American families. Not just family disruption but spiraling rates of interfaith marriages and new types of family units undermine the traditional role of families in sustaining religious life. Moreover, the normative religious expectations of family life have faded despite the rhetoric about a return to "family values" voiced a decade ago. A survey question in our research on the baby boom generation some years back was very revealing in this respect. To tap this changing ethos, we asked: "Is it important to you to attend church/synagogue as a family, or should family members make individual choices about religion?" Fifty-five percent of our respondents said it was important to do so as a family, but 45 percent indicated that family members should make their own choices. A shared faith is still a family ideal, but not by much. We do not have historical data to describe the trend, but it is unlikely we would find as much individual emphasis in previous decades. What such findings underscore is that the family as a traditional bastion of religious unity, long held up as an ideal for the maintenance of faith across the generations, is less able to sustain itself in this manner under contemporary circumstances; consequently, many individuals are left without the religious support and reinforcement that once was found within this institution, and thus now must rely more upon themselves.

Important, too, the current concern with the spiritual is a reflection of a deeply personal search for meaning arising out of broader cultural changes within society, and manifest in worries about the "self" and its well-being. If, as many sociologists argue, religion is about two major foci of concerns – personal meaning and social belonging – then it is around the first of these that religious energies primarily revolve today. Pressures mount in the direction of bringing Bellah's internal religion to the fore. "Firsthand" religion, or its more inward realities, to use William James's (1902/1961) expression, takes precedent over the "secondhand" manifestations of creeds, rituals, and institutions. Surveys show that ordinary Americans are capable of drawing this distinction. For example, in a 1994 poll, 65 percent of Americans reported believing that religion was losing its influence in public life, yet almost equal numbers, 62 percent, claimed that religion was increasing in importance in their personal lives. Attention to the spiritual may indeed represent a healthy response to a felt loss of meaning and a resulting malaise, and especially when as the psychologist Vicky Genia (1997) observes, people find a healthy balance between a structured grounding which is also simultaneously open to the cultivation and expansion of the interior life. Whatever spiritual maturity might mean, it seems apparent that a seismic religiocultural shift is underway in how people, as the ethnographer Robert Orsi (1997: 7) says, "live in, with, through, and against the religious idioms, including (often enough) those not explicitly their own." That is to say, Americans concerned with their spiritual well-being are reaching deeper into their own faith traditions, yet at the same time are not necessarily ruling out the presence of other faith traditions as a possible resource for themselves.

Helpful is Ann Swidler's (1986) notion of "strategies of action." Using a toolbox metaphor of culture, she emphasizes how we selectively draw off religious traditions, although in quite differing ways in settled and unsettled times. In settled times, as with Wuthnow's (1998) "dwellers," people relate to the sacred through their habits; that is, their strategies of action are firmly established within communities. As the historian Dorothy Bass (1994: 172) says, "Living traditions are embodied in the social world in two related ways: Through *practices* and *institutions* where practices are sustained. Individuals can learn and participate in traditions only in the company of others; they do so by entering into the practices and institutions through which particular social groups, versed in specific activities and gathered into specific organizations, bear traditions over time." Practices embedded within tradition reproduce religious memory, essential to its continuing hold upon consciousness. Shared faith and community sustain individuals.

In unsettled times, however, memory becomes more problematic (Hervieu-Léger 2000). Lacking a firm rooting within tradition, as with Wuthnow's "seekers," people devise new strategies of action, or ways of responding to the sacred. This can involve negotiation both with themselves and with others as to the meaning and practice of faith in a given life-situation. Or it may be more radical as with the conscious exploration of religious alternatives and recognition of the "merits of borrowing" symbols, beliefs, and practices from many sources. Drawing from their own experiences and an expanded menu of spiritual resources, people produce discursive strategies toward religion, as reflected in such questions asked by many today such as, "How can I find a deeper spirituality?" "What might faith mean in my life facing the problems we face today?" "Can religion relate to my everyday life in a more personal way than it did when I was growing up?" It is not so much that religion itself changes, but rather the psychological frames that people bring to it.

Alasdair MacIntyre argues that in our time "the unity of a human life is the unity of a narrative quest" (1984: 219). His point is that the task of finding order and meaning to life becomes more of a *reflexive* act in a world where tradition has less of a hold on us. Reflexivity implies an awareness of the contingencies of life, and the necessity for engaging and responding to those contingencies as best one can. All of which is to say that modernity, or late modernity depending on how one defines our era, has given rise to altered relations between the individual and tradition, and therefore to a fundamental change in the process of self-narration itself. Increasingly, individuals discover they must "bring" religious meaning to their lives – that is, they must search for it. Identity becomes inescapably bound up with its narration, and especially so in a quest culture as we know it in contemporary America. We become our stories in the sense that storytelling yields a degree of coherence for our lives. We gain not just upon a heightened self-consciousness but an awareness of the role we play in shaping our own identities. As MacIntyre insists, we are led to think about life and to ask ourselves: "a quest for what?" As I have written elsewhere about MacIntyre, "He forces the hardest question of all, moral in its broadest sense, and having to do with some final *telos* to which life is directed. Quest is not about itself, but about the narration of human intentionality and purpose, ultimately about some object of value and fidelity. His is *the* question modernity forces on all individuals in a 'post-traditional' context where the binding force of tradition is greatly diminished and agreed-upon, culturally embedded answers cannot be presumed from one generation to the next, and where individual choice in such matters becomes increasingly obligatory" (Roof 1999a: 164).

In one reading of the situation, the challenge to narrative unity is apparent in people's use currently of self-reported designations as "religious" or "spiritual." While 74 percent of the people polled in one of our surveys say they are "religious" and 73 percent say they are "spiritual," the two identities are only partially overlapping. Seventy-nine percent of those who are religious claim to be spiritual, but 54 percent of those who are not religious are also spiritual. This points to a healthy balance of the internal and external forms of religion for many Americans, yet we cannot assume that one designation necessarily implies the other. The discrepancy is great enough that in terms of cultural identities, the "spiritual" and the "religious" take on separate meanings. Of interest, too, is the empirical finding that the two types of self-identities relate quite differently to levels of religious individualism. Using a scale measuring religious individualism, we find this latter to be negatively related to defining oneself as religious but *positively* to defining oneself as spiritual. That is, given a high level of personal autonomy in the modern context, the religious consequences appear to be mixed: Religious identity as culturally defined appears to be undermined, but at the same time there is an enhanced self-reflection associated with greater clarity of conviction and ethical and spiritual sensitivities. In this respect we might say that personal autonomy has a double face, one that reflects the dislocations of institutional religious identities in the contemporary world, and a second that mirrors a deeply personal search for meaningful faith and spirituality. This poses an interesting, and potentially very significant problem for the analysis of personal religion.

III

For analytic purposes, it is helpful to cross-classify people's identities as either religious or spiritual. Simple though this may be, such a typology makes problematic the intersection of inner-experiential and outer-institutional identities, and thereby sensitizes us to a wide range of religious, spiritual, and secular constituencies within contemporary society. A brief description of the major constituencies follows from the typology found in my *Spiritual Marketplace: Baby Boomers and the Remaking of American Religion* (Roof 1999a: 178).

Statistically, the largest sector of Americans from our survey fall into the quadrant with overlapping religious and spiritual identities – roughly 59 percent of the total population. This includes the 33 percent who are "Born-again" Christians and the 26 percent who we describe as Mainstream Believers, differing in religious style but not necessarily in spiritual vitality. Here the spiritual is contained, so to speak, in and through existing institutional religious forms. William James's "firsthand" and "secondhand" religion fuse together in a balanced whole. These are Wuthnow's dwellers. The religious world is maintained through shared symbols, beliefs, and practices, and especially through regular interaction and communally based reinforcement. Shared practices presuppose language, symbols, and myth, vehicles all necessary for sustaining a religious thought world and guiding emotional and intentional responses to that world. In this respect, religious dwelling is emblematic of settled times, or settings where prescribed "strategies of action" not only express, but recreate experiences that fit what is generally defined as religious. Religious experience under these conditions is largely derivative; it arises out of practice, or the rehearsing of myth and narrative. In this way the unity of the "religious" and the "spiritual," or of form and spirit, is more or less held together.

But there are serious threats to narrative unity or the "felt-whole" experiences as Herbert Richardson (1967) once called them. Some people are drawn into revering tradition for its own sake, in which case ritual turns into ritualism, doctrine into dogma, and the inherited practices of tradition become encrusted and lifeless. Rapid social and cultural change provoke antimodernist reactions of this sort as evident in fundamentalist and neotraditionalist movements across many faith communities. Being "religious" comes to mean holding on to the outward forms of doctrine, morality, and institution to the point of not having, or feeling, any serious engagement with faith as a living reality. The strategies of action are rigid and literally mandated. People who are religious but not spiritual in this sense are perhaps more common than we presume, encouraged in part by the popular cultural meanings that have come to be attached to these identifying labels. To invoke a "religious" identity as distinct from being "spiritual" emerges as a marker distinguishing conservative fundamentalists from more moderate-minded evangelicals, charismatics, and Pentecostals. Fifteen percent of our respondents fit into this more narrow classification, people we call Dogmatists.

And, of course, there is the opposite combination – the spiritual seekers who report being "spiritual but not religious." This configuration of responses has taken on a particular cultural meaning with the word *spiritual* serving as a unifying label of positive self-identity, and the word *religious* used as a counteridentity, describing who they are not. Here strategies of action are much less established, and often are little more than exploratory attempts at belief and practice that promise to lead to spiritual growth and personal well-being. Because spiritual seeking is largely a private matter involving loosely based social networks, this is more a striving for meaning than for belonging, but the distinction often evaporates in the lived-religious context. Spiritual quests are not necessarily antitraditional; indeed, "old" pasts are often reclaimed as in the case of Wicca, and "new" fabricated pasts get created as with ecospirituality currently. Hervieu-Léger (1994) observes that tradition, or at least a selective reappropriation of it, is so important that people not well-grounded within it are likely to create "imaginary geneologies." In so doing, they lay claim to spiritual lineage and legitimate themselves as yet another constituency in the spiritual marketplace. At the hands of spiritual entrepreneurs who rationalize choices and devise technologies, meaning systems proliferate in an expanding world of metaphysical possibilities. Fourteen percent of those we surveyed fall into this category, described simply as Metaphysical Believers and Spiritual Seekers.

Research shows, as well, that there are people who do not identify as either religious or spiritual. Neither the language of religious heritage nor the inner language of a spiritual self carry much meaning. They may have "flow" experiences of the sort the psychologist Mihaly Czikszentmihalyi (1990) describes, or moments of intense excitement, energy, and creativity, but in describing them they do not turn to the shared language of faith or even to a deeply spiritual-type vocabulary. When asked about influences shaping their lives, they are likely to point to the characteristics they were born with, or their own mastery of destiny. They do not necessarily reject God-talk, but when they engage in such talk God or the sacred is imaged typically in a generalized, and highly individualized way. In many respects they are the polar opposites of the Dogmatists. Often they have explored religious possibilities but over time have worked themselves out of a religious frame of mind; rather than reifying tradition and becoming rigid and exclusivistic, they have moved toward open-mindedness to the point of being inarticulate about what they really believe. Strategies of action are embryonic, if at all evident. One would suspect there is a thin boundary separating those who make use of the word "spiritual" in defining themselves and those unable to make use of the word. Twelve percent of the people we interviewed belong to this category, labeled simply as Secularists.

As pointed out, this typology is at most a heuristic device sensitizing researchers to some crucial dimensions in the analysis of contemporary American religion. It is but a start toward gaining greater clarity and analytic control over James's "firsthand" religion that is often missed by sociologists focusing primarily on its "secondhand" manifestations. If we are to bring the spiritual into our explanatory schemes, we must work toward a more integrated social science building on the insights of psychology and sociology. A more systematic approach drawing more widely across these two disciplines especially promises a healthy balance for the study of religion, and one that very much is needed if we are to make sense of the deep, quite subtle religious and spiritual changes now occurring.

PART THREE

Religion and the Life Course

CHAPTER TWELVE

Religious Socialization

Sources of Influence and Influences of Agency

Darren E. Sherkat

Religious socialization is an interactive process through which social agents influence individuals' religious beliefs and understandings. People interact with a variety of different agents of socialization over the life course, and these individuals, organizations, and experiences channel the beliefs and understandings that constitute religious preferences – and these preferences help inform commitments to religious organizations. Agents of socialization influence individuals only if the source is a trusted and valued connection, and experiences can only inform religious understandings if they are salient for religious faith. Individuals have considerable agency to reject socialization pressure, and to choose which connections guide religious preferences. The temporal ordering of contact with agents of socialization is clearly important. Parents' initial inputs into religious preferences and ties help guide people's interactions with other individuals and organizations (Myers 1996; Cornwall 1989; Sherkat 1998). Parents and denominations also channel peer interactions, and especially spousal choice – both of which motivate religious beliefs and ties. Education and status factors also may influence religious preferences, and religious orientations also direct educational attainment and occupational choice (Sherkat and Wilson 1995; Darnell and Sherkat 1997; Sherkat and Darnell 1999).

In this chapter, I begin by elaborating a theoretical foundation for the study of religious influence and religious socialization. I draw on contemporary theory and research on social movements and the sociology of religion, particularly on the nature of religious preferences and endogenous and exogenous sources of preference change. The nexus between these arenas of social research is crucial for an integrative perspective on socialization geared toward ideologically structured collective action (Zald 2000). Next, I review research documenting the influence of various socialization agents. Finally, I provide a general assessment of the prospects for future research on socialization and how they fit into important theoretical debates in the sociology of religion.

RELIGIOUS PREFERENCES, DYNAMICS, AND CHOICES

John McCarthy and Mayer Zald (1977) provided a definition of social movements that can easily be integrated to the study of religion: Social movements are preference structures for change. McCarthy and Zald (1977) contrast these unmobilized preference structures with mobilized social movement organizations, just as contemporary studies in the sociology of religion juxtapose believing and belonging (e.g., Davie 1994; Stark and Finke 2000). Religious movements have a distinctive character – at least some of the benefits they provide are supernatural explanations and compensators that yield value for those who believe (Stark and Bainbridge 1985,1987; Stark and Finke 2000). Humans find explanations for the meaning of life – and even more trivial things – highly valuable, and are willing to exchange actual rewards (time, money, or other resources) for these explanations. Of course, answers to the meaning of life are typically suspect, and only valuable if they are also taken to be true by trusted others. Hence, these explanations are, to a large extent, collectively produced goods (Iannaccone 1990; Stark and Finke 2000).

Religious socialization is the process through which people come to hold religious preferences. To understand the development of religion at the individual level, we have to know how preferences are formed and how they change. Notably, this view of religious preferences does not equate them with choices of religious affiliation, and instead takes preferences to be separate. Religious preferences are the favored supernatural explanations about the meaning, purpose, and origins of life – explanations that cannot be proven nor disproved. These preferences will help drive choices in the realm of religion – motivating religious devotion, public religious participation, and affiliation with religious organizations. In this section, I will briefly describe the development and dynamics of preferences, and how choices are influenced by both preferences and other social factors. In making religious choices, religious preferences are not the only factors taken into account. Religious decision making is also influenced by social pressures – nonreligious rewards and punishments that are attached to piety or impiety. I will deal with these social constraints on choices separately.

Sociologists interested in the dynamics of preference structures have to engage in the messy task of getting inside people's heads and accounting for tastes (Elster 1983), which contrasts with the view of preferences favored by neoclassical economists (e.g., Stigler and Becker 1977; Iannaccone 1990). Preference structures for supernatural explanations do not spring mechanistically from the events or structural strains that occur at particular time points. This "immaculate conception" view of social movements is rejected by serious historical work (Taylor 1988), and studies in the sociology of religion that privilege macro-social revolutions in religious understandings (e.g., Wuthnow 1976; Bellah 1976; Roof 1993) are unsupported by empirical examinations (Bainbridge and Stark 1981; Sherkat 1998).

As a socialization perspective would suggest, people learn preferences for religious goods, and if religious preferences shift they do so in predictable ways in response to individual experiences or social influences. Beginning early in the life course, parents and valued others promulgate religious beliefs and understandings, and these commitments foster preferences for particular religious goods (Sherkat 1998; Sherkat and Wilson 1995). Parents, friends, spouses, and peers are valued sources of information about collective goods. Social network ties are important for generating shifts in preferences, and close friendships can (although not usually) motivate radical shifts in preferences for collective goods (Stark and Bainbridge 1980; Snow et al. 1986; Rochford 1985). Later in this chapter I will discuss varied agents of socialization at length.

People tend to prefer the familiar, and religious preferences are generally reinforced through routine religious experiences (Elster 1983; Sherkat and Wilson 1995; Sherkat

1997, 1998; Von Weisaker 1971). Religious choices are often driven by adaptive preferences. People are comforted by familiar religious explanations, and they find value and solace in the supernatural rewards and compensators of familiar religious goods. Endogenous preference shifts like adaptive preferences are a function of individual fluctuations in desire that are not a response to social influences on tastes. Instead, people's prior consumption of religious goods makes them more desirous of similar goods – just as when people desire the same sort of soft drink they consume every day. This tendency of preferences to adapt to common alternatives leads to a substantial conservative bias in the development and reproduction of preferences (Sherkat 1998). Iannaccone (1990) explains the inertia of religious choices as a function of the development of human capital, rather than shifting preferences. From the human capital perspective, religious experiences build individuals' stocks of religious human capital. Religious human capital enables the efficient and effective production of religious value in collective settings. Hence, the human capital perspective views preferences as stable; what is seen to change is the ability to produce religious value. Both the theory of adaptive preferences and human capital theory lead to similar conclusions regarding the development and trajectory of religious beliefs and behaviors, and they are not mutually exclusive explanations for religious dynamics. What is also common to both of these perspectives is that they lend agency to individuals making religious choices – adaptive preferences and human capital are not a function of socialization, but instead are generated endogenously by individuals.

Preferences sometimes shift endogenously in a way that promotes change rather than the reproduction of sentiment. *Counteradaptive preferences* occur when people aver from previously desired collective goods, and instead prefer more novel ends (Elster 1983). Hence, people sometimes may gravitate to varied religious expressions and modes of supernatural explanations, while rejecting their formerly preferred religious options. Counteradaptivity is evident in motivations for religious seekership (Sherkat 1997; Roof 1993). As with adaptivity, counteradaptivity is not the result of socialization or preference learning, but is endogenously motivated. Social influences may generate preference shifts in another way as well. People may be coerced or seduced into trying a particular good, and then come to prefer it (Elster 1983). Preference shift through seduction combines dynamic preferences with social influences on choices – which will be elaborated below. Religious seduction is clearly evident in the educational process in seminaries, where students preferring faithful orthodoxy are forced into trying more secular ideologies, which they then come to embrace (Finke and Stark 1992). Forced conversion, like that experienced by African slaves in the United States or indigenous peoples on a variety of continents on contact with Christian, Hindu, Moslem, or Buddhist crusaders, will also follow this pattern if coerced "conversion" genuinely succeeds.

Social Influences on Individuals' Choices

Religious preferences are not the only motivations for making religious choices. Like all decisions about cultural consumption, religious choices have social consequences, and because of this religious decision making may be dominated by social influences on choices. These social influences on choices are not to be confused with socialization – if we define socialization as an influence on preferences as I have above. Instead, social influences provide an explanation for religious dynamics in spite of or in addition to the impact of socialization. Following Amartya Sen (1973,1993), I identify three types of social influences on religious choices: (a) sympathy/antipathy; (b) example setting; and (c) sanctions (Sherkat 1997, 1998; Sherkat and Wilson 1995).

People often participate in religious groups out of sympathy for the feelings of others, despite receiving little or no benefit from the supernatural compensators supported by the collective activities. Adult children may attend church with aging parents to make parents feel better, despite being agnostic or even ill at ease with the collective benefits generated by religious activities (Sherkat 1998). In contrast, individuals sometimes participate in religious groups not because they desire the collective good generated, but instead to antagonize others who are held in disdain – an antipathetic motivation for action. Antipathy seems to direct religious choices for many participants in neopagan and "Satanic" audience cults and cult movements (Stark and Bainbridge 1985). Rather than deriving religious benefits from the actions supporting pagan or Satanist supernatural explanations, most participants seem to relish the negative impact their blasphemy has on devout Christians. Notably, both sympathy and antipathy imply considerable agency for individuals making choices. Here, participants act not because of a mechanistic link between social ties and religious understandings but, instead, as a choice to reward or punish valued or detested others. This avoids the common problem of oversocialized views of actors in cultural theorizing (e.g., Granovetter 1973; Frank 1993).

Example-setting is another potential social motivation for religious choices that does not involve preferences for religious goods. People may affiliate with religious groups and attend religious services because they wish to set an example for others. Parents are likely to join churches and attend religious services not because they find the supernatural compensators and rewards appealing, but instead to set an example for their children. Faculty members at religious schools and public political officials may also participate in order to exemplify pious behavior. However, public religionists may instead be seeking tangible rewards for their hypocritical participation (Heckathorn 1993), or avoiding punishments for impiety. Here, the motivation would not be preferences for the religious goods, nor example-setting or sympathy; instead religious participation is motivated by selective incentives and disincentives (McCarthy and Zald 1977; Hall 1988). If selective rewards or punishments are strong enough, individuals may participate in religious actions that produce collective bads (such as collective suicides, proscriptions that limit members' occupational attainment), and people will engage in the overconsumption of religious goods for the sake of social rewards (Ellison and Sherkat 1995; Phillips 1998; Sherkat and Cunningham 1998).

Religious pursuits are no different from other behaviors in this regard. Social sanctions cause people to buy clothes they do not prefer to wear; to drink repulsive drinks; to smoke cigars; pursue deviant careers; buy expensive, unsafe, and unreliable automobiles; and so on (Akerlof 1997; Bernheim 1994; Bagwell and Bernheim 1996). Religious groups generate nonreligious social rewards by giving participants access to mating markets, contacts for business, friendship networks for children, social status in the community, and the like. Religious consumption may also prevent people from experiencing punishments such as social isolation, economic insecurity, and violent repression. The importance of social rewards and sanctions demonstrates even more clearly that personal preferences are not all that determine religious action. Social influences are not simply through socialization or endogenously changing preferences because choices are not freely made – there is no social vacuum that would allow such freedom. Choices are embedded in social relations that influence both the development and dynamics of preferences, as well as the options available and choices taken (Akerlof 1997; Sen 1973,1993; Sherkat 1997).

Religious commitments are a function not only of socialized preferences but also factors intrinsic to the individual and exogenous to the religious choice. Furthermore, social influences may have nothing to do with the understandings that constitute religious preferences, and hence are not socialization influences even though they may direct individuals' behaviors. In the remainder of the chapter, I will discuss research on agents of influence while keeping in mind the distinction between socialization and social influences.

AGENTS OF INFLUENCE

Parents and Family

Across cultures and history, the family is the primary source of information about supernatural explanations. Parents and relatives teach children understandings about supernatural things, and this source of information has temporal and affective primacy – both of which are important for influencing preferences. Surprisingly, many studies in the sociology of religion contended that parents have limited influence on children's religious commitments (e.g., Hoge et al. 1994). These studies accepted commonly articulated assumptions about growing generational differences in values and commitments – the generation gap thesis that led many scholars to assume that radical shifts in religiosity were on the horizon (e.g., Wuthnow 1976; Bellah 1976). However, most systematic research and more studies employing national samples and longitudinal data from parents and children have demonstrated that parental influences dominate religious beliefs and attachments throughout the life course (Acock and Bengtson 1978; Acock 1984; Willits and Crider 1989; Myers 1996; Sherkat 1998).

Parents and Children

The systematic study of parental influences on children's religious preferences for religion began with Newcomb and Svehla's (1937) study of 558 parents and children – in which they found that mothers' attitudes toward religion explained 34 percent of the variation in sons' religious understandings and 48 percent of the variation in daughters' religious preferences. Since this early work, many studies have concluded that parents have a substantial effect on children's religious beliefs and behaviors (Hunsberger 1985; Acock and Bengtson 1978; Acock 1984; Willits and Crider 1989). Generally, these studies assume that parental influences are limited to earlier periods of the life course and that the crystallization of belief is achieved in the early life cycle. Later researchers borrowed lifelong learning models from political socialization (cf. Sigel 1989) and investigated how parental effects continue over the life course. Parents help shape other social ties, and this channels lifelong socialization. Indeed, life course events may make parents more influential as young adults seek wisdom from parents on how to raise children of their own and deal with stressful life events (Stolzenberg et al. 1995; Myers 1996; Sherkat 1991a). Examinations of parental socialization have tended to focus on religious affiliation and participation – noting how parents' participation early in the life course influences children's participation (Acock 1984; Acock and Bengtson 1980; Willits and Crider 1989). Some, like Myers (1996), mix indicators of religious beliefs and participation to construct measures of religiosity. While this strategy yields common conclusions, it does not allow for an assessment of the relationship between religious understandings or preferences and religious participation.

Studies also have shown how solidarity among parents and feelings of closeness between parents and children influence the socialization process. First, researchers have demonstrated that when parents have divergent religious affiliations, children are less likely to develop religious affiliations common to their parents, and are more likely to switch their religious affiliations or become apostates (Sandomirsky and Wilson 1990; Sherkat 1991b). Second, the presence of parental discord in the family has been shown to lower religiosity, particularly for male children (Nelsen 1981). Youths who report feeling close to their parents are less likely to defect from their parents' religious affiliation (Sherkat and Wilson 1995). Each of these findings suggests the operation of social influences on choices. When parents have different religious values or affiliations, then they place competing pressures on children's (and each other's) religious attachments. Feelings of closeness will also motivate participation out of sympathy for the feelings of parents. Emotional attachment also may be linked to preference development, since strong emotive ties may lead to preferences for interactions and understandings (Collins 1993). Future studies will certainly need to further develop connections between affective ties and both preference development and religious choices.

Following the lead of studies in developmental aging (e.g., Bengtson 1975; Bengtson and Black 1973; Bengtson and Kuypers 1971; Bengtson and Troll, 1978; Hagestad 1982; Rossi and Rossi 1990), a few scholars have pondered how socialization influences between parents and children may be reciprocal (Thomas and Cornwall 1990). Glass et al. (1986) drew on exchange theory to explain how dependencies and developmental stake may lead children to influence their parents' values, particularly later in the life course, when parents may be more dependent on children for critical cues and information. Glass et al. (1986) find reciprocal influences between parents and children across the life course, and I have shown reciprocal influences between parents and children in religious beliefs and religious participation (Sherkat 1991a). Using longitudinal data from the Youth Parent Socialization Panel Study, which interviewed parents and children at three points over eighteen years of the life course, I found that parent-child reciprocal influences are relatively constant over the life course for religious choices – measured in terms of religious participation. Importantly, the magnitude of the reciprocal influences between parents and children exceeds the degree of influence of other factors such as educational attainment, family of procreation dynamics (e.g., marriage, divorce, and childrearing), and denominational influences. Looking at religious beliefs, operationalized by beliefs in biblical orthodoxy, I found a clear developmental trajectory of parent-child, child-parent influence. Parents have more influence on children's beliefs early in the life course (before adulthood), while children then influence their parents as young adults. However, as the offspring reach their thirties, parents once again become more influential.

My findings are based entirely on a U.S. sample at a particular period (1965–82), which may have given more credibility to young adults as sources of valid information regarding the interpretation of the Bible as the word of God – which was the indicator of religious beliefs. What clearly happened in my case is that young adult baby boomers influenced their parents' beliefs in the Bible, leading their elders to become less ortho-dox in their interpretation of scriptures. Later in the life course, older parents pulled the adult children back toward more conservative religious beliefs. A similar pattern might be expected in revolutionary Iran, as young religious activists led their parents and other relatives toward preferring particular Islamic beliefs. Later, as the revolution lost its flare and the realities of living adult life under religious constraints sunk in, older Iranians from more moderate generations probably became more influential in defining their children's religious commitments.

Spousal Influences

Marital ties are also important sources of influence, and religious intermarriage is one of the strongest predictors of changes of religious affiliation (Lazerwitz et al. 1998; Lazerwitz 1995a, 1995b; Sandomirsky and Wilson 1990; Sherkat 1991b). Importantly, however, the direction of switching follows a particular pattern – what Stark and Finke (2000) call "Greeley's law" – that the more religious spouse has more influence over the direction of change. Typically, this has meant that intermarriage with Catholics generates switching into Catholicism, and that people who marry members of exclusive sects tend to switch into the sect. Of course, intermarriage is also related to underlying religious preferences, as people with strong valuations of particular religious goods will be unlikely to marry someone who doesn't share their desires. This selection bias tends to minimize the influence of spouses on religious choices. When people have strong religious preferences they will be unlikely to choose a mate who differs, and those with weak religious preferences who are more likely to intermarry would exert little influence on their partners (McCutcheon 1988; Johnson 1980).

People choose their friends and spouses in accordance with preferences; hence, val-ued others are likely to reinforce existing desires rather than arouse new ones. Because preferences also drive educational and occupational choices, this will tend to consoli-date social ties across varied fields of social life (Darnell and Sherkat 1997; Sherkat and Blocker 1997). Homophily strongly influences the composition of voluntary groups, and social movements of all kinds are populated by people with similar backgrounds and opinions (McPherson and Smith-Lovin 1987). Together, these theoretical expecta-tions and the supporting empirical research suggests that macrostructural connections are less important for the formation of preferences for collective goods, and instead that individuals' preferences drive their connections to social groups (whether families, oc-cupations, neighborhoods, or social movements). Here, I argue against the macrostruc-turalism that dominates explanatory frameworks in social exchange theory (e.g., Lawler et al. 1993), and call for less minimalist conceptions of actors. Thickening the view of actors' motivations will help identify how people choose many of the structures of which they are a part, thus lending agency to the framework and allowing for testable hypotheses regarding the influence of networks on individuals, and of individuals on networks.

Family Research and Socialization

The late twentieth century saw a flurry of sociological research on the religion-family connection, yet data constraints hamper progress in the assessment of how family re-lations influence religious beliefs and commitments and vice versa. Very few studies track both parents and children over the life course, and fewer still have employed even the most rudimentary indicators of religious involvement – and only the Youth Parent Socialization Panel Study has provided a single indicator of religious beliefs. To my knowledge, no study has tracked parents, children, and siblings over the life course, and there is strong theoretical reason for believing that siblings provide ongoing influences on religious preferences and choices. While a few panel studies have examined spouses over short periods of the life course (e.g., the National Survey of Families and Households), the data collected postdate marriage. Familial influences beyond the nuclear family are also likely to be influential (Glass et al. 1986; Sherkat 1998, 1991a). This may be particularly true for subpopulations in which extended family ties are more important for childrearing and other tasks, perhaps especially for African Americans and ethnic immigrant groups.

One important task ahead for sociologists of religion is to begin to examine extended family influences, and the reciprocal influences in families over the life course. Of greatest theoretical importance, and absent from most examinations of religious "socialization" is the separation of preferences from choices. As I discussed at length earlier, families not only inform the religious beliefs and understandings of individuals, they also provide a primary social context in which religious choices are made. Sympathy, example-setting, and sanction are motivations for religious participation and affiliation that are often rooted in the overlapping structural connection between religion and family. Valuations of family ties and their importance drive religious choices, as family schemata are transposed into the religious field. Studies that mix measures of belief and participation cannot hope to identify social influences on choices.

Denominations

In the latter part of the twentieth century, it became fashionable for religious scholars to claim that denominational differences were declining – that variance within denominations somehow meant that denominational influences were waning and that denominations were no longer important. Of course, there has always been variation of belief and commitment within denominations – in part because of internal processes that lead to organizational domination by worldly elites, and the formation of sectarian movements seeking to reestablish tension with the broader society (Finke and Stark 1992; Stark and Bainbridge 1985; Stark and Finke 2000). Despite the variance, denominations remain consequential avenues for the transmission of religious schemata, and they help define the local markets for religious choices. Denominations constitute the vast majority of religious resources, and even the widely touted "nondenominational" special purpose groups are in fact divided by denominational constellations.

Denominations influence individuals through their particular orientations toward beliefs and offerings of opportunities for religious action (Harrison and Lazerwitz 1982). Within denominations, ministers, youth leaders, and Sunday School teachers will transmit the message to parishioners in congregations. Denominational perspectives bound the message transmitted by these denominational agents on supernatural explanations and compensators (Finke and Stark 1992). In a sectarian Protestant group, a Sunday School teacher will quickly be removed if they begin to teach that Jesus was not divine, that there is no hell, or that Christ will not return. Indeed, anyone predisposed to such liberal thinking would not be deemed fit to instruct young people – or adults, since many sectarian groups recognize the importance of lifelong socialization and continue

Sunday School for all ages. In a liberal church, a minister or teacher will be rebuked for claiming that salvation is exclusive to Christians, that there is a real devil, or that good Christians should witness their faith to others. Particularities are also evident in denominational socialization. For example, ministers, deacons, and Sunday School teachers in the Churches of Christ or Southern Baptist Convention would be censured for claiming that the Holy Spirit gives messages to the faithful through interpretations of glossalalia. Agents of the Assembly of God or Church of God in Christ would be sanctioned for claiming that people are not filled with the Holy Spirit, or arguing that evidence of being spirit filled is unimportant for salvation (or evidence of demonic possession!).

Denominational agents also are channeled in their influence on people's preferences by published materials that are generally provided by, or at least approved by, denominational hierarchies. Workbooks for Sunday School, themes for special worship, agendas for denominational age and sex-specific groups (women's groups, youth groups, men's groups) are machinations of denominational elites. Indeed, conflict within denominations is often spurred by denominational literature that is at variance with the preferences of the masses. While the denomination may influence the laity, élite influence is bounded by the agency of individuals, and congregants' abilities to engage in collective action through sectarian movements or schism (Stark and Bainbridge 1985; Finke and Stark 1992).

Denominations also provide distinctive contexts for collective activities, thereby channeling peer influences on religion. Through these collective settings, individuals come to identify with the particular understandings and commitments of a religious body, and may hold these denominational identities as cognitive resources (e.g., Sherkat and Ellison 1999). Of course, within a denomination there will be collectivities with varied identities (Dillon 1999a), but common to each is some understanding of distinctive religious themes. Feminist Catholics retain identification with Catholicism, rather than switching to other traditions that might be more supportive of their political goals or desires for more opportunities within a religious organization. If denominations were not influential, there would be little reason for loyalty, nor motivation to voice opposition for change or support for continuity – exit would be the primary response to variance from personal preferences (Hirschman 1970).

As I noted above, some religious commentators have contended that denominational identities are no longer as salient as they once were, and that boundaries between religious groups have diminished to the point that denominations are less relevant units of analysis. Denominational differences in status, regional distribution, and ethnic identity have arguably decreased (Wuthnow 1988, 1993). The attenuation of demographic differences is presumed to influence the belief systems of denominations – and scholars have asserted that religious beliefs now vary more within denominations than between denominations (Wuthnow 1988: 86–7, 1993: 156–7; Hunter 1991: 86–7). Wuthnow (1993:156) argues, "Over the past half-century, denominationalism has declined seriously as the primary mode of identification in American religion. Indications of this decline include increased interfaith and interdenominational switching, heightened tolerance across faiths and denominational boundaries, ecumenical cooperation, and a deemphasis in many denominations on distinctive teachings and specific membership requirements." Yet empirical research finds no evidence of declining denominationalism.

Most people remain in their denomination of origin, and there is no evidence that rates of religious mobility are increasing over time or across cohorts (Sullins 1993; Sherkat 2001). If people make a switch, it is most often to denominations that are similar in theology and worship style to the ones from which they came (Sullins 1993; Sherkat 2001). General Social Survey data reveal that 45 percent of married people in the United States are wed to someone from the same faith background, when religious traditions are divided into twelve diverse categories (separating Episcopalians from other Liberal Protestants, Lutherans from other moderate Protestants, and Baptists from other sects). Rates of intermarriage have increased somewhat in younger cohorts (homogamy declines to 43 percent in the youngest cohort, when compared to 48 percent in the oldest cohort). However, this is entirely a function of increased intermarriage for Catholics, Jews, and liberal Protestants. Rates of intermarriage for Baptists, sectarians, and Mormons are unchanged across cohorts (Sherkat 2001). As for distinctive beliefs, a host of studies has shown that religious beliefs and practices vary substantially across denominational groups (Hoffmann and Miller 1998; Sherkat and Wilson 1995; Sherkat and Cunningham 1998; Sherkat 1998). The denominational structuring of religious beliefs has a consequential impact on future religious choices about participation and affiliation (Sherkat 1998; Sherkat and Wilson 1995). Rather crude survey research instruments are unable to capture many of the subtleties of the beliefs and identities that differentiate the Churches of Christ from the Southern Baptists (for example), and more systematic qualitative and quantitative research is needed in this area.

As with studies of the family, examinations of denominational influences also have tended to ignore the distinction between socialization influences – effects on religious beliefs and understandings – and social influences on choices. Congregations provide important contexts for social rewards and punishments, and these may significantly motivate religious participation. Friendship networks, occupational ties, neighborhood networks, and kinship connections may also be consolidated in religious congregations (Harrison and Lazerwitz 1982). Given that denominational affiliation is a choice, the distinction between preferences and choices is particularly crucial for the systematic study of denominational influences.

Educational Influences

Scholars have long believed that reason forged through education would drive out myth and superstition – eventually eliminating religion altogether. Surely, secular scholars believed, once exposed by scientific inquiry religious explanations would become implausible and nobody would believe. This type of secularization theory was the dominant theoretical perspective explaining religious change for the first century of the sociology of religion. From this perspective, educational attainment and the quality of educational reasoning is crucial for driving out myth and superstition, and replacing religion with scientific explanation. Despite the prognostications and hopes of secularization theorists, religion has not gone away, or even declined in importance (Stark and Finke 2000; Sherkat and Ellison 1999). One key reason for this is that science and education have nothing to say about the supernatural explanations provided by otherworldly religious groups. Science will never prove that there is no god, no heaven, or no hell. Hence, educational influences on religious preferences and choices are going to come instead from cultural orientations fostered in dominant educational institutions. When secular education makes an attempt to drive out religious belief and sanction religious commitment, it may have an influence on religious preferences and choices. However, religious preferences and religious organizations can counter secularizing influences by leading individuals away from antireligious education and by developing alternative educational institutions (Darnell and Sherkat 1997; Rose 1990; Sherkat and Darnell 1999). The transposition of religious values into the educational field prevents secular education from dominating religious understandings and choices.

The separation of preferences (religious understandings) from choices (religious commitments) helps make sense of how education may influence religious factors. First, educational attainment is generally going to indicate exposure to secular education. Primary and secondary educational institutions are not generally hostile toward religion; however, in higher education, and in particular educational disciplines, antireligious sentiment is common, and religious orthodoxy is viewed in a negative light. This is evident in the religious preferences and choices of educators. Stark and Finke (2000) summarize consistent research over several decades showing that among college professors, hard scientists – physicists, mathematicians, biologists, engineers, and so on – tend to express orthodox religious beliefs and they attend church and maintain religious affiliations. This evidences the compatibility of reason and faith. Yet, college professors from the humanities and social sciences are much more prone to atheism, and lack commitment to religious organizations. Scientific inquiry and discovery are unlikely to confront faith, much less displace it. In contrast, secular philosophies and cultural movements that dominate the humanities are often based on open hostility to religious faith, and seek to root it out.

Not surprisingly, systematic research has found that educational attainment reduces preferences for orthodox religion, promotes atheism, and is linked to religious disaffiliation (Hunsberger 1985; Johnson 1997; Sherkat 1998; Roof and McKinney 1987; Wilson and Sherkat 1994; Wuthnow and Mellinger 1978). Interestingly, Johnson (1997) finds that the effect of education on religious beliefs is less negative for Catholics, and Greeley and Hout (1999) show that education has a positive impact on beliefs in life after death among Catholics. Cornwall (1989) shows that education has a positive impact on commitment and church attendance among Mormons. In each case, this suggests how religious education counters negative influences of secular education on religious preferences and choices. More generally, Stolzenberg et al. (1995) show that education has a positive impact on the probability of church membership. This finding likely reflects the fact that more educated respondents are more able to maintain affiliations with a variety of voluntary organizations, including religious ones (Wilson and Musick 1997).

Indeed, the relationship between educational attainment and religious understandings is not unidirectional. Religious groups with strong belief systems recognize the corrosive power of secular education and seek to insulate their members from these social forces. In the West, Catholics have successfully met the challenge of Protestant hegemony by forming their own educational institutions. Indeed, in the United States, Catholic education was developed in an overt effort to counter the influence of Protestant dominated public education. As public education became more secular and more openly antireligious, conservative Protestant sects began to form their own school systems, or to advocate home schooling (Rose 1990). Most of all, conservative Protestant religious activists have warned parents against the pitfalls of postsecondary education, advocating Christian private schooling instead. Indeed, research has demonstrated that conservative Christian parents dissuade their offspring (particularly those weak in faith) from going to college (Sherkat and Darnell 1999). Young people who hold conservative religious beliefs avoid college preparatory high school coursework and have lower levels of postsecondary attainment net of the socioeconomic and ascriptive (gender, race, region) factors that influence educational attainment (Darnell and Sherkat 1997).

The connection between education and religious preferences and choices is of continuing importance for sociologists of religion. The dramatic growth of private Protestant schools and the increasing popularity of home schooling could have a tremendous impact on the solidification of conservative religious preferences and commitment to sectarian religious organizations. The recent push to provide tax credits and other state support for these educational options will only bolster their growth. More globally, there are similar developments in Islamic nations and in Hindu strongholds in India. Religious institutions are recognizing and countering the impact of secular education on future generations of devotees.

RETROSPECT AND PROSPECT

While most influential works in the sociology of religion focus on grand themes of macrocultural transformation, the explanatory mechanism for religious dynamics is inherently at the individual level. Religious change will only occur if large proportions of individuals change their preferences for religious goods and alter their religious choices. Ideologically structured action must be maintained through normal processes of socialization and influence (Zald 2000), and to understand this we must focus on family processes, denominational ties, friendship and kinship networks, and other institutional influences such as education. There are many things we have learned about religious socialization. However, there are other important questions that have gone unaddressed. First, we know that the family remains the primary influence on religious preferences and choices. Families of origin instill preferences and channel commitments, while families of procreation tend to reinforce preferences and choices. Religious denominations have a consequential impact on the nature of religious preferences and the dynamics of religious choices. While secular education undermines traditional religious faith, religious individuals and institutions counter this influence by removing themselves from hostile academic climates and by generating religious alternatives to secular education.

Unfortunately, we do not know enough about family dynamics and religious preferences and choices. There are too few studies that examine families of origin over the life course and include adequate measures of religious understandings and commitments. We know very little about spousal effects and extended family influences, even less about the impact of children on parents, and virtually nothing about the influence of siblings on religious preferences and choices. Family and life course transitions will also have an impact on religious preferences and choices. We know quite a bit about how divorce and childrearing impact religious choices (affiliation and church attendance) but very little about how these events might alter religious tastes. Perhaps more important, there are no serious studies of how experiences of death and serious illness might impact religious desires and choices. Studies addressing these issues may help us better understand the connection between aging, life course transitions, and religious understandings and commitments.

Sociological investigations of religious socialization are also underdeveloped in how they address denominational and congregational influences. Few studies explore distinctive religious preferences of particular denominations, and there are no studies demonstrating congregational influences on individuals' preferences. While congregational studies have proliferated in religious sociology, it has generally meant a shift of focus to the organizational level of analysis. Ideally, we would have multilevel longitudinal data that would allow us to sort out the impact of family, congregations, denominations, and peer influences. However, this is a tall order to fill in an era of declining research support and in a subspecialty with an applied focus and strong religious agendas in many funding agencies. To explore the nuances in religious understanding and commitment, systematic ethnography would be ideal. We do have a few good examples, largely on socialization into new religious movements (e.g., Rochford 1985), but most ethnographic treatments in the sociology of religion have failed to deal with issues of socialization and tend to lack a rigorous approach to sampling and interviewing. Also, there are no longitudinal ethnographic works on religious socialization or commitment over the life course (but see Dillon and Wink, Chapter 14, this volume).

Gender differences in socialization are also of immense importance. Scholars have long assumed that gender differences in religiosity are a function of variations in socialization, and that gender divides spheres of influence among parents (cf. Nelsen and Potvin 1981; Suziedelis and Potvin 1981; Acock and Bengtson 1978; De Vaus and McAllister 1987). Yet, no study has rigorously tested this – particularly by investigating the effects of specific socialization efforts on siblings. Recently, scholars have claimed that gender differences in religiosity may instead be a function of risk preferences that may or may not be a product of socialization (Miller and Hoffman 1995; Miller and Stark 2002). This is an intriguing proposition, which also calls into question the scope of socialization models for explaining individual differences in religiosity. Perhaps in the future we will be able to investigate further the biopsychosocial foundations of religiosity (Gove 1994; Stark 2000). Such a perspective may well be a valuable tool for explaining gender and sexuality differences in religious commitment.

CHAPTER THIRTEEN

In Rhetoric and Practice

Defining "The Good Family" in Local Congregations

Penny Edgell

Throughout American history, religious institutions and families have been linked together through relationships of dependency and control. Religious leaders and organizations in the United States generally promote norms of stable, monogamous, and faithful marriage; uphold the nuclear family with children as an ideal; and provide a venue for the religious and moral socialization of children. For individuals, religious participation is associated not only with traditional family forms and practices, but also with happiness and satisfaction in marriage and parent-child relationships. Religious institutions depend on families to pass on the religious tradition and for the resources – money, time, membership – that enable them to survive (Christiano 2000; Sherkat and Ellison 1999).

The relationship between religion and family is constituted and defined by the production of religiously-based familistic ideologies. Religious familisms in the United States have varied somewhat over time and social location, but all versions have shared certain fundamental characteristics. They define the family as the precious, central organizing unit of society and teach members that conforming to normative expectations about family life is a form of patriotism, good citizenship, or moral worth (cf. Christiano 2000; D'Antonio 1980; McDannell 1986).

Because religion and family are tightly linked and interdependent institutions, rapid and fundamental changes in one institutional arena may trigger responsive changes in the other (Friedland and Alford 1991). This chapter explores the effects of recent changes in work and family on local congregations. I argue that congregational responses are largely filtered and shaped by rhetorical frameworks anchored in a traditional nuclear family schema that was widely institutionalized in the religious expansion of the 1950s. This means that, across religious traditions, many changes in work and family are "filtered out" or are acknowledged in ways that buffer the institution's core tasks and core ideology from change. There is incremental adaptation, but little radical transformation (cf. Greenwood and Hinings 1996). The exception occurs in a few large, innovator congregations that are organized around a

This research was supported by the Lilly Endowment, grant # 1996 1880–000. The author would like to thank Pawan Dhingra, Elaine Howard, Heather Hofmeister, Evelyn Bush, Sonya Williams, and Ronald Johnson for research assistance.

newer family schema that is more open to alternative family forms and work-family strategies.

This analysis sheds light on questions that occupy sociologists across the subfields of religion, culture, and organizations. For sociologists of religion, this confirms that the culture-wars thesis does not provide an adequate map of the cultural and moral cleavages that structure local religious life (cf. Becker 1999, 1998, 1997; Wedam 1997). The dominant family schema in these congregations cross-cuts the liberal-conservative divide, reducing the impact of this ideological division on family rhetoric and family ministry. The production of religious ideology at the local level is shaped by official ideology and discourse, and also by the institutional and contextual embeddedness of local religious practices, and other sources of discourse that can be creatively blended with religious discourses at the local level to bring about ideological change (cf. Bass 1994).

For sociologists of culture and those who take an institutional approach to the study of organizations, this analysis provides an important specification of the level of analysis at which anchoring schema operate and outlines the mechanisms through which schema serve as filters on organizational change within a particular institutional arena (Sewell 1992; Greenwood and Hinings 1996). A focus on anchoring schema as institutional filters also enables a critique of market-based analyses of religious institutional change by identifying cultural models that do more than shape supply and demand, but also organize action within some portions of the field in ways that embody a value-rational approach to action (cf. Stark and Finke 2000).

The Family as Anchoring Schema

In the 1950s, the growing economy, the rapid expansion of the postwar suburbs, and the beginning of the baby boom all contributed to century-high levels of church attendance. This was the decade when Will Herberg (1960) could argue that an ecumenical spirit had triumphed over earlier sectarian divisions and that being a Protestant, a Catholic, or a Jew were three legitimate ways to express an American identity. More specifically, these became three ways to express a white, middle-class American identity or identity-aspirations, along with the social status and legitimacy thereby implied.

The 1950s was a decade of prosperity, expansion, and rapid institution-building for the largely white denominations of which Herberg wrote (Ellwood 1997; Hudnut-Buemler 1994). In the postwar suburbs of white America, record numbers of families attended weekly worship. These families used congregations, along with schools and other voluntary groups, as part of a larger institutional repertoire for constructing a life that embraced the nuclear, male-breadwinner family model and the lifestyle associated with it (Dobriner 1958). This pattern of church attendance spanned middle-class and working-class communities, promoting the male-breadwinner family as an ideal, if not an actual fact[1] (Bell 1958; Dobriner 1958; Fishburn 1991; May 1999; Mowrer 1958; Nash and Berger 1962; Thomas 1956; Warner 1962a, 1962b).

---

[1] Of course, even in the 1950s, with a century-high peak in nuclear family households, most families' lives did not fit this ideal, and some have argued that this model of the family was from the beginning a form of nostalgic cultural construction (Coontz 1992; Meyerowitz 1994; Skolnick 1991).

The significance of this family model is not simply in how widespread it was in popular culture, the sentimentality surrounding it, or its link to other cultural ideals of prosperity and patriotism. It is also significant because it became the anchoring schema[2] for institutional routines of practice across many arenas, constructing an interlinked institutional matrix that supported the growth of a particular work-family lifestyle.

Since the 1950s, there have been rapid and fundamental changes in family life in our society. Furstenberg (1999) identifies several as being of particular importance: The rising numbers of dual-earner, single-parent, and blended families, the increasing visibility and legitimacy of gay and lesbian lifestyles, the increasing numbers of long-term singles and childless couples, and the decoupling of family formation from other transitions into adult status (cf. Treas 1999). This has led to increasing cultural and structural pluralism in the family (Skolnick 1991).

The cultural pluralism means that newer, alternative family schema are widespread, readily available, and increasingly legitimate. As Sewell (1992) argues, the multiplicity of available schema is one source of structural change, because agents may draw on new schema to bring about a more favorable organization of resources within an arena of action (cf. Friedland and Alford 1991; Fine 1987). This implies that a period of increasing cultural pluralism in one arena (the family, for example) may trigger accompanying changes within linked social arenas that draw on it for the anchoring schema that organize routine institutional practices. Historically and institutionally, the family has served as a source of anchoring schema and symbols for religious life in the United States (Christiano 2000; Lakoff 1996).

From this perspective, the richness of the available and legitimate cultural repertoire for thinking about the family does not guarantee changes in other social arenas, but it does introduce one source of potential change. However, it is important to emphasize that when they are faced with changes in the family, religious leaders and organizations have several choices. They can ignore the changes, or actively resist them. They can adapt in some incremental way, or they can fundamentally transform the institution (Ammerman 1997a; Greenwood and Hinings 1996). Change is not automatic, nor is it uniform if it does come about.

Beyond the Culture War

The importance of a left-right "culture-wars" divide in determining religious responses to changes in the family is taken for granted throughout the sociological literature (Christiano 2000; Glock 1993; Hunter 1991; Lakoff 1996; Woodberry and Smith 1998). In particular, evangelicals and fundamentalists have received a great deal of attention for how they buffer their core family ideology – with its emphasis on male headship in the home – from changes in gender roles within marriage, thus maintaining religious authority and resisting accommodation to the corrosive effects of ongoing modernization (see Sherkat and Ellison 1999; Woodberry and Smith 1998).

Most of these studies have either focused on elite discourse and social movement rhetoric or on individual-level attitudes and behaviors regarding family, gender, and

---

[2] I view anchoring schema as cultural models that organize resources and practices within an institutional arena at a given time and place; that is to say, schema are a specific subset of a more general phenomenon, the cultural model (cf. Douglas 1986; Sewell 1992).

sexuality (Glock 1993; Hunter 1991). Missing from this analysis is any sustained focus on local religious communities and organizations and how they respond to changes in work and family (see Ammerman and Roof 1995). This oversight is particularly unfortunate because the relationships of dependency and control between religious institutions and the family are enacted, reinforced, and changed primarily through face-to-face interaction in two arenas: The family and the local congregation. Yet there are relatively few studies of congregations that address these questions, and those that have been done privilege the importance of a left-right dichotomy and the teleology of modernization and religious decline on which it is based.[3]

Other work suggests that, within local religious communities, a left-right dichotomy may not be the dominant or organizing distinction, even on "hot button" issues such as the family, gender roles, and sexuality (Becker 1997; Wedam 1997; Williams 1997a). The practices of local congregations are organized around upholding religious truths, and are informed by religious ideology. But they also are organized around a kind of pragmatic imperative to provide a caring community for members and compassionate outreach in the broader community (Ammerman 1997b). This can lead to more commonality in local congregational rhetoric and practice across traditions than a culture-wars thesis would predict (Becker 1999, 1998, 1997).

This new emphasis on congregational culture is part of a larger intellectual turning toward the study of lived religious experience as a way to refine theories of religious commitment, symbolic life, and organization that have been based heavily in studies of official religious culture and discourse (Becker and Eiesland 1997; Hall 1997). This parallels the shift in the sociology of culture away from studying culture as subjective, discursive, and symbolic and toward understanding culture as practice, code, and institutional routine (DiMaggio 1994; Jepperson and Swidler 1994). Taken together, this newer work suggests a focus on local religious practice as a way to examine the production of ideology while at the same time exploring other factors that influence how congregations respond to social change on even "hot button" issues like changes in the family.

Based on a comparative study of 125 congregations in four upstate New York communities, I show that, despite vast differences in official family ideology, the practice of ministry in most local churches is still organized around a neopatriarchal nuclear family with children. The cultural schema of the family institutionalized in the last great religious expansion provides a powerful filter on how changes in the family affect congregational life, and congregations remain strong exponents of a relatively traditional familism in the era of what Furstenberg (1999) has called the "postmodern family." The exceptions are a few congregations organized around radically different, and newer, family schema. These innovators, although small in number, are quite large in membership and are influential in the local religious ecology, giving them a disproportionate influence, and lending a legitimacy to the newer forms of ministry they are developing.

---

[3] Demmit (1992) studies an evangelical congregation that maintains an emphasis on male "headship" in rhetoric while accommodating dual-earner families in practice. Marler (1995) studies a liberal Protestant church which exhibits what she calls a "nostalgia" for the male-breadwinner family of the past, and has accommodated work-family changes in ways she argues are problematic for long-term growth and vitality.

The Religion and Family Project

The following discussion is based on data collected between 1998 and 2000 in four communities in upstate New York as part of the Religion and Family project. The communities are:

Liverpool. A metropolitan, white, professional/middle-class suburb outside of Syracuse.

Northside. A metropolitan, working-class neighborhood in Syracuse.

Seneca County. A nonmetropolitan county with a stable agricultural base and a largely working-class population.

Tompkins County. A nonmetropolitan county with a large central town that is economically prosperous and a largely middle-class, professional population.

For this analysis, I draw on a telephone survey of pastors across all four communities ($N = 125$, response rate 78 percent). Each telephone survey lasted between an hour and an hour and a half. In addition to the survey, the project research team conducted participant-observation and in-depth interviews with lay members in sixteen congregations, four in each community. Focus groups of pastors were also run in each community, with a total of forty-seven pastors participating. In this chapter, the qualitative work is used in two ways. It provides a comparison between informal rhetoric and the formal discourse that is revealed through the survey responses. And it allows me to validate and interpret the survey results.

These communities are in no sense a "microcosm" of American religion. The communities are, on average, 94 percent white. There are four synagogues and only a few congregations in historic black church traditions, and no predominantly Latino congregations. There are several congregations with significant proportions of immigrants, mostly from Asian countries. Moreover, if one were to design a study to be a microcosm of American religion today, it would have to include not only congregations but also the small groups, new religious movements, and loosely organized networks of religious practice that constitute the broader "spiritual marketplace," and that are not represented in this sample (Roof 1999a; Wuthnow 1998).

These communities do, however, provide a good sample through which to examine how a specific set of white, middle-class religious institutions, dominant in the 1950s, have adapted to changes in work and family. These institutions of American mainline religion comprise a large majority of those who are active participants in organized religion in the United States, and they have retained a cultural dominance that has given them influence far beyond their own membership (cf. Roof and McKinney 1987; Wuthnow 1988). Comparisons with national data, where available, suggest that the congregations in these four communities are similar to congregations across the country both in size and in the distribution of programming.[4]

---

[4] Based on comparisons with National Survey of Congregations data and with data from the Faith Communities Today project at Hartford Institute for Religion Research. See Becker (forthcoming), Chapter 6, for details (also available on request.)

The Good Family in Rhetoric and Practice

Ideology is a matter of both rhetoric and practice, and the survey gathered data on both dimensions of familism. Pastors were asked to agree or disagree with a number of items concerning their own beliefs about gender and family, and additional items were included to elicit the pastor's interpretation of the faith tradition's stand on gender roles and family forms. Extensive information on congregational ministry practices and programming was also gathered for each congregation.

Tables 13.1 and 13.2 contain more information about the specific items on the survey. These tables are organized by religious tradition.[5] For Protestants, this organization allows for a quick assessment of the degree to which a congregation's stand on a liberal/conservative continuum influences the symbolic and pragmatic dimensions of family ideology. It also allows an assessment of whether a liberal/conservative categorization is a useful one with which to understand the family ministry and rhetoric of local Catholic parishes in these communities.

Both tables suggest that familism is a central element of congregational life and rhetoric in these communities. Table 13.1 reveals that virtually all pastors view the family as "in crisis." In focus groups, over 95 percent of pastors told us that changes in work and family were among the most important issues facing their congregation today.

Focus groups with pastors and participant-observation within congregations revealed that pastors are responding to the perceived crisis in the family in a variety of ways designed to be more inclusive of those who do not fit the nuclear family ideal. In the basement of a little church at a crossroads in Seneca County one afternoon, the pastor of an independent Baptist congregation talked at length about his church's decision to make the annual Mother-Daughter banquet into a Women's banquet that celebrates women's contributions to the family, the congregation, the broader community, and the workplace. He said they did this to make working women, single women, and childless women feel welcome at the most important and well-attended women's event on their church calendar. This kind of rhetorical, symbolic inclusion is common across congregations, as indicated by the second-to-last line of Table 13.1.

But if congregations are moving to provide a more caring and inclusive atmosphere for those who do not fit the nuclear family "ideal," they differ sharply in their willingness to affirm the ideal itself, or to uphold the nuclear family as a normative model for family life today. And to some extent, this difference is organized according to a left-right "culture-wars" divide, as shown in Table 13.1. Evangelical Protestant pastors were by far the most likely, in our telephone survey, to affirm the importance of male spiritual headship in the home, a traditional division of labor between husband and wife, and the importance of obedience in children.

In focus groups, evangelical Protestant pastors, along with some Catholic priests, would employ a language of symbolic inclusion and talk about the need to minister to all members regardless of their family situation while at the same time affirming the neo-patriarchal family as the ideal kind of family. Evangelical pastors may be openly

---

[5] Categorized according to the Appendix in Smith 1990, which yields a classification very similar to that proposed by Steensland et al. 2000.

Table 13.1. Family Rhetoric[1]

	Liberal Protestant[2]	Moderate Protestant	Conservative Protestant	Catholic
N	22	21	59	18
Progressive Items – % Agreeing[3]				
Reject "family ministry" as exclusive term	46%	53%	13%	0
Wrong to think only one kind of family is a good family	73%	81%	65%	83%
There have been all kinds of families throughout history, and God approves of many different kinds of families	86%	90%	0	85%
Affirm congregation has gay/lesbian members[4]	55%	29%	10%	33%
Teach kids to think for themselves	68%	44%	0	57%
Mean on Progressivism Index	*3.00*	*2.76*	*.91*	*2.33*
Traditional Items[5] – % Agreeing				
It's better for all if man earns $, woman takes care of home/children	0	14%	78%	38%
It's God's will that the man is the spiritual head of the family	14%	0	91%	14%
We teach kids to trust, obey parents, teachers, the pastor	32%	56%	93%	43%
Mean on Traditionalism Index	*.50*	*.67*	*2.50*	*.78*
Other Items				
Changed Family Rhetoric/Symbols in Last five years	55%	57%	24%	40%
Families Today are In Crisis – Agree (Strongly Agree)	57% (38%)	67% (24%)	31% (67%)	61% (39%)

[1] The items "It's God's will that the man is the spiritual head of the family" and "There have been many different kinds of families throughout history, and God approves of many different kinds of families" refer to the larger faith tradition; pastors were asked to choose which one best characterizes their faith tradition's "official" stance. The items about children (obey versus think for themselves) refer to what the congregation tries to teach children through its religious education activities. All other items refer to the pastor's own views. Taken together, the items provide a broad picture of the official sources of congregational rhetoric about the family.

[2] Denominations classified following Smith 1990; resulting classification is virtually identical to Steensland et al. 2000.

[3] When summed, the progressive items form an index with an alpha = .7, a mean of 1.86 and a standard deviation of 1.39.

[4] Pastors were asked whether or not the congregation has lesbian or gay members. This is treated as a rhetorical item because it is unlikely that this constitutes an accurate report of which congregations actually contain gay and lesbian members. Rather, this item is an indicator of the willingness of lesbian and gay persons to be "out" within the congregational context and of the pastor's willingness to affirm the presence of lesbian and gay members.

[5] When summed, the traditionalism items form an index with an alpha = .8, a mean of 1.54 and a standard deviation of 1.24.

critical of their own tradition's history of dealing with family change, saying things like:

> A lot of times, a family-oriented church means mom and dad, three kids and the dog, and this can turn away those who don't have this type of family."[6]

But they would also say that "God describes a humanity that is broken and lost,"[7] and they would refer to those in single-parent families, the divorced, or gays and lesbians as being broken or lost.

Catholics and mainline Protestants, by contrast, affirm that "God approves of many kinds of families" (see Table 13.1). They score higher on all of the measures of "progressive" family ideology, in our survey, than do evangelical Protestants. And these views were echoed in the focus groups, as well, where pastors from these traditions spoke positively about gay and lesbian lifestyles, and outlined their ideal of a nurturing family that fosters self-expression and mutual care over any rigid division of labor or strict within-family roles. As one Presbyterian pastor explained to us in the Tompkins county focus group,

> I think it's fair to say that we have changed our thinking as to what constitutes family, in our churches, to get up to speed with society. I shudder to think what was considered a family when I was growing up in the church. (6/6/00)

Mainline Protestant congregations, and many Catholic parishes, see a consistency between the local rhetoric of symbolic inclusion as it is applied to actual persons and the official rhetoric about the ideal family. There is not the decoupling of ideal from practice found in evangelical churches.

Nevertheless, pastors in many mainline Protestant and Catholic congregations do use other rhetorics about contemporary family life and the source of the "crisis" in the family that undercut the progressive message behind their official views about what constitutes a good family. In particular, comments about the large numbers of dual-earner couples in these communities were couched in a time-bind rhetoric pervaded by nostalgic references to the male-breadwinner family of the past – and the corresponding availability of women's volunteer labor in the church.

During fieldwork in one otherwise progressive Catholic parish, I asked the director of family ministry to tell me how recent changes in work and family had affected her church. She responded immediately, with a time-bind rhetoric, as shown in the excerpt from my fieldnotes, below:

> The biggest change over the last fifteen years or so is the lack of time that families have now. She said that's much bigger, more important, than any other change, "more than single parents, more than divorce. It's time. The women, *all* the women, went to work. And they have no time for parish activities, to bring the kids to activities." (11/16/98)

She went on to blame the loss of traditional priorities – a life centered on home and church, women being the mainstay of both arenas – on the rise of the dual-earner couple and on the time-bind that such families face on a daily basis.

---

[6] Pastor of an independent Baptist church, Tompkins County focus group, 11/20/1997.
[7] Pastor of a Missouri Synod Lutheran church, Northside focus group, 6/14/2000.

This sentiment was echoed in pastor focus groups by mainline Protestant ministers and some Catholic priests, as well. Using a larger "time-bind" rhetoric, these pastors had developed a critique of the speed-up of contemporary life, the long hours spent at work, the competition from the increasing numbers of other organized activities for church-members' time, and the materialism of a dual-earner lifestyle.

This rhetoric is not part of any church's "official" views, but is taken from a combination of popular media accounts and scholarly works such as *The Time Bind*, by Arlie Hochschild (1997). It conveys a nostalgia for the male-breadwinner family of the past, a family remarkably like the family that evangelical pastors would find to be both ideal and biblically endorsed. And just as the rhetoric of "brokenness" in evangelical congregations undercuts the more progressive implications of having ministry for single parents or divorced members, the time-bind rhetoric in many mainline Protestant and Catholic churches undercuts the more progressive implications of their official rhetoric about gender and the family. Across religious traditions, the neopatriarchal nuclear family schema dominant in church life in the 1950s retains influence on either the official or the unofficial rhetoric about family life.

Family schema are embedded in rhetorics, but they are also embedded within and guide the routine practices of organizational life. For example, the decision to have a Sunday School says something about the importance that a church places upon the religious socialization of children. The decision to organize the Sunday School into age-graded, gender-specific classes with women teaching the girls and men teaching the boys says something additional about the gender ideology of the congregation. The routine practices of ministry in a congregation, the programs that are in place, and how they are organized, are a location for the production of family ideology (cf. Marler 1995; Demmit 1992).

Table 13.2 gives information about the practice of ministry directed to families in these congregations. Most offer babysitting during meetings and other congregational activities. Focus groups suggest this is largely in response to dual-earner couples who have a hard time managing multiple and conflicting family schedules in order to have one parent home for childcare on a weeknight. It also helps single parents participate in congregational life. Intergenerational ministry is also common, and so is informal marriage and family counseling.

Table 13.2 also shows some differences between the religious traditions. Daycare is offered by Catholics and mainline Protestants, while Catholics and evangelicals have done the most to experiment with the time and timing of family-oriented programs, and evangelicals do more programming for single parents. In analyzing the combined rhetoric about the family and the practice of family ministry, it is apparent that each religious tradition has an overall style of family ministry.

Conservative Protestants embrace a patriarchal rhetoric of the family that favors traditional gender roles and an emphasis on obedience in children. They construct the heterosexual, nuclear, intact two-parent family as an ideal. Focus groups with pastors show that gay and lesbian unions are not recognized as "families" in evangelical Protestant congregations.

Evangelical congregations have some typical ministry practices. Flexible about timing and organization, they experiment to find a way to make programs fit members' schedules. And they target men as part of an explicit rationale for strengthening the family, seeing ministry to men as the key element in keeping families intact. Men's

Table 13.2. Programming by Faith Tradition

	Liberal Protestant	Moderate Protestant	Conservative Protestant	Catholic
N	22	21	59	18
Change time/timing of programs	23%	38%	54%	65%
Move programming off-site, closer to members' homes	9%	5%	32%	11%
Programs that help people cope with work-related stress	27%	14%	29%	17%
Counseling – domestic violence	23% (40%)	24% (40%)	27% (19%)	22% (67%)
Counseling – family or marital	73% (25%)	62% (15%)	83% (12%)	50% (22%)
Daycare for members	23%	33%	5%	33%
Babysitting during meetings/activities	86%	81%	85%	61%
Babysitting/nursery during worship	96%	76%	83%	50%
Programs for single parents	10%	0	33%	17%
Programs for divorced members	18%	19%	25%	22%
Parenting classes	32%	19%	36%	33%
Intergenerational programming	68%	81%	68%	54%
Total # of programs organized by gender and life- stage – mean (mode)	6.5 (5)	5.1 (5)	7.4 (6)	6.8 (5)
Total # of formal programs organized by gender and life- stage – mean (mode)	4.6 (5)	4.1 (3)	4.2 (4)	5 (2)

Note: Denominations classified following Smith 1990; The numbers (in parentheses) indicate the percentage of those who, offering the program, do so in a formal/regular way, instead of on an ad-hoc or case-by-case basis.

fellowship activities often include structured dialogue on men's roles as husbands and fathers, and pastors work hard to establish one-on-one counseling relationships with men who feel troubled about their marriages or children.

Ministering to those who have experienced family disruption is also a high priority for evangelical Protestant congregations, and over a third make some effort to develop ministry for divorced members or single parents. In focus groups, evangelical pastors talked about the congregation's role in providing healing for members having gone through family crisis or dissolution. This rhetoric corresponds to a larger evangelical discourse that views all members as being "broken" by sin and in need of the healing offered through Christ and through the fellowship with other believers. Interviews with single parents in several evangelical congregations suggest that this rhetoric resonates with members' own theology and with their own felt need for healing, and is not experienced as stigmatizing.

Overall, there is a discernible mainline Protestant familism, as well, but there are some differences between congregations from more liberal traditions and those from more moderate traditions. In official rhetoric, liberal Protestants embrace a nurturing view of the family that favors egalitarian gender roles and self-expression in children. Moderate Protestants are similar to liberal Protestants, but more moderate Protestant pastors endorse traditionally gendered roles within marriage, and say their congregations try to encourage obedience in children. All mainline Protestant pastors define the "good family" according to the quality of the relationships among the members, and they do not equate the ideal family with any particular family form. They are the most likely to be affirming of single-parent families and of gay and lesbian unions.

However, the progressivism of mainline Protestant congregations is largely a matter of official rhetoric, and not of informal rhetoric and practice. These congregations are the least likely to have changed the time or timing of their programs to meet the needs of dual-earner couples or those facing alternate-weekend custody arrangements. They are the least likely to minister to single parents, either through programs for these groups or through the kind of one-on-one visitation to bring such members into other congregational programming that Catholic and evangelical pastors report doing on a routine basis. Focus groups suggest that, by and large, the organization of ministry in these congregations exhibits a kind of nostalgia for the male-breadwinner family of the past, and many mainline pastors still lament the loss of volunteer labor that occurred in the 1970s when large numbers of their female members "went to work" in the paid labor force.

Catholic congregations incorporate elements from both ends of the ideological spectrum in their rhetoric about the ideal family. While being genuinely open to those in single-parent families, blended families, and gay and lesbian unions, Catholic parishes also embrace more traditional gender roles than do mainline Protestants. And Catholic pastors are the most likely, in these four communities, to develop a well-thought-out critique of the dual-earner lifestyle, especially for middle-class members, and to argue that mothers who do not need the money should stay home with their young children.

Catholic parishes also adopt some of the flexibility and pragmatism in organizing ministry that evangelical congregations show, especially in changing the time and timing of their family programs. Focus groups and fieldwork suggest that this is because the proliferation of organized activities for children, along with alternate-weekend custody arrangements, have had the most severe impact on Catholic religious education, especially the tradition of having ten to twelve weeks of sacrament preparation classes on successive weekends.

These differences between religious tradition are persistent and continue to hold in multivariate models that control for other factors.[8] Large congregations in which more than 50 percent of the members are in nuclear families with children have more of all kinds of "traditional" family programming – programs for women, children, and teens, parenting programs, and "family nights." But controlling for size and membership composition, so do conservative Protestants. The likelihood a congregation will have programs for divorced persons or single parents increases as the size and budget increase. It also increases if more than 50 percent of the members are within nuclear families with children. But controlling for these factors, there is still a statistically significant relationship between being conservative Protestant and having these programs.

A congregation that is large (250+ members), has a female pastor, and a better-educated pastor is more likely to have a daycare center and is also more likely to have other forms of innovative family programs. But in models controlling for these factors, religious tradition is still significant, with mainline Protestant and Catholic churches

---

[8] Discussion based on multivariate models using both single items as outcomes (daycare) and also scales that combine items (e.g., the total number of "innovative" programs a congregation reports). See Becker (forthcoming), Chapter 6, for details. Models are available on request.

having more programming for dual-earner couples, for gay and lesbian members and families, and more intergenerational programming that does not take a nuclear family with children as the organizing unit.

There is a fundamental irony here. There is diversity in family rhetoric and, among Protestants, this is organized along a left/right "culture-wars" dynamic. Religious tradition is also strongly associated with some differences in the practice of family ministry. More conservative traditions have congregations that are the most flexible in how they organize their programs, and evangelical Protestants do more ministry for nuclear families with children, as well as more ministry for those experiencing painful family disruption. Liberal traditions encourage daycare, lesbian and gay members, and official rhetoric that sends the message that "God approves of all kinds of families."

However, in practice the vast majority of local congregations of all traditions organize much of their ministry – programming and practice – around the nuclear family with children. The last two lines of Table 13.2 show that most congregational programs are still organized around gender and life stage groups, and most often these are traditional life stage divisions that foster movement through a traditional life course with the nuclear family with children at the apex. The only widespread changes in family ministry have to do with accommodating dual-earner and blended families with children, both widespread contemporary forms of the nuclear family (with babysitting, daycare, changing the time and timing of programs, and counseling for couples directed at keeping the family intact).

And informal rhetoric indicates that across the board, the traditional nuclear family with children is still considered ideal for many members and leaders. Intergenerational programming brings members together regardless of family type, but focus groups suggest that this is often done to make families with small children feel more connected to broader, extended-family-like connections. Evangelicals minister to the divorced and single parents while using a language of "brokenness" that affirms the nuclear family ideal. Liberal Protestants affirm they have gay and lesbian members, but very few provide formal ministries directed to these members, or offer joining ceremonies or other symbolic affirmations of gay and lesbian lifestyles. And the time-bind rhetoric exhibits a nostalgia for the ideal family of the 1950s and early 1960s that many women in our survey of community residents named as something that either keeps them out of a local church or has sent them searching in the past for a more supportive congregation.

With some variations, the nuclear family with children still serves as a kind of "anchoring schema" for local congregational life within the mainstream religious institutions which embraced the familism of the postwar suburbs in the 1950s (cf. Sewell 1992; Lakoff 1996). And, even in traditions in which the official rhetoric rejects the male-breadwinner form of this family as an ideal, informal rhetoric embraces this more traditionally gendered version of the family.

Looking at the distribution of programming and ministry practice by congregation, rather than across religious tradition, this becomes even more clear, and reveals three profiles of family ministry in the congregations of these four communities:

"Standard package" (15 percent). These congregations have the standard package of ministry that was in place in the 1950s, with Sunday School/religious education, some kind of youth- or teen group, and a women's ministry (cf. Nash and Berger 1962).

"Standard package plus" (70–75 percent). This is the largest group, and it is made up of congregations that have the standard package of family ministry, with one or two additions. A conservative Protestant congregation might have the standard package plus a men's ministry or a program for divorced people, and a liberal Protestant congregation might have the standard package plus a daycare center or a work-stress program.[9] A Catholic congregation might have the standard package and offer babysitting and counseling.

"Innovators" (10–15 percent). This is a small group of congregations that has the standard package plus multiple other programs, offered both formally and on an informal, as-needed basis. Innovators tend to be large, and most of them are liberal or moderate Protestant, but there are some conservative Protestant and Catholic innovators, too. Innovator congregations are the only ones not organized around the nuclear family with children. These congregations are almost all large, with more than 250 members and very good financial resources. They have all hired pastors committed to activism and change, and they are all congregations with a history of innovation in other areas, not just family ministry. The kind of radical innovation that displaces the nuclear family from the center of congregational life is rare in these communities, and it takes place out of conscious intention, and takes significant resources to sustain.

Religious Familism Today

It has become common, in studies of evangelical Protestants, to talk about the "loose coupling" that allows for an emphasis on male headship in the official rhetoric of the church to coexist with egalitarian and nurturing relationships in practice within the family (Woodberry and Smith 1998). Within the life of local congregations, this loose coupling of the official ideology and the practice of ministry is not just a feature of an evangelical religious culture. It characterizes the family ministry of congregations across mainstream, white religious traditions.

In focus groups, pastors of mainline Protestant and Catholic congregations would talk about the need to be inclusive of all individuals, regardless of family situation. Going beyond the desire not to exclude anyone who does not "fit" with the nuclear family model, these pastors would avow a feminist analysis of the harm and injustice – to women, children, and men – fostered by patriarchal family structures. In the same group discussions, however, these pastors would lament the lack of time contemporary families have for congregational participation, and would talk fondly of the congregations of their childhood, where "Mom stayed home" with the children, and took responsibility for making sure the whole family was in church on Sunday. And the practice of ministry in these churches does little to include those not fitting the two-parent-with-children ideal. These congregations also routinely decouple their official views on the family from unofficial discourse and daily practice.

"Ozzie and Harriet" were the 1950s ideal family, with Harriet at home raising the children and doing volunteer work in the community, and Ozzie being the "organization man" who worked during the day to support the family's suburban lifestyle.

---

[9] In all cases, conservative Protestants offer more programs and services on an informal/as-needed basis; others are more likely to have formal programs.

Churches in the 1950s were organized largely around the Ozzie and Harriet lifestyle. Today, middle-class families are like the Huxtables, with two working parents, overachieving children, and a sense of tenuousness that Ozzie and Harriet never felt. Working-class families have never fit the Ozzie and Harriet ideal to begin with. Single parents, adults who live singly for long stretches of their lives, married couples who choose not to have children, and gay and lesbian unions – these are not even on the map in the Ozzie and Harriet world.

Lakoff (1996) argues that cultural models of the family provide anchoring schema that organize other social and political divisions throughout our society, and that structure many of our institutions. Sewell (1992) makes a similar theoretical case for the role of schema in anchoring social structures and in serving as filtering mechanisms through which new information – including the effects of social change – are interpreted. For the religious institutions that expanded so rapidly in the postwar era by organizing ministry around the nuclear, male-breadwinner family, this remains an anchoring schema for congregational life. Most congregations that have adapted to changes in work and family have done so in a partial, incremental way, and most innovations revolve around facilitating new nuclear family arrangements.

The categories of "liberal" and "conservative," although helpful for understanding the official beliefs, doctrines, and theology that inform pastors' views of the family, prove less helpful in understanding informal, locally based rhetorics about family life or the daily practice of family ministry. Local practices, and the interpretive frameworks applied to them, are rooted in a common family model that lends a fair amount of uniformity to local ministry and local culture. At the local level, both liberals and conservatives buffer their ministry not only from the more fundamental changes in family life that have occurred since the 1950s but also from the more radical implications of their own traditions' theology and family ideology.

This buffering takes place because of the dependencies fostered by interinstitutional linkages. This dependency, however, is not just a matter of resource flow. Interinstitutional dependencies are a source of anchoring schema and, in turn, a source of limitation on how adaptation to social change occurs within an institutional arena. Such interdependencies may be decoupled from "official" discourse, to be expressed at the level of analysis at which the practical interdependency is most acutely felt. In this case, that is the local congregation, the arena where religion and family are most tightly intertwined. Such practical interdependencies can shape how official beliefs, core values, and ideologies are expressed – or fail to be expressed – in the institutional routines within any given set of organizations, and thereby have an effect on the larger institutional field.

Sociologists of religion need to study local religious rhetoric and practice, and in so doing, incorporate the insights gained from such analyses into the field's dominant theoretical frameworks. The reactions of these local congregations to changes in the family exhibit none of the dynamism and responsiveness of a market, nor do they exhibit a kind of means-ends instrumental rationality (Stark and Finke 2000). Rather, evangelical Protestants respond to change in the family with a kind of value-rationality that resists any fundamental reworking of the ideal family they believe is based in Scripture. And mainline Protestants and Catholics exhibit the kind of "habitual" rationality of the bureaucracy, valuing past ways of doing things for their own sake. Our theories of the religion field need to account for the multiple forms of rationality, and multiple logics of action, within the field (cf. Friedland and Alford 1991).

Of course, upstate New York is a particular place, and this study sheds little light on the familism of other religious traditions. It is not very helpful in understanding the familism in immigrant communities, including the large and growing Latino religious community in the United States. And it is likely that congregations in the black church tradition do not exhibit either a nostalgic longing for the male-breadwinner family ideal of the 1950s, or a ministry so exclusively organized around a nuclear family unit in practice. But this community does provide a useful sample through which to analyze how anchoring schema filter the effects of social changes on local religious communities' rhetoric and practices. This suggests that a focus on schema is useful for understanding larger questions about institutional dependencies, social change, and the production of ideology.

CHAPTER FOURTEEN

Religiousness and Spirituality

Trajectories and Vital Involvement in Late Adulthood

Michele Dillon and Paul Wink

Americans today are living longer and healthier lives than earlier generations. Currently 13 percent of the U.S. population is aged sixty-five or over (Kramarow, Lentzer, Rooks, Weeks, and Saydah 1999: 22), and this expanding sector is experiencing lower rates of functional disability than was the case even a few decades ago. These trends and the aging of the populous baby boom generation understandably focus attention on the factors that are conducive to purposeful and socially engaged aging. The focus of current research is thus beginning to move beyond questions of physical health and mortality to give greater attention to the quality or character of older persons' everyday lives.

In the pursuit of "successful aging" some social scientists have begun to investigate characteristics that become particularly salient in the second half of adulthood such as wisdom (e.g., Wink and Helson 1997) and spirituality (e.g., Tornstam 1999). Other researchers have explored characteristics that are not necessarily specific to older adulthood but that nonetheless play a vital role in the negotiation of the aging process. Religiousness is one such factor because although it is positively associated with social functioning throughout adulthood, it takes on increased significance in the second half of the adult life cycle (e.g., Hout and Greeley 1987).

This chapter explores adulthood patterns of religiousness and spirituality and their association with social functioning in older adulthood drawing on our research with a longitudinal study of men and women that spans adolescence and late adulthood. We first briefly discuss our conceptualization of religiousness and spirituality. We then introduce our sample, focus on whether religiousness and spirituality increase in older age, and discuss their relations to various indicators of social functioning in late adulthood.

RELATION BETWEEN RELIGIOUSNESS AND SPIRITUALITY

While just a few decades ago it made little sense to differentiate between religiousness and spirituality, such a distinction now seems to have become part of everyday

We are grateful to the Open Society Institute whose grant to the second author facilitated the data collection in late adulthood, and for grants to both authors from the Louisville Institute and the Fetzer Institute for our research on religiousness and spirituality.

conversation (Marty 1993; Roof 1999a, Chapter 11, this volume; Wuthnow 1998). There is a lot of ambiguity, however, about the meaning and use of these terms and their interrelation. The term spirituality is used in multiple and divergent ways with the result that it can be applied equally aptly to describe a pious individual who expresses his or her devotion through traditional religious practices (e.g., church attendance), someone who has no religious affiliation but believes in God or a Higher Power, a New Age seeker who borrows elements of Western and Eastern religions, and a person who is prone to mystical experiences. Obviously, the nature of the relation between religiousness and spirituality shifts depending on the definitions being used and the cultural and socio-biographical context in which they are being investigated (Wulff 1997).

In our research on religion and the life course, we have conceptualized religiousness and spirituality as two distinct but partially overlapping types of religious orientation following Wuthnow's (1998) distinction between dwelling and seeking. We have defined *religiousness* in terms of the importance of institutionalized or tradition-centered religious beliefs and practices in the life of the individual. Highly religious individuals are those for whom belief in God and the afterlife and organized religion (e.g., church attendance) play a central role in life; they are *dwellers* whose religious practices and experiences are based on derived and habitual forms of religious behavior typically performed in a communal setting. In contrast, we operationalize *spirituality* in terms of the importance of noninstitutionalized religion or nontradition centered beliefs and practices in the life of the individual. Highly spiritual individuals are those for whom a personal quest for a sense of connectedness plays a central role in life; they are *seekers* who engage in practices (e.g., prayer, meditation) aimed at deriving meaning from, and nurturing a sense of interrelatedness with, a sacred Other. Importantly, in this schema, to be coded high on either religiousness or spirituality requires that the individual intentionally and systematically engage in practices aimed at incorporating the sacred. (For a detailed explanation of the study's definitions and coding procedures, see Wink and Dillon 2002; in press.)

THE IHD LONGITUDINAL STUDY

Our research uses a longitudinal representative sample drawn by the Institute of Human Development (IHD), University of California, Berkeley, in the 1920s. Participants in the IHD study were born in the 1920s and they and their parents were studied during the participants' childhood and adolescence. Subsequently, the participants were interviewed in-depth four times in adulthood: in early (age thirties; 1958–9), middle (age forties; 1970), late middle (age fifties–early sixties; 1982), and late adulthood when they were in their seventies (1997–2000). At each interview phase the participants were asked detailed open-ended questions about all aspects of their lives including religious beliefs, attitudes, and practices. We are therefore able to explore changes and continuities in religious values and habits across the life course and without having to rely on interviewees' retrospective accounts. Moreover, because the participants talked extensively about religion in the context of a lengthy life-review interview it is likely that their accounts are less biased by the overreporting of involvement that may be a factor in opinions polls of the general population (e.g., Hadaway, Marler, and Chaves 1993). The current sample (N = 181) represents 90 percent of the original sample who were available for follow-up in late adulthood. Fifty-three percent of the current sample are women and 47 percent are men. In late middle adulthood, 59 percent of the participants (or their spouses) were upper-middle-class professionals and executives, 19 percent were lower middle class, and 22 percent were working class. All but six of the participants are white. The majority of the sample (73 percent) grew up in Protestant families, 16 percent grew up Catholic, 5 percent grew up in mixed religious (Protestant/Jewish) households, and 6 percent came from nonreligious families. In late adulthood, 58 percent of the study participants were Protestant, 16 percent were Catholic, 2 percent were Jewish, and 24 percent were not church members. Forty-eight percent said that religion was important or very important currently in their lives, 83 percent still resided in California, 71 percent were living with their spouse or partner, and 89 percent reported their general health as good. Using our practice-oriented definitions of religiousness and spirituality, 40 percent of the participants were rated high on religiousness and 26 percent were rated high on spirituality. The intercorrelation between independent ratings of religiousness and spirituality for the sample in late adulthood was moderate (mean $r = .31$).

CHANGES IN RELIGIOUSNESS AND SPIRITUALITY IN THE SECOND HALF OF ADULT LIFE

Changes in religiousness. It is typically assumed that religiousness increases in older adulthood. This view is premised on the idea that aging confronts the individual with concerns over death and dying that increase existential angst and threaten the person with despair (e.g., Becker 1973). A natural response to this involves turning to worldviews and institutions that are sources of meaning and security, and religion has traditionally fulfilled this function. The turn toward increased religiousness may be further enhanced because individuals in the postretirement period have more free time and fewer social roles (Atchley 1997). It is thus assumed that religious participation should increase from the preretirement to the postretirement period only to decline in old-old age (eighty-five-plus) when physical problems make it increasingly harder to attend places of worship (McFadden 1996).

Although theories of aging and cross-sectional empirical data support the view of religion as a life cycle phenomenon that increases with age (e.g., Greeley and Hout 1988; Hout and Greeley 1987), this thesis has not been investigated using longitudinal data gathered from the same individuals over an extended stretch of the life span. There are very few longitudinal studies that follow participants across the life course, and a number of studies that span adulthood have not paid attention to religion. Longitudinal studies that have focused on religion such as Shand's (1990) forty-year followup study of male graduates of Amherst college and the Terman study of intellectually gifted persons (e.g., Holahan and Sears 1995) report stability rather than an increase in religiousness in the second half of adulthood. The generalizability of these studies' findings, however, is limited because the samples comprise rather elite and homogeneous groups of individuals and, or, rely on retrospective accounts of religious involvement (Holahan and Sears 1995).

In contrast to a pattern of stability, studies using cross-sectional, representative samples of the American population confirm the hypothesis that religiousness increases in older adulthood (Hout and Greeley 1987; Rossi 2001), although there is uncertainty about the age interval when the greatest increase occurs. The public opinion data

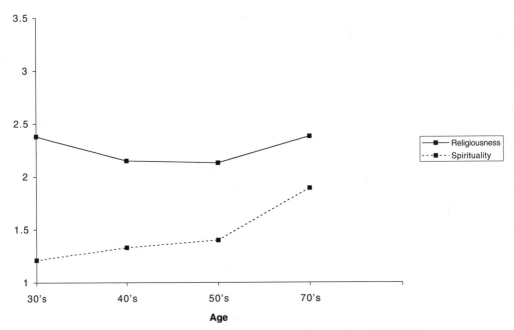

Figure 14.1 Mean Changes in Religiousness and Spirituality over the Adult Life Course.

analyzed by Hout and Greeley suggest that the steepest rate of increase occurs between ages forty-five and fifty-five, thus placing it in the pre-retirement phase, a time when individuals may begin to have more time as a result perhaps of occupational commitments being less demanding and children having left home. In contrast, Rossi's (2001: 124) survey data indicate that the sharpest increase occurs when individuals are in their fifties and sixties.

The pattern in the IHD longitudinal data fits with the findings of cross-sectional studies demonstrating an upward trend in religiousness in the second half of the adult life cycle. The IHD participants increased significantly in religiousness from their fifties to their seventies, although the magnitude of the change was small (less than a quarter of one standard deviation (see Figure 14.1) (Wink and Dillon 2001). The increase in religiousness in later adulthood was true of both men and women, of individuals from higher and lower social classes, and of Protestants and Catholics. The increase in religiousness in late adulthood was preceded by a decrease in religiousness in the first half of adulthood: For women, the decline occurred between their thirties and forties, whereas for men the decline occurred between adolescence and early adulthood. The women participants were in their thirties during the 1950s and thus were engaged in the religious socialization of their schoolage children at a time coinciding with the peak in American religious devotion and the cultural expectation that women were primarily responsible for children's religious socialization. Their midlife dip in religiousness, therefore, is likely to have been accentuated by the confluence of life stage (the relative absence of child socialization pressures) and historical effects. The initial decline in religiousness from early to middle adulthood just as the increase in later adulthood, although significant, was of relatively small magnitude.

How are we to interpret the increased religiousness of the IHD participants from middle to late adulthood? Although we cannot exclude the possibility of a cohort effect, the fact that our findings coincide with national cross-sectional trends (e.g., Hout and Greeley 1987; Rossi 2001) minimizes this explanation. Although it is possible that increased religiousness in older age is a strategy to try to fend off death anxiety prompted by specific reminders of mortality that become increasingly prominent from late middle age onward (e.g., the death of one's parents, spouse, or close friends, or personal illness), there are two factors arguing against this explanation. First, death anxiety tends to decline with age and older adulthood is a time when concern about death (although not about the process of dying) is at its lowest (e.g., Fortner and Neimeyer 1999).

Second, although the IHD participants increased in religiousness from their fifties to their seventies, the sample also showed high levels of rank order stability in scores on religiousness across this same interval (r = .82; Wink and Dillon 2001). What this means is that whereas the IHD participants as a group increased in religiousness from late middle to older adulthood, the individuals in the study tended to preserve their rank in terms of their religious involvement relative to their sample peers. In other words, those individuals who scored comparatively higher in religiousness in their fifties also tended to score higher in their seventies. The very high correlation between individuals' scores on religiousness from their fifties to their seventies means that very few individuals experienced radical changes in religious behavior. In addition, similar to Rossi (2001), who used a retrospective measure, we have evidence indicating that the religious atmosphere (defined in terms of practices and values) in the respondent's family of origin (assessed using data collected from the participants and their parents in adolescence) is the single best predictor of religious involvement in late adulthood. Taken as a whole, these findings suggest that the overall increase in religiousness observed for the IHD participants from their fifties to their seventies was much too orderly to be a response to personal crises associated with such life events as the death of a spouse or a life threatening illness. The increase is more likely attributable to socially normative trends in the sample such as the increased time available in the post retirement period, the increased freedom attendant on having fewer social roles, and perhaps a generalized awareness of the finitude of life.

Changes in spirituality. Unlike religiousness that tends to be salient in the life of "religious" individuals throughout the life cycle, spirituality has been typically described as a midlife and post–midlife phenomenon. In this sense, similar to postformal stages of cognitive development (e.g., McFadden 1996; Sinnott 1994), it can be described as an emergent characteristic of aging. According to Carl Jung (1964), it is around midlife that individuals begin to turn inward to explore the more spiritual aspects of the self. Prior to this stage, the external constraints associated with launching a career and establishing a family take priority, but the increased awareness of mortality that tends to come at midlife reduces the self's emphasis on this-worldly success and facilitates greater spiritual engagement. Cognitive theorists (e.g., Sinnott 1994) share with Jung the idea that spirituality is the outcome of adult maturational processes. Having experienced the contextual ambiguities and relativity of life, middle-aged and older adults tend to go beyond strictly logical modes of apprehending reality to embrace paradox and feelings in making evaluative judgments. This process, in turn, is seen as conducive to spiritual growth. McFadden (1996) argues that spirituality may be especially meaningful in old age because of the many losses and difficulties encountered in later life. Following Stokes (1990: 176), who argues that changes in the "process of making sense of life's meaning and purpose" occur more frequently during periods of transition and crisis than stability, spiritual development may be related to aging because although crises are not age-specific, the chance of having experienced personal crises clearly increases with age.

As far as we know there are no longitudinal data testing the hypothesis that spirituality increases in the second half of adult life. Support for the theory comes from cross-sectional survey data (e.g., Fowler 1981; Tornstam 1999) and individual case studies (e.g., Bianchi 1987) that rely on retrospective accounts. In the IHD longitudinal study we found support for the hypothesis with the participants increasing significantly in spirituality from their fifties to their seventies (see Figure 14.1). As with religiousness, the significant increase was true of both men and women, of Protestants and Catholics, and of individuals from higher and lower social classes (Wink and Dillon 2002).

Although the pattern of mean changes in spirituality in the second half of adulthood was similar to that observed for religiousness, there were three notable differences. First, the magnitude of the increase in spirituality from late middle to late adulthood was much greater, with the total sample increasing by more than one-half of a standard deviation and women increasing by close to three quarters of a standard deviation. Because of this sharper rate of increase, women were significantly more spiritual than men in older adulthood. Second, whereas the mean scores on religiousness across adulthood indicated that many of the IHD participants had been religious all their lives, the mean scores on spirituality indicated that spirituality played virtually no role in the lives of the study participants prior to midlife. Third, whereas the high rank order stability of religiousness from early adulthood onward indicated very little individual variability or change over time in who was religious and who was not, the rank order stability of spirituality was much lower suggesting that there was considerable interindividual change in who scored high and who scored low on spirituality over time.

Our results confirming the hypothesis of spirituality as a post-midlife phenomenon do not mean, of course, that spirituality is nurtured solely by life-cycle maturational processes. The post–midlife trajectory we document also may clearly have a cultural explanation. Because the study participants entered middle adulthood in the 1960s, their negotiation of midlife identity during this time of cultural change may have primed their openness to the new spiritual currents that were taking hold in American society. As noted, the 1970s witnessed an explosion of interest in Jungian psychology, Eastern philosophies and practices, and a variety of self-help therapeutic groups and manuals addressed at satisfying the inner needs of Americans (Roof 1999a; Chapter 11, this volume; Wuthnow 1998). These newly accessible spiritual vocabularies and resources could be drawn on to enhance a preexisting disposition toward a journey of self discovery or, independently, to generate new spiritual interests among individuals who were attracted to this novel aspect of public culture (irrespective of any intrapsychic motivation). Thus the greater salience of spirituality for our study participants from late middle age onward is likely to be the result of a confluence of an expanded and publicly accessible spiritual marketplace, especially in California, where most of the participants were living, and chronological age or stage in the life cycle.

Because spirituality demonstrated low rank order stability across the adult life course (mean r = .47 across four time points in adulthood, as opposed to r = .74 for religiousness), it makes good sense to inquire into the factors that are conducive to its development. In the IHD sample we found that spirituality was highest among women who in early adulthood were introspective and religious, and who in their thirties and forties experienced stressful or negative life events (such as death of a spouse or child, divorce, psychological turmoil). Our data indicated that it is the interaction of introspection and negative life experiences that is particularly conducive to the subsequent spiritual growth of women. In the case of men, spiritual development in older adulthood was associated with early adulthood religiousness and introspection but was unrelated to negative life events (see Wink and Dillon 2002).

VITAL INVOLVEMENT IN LATE ADULTHOOD

Having reviewed findings showing that religiousness and spirituality are likely to increase in older adulthood, we now turn our attention to the relation of religion to individual meaning and social participation in late adulthood. In doing so, we find it useful to adopt Erik Erikson's (Erikson, Erikson, and Kivnick 1986) concept of vital involvement because it moves the assessment of the positive role played by religiousness and spirituality away from a narrow focus on life satisfaction to include how individuals cultivate purposive and socially responsible lives (Bellah et al. 1991: 273–7). Erikson theorized that successful functioning in old age includes the ability to maintain a vital involvement in life despite suffering the multiple losses associated with later adulthood (e.g., bereavement, illness, fewer social and occupational roles). The investment of the self in purposeful and enriching activities that is the hallmark of vital involvement demonstrates a sense of basic trust in the world and in other human beings. This disposition, in turn, injects a sense of social trust, reciprocity, and optimism among the younger generations who witness it (Bellah et al. 1991; Erikson 1964; Putnam 2000). One way of being vitally involved is through engagement in caregiving activities that show a selfless concern for the welfare of future generations (what Erikson called generativity). One also can be vitally involved in everyday activities or pastimes that may or may not be explicitly generative but that nonetheless allow individuals to give attention to the present and to "live as fully as possible" (Bellah et al. 1991: 275).

It is important to know whether there is a link between religiousness, spirituality, and vital involvement in older adulthood for a variety of reasons. On the most general level, in view of the graying of American society there is increased interest in identifying the factors that are conducive to enhancing the participation and trust of older age persons in social relations and in the world that they will pass on to future generations. More specifically, the growing number of healthy older adults who are outside the work force constitute a potentially productive national resource in terms of caring for the welfare of individuals and of society as a whole. It thus becomes of increased practical importance to know whether religiousness or spirituality enhances older age individuals' engagement in social and community activities. A third reason for investigating the links between religiousness, spirituality, and vital involvement has to do with the ongoing cultural debate about the potentially narcissistic turn in American society. Many authors have argued that, especially since the 1960s, a narcissistic individualism has attenuated Americans' communal obligations and their commitment to religious

Table 14.1. The Relations Between Religiousness,
Spirituality and Vital Involvement in Late Adulthood

Variables	Religiousness	Spirituality
Generativity		
Interpersonal Engagement	+	O
Broad Societal Perspective	O	+
Life Tasks		
Social/Communal	+	O
Creative/Cognitive	O	+
Narcissism	O	O

Note. This table summarizes findings presented in Wink and Dillon
in press. + refers to statistically significant standardized beta co-
efficients in regression analyses controlling for gender, social class,
and the overlap between religiousness and spirituality. Generativity was measured using the California-Q-Set Generativity scale
(Peterson and Klohnen 1995); involvement in everyday activities
was assessed using Harlow and Cantor's (1996) measure; and narcissism was measured using the CPI Narcissism scale (Wink and
Gough 1990).

and civic traditions (e.g., Bellah et al. 1985, 1991). In this view, a socially responsible
individualism is being displaced by an expressive and therapeutic individualism (Rieff
1966) that sees communal involvement not as a social good in its own right but only
worthwhile insofar as it fulfills the transitory needs of the self.

Bellah and coauthors' (1985) critique of American individualism highlighted a self-
centered spirituality that was autonomous of the social commitments that are fostered
by traditional forms of religious involvement. The social trust that for so many generations has been bolstered by the strong association between church participation,
interpersonal networks, and social and community involvement (e.g., Putnam 2000;
Rossi 2001; Verba, Scholzman, and Brady 1995), is now seen as being undermined by
an individualized spirituality. The concern, therefore, is that it is becoming increasingly
difficult for Americans to give attention to cultivating the interests and activities that
give purpose to life and that in the process serve both the individual and the common
good (e.g., Bellah et al. 1985, 1991; Putnam 2000; Wuthnow 1998).

For the IHD sample, we found that both religiousness and spirituality were related
to scores on an observer-based measure of generativity in older adulthood (Dillon and
Wink in press; Wink and Dillon in press). In other words, both highly religious and
highly spiritual individuals were likely to show a deep and genuine concern for the
welfare of future generations. We also found that both religiousness and spirituality
correlated positively with involvement in a variety of everyday activities and pastimes
such as socializing with family and friends or doing arts, crafts, or wood work.

Although generative and purposeful everyday activities were common to both religious and spiritual individuals, the nature of their emphases differed. As summarized
in Table 14.1, religious individuals, for example, were more likely than spiritual individuals to express their generativity in a communal way by caring for family members
or friends and, in general, through interpersonal relations. They tended to be described

by observers as giving, sympathetic, protective of others, and warm. Similarly, the everyday routines characteristic of highly religious individuals showed a stronger involvement in spending time on social activities (e.g., visiting or entertaining family members and friends) and in community service done with a group (Wink and Dillon in press; Dillon and Wink in press).

In contrast, the generativity of spiritual individuals was more likely to be expressed through involvement in creative projects and in social activities that would make an impact beyond the domain of family and friends and that might leave a legacy that would "outlive the self" (Kotre 1984). The generative concerns associated with spirituality tended to show a broad societal perspective and incisiveness into the human condition rather than an emphasis on interpersonal relations (Dillon and Wink in press). In terms of everyday pastimes, highly spiritual individuals were more likely to work on creative and knowledge- or skills-building projects than to socialize with friends or family. The different, more self-expanding focus of individuals who were spiritual was not, however, excessively narcissistic. In fact, we found no relation between spirituality and a well-validated measure of narcissism (Wink and Dillon in press). Importantly, then, when spirituality is linked to systematic practices (as our measure is) it does not appear to have the negative features that cultural analysts (e.g., Bellah et al. 1985) are concerned about.

Longitudinal analyses showed that the connection in late adulthood between religiousness and vital involvement, including participation in family, social, and community activities, could be predicted from measures of religiousness scored in early adulthood and onward. In contrast, the significant relation between spirituality and involvement in everyday creative and other productive endeavors found in late adulthood could be predicted only from late middle adulthood (age fifties) onward. All of the longitudinal relations between religiousness, spirituality, and the various measures of generativity and everyday involvement continued to be significant after controlling for the gender and social status of the IHD participants (Wink and Dillon in press).

The longitudinal evidence in our study in favor of the long-term impact of early religiousness on social and communal involvement later in adulthood fits with the findings of studies on social responsibility that employ retrospective measures of early religiosity (e.g., Rossi 2001). The fact that spirituality was a significant predictor of generativity and of involvement in everyday activities only from late middle adulthood onward is because, as already indicated, spirituality is primarily a post-midlife phenomenon in the IHD sample. Taken as a whole, the IHD data show that for older age individuals – the parents of the baby boomers – both religiousness and spirituality enhance successful aging by providing mechanisms for maintaining vital involvement in life. These findings may thus suggest that the aging of the more spiritually than religiously attuned baby boom generation does not necessarily augur a decline in the salience of Americans' communal and societal commitments.

RELIGION AS A BUFFER AGAINST ADVERSITY IN LATE ADULTHOOD

We now turn to consider the effect of religiousness on life satisfaction and its ability to buffer individuals in times of adversity. Although there is a large body of research documenting the positive impact of religiousness on mental health or life satisfaction (e.g., Ellison and Levin 1998: McCullough et al. 2000), there is ambiguity as to whether this effect is evident among older adults in general or whether it is restricted to samples who have experienced illness or other personal crises. In other words, there is uncertainty in the literature whether religion buffers life satisfaction both when things go well and when things go poorly in life or whether it is only in the latter circumstances.

In exploring this question in our relatively healthy sample of older adults we found that religiousness did not have a direct effect (either positive or negative) on life satisfaction in late adulthood (Wink and Dillon 2001). This finding may have emerged because most of the participants were highly satisfied with their lives and were in relatively good physical health, thus indicating perhaps a ceiling effect in statistical analyses exploring the direct relation between religiousness and life satisfaction.

There was support, however, for the hypothesis that religiousness exercises a buffing effect on life satisfaction in times of adversity. The IHD data showed that among individuals who were in poor physical health, those who were religious tended to be happier and more optimistic about the present and the future than those who were not religious. Moreover, the buffering effect of religiousness on life satisfaction in late adulthood could be predicted from religiousness in late middle adulthood (age fifties) even after controlling for physical health in midlife. By contrast, among individuals who were in good physical health – the majority of the IHD sample – whether an individual was or was not religious did not make any difference to levels of life satisfaction. In fact, the two groups of healthy individuals (religious and nonreligious) had the same level of satisfaction as the group of individuals who were in poor health and who were religious. In preliminary analyses, spirituality had no direct effect on life satisfaction in late adulthood and nor did it have the kind of buffering effect for individuals in poor physical health that was observed for religiousness. Spirituality did, however, buffer the IHD participants, especially women, against a loss of personal mastery and control in response to physical illness. Therefore, while spirituality does not necessary dampen negative feelings, it may help to preserve a sense of competence and meaning in times of personal adversity.

CONCLUSION

This chapter has focused on religiousness and spirituality in the second half of the adult life cycle and their relations to various aspects of social functioning in older adulthood. The IHD study's findings are based on research with a cohort of Americans born in California in the 1920s and thus are limited in their generalizability. It would be interesting for future studies to investigate whether broadly similar patterns of results would emerge in more ethnically, geographically, and religiously diverse samples and for different age cohorts. It is also important to investigate how other conceptualizations of religiousness and spirituality relate to everyday social functioning.

Nonetheless, the IHD study's longitudinal interview data, available for the same individuals over such a long span of time in which life cycle and cultural changes intersect, offer an important resource for understanding the contextual relation between religion and aging. Our results underscore the basic sociological point that religion matters in people's lives. More specifically, the fact that both women and men increased in religiousness and spirituality from their fifties to their seventies highlights the relevance of religion in the lives of older age Americans. Gerontological and life course studies that give short shrift to the place of religion in late adulthood are thus likely to miss out on understanding a substantial part of the lives of older persons. Whether it involves traditional forms of religious participation or newer spiritual practices, or a combination of both, religion is a salient dimension in many older individuals' routines.

Religion is not just meaningful to older age individuals in and of itself, but as indicated, it provides an important bridge to purposeful aging. Religiousness and spirituality are associated with generativity and with participation in the everyday activities that make late adulthood a season of vital involvement in life rather than an inconsequential, liminal stage wherein individuals relinquish purpose in life while awaiting its end. To adapt a well-worn phrase, summer's bloom passes but the winter of life is not necessarily harsh (cf. Weber 1919/1946: 128). The IHD participants lived through much of the twentieth century, experiencing firsthand its economic and technological transformations and its major historical events (e.g., the Great Depression, World War II, the Korean War, the Sixties, Vietnam, the collapse of the Berlin Wall). Yet, at century's end, and toward the end of their own life cycle, religion continued to be a meaningful part of many of the participants' lives. From a secularization perspective, this finding in itself testifies to the power of religion to maintain relevance and to endure through the life course and societal changes.

CHAPTER FIFTEEN

Religion and Health

Depressive Symptoms and Mortality as Case Studies

Michael E. McCullough and Timothy B. Smith

Most scholars who study the links between religion and health – whether they specialize in sociology, psychology, gerontology, epidemiology, or some other field – rely heavily on sociological foundations. As Idler and Kasl (1997) succinctly explained, Durkheim's (1897/1951) sociological study of suicide and Weber's (1922/1993) sociology of religion have described three pathways by which religion might affect human health and well-being. First, Durkheim noted that religion tends to provide, in Idler and Kasl's (1997) words, a *"regulative function"* (p. S294). Many religions provide rules that are considered by adherents to be binding not only in religious, spiritual, and ethical matters, but in the most basic human concerns, including eating, drinking, and sexual intimacy. Indeed, it seems uncanny how discoveries in biomedical science concerning the major vectors for the greatest health problems of the modern world (e.g., cardiovascular disease, cancer, diabetes, obesity, HIV/AIDS) have shown the great practicality of the prescriptions and proscriptions of many religions regarding alcohol, tobacco, food, and sex.

Idler and Kasl (1997)) additionally pointed out that Durkheim supposed that religion also can have an *"integrative function"* (p. S294), providing people with meaningful and tangible connections to other people, fostering the transfer of social capital. Not only can these social connections provide people with a subjective sense of belonging to a group and the perception that they are loved and cared for by other people, they also can put people who lack specific tangible resources (e.g., food, housing, clothing, safety, money, transportation, job prospects) into contact with people who are willing and able to help them acquire these tangible resources. A more indirect but no less tangible way that religion might serve an integrative function is by promoting the creation of new institutions (e.g., hospitals, clinics, hospices, shelters, after-school programs for children) or the rehabilitation of existing ones (e.g., safer and cleaner neighborhoods and housing options) so that the environments in which people live are less dangerous and more conducive to health and well-being. It is interesting to note that insofar as religion is successful in promoting such broad improvements to people's living and working environments, and insofar as these improvements are equally available to people of all religious persuasions, these improvements should actually minimize

Preparation of this chapter was generously supported by a grant from the John Templeton Foundation to the first author and a grant from the Religious Research Association to the second author.

health differences among people of varying degrees of religiousness or varying religious persuasions.

Finally, Idler and Kasl (1997) described Weber's (1922/1993) notion that religion can provide meaning and coherence to people's understandings of their lives and their worlds. Coherent worldviews might be especially valuable when people endure personal stress or undergo developmentally significant changes in life, such as illness, bereavement, job loss, or transition to long-term care. Specifically, religion might help to relieve emotional suffering by providing religious interpretations for people's physical or mental suffering, thereby helping them to maintain coherent life narratives. Also religion can provide consolation during such times of stress by encouraging people to look forward to ultimate and divine resolutions of their problems – either in this life or the next. As George, Larson, Koenig, and McCullough (2000) pointed out, however, religion can also lead to malevolent religious explanations for suffering, which appear to exert a negative effect on health (e.g., Pargament, Koenig, Tarakeshwar, and Hahn 2001; see also Pargament 1997).

In the decades that have passed since Durkheim's and Weber's works were published, many investigators have examined one or more aspects of the links of religion to mental and physical health, typically invoking one or more of the explanations that Durkheim or Weber offered so many years ago. Indeed, while preparing a recent handbook specifically devoted to the topic (Koenig, McCullough, and Larson 2001), we identified hundreds of studies investigating relationships between religion and health. These studies were remarkably diverse in scope, quality, and objectives, reflecting the fact that scholars have presumed that religious considerations are potentially relevant to nearly every important aspect of health and well-being. Indeed, Koenig et al. (2001) devoted individual chapters to eight specific dimensions of mental health or interpersonal functioning (well-being, depression, suicide, anxiety disorders, schizophrenia and other psychoses, alcohol/drug use, delinquency, and marital stability) and nine dimensions of physical health (heart disease, hypertension, cardiovascular disease, immunity, cancer, mortality, disability, pain, and health behaviors).

Because no single chapter could present an in-depth review of the entire body of research on religion and health, in the present chapter we focus on the relationships of religiousness to one measure of physical health – mortality – and one measure of mental health – depressive symptoms. We use our recent meta-analyses of the research regarding the association of religion with these two health issues (McCullough, Hoyt, Larson, Koenig, and Thoresen 2000; Smith, McCullough, and Poll 2002) to illustrate what modern research has revealed regarding the religion-health relationship more broadly. We then discuss some issues raised by the existing research that, we believe, deserve further attention in the years to come.

RELIGION AND MENTAL HEALTH: DEPRESSION AS A CASE STUDY

Researchers have investigated the links between religion and mental health in hundreds of studies, and several major reviews have been published during the past decade (e.g., Batson, Schoenrade, and Ventis 1993; Gartner 1996; George et al. 2000; Koenig et al. 2001; Payne, Bergin, Bielema, and Jenkins 1991). Although the findings are complex and sometimes inconsistent, many empirical studies indicate that people who are religiously devout, but not extremists, tend to report greater subjective well-being and life satisfaction, greater marital satisfaction and family cohesion, more ability to cope with stress and crises, less worry, and fewer symptoms of depression. For the purposes of this chapter, the research on religious involvement and depression provides a case study for this corpus of research.

Studies Establishing a Relationship

Several recent studies (e.g., Braam et al. 2001; Murphy et al. 2000) indicate that certain aspects of religiousness (e.g., public religious involvement, intrinsic religious motivation) may be inversely related to depressive symptoms. Notably, Braam et al. (2001) reported that public religious involvement (viz., church attendance) was inversely related to depression among the elderly individuals from European countries who were included in the EURODEP collaboration. These results were similar at the individual and national levels, with the effects being strongest among women and Roman Catholics.

Murphy et al. (2000) found that symptoms of depression among 271 clinically depressed adults were negatively correlated with religious beliefs, even after controlling for age, race, gender, marital status, and educational level. A path model indicated that religious beliefs had both a direct effect on symptoms of depression and an indirect effect when symptoms of hopelessness were included as a mediator.

Schnittker (2001) examined the association of religious involvement with symptoms of depression using a nationally representative longitudinal data set of 2,836 adults from the general population. He found that although religious *attendance* had no significant relationship with symptoms of depression once demographic and physical health variables were controlled, there was a significant curvilinear association between religious *salience* and symptoms of depression. Specifically, individuals who did not see themselves as religious and individuals who saw themselves as extremely religious had higher symptoms of depression than those who considered themselves moderately religious. Moreover, he also found evidence that religious beliefs acted as a buffer against distress. The negative correlation between religiosity and symptoms of depression was of greater magnitude for individuals who experienced multiple life stressors compared to other individuals.

Koenig et al. (1998) reported that among eighty-seven clinically depressed older adults who were followed for one year beyond the onset of depression, intrinsic religiousness was directly proportional to the speed with which their depressive episodes abated. Specifically, Koenig et al. estimated that every ten-point increase in people's raw scores on a self-report measure of intrinsic religious motivation was associated with a 70 percent increase in the speed of remission of depressive symptoms. This association appeared to be even stronger among subjects whose physical disabilities did not improve over the follow-up period. This association persisted even after researchers controlled for several important potential confounding variables.

Conclusions from a Meta-Analytic Review

Because so many studies have addressed the associations of religious involvement and depression, we (Smith, McCullough, and Poll 2002) recently completed a meta-analytic review of these studies. We located 150 studies (involving nearly one hundred thousand participants total) that had addressed the cross-sectional association of one or more measures of religiousness with one or more measures of depressive symptoms. Among these studies, the mean association of religiousness and depressive symptoms was a modest $r = -.126$, suggesting that people with high levels of religiousness have slightly lower reports of depressive symptoms.

As is typical in meta-analyses, our main conclusions did not apply equally to people from all backgrounds. Although the religiousness-depression relationship was approximately the same size for women (mean $r = -.126$) as for men (mean $r = -.125$), we did find evidence that religiousness may be associated more negatively with depressive symptoms for African Americans (mean $r = -.121$) than for European Americans ($r = -.085$). However, our ability to detect ethnic differences was rather limited.

We also found some rather complex age trends: The religiousness-depression relationship was very small during adolescence and the college years (mean $rs = -.06$ and $-.13$), then reached a local minimum (i.e., mean $r = -.17$) during early adulthood (i.e., ages twenty-five–thirty-five). The association then appeared to decrease in strength again through mid-adulthood (mean $r = -.11$ for adults ages thirty-six–forty-five, mean $r = -.051$ for adults ages forty-six–fifty-five, and mean $r = -.07$ for adults ages fifty-six–sixty-five). In older adulthood, the association strengthened again to $r = -.18$ for adults ages sixty-six–seventy-five and $r = -.21$ for adults ages seventy-six and older. Thus, the association of religiousness and depression appeared to be most strongly negative for people in early adulthood and those beyond age sixty-five.

In addition, we found evidence for some interesting differences in the religiousness-depression relationship as a function of how religion was measured. In particular, measures of intrinsic religious motivation (i.e., the extent to which one views religion as the "master motive" in one's life; Allport and Ross 1967) and measures of "positive" religious coping (e.g., Pargament et al. 1997) were moderately negatively related to depressive symptoms ($rs = -.197$ and $-.177$, respectively), whereas extrinsic religious motivation (i.e., involvement in religion as a means to other ends) and negative forms of religious coping were related *positively* to depressive symptoms (mean $rs = +.145$ and $+.140$, respectively). These findings suggest that assessment of the motivational aspects of religiousness as well as the specific ways people use religion to cope with stress may provide particularly useful windows for examining the possible impact of religious involvement on depressive symptoms.

Relatedly, we found some evidence that the association of religiousness and depression was most strongly negative in studies in which participants could be assumed to be under severe levels of life stress. We read descriptions of the participants of the study to infer the amount of life stress that the participants in each sample were likely to be experiencing (minimal, mild to moderate, or severe). Among samples of people whom we perceived to be undergoing minimal life stress, the expected association of religiousness and depressive symptoms was $r = -.10$. Among samples of people whom we perceived to be undergoing mild to moderate life stress, the correlation dropped to $r = -.17$, and among samples of people whom we perceived to be undergoing severe life stress, the correlation dropped slightly further to $r = -.19$. Thus, we think there is good reason to believe that the so-called protective effects of religious involvement against depressive symptoms are at their strongest when people are undergoing highly stressful life events (Cohen and Wills 1985; Schnittker 2001). Given that stress contributes to the onset and exacerbation of nearly all physical ailments, the finding of a stress-buffering effect in the research specific to depression has potentially strong implications for the relationship between religion and physical health.

RELIGION AND PHYSICAL HEALTH: MORTALITY AS A CASE STUDY

Recent scholarship that is increasing in both quantity and quality has indicated that religiousness can promote physical health and well-being. Religion has been found to be a factor in deterring nearly every malady, from cancer to heart disease (Koenig et al. 2001). McCullough et al. (2000) reasoned that if religiousness promotes physical health, then there should be evidence that religiousness is consistently related to the ultimate measure of physical health – length of life. Several investigators have found measures of public religious involvement, such as frequency of attendance at religious services or other forms of public religious activity, to be associated with lower mortality, both in U.S. samples (Comstock and Tonascia 1977; Seeman, Kaplan, Knudsen, Cohen, and Guralnik 1987; Goldman, Korenman, and Weinstein 1995; Hummer, Rogers, Nam, and Ellison 1999; Oman and Reed 1998; Strawbridge, Cohen, Shema, and Kaplan 1997) and elsewhere (e.g., Goldbourt, Yaari, and Medalie 1993).

Studies Establishing a Relationship

Strawbridge, Cohen, Shema, and Kaplan (1997) conducted a twenty-eight-year longitudinal project with data from the Alameda County study to examine the relationship between religious attendance and all-cause mortality from 1968 to 1994. They found that frequent religious attendance in 1968 was related to lower hazard of death during the ensuing twenty-eight years. Although adjustments for baseline health status accounted for some of the religious attendance-mortality relationship, the adjusted relationship was still significant, with a relative hazard = .67 (i.e., the probability of dying in any given year, given the number of respondents alive during the previous year, was only 67 percent as large for people who frequently attended religious services as it was for people who attended less frequently). Strawbridge et al. also found that people who frequently attended religious services in 1968 were less likely to smoke or drink heavily than were people who attended religious services less frequently. Religious service attenders also had more social connections than did infrequent religious service attenders.

   An important finding of Strawbridge et al. was that those who attended religious services frequently were more likely to improve their health behaviors during the twenty-eight years that ensued. Even after adjusting for initial differences in health behaviors, frequent attenders were more likely than were infrequent attenders to (a) quit smoking, (b) reduce their drinking, (c) increase their frequency of exercising, (d) stay married to the same person, and (e) increase their number of social contacts. Thus religious attendance was related to *positive changes* in the study population's health behaviors, changes that might have been in part responsible for the relationship of religious attendance and mortality. It was interesting that religious people were significantly *more* likely to become obese during the twenty-eight years of the study – a finding that has been replicated by Oman and Reed (1998) and others. [Koenig et al. (2001) noted that obesity is a behavioral risk factor for which religious people have a consistently elevated risk.]

A recent prospective study of 3,968 community-dwelling older adults from the Piedmont region of North Carolina (Koenig, Hays, Larson, George, Cohen, McCullough, Meador, and Blazer 1999) yielded evidence that frequency of attendance at religious services was related to significantly reduced hazard of dying over the six-year study period. After controlling for potential sociodemographic and health-related confounds, Koenig et al. found that the relative hazard of dying for frequent attenders of religious services remained relatively low (for women, RH = .51, CI = 0.43–0.59; for men, RH =.63, CI = 0.52–0.75). After adjusting the association for explanatory variables such as social support and health behaviors (including cigarette smoking, alcohol consumption, and body mass index), the religion-mortality association became appreciably weaker (for women, RH = 0.65, CI = 0.55–0.76; for men, RH = 0.83, CI = 0.69–1.00). These results indicate that being involved in public religious activity – namely, attendance at religious services – was associated with a reduction in mortality. Part of this association was attributable to potential confounds (e.g., gender, ethnicity, education, number of health conditions, self-rated health), and part was attributable to the influence of church attendance on well-established risk factors for early death.

In what is perhaps the most far-reaching study on religion and mortality to date, Hummer, Rogers, Nam, and Ellison (1999) followed a nationally representative sample of over twenty-one thousand adults from 1987 to 1995. In 1987, respondents completed a single-item measure of frequency of attendance at religious services, along with a variety of other measures to assess demographics, socioeconomic status, health, social ties, and health behaviors. Hummer and his colleagues found that frequent religious attendance was positively related to length of life. People of both sexes who attended religious services more than once per week were estimated to live for 62.9 years beyond age twenty. For those who attended once per week, life expectancy beyond age twenty was 61.9 years. For those who attended less than once per week, life expectancy beyond age twenty was 59.7 years. Finally, for those who reported never attending religious services, the life expectancy beyond age twenty was 55.3 years. This represents a 7.6-year survival differential between the frequent attenders and the nonattenders.

After controlling for a variety of potential confounds and mediators that could explain the association of religious involvement and longevity (including age, gender, health, social status, social support, cigarette smoking, alcohol use, and body mass index), people who frequently attended religious services still appeared to survive longer than did those who did not attend. Indeed, people who reported never attending religious services had an 87 percent higher risk of dying during the follow-up period than did people who attended religious service more than once per week. People who attended religious services, but less frequently than "more than once per week" also experienced longer survival than did those who did not attend.

Because Hummer et al. (1999) worked with such a large data set, they were able to explore the association of religious involvement with death from specific causes including circulatory diseases, cancer, respiratory diseases, diabetes, infectious diseases, external causes, and all other causes. Religious attendance was associated with lower hazard of death from most causes, including circulatory diseases, respiratory diseases, diabetes, infectious diseases, and external causes. One notable exception was that religious attendance did not appear to be related to a reduced risk of dying from cancer. When demographics, health, socioeconomic status, social ties, and health behaviors were controlled, most of these survival differences became statistically nonsignificant, although the direction of the associations still indicated that frequent attenders were living slightly longer lives than were nonattenders. The fact that religious involvement was related to reduced mortality by so many causes led Hummer and colleagues to propose that religious involvement might actually be one of the "fundamental causes" of longevity: Because each of the major causes of death has its own specific etiology, the so-called effects of religious involvement on mortality must influence mortality through a variety of casual patterns; thus controlling any single mechanism or cause of death should not cause the religion-mortality association to disappear.

Is the religion-mortality association a strictly American phenomenon? Perhaps not, although the data from other places in the world are scant and preliminary. Goldbourt, Yaari, and Medalie (1993) followed a sample of 10,059 male Israeli government workers for twenty-three years to examine the predictors of mortality. They assessed religious orthodoxy using a three-item measure consisting of (a) whether the respondent received a religious or secular education; (b) whether the respondent defined himself as "orthodox," "traditional," or "secular"; and (c) how frequently the respondent attended synagogue. Unadjusted data indicated that each standard unit increase in orthodoxy was associated with a 16 percent increase in odds of survival through the twenty-three-year follow-up period. (These data were adjusted for age, but were not adjusted for other demographic, biomedical, and psychosocial variables.)

Of course, not all investigations of the association of religious involvement and mortality have revealed favorable associations (e.g., Idler and Kasl 1992; Janoff-Bulman and Marshall 1982; LoPrinzi et al. 1994; Pargament et al. 2001; Reynolds and Nelson 1981). For example, Koenig et al. (1998) studied whether the use of religion as a source of coping was a predictor of all-cause mortality in a sample of 1,010 older adult males who were hospitalized for medical illness. These 1,010 patients were followed for an average of nine years. At the beginning of their involvement in the study, patients completed a three-item measure of the extent to which they used their religion to cope with stress. In both bivariate analyses and multivariate analyses in which the investigators statistically adjusted for demographic, social, and medical differences among the patients, those who relied heavily on religion for coping did not live any longer than did patients who did not rely heavily on religion for coping. Idler and Kasl (1992) reported similar results from analyses of a sample of basically healthy, community-dwelling older adults.

Moreover, Pargament et al. (2001) recently reported that in a sample of medically ill adults people who believed that their illnesses were signs that God had abandoned them or was punishing them, or who believed that the Devil was creating their illnesses, had *shorter* lives, even after controlling for a variety of demographic, physical health, and mental health variables.

Conclusions from a Meta-Analytic Review

After conducting an extensive search, for published and unpublished studies relevant to the topic (using electronic databases, searches through the reference sections of relevant studies, and leads from other investigators), we retrieved forty-two independent estimates of the association, or *effect sizes*, for religious involvement and mortality, incorporating data from 125,826 people. We coded these forty-two effect sizes for a variety of qualities, including (a) how religiousness was measured; (b) percentage of males and females in the sample; (c) number of statistical adjustments made to the association; and (d) whether the sample was composed of basically healthy community-dwelling adults or medical patients. We also determined whether each of fifteen putative confounds and mediators of the religiousness-mortality association were controlled: Race, income, education, employment status, functional health, self-rated health, clinical or biomedical measures of physical health, social support, social activities, marital status, smoking, alcohol use, obesity/body mass index, mental health or affective distress, and exercise.

Using these forty-two effect sizes (which were adjusted for a variety of covariates of religion and mortality in the studies from which we derived them), we found an association of religious involvement and mortality equivalent to an odds ratio (OR) = 1.29, indicating that religious people had, on average, a 29 percent higher chance of survival during any follow-up period than did less-religious people. Another way to describe this association is to say that religious people had, on average, only 1/1.29 = 77.5 percent of the odds of dying during any specified follow-up period than did less religious people.

A major concern with meta-analysis is the possibility that the studies included are a biased sample of the population of studies, and thus might fail to represent accurately the population estimate. To examine the sensitivity of our meta-analytic conclusions to this particular threat to their validity, we calculated a fail-safe N (Rosenthal 1979), which indicated that 1,418 effect sizes with a mean odds ratio of 1.0 (i.e., literally no relationship of religious involvement and mortality) would be needed to overturn the significant overall association of religious involvement and mortality (i.e., to render the resulting mean effect size nonsignificant, $p > .05$, one-tailed). The large number of nonsignificant results that would be needed to overturn these findings makes it extremely unlikely that our estimate of the association of religiousness and mortality was solely due to having worked with an uncharacteristically favorable set of studies in our meta-analysis, since it seems rather improbable that so many studies yielding, on average, null results could have been conducted but not published.

Nonetheless, there was a considerable amount of variability among the forty-two effect size estimates included in our meta-analysis. Through a series of subsidiary analyses, we identified several variables that helped to explain these variations in effect size.

First, studies that used measures of public religious involvement (e.g., frequency of attendance at religious services, membership in religious social groups, membership in religious kibbutzim versus secular kibbutzim) tended to yield larger effect sizes than did studies that focused on measures of private religious practice (e.g., frequency of private prayer, use of religious coping), measures that combined indicators of public and private religious activity, and measures that could not be identified due to insufficient information in the study reports. Indeed, studies that used measures of public religious involvement yielded an omnibus effect size of OR = 1.43: that is, after researchers controlled for covariates, they found that people high in public religious involvement had 43 percent higher odds of being alive at follow-up. In contrast, the association of religious involvement and mortality for effect sizes that used nonpublic measures of religious practice was nearly zero (OR = 1.04). This finding suggests that mortality is linked to involvement in public religious activity to a much greater extent than to measures of other dimensions of religiousness.

Another important predictor of effect size was the percentage of males in the study sample. We estimated that a sample with 100 percent males would yield an effect size of OR = 1.33, whereas a sample of 100 percent females would yield an effect size of OR = 1.59. Thus, women involved in religion appear to gain considerably more protection from early death than do men involved in religion.

Finally, the degree of statistical control exerted over the religion-mortality association was negatively related to effect size. Not surprisingly, better-controlled studies (i.e., those including more covariates or copredictors) yielded smaller associations. In a final set of analyses, we estimated how strong the relationship between public religious involvement and mortality would be if researchers were to conduct a study that controlled for all fifteen of the potential covariates, mediators, and confounds that we identified. In such a study, one would expect an odds ratio of 1.23, which indicates that people highly involved in public religious activities would be expected to have 23 percent higher odds of survival than would people who are less involved in religious activities, *even after controlling for a huge array of potential confounds and mediators*. In this final set of analyses, the odds ratio of 1.23 was not statistically significant, a point that has been debated recently (McCullough, Hoyt, and Larson 2001; Sloan and Bagiella 2001). As we noted, the nonsignificance of this estimate was probably caused by the fact that we were playing into the weaknesses of multiple regression by estimating parameters for a relatively large number of highly correlated predictor variables with a relatively small number of effect sizes. Indeed, the fifteen predictor variables were so highly intercorrelated that it was mathematically impossible to arrive at a solution without throwing three of them out of the prediction equation altogether! Thus, we have argued that it is a red herring to focus very much on that particular test of statistical significance. Instead, we think the most important point from this meta-analysis is that even if much of the religion-mortality relationship can be explained in terms of other psychological or behavioral factors, it appears to be "real" and important for sociological theory and research – a point to which we now turn.

ASSOCIATION OF RELIGION WITH HEALTH: HOW IMPORTANT? HOW REAL?

Based on these two meta-analyses, we have concluded that the evidence supports many researchers' perceptions that some aspects of religiousness are indeed related to better functioning on some measures of mental and physical health. It does seem to be the case that people involved in religious pursuits, on average, live slightly longer lives and experience slightly lower levels of depressive symptoms than do their less religious counterparts. However, the simple presence of a statistical relationship between two constructs does not tell us all that we need to know to put these relationships into perspective. In particular, we need to concern ourselves with at least two additional sets of questions: First, we must ask how important the associations between religious involvement and health are; second, we must ask whether these associations are "real."

How Important Are the Associations of Religion and Health?

As most social scientists acknowledge, statistical significance is but one criterion for judging the importance of a relationship between two variables (Howard, Maxwell, and Fleming 2000). While null hypothesis significance testing has certainly been valuable in the evolution of social science (Krueger 2001), statistical significance fails to tell us anything about the practical importance of an association. However, we can gain an appreciation for the importance of the religion-health association by comparing the mean effect sizes for the association of religiousness with a given health outcome to the effect sizes gleaned from meta-analytic literature reviews that have examined other factors also thought to be predictors of the same health outcome.

One helpful way to portray the association of religious involvement and mortality is the binomial effect size display (BESD; Rosenthal 1990, 1991), a statistical simulation that can be used to portray effect sizes in terms of the difference between two groups (e.g., one hundred people high in religiousness, one hundred people low in religiousness) in the odds of dying when the base mortality rate is 50 percent. If the odds ratio of 1.23 derived from our meta-analysis (the most conservative estimate of the association of religiousness and mortality) is portrayed using the BESD (see McCullough, Hoyt, and Larson 2001), one finds that approximately forty-eight of the one hundred people in the "highly religious" group would be dead at follow-up (52:48 odds in favor of surviving), whereas approximately fifty-two of the one hundred people in the "less-religious" group would be dead at follow-up (48:52 odds against surviving). Thus among a group of one hundred "religious" people and a group of one hundred "less-religious" people, we would expect four more of the religious people to be alive at the point in time when 50 percent of the sample had died.

The BESD obtained for the association of religious involvement and mortality can be compared to the BESDs for the relationship of other psychosocial variables or medical interventions to all-cause mortality. Based on prior meta-analytic findings, McCullough (2001) estimated that hazardous alcohol use and postcardiac exercise rehabilitation programs account for ten and eight deaths per two hundred people, respectively. Saz and Dewey (2001) reported a meta-analysis in which they synthesized the existing evidence regarding the relationship between depression and mortality in the elderly. They found a mean association of Odds Ratio = 1.73. This odds ratio, when converted to a BESD, corresponds to fourteen outcomes per two hundred people accounted for by diagnoses of depression.

Strawbridge, Cohen, and Shema (2000) adopted a similar comparative approach, although they conducted their comparative analyses of the association of religious involvement and mortality with the Alameda County data set that we described previously. Using nearly three decades of longitudinal data for 5,894 adult residents of Alameda County, they compared the strength of the association of religious service attendance with mortality to the strength of the associations of four other well-known predictors of mortality – cigarette smoking, physical activity, alcohol consumption, and nonreligious social involvement. They computed these associations separately for men and women, after controlling for age, education, self-reported health, and number of chronic health conditions. For men, weekly religious service attendance was associated with reduced mortality (relative hazard = 0.84). In other words, the likelihood of death in any given year for someone who attended religious services weekly was only 84 percent of the likelihood of death for someone who never attended religious services. The relative hazards for abstaining from cigarette smoking (relative hazard = 0.49), frequent physical activity (relative hazard = 0.58), moderate versus heavy alcohol use (relative hazard = 0.76), and individual and group social involvement versus social isolation (relative hazard = 0.58) were all considerably stronger (smaller relative hazards imply lesser probability of dying for people who possess high scores on the variable in question). Thus, for men at least, the protective effects associated with religious involvement seemed relatively modest in comparison to the protective effects associated with abstinence from smoking, frequent physical activity, moderate alcohol use, and social engagement.

For women, in contrast, weekly public religious attendance appeared to be substantially more protective (relative hazard = 0.63), which is an effect comparable to those for never smoking (relative hazard = 0.53), frequent physical activity (relative hazard = 0.68), moderate versus heavy alcohol use (relative hazard = 0.58), and individual and group social involvement vs. social isolation (relative hazard = 0.58). Thus Strawbridge et al.'s (2000) data are consistent with the findings of our meta-analytic review, linking regular religious attendance with a survival advantage that is comparable, at least for women, to the survival advantages associated with other well-established psychosocial predictors of mortality.

In light of these comparisons, we think it is fair to say that the religiousness-mortality association is probably somewhat weaker (certainly for men, perhaps less so for women) than are the associations of other important psychological variables (including depression, excessive alcohol use, and physical exercise). However, the predictive power of many of the variables that society has deemed "important" risk or protective factors against early death is of the same magnitude as the association of religiousness with mortality (most of them, including religiousness, accounting for fewer than fifteen outcomes per two hundred). Moreover, given the complex multivariate nature of the causes of such outcomes as mortality and depression, even small effects can be considered "impressive" (Prentice and Miller 1992). Thus religiousness certainly may be a factor, albeit a small one, in predicting mortality. Moreover, for women at least, the so-called protective effects of religiousness may be nearly as strong as are those for other well-established risk and protective factors.

In our meta-analysis of studies on religion and depression, the mean overall effect size was estimated as $r = .126$, suggesting that measures of religiousness typically account for $(.126)^2 = 1.6$ percent of the variance in the severity of depressive symptoms in the population. Even though an association of this size is typically considered "small" (J. Cohen 1988), this small correlation need not be dismissed entirely. For comparison, one might consider that the association between gender and depressive symptoms (i.e., women tending toward more severe depressive symptoms than do men) is frequently on the order of $r = .10$ (e.g., see Nolen-Hoeksema, Larson, and Grayson 1999, Table 1; Twenge and Nolen-Hoeksema 2001). Although the gender difference in depressive symptoms is "small" statistically, and although it belies a considerable gender difference in the odds of depressive disorders (Culbertson 1997), this gender-depression association is reliable and has considerable scientific and social importance. Moreover, the gender difference in depressive symptoms has led to theoretical advances regarding the nature of depression itself (e.g., Nolen-Hoeksema et al. 1999). With the gender differences in depressive symptoms as a benchmark for how "small" associations can be important (see also Prentice and Miller 1992), we also conclude that despite the modest statistical strength of the association between depressive symptoms and religiousness, it may have important implications.

How "Real" Is the Religion-Health Association?

Is the religion-health association "valid"? Contemporary investigators of the religion-health association have worked diligently to appraise its validity (see Levin 1994, for a review). To address the first of these concerns, investigators have adopted two major strategies. The first strategy has involved conducting studies in which the association of religiousness with a given health outcome (e.g., mortality) was assessed only after controlling statistically for every other variable that might conceivably account for variance in the health outcome (e.g., age, gender, socioeconomic status, health status, social support and social activity, and other psychosocial factors). The logic behind this "subtractive" method is not to determine whether religiousness accounts for variance in a given health outcome, but rather to determine whether religiousness accounts for "new" variance in a given health outcome. The concern here, obviously, is with improving society's ability to predict, for example, who dies or who gets depressed, with the logic that a new innovation (i.e., a relatively new health factor like religiousness) should be considered important only if it *improves* society's ability to predict health outcomes. This subtractive method is indeed useful if the goal is to arrive at a maximally efficient set of risk factors and protective factors for predicting a particular health outcome. Thus, we contend, the subtractive method is used in the service of a *technological* goal (applying health-related empirical knowledge to the prediction of health and well-being in the real world).

Despite its practicality, the subtractive method is deficient from a purely scientific perspective because it focuses solely on evaluating whether religiousness exerts a so-called direct effect on a given health outcome. By doing so, the subtractive method fails to shed light on the indirect routes through which religiousness might exert influence (see Levin 1994). A better method would be to evaluate a series of hypotheses that allow for several different perspectives on the religion-health association to be considered simultaneously (a method used both by Hummer et al. 1999, and in the meta-analysis by McCullough et al. 2000). First, it is scientifically useful to know simply whether an association exists. This involves estimating the bivariate association between a measure of religiousness and a measure of health, with no other variables controlled.

Second, it is helpful to know whether the religion-health association is spurious, thus determining whether variables that cause both religiousness and the health outcome can be credited with the apparent religion-health relationship. For example, gender is a known correlate of religiousness and longevity, and because gender is causally prior to both religiousness and longevity (i.e., it cannot be influenced by religiousness or longevity), its ability to account for variance in the religion-health relationship should probably be interpreted as evidence for confounding. Such confounds should be observed and evaluated, and estimates of the religion-health association adjusted downward accordingly.

Third, variables should be identified that might serve as mediators of the religion-health relationship (e.g., factors associated with the regulative, integrative, and coherence functions of religion à la Durkheim and Weber; see Idler and Kasl 1997). Once conceptualized, these mediators should be evaluated as such, using appropriate statistical modeling. One would expect the associations of religiousness with the specified health outcomes to become smaller as more and more of the mediators through which religiousness exerts its effect are controlled statistically. By the time that all of the putative mediators of religiousness and all potential confounds are controlled statistically, what remains is the parameter estimate that proponents of the subtractive method would want to see anyway: the net association of religiousness with the given health outcome after all other possible predictors have been controlled. Through a sequence of hypothesis tests, the goals of technology (i.e., evaluating whether religious information improves our ability to predict health outcomes in the population) and the goals of science (evaluating the religion-health association and exploring its putative causal mechanisms) can be served simultaneously.

We think another good method for determining whether the religion-health association is causal is to conduct experimental research, rather than relying exclusively on the interpretation of nonexperimental data. Although some investigators have cast serious doubts on the ability of science to manipulate religiousness experimentally for the purpose of experimental research, we believe that investigators who are motivated to think creatively about this problem may arrive at feasible and ethical means for modifying dimensions of people's religiousness, at least in the short term, to examine whether specific dimensions of health improve in response.

Is the religion-health association generalizable? A second way of asking whether the religion-health relationship is "real" is to ask questions about the limits on its generalizability. If the religion-health association is a "human" phenomenon, rather than a phenomenon that is specific to a single era in history, a specific culture, or a specific gender, then we might make more of its significance than if it appears to be simply a local phenomenon. The meta-analytic approach is extremely useful in this regard because meta-analysis allows investigators to search explicitly for the facets (i.e., elements of study design, characteristics of samples) that create heterogeneity in the results that investigators have obtained over the years. From our own work, we know that the religion-mortality relationship is stronger for men than for women, for example, and that the religion-depression relationship is stronger for African Americans than for European Americans. Other creative approaches to meta-analysis (e.g., Mullen, Muellerleile, and Bryant 2001) would allow for the investigation of whether an apparent association between religiousness and health is stable across time. The facets of generalizability can be explored by any researcher working with primary data, however, by simply examining whether any apparent associations generalize across the major categories of human variation (e.g., at a minimum, gender, age group, and ethnicity).

UNIFYING MODELS OF RELIGION AND HEALTH: FROM GENERAL TO SPECIFIC

Many scholars have articulated general models for explaining how and why religiousness might be related to health. (For a meta-theoretical overview, see Levin and Chatters 1998.) The elegance, scope, and apparent explanatory power of the mechanisms for the religion-health association that Durkheim and Weber introduced so many years ago (i.e., religion's regulatory, integrative, and coherence functions) may have contributed to this tendency for grand theorizing in the literature on religion and health. Efforts at grand explanatory systems are no doubt useful from a pedagogical perspective, and they may be useful to investigators in designing analytic strategies for examining religion-health relationships in specific data sets. We wonder, however, whether they are the best approach to fundamental insights about religion and health that can unify multiple levels of scientific explanation. In particular, we doubt that a single model – no matter how grand – could account for all of the religion-health relationships in a way that unifies sociological, psychological, and biomedical perspectives on the etiology of health and disease. The number of causal factors involved in creating health and illness are enormous and, of course, vary across different types of disease. The etiology of alcoholism is completely different from the etiology of chronic obstructive pulmonary disease, or of colon cancer, or of suicide. Is it really scientifically useful to define a single theoretical model to address the associations of religion with health outcomes as diverse as these? Attempts to explain all of these associations in a single model that integrates sociological, psychological, and biological insights would likely be bland recipes indeed.

However, it may be possible to design powerful scientific models on a smaller scale that can integrate such insights from other relevant sciences. Elsewhere, it has been suggested that "lack of specialization leads to bland generalizations" (McCullough and Larson 1998: 97). For the field to progress toward unifying the scientific study of religion with the scientific study of health and illness, we believe that theorists and researchers must dedicate themselves to uncovering the links of religion with specific diseases: Depression, heart disease, lung cancer, or alcoholism, to name a few. The next generation of theories, in our opinion, will be most fertile if social scientists join hands with specialists in the medical sciences, life sciences, and perhaps even natural sciences to develop models that address the etiology of particular diseases in ways that unify these many possible levels of explanation. Such an approach would allow investigators to make the most of sociological, psychological, and biomedical insights, taking the etiology of particular diseases, their interactions with the life course, and the sociocultural contexts in which they manifest themselves into account. Models with such scope and specificity would be, in our opinion, grand models indeed.

SUMMARY

The existing evidence, which has been accumulating over the course of decades, leads us to the conclusion that religious involvement is associated with some measures of health. These findings suggest that religious involvement may indeed promote some aspects of health and deter some forms of disease – probably through a multiplicity of routes that are specific to particular dimensions of health and particular types of disease. It seems unlikely that religion is salutary vis-à-vis all measures of health and disease, and many questions remain. If the literatures on depression and mortality are any clue as to what future studies will reveal, we can predict that the associations of religion with various health outcomes will be, on average, small in magnitude, but they may be practically and theoretically important nonetheless.

Many of the insights one might gain from the existing research on religion and health are consistent with the grand theoretical insights of sociologists such as Durkheim and Weber. Much more work remains, however, to integrate these insights into coherent theoretical frameworks that make the most of what sociology, as well as the other social sciences and the life sciences, can offer in understanding how religion might influence health and disease.

In this chapter, we have focused on a very thin slice of the religion-health field – the possible causal associations between measures of religiousness and measures of health. However, investigators have been asking a variety of other interesting questions for many years, including questions about how religious holidays may postpone death for days or even weeks, how religiousness may moderate the effects of testosterone upon the initiation of coitus in adolescent females, and how approaching death may influence people's religious beliefs and behaviors, to name but a few. To readers who have enjoyed the modest sampling of the religion-health literature that we have offered in the present chapter, we might also recommend a broader sampling from the full menu.

PART FOUR

Religion and Social Identity

CHAPTER SIXTEEN

Religious Identities and Religious Institutions

Nancy T. Ammerman

For modern social theory, as well as for many ordinary people, religious identities have been a problem.[1] Just what does it really mean to claim a Jewish or Christian identity? To think of oneself as Presbyterian or Baptist? What do we know of that new church down the road that simply calls itself "Fellowship Church"? And do any of those things have anything to do with how we might expect someone to perform their duties as a citizen or a worker? As modern people have loosened their ties to the families and places that (perhaps) formerly enveloped them in a cocoon of faith (or at least surrounded them with a predictable round of religious activity), they can choose how and whether to be religious, including choosing how central religion will be in their lives. Religious practices and affiliations change over a complicated lifetime, and the array of religious groups in a voluntary society shifts in equally complex ways. If religious identity ever was a given, it certainly is no longer.

In his influential work on religion and personal autonomy, Philip Hammond posits that, given the mobility and complexity of the modern situation, individual religious identities are of various sorts – either ascribed (collectivity-based) or achieved (individual) and either primary (a core or "master" role) or secondary (Hammond 1988). In the premodern situation, religion was presumably collective and core.[2] In the modern situation, taking up a collective, core religious identity is a matter of (exceptional) choice, not determinism.[3] We neither all share one religious identity nor know quite what to make of the many identities with which we are surrounded.

While social theory has taught us that maintaining a religious identity is a problem in the "mainstream" of culture, at the margins, religious identities seem still to play a role. Indeed, much of recent research on religious identity has focused on the margins and the interstices, on the times and places where religious identities clash and/or must be remade. Lively work is now underway, for instance, on the struggle to

---

[1] Classic theories predicting religion's demise include Marx (1878/1964) and Weber (1904–5/1958), with Berger (1967) providing the most elegant theoretical formulation and Lechner (1991) among the most cogent current defenders.

[2] Mary Douglas (1983) debunks the notion that premodern people were thoroughly religious.

[3] John Hewitt (1989) uses the example of the totally dedicated fundamentalist or orthodox person to illustrate the uncommon modern identity strategy of "exclusivity."

maintain or recreate immigrant religious identities.[4] Circumstances and demands in a new culture inevitably reshape the beliefs and practices that were taken for granted in a home country. Thrown together both with "anglo" hosts and with more proximal, yet often strange, ethnic compatriots, immigrants use religious gatherings as places to sustain old cultural ways, but also as places where new ways are hammered out (Warner and Wittner 1998). The clash of cultures is across generations, as well, as second and third generations arrive at their own relationships to ethnic and religious traditions.

Two earlier sets of immigrants now fuel another stream of writing about religious identity. Both American Catholics and American Jews have, in the last generation, passed into the mainstream of culture, have begun to experience high rates of intermarriage, and have consequently generated a good deal of identity anxiety among their leaders. Can religious institutions support distinct ways of life that are both ethnic and religious in American middle class society? Researchers have attempted to disentangle the beliefs, practices, relationships, institutions, and conscious self-identity that may or may not be essential to perpetuating community and tradition. Whether the object of study is independent-minded post–Vatican-II Catholics or intermarried nonreligious Jews, questions of religious identity have emerged in both practical and theoretical discussions.[5]

Another set of questions about religious identity is raised by seemingly incongruous religiosocial pairings (Warner 1997). Where significant collective identities stand in opposition to one another, individuals who find themselves in both warring camps at the same time must engage in active identity work. Thumma (1991) examines, for instance, the case of gays who are also evangelical. He demonstrates that special purpose organizations can engender both the rationale and the practices by which a "gay evangelical" identity can be built and sustained, but such practices take intentional work. By replicating much of evangelical culture, but within a gay environment, people create and try out new religious solidarities.

Equally interesting has been the attempt to understand conversion. Especially at the height of sociology's attention to new religious movements, we had opportunities to see actions and affiliations transformed in ways that brought identity construction visibly to the fore (e.g., Bromley and Hammond 1987; Robbins 1988). Here were people who chose, in a thoroughly modern way, a seemingly pre-modern absorption in a religious community, trading a multilayered and complicated modern identity for one organized around a single set of core religious beliefs, practices, and associations.[6]

Among the most helpful of the work on conversion that emerged from that era was Mary Jo Neitz's portrayal of the process by which charismatic Catholics gained that new identity (Neitz 1987). She describes conversion as the gradual building up of a new "root reality" (Heirich 1977) at the same time that the old one is being discarded. The change is made as people engage in a kind of practical/rational process

---

[4] See, for example, Chong 1998; Kim 2000; Lawson 1999; Peña and Frehill 1998; Yang 1999.

[5] Hoge (2000) has recently made this argument . Among the key recent studies of Jewish identity are Davidman (1990), Heilman (1996), and Goldstein and Goldstein (1996). For Catholics, see Dillon (1999a) and McNamara (1992).

[6] Even that construal is, of course, more "ideal typical" than real. Even the most tightly bounded new religious movement still retained complex layers of involvement and dissent and therefore complex versions of identity. See, for example, Barker (1984).

of testing faith claims against their everyday experience to see what makes practical sense. She notes that conversion can take many forms, given that we all live with varying degrees of complexity in our worlds and begin from different degrees of religious salience. To move from a high-salience Catholic to a low-salience Catholic is a process to be explained no less than the move from a low-salience Catholic to a high-salience charismatic. And her insistence that we take practical reason into account moves us helpfully into questions of the social conditions under which religious actors, ideas, and relationships become salient within the complicated lives of modern persons.

Two things are striking to me about this literature. First, much of it proceeds with little attention to a definition or theory of identity. The assumption seems often to be that "we know it when we see it." Even careful ethnographers charting the process by which identities are under siege or being remade, write a text between the lines that asserts identity (especially an authentically religious one) to be a singular guiding "core" that shapes how others respond to us and how we guide our own behavior. We either have it or we don't. Other identities may be partial, but "real" religious ones surely must be total. The task in transitional and contradictory situations, this subtext reads, is to get the core back together again. In what follows I want to question and nuance that basic assumption.

The second thing that strikes me is that so little of our thinking about religious identity has taken the everyday world of ordinary people into account. In looking – understandably – at the places where identity work was obvious, we have perhaps avoided the basic questions about social life that ought to inform any attempt to understand the place of religion in it. How and why do people act as they do? What guides and constrains that action? Under what conditions do people orient themselves toward religious institutions and realities? By beginning with a look at recent thinking about social identity – both personal and collective – I hope to move our discussion of religious identity to include such questions.

CONSTRUCTING AND DECONSTRUCTING SOCIAL IDENTITY

Zygmunt Bauman (1996) posits that the very notion of identity is a modern preoccupation. Only when human beings begin to be disembedded from traditional spaces and relationships, long-accepted rhythms of time and well-established activities of survival, do we begin to ask such questions as "Who am I?" and "Where do I belong?" The notion of constructing a self makes sense, he argues, only when the materials for such construction have had to be gathered from far and wide, piled up out of the deconstruction of existing social worlds. Only then do we begin to worry – either existentially or theoretically – about the coherence of our biographical narratives or the bases for our group memberships (Giddens 1991).

John Hewitt (1989), by contrast, points out that the tenuousness of personal identity is simply part of the human condition. All identities include elements of continuity (being the same person over time), integration (being a whole person, not fragments), identification (being like others), and differentiation (being unique and bounded). And every human situation, not just modern ones, places identity in jeopardy. Most basically, no situation is every fully routine; there are always surprises. Every situation gives others the opportunity to evaluate whether we are who we have been believed to be, whether our actions fit the roles we have assumed. And every situation carries a tension between assuming those roles, fitting in, declaring our identification with the group, and, on the other hand, doing something that emphasizes our uniqueness, our differentiation. Whether because our actions arouse doubts in others or because we ourselves seek to declare our independence or because the situation challenges existing assumptions, human society has never allowed identity to be unproblematic. Modern society is different in the number of roles and communities available for the choosing, but not different in these basic dynamics of identification and differentiation.

More than a generation ago, Goffman (1959; 1967), Garfinkel (1967), and Berger and Luckmann (1966) began the task of theorizing how persons construct, present, and conspire to protect the fragile stability of each other's selves. Their work began to lay out the ways in which each social situation calls for the creative work of its participants, each picking up the strands of the drama as it unfolds. Players take roles that make sense to and of themselves and others (Mead 1934), aligning their actions with scripts and categories that will be recognized and can be responded to by the other players. More recently, Hall, among others, has pointed to the ways in which we identify with and "perform" the positions to which we are assigned, talking our way into ongoing stories that are always partial and incomplete (Hall 1996). The ability to align our actions with the actions of others, mutually defining and working within a recognized script, marks us as sane and competent members of our society. To break character or to challenge the basic story line of the script, these theorists taught us, is to risk insanity or to incite revolution. Although scripts and characters are constantly remade by the small dramas of everyday life, those dramas are also the agents that keep existing social structures in place.[7]

In the generation since, the "postmodern" fragmentation of everyday life has prompted many to speculate about the increasing complexity of identity construction, emphasizing the incoherence of the scripts, rather than their solidity. Even before adding relationships built in cyberspace to the mix, many have posited a fluidity of identity that makes coherence seem obsolete.[8] Bauman and others argue that the notion of any "core" self is impossible, that we are tourists and vagabonds, rather than pilgrims with a sense of destination (Bauman 1996). We have no core itinerary guiding our movement through the world. A tentative step in the direction of order is taken by the French theorist Michel Maffesoli, who describes our postmodern situation as a new "time of tribes" (Maffesoli 1995). He argues that "we [social scientists] have dwelled so often on the dehumanization and the disenchantment with the modern world and the solitude it induces that we are no longer capable of seeing the networks of solidarity that exist within" (p. 72). Leaving aside the traditional institutions that are presumed to hold society together and define its citizens, he turns his focus to the solidarity created in everyday gatherings. Sounding often like Durkheim (1912/1976), he looks for the affective force of sociality and custom (a "religion of humanity") that binds people together in ever-shifting gatherings. Local face-to-face groups, as seemingly anonymous as the passengers on a bus, constitute, he proposes, a "neo-tribalism characterized by

---

[7] Their insistence on the power of the scripts is echoed in Pierre Bourdieu's notion of "habitus," a set of practical dispositions or master patterns into which we are socialized so that our actions in any situation are exactly suited to our position in that field of interaction. See Swartz (1998).

[8] This is a form of community and identity that needs much more attention. See Cerulo and associates (1992) for an excellent treatment of the subject.

fluidity, occasional gatherings and dispersal" (p. 76). Faced with the fluidity of bound-aries that brings ever-changing arrays of people together, we use theatrical displays of clothing and body art to found and reconfirm communities and recognize ourselves in them.

His is an attempt to find a new way of understanding the order that still exists in the midst of the seeming chaos, a chaos that appears to leave each of us to invent a new self for each new situation and each group to an arbitrarily defined fight for recognition. While not everyone is so sure that emerging "tribes" are potentially benign, Maffesoli is not alone in pointing to fluidity of boundaries *and* to the strength of sociality and custom. Neither selves nor groups are utterly reconstituted with each new encounter. Some continuity clearly prevails at the same time that a complex society continually challenges that continuity.

The tension between order and chaos, between continuity and revision, is reflected in differing emphases in thinking about identity.[9] Some focus on fluidity and agency, on the ways in which each new encounter leaves the world or the identity slightly (or radically) changed. Others, following especially in the footsteps of Bourdieu (e.g. 1987), focus on the ways in which every interaction is structured by and reinforces patterns of difference, hierarchy, and domination, especially through categories of class, race, and gender (Lamont and Fournier 1992).

But either such view of identity seems to me inadequate. I am unwilling to discard the possibility that persons seek some sense of congruence within the complexity of their lives. Nor do I believe that structured categories exist untouched by the actions and resistance of the actors who inhabit them. What seems essential is to move beyond the notion that any single category of experience – even race, class, or gender – defines identity or action. Identity is not an essential, core, category, nor is it well-conceived in binary either/or terms.[10] To be feminine does not preclude being also masculine, nor does being "American" preclude being also "Irish" or "Hispanic." What we need is a way to talk about who we are and how we behave without reducing ourselves either to a single determining structural essence or to complete chaotic indeterminacy. While the realities of the late modern situation make analysis (and life itself) immensely complex, any adequate account of identity needs an account of the ongoing coherence that is constructed by human consciousness and the solidarity that is created by social gatherings, however temporary. In Giddens's words, "The reflexive project of the self...consists in the sustaining of coherent, yet continuously revised, biographical narratives" (Giddens 1991: 5). Both the coherence and the revision are central to the process. This task is made challenging by the pluralization of our life contexts and the diversity of authorities and power present in any society, but neither the life project nor the analytical task can be set aside in the face of complexity.

IDENTITY AS A PROBLEM OF AGENCY AND STRUCTURE

At its root, differences over fluidity and constraint in the formation of identity grow out of different understandings of agency and structure. To what extent and in what ways

---

[9] Cerulo (1997) calls these two camps the "constructionists" and the "postmodernists."

[10] Minow (1997) is especially helpful in examining the political difficulties of insisting on this middle ground between essentialism and constructionism.

do we understand the human person to be an agent in the creation of her or his own persona? Are groups free to define themselves, or are they defined by powerful others? The answer to those questions begins with the recognition that social action is guided by patterned regularities, social-constructed categories that organize our experience and thinking. We simply respond to the world in terms of what we think we already know about it. There are cognitive and psychological reasons, as much as social ones, for the fundamental way in which human thinking depends on socially constructed categories (DiMaggio 1997).

Agency is located, then, not in freedom from patterned constraint but in our ability to invoke those patterns in nonprescribed ways, enabled in large measure by the very multiplicity of solidarities in which we participate. Sewell (1992) locates agency in the fact that actors always occupy multiple structures and can import resources and schemas ("rules" or categories of understanding) from one to another – what he calls transposability. The rules that tell me who I am at work are not the same rules that guide my behavior at home or at church. Minow observes similarly that all identities are "intersectional," that we are always many things as once – female, white, Catholic, disabled, daughter, and the like (Minow 1997: 38ff). Indeed, part of the experience of education is to gain access to the schemas of cultures in distant times and places, adding other voices to the conversation about how life should proceed.

Emirbayer and Mische (1998) locate agency in the play of structures across time, as well as across institutions and space. They point to the human ability to bring past, present, and future into play at any given moment and to choose which "past" is the relevant one. They call this the "iterational element" of action. It is located in our ability to categorize (if this is an X, then I do Y) and in our necessary formation of habits, which are not automatic but *are* shaped into "settled dispositions." These theorists take very seriously, then, the real power of existing schemas and their ability to produce predictable "strategies of action" (Swidler 1986), but the equally real ability of actors to invoke those strategies in unpredictable ways.

The movement across institutions and time is not, of course, done on a perfectly level playing field. Some actors have a disproportionate ability to mobilize human, symbolic, and material resources in the service of perpetuating or altering patterns of interaction. Sewell, like Bourdieu, points out that some actors can simply manipulate situations and conversations to their own symbolic and material advantage (Sewell 1992). Still, because we do not live in an enclosed world with only one pattern of resource allocation, no single situation is fully determined by itself. We constantly import rules from one situation into another new or unfamiliar one. Identities, then, need to be understood as structured by existing rules and schemas, constrained by existing distributions of resources and power, but also malleable in the everyday reality of moving across institutional contexts and among symbolic worlds.

What each of these theorists has provided is explication for the dynamic nature of each social encounter. We never arrive on the scene as a single identity, but always carry with us the multiple entanglements of our past and present. The very multiplicity of our identities makes agency possible (cf. Coser 1991). Acting within and between structures, across time and space, we cumulatively build up a persona and collectively shape the solidarities of which we are a part. Those personas and solidarities are themselves, then, both structures that constrain future action and sites for continuous revision and improvisation.

IDENTITY AS A NARRATIVE CONSTRUCTION

What is already implied in these discussions of action and agency is the way in which "narrative" may prove a helpful metaphor for understanding the nature of identities. Studies of identity have long taken conversation and language as key sites for analysis. Indeed, the ability to use a group's language is basic to what we mean by membership and identity. To participate in the "discourse" of the group is to enter the social world that the group has constructed (Brown 1993). Our understanding of ourselves, including our incorporation of categories that keep us in dominated positions, is worked out in communication and language. As George Herbert Mead (1934) suggested, identity construction can be viewed in terms of the words we use – words that categorize, words that imply relationships (and often the unequal power inherent in them).

It is, however, critical to move past the words themselves. What narrative analysis offers us is attention to the *relationships* and *actions* that give words their meaning. If we are to understand the nature of identity in a complex world that involves multiple solidarities that both constrain and are continually reconstructed, we need a dynamic mode of analysis that moves beyond categorizing words and analyzing syntax. "(A)ll of us come to be who we are (however ephemeral, multiple, and changing) by being located or locating ourselves (usually unconsciously) in social narratives...," claims Margaret Somers (1994: 606). Narrative, she goes on, renders an event understandable by connecting it to a set of relationships and practices – historically and spatially, particular people doing socially patterned things.

Narrative takes an event and makes it part of a plot, that is, an action-account. The event cannot do this for itself, but must be "emplotted" by the actors who must evaluate the various possible scenarios available to them.[11] The events that become part of a narrative are selected from all that we know of the world. They are placed in a temporal order that implies causation and provides closure. And they are placed in a structure of relationships. As Ewick and Silbey (1995) point out, the process of emplotment is an inherently moral exercise, giving meaning at the same time that it creates explanation and order. This process of emplotment need rarely be conscious; internalized narratives guide most action through habit. Nor are narratives grand stories that explain the world. They need only be unspoken accounts that take an event and give it meaning by making it part of an implied episode or chapter, accounts that identify the characters in the event as part of a larger cast and that situate the event in a meaningful setting.

Among the narratives at play in identity construction are, according to Somers (1994), four types. What she calls "ontological narratives" are the socially constructed stories that are carried by the individual actor as a way of orienting and emplotting the actor's own life. This is her way of reinstating some notion of "core" or "coherence" in the face of arguments about the self as vagabond. To avoid the presumptions of immutability contained in the notion of an "ontological" self, however, I would prefer to capture this idea as "autobiographical narratives," instead. Choices about how to act

---

[11] Emirbayer and Mische's (1998) notion of agency is very compatible with a narrative analysis. Every action, they claim, contains, in addition to the "iterative" (past patterns), an imagined future, and an improvised present; and creative selection is involved in all three dimensions. The "imaginative element" in agency is the human ability to generate future trajectories of action (plots), to imagine what may happen as a result of my action.

depend as much on the internal themes and plots of this autobiographical narrative as on the situation and cultural plots we imagine to be in play. The core self is constantly being negotiated in the various social contexts of a life, but it retains certain themes against which new events and episodes are weighed. Persons understand themselves as certain sorts of characters who are capable of acting in certain ways and incapable or unwilling to act in others.[12] An autobiographical narrative makes possible the predictability with which we respond to each other and imparts a certain trustworthiness and integrity to our action.[13]

It is important to note here that individual internal narratives may be at odds with the story projected to others. Persons are quite capable of acting strategically and/or without sincerity, creating a narrative more suited to what they think others will reward than to their own conscious autobiographical narrative. Likewise, those internal narratives may include characters and episodes that are never recognized by others as "real." Whether the voices heard by a schizophrenic or the visions of a mystic or the body images that tell an anorexic she is fat, autobiographical narratives may guide behavior in ways that do not include the "rational" assessment and critique of the larger community.

But much of identity *is* guided by those community assessments. In addition to autobiographical narratives, Somers posits the "public narratives" which are attached to groups and categories, cultures and institutions.[14] Whether it is the court system or shopping malls, ethnic group or gender, these social institutions and categories provide recognized "accounts" one can give of one's behavior, accounts that identify where one belongs, what one is doing and why (Mills 1940; Scott and Lyman 1968). These are publicly constructed and shared, existing beyond the agency and consciousness of any single individual. Some have enormous strength and widespread recognition; others seem more malleable and/or more narrowly recognized. The strength of an institution can, in fact, be measured by the degree to which its narratives are available in the culture, the extent to which its stories are used to emplot actions across many settings.

Finally, Somers lists metanarratives, which are overarching cultural paradigms for how stories go – a narrative of progress or Enlightenment, for instance – and "conceptual narratives," that is, those constructed by scientists for the sake of explanation. In making the determination about how to emplot an event, then, we evaluate possible story lines according to whether they fit with existing themes – both internal and external – that guide those plots. That process is not utterly free, of course, and is often constrained by the power of certain actors to keep dominating stories in place.

Narrative theories posit that action proceeds, then, from the specific place and time in which it is situated, including thereby all of the available culturally constructed stories in that place. It proceeds, as well, from the relationships embedded in the situation,

---

[12] Teske's (1997) work on the construction of activist identities makes clear that it is possible for individuals to construct a schema to describe themselves that can then shape the action they perceive as inevitable and necessary.

[13] The moral dimensions of the human construction of a self are taken up by Shotter (1984), Niebuhr (1963), and others. Much of "virtue" or "character" ethics has these issues as a central concern.

[14] These public narratives reside in what Bourdieu would call "fields," the operative arena that determines which forms of cultural capital and which habitus will come into play. See Swartz (1998).

including the specific institutional context of rules and practices in which it is located (Lewin 1996). And it proceeds from the individual (but socially constructed) autobiographical narratives of the actors. Action takes place in a relational setting, which is composed of institutions (recognized, patterned structural relations), public narratives, and social practices, all of which are both patterned and contested – constructed and constrained.

Somers and other narrative theorists go a long way toward providing the sort of dynamic and layered mode of analysis needed in understanding identities, but at least one more layer remains. While they acknowledge the way in which narratives are situated in particular places and times, they often forget that they are also enacted by actual physical bodies in material environments. The metaphor of narrative runs the risk of allowing us to reduce social action to texts and words, when the habits that guide us, as well as the experiences that disrupt those habits, are often carried by affect more than thought, by deeply sensual memories and impulses as much as by plot lines. I am convinced that embodied practices are crucial. Gestures, postures, music, and movements tell the story and signal our location in it. There has been a good deal of attention to the way social situations define bodily meaning and experience (Collins 1992; Giddens 1991; Young 1989), but less attention to the physical self as agent in defining identity and membership. Here students of ritual may have something to contribute to the analysis of other forms of social interaction (Comaroff 1985; Soeffner 1997).

INGREDIENTS FOR UNDERSTANDING IDENTITY

We may understand identities as emerging, then, at the everyday intersections of autobiographical and public narratives. We tell stories about ourselves (both literally and through our behavior) that signal both our uniqueness and our membership, that exhibit the consistent themes that characterize us and the unfolding improvisation of the given situation. Each situation, in turn, has its own story, a public narrative shaped by the culture and institutions of which it is a part, with powerful persons and prescribed roles establishing the plot, but surprises and dilemmas that may create gaps in the script or cast doubt on the proffered identity narratives of the participants. Both the individual and the collectivity are structured and remade in those everyday interactions.

We are situating the study of identity, then, in the socially structured arenas of interaction present in everyday life.[15] Those everyday arenas have two key characteristics we must recognize. First, they are *both structured and constructed*. Our mutual storytelling is both patterned and improvised. Entrenched habits and powerful actors may maintain existing templates for action, reinforcing the reality of social categories that define us. Nevertheless, stories and characters are constantly being revised. An adequate understanding of both personal and communal identity requires attention to the reality of both agency and structure, both revolution and hegemony.

It also requires attention to the *intersectionality* of the situations out of which identities are constructed. Actions arise out of the multiplicity of public narratives available to modern actors. Because no situation is rigidly bounded, multiple public narratives

---

[15] These are Marx's "social relations of production," the occasions for socially constructed actions and ideas that constitute the basis for society (Marx 1844/1964).

are always present, and no institutional field is defined utterly in its own terms. All situations are characterized by a fluidity of boundaries and the presence of story lines gleaned from the multiple contexts in which modern and postmodern persons live. While some visible signals, such as race, class, or gender, may act as powerful narratives across settings, in our own minds and in the actions of others toward us, no single story and no single context is an adequate account of an identity. All identities are intersectional, oriented toward the multiple stories of which they are a part.

LOCATING RELIGIOUS IDENTITIES

If we are to understand religious identities, then, we must begin by attending to episodes of social interaction (whether face-to-face or mediated) that are emplotted in a *religious* narrative – one in which "religious" actors, ideas, institutions, and experiences play a role in the story of who we are and who I am. An interaction takes on a religious character when it directly or indirectly invokes the co-participation of transcendence or Sacred Others, invoking a narrative in which they play a role.[16] Action may directly reference the words, actions, or presence of a Sacred Other, but the religious narrative may also be more implicit. Once experiences of transcendence have been institutionalized in rituals, stories, moral prescriptions, and traditions, those practices are then recognized as religious, whether or not the participants experience them as direct encounters with the Sacred (or even believe Sacred Others to exist). Participating in practices that have been handed down through a religious tradition (lighting Sabbath candles, for instance) invokes thereby religious narratives, whether or not the participants understand their action to directly involve a Sacred Other. When I say I am a Baptist, you recognize that as a religious identity (with more or less accurate expectations about how Baptists behave) simply because of the implied connection to religious institutions and traditions I am invoking. Here the distilled and institutionalized symbols of religious experience evoke religious narratives, whether or not particular individuals believe in or experience them. Likewise, within institutionalized religious contexts, given episodes of social interaction will be governed by accepted strategies of action that may or may not directly involve transcendent ideas or experiences, may or may not invite direct participation by Sacred Actors. Religious narratives – the building blocks of individual and collective religious identities – are activated, then, by settings in which they are implied and by actions into which they have been distilled, as well as by overt experiences and direct references.

In modern, functionally differentiated societies, religious experiences of any sort have been assumed to be confined either to a recognized religious institution or to the privacy of one's own ecstasy. Religious institutions have become the sole social repository of mystery, according to this view, keeping it safely domesticated and out of public view. I would argue, however, that this is a very incomplete inventory of the presence of religion in society.[17] *If we take structured-yet-improvised episodes of social*

---

[16] Berger (1974) argues for a substantive definition of religion that depends on the presence of a socially recognized Sacred Other. This is basic to his disagreement with Luckmann, who uses a functional definition. However, Luckmann (1991) also recognizes the role of "great transcendences," the sorts of extra-empirical actors referenced here.

[17] In what follows I am seeking to expand the modern social territory seen as potentially religious. Berger (1992) makes a similar move in expanding the modern cognitive territory for religion.

interaction as our basis and recognize the necessary intersectionality of all such episodes, there is no a priori reason to assume that religious episodes will only happen in religious institutions or in private seclusion. If it is true that all social contexts contain multiple narratives, that schemas from one social arena can be transposed onto another, then it must be true that under certain conditions religious narratives may appear in settings outside officially religious bounds. No matter what the presumed functional arena, narratives of transcendence might intervene.

Rather than making assumptions of religious absence based on the meta-narrative of secularization, or assuming that religious narratives can only be plausible if they have no competition, our task as social scientists ought to be the examination of ordinary episodes of social interaction to determine the presence or absence of religious narratives and practices (Ammerman 1994). If we do not begin with a conceptual narrative that assumes a radical functional differentiation between religious and nonreligious (or between "public" and "private"), we may be able to ask important questions, then, about the circumstances under which religious narratives of identity come into play. Once having removed our conceptual blinders we can begin to ask more basic questions about the social organization of religious identities, analyzing them as potentially part and parcel of the multiple narratives that shape all of social life. Situations where religious identities seem to clash with other identities (e.g., gay evangelicals) or where identities are being remade in new contexts (e.g., immigrants) remain theoretically interesting, then, not because they are anomalies, but because they are exemplars. They provide models that can inform the study of religious identities of a more common sort.

RELIGIOUS ORGANIZATIONS AND NARRATIVES OF IDENTITY

That conceptual turn should not, however, lead us to neglect explicitly religious organizations, places where the society has indeed institutionalized an expectation that religious interaction will take place. Religious organizations *are* important sites for religious experience and for the constructing of religious identities. They are suppliers of "public narratives," accounts that express the history and purposes of a cultural or institutional entity (Somers 1994: 619). These organizations create widespread social arenas in which religious action can occur, and they supply structured religious biographical narratives – the saved sinner, the pilgrim – within which the actor's own autobiographical narrative can be experienced.

Religious organizations establish such narratives through elaborate sets of roles, myths, rituals, and behavioral prescriptions that encourage participants to perceive Sacred Others as their coparticipants in life. They establish a "grammar" for the stories people tell about the world (Lindbeck 1984), a grammar that extends to the body, as well as to language (Hervieu-Léger 1993). As Warner points out, music, posturing, rhythmic movement, and eating are human experiences that create community, define boundaries and identities, but also sometimes allow the bridging of those boundaries (Warner 1997).[18] Simple melodies and the deep resonance of sound, he argues, create an

---

[18] Although Bartkowski (2000) focuses primarily on discourse, he also has paid attention to the use of space, physical contact, and gesture, and other ways in which Promise Keepers have remade male identities.

experience beyond words and ideas that is inherently communal and identity defining. Similarly, rhythmic common movement is a powerful bonding force that creates community and establishes practices that become part of a member's repertoire of action (see Bellah, Chapter 3, this volume). By supplying and reinforcing habitual gestures and actions, religious organizations orient their participants toward the sacred dimensions of experience.

While religious organizations generate and sustain powerful narratives, the intersectionality of identities and the permeability of modern institutional boundaries guarantee that these narratives will not remain singular or untouched. Even institutional religious participation is not always limited to a single organization or tradition. Nancy Eiesland describes one such multiple-religious family, residents of an Atlanta exurb (Eiesland 2000). While they are members of the local United Methodist Church, the wife attends meetings of a "Grief Relief" support group at the nearby Baptist megachurch. She has siblings who are Presbyterian and Catholic, respectively. Her husband grew up with little attachment to any faith, and neither of them had been part of a Methodist church before joining this one. The religious narratives in which they participate include elements from all these ties at once. It would be a mistake to say that they "are" Methodist. They are constructing religious identities that weave together stories from all these experiences of religious community and faith.

Given that members participate in multiple public narratives, from both religious and secular institutional sources, we can ask which religious institutions supply the most robust and portable plot lines. The narratives supplied by religious organizations may be more or less richly nuanced, allowing them to address wider or narrower ranges of human existence. They may also be more or less able to incorporate counter-narratives, making sense of the very events that would seem to challenge their plausibility.[19] Part of the analyst's job is to assess the degree to which any given religious organization is generating, nurturing, and extending the language, grammar, gestures, and stories that are capable of surviving in the everyday practical competition among modern identity narratives.

Over the last forty years, for instance, liberal Protestant traditions have notoriously neglected their unique narratives, creating a time of "vanishing boundaries" (Hoge, Johnson, and Luidens 1994). Higher education has led to increasing knowledge about multiple religious traditions and to increasing contact (including intermarriage) with persons from those traditions (Wuthnow 1988). The typical period of youthful exploration has extended well into adulthood, and increasing numbers of liberal Protestant youth have simply never returned. Whatever religious accounts they may have learned as children are now buried beneath layers of new experience that may or may not extend those childhood stories. Even their parents are hard-pressed to give an account of their religious identity that extends beyond an attempt to "do unto others as you would have them do unto you" (Ammerman 1997b).

Our recent research found, for instance, that barely one-third of the members of the Episcopal and United Church of Christ congregations we surveyed had grown up as Episcopalians or Congregationalists (or in the other denominations out of which the merged UCC was formed), respectively. Not surprisingly, persons who are

---

[19] Christian Smith (1998) argues that it is precisely this ability to explain its enemies that has rendered American evangelicalism so robust.

not maintaining a lifelong religious tradition are less likely to describe their current denominational identification as important to how they think about themselves. All the church attenders we surveyed – from the Church of God members to the Presbyterians and Lutherans – chose, on average, "spiritual person" and "devout Christian" as more important to them than their particular denominational identity. But for noncradle members the margin was much wider than for cradle members, and "spiritual person" was a more popular self-designation than "devout Christian." Having been exposed to numerous religious narratives, they have developed a less particular way to describe themselves. While "religious seeker" is not the term they most often chose, their journey has nevertheless been incorporated into an autobiographical narrative more "spiritual" than "religious" (Roof 1999a; Wuthnow 1998). In turn, congregations in which "switchers" dominate are less likely to describe themselves as strongly attached to their denomination's traditions. Congregations full of "switchers" often report that they have given up on maintaining the narratives of the denominational tradition, emphasizing a more generic Christian story (Sikkink 1999).

Some switcher congregations, however, have adopted a different narrative strategy. They emphasize practices intended to introduce new adherents to the stories and traditions of the denomination. They teach newcomers their distinctive modes of worship, introduce children and adults to denominational ideas and stories through Christian education programs, and tell tales of the great deeds done through the cooperative efforts of the churches that share their denominational identity. As a result, in these churches the tie between the congregation's identity and that of the denomination remains strong in spite of the mixture of religious stories represented by those in the pews (Ammerman 2000). Theirs is an active process of narrative construction, of bringing individual stories into a new communal context at the same time that a tradition is being passed on and thus modified (Bass 1994). Within some religious organizational contexts, then, religious identities are being constructed in rather intentional ways out of longstanding narratives. Tradition becomes more a verb than a noun (Calhoun 1991), supplying and introducing accounts and characters to new cohorts of religious actors. By telling the stories, practicing the rituals, and celebrating the heroes, these congregations consciously keep a genre of denominational public narratives alive.[20]

It is important to note that the narratives derived from religious tradition are not static. Sacred stories, no less than any others, are both structured and improvised, determined by tradition and created out of human appropriation of that tradition. Indeed, primal religious narratives that involve episodes of transcendence are inherently unstable, disrupting existing scripts.[21] "Sacred Others" are notoriously unpredictable. If we recognize religious identities as both structured and emergent, then one of the most interesting questions we may ask is about the conditions under which religious episodes emerge in surprising ways, redefining the expectations of the actors in them. To use

---

[20] Hervieu-Léger (2000) argues that posttraditional religious institutions must mobilize a combination of emotional belonging and rational appeals to an "ethicocultural heritage." For example, pilgrimages involve the experience of a long journey, the exhilaration of being part of a large throng, recognition by international media, rituals in which potent symbols (like the Pope) are mobilized, exposure to sites in which traditional stories are embedded, and participation in didactic efforts to pass on those stories.

[21] Berger's (1967) discussion of "exstasis" and "dealienation" is a particularly provocative suggestion of the way in which religious experience can threaten established orders.

Weber's (1925/1978) terms, when does "charismatic" authority trump "rational-legal" or "traditional" rules? A variety of students of religious ritual have attempted to assess the ability of ecstatic experiences to alter the narratives participants take with them into the more mundane world.[22] Others have noted that religious experience has its own ordered "flow" (Neitz and Spickard 1990). A deeper understanding of religious identities would surely take up the question of these tensions between everyday order and transcendent chaos. How is that everyday order maintained, and when are glimpses of transcendence allowed to intrude?[23] While religious organizations are primary sites for locating religious narratives, they are by no means passive repositories.

RELIGIOUS NARRATIVES BEYOND RELIGIOUS BOUNDARIES

A given autobiographical narrative may contain plot lines derived from numerous religious organizational contexts and from both structured traditions and emergent experience. But it is important to look for religiously oriented narratives in other social contexts, as well. There are enormous numbers of opportunities for encounters with transcendence and equally pervasive religious plot lines available in contexts as varied as mass media, small study groups, voluntary social service activity, even corporate retreats.[24] Popular music, television programs, and movies often use religious images and stories, both borrowing from existing traditions and inventing new ones. Incorporated into the telling of stories about love and life, writers and artists invoke sacred actors and images.

In addition, myriad religious sources beyond official institutions supply us with signals by which we can recognize religious coparticipants. So-called New Age practices make their way through a loose network of bookstores and conventions, movies and Internet sites. But New Age is only one small stream within the eclectic flow of religious products and experiences present in every corner of late modern culture. Far more pervasive – but also largely outside the bounds of traditional congregations and denominations – are the narratives supplied by conservative Christian preachers, family advisors, clothing manufacturers, event producers, broadcasters, politicians, and missionaries. But, within every religious tradition, entrepreneurs in the cultural marketplace offer prescriptions and exhortation on how to live out a properly religious life.

These extrainstitutional religious producers are often just that – *producers* of goods and services that create a material world that supports and expresses the narratives of those who inhabit it. Whether it is a New Age t-shirt or a Conservative Christian coffee mug, clothing and props are used to signal religious identities to whatever community or potential community may observe them. In mass culture, jewelry and bumper stickers can tell a story that signals the membership of some and the exclusion of others.[25]

---

[22] See, for example, Alexander (1991), Neitz (2000), McRoberts (Chapter 28, this volume), and Nelson (1997) for recent analyses of the way religious experience constructs reality.

[23] Berger's more recent musings on these subjects can be found in *A Far Glory: The Quest for Faith in an Age of Credulity* (1992).

[24] On mass media, see Hoover (1997); on small groups, see Wuthnow (1994); on volunteering, Wuthnow (1991); and on religion in business, Nash (1994).

[25] Maffesoli (1995), Soeffner (1997), and others have paid attention to "punk" bodily displays, but few have noted the way Christian clothing and jewelry functions analogously to create an implied community of evangelicals within public spaces. An exception is McDannell (1995). Read and Bartkowski (2000) pay attention to the role of clothing for Muslim women.

The interactions of those who thereby recognize each other as coparticipants in a story extends and elaborates that same story.

Religious clothing is one example of the ways in which religious narratives and practices cross institutional lines. Privatized religious identities may, of course, be at work in any setting. Individuals for whom religious narratives play a central role may weave religious accounts together with the experiences of everyday life. Recall Neitz's study of converts to charismatic Catholicism (Neitz 1987). As they experience the stresses and strains of everyday work and family life, they "try on" the accounts provided by the charismatic community. Those who finally identify with the prayer group are those for whom everyday autobiographical narratives and public religious narratives begin to be consonant. It is not just that they have learned to experience God's presence in weekly prayer meetings, but that they have learned to see God's hand at work in the most mundane of everyday events, whether or not other participants in those events see the story in a religious light. While their conversion is obviously encouraged and shaped by a religious organization, the stories it engenders cross institutional boundaries – at least by way of the private experiences of participants.

But sometimes religious narratives and practices cross institutional boundaries in much more publicly accessible ways. Both Mary Pattillo-McCoy (1998) and Richard Wood (1999) have offered persuasive accounts of the ways in which religious idioms can enable social movement activity. Prayer, hymn singing, and biblical storytelling can exist alongside economic and political rhetoric in attempts to mobilize citizens for action. In so doing, the activist identity that is constructed is infused with religious meaning. The symbols and rituals of "civil religion" are less oriented toward change, but they, too, offer a transcendent account of collective identity (Bellah 1967). Similarly, businesses of all sorts may tell religious stories about their founding and purpose, encouraging religious identification among their workers and customers (Bromley 1998b).

Even when the organization itself does not claim any sort of religious narrative, units within it may be dominated by coreligionists who establish an environment in which they carry on a religious narrative about who they are and what they are doing. At the church I call Southside Gospel Church, several members recounted their successful efforts to get church friends hired at their workplaces (and/or to convert coworkers), resulting in a "Christian" workplace in spite of the secular structures in which it was lodged (Ammerman 1987). Woven throughout the activity of producing and selling commercial products was a narrative of God's activity in their lives, guiding and reflecting on those transactions, sometimes breaking into their conversations with outsiders, as well. A similar pattern is emerging in our recent research with social service providers. While some aspects of their organizations and interactions are defined by structures of governmental or economic necessity, other signals emerge, as well. Their stories of individual "vocation" and organizational "mission" are full of religious symbols, and their communities of solidarity and support are populated by religious actors.[26]

It is not, however, always possible to bring religious narratives into play. In many settings, official or unofficial rules prohibit any but the most privatized engagement with religious experiences or ideas. Individuals may bring their faith to work, for instance,

---

[26] Ongoing analysis from the "Organizing Religious Work" project, Hartford Institute for Religion Research, Nancy Ammerman, principal investigator.

but it is often prohibited from escaping their own private musings. As with any other identity, we cannot understand the nature of religious identities without asking questions of institutional power and hegemony. We need to know what the existing rules are and what resources various actors bring to the task of identity construction and maintenance.

But religious narratives are also often excluded because they violate the meta-narrative of rationality. Where social institutions depend for their legitimacy on a myth of reason, events and interaction defined as religious are unlikely and unwelcome. Under that meta-narrative of modern progress and Enlightenment, individuals and institutions have learned to separate episodes and chapters in their lives into separate narratives, submerging experiences that seemed to violate the larger narrative's prescriptions. When relationships with a Sacred Other threatened to intrude in contexts not deemed appropriate, those relationships were stuffed back into the closet. Indeed, as this metaphor suggests, the analysis of religious identities could learn a good deal from analysis of the ways in which gay identities have been suppressed (Butler 1990; Rahman 2000). Whether the mechanisms are psychological denial or subcultural seclusion, dominant cultures can suppress identity narratives that violate the basic rules by which power is distributed or orderly meaning maintained. Attention to all the ways in which cultural elites shape the available narratives is a critical project for those who wish to understand the formation of religious identities.

One of those elite sectors, of course, is located in the modern nation-state. Here we find that religious identities have been excluded (except as expressions of individual preference) because bitter experience has taught us the dangers of linking God to temporal powers that tax and kill (Casanova 1994). The particular history of negotiation between "church" and "state" in the Western world has framed a story that casts religion as a dangerous character to be avoided at all cost. Throughout the middle of the twentieth century, courts in the United States struggled with the ways in which religious identities could and could not be recognized in various public settings, ranging from schools and hospitals to zoning decisions and presidential politics. In the midst of the arguments, many in U.S. society came to perceive that all public shared spaces must be kept free of religious events, actors, ideas, and symbols. More recent arguments have begun to question and criticize those assumptions (Carter 1993). It is simply not clear when the power of the state can and should be brought to bear on the ability of persons and organizations to invoke religious narratives and rationales for their public behavior. Nor is it clear when or if public religious behavior violates necessary norms of civility. The meta-narratives of modern civility are being challenged and remade, and these meta-narratives play a powerful role in the ability to bring religious narratives to bear outside religious institutions.

CONSTRUCTING RELIGIOUS IDENTITIES

Every social interaction, then, provides an opportunity for the expression and elaboration of narratives that come from the variety of settings and memberships represented by the participants. The construction of religious identities is a multilayered exercise that takes place in specialized religious settings, but also in every other institutional context. Autobiographical narratives are constructed in a world where episodes of transcendence can occur anywhere; no interaction is utterly secular or utterly sacred. The permeability of boundaries and the intersectionality of identity require more subtle tools of analysis than the categorical checklists of old. It requires tools that will let us move beyond either/or assumptions about religious identity.

We might begin with a not-so-simple catalogue of religious narratives, looking for the chapters and themes that are most common in different social locations. To what extent does a person use various religious stories as organizing frames for the episodes of a life? Do those stories come from and resonate with specific religious traditions? What narratives occur most commonly as markers of membership in various religious collectivities? And how are religious narratives and social action implicated in each other across institutional boundaries? Both the cataloguing and the organizing are basic tasks mandated by the multiple arenas and permeable boundaries of the late modern world.

As with any other identity, however, we cannot understand the nature of religious identities without also asking questions of institutional power and hegemony. We need to know what the existing plot rules are and what resources various actors bring to the scene. Under what conditions, for instance, are glimpses of transcendence allowed to intrude on everyday, ordered, reality? How and where does the meta-narrative of rationality, progress, and Enlightenment, exclude accounts that reference sacred actors and experiences? How is the idea of a secular state being renegotiated to include (perhaps) new public arenas in which religious narratives can be voiced (Casanova 1994; Carter 1993)? Attention to all the ways in which cultural (and religious) elites shape the available narratives is a critical project for those who wish to understand the formation of religious identities. We need attention to the various ways in which mechanisms of culture and state make some narratives more available and permissible than others. Questions of power and domination are central to the construction of religious identities no less than to any other sort.

It is important to note that the structures that shape religious identity formation are not only those imposed by powerful secular authorities. They are also the very religious institutions that claim legitimate authority to determine who may give voice to their narratives. By the stories they tell and the people they valorize, religious institutions highlight some life plans and ignore or denigrate others (Nason-Clark 1997). Mostly these messages are carried by the routine activities and habits of the participants, but overt sacred authorities can step in, as well. Whether silencing a Southern Baptist woman who entertains the possibility of a clergy identity or excluding a Methodist man who constructs a story in which he and a partner live in a religiously blessed union, religious institutions intervene to control the stock of identity narratives available to their participants.

But even religious authority is not unchangeable. All narratives of identity – both individual and collective – are both constructed and constrained. We listen for the public narratives we recognize and tell the personal stories that have shaped us. And in the midst of those intersecting narratives, we continually recreate an autobiography that is "coherent, but constantly revised" (to return to Giddens's [1991] words). While powerful authorities keep existing stories in place, new narratives are constantly emerging. Ongoing stories are disrupted by unexpected events and deliberate innovation. Accounts from one arena are imported into another, as new participants carry plots from place to place. The study of religious identity is not the study of external assaults on an unchanging religious core. Rather, it is the study of religious narratives that are themselves the product of ongoing interaction, both among the diverse human participants in the drama and between them and whatever unpredictable sacred experience they recognize in their midst.

If we posit that at least some individuals and some social settings can and do generate experiences of transcendence, then the study of religious identities should take place at that intersection where individual and social meet the sacred. Given the human propensity for ordering our world, we may expect such intersections to occur in patterned and institutionalized ways. But given the equal human propensity for imagination, invention, and disruption, we can also expect both internalized and externally structured religious narrative patterns to shift over time. The transcendent referent that makes an identity narrative a religious one is neither a fixed set of institutional symbols nor an utterly chaotic experience in which selves and situations are redefined by divine fiat. It is at once both structured and emergent.

Individuals improvise religious narratives out of past experience and interaction, the other times and places in which sacred actors and institutions have had a role. Their culture and its institutions create situations that are more or less open to religious action. From both the existing themes of an individual autobiography and the available themes in the situation, episodes emerge and are "emplotted." Describing religious identities is not a matter of asking a checklist of categorical questions, but a matter of analyzing a dynamic process, the boundaries of which cannot be assumed to fall neatly within private or personal domains. Intersectionality means that no situation or identity is ever utterly devoid of multiple narratives, both public and private, sacred and secular. People can signal the presence of religious ideas, symbols, story lines, and sacred coparticipants within a wide range of social contexts, both to themselves and to others, invoking religious narratives of widely varying scope and robustness. Wherever those religious signals are being generated and received, new narratives are being created and old ones retold. Understanding religious identities will require that we listen for stories in all their dynamic complexity, situating them in the multiple relational and institutional contexts in which contemporary people live their lives.

CHAPTER SEVENTEEN

Religion and the New Immigrants

Helen Rose Ebaugh

Changes in U.S. immigration laws in the past four decades have had far-reaching consequences for American religion. Even though the majority of the new immigrants are Christian (Warner and Wittner 1998; Ebaugh and Chafetz 2000b), the practices, symbols, languages, sounds, and smells that accompany the ethnically and racially diverse forms of practicing Christianity, brought by immigrants from Latin America, the Caribbean, the Philippines, China, Vietnam, India, Africa, and elsewhere challenge the various European practices of Christianity that have predominated in the United States since its founding. As Maffy-Kipp (1997) argues, rather than immigrants "de-Christianizing" religion in America, they have, in fact, "de-Europeanized" American Christianity. In addition, the new immigrants have brought religious traditions, such as Buddhism, Hinduism, Islam, Zoroastrianism, Sikhism, Vodou, and Rastafarianism, that were unfamiliar to Americans prior to the mid-1960s. Today many American neighborhoods are dotted with temples, mosques, shrines, storefront churches, Christian churches with foreign names, guadwaras, and botannicas.

THE HISTORICAL CONTEXT

The "new immigrants" refer to those who entered the United States after the passage of the Hart-Cellar Immigration Act of 1965. The abolition of the country-of-origin quotas established in 1924, and the dramatic increase in immigration visas provided to people from Asia and Latin America, in particular, significantly altered the racial and ethnic backgrounds of immigrants. For example, the number of Asian immigrants living in the United States rose from about 150,000 in the 1950s to more than 2.7 million in the 1980s, while the number of European immigrants fell by more than one-third. Likewise, during the 1950s, the six hundred thousand immigrants who came from Latin America and the Caribbean accounted for one in four immigrants, while three decades later, the 3.5 million immigrants who arrived from these areas accounted for 47 percent of all admissions (Miller and Miller 1996). Of the five million immigrants who arrived between 1985 and 1990, only 13 percent were born in Europe, Canada, Australia, or New Zealand, while 26 percent came from Mexico, 31 percent from Asia, and 22 percent from other parts of the Americas (Chiswick and Sullivan 1995: 216–17). In addition, per country limitations on legal flows have increased the national diversity of the immigrant population. In 1960, for example, the top ten countries accounted for 65 percent of the legal immigrant flow, but only 52 percent in 1990, and the number of countries with at least one hundred thousand foreign-born residents in the United States increased from twenty in 1970 to forty-one in 1990 (Fix and Passel 1994).

Along with increased diversity in national origins, the new immigrants are creating greater religious diversity in the United States as they transplant their home country religions into their new neighborhoods. As a result, the religious landscape of the United States is changing (Warner 1993; Eck 1997). Not only are ethnic churches, temples, and mosques springing up around the country, but many established congregations are struggling to incorporate these new ethnic groups into their memberships. As Ammerman describes in *Congregation and Community* (1997a), ethnic changes in a neighborhood often mean changes in the composition of local churches, a shift that is frequently threatening to established congregants who may have built and nurtured the church for decades.

While we know much about the new immigrants in terms of their countries of origin, socioeconomic backgrounds, labor force participation, educational achievements, family patterns, reasons for migration and the role of social networks in their patterns of settlement, we know relatively little about their religious patterns. Immigration scholars have ignored religion as a factor both in the migration process and in their incorporation into American society. A number of reasons have been posited for this lack of attention. Most important, as Warner (1998) has pointed out, immigration researchers rely primarily on data gathered by governmental agencies (e.g., Bureau of the Census, the Immigration and Naturalization Service [INS], the Bureau of Labor Statistics, and boards of education), which are restricted from asking questions about religion. Their other source of data is surveys such as those conducted by the National Opinion Research Center, which employ random samples of the U.S. population that do not contain sufficient respondents from small subpopulations, such as Muslims, Jews, or Buddhists, to effectively analyze. Kivisto (1992) also has suggested that it is frequently insiders who study their own immigrant groups and that many groups lack a critical mass of such scholars who are interested in religion. A third explanation is the antireligion bias that exists in much social science literature, based on the assumption that religion deals with value-laden issues that are not amenable to empirical analysis. In addition, many social scientists have uncritically accepted secularization theory, which argues that religion is becoming increasingly unimportant in modern industrial societies. For whatever reason, religion is missing in the work of immigration scholars, as evidenced in the fact that four recent special issues of social scientific journals on immigration (*International Migration Review*, Vol. 31, Winter, 1997; *Sociological Perspectives*, Vol. 40, No. 3, 1997; *American Behavioral Scientist*, Vol. 42, January 1999; and *Racial and Ethnic Studies*, Vol. 20, January 1999) include no article on religion. Likewise, the recent *Handbook of International Migration* (Hirschman et al. 1999) has no index entry on religion.

Until the mid-1990s, scholars in the field of religion had also, by and large, neglected the study of new immigrants. Christiano's (1991) analysis, as well as that of Kivisto (1992), bemoaned the lack of research concerning religion and the new immigrants. The bulk of the social scientific research on religion in the latter decades of the twentieth century was devoted to issues of denominationalism, the rise of conservative Protestantism, new religious movements and the disenfranchisement of disadvantaged groups such as women, African Americans, and Hispanics. Again, the relative lack of immigrant scholars fluent in both the language and culture of their respective groups no doubt limited access and interest in studying immigrant religion. The decline of denominationalism and the renewed interest in congregational studies in the decade of the 1990s, as evidenced in the two-volume *American Congregations* book (Wind and Lewis 1994) and Ammerman's (1997a) *Congregation and Community,* focused attention on the local level of congregational life and pinpointed the demographic changes that were occurring within congregations. With these publications, it became evident that immigrants were beginning to change American congregationalism.

In addition to thousands of informal places of worship, including house churches, scriptural study groups, paraliturgical groups, domestic altars, and neighborhood festivals, immigrants have established many of their own formal places of worship. The task of obtaining an accurate count of these religious institutions and the immigrants who are members is almost impossible due to a number of issues that Numrich (2000) elaborates. Many estimates come from local-level ethnic communities whose self-interest is served by robust counts. In addition, accounting methods differ greatly, from registered membership in some institutions to ascribed status in an ethnoreligious population in others. Census and INS data on ancestry, country of origin, and language is often used to extrapolate estimates of religious identification, an exercise fraught with questionable assumptions. Data gathered from various polls and surveys, such as the General Social Survey (GSS) or the National Survey of Religious Identification (NSRI) (Kosmin and Lachman 1993), are based on random samples that include insufficient numbers of small subpopulations to make accurate generalizations. The best estimates to date of immigrant congregations are those generated by Warner (1998): (a) over thirty-five hundred Catholic parishes where Mass is celebrated in Spanish, and seven thousand Hispanic/Latino congregations, most Pentecostal or Evangelical, and many others nondenominational; (b) in 1988, the last count available, 2,018 Korean-American churches; (c) and in 1994 approximately seven hundred Chinese Protestant churches; (d) in the early 1990s, between one thousand and twelve hundred mosques and Islamic centers; (e) fifteen hundred to two thousand Buddhist temples and meditation centers; and (f) over four hundred Hindu temples.

While variations exist in the organizational structures in the religious institutions created by new immigrants, Warner (1994) used "congregation" as an umbrella term to indicate "local, face-to-face religious assemblies." In our work, we (Ebaugh and Chafetz 2000b) also use congregation in this sense, rather than its traditional Protestant reference to a type of church polity.

What, if anything, is really "new" about the most recent wave of immigration to the United States? This question is currently receiving the attention of, and the focus of debate among, many who study post-1965 immigration (Glick-Schiller 1999; Perlmann and Waldinger 1999; Levitt 2000). As we indicate in the final chapter of our book (Ebaugh and Chafetz 2000b), we found far greater similarities than differences across time in the types of congregations that immigrants establish, as well as the roles that religious institutions play in their lives. Nineteenth-century immigrants, like those today, built their places of worship on a congregational model, emphasizing voluntary membership, lay initiative and participation in administrative functions, and the expansion of worship sites to encompass community centers. The accounts of the functions served by nineteenth-century ethnic churches (e.g., Thomas and Znaniecki

1918; Dolan 1975; Green 1975; Tomasi 1975; Mohl and Betten 1981; Dolan 1985; Alexander 1987; Papaioannou 1994; Sarna and Goldman 1994) read very much like those discussed in case studies of contemporary ethnic congregations (Kim 1981; Orsi 1985; Kwon et al. 1997; Warner and Wittner 1998; Ebaugh and Chafetz 2000b). Then, as now, ethnic places of worship served the dual purpose of reproducing the group's cultural and religious heritage while assisting immigrants in the process of adapting to a new society. Even lines of cleavage and conflict within congregations are very similar. Language debates were as fierce in earlier periods as they are in congregations today (Bodnar 1985; Dolan 1985; Ebaugh and Chafetz 2000b). The introduction of English as a response to the demands of youth born and raised in this country is common across religions, ethnic groups and time periods.

Multiethnic congregations were as common and conflict ridden in earlier immigrant communities as they are today. Nineteenth-century immigrants did not stay forever in their original ethnic enclaves; as their socioeconomic status improved, they moved to economically better neighborhoods, leaving their old neighborhoods and churches for a succession of new, less privileged groups. In that interim period of residential succession there were often several ethnic groups sharing congregations, a situation that frequently raised contentious issues regarding language, style of worship, patron saints, and social customs. Also, like today, conflicts arose among groups that shared the same religion but came from different nations, such as German and Polish Catholics (Shaw 1994) and Dutch and German Jews (Sarna and Goldman 1994). Issues of accommodation and contention closely resemble those faced by Taiwanese, Hong Kong, and mainland Chinese members of the same Buddhist temple (Yang 2000b) or Hispanic, Vietnamese, and Nigerian Catholics who attend the same parish church (Sullivan 2000b).

Contemporary immigrants are entering a society that is more accepting of ethnic pluralism, unlike earlier waves that confronted demands that they "Americanize" (Alba and Nee 1997). They are also entering a different labor market than that of the nineteenth century (Levitt 2000) and are better able to remain part of transnational communities, expedited by the expansion of modern technologies of communication and transportation (Portes 1996; Glick-Schiller 1999). The multiculturalism of the post–civil rights era that new immigrants enter embraces both a wider array of types of Protestant churches and numerous non-Christian religions virtually unknown in the United States during the earlier immigrant waves. Despite this organizational diversity, however, we see repeated in the case studies of contemporary immigrant religious groups many of the same patterns and issues that characterized the "old" immigrant churches. Religion appears to be persistent in its centrality in the lives of immigrants, as a means to cope with the challenges of relocation, a way to reproduce and pass on culture, a focus for ethnic community and a way to provide formal, and especially, informal assistance in the settlement process.

RECENT RESEARCH ON RELIGION AND THE NEW IMMIGRANTS

Most of the research on religion and the new immigrants, until very recently, consisted of case studies, either of one or a few immigrant religious institutions or of one specific ethnic group. Among the case studies of congregations are Numrich's (1996) study of two Theraveda Buddhist temples, Waugh's (1994) description of a

Muslim congregation in Canada, and Yang's (1999) analysis of several Chinese Christian churches in Washington, DC. Even more numerous are studies of religious institutions among one specific ethnic or nationality group. These include Mullins's (1987) study of Japanese Buddhists in Canada; Williams's (1988) description of the religions of Indians and Pakistanis; Fenton's (1988) research on Asian Indian religious traditions in the United States; Denny's (1987), as well as Haddad and Lummis's (1987), analysis of Islam in the United States; Diaz-Stevens's (1993a) description of Puerto Rican Catholicism in New York; Kashima (1977), Lin (1996) and Fields's (1992) work on Buddhism in America; Orsi's (1985) study of Italians and Haitians in Harlem; and the numerous studies of the Korean Christian church in America (I. Kim 1981; Hurh and Kim 1984; Shin and Park 1988; Min 1992; Kwon 1997; Chai 1998; Chong 1998).

In the mid-1990s, a number of research projects on religion and the new immigrants were initiated, fueled by grants from the Lilly Endowment, the Pew Charitable Trusts, and the newly established initiative in religion by the Ford Foundation. The first of these was Warner's NEICP (New Ethnic and Immigration Congregations Project) study that funded twelve doctoral and postdoctoral fellows to study immigrant religious communities across the United States. In addition to providing rich ethnographies on Christian, Hindu, Jewish, Rastafari, and mixed Vodou-Catholic congregations, the NEICP experience was a training ground for newly minted scholars interested in the study of religion among new immigrants. Individual books and articles on the various immigrant religious communities began to filter into the sociology of religion literature and to fill the lacunae that had earlier been identified.

Building on Warner's work, in 1996 I initiated the RENIR (Religion, Ethnicity, New Immigrants Research) project in Houston, Texas. Rather than a series of ethnographies, my research design was a comparative one in which I focused on thirteen religious congregations within the same city. These congregations included two Roman Catholic churches (one overwhelmingly Mexican, the other composed of seven formally organized nationality groups); a Greek Orthodox church; a Hindu temple; a Muslim mosque that was mostly Indo-Pakistani in membership; a Zoroastrian Center, most of whose members also came from India and Pakistan; two Buddhist temples (one Chinese and one Vietnamese); and five Protestant churches (one whose members represent forty-eight nationalities, one dominated by Argentines, one mostly Mexican, one totally Korean, and one totally Chinese). By conducting focus groups in the immigrant community in Houston, we were able to develop research questions that were grounded in the experiences of those we were to study. Focus group members also helped us to identify immigrant congregations to study. We spent three to six months in each congregation, conducting observations of worship services and other activities that take place in the congregational setting. We also conducted interviews with clerics, lay leaders, immigrants, nonimmigrants and youth in each setting, utilizing the same observation protocols and interview schedules, thereby generating comparable data (see Ebaugh and Chafetz 2000b for a comprehensive description of the findings of this study).

In 1997, the Pew Charitable Trusts approved a $5 million new initiative, entitled "The Gateway Cities Projects," whose purpose is to facilitate the examination of the role of religion in the current immigrant experience in the United States and how it relates to the incorporation of immigrants into American society. Six gateway cities (New York, Washington, DC, Chicago, Los Angeles, San Francisco, and Miami), the largest immigrant points-of-entry cities in the United States, were selected, in addition to the earlier funding for the study in Houston.

There is no doubt that Religion and the New Immigrants became a "hot topic" for research during the 1990s (there were some twenty-five papers at the 2000 Society for the Scientific Study of Religion meetings in Houston, Texas) and that the interest will continue, in part stimulated by the cohort of young scholars and graduate students who have participated and are participating in the research projects focused on the topic. Monographs and professional papers from the Gateway Cities Projects will, no doubt, appear throughout the first decade of the new millennium, thus sustaining interest in the area.

THEMES AND ISSUES

From the increasing body of research published in the 1990s, a number of central issues arose, along with tentative generalizations concerning: (a) the central role religious institutions play in the reproduction of ethnic identity; (b) the role of religion as an agent in the incorporation of immigrants into American society; (c) congregationalism as the primary form of organization; (d) conflict and segregation within multiethnic congregations; (e) the relationship between the second generation and immigrant religious institutions; (f) the role and status of immigrant women as impacted by their religious congregations; and (g) transnational religious ties between immigrants in the United States and their home communities.

The Reproduction of Ethnic Identity

Religious institutions provide social and physical space and social networks that help the immigrants reproduce and maintain their values, traditions, and customs in the midst of an often alienating and strange American society. Religion is intricately interwoven with cultural values and practices so that it becomes a way of reproducing many aspects of immigrants' native cultures for themselves and their children. Collective memory and symbolic rituals are major strategies for maintaining and passing on cultural values, norms, and practices (Cook 2000; Hervieu-Léger 2000), and it is within ethnic congregations that symbolic representations are often most evident.

In reflecting on the immigrants who came to America in earlier waves, Will Herberg (1960) argued that immigrants were expected to give up virtually everything they brought with them (e.g., language, nationality, manner of life) except their religion. In fact, religious identity often replaced ethnic identity and became more important to them in their new country than it was in their homeland. Similar patterns exist for the new immigrants, who frequently comment that they are more "religious" in the United States than they were prior to immigration (Conzen 1991; Pozzetta 1991; Abusharaf 1998; Kurien 1998; Warner 1998; Badr 2000). In addition to immigration itself being a "theologizing" experience (T. Smith 1978), being part of a minority religion in an overwhelmingly Christian country often makes immigrants more conscious of their religious identity and practices (Yang and Ebaugh 2001).

As well as using native languages, one major way that congregations reproduce ethnicity is by physically reproducing aspects of home-country religious structures, such as temples, pagodas, golden domes, statues, ikons, steeples, and the use of native construction materials. Many immigrant groups, such as Chinese, Vietnamese, and

Laotian Buddhists, Indian Hindus, and Greek Orthodox, go to great effort and expense to import building materials, architects, and artisans to recreate physical structures from the home country. For example, members of a South Indian Hindu temple brought dozens of artisans to Houston over several years to carve the images that grace the white stone pillars in the temple. During the dedication ceremony, twelve priests were brought from India to bless the temple in traditional Hindu ceremonies (Jacob and Thakur 2000). Likewise, a Vietnamese Buddhist center in Houston imported statues of buddhasatvas, as well as tiles for the temple's roof, to create a sense of "home away from home" for temple members (Huynh 2000). When these visual images are combined with the sound of native vernaculars, home-country musical instruments and songs, the smell of incense and native foods, the feel of oils and sacred objects, most immigrant congregations flood the senses with physical reminders of the native lands from which their members came.

By incorporating ethnic practices and holidays into formal religious ceremonies, immigrant congregations help their members feel more "at home" in a strange land. The familiar ancestral altars and ash houses, as well as traditional Buddhist customs that accompany the forty-nine days of mourning for a deceased person, remind members of both their religious and ethnic roots. Holidays such as the Chinese New Year and 'Id al-Fitr, the Islamic feast of fast-breaking during Ramadan, are widely celebrated in temples, churches, and mosques across the country and create a sense of ethnic pride within many immigrant communities. The diverse images of the Virgin Mary among Hispanic immigrants stem from their home country images and devotions (Díaz-Stevens 1993a; Flores 1994; Tweed 1997; Díaz-Stevens and Stevens-Arroyo 1998; Wellmeier 1998; Sullivan 2000b).

Furthermore, most immigrant congregations sponsor secular activities, such as meals, festivals, holiday celebrations, fundraisers, language classes, citizenship classes, and youth activities. One way in which immigrant religious institutions often differ from those in the home country is that they develop community centers, along with places of worship, social spaces, and activities whose function it is to maintain social ties among members and the passing on of both religious and ethnic culture to the next generation (Ebaugh and Chafetz 2000c).

The serving of ethnic food in immigrant congregations is another way in which members celebrate and pass on their culture. Communal eating is a regular and frequent feature of congregational life, enjoyed at the central worship site, at homes after fellowship, cell, or religious study meetings, and as part of domestic religious celebrations (Flores 1994; León 1998; McGuire and Spickard 1998; Ebaugh and Chafetz 2000b). In many cases, women provide most, if not all, of the work of securing supplies, preparing and cooking the food, and then serving it. The preparation of the traditional food often provides women with the opportunity to instruct their daughters in ethnic customs (Orsi 1985; Ebaugh and Chafetz 1999).

Alongside community-based religious practices, many immigrant religions center a substantial part of their religious observances on domestic rituals practiced at home shrines or altars. In addition to daily prayers said at these sacred domestic spaces, in many instances life cycle events, such as infant blessings, engagements, weddings, and remembrances of the dead, are enacted there (Brown 1991; Wellmeier 1998; Huynh 2000; Rustomji 2000). These domestic religious practices function to reproduce traditional culture for family members.

Religion and the Incorporation of Immigrants into U.S. Society

Immigrants' congregations also help their adaptation to American society by providing much of the information and services required in the course of settlement in a new
country. While some churches, in particular Catholic and mainline Protestant ones,
offer an array of formal social services, such as food pantries, clothes closets, emergency financial assistance, job hotlines, immigration status assistance, and ESL, GED,
and citizenship classes, the use of informal networks among congregational members
is far more common (Ebaugh and Pipes 2001). Religious institutions provide places
where immigrants meet one another, discuss their needs, and share information about
resources that are available in the community.

There are two major reasons that most immigrant congregations offer few formal
social services. First, most members of many immigrant groups arrive in the United
States with high levels of education and jobs already lined up and therefore have little
need for such services or are capable of purchasing any that might be required. Second,
both religious leaders and most members of several religions (e.g., Hindu, Buddhist)
define formal social service delivery as outside the scope of religious institutions. Many
Asian groups, in particular, look to family, kin, and close friends for material assistance
and are embarrassed to have to resort to outside agencies, including religious institutions. Many immigrant populations largely take care of their own members, turning
infrequently to religiously based service providers outside of the informal networks that
exist within their immigrant congregations (Ebaugh and Chafetz 2000b; Ebaugh and
Pipes 2001).

While few immigrant congregations have formal structures to assist their members,
immigrants are being assisted by larger formal bodies such as interfaith coalitions. These
groups consist of local congregations, comprised mostly of native-born members, that
join together to provide social services for the needy and are part of the faith-based
organizations that are now eligible for "charitable choice" monies provided by the
Ashcroft provision of the Welfare Reform Act of 1996 (Cnaan 1997; Cnaan 1999; Ebaugh
and Pipes 2001). These coalitions are financed primarily by member congregations,
usually mainline Protestant ones, and by resale shops that are run by volunteers from
participating congregations.

By providing the social space for immigrants to gather and engage in shared religious
services, immigrant congregations facilitate the informal networks that constitute the
major pathway to learning about and accessing services that are essential in their settlement. Frequently, when new immigrants arrive in the United States they turn first to
an ethnic congregation where they are assured they will encounter fellow-countrymen
and women who will understand not only their native language but the challenges
they face as newcomers in a strange and foreign country (Kwon 1997; George 1998;
Wellmeier 1998).

Congregationalism as a Form of Organization

Immigrant congregations often differ substantially from the ways in which they were
structured and functioned in their homelands. These differences occur as a response
to the adaptations required in the context of a new land and social environment. In
particular, immigrant religious institutions tend to become more congregational in the

United States, following the model of the majority Protestant/Catholic faiths (Warner 1994, 1998). The congregational model has the following characteristics: (a) a formal list or roster of members; (b) who elect a local governing body, composed of lay members, that makes policy for and administers the affairs of the institution; (c) committees/ministries composed of lay members who conduct the work of the institution; (d) clergy who are selected by the local organization; and (e) a financial structure whereby most of its operating funds are raised from its own local members (Ebaugh and Chafetz 2000c). Congregationalism was the primary organizational form established by earlier eighteenth- and nineteenth-century immigrants. Even though some of the earlier immigrant groups came from countries that were dominated by state religions (e.g., Italy, England, Russia) and/or powerful clergy (e.g., Ireland), many of these groups became more lay dominated and congregational as they adjusted to the American religious landscape. In fact, some historians (Dolan 1985; Jones 1992; Wyman 1993) describe the displeasure felt by religious leaders in home countries regarding the "Americanization" (i.e., lack of respect for the authority of the official clergy) of immigrant churches in the United States.

Although the congregationalism of American churches was often more pronounced than those in Europe, the model was not totally foreign to most immigrant groups who were at least somewhat familiar with characteristics such as membership rosters, lay committees, and lay involvement with the selection of clergy. For many of today's immigrants, especially non-Christians, congregationalism represents a new and unfamiliar way of organizing a religious institution. Most Asian Buddhists, for example, were not used to maintaining lists of members, having strong lay control of temple matters or operating on the basis of lay committees. The fact that most immigrant groups tend to establish congregational structures in this country is a testimony to their adoption of the established congregational model (Numrich 1996; Kurien 1998; Zhou and Bankston III 1998; Ebaugh and Chafetz 2000c).

Along with structures for worship and administering the religious institution, immigrant congregations tend to expand their facilities to include community centers where they can socialize and provide education, recreation, and other activities for themselves and their children. Such centers are usually unnecessary in home countries, where the religion may be the majority one, in some cases state supported. In the United States, however, where they are often minority religions (Yang and Ebaugh 2001), community centers provide space for socializing among fellow ethnics, reinforcing religioethnic identity, and a place where needed secular services such as medical and legal help, information, GED and citizenship classes, and emergency services are provided.

Conflict and Segregation within Multiethnic Congregations

Whereas many immigrants join ethnic congregations in the United States, others become members of existing congregations that have members from more than one immigrant/ethnic group. Multiethnic congregations face a number of challenges in their efforts to create unity, and to discourage discord, among the ethnic/nationality groups. Among the major challenges that they face are issues related to: Language usage, incorporation of ethnic customs, and participation in the administration of congregational affairs.

Language usage in immigrant congregations is often a highly contested issue and one that poses dilemmas for the clerical and lay leaders responsible for congregational policy (Ebaugh and Chafetz 2000a). On the one hand, the use of an old-country language enhances a sense of commitment and comfort for immigrants while, on the other hand, differences in native language, and in dialects of the same language, often constitute the bases for segregation among congregational members and, not infrequently, for intergenerational strains and tensions. A major issue revolves around the language used in worship services. While some religious traditions, such as the Greek Orthodox, Zoroastrians, Hindus, and Muslims, require that worship services be conducted in a holy language, others, such as Christian churches and many Buddhist temples, allow for vernacular languages. Which native language is to be used, however, when multiple ethnic groups are involved? The use of native language at different worship services often creates "parallel congregations" (Numrich 1996) rather than one congregation. Even in instances where English is the language used for formal worship services, there is a strong tendency for native language speakers to self-segregate at social and other informal occasions held at the religious site.

The incorporation of ethnic customs in the formal and informal activities of a congregation is another strategy to be broadly inclusive and to make immigrants feel comfortable in the religious setting. For example, the display of icons, statues, or pictures of patron saints or religious figures from home countries creates a sense of ethnic identity and comfort for immigrants, as does the use of native music, food, and dress. However, emphasis on ethnic differences in multiethnic congregations also has the potential for ethnic segregation and the alienation of members who are uncomfortable with such customs.

Ethnic representation among clerical leaders, on administrative boards, and in the lay leadership who direct the major ministries of the congregation is also a major challenge, especially in congregations that have existed and been run by Anglos for a long time. The acceptance of "new immigrants" into these positions indicates that these newcomers are not just guests who benefit from being in the congregation but are part of the decision makers who are creating the future of the congregation, a fact that is often difficult to accept on the part of old-timers who may have built and sustained the congregation for generations.

The Second Generation

Because religious and ethnic identities are often closely intertwined, immigrants look to religious institutions as the place to reinforce and pass on the native language and ethnic values, traditions, and customs to the next generation. The symbols, stories, rituals, and native language that are part of immigrant religions often provide the context within which parents hope that their native culture will become that of their children. While many parents are grateful for the opportunities provided in this country for their offspring to achieve educationally and occupationally, they also worry about the influence of what they define as "amoral" American society on them (Kurien 1998; Sullivan 1998). They hope that their children will be protected against these influences by associating with fellow ethnics in religious settings.

Beyond childhood and the ethnoreligious classes in which youngsters are involved in their religious institutions, teenagers and young adults are infrequently present in most immigrant congregations, with the exception of evangelical Christian churches that tend to attract young people (e.g., Chinese Christian [Yang 2000a]; Korean Christian [Chai 1998]; and evangelical Hispanic churches [León 1998; Sullivan 2000a]). In fact, the issue of the second generation and its lack of interest in participating in ethnic congregations is one of the major concerns in most congregations. The future of these religious institutions rests on the participation and involvement of the next generation in congregational affairs, yet the youth are not present in large numbers.

There are four major problems that second generation members confront within their parents' congregations: (a) many feel estranged by the ethnic ambiance of the immigrant congregation, including the heavy use of an old-country language; (b) in some cases, the young people adopt Americanized attire and/or demeanor that the older generation defines as improper and often comment on negatively; (c) sometimes the religious services themselves are defined by youth as too rigid and old-fashioned, although in most congregations, English services designed for the second-generation incorporate aspects of American youth culture such as rock music, and are less formal than the services their parents attend; and (d) in some religious institutions, adult second-generation members are denied meaningful participation in congregational affairs and access to authority roles to which they think they are entitled. These issues cut across case studies of different religions and ethnicities and are widespread (Chai 1998; George 1998; León 1998; Ebaugh and Chafetz 2000b).

The participation of second-generation youth in evangelical, often nondenominational ethnic Christian churches provides an interesting exception that gives clues regarding what is meaningful and attractive to them. First, these churches emphasize the provision of special youth worship services in English, with a youth pastor who can relate to that age group, and that incorporate modern versions of hymns and musical instruments (Mullins 1987; Goette 1993; Kwon 1997; Chong 1998). Second, they emphasize social and group activities for young people in which they can interact on an informal basis, such as youth retreats, cell groups based on age, community projects, socials, and so on (George 1998; Yang 2000a). Third, youth play central roles in planning, executing, and evaluating these activities so that they, in fact, feel that they "own" them and are responsible for them (Chai 1998).

The future of immigrant congregations rests substantially on whether they can maintain the interest and commitment of the second generation. Since the majority of second-generation members among the new immigrants are only now in college or beginning their adult lives, there is little longitudinal research on their religious patterns. Large-scale studies of the second generation, including variations in degree of religious involvement, such as the current one being conducted by Mollenkopf, Kasinitz, and Waters in New York, will hopefully provide the kinds of data needed to understand the future of religion among immigrant youth.

The Role/Status of Women in Immigrant Religious Institutions

While women play a central role in reproducing cultural traditions in immigrant religious institutions, they are also beginning to assume more leadership roles and greater "voice" within them than is often the case in counterpart institutions in their homelands. Their role in reproducing traditional culture, a conservative role that women frequently play in many cultures, occurs in three basic ways: (a) by preparing and serving ethnic foods for social events both at the central religious site and at home for religiously connected practices (Orsi 1985; Flores 1994; León 1998; Ebaugh and Chafetz 1999); (b) as central actors in domestic religious practices (Orsi 1985; Brown 1991; Jacobs 1996; Orsi 1996; Peña and Frehill 1998); and (c) as teachers of children in ethnoreligious classes (e.g., Sunday school; J. H. Kim 1996; A. R. Kim 1996; Hepner 1998; Ebaugh and Chafetz 1999).

In addition, in many cases, women are organized into gender-segregated women's groups or ministries that serve as mutual support groups (Abusharaf 1998; Ebaugh and Chafetz 1999). These groups are especially helpful for newly arrived immigrant women, many of whom do not speak English and are not working outside the home. In addition to assisting these women adjust to American society (e.g., find schools for their children, locate ethnic stores, learn to use public transportation), over time some often create consciousness-raising among the women as they share common experiences, especially regarding their role within their religious institutions.

As immigrant religious institutions become more congregational in structure and establish community centers, the number and scope of lay roles expand to the point where women's active participation in formal roles is needed, whether or not such participation is permitted in the old country (Ebaugh and Chafetz 1999). Simultaneously, immigrant women and especially their daughters are increasingly becoming well educated and employed outside the home, providing them with the skills and self confidence required for performing leadership roles. One significant factor in the pace at which women enter such roles is men's desires to play them. To the extent that immigrant men suffer downward mobility in the process of immigration, such as is frequently the case with Koreans (Min 1992; Kwon et al. 1997) and sometimes Indians (George 1998), they try to recoup their sense of worth by filling prestigious congregational roles. Traditional cultural norms provide them preferential access to such roles, and women are left with whatever roles men cannot fill. Whether the daughters and granddaughters of immigrants will challenge this situation remains to be seen.

Transnational Religious Ties

Within the past decade there has been increasing awareness of the fact that immigrants often remain part of transnational communities in so far as they "forge and sustain multi-stranded social relations that link together their societies of origin and settlement" (Basch et al. 1994: 7). These economic, political and social ties are sufficiently enough widespread and sustained to lead Glick-Schiller (1999) to propose transnationalism as a new paradigm for the study of migration across the borders of nation-states and to argue for the existence of transnational communities (Nagengast and Kearney 1990; Rouse 1992; Smith 1994; Goldring 1996; Portes 1996; Levitt 1998).

The existence of religious ties between immigrants in the United States and both individuals and religious institutions in their home countries is just beginning to be documented (Levitt 1998, 2000; Popkin 1999; Ebaugh and Chafetz 2000b). As was the more general case for research on the role of religion among the new immigrants, the study of the role of religious ties in forging transnational communities has also lagged behind the documentation of political, economic, cultural, and social ties. Levitt (1998) traces local level religious ties between Catholic Dominicans in Boston and their home community of Miraflores, in the Dominican Republic. In her current research, she is expanding the study of transnational religious communities to other immigrant groups in Boston (e.g., Irish, Brazilians, Gujarati Indians). For the past two years, I have been conducting research on religion and transnational ties among Mexican, Argentine, Chinese, Vietnamese, and Guatemalans in Houston and their home communities, funded by The Pew Charitable Trusts. Several of the Gateway Projects, described earlier, also have transnational components.

While the technological advances of e-mail, fax, rapid telephone exchanges, videos, and modern modes of travel have facilitated the rapidity and ease of maintaining transnational ties, it is important to keep in mind that earlier, nineteenth-century immigrants were also transmigrants. As a number of scholars have documented (Bodnar 1985; Alexander 1987; Morawska 1989; Chan 1990; Wyman 1993; Gutierrez 1997; Glick-Schiller 1999), seasonal migrants who came to the United States to work were a major source of capital investment on their return. Steamships, telegraph, and postal services made it possible to circulate between two societies (Rouse 1992; Glick-Schiller 1999). Remittances sent by immigrants in the United States to home communities were frequently a major source of income for both families and local churches that depended on the help of immigrants to survive (Bodnar 1985; Dolan 1985; Wyman 1993). Likewise, there were numerous organizational ties between churches in the United States and in sending communities (Wyman 1993). It is important, therefore, in analyses of transnational religious communities not to assume that the phenomenon is new. Rather, the challenge is to specify the nature of the pathways that current transnational ties take and their impact on religious institutions in both sending and receiving countries.

FUTURE RESEARCH

The recently increasing number of studies that focus on religion and the new immigrants has established the fact that religious institutions are central in the lives of immigrants. In addition, these studies have indicated the roles that religion and religious institutions play in helping immigrants to maintain their ethnoreligious identity while at the same time adapting to American society. Simultaneously, research has focused on challenges which established religious institutions face in incorporating immigrants, many of them becoming multiethnic in the process. While religion is beginning to take its place in the broader analysis of immigration, there are a number of directions on which I think future research needs to focus.

As indicated earlier, research on new immigrants that was done prior to the 1990s focused primarily on case studies of religion in specific ethnic or religious groups. These studies were valuable in delineating the centrality of religion in the lives of these immigrant communities and describing the functions that religion served in the settlement processes. The NEICP (Warner and Wittner 1998) and RENIR (Ebaugh and Chafetz 2000b) projects focused on comparisons of patterns among ethnoreligious groups. By the time the Gateway Cities Projects were funded, literature existed on the major themes that characterize immigrant religions and the conditions under which various patterns seem to emerge. The major challenge in future projects is to move beyond idiosyncratic cases and to continue comparative study across a number of ethnic and religious groups, with the goal of furthering our understanding of the cultural, social, theological, historical, and structural conditions that impact the settlement process. Hopefully, by discerning patterns of religious adaptation, we can develop generalizations that go beyond endless descriptions of specific cases and arrive at conclusions that are testable.

One of the outcomes of a strategy to develop generalizations is the ability to construct meaningful survey questions that can be utilized in broader immigration studies. Religion items could then be correlated with sociodemographic characteristics of respondents as well as their immigration histories, occupational and socioeconomic aspects of their settlement in the United States, and social networks that serve as support structures. In addition, such general surveys would provide comparisons of immigrants who are involved in religious institutions with those who are not. The inclusion of religion items in surveys, as well as in other immigration studies, would, no doubt, increase the awareness of immigration scholars of the importance of including religion in their analyses of immigrant settlement and incorporation.

Another area for future research is greater focus on religious institutions in the context of other community institutions that service the needs of immigrants, such as cultural societies, political groups, neighborhood associations, social service agencies, and home-town associations. The work of Eiesland (2000) on the social ecology of a neighborhood, as well as Becker's (1999) study of Oakland Park, are models of the ways in which religious institutions and their members interact within a larger community context.

One difficulty with using religious congregations as the unit of analysis, as is the case in both the NEICP and RENIR projects, is the self-selection of respondents, that is, a focus on those who are part of religious institutions. What is lacking in these studies are data on immigrants who do not use religious institutions to facilitate their settlement, including those who use nonreligious organizations.

The study of transnational religious communities is in its infancy and calls for much more extensive work both in terms of individual and institutional ties between the United States and home countries. In addition to focusing on direct transnational ties, more research is needed on religious organizational networks that facilitate and coordinate religious activities between home countries and those in which immigrants have settled.

Most of the work being done on transnational religious communities focuses upon immigrants in a specific sending and receiving country. We know, however, that immigrant streams seldom follow one geographical path; rather, immigrants tend to settle in various receiving countries and communities simultaneously (Ong and Nonini 1997; Laguerre 1998). A major research question arises: What variations evolve as immigrants from the same country of origin adapt their religion to different social contexts? Are there global influences that impact not only religious ties between home and host countries but also among religious communities in various nations?

In conclusion, during the past decade the study of religion among the new immigrants has become a major research topic in the social scientific study of religion. A body of literature is developing that demonstrates the central role that religion plays in the settlement of new immigrants in the United States, as well as the impact that the new immigrants are having on American religion. In addition to providing comfortable and familiar ways of worshiping, immigrant congregations today, as they did in the past, are providing ways in which their members can reproduce and pass on to their children cultural values, customs, and language. They create a "home away from home," a social space in which immigrants can share ethnic and religious customs with fellow immigrants while they develop informal social ties that facilitate their settlement into American society. Given the congregational model that most immigrant groups use in establishing their religious institutions in the United States, immigrant congregations are also places where newcomers learn the civic skills necessary to participate in American democracy. Simultaneously, new immigrants are impacting established American churches as they join multiethnic congregations and challenging them to incorporate new languages, styles of worship, and social customs.

Social scientists are beginning to accumulate the types of data that indicate not only the major issues in new immigrant congregations, but generalizations about the conditions under which various patterns arise. The challenge now is to continue the kind of comparative analyses that can lead to generalizations regarding patterns of religious adaptation of new immigrant groups, not only in the United States but as global diasporic religious communities.

CHAPTER EIGHTEEN

A Journey of the "Straight Way" or the "Roundabout Path"

Jewish Identity in the United States and Israel

Arnold Dashefsky, Bernard Lazerwitz, and Ephraim Tabory

Jewish identity has not remained the same throughout the four millennia, which span the development of Jewish civilization. Nor is Jewish identity identical in all of the societies of the contemporary world in which Jews find themselves. It therefore may be useful to conceive of Jewish identity as a journey, which for some has been a "straight way" (figuratively the traditional trajectory embodied in Jewish religious law or "*halakhah*"), and for others a "roundabout path,"[1] embodying a more circuitous byway to being Jewish (whose entry points do not necessarily follow the traditional road traveled but, rather, individual choices). This distinction highlights the difference between the historic approach in Jewish civilization giving greater weight to communal responsibility vis-à-vis individual rights as compared to the reverse emphasis in modern American and European civilizations.

In this chapter, we will focus on understanding Jewish identity as it dawns in the twenty-first century by focusing on the two largest concentrations of Jewry in the world: The United States with approximately six million Jews, who represent only about 2 percent of the total population,[2] and Israel with approximately five million Jews, where they represent about 80 percent of the population. Most of the remaining more than two million Jews worldwide are scattered in various countries in Europe

---

[1] This phrase first appeared in Hebrew Scriptures in *Judges* 5:6 "... caravans ceased and wayfarers went by *roundabout paths*" (Heb: *orahot akalkalot*) although it applies to a different context.

[2] According to Schwartz and Scheckner in the *American Jewish Yearbook* (1999), the official estimate is 6,041,000 million or 2.3 percent of the American population, an increase from the 5.5 million (or 2.2 percent of the population) reported in the 1990 National Population Survey (NJPS), a nationwide probability sample. Some scholars would dispute this increase; but the results of NJPS 2000, which will be available in 2002, will clarify the matter.

This is an equally coauthored chapter. A few paragraphs from pages 4 to 8 of Dashefsky and Shapiro (1993/1974) have been condensed and adapted for this chapter and are used with permission of the publisher and coauthor. An abbreviated version was presented at the Annual Meeting of the American Sociological Association in Chicago, August 2002. Thanks are due to Mira Levine and Rebekah Shapiro Raz for their research assistance and to Jeanne Monty for her technical assistance in the preparation of this manuscript. We also would like to thank Stuart S. Miller, Dianne Tillman, and J. Alan Winter for their very helpful comments on previous drafts. Finally, special thanks are extended to Howard M. Shapiro, who helped nurture an initial interest in this topic.

and the Americas.[3] We begin with a review of the evolution of Jewish identity within Jewish civilization, go on to examine the conceptualization and measurement of that identity in sociology and the social sciences, review the sources (with special reference to gender) and consequences as well as the role of denominations in shaping identity, and finally offer some concluding thoughts and implications for further research.

EVOLUTION OF JEWISH CIVILIZATION AND IDENTITY

Jewish identity has generally been regarded throughout the evolutionary history of the civilization of the Jewish people[4] as the result of two forces: "The consensus of thinking or feeling within the existing Jewish community in each age and the force of outside, often anti-Jewish pressure" (Hertzberg 1971: 53). The formal definition of Jewish identity that is most long lasting and harking back about two millennia is provided by religious law or *halakhah* (literally the "way" or the "walk" of Jewish life), namely, one is Jewish who is born of a Jewish mother or is converted to Judaism (see Zohar and Sagi 1994). As Hertzberg (1971) pointed out, this is not the oldest definition, nor the only definition, that has existed since ancient and medieval times; and later, we will compare this definition to that of social scientists.

The conceptualization of Jewish identity (and its oscillation through time and space) requires an understanding of the transformation of Jewish civilization across the multiple millennia of the existence of the Jewish people, but the need for brevity limits this discussion. (For a concise review of Jewish history, see Ben-Sasson 1971.) Suffice it to say that powerful economic and political forces in the social sphere have transformed the cultural (i.e., religious and literary traditions) as well as the personal sphere (i.e., familial and individual identities) of the Jews throughout the development of Jewish civilization from the biblical to the contemporary period.[5] Jewish identity, which in biblical times, was transmitted through patrilineal descent, was changed during the rabbinic period to matrilineal descent. Deviations from this normative Jewish identity, such as the Marranos or secret Jews of Spain after the exile in 1492, were treated differently by various rabbinic authorities during the medieval period. Subsequently, modernity was ushered in by the French Revolution at the end of the eighteenth century, which paved the way for the collapse of the physical and social ghetto in which many Jews had lived in medieval European societies. This emancipation created opportunities to give religious identity a variety of expressions through the development of denominations, especially in the Diaspora. New social contacts developed and intermarriage increased in Western countries, resulting in the notion of Jewish identity being divided between a strict *halakhic* religious definition as well as a non-*halakhic*, ethnic definition, which emerged in Israel and the Diaspora.

---

[3] By contrast, there were an estimated eighteen million Jews in the world in 1939 on the eve of World War II and the ensuing Holocaust, and they represented eight tenths of one percent of the world's population. The more than thirteen million Jews today represent a mere two tenths of one percent of the world's population, a proportional decline of three fourths.

[4] See Eisenstadt (1992) for an elaboration of this theme.

[5] The approximate time frames for the five periods of the development of Jewish civilization are as follows: 1. Biblical (origins in the fourth millennium removed from the present to the fourth century Before the Common Era or B.C.E.), 2. Second Temple/Talmudic (fourth century B.C.E. to the fifth century); 3. Medieval (fifth–eighteenth centuries), 4. Modern (later eighteenth to mid-twentieth centuries); and 5. Contemporary (mid-twentieth century to the present).

CONCEPTUALIZATION OF JEWISH IDENTITY

Identity and Identification

Identity is probably the most widely used concept to define and describe the individual's sense of who he or she is. However, in the many works dealing with identity in general (or Jewish identity in particular), different uses frequently appear. "*Identity* may best be understood if it is viewed first as a higher-order concept, i.e., a general organizing referent which includes a number of subsidiary facets... measurements of identity are carried out in terms of self-reported statements or placement in social categories, such as age, sex, and race" (Dashefsky 1972: 240).

There are two major sources of a person's identity: the social roles that constitute the shared definitions of appropriate behavior and the individual life history. Both the person and others base their conception of identity on these two sources. Combining these two dimensions (the *sources of definition*, social vs. individual, and the *act of definition* by self and others yields four facets of identity: *Social identity, self-conception, personal identity, and ego identity*. Thus the facets of identity are rooted in both internal, subjective perceptions and external, objective characterizations as noted also by Horowitz (2000) and Waxman (2001) in reference to Jewish identity.

The concept of *social identity* refers to how others identify the person in terms of broad social categories or attributes, such as age, occupation, or ethnicity. By contrast, *self-conception* is a cognitive phenomenon, which consists of the set of attitudes an individual holds about himself or herself (see Fiske and Taylor 1991:195ff.). It has been operationally defined by Kuhn and McPartland (1954) through asking respondents to answer the question "Who am I?"

The concept of *personal identity* refers to how others define the person in terms of a unique combination of traits that come to be attached to the individual. Basically these are biographical data. By contrast, *ego identity* is an intrapsychic phenomenon that consists of the psychological core of what the person means to himself or herself (Erikson 1963: 261–2).

The semantic confusion that envelops the term identity, is no less clear with regard to the term identification, as Winch noted long ago (1962). "Identity in any one of its facets... is built up through a series of identifications" (or linkages to) "others in an organizational sense... or in a symbolic sense" (Dashefsky 1972: 242). "Identity thus is not the sum of childhood identifications, but rather a new combination of old and new identification fragments" (Erikson 1964: 90). *Group identification* is a "generalized attitude indicative of a personal attachment to the group and a positive orientation toward being a member of the group" (Dashefsky 1972: 242). The basis of the group may be religious, ethnic, and so on. In sum, it may be concluded that ethnic identification "is both a *process*... and a *product*..." (Dashefsky 1972: 242).

JEWISH IDENTITY AND GROUP IDENTIFICATION

Having reviewed the definitions of identity and identification, let us examine whether these social psychological notions are relevant to the understanding of Jewish identity in contemporary Jewish civilization. In 1970, the Israeli Supreme Court rendered its judgment in the case of Lieutenant Commander Benjamin Shalit. Commander Shalit had sought to register his children as Jews by nationality *but without any religion.* This did not conform to Israeli regulations based on Jewish religious law. The children did not meet the criteria of being born to a Jewish mother or one converted to Judaism. The mother, Anne Shalit, was of Scottish and French Christian origin, but the family professed no formal religious beliefs. The ruling handed down by the Court permitted the children to register as Jews by nationality without declaring a religion. Thus one could be a Jew in Israel if one defined oneself as such in a secular, cultural, or national sense even though not defined as one in a religious sense (Roshwald 1970).

Could this be extended to include a person who considered himself or herself a Jew by nationality, and, a non-Jew by religion? This question had already been brought before the Israeli Supreme Court in the Brother Daniel case several years before the Shalit decision. Oswald Rufeisen was born a Jew in Poland in 1922 and was active in a Zionist youth movement. World War II erupted as he was preparing to emigrate to Palestine. He twice escaped from imprisonment. While hiding in a monastery, he converted to Catholicism and he later became a Carmelite monk. Brother Daniel, as he was known in his monastic order, eventually migrated to Israel in 1958 and applied for citizenship under the Law of Return, which grants citizenship virtually automatically to any Jew who settles in Israel. He claimed that he was a Jew by nationality and a Catholic by religion. The ruling of the Supreme Court did not permit him to attain citizenship under the Law of Return, arguing that a Jew who converted to another religion severed ties to Jewry as well as to Judaism. He was, however, allowed to become a naturalized citizen (Roshwald 1970).

How do these two cases bear on Jewish identity? First, they point out the complexity of defining what it is to be a Jew. Second, they suggest that being a Jew depends on the congruence of one's own definition and that of others. As Sartre (1948) and Eisenstadt (1970) have suggested, a Jew is someone who considers himself or herself to be Jewish and is considered by others to be one. In social psychological terms, as we have pointed out, there is some correspondence between one's social identity and one's self-conception. Third, these cases indicate that Jewish group identification reflects loyalty to the Jewish people, not specifically to its religious precepts, although formally adopting another religion severs the ties of peoplehood. These rulings tend to give juridical support to the linguistic overlap of the same Hebrew word, *Yahadut,* which stands for both Jewry and Judaism.

This complexity of Jewish identity as understood in the behavioral sciences, was first alluded to by the psychologist Kurt Lewin, who helped to bring the study of Jewish group identification to the attention of social scientists. He observed that it is "one of the greatest theoretical and practical difficulties of the Jewish problem that Jewish people are often, in a high degree, uncertain of their relation to the Jewish group, in what respect they belong to this group, and in what degree" (1948: 148). Indeed, this confusion may be understood in terms of the fact that Jewish identity contains both elements of a sense of peoplehood as well as religion and the relative balance between them varies depending on the society in which Jews live. As Elazar (1999) noted, Jews in Israel consider themselves a "nation;" in the United States, a "religion"; and, in other parts of the world, an "ethnic group." This emphasis on religion among American Jews represents a shift away from ethnicity but is supported by Lazerwitz et al. (1998: 71–2) in their study of American Jewish denominationalism.

INTERGROUP RELATIONS AND ANTISEMITISM

The traditional sociological approach to studying religioethnic identity and identifi-cation has been to focus on intergroup hostility and prejudice and discrimination. According to a formulation by Rose and Rose, group identification occurs when "the members feel that they are the objects of prejudice and discrimination" (1965: 247). In the same vein, the authors of a classic textbook in the sociology of minorities argued that group identification is the product of discrimination (Simpson and Yinger 1972). The consequence of this approach may be to define minority group identity as simply the result of negative forces without any countervailing positive influences. Thus, as Schoenfeld observed, "In popular culture, Jews seem to be represented as either vic-tims, neurotics, or exotics. Consequently, Jewish identity is either a curse, an illness, or something foreign – a source of shame" (1998: 111).

This theme was also readily apparent in the sociological literature about American Jewry. Consider the following statement by Goldstein and Goldscheider: "Even if the social exclusion of the Jew is declining, the fear of discrimination, and concomitant insecurity, may be a powerful factor in the identification of Jews with their own group" (Goldstein and Goldscheider 1968: 10). An even earlier formulation was provided by Wirth in *The Ghetto*: "What has held the Jewish community together...is...the fact that the Jewish community is treated as a community by the world at large" (1928: 270).

Wirth continued in a prescient manner: "In the past, it was the influx of a constant stream of Orthodox Jews that was relied upon to hold the community together and to perpetuate the faith. Today, however, this force can no longer be depended upon" (1928: 279). Outgroup hostility, then, clearly must be considered in the study of Jewish identity and identification, but its relative contribution may be overstated especially in the contemporary period. This point is emphasized by Lipset and Raab (1995: 199) who assert that the ethnic (or "tribal") identity of American Jews has been weakened by the "inexorably integrative forces of American society" associated with the decline of antisemitism.

MEASUREMENT OF JEWISH IDENTITY

Farber and Waxman (1999: 191) cited a *Los Angeles Times* survey of 1988, which re-vealed the various conceptions of Jewish identity held by American Jews. The most popular expression of the personal importance of Jewish identity reported by the re-spondents was a commitment to social equality (54 percent), followed by support for Israel (16 percent) and religious observance (15 percent). For most of the rest, there was nothing specific they could report as to what was important to their Jewish identity: "Rather it is just there, a part of them. They *feel* Jewish."

Behavioral Dimensions

Popular conceptions of feeling Jewish, notwithstanding, social scientists have offered a more detailed understanding of the dimensions of Jewish identity. Thus, a move from a theoretical discussion of Jewish identity to empirical research requires operational measurement of such involvement. Before one can assess the complex elements that define Jewish identity, one has to have an operational measure of who is a Jew. Social scientists are not limited in such definitions by rabbinic judgments or rulings by the Supreme Court of Israel as discussed in previous sections. Thus, the National Jewish

Population Survey (NJPS 2000), relying on questions asked in NJPS 1990, arrived at a definition of who is a Jew based on whether the respondent had a religious affiliation, had a Jewish mother or father, was raised Jewish, and considered him/herself Jewish for any reason (Schwartz and Amir 2001).[6]

Once the population is defined, then it is possible to examine the operational, quantitative measures of the elements of Jewish identity, which are often based on four dimensions: (a) childhood family religious and ethnic background and the extent and intensity of religious education during childhood; (b) religious participation; (c) involvement of one's family during childhood; and (d) children's socialization. Note that these variables are products of social institutions. They derive from one's family of orientation and procreation; the religious institution; the social characteristics of one's community; its network of voluntary associations – both general and ethnic; and the characteristics of primary and secondary social groups.

Phillips (1991) provided a summary of the major sociological studies of Jewish identity that emerged in the post–World War II era as Jews began to participate in the suburbanization movement. (See also Segalman's early 1967 report on Jewish identity scales and Schoenfeld's 1998 review of theory and method in the study of Jewish identity.) Phillips (1991) sought to present the traditional measures of Jewish observance based on the most well-known monographs on Jewish identity covering the 1960s to the 1980s.[7] These behavioral measures of Jewish identification also may be supplemented

---

[6] Based on these questions, the researchers operationally defined a Jew as "a person who (a) says s/he is Jewish by religion, or (b) considers him/herself Jewish and has/had at least one Jewish parent, or (c) considers him/herself Jewish and was raised Jewish."

[7] These Jewish observances (adopted from Phillips 1991: 7) included:

1. *Sabbath*
   Light Sabbath candles (Sklare and Greenblum 1967; S. Cohen 1983, 1988, Goldstein and Goldscheider 1968; Bock 1976);
   Special/Sabbath meal on Friday night (Sklare and Greenblum 1967, Dashefsky and Shapiro 1993/1974);
   Kiddush on Friday night (Sklare and Greenblum, Bock);
   No smoking allowed in house on Sabbath (Sklare and Greenblum);
   Carries no money on the Sabbath (S. Cohen 1988);
   Observed the Sabbath (Dashefsky and Shapiro).

2. *Kashrut*
   Bacon or ham never served (Sklare);
   "Kosher meat bought regularly"/"kosher meat" (Sklare and Greenblum; Goldstein and Goldscheider);
   Kasher the meat (Sklare and Greenblum);
   Has two sets of dishes for meat and dairy/separate dishes (S. Cohen 1988; Goldstein and Goldscheider);
   Kept Kosher (Cohen 1983; Dashefsky and Shapiro).

3. *Passover*
   Seder on Passover/attends Passover seder (Sklare and Greenblum; Cohen 1983, 1988; Dashefsky and Shapiro; Goldstein and Goldscheider)
   No bread eaten in home on Passover/ate only special food on Passover (Sklare and Greenblum; Dashefsky and Shapiro).

4. *Yom Kippur*
   Either or both parents fast on Yom Kippur/fasts-fasted on Yom Kippur (Sklare and Greenblum; S. Cohen 1983, 1988; Dashefsky and Shapiro).

5. *Hanukkah*
   Candles lit/lights Hanukkah candles (Sklare and Greenblum, S. Cohen 1988; Goldstein and Goldscheider).

by measurements of affiliation and attachment as well as attitudinal measures,[8] which Bock (1976) and Dashefsky and Shapiro (1993/1974) utilized.[9]

POSTMODERN INSTABILITY OF JEWISH IDENTITY

These conceptualizations and measures of Jewish identity discussed have been challenged at the turn of the twenty-first century. As American Jewry has become transformed by a postmodern, individualistic, multicultural society, so Jewish identity and its measurement have been altered from relying on more external, objective measures (corresponding to the "straight way") to more subjective ones (related to the "roundabout path"). This shift has led to even less consensus as to what Jewish identity means to American Jews and has complicated its measurement by researchers as well.

---

[8] Religious affiliation behaviors (adapted from Phillips 1991: 14) included:
  1. *Synagogue membership:* (Cohen 1983, Goldstein and Goldscheider 1968, Dashefsky and Shapiro 1993/1974; Sklare and Greenblum 1979/1967).
  2. *Attendance at services*:
     Service attended? (Cohen 1983);
     Attends(ed) services on High Holidays (S. Cohen 1988; Sklare and Greenblum; Dashefsky and Shapiro);
     Attended services on Sabbath (Dashefsky and Shapiro);
     Attended services on other occasions (Dashefsky and Shapiro);
     Attends services monthly or more (S. Cohen 1988).
  3. *Denomination:* (S. Cohen 1988; Goldstein and Goldscheider; Sklare and Greenblum).
  4. *Jewish study/Jewish education*:
     Received Jewish education (Goldstein and Goldscheider).
     Attended Jewish camp (Dashefsky and Shapiro);
     Discussed topics with Jewish themes (Dashefsky and Shapiro);
     Studies Hebrew (Dashefsky and Shapiro);
     Studies Yiddish (Dashefsky and Shapiro);
     Studied Jewish sacred texts (Dashefsky and Shapiro);
     Studies Jewish history (Dashefsky and Shapiro);
     Studied Jewish customs and ceremonies (Dashefsky and Shapiro);
     Detailed chapter on Jewish education (Sklare and Greenblum);
     Reads Jewish newspaper (S. Cohen 1988).
  5. *Jewish organizational and communal memberships*:
     Member of/belongs to Jewish organization (S. Cohen 1983, 1988; Goldstein and Goldscheider; Dashefsky and Shapiro; Sklare and Greenblum);
     Jewish giving (Cohen 1983, 1988);
     Nonsectarian organization member (Cohen 1983);
     Nonsectarian giving (Cohen 1983);
     Has Jewish friends (S. Cohen 1983, 1988; Dashefsky and Shapiro; Sklare and Greenblum).
  6. *Israel*:
     Has considered aliyah (S. Cohen 1988);
     Has visited Israel (Cohen 1988; Dashefsky and Shapiro);
     Studied in Israel (Dashefsky and Shapiro);
     Danced Israeli dances (Dashefsky and Shapiro).
  7. *Intermarriage*:
     Couple is intermarried (Cohen 1983).
[9] Stern (2001) a psychologist, added a number of psychologically oriented attempts at measurement of dimensions of Jewish identity, including works by Geismar (1954), Brenner (1961), Zak (1973), Tzuriel and Klein (1977), Elias and Blanton (1987), London et al. (1988) and his own work (Stern 2001) as well as more recent sociological and social psychological studies, subsequent to Phillips (1991), including Cohen (1997) and Horowitz (2000).

Such a change has led Charles Liebman (2001) to suggest that American Jews have become less Jewishly identified in the past half century, but modern scholarship, he argued, has reformulated Jewish identity as "multivalenced" without a central core of mandated obligations thereby muting this decline in identity. Thus, American Jewish identity becomes a mere personal experience rather than a communal attachment, leading to a diminution of Jewishness (as ethnicity) and accentuation of Judaism (as religion) but without normative standards.

Prell (2001) replied to Liebman that the transformation in conceptualizing Jewish identity is not the response of scholars who seek to toady to the whims of Jewish communal leaders and a "feel good" "anything you want to be" Jewish identity as some have suggested. Rather, Prell argued for a "need to conceptualize a 'developmental Judaism', a focus on the life course, and the continuation of Judaism over time for the individual" (Prell 2001: 122). Prell continued: "Rather than finding 'packets,' easily identifiable behaviors and attitudes that might be placed in one or another container, this scholarship pays attention to narrative, biography, and life history, and does suggest a powerful role for subjectivity and individual choice (Prell 2001: 122).

Even in Israel, Jewish identity has changed. As Liebman has suggested referring to the time period shortly after the founding of the State of Israel in 1948:

> Fifty years ago we could distinguish a small religious public with a strong Jewish identity for whom Jewishness and Judaism (the terms were synonymous) meant religious observance and commitment to the welfare of the Jewish people.... The non-religious majority, that is the secular Zionists, all shared a strong Zionist or proto-Israeli identity and reservations if not hostility toward religion. However, the older generation possessed a strong Jewish identity. (2001: 33–4)

For the present era, Liebman noted that a strong Israeli national identity has weakened among the secular Jews in Israel and gained strength among those with a strong religious identity (2001: 36). Citing the work of Herman (1970a, 1970b), who reported that a strong Jewish identity led to a strong Israeli identity, Liebman argued that the finding is more true in the present.

SOURCES OF JEWISH IDENTITY IN THE UNITED STATES AND ISRAEL

Static Model

Lazerwitz (1973) was one of the first scholars to seek to build a multivariate model of Jewish identification following the work of Lenski (1961) and Glock and Stark (1965), among others. The model, based on a probability sample of Jews and Protestants in Metropolitan Chicago, stressed the social and institutional bases in defining Jewish identification by examining the biosocial and socioeconomic factors along with religious, organizational and communal determinants.

The main thrust of the findings were:

1. There is no separation of religion from Jewish communal life...
2. There does exist a mainstream of Jewish identity which flows from Jewish childhood background to Jewish education to religious behavior to pietism to Jewish organization activity to Jewish education for one's children...

3. Both Jewish education and to a lesser extent, Jewish background operate through their indirect effects...
4. ...Jewish childhood home background and, then, religious behavior dominate the identity block. (Lazerwitz 1973: 213)

Complementing this approach was that of Dashefsky and Shapiro (1993/1974), who investigated Jewish group identification as a function of specific socialization experiences and interpersonal interaction for two generations of American Jews. Unlike those who argued that Jewish identification was the result of the intensity of outgroup hostility in the form of prejudice and discrimination, they argued that Jewish identification was formed at the interpersonal level through a process of socialization and social interaction with significant others. Their study, one of the first monographs in the field, that utilized multivariate regression analysis to examine the formation of group identification in two generations of the Jewish community of metropolitan St. Paul, Minnesota (n = 302), found that three main socialization factors (family, peers, and Jewish education) produced independent effects on Jewish identification, with the family three times as powerful as peers and four and a half times as powerful as Jewish education. Despite the latter finding, this study was also one of the first to suggest that Jewish education produced a significant *independent* effect on Jewish identification.[10]

Because Dashefsky and Shapiro developed a two-generational analysis that focused on comparing a group of young men between the ages of twenty-two and twenty-nine to a group of fathers, it was difficult to study comparisons of mothers and daughters because of the frequent name changes after marriage prevalent at that time. Strauss, however, studied one hundred and three young Jewish men and women between the ages of twenty-one and twenty-nine living in Toronto, Canada, and reported that "there was strong evidence that the two male groups of subjects [Toronto and St. Paul] were alike" (1979).[11]

Socialization creates a pattern of social interaction that puts children and adolescents on a certain path, but whether they remain on that path throughout the life course depends on the way they are structurally integrated into the larger Jewish community as adults. Dashefsky and Shapiro (1993/1974) examined the combined influences of socialization and structural integration factors for two generations. With regard to the younger generation, they found that synagogue involvement and income produced independent contemporary structural integration effects in shaping Jewish identification.

---

[10] By comparison in the older generation, the socialization effects documented were more limited with the family accounting for 20 percent of the variance explained and peers contributed 6 percent for a total of 26 percent of the variance explained. Jewish education failed to produce an independent effect. This was probably the case in this generation because Jewish education was not as extensive for the second generation who were educated in the pre–World War II era. The greater assimilation of the younger generation had led to Jewish education having a more pronounced and independent effect on Jewish identification for them.

[11] Strauss relied on Dashefsky and Shapiro's questionnaire, and her findings for the sources of Jewish identification were similar to Dashefsky and Shapiro for the males among her respondents. However, there were some differences that emerged with respect to her female respondents. With respect to males, for example, both Strauss and Dashefsky and Shapiro found that father's religiosity was the most important variable, followed by friends' expectations, Jewish education, and activities with parents. For females, however, Strauss found activities with parents was the most important, followed by Jewish education, friends' expectations, and father's religiosity.

Of the total of 40 percent of the variance explained, 24 percent came from current syn-agogue involvement, and 2 percent came from current income. The remaining 14 per-cent of the variance explained resulted from socialization factors, including 9 percent from family influences, 3 percent from Jewish education, and 2 percent from peers. They concluded: "The data indicate that socialization factors had an indirect effect on Jewish identification by affecting current religiosity and adolescent experiences pro-vided a basis for later adult activities" (1993/1974).[12] Nevertheless as Sklare had already observed, "The changing significance of the family, and . . . declines in frequency and intensity of interaction with the kinship group, means that identity can no longer be acquired solely through this traditional institution" (1971: 98).

DYNAMIC MODEL

As American Jewry, in particular, has become transformed by postmodern, multicul-tural society, so, too, has Jewish identity as well as its measurement. Thus, the concep-tualization and measurement of Jewish identity need to be broadened to encompass a new empirical reality. An example of this line of research is illustrated in the work of Horowitz (2000), who gathered her data through face-to-face interviews, telephone surveys, and focus groups with "Jewishly connected" adults aged twenty-two to fifty-four, in metropolitan New York (n = 1,504). In this study, Jewish identity was measured both attitudinally ("Subjective Jewish Centrality") and behaviorally ("Religious Ritual Activity" and "Cultural-Communal Activity"). Horowitz (2000: 185–9) found that Jew-ish identity is not necessarily declining but "persists and is reinvented," it is diverse in levels of engagement ranging from those who are "indifferent" to those who are "tradition oriented," and for some it changes over the life course, whereas for others there is stability of engagement (either high or low). Horowitz (ibid.: 190–2) identi-fied parental relations as a powerful source in shaping Jewish identity, but also found that other significant relationships, experiences, and events had a significant impact on Jewish identity. Overall, Horowitz's (2000) study revealed that the Orthodox tend to follow the "straight way" and demonstrate a more predictable outcome than the non-Orthodox who tend to follow the "roundabout path" with less predictable outcomes as supported by the greater amount of variance explained for the former than the latter group.

GENDER AND JEWISH IDENTITY

Gender also comprises an important factor shaping Jewish identity. This is symbolically indicated in the daily prayer service. Orthodox Judaism has women thank God for "making me according to His will." The parallel blessing for men thanks God "who has not made me a woman" (Tabory 2001). The questions raised about traditional gender divisions in Judaism are having a profound impact on Judaism and Jewish identity in the contemporary period.

---

[12] In regard to the older generation, a similar pattern emerged albeit with a more limited range of significant variables. Current synagogue involvement accounted for 23 percent of the total of 35 percent of variance explained, with 7 percent for peers, and only 5 percent for family influences. Jewish education offered no independent contribution as noted in footnote 10.

Men have always played the dominant, higher status role in organized Jewish life. The rationale for women's more limited roles has often been interpreted in a way that ascribes to them tasks of great importance that focus on raising and educating the younger generation. These "important" jobs excuse women from a variety of time-dependent ritual requirements that could undermine their devotion to the tasks that they "have" to do as women. The high status activity of Jewish learning also has been restricted to men. Even now, learned, fervently Orthodox women have to hide their knowledge and manifest self-deprecation before their husbands (El-Or 1992).

Improving the status of women in Judaism went hand-in-hand with the formation of Reform and Conservative Judaism. The civil equality adopted by the Jews of the Emancipation also led to a more positive self-concept among Jewish women (see Hertz 1998). The changing role of women in Judaism was still relatively slow in the non-Orthodox movements, because it was the slowly changing identity of women in society that trickled down to the identity of women in Judaism (see Kaplan 1982; Burman 1986).

Changes that came about in non-Orthodox Judaism included the inclusion of women as part of the synagogue service quorum and their right to receive the same Torah honors that had traditionally been restricted to men. The last bastion of formal separation of men and women is related to clerical ordination. The Conservative movement joined the Reform denomination in admitting women to its rabbinical studies program only in the 1980s. Clearly the social environment of the United States that affected the social identity of women and the development of a strong feminist movement had its consequences in the Jewish world as well. For some Reform women, and for a larger number of Conservative women, the combination of a modern secular orientation together with a traditional Jewish identity considerably moderates the degree of feminist expectations. Some women, for example, support the principle of equality, even as they do not necessarily want to personally benefit from the greater roles available to them because of a lingering conservative Jewish identity (Tabory 1984). The relative importance attributed to the male in Judaism is also manifested by some women adopting the male dress pattern of wearing a skull cap and prayer shawl in the synagogue.

The greatest impact of feminism is being felt in the Orthodox community. Reform and Conservative Judaism try to accommodate themselves to the surrounding society. Feminism is part of that culture. Orthodox Judaism by and large tries to segregate itself from secular influences. Orthodoxy involves a total life style. Those Orthodox Jews who take part in secular society must compartmentalize their identities, but they are doing this as a member of a denomination that does not make such separation easy. An Orthodox Jew in the secular world has to try to manage his or her dress, Jewish dietary restrictions, and limitations regarding work and travel on the Sabbath and Festivals (see Frank 1975). In this respect, accommodation works from the inside out – as the internal requirements of Judaism affect life outside Jewish society. The impact of feminism is in the opposite direction, as the ideology of the general society is carried inward to the Jewish world and affects the identity of Orthodox women caught up in a dual value system. (See Greenberg 1981 for a very interesting attempt to reconcile feminism and Orthodox law.)

The traditional division between men and women in the Orthodox world affects many facets of life, including areas of religious study. Even in the twenty-first century, when Orthodox women undertake religious studies, they are exposed to a different, less prestigious curriculum than men. Orthodox males in Israel can receive an exemption from military service as long as they commit themselves to full-time religious study. Orthodox females can receive an exemption from compulsory conscription by merely declaring their religious identity.

A change is taking place in the religious identity of Orthodox girls in Israel, and even more so in the United States. Many Orthodox women now receive high quality secular education as a consequence of the principle of gender equality found in the Western world. This exposure shapes their identity as Jewish women. They are not demanding radical change; that would go against their perception of Orthodox Judaism as the legitimate manifestation of organized Jewish religion. (Many women who are totally disillusioned and want to leave the fold of Orthodoxy do so if they can gather the personal strength to overcome the social pressure against their move.) The interesting impact of feminism on Orthodox identity relates to genuinely Orthodox women who want a greater religious experience that involves, ipso facto, greater equality. Some Orthodox women seek to participate in women's prayer groups, for example, and study the same types of texts as the men do because such behavior will enrich their Jewish lives. In fact, their initial desire is affected by broader social norms, and it is therefore no wonder that the movement for more religious participation has been stronger in the United States than in Israel, where feminism is relatively less of an issue (Yishai 1997; Herzog 2000). At the same time, the women who are affected by the wider social values system do not really recognize those norms as undermining their traditional religious identity. They are not trying to consciously revolutionize Orthodox Judaism but to express their identity as Orthodox women in the contemporary world.

While the motivation of the women may be innocent, some Orthodox leaders (most of whom happen to be men) reject their acts as undermining *halakhic* Judaism. Religious fundamentalists are more opposed to change than are "modern" Orthodox Jews. The latter accept some form of accommodation even if religious law has to be somewhat stretched (cf. Frimer and Frimer 1998). Pararabbinic functions for women have even been approved in Israel by the state authorities, although the women involved have not met total acceptance from all Orthodox authorities. It is not inconceivable that Orthodox women may eventually be ordained as rabbis as there is no apparent prohibition in Jewish religious law, but quite a few revised editions of this handbook will likely appear before that day comes.

CORRELATES AND CONSEQUENCES OF JEWISH IDENTITY

Contrasting the Religiosity of American and Israeli Jews

An interesting comparison arises when contrasting the correlates of Jewish identity by examining the differences in religious involvement in Israel, where Jews are the dominant group, and the United States, where they are a small minority. Two surveys, NJPS 1990 for American Jews and the Israel Central Bureau of Statistics Survey (1995) for Israeli Jews, permit a comparison of religiosity.

Table 18.1 contrasts American Jewish religiosity with its Israeli equivalent. It is feasible to combine those in Israel who consider themselves very religious or religious and to consider them as equivalent to American Orthodoxy. When done, this indicates

Table 18.1. Contrasting Jews of America and Israel on Religiosity Orientation

American Jews			Israeli Jews		
			European Descent	Middle Eastern Descent	All Israeli Jews
Orthodox	6%	Very religious and religious	14%	16%	14%
Conservative	40%	Traditional-religious orientation	5%	20%	11%
Reform	39%	Traditional, but nonreligious orientation	25%	45%	34%
No denominational preference	15%	Not religious	56%	19%	41%
Total	100%	Total	100%	100%	100%

Sources: For American Jews, Lazerwitz et al. 1998; for Israeli Jews, Israel Central Bureau of Statistics Survey 1995.

that the "Orthodox" group in Israel is more than twice as numerous as in the United States. If one regards the religiously oriented traditionalists as akin to the American Conservative denomination, it shows that this orientation is weak within Israel. The U.S. Reform and the Israeli traditional, but not religious, category are just about equal. The "not religious" grouping within Israel is about three times as numerous as the no denominational preference group in the United States.

There are also major differences between Jews of European and Middle Eastern descent. The Middle Eastern country descendant group has a much smaller percentage declaring themselves to be not religious. Instead, this group has almost twice as many who opt for the traditional but not religious orientation as do the Jews of European descent and four times as many in the traditional with a religious orientation than has the European descendant group. All told, a majority of the European Jewish group regard themselves as not religious, while almost two-thirds of the Middle Eastern Jewish group fall into either of the two traditional categories.

Table 18.2 contrasts the groups on synagogue attendance. While the question on synagogue attendance was coded differently on the two surveys, it is possible to contrast the American category of several times a month or more with the Israeli categories of most Sabbaths or daily attendance. This contrast shows both national groups are relatively similar on the frequently attending categories. At the other end of the scale, the Americans have 51 percent stating they attend around three times a year or less in contrast to the European descendant Israeli group with 46 percent attending seldom or never and 30 percent of the Middle Eastern country descendant Israelis attending seldom or never.

Table 18.3 provides data on religious observances, including the extent to which families observe the religious laws of keeping kosher by having separate dishes for meat and dairy foods and also the degree to which respondents observe the Yom Kippur fast, which takes place outside the synagogue. About three times as many Israeli Jews keep separate meat and dairy dishes as do American Jews. Then, in contrast to American

Table 18.2. Contrasting Jews of America and Israel on Synagogue Attendance

American Jews		Israeli Jews		
		European Descent	Middle Eastern Descent	All Israeli Jews
Several times a month or more	16%	Almost daily	6%	6%	6%
Once a month	11%	On most Sabbaths	9%	19%	13%
A few times per year	22%	The nine major religious holidays	39%	45%	42%
1–2 times per year or high holidays	35%	Seldom or never	46%	30%	39%
Doesn't go	16%				
Total	100%	Total	100%	100%	100%

Sources: For American Jews, Lazerwitz et al. 1998; For Israeli Jews, Israel Central Bureau of Statistics Survey 1995.

Table 18.3. Contrasting Jews of America and Israel on Observing Kosher Law and the Yom Kippur Fast

Religious Variables	American Jews (n = 1905)	Israeli Jews		
		European (n = 1258)	Middle Eastern (n = 956)	All Israeli Jews (n = 2214)
1. Keeps separate sets of dishes for meat and dairy				
Yes	17%	34%	64%	47%
No	83%	66%	36%	53%
Total	100%	100%	100%	100%
2. Fasts on Yom Kippur				
Yes	59%	60%	81%	74%
No	41%	40%	19%	26%
Total	100%	100%	100%	100%

Sources: For American Jews, Lazerwitz et al. 1998; For Israeli Jews, Israel Central Bureau of Statistics Survey 1995.

Jews, about four times as many Israelis having Middle Eastern country descent keep separate dishes as do about twice as many European descendant Israelis. In contrast, American and Israeli Jews of European descent report equivalent fasting percentages. However, Israeli Jews of Middle Eastern country descent have one-third more reporting the observance of the Yom Kippur fast. In summary, on the religiosity measures thus far introduced, one finds those Israeli Jews of Middle Eastern country descent being the most religious followed by Israeli Jews of European descent with American Jews coming close behind.

Even the not religious, European descent Israeli Jews have more home religious practices than do the equivalent American "no denominational preference-no synagogue membership group." In the Israeli not religious group, 10 percent claim separate dishes and 41 percent claim to fast on Yom Kippur. The American equivalent group has just 4 percent claiming separate dishes at home and just 15 percent claiming to fast on Yom Kippur. Thus in many ways, the identity aspects of Jewish life in Israel are equivalent to Protestant identity in the United States.

As just seen, being not religious in Israel involves a different type of behavior than it does among the Jews of the United States. The not religious group in Israel performs more home religious practices than the American no denominational preference group without a synagogue affiliation, or those who prefer the Reform denomination but are not members of Reform synagogues and who do little in the way of home religious practices. Both in Israel and the United States, these Jewish groups seldom attend synagogue services. This comparison highlights the differential effects for Jews who live in a society where they are a small minority (e.g., the United States) as compared to the one society where they constitute the dominant group (Israel).

INTERMARRIAGE

No social science study focusing on American Jewry in the recent past has had the effect on public discourse that the NJPS 1990 (Kosmin et al. 1991) has had. This survey helped to show that 46 percent of recent marriages (1970–90) were mixed marriages involving a couple who, at the time of their marriage, consisted of one Jewish partner and one partner of another faith (Lazerwitz et al. 1998: 99). Furthermore, a corollary finding of this study revealed that only 38 percent of those who were in mixed marriages were raising their children as Jews (1998: 108–9). These findings represented the stimulus that led many Jewish communities in North America to initiate commissions which investigated how they could respond to what they viewed as a severe challenge to Jewish continuity (see Dashefsky and Bacon 1994).

Jewish-gentile intermarriage had already been studied in Europe in the first quarter of the twentieth century with the finding by Engelman (1928) that both Jewish men and women in Switzerland were out-marrying at a higher rate than they were in-marrying.[13] By the middle of the twentieth century in the United States, some early signs of increasing intermarriages were becoming evident. *Look* magazine ran an article on "The Vanishing American Jews" in the early 1960s, which alluded to increased rates of intermarriage. Perhaps most people did not take this observation very seriously because *Look* magazine vanished before American Jewry showed much signs of disappearing!

A more scholarly article was published by Rosenthal (1963), who documented higher rates of intermarriage in states such as Iowa where there was only a very small proportion of Jews and also showed increasing rates of intermarriage by generation in the Jewish community of Washington, D.C. Again, not much serious attention was paid to this, because most Jews did not live in states like Iowa, where the Jewish population was very small, nor in cities like Washington, DC, which was characterized by

---

[13] This study by Engelman is the earliest reported on this subject accessed by computer-assisted searches of the social science literature.

a high degree of residential migration and mobility. Research based on the 1990 NJPS revealed that intermarriage was highest among Reform Jews, followed by Conservative and then Orthodox Jews, a pattern that corresponded to the popularity of denominational preferences of American Jews (Lazerwitz et al. 1998:101).

While Jewish-Gentile intermarriage exists primarily as a phenomenon of diaspora Jewish life, it has appeared within Israeli society. As there is no possibility of civil marriages in Israel, there is no official, legal evidence of such marriage. This proportion will likely increase with the emergence of civil marriage in Israel, the globalization of the world economy, the breakdown of barriers of cross-national communication and transportation, the influx of non-Jewish immigrants and Gentile migrant workers, and the opportunity for eventual peaceful relations between Israel and her neighbors as well as a breakdown of barriers between Israeli Jews and Arabs. This likely small initial increase in intermarriage will introduce some of the complicated issues surrounding Jewish identity which are already manifest in diaspora Jewry with one major difference. All of the tensions surrounding Jewish identity among the intermarried for the partners themselves and for their children take place within the context that the Jews are very small minorities (about 2 percent or less of the population) in all of the diaspora countries. In Israel, nevertheless, Jews will likely continue to reside in a country, where over three-fifths of the population will be Jewish and the society will likely continue to be imbued with a culture and calendar rooted in the continuously evolving Jewish civilization. Thus, the children of such mixed couples in Israel will likely become Israeli Jews without religious affiliation.

It is in the diaspora, however, where the empirical research on Jewish-Gentile intermarriage has grown, especially in the United States with the appearance of the National Jewish Population Survey of 1990. As Medding, Tobin, Fishman, and Rimor argued about intermarriage: "The size of the Jewish population, the vitality of Jewish life, and the future of the American Jewish community all depend upon a clear understanding of the phenomenon and appropriate actions by individual Jews, scholars, and communal bodies" (1992: 39). What can we learn from this research that helps us to understand the nature of Jewish identity?

Phillips (1997) suggested that it is useful to see the intermarried not as a homogenous but as a heterogeneous group. Based on interviews of both the Jewish and Gentile partners in 1994 and 1995 (as a follow-up to the 1990 NJPS), Phillips identified six categories of intermarried couples: Judaic (14 percent), Christian (28 percent), Christocentric (5 percent), Judeo-Christian (12 percent), Interfaithless (10 percent), and Dual Religion (31 percent). Given this classification, the identity of the Jewish and Christian partners in the mixed marriage is better understood "according to the balance of religious commitments in their homes" (Phillips 1997: 77).

In addition, Phillips found that about one-fifth of adult Jews who were the products of intermarriage and who have themselves intermarried have stated their intention to maintain their Jewish identity (Phillips 1997: 78). Furthermore, Phillips uncovered a pattern of "return in-marriage," that is, Jews who are products of intermarriage who marry a Jewish spouse. Indeed, it is the murky issue of intermarriage that so clearly reveals that, for many American Jews, their Jewish identity is a journey on the "roundabout path" rather than the "straight way."

As is to be expected in the highly individualistic religious climate of the United States, intermarriage has a variety of outcomes with respect to whether the children of such marriages are raised as Jews (Mayer 1985: 245–7). A crucial factor for the religious socialization of children of an intermarried couple is whether the originally non-Jewish parent later identifies as a Jew (Mayer 1985: 253). In the 1990 NJPS, 97 percent of conversionary couples with children in their homes were raising their children as Jews. Among the mixed marriages (those marriages in which the non-Jewish spouse remained as such), just 38 percent were raising their children as Jews where the non-Jew is Christian and 37 percent where the spouse is of another religion or has none at all (Lazerwitz et al. 1998).

The gender of the Jewish spouse also makes a difference as to whether children in an intermarriage are raised as Jews. When it is the wife who has a Jewish background, a majority (52 percent) report raising Jewish children; when it is the husband who has a Jewish background, only a minority (25 percent) are raising their children as Jews. The perpetuation of the Jewish population, then, is not threatened by intermarriage *per se*. Fewer than 1 percent of respondents (25 of 1,905) reported converting from Judaism to some form of Christianity. Nevertheless, the decision of those who are intermarried, even though they themselves remain Jewish, not to raise their children as Jews does pose a threat to the perpetuation of the Jewish population in the United States. The absorption of those with a Jewish heritage into the non-Jewish world occurs not so much with the intermarriage of parents as with their decisions about how to raise their children.

DENOMINATIONALISM AND JEWISH IDENTITY

The Relations Among Jews of Different Denominations

The relationship between the evolution of Jewish civilization and the conceptualization and measurement of the sources, correlates, and consequences of Jewish identity are especially evident in the emergence of Jewish denominationalism. The willingness of the Jews to continue to adhere to the restrictive practices of Judaism was affected by political emancipation in Western and central Europe (Katz 1961). Increased social contact with non-Jews and acceptance of the Jews as equals led many Jews to incorporate the values of their national societies in their own lives (Yinger 1970: 232–3). Many persons felt that traditional religious symbols, suitable for a closed, segregated subgroup had to be modified if the Jews were to become part of general society. The "enlightened" upper-class Jews of nineteenth-century Germany who were uncomfortable with their ambiguous status as Jews and as Germans preferred to deemphasize the national, cultural, and ethnic aspects of Judaism and to define Judaism only as a religion. The development of Reform Judaism in Germany in the nineteenth century thus involved a redefinition of the nature of Judaism as a religious collective (Philipson 1967). By limiting the scope of Jewish ritual, Reform Judaism enabled its adherents to aspire to acceptance as equal citizens with non-Jews, and yet to retain a Jewish identity as members of the Mosaic faith (Glazer 1957/1989).

Whereas the Reform movement became one of the largest Jewish denominations in the United States, Israelis perceive Reform Judaism as inauthentic because of its rejection of traditional Judaism and its initial negative attitude toward Zionism. While Reform Judaism's anti-Zionist orientation has undergone change – the movement affiliated with the World Zionist Organization in 1975 – the effect of its initial stance still lingers. The Association of Reform Zionists of America (ARZA), which held its first national assembly in 1978, warmly supports Israel and calls on its members to visit Israel and even move there.

Conservative Judaism developed in reaction to Reform Judaism. It was established by people who wanted to allow innovative religious change, but in a manner that still recognized the basic legitimacy of the Jewish legal system of *halakhah*. With regard to ritual observance, Conservative Judaism falls between Orthodox and Reform Judaism. From a peoplehood aspect, it is closer to Orthodox Judaism. Conservative Judaism had a much easier time recognizing Zionist aspirations and its adherents were less fearful of being accused of loyalty to two separate peoples. The formation of Conservative Judaism completed the division of contemporary Judaism into three major denominations competing for adherents.[14] Conservative and Reform Judaism recognize pluralism in Judaism but Orthodox Judaism continues to deny the legitimacy and religious authenticity of all non-Orthodox movements.

THE DENOMINATIONAL SITUATION IN THE UNITED STATES AND ISRAEL

The separation of religion and state in the United States makes the mutual recognition of the movements in that country a relatively moot question. While there is some friction between Orthodox and non-Orthodox Jews (Freedman 2000), state authorities recognize the religious actions (such as marriage ceremonies) of all rabbis. In Israel, however, there is an Orthodox state Rabbinate that is accorded official status by the civil authorities. Only Orthodox performed weddings and conversions are recognized when conducted in Israel. This sole authority, granted to the official (Orthodox) Rabbinate to undertake conversions to Judaism (an issue that is subsumed under the heading of "who is a Jew"), has led to various political crises in Israel and tension with the Reform and Conservative movements in the United States.

The issue of "who is a Jew" relates to the question of which rabbis are granted recognition as authentic clergy (Samet 1985, 1986), but questioning the authenticity of Reform and Conservative rabbis in Israel undermines the legitimacy of the Jewish identity of Reform and Conservative Jews everywhere. The message received by non-Orthodox Jews is that their beliefs and identity are not authentic, and that if one wants to be part of the Jewish religion, one has to accept the premise of Orthodoxy as the yardstick of religious belief and practice (Tabory 2003a).

The relationship between Jews within Israel is affected by the fact that Jews constitute the majority (80 percent) population. In contrast with societies in which Jews are but a small minority, little consideration has to be given to Jewish identity in Israel. It is largely taken for granted. Herman (1970b) found that religious (or Orthodox) Jews in Israel give some prioritization to their Jewish identity and nonreligious or secular Israelis give some preference to their Israeli identity, but there is nevertheless considerable overlap between the two identities. One of the reasons for this is that many Jewish Israelis seem to accept the Orthodox definition of Jewish identity, even if they are not themselves observant. The degree of observance is used to indicate whether one is

---

[14] Newer approaches, such as the Reconstructionist denomination, the Renewal Movement, and Humanistic (secular) Judaism, have not yet been widely studied and are too small as of now to produce large enough sample sizes in demographic and social surveys in the American Jewish community.

"religious," "traditional," or "nonreligious," but not whether one is Jewish. Israeli Jews by and large do not need to affiliate with a synagogue in order to identify as a Jew, let alone affiliate with one that is non-Orthodox (Tabory 1983, 1998).

Jewish identity is undergoing change in Israel, with implications for the relationships between Jews. There are an increasing number of persons for whom Jewish identity is irrelevant and who are disillusioned with the "in your face" attitude of the Orthodox establishment that seeks to impose its will with regard to mandatory religious observance that infringes on the personal rights of the population (Cohen and Susser 2000; Tabory 2003b). The regulations regarding religious observance include the proscription of public transportation and the opening of stores on holy days, the observance of religious dietary laws, and the question of who is a Jew. A new breed of Israelis is beginning to ideologically identify as secular Jews reflecting their nonbelief in a traditional god (Tabory and Erez 2003), and they oppose the condescending attitude of Orthodoxy that views them as sinners who would change their ways if they had not been the victims of modernity. The attitudes of these persons suggest that assimilation is possible even in a Jewish state (Schweid 1999). This also raises the question, posed by Susser and Liebman as to whether adversity – an ideology of affliction – is enough to ensure the continuity of the Jewish people:

> The essential guarantor of contemporary Jewish survival is not to be found outside in the Jewish world. It is what Jews think rather than what Gentiles do that is decisive. If the will to live rooted in a commitment to Jewish ideas, values, and practices perishes, nothing can – perhaps nothing should – retard the natural death of the Jewish people. (1999: 175)

CONCLUDING OBSERVATIONS AND IMPLICATIONS FOR FURTHER RESEARCH

The Study of Jewish Identity in Sociological Context

The study of Jewish identity within sociology emerged in the United States during the transformation of Jewish civilization in the 1940s as a result of the destruction of the Holocaust and subsequent creation of the State of Israel. Seminal studies in this era were Glazer's sociohistorical account of American Judaism (originally published in 1957) and Sklare and Greenblum's study of Jewish identity in "Lakeville," (originally published in 1967). By the 1960s, the sociological study of intergroup relations based on the Park (1950) model of the inevitability of assimilation began to be challenged and refuted in the work of Gordon (1964) and Glazer and Moynihan (1963). They argued that assimilation was multifaceted and not inevitable and that ethnic groups might alter their character but not necessarily disappear. These influential sociologists of ethnicity in general and Jewry in particular were read by a generation of students who received their doctorates in the late 1960s and 1970s and built on their work to create a new subfield of the sociology of Jewry, which included a professional association (Association for the Social Scientific Study of Jewry) and journal (*Contemporary Jewry*), as well as to develop undergraduate and graduate courses (see Porter 1998). Furthermore, the National Jewish Population Surveys conducted by the Council of Jewish Federations (in 1971 and 1990) and its successor organization the United Jewish Communities (in 2000), together with local Jewish community population surveys (see Sheskin 2001), added to a growing database through which studies of the dimensions of Jewish identity increased.[15]

For Further Research

As mentioned earlier in this chapter, there are two major trends among American Jews that ought to be among future research concerns: decreasing ethnicity and increasing religiosity. First of all, American Jews continue to assimilate and are becoming more and more like other citizens of the United States. This development appears as a decreasing sense of ethnicity. What differentiates Jews in the United States from others are their religious activities and ideology. How these trends – reduced ethnicity and gradually increasing religiosity – develop in the coming years ought to be a concern for researchers in the sociology of religion.

Meanwhile in our judgment, a similar trend with an opposite effect is occurring among the Jews of Israel. As the major ethnic subgroups of Israel's Jewish society assimilate as well and become more alike and marry among one another across traditional Jewish ethnic divisions, it will become less and less a matter of concern over whether one's immediate forebearers came from European or Middle Eastern countries. Along with this trend toward the mixing of ancestry is the negative reaction to Israeli religious orthodoxy, which leads to a decreased religiosity and increased ethnicity in Israeli Jewish life. How will the Jews of Israel handle the differences between the highly Orthodox and the highly secular? Etzioni-Halevy (2000) describes the situation as an unbridgeable rift. What implications does this have for the identification of American Jews and their identification with Israel? What religious shifts will occur in the near future? Will versions of American Conservative and Reform Judaism grow to numerical importance in Israel?

Future research should include a focus on the family as a whole.[16] Too often, current and past researchers have focused their surveys upon individual adults, usually the head of household. This has led to getting information on religious rituals, usually at home, that are basically family activities. We think it wise to obtain information on both partners in a household. Thus, one can also determine how couples from differing denominational and religious backgrounds resolve their differences. This would expand research and yield more reliable data on interfaith and interdenominational marriages.

Finally, our review of Jewish identity in the United States and Israel began with the metaphor of Jewish identity being a journey. For some (the more traditional and the Orthodox in the United States and even more so in Israel), the journey follows the straight way based on the traditional trajectory of Jewish religious law.[17] For a growing number of Jews in America and to a lesser extent in Israel, they follow the roundabout path, which embodies a more circuitous route to developing and maintaining Jewish identity (see Davidman, Chapter 19, this volume). Therefore, it is important

---

[15] The National Jewish Population Survey of 1990 spawned a series of monographs on varying topics which were all concerned with Jewish identity in a significant way. See Goldstein and Goldstein (1996) on mobility; Hartman and Hartman (1996) on gender; Lazerwitz, Winter, Dashefsky, and Tabory (1998) on denominations; Keysar, Kosmin, and Scheckner (2000) on children; Elazar and Geffen (2000) on the Conservative denomination; Waxman (2001) on baby boomers; and Fishman (2000) on identity coalescence.

[16] Fishman (2000) has demonstrated the significance of such an approach.

[17] See Cohen and Eisen (1998) for an innovative documentation of the moderately affiliated Jews.

to rely on multiple research strategies incorporating both qualitative and quantitative methods to ascertain the more complete truth. As Horowitz noted, Jewish identity is not a unilinear phenomenon but one that is multiplexed, "moving in a variety of historical as well as structural directions. To discuss the Jewish condition is to examine religiosity, nationality, and culture all at once as well as one at a time" (1998: 3).

Final Thoughts

Jewish identity incorporates dimensions that carry across time and space. Many Jews view their ancestry and origins as integral parts of their identity. Moreover, a sense of Jewish peoplehood also ties Jews around the world together. The feeling of Jewish unity involves a communal identification that is surely related to Jewish practice, but is even more affected by Jewish ethnicity. Both push and pull factors have operated to link Jews around the world together as a people. Anti-Jewish sentiment and attitudes, discrimination, pogroms, and genocide are very effective in leading people to identify themselves as members of a common group. The central role of Israel as a component of Jewish identity is not unrelated to the feeling that "the whole world is against us," but it also incorporates positive feelings of pride in identifying with the Jewish state.

All this is changing in modern society. In an age of globalization, when everything is related, there is little to distinguish one group from another. In an age of cultural relativism, when everything is legitimate, there is little to justify the perception that one's unique group is better than the others. Rather than serving as a source of pride, group identity stigmatizes and labels minority group members as different. Rituals that distinguish a group are dropped or moderated in a manner that is in keeping with the dominant group. Sklare and Greenblum (1979/1967) have found this to be the case with regard to the Jews of the United States. With little internal belief about the correctness of one's ways, why should group identity become a focal concern for continuity? The question is rarely openly mouthed among Jews, but by default many of them are asking what difference does it really make if the Jews (or any group for that matter) disappear? The response has been framed in popular works such as Wolpe's *Why Be Jewish* (1995) and Jewish communal policy makers' efforts at Jewish continuity, renaissance, and renewal.

For social scientists studying American Jewry in particular, the issue of whether Jewish identity can persist and Jewish continuity endure for yet another century (or millennium) is debated by the optimists and the pessimists (see Cohen and Liebman 1987). Perhaps the most appropriate response as to whether Jewish identity will endure is neither full-blown optimism or pessimism but agnosticism; namely, it is difficult to know for certain, in which case, cautious optimism (see Goldstein 1994) may be the most prudent response.

CHAPTER NINETEEN

Beyond the Synagogue Walls

Lynn Davidman

For most of the twentieth century, the study of religion in the United States has focused on institutionally and denominationally based religious groups, behaviors, and beliefs. By keeping institutional religion at the center of our research, students of religion have limited the understanding of the various meanings that individuals may attribute to their religious practices. An institutional focus marginalizes the diverse and syncretic nature of individual religious behavior. Recently, sociologists and anthropologists of religion have begun to recognize that religious practices and expression are not limited to the sanctioned forms and loci provided by the major traditions and denominations. Nor are they fully encompassed by the studies of "new religious movements" that dominated the sociological study of religion in the 1970s and 1980s. Recent volumes edited by Robert Orsi (1999) and David Hall (1997), for example, direct attention away from institutional religion to the study of "lived" religion, and religion outside of institutions, that is, the various and complex ways that people act to create meaning and new practices within the fabric of their everyday lives. By adapting a radically empiricist methodology, the study of lived religion focuses on those subtle ways that people "in particular places and times, live in, with, through and against the religious idioms available to them in culture – all the idioms, including (often enough) those not explicitly 'their own'" (Hall 1997: 7).

The practice of religion is not fixed, frozen, and limited, but can be spontaneous, innovative, and assembled by cultural bricolage (Orsi 1997). To put this otherwise, prescriptive texts don't tell the whole story, or even a very accurate story. Learning about the many imaginative ways individuals create the sacred and construct meaning in their everyday lives requires us to expand our understanding of what religion is and what it means to be "religious." The concept of lived religion is not necessarily only about practices per se but also about how people understand and live out their identities as members of a religious/ethnic community on an everyday basis. As David

I gratefully acknowledge the financial support this research received from the Lucius Littauer Foundation, the Salomon Research Grants at Brown University, and the Memorial Foundation for Jewish Culture. The chapter has benefitted considerably from careful readings by Shelly Tenenbaum, Larry Greil, and the religion and culture workshop at Princeton University in the Fall of 2001. I gratefully acknowledge the superb work of my research assistants, Elaine Farber and Judith Rosenbaum.

Hall has written, the term *lived religion* is not "confined to what people do," (1997: ix) but rather, it is about *"meaning and ritualization"* (1997: x).

This chapter unpacks the meaning of "lived religion," through a case study of twenty-eight Jews who do not belong to synagogues. By focusing on Jews who do not participate in the institutional Jewish religious life of synagogues, this sample selects for those who create and maintain their Jewish identities through practices that fall outside of traditional Jewish ritual but that elucidate some of the modes of lived religion among Jews. These Jews have largely been invisible in studies of American Jewish life because they are not representative of the approximate majority of American Jews, most of whom join synagogues at some point in their adult lives, particularly when their children are young (Cohen and Eisen 2000). Their invisibility is also shaped by their not fitting into any institutional model. It is precisely this factor, however, that makes them interesting as an example of lived religion. Jews, in general, may provide an especially fascinating exemplar of lived religion because within contemporary American Judaism, one does not have to belong to a community, believe in God, or even do any practices to consider oneself Jewish. Jewish identity and Jewish practice in contemporary America does not necessarily take the form of participation in recognizable rituals of religious observance. American Jewish identities are constructed along a continuum and through various combinations of religion and ethnicity. The construction of ethnic Jewish identities is a particularly important part of American Jewish practice for those Jews who choose not to join religious institutions. The study of lived religion can fruitfully be applied to their various attempts to create these identities that are on the slippery slope of religion and ethnicity. This chapter highlights the ways some American Jews construct themselves as Jewish outside institutional frameworks. It reveals that for some Jews religious practices and ethnic identities are experienced as distinct, whereas for many others, there is blurring of "purely" ethnic identifications with historically religious practices.

Sociologists of American Jewish life, like their peers who study Christians, have focused on institutional participation and adherence to officially sanctioned beliefs and practices. Over the past three decades, statistical studies have dominated the field although some qualitative studies have emerged as well.[1] This is because Jewish federations, concerned with the policy implications of the information gleaned, often fund quantitative researchers, who can give them facts about the beliefs and practices of large numbers of Jews. These studies have inquired into rates of ritual observance and levels of faith among the Jewish population. They have revealed that most American Jews celebrate the High Holy Days, Hanukkah, and Passover; that the majority of Jewish parents circumcise their sons and that few light Sabbath candles, keep kosher, or attend synagogue regularly (Cohen 1991). The 1990 National Jewish Population Survey has revealed many interesting statistics about the contemporary American Jewish community including: There are 6.8 million Jewishly identified people in the United States; 72 percent of Jews by birth[2] are married to other Jews (either by birth or by conversion); Jews

---

[1] Some of the major quantitative studies include Cohen and Horenczyk 1999, Goldscheider 1986, Goldstein 1996, and Heilman and Cohen 1989; see also Dashefsky et al., Chapter 18, this volume. Some of the ethnographic studies include Cohen and Eisen 2000; Davidman 1991; Heilman 1996; Horowitz 1998, 1999; Kaufman 1991. *Contemporary Jewry* 21: (2000) discusses the merits of qualitative research in this field.

[2] All data on "Jews" cited from this study will be referring to Jews by birth.

considered to have stronger identities have higher incomes on the average; 41 percent live in the North East; and 43 percent of Jews who are religiously identified are politically liberal compared to 57 percent of those considered "secular." In terms of denominational affiliation, 6.6 percent are Orthodox, 37.8 percent are Conservative, 42.4 percent are Reform, 5.4 percent are "Just Jewish" and the remaining 7.8 percent were split between Reconstructionist, nonparticipating, something else, and don't know. Although these numbers tell us something about overall patterns and trends, they reveal nothing about the *meaning* of religious practices and identifications for the individuals who claim them. Nor do they inform us about the alternative ways that contemporary Jews in the United States, a minority (7.8 percent) of whom do not affiliate with any major Jewish institutions, might construct Jewish practices and identities outside of the boundaries of organized Judaism. The focus on institutionalized Jewish religious practice has, perhaps unintentionally, rendered invisible other forms of expression of Jewish identity and practice.

The majority of studies of American Jews in the past twenty years have highlighted the issue of Jewish continuity. Questions of survival dominate the field in the wake of the Holocaust and the destruction of a third of world Jewry. Sociologists of American Jewry are haunted by the question of whether modernization weakens the Jewish community, threatening its survival, or whether the changes brought about by modernization simply mean that new, vital forms of Jewish cohesion and expression have emerged.[3] These studies have generally been oriented toward setting policy goals for Jewish leaders and Federations. Within this focus on continuity, Jews who do not belong to synagogues are seen as powerfully threatening to survival and as such become a residual category in studies of contemporary Jewish life.

A significant subset of the sociological research on American Jews has focused on particular denominations. While these works reveal new understandings of the meaning of religious practices and identities, the denominational focus maintains and reinforces the dominant institutional and traditional locus of research. One such study (Heilman and Cohen 1989), which examined how Orthodox Jews live in the modern American context, ranked respondents by levels of observance and analyzed them based on these rankings. In another study with a strong institutional component, based on interviews with Conservative Jews, Heilman argued that there was often a synergistic relationship between the individual's connection to the synagogue and to the Conservative movement as a whole (Wertheimer 2000: 183). By focusing both on institutionalized forms of practice and on the relationship between synagogues and their members, the individual paths of the people interviewed were often left out.

In the past five years, some scholars of the American Jewish community have begun to recognize the need to understand the pathways to Jewish identity of the marginally affiliated and even the unaffiliated. For example, Bethamie Horowitz has analyzed the indicators of Jewish identity in existing research, pointing out that indicators such as denomination, affiliation, exposure to Jewish education, and generation in America do not address the subjective experience of Jewish identity (1998: 2–10). Horowitz uses the narratives of individuals to rethink some of the dominant paradigms in communal policy discussions about American Jewish identity and Jewish continuity, suggesting the

---

[3] This emphasis on modernization and survival has been criticized by several sociologists, including Davidman and Tenenbaum (1994), Horowitz (1999), and Tenenbaum (2000).

incorporation of new questions that explore the meaning and nature of actions and rituals and address individuals' self-perception of Jewish identity. She argues against models that highlight continuity motifs, claiming that despite "Jewish communal expectations of 'erosion,'" she has found "evidence of persistence and invention in American Jewish identification" (1998: 17). Although the findings of her study affirm that affiliational connection is less meaningful than it used to be, many contemporary Jews are discovering entry points into Judaism through approaches other than traditional institutions. For example, she describes a secular Jewish jazz musician whose identity was strengthened through encountering klezmer music. Interestingly, a Jewish institution, the Mandel foundation, funded her study. It, and others like it, may be beginning to recognize the growing number of Jews for whom institutional affiliation is on the decline (particularly through intermarriage) and thus these institutions' policy concerns include seeking ways to establish "outreach" to the unaffiliated.

Moderately affiliated Jews have recently been recognized as a separate category of study that may provide important data about the nature of Jewish identity and changing attitudes toward Jewish practice in America. The first book focusing on the moderately affiliated, *The Jew Within* (Cohen and Eisen 2000), defines its subject as those Jews who are members of Jewish institutions such as synagogues, Jewish Federations, Jewish community centers, and other Jewish agencies, but who are not activists within these institutions. The authors argue that 50 percent of American Jews fall within this category (ibid: 5). Their analysis, based on approximately fifty in-depth interviews with the moderately affiliated as well as one thousand mail-back questionnaires from households with at least one Jewish adult member, highlights the role of American individualism in shaping the choices of their respondents. The members of this group see themselves first and foremost as individuals who are free to use their own authority when deciding about the ways they express their Jewishness. Many of their interviewees agreed that being a Jew is not a choice but that what one does with that identity is a personal decision; Cohen and Eisen refer to this perspective as "choosing chosenness" (2000: 22). In other words, Jewish identity is simultaneously a given from birth – an ascribed identity – as well as a choice one makes – an achieved status. Within the traditional and historical confines of Jewish culture, then, there is actually great room for individual autonomy.

For generations, Jews have struggled with their differences from the larger American population and regarded Jewish distinctiveness with great ambivalence. Since their arrival in the United States in great numbers in the nineteenth and early twentieth centuries, Jews have sought economic and social mobility as well as white racial identity (Brodkin 1998: 139–40). Some gave up the traditional observances that they saw as hindrances to fitting in (possibly at the much-lamented cost of Jewish continuity), while others went so far as to adopt popular Christian practices, such as having a Christmas tree. Cohen and Eisen show that this is no longer true of most of the people they studied, who seem to see no contradiction between being Jewish and being American. Christmas is not celebrated by Jews nearly as much as it was a generation ago – at least partially – because Jews are interested in declaring that being Jewish is being not-"them" (Cohen and Eisen 2000: 82, 99). Thanksgiving is taken seriously and "celebrated nearly universally" because one is made no less Jewish *or* American by "the hyphen in one's identity" (ibid.: 99). In some ways, this increased acceptance of dual or multiple identities in America has given free reign to and validation of the personal choices about religious identity and observance that Jews now feel comfortable making.

While Cohen and Eisen's research adds a great deal to our knowledge of the lived religion of Jews in the United States today, it continues the dominant pattern of study- ing primarily Jews who are institutionally affiliated in some way (whether or not they are active participants). In contrast, my research attempts to illuminate some of the interesting features in the Jewish lives of those who self-identify as unaffiliated with one of the most major of American Jewish institutions – the synagogue. This marginal but diverse group can broaden our understanding of what it means to be Jewish in America, highlighting those normally outside of the spotlight. Attempting to define the contents of Jewish life outside of mainstream Jewish institutions, these Jews may, in fact, need to reflect on the meaning of Jewishness more than do affiliated Jews. My training as a sociologist of religion, rather than solely as a Jewish studies scholar, allows me to bring a fresh perspective to the study of contemporary Jewish life. By drawing on the current sociological and anthropological emphasis on lived religion outside of institutional boundaries, I hope to shed new light on the constructions of Jewish prac- tice, identity, and meaning among a group of Jews who consider themselves marginally affiliated.

This study is based on twenty-eight interviews in the Providence (Rhode Island) area. I gathered the sample by placing an advertisement in the local newspaper, *The Providence Journal*, calling for Jewish women and men who do not belong to a syna- gogue. I selected the interviewees from among the fifty callers who responded to my ad in order to have an equal number of women and men, and an age range that spanned people in their thirties through their seventies. Individuals younger than age thirty generally have not reached the life-cycle stage in which most American Jews join syna- gogues, so I excluded them from the sample. In general, I interviewed only those who had never belonged to a synagogue, with only two exceptions of individuals who did not disclose in our telephone conversation that they had belonged to synagogues in the past. Although individuals who answer ads are not representative of anyone other than those who feel they have something they would especially like to say on the subject, such individuals nevertheless provide narratives that can suggest insights about others in similar situations. My interviewees emphasized various reasons for not belonging to synagogues, especially that they hated the emphasis on money (i.e., dues and dona- tions) in synagogues and that synagogues have become heartless businesses; that they find service "boring"; that they do not respect the rabbis in their communities; and that they find no meaning in synagogue attendance, especially in the worship services.

These interviews as a whole revealed that Jews who consider themselves marginally affiliated cannot rely upon any readily available, institutionally defined scripts through which they can create narratives about the meaning of Judaism in their lives. Instead, they each struggled to create coherent narratives of identity, in which they strove to clarify the distinctions they make between religion and ethnicity, and religious practices and cultural traditions. In constructing their narratives, my informants developed their stories by drawing on a wide variety of – and sometimes even conflicting – available sources and cultural scripts. My interviewees' sensibilities as Jews are shaped by their family backgrounds as well as their own personal experiences and can be highly id- iosyncratic. Each interviewee, in telling her or his own story, is attempting to create a sense of balance for her/his self. The very notion of balance, however, does not imply some preconceived notion that to be Jewish one must follow a recipe – one ounce of law, two tablespoons of text, a pinch of tradition, some values and voila! While creating individual identities in the postmodern world is always a highly complex and ever-changing process, creating an identity as a Jew may be particularly complicated by the question of what Judaism actually is, a religion, ethnicity, culture, or history. Thus, creating an identity as a Jew is never achieved through a formula in contrast say, to the identities established in identity transforming organizations such as Alcoholics Anonymous.[4]

Nevertheless, the popularization of Jewishness, through the mainstream media, especially and through consumer culture in general, means that America itself offers a variety of ways to be Jewish without affiliating with a synagogue. Here, for example, I am referring to widely viewed movies on Jewish life and identity such as Spielberg's *Schindler's List*; *Shoah*; or Streisand's performance in *Yentl*; popular literature by writers such as Chaim Potok; and various memoirs exploring newly discovered Jewish roots, as well as the availability of Hallmark cards to mark every Jewish occasion. Similarly, the prominence of Israel in daily news in America also offers a way of identifying as a Jew without any particular affiliation or engaging in traditional religious practices. These popularized ways of expressing "Jewishness" are etched into the very notion of a multicultural nation – one that, at least in some ways, values differences and tolerates and even encourages, identity politics. Living in a post-Shoah age also has a significant impact on contemporary Jewish identity and the ability to call oneself a Jew without belonging to a larger Jewish community. Jews today are aware that they would have been persecuted as Jews by the Nazis despite their lack of affiliation with institutional Judaism, and this knowledge creates the possibility for a new category of Jewish identity, independent of traditional Jewish observance or institutional participation.

Thus, there is an intricate dynamic going on for my respondents. On the one hand, they have to do the personal and cultural work of fixing their identity in a coherent way that allows them to make sense of the contemporary disruption of religious and ethnic cultures. On the other hand, they are also exposed to other identity making tools – through movies, books, articles in the press, political ideologies – all of which give them, in a sense, a "cultural tool kit" (Swidler 1986) that aids them in creating a Jewish identity.

The Jews I am studying are establishing and creating some form of connection with their roots. Although my respondents do establish their identification with the history and culture of the Jewish people through some of their lived religious practices, they themselves see their practices as ethnic, cultural, and familial and not religious. In trying to understand the meaning, practices and establishment of "lived religion" among Jews, I am taking what my respondents say about what they are doing at face value and avoiding the debate about functionalist vs. exclusivist definitions of religion.

In this chapter, I illustrate the various ways that my respondents create ethnic as opposed to what they consider "religious" identities by weaving together certain practices that they can define as historical, cultural, or familial, with a sense of Judaism as an

---

[4] In reference to AA, however, even here it is important to note that individuals can, and do deviate from the prescribed blueprints. Modern and postmodern identities, in general, are difficult to construct in narratively coherent ways.

ethnic identification. For these unaffiliated Jews, the process of constructing a Jewish identity is itself a Jewish practice and one of the primary ways in which they live their religion, even if they define this identity in nonreligious terms. An interesting contrast between my study and the one conducted by Cohen and Eisen is that they found that 80 percent of their sample population identified being Jewish as a religious identity, whereas in mine, only ten of the twenty-eight interviewees did so. For many, ethnic pride was an important component of their Jewish identities. They emphasized how "immensely proud" they are of being Jewish and of the numerous accomplishments of Jews, such as the percentage of Nobel laureates, and the sheer raw ability to survive over millennia of persecution. For my respondents, this was an important reason to claim an identity as Jews, even if they do not see themselves as religious. These interviewees have a sense of awe for the history and accomplishments of Judaism and the Jewish people and want to feel tapped into that. And their narration of ethnic pride allows them to establish connections with this tradition and heritage they perceive as great, without their having to engage in any particular religious behaviors.

In one interview with a retired, nonpracticing seventy-year-old man named Mark, I asked, "What does it mean to you to be a Jew?" He answered:

> It makes me immensely proud. I think that the contributions that Jews have made to the world, to society, and to culture, are just staggering. Um, I'm so proud to be a Jew. I think about who won the most Nobel Prizes. Who's fought incredible odds against every kind of horrific enemy and condition and not just survived, but flourished and went on to do all these magnificent things. I mean, I just swell with pride when I think about it. I feel so badly when I hear all these stories about all these American Jewish kids who have no idea who they are, or what they are, or what they've come from. I remember somebody talking in the sixties about kids wanting to become, I don't know, Buddhist or Maoists, who were Jews who had no idea who they were or what they were, the incredible, fabulous legacy, because they had had a bad way of being exposed to that, if at all. I'm lucky I was able to go forge my own way of learning about all that.

Most fascinating to me was the fact that nineteen of my twenty-eight interviewees explicitly emphasized a genetic notion of Jewishness. They stated that being Jewish is something one is born into and that has a hardwired genetic truth to it. Cohen and Eisen's respondents, too, argued that Jewishness was not dependent on observance or education; "they are Jews because they are Jews, period" (2000: 101). Highlighting the genetic dimension is a particularly powerful way of claiming a link with this great tradition and people, without having to engage in any particular religious or other behaviors – it is simply seen as a native part of oneself. There is a fascinating slippage here between ethnicity and biology. Many of my respondents started out defining Judaism, for them, as an ethnic or cultural identity, but when asked to flesh out what they meant by that, they returned to some level of biological essentialism.

In my conversation with Mark, I asked him, "Is Jewishness, or Judaism, or being Jewish something you're born with?" He responded as follows:

> Yes. Well, I think ethnically, everybody's born Jewish. And I think we know about genetics. Certain things are going to have a tendency to be passed along, like intellect. I mean, since we are the people who first created the idea that to be holy you had to be, if you will, cerebral. Have you ever seen Fiddler on the Roof? My favorite

part . . . the best part, and I almost missed it, but when Tevya sings that stuff about if I were a rich man, and he says at the end, about if he could just study all day, if he could just study the Holy Books. . . . I'm getting goose bumps as I say this, and Tevya said, 'That would be the greatest gift of all.' That's what makes Tevya such a great guy. That's why you're so drawn to him. He . . . I know it's almost like a cartoonish figure, but it's almost like the embodiment of the Jewish spirit. Yep. So I think that one can be born with those kinds of traits. Who we are has come through. I mean, there are people who have been Cohens [the name for individuals who are heredi- tarily members of the priestly caste] for thousands of years. So maybe there is, I don't know, like a collective spirit. Who is it? Was it Jung that talked about that? The idea about collective spirit.

Cindy, a thirty-year-old single teacher, also expressed a "genetic" view of Jewish identity: "Yeah, I do think that we are better. I do have the notion in my mind growing up where on the one hand I was embarrassed to be Jewish, but I do think there is a supremacy thing, even though that is also a horrible thing to say . . . especially after what the Germans did to the Jews."

In this quotation we see her ambivalence about a genetic argument. On the one hand, she feels that Judaism is inherited genetically and that Jewish accomplishments through the ages suggest Jewish superiority, but, on the other hand, she understands that such an argument can lead to profound racism.

One particularly sensitive issue in this genetic/ethnic view of Judaism is the question of conversion and whether, if Judaism is indeed inborn, a convert can ever truly be a Jew. Belinda, a fifty-year-old businesswoman, expressed this tension as follows: "Well, I don't really think somebody can convert to Judaism. . . . They can convert to the religion, but they can't convert to being a Jew, I don't think." Cindy, the thirty-year-old teacher mentioned earlier, similarly expressed uncertainty about the meaning and nature of conversion as an index of "real" Jewish identity. When she told me that she feels she has "something in common with all Jews," I asked her what that was. She replied, "History, genetics, very specific genetics." When I queried her in return about whether Judaism is something you're born with she responded in a confused manner. "Unless you convert. There are some people who convert who are more religious than me. But they don't have the genetics and I think that one of the important parts of being Jewish is the genetics. And it can get watered down, and then once it's watered down, it's less Jewish." I asked, "So do you think if a Jew marries a non-Jew and they have children, the children have watered down genetics?" In response, she said, "Well yes, and no . . . I mean, yes and no. Yes and no." Here, she demonstrated her lack of certitude by wavering back and forth three times! She continued, "Yes, but I guess it depends on the father and mother. If it's the father who is Jewish, then yes, but if it's the mother, then no." In the end, she resolved her own tensions and contradictions in favor of the traditional perspective on Jewish heredity.[5]

One *possible* interpretation for this emphasis on genetics is that those who are unattached to a Jewish community put far more stock in being biologically Jewish – Jewish because they were born that way – than those who see their Jewishness mediated

---

[5] In traditional Jewish law, religion is passed down though the mother. Therefore a child born to a Jewish woman and a Gentile man is Jewish, whereas a child born to a Jewish man and a Gentile woman is not.

through institutionally defined religious activities, practices and, beliefs. Although they are not making any efforts to participate in any distinctly Jewish institutions that might shape their identities as Jews, "genetics" allows them to still identify as Jewish and have a sense of belonging to the group they refer to as "the Jewish people."

In contrast to my respondents' ideas of religion/ethnicity as inscribed aspects of identity, Steven Warner's (1993) important article offering a paradigm shift in the sociology of religion argues that religion is actually an *achieved identity*, a product of upbringing, social factors and personal identity development. The fascinating tension for my respondents is that although they claim ascriptive identities, they are also highly aware that religious or ethnic identities are also achieved. In fact, they themselves seek to construct these identities in ways that are different from the traditional definitions; they pick and choose from the available options in their traditions to craft new versions of the meaning of Judaism. The achievement component of identity is revealed in the multiple, varied ways individuals construct themselves as Jewish. Despite defining Judaism as an innate identity, independent of specific observances and religious beliefs, "ethnically identified" Jews can be seen as living their religion through their ongoing construction of ethnic identity. In a context in which simply "being Jewish" supplants particular ritual observances as the central meaning of Jewish identity, defining what "being Jewish" actually means is a complex and ongoing process. Negotiating the many, contested ways to be Jewish in contemporary America and creating their own understanding of the basis of Jewish identity becomes for these ethnically identified Jews a ritual of American Jewish practice.

My respondents' claims about the centrality of genetics are being espoused in a social context in which many types of individuals, such as antiracists and feminists, are challenging essentialist views, arguing that identities are actually socially constructed. There are great political and economic stakes in the current sociological and political debates between the social construction of identities, such as race, gender and sexuality, and the essentialist view of these elements of identity. It is notable that in this era in which the role of genetics is an important and fiercely contested issue – for example, the contemporary dominance of sociobiology as a major paradigm in biological research and theory, and the widely debated reaction to the book, *The Bell Curve* (Herrnstein and Murray 1994) – my respondents nevertheless feel comfortable in claiming a genetic essence to their Judaism. This ongoing social dispute about the genetic components of identity nevertheless may further complicate my respondents' attempts to define the roots of Jewish identity. In their study, Cohen and Eisen uncovered ambivalence toward the idea of an essentialist Jewish identity; while the respondents downplayed their sense of distinctiveness as Jews in their responses to the survey, it was revealed in the extended interviews. Despite some ambivalence about the source of Jewish identity, my respondents are clearly adapting the essentialist claim that "genetics" or history rather than rabbis or researchers define who and what is Jewish. By claiming their identity is ascribed, they are stating that the individual cannot be held responsible for it. This is how the gay Catholics in Michele Dillon's (1999a) study of nonconformist Catholics talk about their sexuality – if it was simply a "construction," then it could easily be changed.

The view that Jewishness is genetic stands in contrast to the argument articulated by about ten of my respondents that although being Jewish is not necessarily about religion, it is *also* not about race.[6] Several stated this position quite explicitly, while others referred to it through scoffing at the idea that there is such a thing as "looking Jewish." A respondent named Judith, in response to my question, "Do you think of Judaism as a religious tradition, a culture, or an ethnicity?" expressed this idea as follows:

> All of those things. There are two ways. Ethnicity is a good thing, a good word for what I had said before, that there were two ways of being Jewish. One is religious and the other is ... well, some people say race, but I think the real way it should be looked upon is as a religion, or an ethnicity, because there will be less racism and hatred that way. If anyone can choose what religion they want to be [thus taking away the racial, genetic components] then you get rid of killing the way Hitler wanted to kill the Jews because they had Jewish ancestry.

However, it is significant that this same respondent, while acknowledging the danger of defining Jewish identity as a racial identity, also expressed (ambivalent) belief in a genetic component to Jewish identity. She said,

> I feel to be a Jew is to be superior. That's a terrible thing to say ... I think if you take the average Jew, we're much better educated. We're much more knowledgeable about other religions. Many subjects. It's incredible what people don't know. I mean, maybe it's because I'm Jewish that I think that Jews are that way, but I know from when I went to school, and from when my children went to school, that the most intelligent people were almost always Jewish, and I don't know why that is. I don't know if it's genetics. My mother-in-law, who wasn't born Jewish, and my sister-in-law, who wasn't either, they're both very intelligent people, too. So I don't know if it's genetics or if it's upbringing.

These contradictory remarks – rejecting the idea of a racial Judaism but holding on to the possibility that Jews may be smarter than non-Jews – reveal a deep ambivalence about the source of Jewishness and highlight the discomfort that many Jews feel about the role of genetics in Jewish identity.

In terms of lived religion as worldview, I have found that religion and ethnicity, as described by my informants, are clearly not one and the same, although they are often construed as such in common parlance, theoretical models, and historical studies. My respondents have said, in effect, I may not be very Jewish if it means keeping kosher and attending synagogue, but if it means having a worldview informed by Jewish culture/history/values, then yes, I am. In other words, they are conscious that there are multiple ways of being Jewish and of defining the nature of Jewishness in contemporary American society. And they claim a sense of interpretive authority over Judaism which allows them to connect so many of their diverse experiences to it.

In this next section of this chapter, I focus on the practice dimension of lived religion. Whether or not my respondents see Judaism as genetic (although the large majority do), all of my respondents have found ways to practice their Jewishness through behaviors that lead them away from religion and closer to those that emphasize culture,

---

[6] While nineteen respondents expressed their belief in a genetic component to Jewishness, only three of these respondents used the word "race" to describe Jewish identity. This suggests the weight of the term race in our society and a general hesitance to use the word, even if implying genetic components of identity. No one used the word race who did not also use the word genetics.

history, and memory. For example, many of my respondents described reading Jewish books, or leaving Jewish books out for their children to pick up and peruse as ways they maintain their connection to Judaism. Renee, the mother of two young sons, described this in some detail: "What I do is put Jewish books out. They love to read when they're eating breakfast or eating lunch. If we're not as a family around the table, I let them read. Like one book was called *I Never Saw Another Butterfly*. It's a book of poems and drawings by children during the Second World War. Very beautiful. Or just articles. I put things out so they get it that way."

In general, my respondents were most likely to take on those ethnic practices that particularly involve memory, family, and historical and cultural traditions. For example, they mentioned practices including studying texts, liking Jewish language and songs and music, displaying Jewish objects in their home, or having nontraditionally Jewish rituals (for example, making every Friday night a "pizza night"). Such a lived religious practice continues the historical notion that Friday night is traditionally very important in Jewish religion but instead of observing it in the traditionally religious way (with blessings over candles, wine and Hallah [special bread] they reinvent the evening to satisfy their own contemporary familial needs. These practices are consistent with Robert Bellah et al.'s notion of participating in a "community of memory;" however, for my respondents this community is a historical and cultural one, not a distinctly religious one (Bellah et al. 1985). Here I choose to take my respondents at their word, without placing them into sociological debates about what religion *really* is.

Singing Jewish songs, even without understanding their meaning or context, is another practice of my respondents that makes them feel essentially linked to Judaism. Julia, a mother of one in her thirties, said that she sings Jewish songs to her little girl, "just because . . . just some songs I like." When I asked her which songs, she replied,

> Oh, I don't know, one called Adon Olam [a traditional prayer from the Saturday services called Adon Olam], I don't even know them by name . . . different parts of Saturday morning services that stay with me, just songs that I remember. And just because they have a lullaby effect, I would sing them to her when I was putting her down when she was little. I'll sing them and it reminds me that I'm connected to this larger body, although I don't have the beliefs, I'm connecting to that culture of the Jewish people.

Food rituals were mentioned, particularly by the women, as ways they keep their ethnic identification alive. Two women, for example, specified that they try to keep Friday night as family dinner night, although because they are so tired from the week their ritual is to serve pizza rather than the more traditional home-cooked meal. As Laura, a social worker in her fifties said,

> We actually have . . . a year ago we started the ritual of Chinese food every Friday night, because I was too tired to cook dinner on Fridays. My husband declared, now that my oldest daughter is in college, that he's sick of Chinese food so now, for the past two weeks, the ritual has become pizza.

Lisa, a woman in her sixties, confided that when she was a stepmom and had kids,

> they loved pork and I would buy it but I never learned what to do with it. My husband would cook it because I didn't eat it. So, even though I'm not religious, certain things remain for me and they are part of being Jewish that I got from my parents, even though I have no way to connect it and make sense of it.

As we have seen, my interviewees do not perceive traditional Jewish law as authoritative. They feel a great deal of freedom to decide what to observe and what not to
observe from the gamut of traditional practices. Indeed, some even claim a link between
practices derived from other aspects of contemporary culture (such as the New Age), or
other religions (such as Eastern traditions), with the ways they construct themselves as
Jewishly identified.

Sheryl, a single woman in her thirties, provides an interesting example of such
religious bricolage. In response to my question of whether there are any rituals, of any
kind, that are important in her life, she said,

> Well, right now I am doing, I don't know if you've heard of the book, *The Artists'
> Way* – it's a book to kind of help unblock your creativity and one of the things
> that they recommend that you do is morning pages. That when you get up in the
> morning you write three, non-stop sort of stream of consciousness to get all that, it's
> like a brain dump, to get all that stuff that's on your mind out onto the page and
> I've been doing that, it's kind of odd, I started doing that and then I was reading
> the book about Rosh Hashanah and Yom Kippur and somewhere in the book they
> talked about at the beginning of the month before Rosh Hashanah how religious
> men would get up at midnight and start to pray because that's when their minds
> would be the most clear. And I realized as I was reading that I had kind of started my
> morning papers on the first day of the month.... It is a very weird coincidence and
> doing them has really um made me see a lot more coincidence in my life, and I don't
> mean necessarily I believe it's coincidence. And that I continue to do this daily, it's
> like the Jewish morning prayers.

Here she describes an example of a daily ritual practice that she links with Jewish
memory and ritual although it does not derive from a specifically Jewish source.

Another important dimension of the ways many of my respondents construct their
sense of ethnicity as Jews is by attributing their worldviews, values, and philosophy
to insights from Judaism or Jewish culture. The interconnectedness between ideas and
practices is explicit here, because respondents linked their worldviews and values to
their daily activities. Several people related their leftist politics to their Jewish heritage,
stating that Judaism is about a sense of social justice. A wonderful example of this can
be seen in the story of a man named Ted. He was an extremely left wing political activist
for much of his life. When talking about his life choices and Judaism, he framed it as
follows:

> So, you know...and like I said, my grandfather was active in the 1905 Revolution
> as one of the People's Police. And he used to tell me about the 1905 Revolution and
> how it failed, but how it was wonderful when it was...when the people took over,
> it was like Nirvana, Utopia, whatever. I mean, it was the first time the Jews were
> free. And you know, what a wonderful time that was. And so what happened in
> the sixties to me was a replay of what my grandfather used to tell me, because there
> were occasions where we freed areas. We fought National Guard troops, we did...
> there were lots of...I mean, I was reliving my grandfather's life in a lot of ways.

Ted also related his activism to a Jewish value structure, saying:

> It seems to me, and you probably know more about this than I do, that this idea
> about doing good deeds while you're alive, that that's all there is. First of all...well,

that's one of the things. There's no belief in afterlife as I understand in Judaism. People who have an afterlife belief that are Jewish are, to me . . . that's not Judaism I believe in. It's that we are here and we're now. That we're conscious beings and have an opportunity to do things that other people might consider good.

Yet even among those who did not espouse leftist political views, the majority of my respondents stated that being Jewish is about being a "Good Person." They explained what it means for them to be a good person by describing practices such as volunteering at soup kitchens, with elderly people, and/or giving to a wide range of charities. Although being a good person is, of course, not *necessarily* a distinctly Jewish value, when pressed to draw connections between their values and being Jewish, they related them to a particularistic Jewish upbringing.

One such example can be seen in my conversation with Henry, a man in his forties. When I asked him, "What does it mean to you to be a Jew?" he replied, "It means it's my culture and my background, if not my practicing religion. It's still my culture and my background." I then asked, "Can you say something more about what you mean by culture?" and he said:

> We're getting down to the down and dirty. By culture, um . . . [long pause] . . . I think it means having been given the identity of oneself as a Jew in all that that means, both as um, being Jewish and being set apart from other people in some ways. Certainly more as a child I felt that, and as a teenager. The teachings of what, um . . . I think by what our family expected of . . . . The way they expected us to live, which was in an honorable manner, and although they didn't call it that, living by the Golden Rule. Um, helping others, doing mitzvahs, things for which you . . . I would say that's another part of my life, of doing things for which I expect and want no reward, that kind of thing. So I would say those are things, although I think maybe other people of other cultures could say that, but I say that as a Jew because I was raised as a Jew. But why is it special because it's Jewish? That I don't know. It's just my background.

These comments, which sound like "Golden Rule Judaism," make me wonder whether in this respect Judaism is distinguishable from Golden Rule Christianity, a concept discussed by Nancy Ammerman (1997b). She argues that a significant number of Christians in the United States define the importance of religion in their lives as centered on their idea of the "Golden Rule." This "Golden Rule" is an injunction to treat people well, to care for others, and to help those in need. They base their everyday values and actions on this principle and derive from its benevolence a basis for faith in God. My respondents' references to the Golden Rule as a central Jewish value raise the question of whether being a good person as a Jew is necessarily distinct from what the Christians might claim characterizes the good person. In the 1950s, President Eisenhower was quoted to have said that he didn't care what religion a person was, as long as s/he had a religion, thus suggesting a possible blurring of religious boundaries. Peter Berger, too, argued in the 1960s that because religions in a secular society are competing for the same audiences, who are free to pick and choose among available alternatives, their distinct contents and modes of presentation become blurred and less precise (Berger 1967).

In showing the ways individuals rely upon their own conventions, authority, and practices to establish their sense of Jewish identity, this chapter raises an interesting sociological question about whether these multiple ways of being Jewish can be understood to be "really" authentically Jewish, or whether there is such a thing as a critical, essential "core" identity or a connection to specific ideas and/or practices that people must actively maintain if they are to call themselves Jewish. This also leads to the question of whether there is a *core* to any religion. As Robert Orsi has argued (quoted by Hall, 1997: 18) "The study of lived religion risks the exposure of the researcher.... Working on this intimate level, it is harder to avoid the question 'so what do you think about all this *'really'*?" Clearly, the answer to this question depends on the perspective of who is being asked. There are important and interesting differences between the ways the custodians of religion, such as rabbis, priests, and ministers, frame the religion and how ordinary folks do so in their lived religion in everyday life. As a sociologist, I myself steer away from this question, recognizing the important influence that social location plays in any answer to this question.

What is clear from my research is that the religious and ethnic components of Judaism are not easily disentangled. Even those who do not meet the religious and institutional criteria (and what these criteria are is itself contested territory) for being a "good Jew" nevertheless create a lived Jewish experience and identity for themselves from their sense of an ethnic, cultural, historical, and familial heritage. Their self-identification as Jews, and even as good Jews, is no less real than that of more traditional, affiliated Jews.

Within Judaism, there are critical issues at stake here, such as the question of "Who is a Jew" and how it defines who can become a citizen of Israel under the Law of Return (the policy that all born Jews can automatically become citizens of the state). In the United States, such issues are hotly contested among the Orthodox and the other denominations, with Orthodox rabbis not recognizing ordained Reform Jews as rabbis. This debate takes on great import in the case of conversion, for example, because if a woman is not "properly converted" according to an Orthodox standard, the Orthodox community may call into question the Jewishness of her children and whether these children can properly be married to other Jews! Obviously, the rabbis have a particular stake in the matter, which is framed by their dire concerns about Jewish survival in a country where intermarriage rates are rising. Individuals' concerns, however, are about how they themselves and their children can live out their Jewishness, rather than about the legal aspects of religious continuity according to Jewish law.

For both the traditional rabbi and the unaffiliated Jew, the relationship between practice and identity is at the center of the search for Jewish meaning, although the nature of this relationship is interpreted differently by each. While the custodians of religions emphasize traditional practices and their observance as if these practices determine a fixed identity, such practices are in fact ways that people perform the identities that they are trying on. Identities are always in a process of construction, as each person continuously works to create the most salient meanings for their lives. What my research points out is that the relationship between Jewish practice and Jewish identity is mutually constitutive. While practices serve as a way for individuals to perform identity, the process of negotiating identity itself becomes a significant form of Jewish practice, particularly for those who are unaffiliated and for whom being Jewish is unconnected to traditional Jewish rituals and observance. Obviously, these processes of identity formation are not "rituals" in the same way that we normally understand the term; they are often less concrete. Nevertheless, the ways in which unaffiliated Jews create and interpret their sense of being Jewish are themselves innovative Jewish practices – lived religion – outside of institutional structures. By including these rituals within our study of American Jewish practice, we succeed in broadening sociological conceptions of religious rituals to include those practices of lived religion.

CHAPTER TWENTY

Dis/Location

Engaging Feminist Inquiry in the Sociology of Religion

Mary Jo Neitz

The impact of feminism and feminist scholarship on the field of sociology has been much debated. This essay extends that debate to the sociology of religion and spirituality. I argue that those women sociologists who identified with the women's movement experienced a dislocation when they tried to move between their experiences as women and their experiences in the world of sociology. This chapter emphasizes one response, the call for a sociology for women, a radical rethinking of how we know what we know and for whom we undertake this project of knowledge production. I begin with a short discussion of feminism both inside and outside of the academy, and then I review a broad range of studies that contribute to making women visible and explore questions of gender and religion. Next I outline a method of inquiry that comes out of the work of Dorothy Smith and Patricia Hill Collins. It is a feminist theory that begins with an alternative epistemology, and posits a feminist sociology that takes as its core assumption the idea that all knowledge is located and interested. I end with three works that exemplify located, feminist research.

DEBATES ABOUT/WITHIN FEMINISM

Sitting down at my wordprocessor, I ponder the task before me. The idea of writing an essay on "feminist theory and the sociology of religion" seems so much more problematic than it did even ten years ago when I agreed to take on a similar task.[1] What it means to talk about feminism and what it means to talk about theory has been "complicated" by a decade of deconstruction. What do I say? Where do I begin? Feminists do not speak with a single voice, and feminist theory never was, and certainly is not now, a single perspective. What I write reflects my own passions, my own intellectual

---

[1] In the review essay "Inequality and Difference," I reviewed research on women and religion in the sociology of religion published before 1990 (Neitz 1993). This essay will address work published since that time. I also am looking primarily at research by sociologists. There are now large literatures looking at this topic by scholars in history, anthropology, and religious studies. These literatures are not included within the purview of this essay.

My deep appreciation to the many people who helped me think about this chapter and who read various drafts: Mimi Goldman, Janet Jacobs, Nancy Nason-Clark, Karen Bradley, Kevin McElmurray, and Ann Detwiler-Breidenbach, and special thanks to Lynn Davidman and Peter Hall.

journey, my own discoveries, my own engagement with questions raised by discourses in the sociology of religion, feminist thought, and the particular groups I have studied – and puzzled about – over the years.

Perhaps a first question is to ask whether we are not now "postfeminist." In both popular and academic cultures I sometimes encounter the claim that feminism is something that has come and gone. Popular news magazines such as *Time* and *Newsweek* have featured the death of feminism in cover stories in 1990 and 1998, respectively. At the same time, second-wave feminists continue to pursue such goals as equality in employment, health care for women, reproductive freedoms, and an end to violence against women. The new generation of "third-wave" feminists write their own *Manifestas* (Baumgardner and Richards 2000), run Internet sites, and organize for their own feminist goals.[2] Likewise, feminist graduate students in the 1990s were likely to be told that feminism was over as a movement of import for sociology: Feminists had some insights, but sociology had learned what there was to be learned from feminism. And moved on. While gender might be considered a variable, feminism was not theoretically *interesting*.[3] I, and the approximately one quarter to one third of American women who label themselves feminist in national opinion polls, disagree with this assessment.[4] Yet, it is also the case that long-term movements are not static. Second-wave feminists raised their children, girls and boys, in a different world from the one in which they had grown up. Rather than feminism being a revelation, for many third wavers, "Feminism is like fluoride...it's in the water," (Baumgardner and Richards 2000: 17). Early successes (and failures) produced changes in the frames that recruit later participants. Third-wave feminists do not necessarily look or talk like second wave feminists did. The 1990s' feminist zines, such as *Bust* (first published in 1993) and *Bitch* (first published in 1995), offer different content for a mostly younger audience from the still existing feminist publishing ventures of the 1970s, *Off Our Backs* and *MS.*, but the difference does not signify the death of feminism.

The idea of an ongoing social and cultural movement is captured by the notion that feminism is a discourse. Jane Mansbridge speaks in terms of the movement as "accountability":

> Most politically active feminists in any country work in occupations whose primary goal is not to advance feminism. When their work affects women, these feminists turn for conscious inspiration to the women's movement. They also feel accountable to that movement. The entity... to which they feel accountable is neither an aggregation of organizations or an aggregation of individuals. It is a discourse. It is a set of changing, contested aspirations and understandings that provide conscious goals,

---

[2] One example is the creation of feminist.com. For a list of organizations, as well as electronic and print resources, see Baumgardner and Richards (2000).

[3] For one account of graduate school in the 1990s, see Becker (2000).

[4] The political scientist Jane Mansbridge has looked at the poll data and reports the following: "If an interviewer from a national survey organization phones and asks the question, 'Do you consider yourself a feminist?' from a quarter to a third of American women these days answer 'yes'. This percentage is not much smaller than the percentage who consider themselves Democrats or the percentage that consider themselves to be Republicans. Nor does it seem to vary dramatically by race or class. In 1989, when a survey asked a representative sample of women in the United States, 'Do you consider yourself a feminist?' 42% of Black women said 'yes' compared with 31% of white women. As many working class women as middle class women said 'yes'" (1995: 27).

cognitive backing, and emotional support for each individual's evolving feminist identity. (1995: 27)

This view of feminism as changing and contested signals an openness and unbound-edness, a yeastiness essential to the bread and beer of feminism.

Academic feminists are a part of this discourse. Starting with the problem of inequal-ity between men and women, the discourse shifted as writers came to realize that we also needed to understand inequalities among women. We needed to think about how race and class and gender intersect in particular ways for different groups of women, creating different oppressions and opportunities (Collins 1991). Postcolonial writers reconfigured boundaries and brought feminist thought into the borderlands (Spivak 1988; Trinh 1988; Anzuldua 1987). Postmodern queer theorists questioned the stability of gender categories (Butler 1990). From a beginning in which second-wave feminists sought to examine and explain women's common oppression, some feminists have moved to deconstructions of the category of "woman" itself (Wittag 1981/1993). Femi-nist researchers working today do not assume that "woman" has a universal meaning.[5] Yet, feminism, much changed, with and without modifiers, persists as the most useful word to identify a way of thinking that begins with questions about the status and experiences of particular groups of women.

All of this ferment has produced new knowledge and new ways of thinking about women, men, and the relations between/among them. Although that thinking has been incorporated unevenly into the academic disciplines, there is now a considerable body of literature that examines gender in relation to religion. Women are now visible in a way that they were not before 1970. Feminism as discourse had an impact on academic life as well as in the popular culture.

In the 1970s those of us hoping to make a feminist revolution in academia spoke of three approaches to studying women. We acknowledged that the first question was likely to be "Where are the women?" Because women were, for the most part, invisible, early feminist writing largely took the form of critiquing male knowledge on this basis (e.g., Wallace 1975). The second approach was a response to the first: We called it "add women and stir." In this approach scholars take women as the object of study, using conventional disciplinary concepts and frameworks. This approach produces new knowledge about women and gender relations, but not necessarily new questions (e.g., England 1993). Some feminists suggested a third approach: They asked, What questions would emerge if we put women's experience at the center of the analysis, as active subjects and as knowers? How would our concepts and theories be disrupted? How does beginning in the location of women present new ways of thinking about key processes and institutions?

What difference can it make to begin with the location of women? The historian Ann Braude provides an example. Her analysis suggests a rethinking of the concept of secularization.[6] Braude examines the historical claims that religion declined in the United States during the colonial period, was feminized during the Victorian period,

---

[5] To see the multiplicity of current issues and framings among feminist researchers, see *Feminisms at the Millennium*, a special issue of *Signs*, Volume 25, Number 4.

[6] For a recent review of this concept in sociology, see Swatos and Christiano (1999). Their essay is an introduction to a special issue of the journal *Sociology of Religion* on the secularization debates.

and gave way to a secular order in the twentieth century. She states that "attention to gender helps to explain why these motifs, and the historical claims which ground them have held such explanatory power for historians, even though, from an empirical perspective, they never happened" (1997: 87). The received view, a tale of the growing absence of religion from the public sphere, reflects the theological views of a particular group of Protestant men, who observed the growing absence of mainline Protestant (male) ministers from the public realm. The story told from the location of women looks quite different. In her essay, Braude outlines a story that begins with the fact that women have always constituted a majority of participants in American religious life. The story she tells is organized around the *increasing involvement* of women. In her version of the story, given their numerical dominance, it is women's exclusions from the conventional narrative that must be explained. This places women's participation in the context of male power. Braude's story differs from the story about decline that dominates the literature: The common understanding of secularization "incorporates into the story of American Religion assumptions about women's powerlessness" (1997: 97). If women's power were considered in a positive light, then the dominant story would assume that the decline of mainline male participation in the public realm meant the decline of religion itself. Putting women at the center of the analysis changes the questions as well as the answers.

BECOMING VISIBLE: WOMEN AND GENDER

The last decade has seen a tremendous increase in the visibility of women. Increasing numbers of studies incorporate questions about women and gender. In looking at this literature, we can see instances where conventional approaches fold in women, but there also are instances where studying women leads scholars to ask new questions. In this section, I review a large literature that increasingly shows us where the women are and demonstrates how gender matters to sociologists studying religion.

Critiques of Androcentric Biases

Early and often, Ruth Wallace has raised the question, "Where are the women?" in the sociology of religion. The question has had a number of meanings in her work: She has questioned both the absence of research conducted from a feminist perspective and also the lack of opportunities for women in leadership positions, in both the organizations we study and the organizations through which we report our studies. She has been concerned about the relative absence of opportunities for women as leaders in religious organizations, especially the Roman Catholic Church in the United States (1975, 1992, 1997). She also has been concerned about the absence of women leaders in organizations where gender and religion are likely to be studied (2000). Several other scholars have examined the androcentric biases in the work of particular theorists. Erickson (1993) examines the work of Weber and Durkheim in the founding generation, and Otto and Eliade, from subsequent cohorts, on the distinction between the sacred and profane. The use of rational choice theory in the sociology of religion also has been criticized for androcentric biases from a feminist interpretivist perspective (Neitz and Mueser 1997) and from a critical perspective that borrows from Gramsci and Freud (Carroll 1996).

Gender as a Variable

Conventional sociology takes on the interest in gender with least disruption to main-stream methods and theories in standard variable analyses that use a person's status as male or female to explain some aspect of religiosity, for example having positive atti-tudes toward Christianity (Francis and Wilcox 1998) or seeking consolation in religion for health problems (Ferraro and Kelly Moore 2000). Miller and Hoffman (1995) offer an interesting variation on this type of study, in that they argue that preference for risk is what explains religiosity, with less risk averse people tending to be less religious. Women are more religious, they argue, because women are more risk averse. Others use gender and religion to explain other attributes such as educational attainment (Sherkat and Darnell 1999; Keysar and Kosmin 1995) or beliefs about suicide (Stack, Wasserman, and Kposowa 1994). For some, gender as the explanatory variable is not one's status as male or female, but rather how masculine or feminine one is according to measures on a personality inventory. Mercer and Durham (1999) suggest that more feminine scores predict greater disposition toward mysticism. Two studies in England among Anglicans and Methodists have also suggested that more feminine men and more masculine women are attracted to ministry as a vocation (Robbins, Francis, Haley and Kay 2001; Robbins, Francis and Rutledge 1997).

Women in the Protestant Mainline

Over the last two decades considerable research on women in mainline Protestant traditions has take women clergy as its focus. In a recent review of this literature, Chang (1997) notes three dominant themes: First, labor market approaches to clergy careers; second, public perceptions of female clergy; and third, gendered ministry styles. We know about the experiences of women clergy in congregations (Charlton 1997; Wessinger 1996), and women's career paths both within (Prelinger 1992) and across denominations (e.g., Zikmund et al. 1998; Nesbitt 1997; Chaves 1997). Research on gender differences in clergy values and styles offers some evidence that women are less hierarchical, more likely to use an intuitive style, and to have developed an ethics based on "responsible caring" (Finlay 1996; Lehman 1993; Wallace 1992). Olson, Crawford, and Guth (2000) showed sustained interests in social justice issues among women clergy in mainline denominations. Konieczny and Chaves (2000) use data from the 1998 National Congregation Study to add to our knowledge of demographic characteris-tics of congregations led by female pastors. Because the sample is the first nation-ally representative sample of congregations, it enables us to look beyond the mainline Protestant denominations which have been the focus of most of the work on women clergy. In contrast to earlier studies, Konieczny and Chaves find that the proportion of women pastors in urban and rural areas is nearly the same. Female-headed urban con-gregations, however, are likely to be predominately African American, and to have no denominational identification.

In a departure from the focus on clergy in much of the literature on mainline denom-inations, Julie Manville (1997) has applied a feminist analysis of gendered organizations to an Anglican parish in Australia. Manville examines the gendering processes which create and maintain a female "church within a church." Manville then shows how the separate domain of women could be – and was – dismissed by the priest and vestry. Women who crossed the boundaries into male domains experienced sexual teasing and harassment. Some women successfully cross the boundaries, but "at the expense of risking being labeled a man" (1997: 37). Manville's study suggests the fruitfulness of looking at the ways organizational practices produce and reproduce gender.[7]

Protestant Evangelical Women

Outside the Protestant mainline, ordination of women is less common, and studies are likely to focus on members rather than clergy (but see Wessinger 1993). A number of important ethnographies in the 1990s, beginning with Stacey and Gerard (1990) have helped readers to understand women's complicated participation in the evangel-ical cultures. For example, Ozorak (1996) explored the question of whether women felt empowered by religious participation. She found that women did not have access to power in conventional ways through religious participation, but that they received valued relational rewards from participation. With case studies of two large congrega-tions from Calvary Chapel and Hope Chapel parachurch movements, in *Godly Women* (1998) Brenda Brasher helps us understand how these women understand their partic-ipation in a context of male dominance. She finds that women accept gender polarity in congregations as a whole and establish separate women's ministries. But they claim that gender does not matter when it comes to God's message; the preaching, teaching, and healing is for everyone. Marie Griffith's (1997) study of Women's Aglow Fellow-ship, *God's Daughters*, describes the changing meaning of "submission" for evangelical women when most of them, by the 1990s, were not full time homemakers.

Gender and American Jews

In 1991, Lynn Davidman and Deborah Kaufman published much cited books about newly Orthodox Jewish women, in which feminist authors asked how modern women could make sense out of living in the Orthodox world. In contrast, Dufour (2000) looks at how women who identify as both Jewish and feminist "sift through" their options to create identities, combining elements of Jewish and feminist practices in such a way that they experience minimal conflict between the two (see also Davidman 1994). Jacobs also looks at the construction of Jewish identities, although in a very different context. In her research on the modern descendants of crypto-Jews, Jacobs investigates the gendered relationship between ethnicity and spiritual development (2000), and the role of women in preserving crypto-Jewish culture (1996).

Other researchers have examined issues of conflict among Jews over gender roles. In one extreme case, it resulted in a schism in a synagogue (Zuckerman 1997). Hartman and Hartman (1996) analyze data from the 1990 National Jewish Population Survey to examine inequality between American male and female Jews, according to their degree of participation and their denominational affiliation. One interesting finding is that gender inequality between spouses does not vary by denomination. In her study of con-servative Catholics, Evangelical Protestants, and Orthodox Jewish women, Manning

---

[7] See also Zoey Heyer-Gray's (2000) suggestive comment on the religious work women do.

(1999) broadens the questions about relations between feminist and religious values by looking across these religious families. In her sites, the meanings of both orthodoxy and feminism are contested, and this work serves to remind researchers of the benefits of problematizing both categories, rather than taking them for granted.

Gender and New Religious Movements

Gender relations in new religious movements, which include both religions new to North America and newly founded religions, continue to be a source of interest to sociologists of religion. Susan Palmer's controversial work argued, among other things, that new religions are places where women experiment with gender roles and sexuality (1993). In an interesting comparison of Brahma Kumaris in India and in Western countries, Howell (1998) contests and clarifies some of Palmer's claims. Marion Goldman's (2000) study of women followers of Bhagwan Shree Rajneesh investigates the psychological as well as social and cultural reasons why followers were disproportionately high achieving women. Goldman and Isaacson (1999) offer a too rare comparison of gender role ideologies in Christian and non-Christian based new religious movements.

Anglo-Roman Catholic Women

Feminist research on white Roman Catholic women has several strands, starting with those documenting the continuing feminist resistance to the male leadership of the church hierarchy. Katzenstein (1995, 1998) examines feminist organizations within the Catholic church, including Woman Church and the Women's Ordination Conference, in terms of practices of a discursive politics through which activists "are engaged in the construction of a knowledge community whose view of the institutional church and of the society is self-consciously at odds with the present day Catholic hierarchy" (1998: 107). Michele Dillon (1999a) also studied the Women's Ordination Conference and along with Catholics for a Free Choice, and Dignity (an organization supporting gays and lesbians within the Catholic church) examined these organizations within a broader emancipatory project initiated by the Second Vatican Council which located the authority within the Roman Catholic Church among the "People of God." Dillon shows how the people she studied use the church's own doctrines to dispute the reasonableness of positions taken by church authorities, and argues that these groups' contestation of Vatican authority offer evidence for pluralism within the Catholic Church.

Several writers tell the story of the opportunities and constraints experienced by women in Roman Catholic communities of sisters (Ebaugh 1993; Wittberg 1994; Wallace 2000). Others study lay women and their participation in congregational life. For example, Manning (1997) looks at how liberal and conservative Catholic women talk about reproductive choice and women's ordination. She suggests that, unlike Protestants and Jews who choose a denominational affiliation corresponding to their liberal or conservative leanings, the Catholic women must deal with each other in the same organization. Yet she is unsure whether this "moderating tendency" is enough to counter the polarized viewpoints of the two camps of women. Thus, the research on both lay women, sisters, and on leaders of resistance movements portrays a church that is polarized over gender issues.

Latina Women

Much of the work on Latina women also has focused on Catholic traditions (but see Jacobs 1996, 2000), although often those that are domestic and informal. Ana-Maria Diaz-Stevens (1993) has focused on the importance of cultural identification and ritual activity carried out away from the institutional church. Detwiler-Breidenbach (2000) presents a case study of a pastor's wife, whose quasi-official role bridges the public and private, as well as the Anglo and Hispanic communities. Ebaugh and Chafetz (1999) argue that women in immigrant communities have an "ironic role": They both reproduce traditional cultures and produce change. Peña and Frehill (1998) argue for more cultural measures that assess embeddedness. They find that Latina women who are embedded in a Latina culture engage in religious practices that are often missed by researchers, but that produce a culture of resistance that helps them take a stance against both dominant societal institutions and Latino ones.

African-American Women

In the sociology of religion, black women are still largely invisible as pastors and as members of congregations, despite the common recognition that black churches are central to the African-American community, and that women are central to black churches. Part of this invisibility is due to the heavy Euro-American focus of the scholarship in the field. But this is compounded by the fact that the places where black women are most likely to be found are also less visible in the literature. Although there are recent signs of change (Gilkes 1998), the traditionally African-American denominations, including the AME and COGIC, have been slow in ordaining women (Dodson, 1996, 2002; Gilkes 2001). The nondenominational storefronts, where black women preachers are over represented, are virtually invisible to sociologists who study denominationally based religion (but see Baer 1993). Works looking at "church food" (Dodson and Gilkes 1995) or a reading of spiritual song traditions as alternative understandings of Bible stories that are liberating and egalitarian (Gilkes 1996) move into the realms of culture and lived religion. As I discuss later, in order to have the fuller, more inclusive understanding of American religion, it is necessary to start in places where those people who are outside of the organizational hierarchies are to be found (see also Davidman, Chapter 19, this volume).

Global Feminism in the Sociology of Religion

Unfortunately it is still the case that most feminist work in the sociology of religion continues to take the United States, and to a lesser extent Canada, as its universe. The increasing interest in Latin America and migrations is an exception. There is also a growing interest in Islam. Articles such as those by Meyer, Rizzo, and Ali (1998) on citizenship rights for women in Kuwait, and Moaddel (1998) on Islamic modernism in Egypt and India versus Fundamentalist Islam in Iran illustrate the usefulness of analysis of societies outside North America. Gerami and Lehnerer (2001) look specifically at how Iranian women negotiate the patriarchal practices of Islamic Fundamentalism.

Religion and the Body

Movement toward thinking about religious practices instead of religious organizations, and religion outside the institutions instead of within formal religious organizations, has led to a new body of research that looks at religious practices in relation to possibilities and constraints linked to embodiment as female bodies. Looking at lived experience allows us into the presence of women, but what we see is full of cultural contradictions. Of particular note is the new work that begins to look at the social/cultural regulation of reproduction, sexuality, and violence and abuse of women. This is relatively new terrain because sociologists are only beginning to think about embodiment. Klassen's study of home birth (2001) brings together an understanding of lived religion and embodied religion, disrupting conventional views of both religion and childbirth. Susan Sered (2000) in *What Makes Women Sick?* addresses what she calls the cultural politics of somaticization. Through a series of specific investigations – of abortion, childbirth, infertility, breastfeeding, rape in military contexts, ritual purity, and body image – we see religion as a site for resistance as well as a site for oppression for women in Israel. But, Sered argues, the forms of resistance religion offers largely use women in iconic ways rather than offering women agency. In addition, Sered shows the intersection of different institutional sources of oppression. Time and time again in this book, Sered demonstrates connections between culture, religion, and politics. Marion Goldman extends these questions to the male experience, looking at the connections between the culture of elite Protestants in the 1950s, and body and spirituality at Esalen Institute. Goldman argues that while Esalen has consistently emphasized body-mind connections, these have a gendered aspect: Women focused on healing aspects of body work, but for many elite Protestant men, Esalen made available the idea of sport as a "structured, embodied spirituality" (2000: 9). The religious practices developed at Esalen could be perceived as manly, by virtue of the link with sports.

Nason Clark (1997, 2000) has been a leader in both investigating church people's response to abused women, and in counseling pastors to take a leadership role in attending to issues of sexual violence among members of their congregations.[8] Studies of sexual abuse survivors, with samples of inner-city minority women and of Mormon women, suggest that spirituality can be a resource for counseling women for whom religion is a cultural resource (Kennedy, Davis, and Taylor 1998; Pritt 1998). Another approach is to investigate religious organizations' complicity in matters of sexual abuse. Essays in a collection edited by Shupe, Stacey, and Darnell (2000) examine sexual abuses by religious leaders, as well as ways that organizational structures can inhibit such behaviors, or conversely, protect and hide the perpetrators. Others have studied how religious belief systems are internalized and then used by victims of wife abuse and sexual abuse (Lundgren 1998; Jacobs 1995).

God is a Woman

Feminist goddess religions imagine female deities. This disruption of tradition raises issues of religion and the body in a quite different way. A number of writers have shown how women practitioners of contemporary witchcraft find goddess imagery a

---

[8] To be discussed in more detail later.

source of empowerment (Griffin 2000; Foltz 2000; Neitz 1990). Looking at female and male countercultural spiritual seekers who were unaffiliated with Goddess worshipping groups, Bloch (1997) found that women spoke about finding validation through Goddess imagery, and both women and men spoke of the need for balance between God and Goddess. Men did not speak about gender inequalities, but rather about seeing the Goddess "in terms of nurturing and assistance" (1997: 189). Berger (1998) discusses the ramifications of reimagining deity as God and Goddess for gender relations and child rearing in a neopagan community. Neitz (2000) further explores the ramifications of neopaganism for gender identity and sexuality. The essay "Queering the Dragonfest" looks at gender-bending and the disruption of heteronormitivity that occurs among witches with a postpatriarchal ideology. The essay narrates a story about witches who create a religion in which sexuality is sacred, and remove from it assumptions of patriarchy. In so doing, they create the possibility for a "queering" of heterosexuality allowing for play with and among sexualities and genders.[9]

Feminist perspectives constitute a reference point for the authors of the studies reviewed here. The studies themselves are a part of an ongoing conversation about women and gender in the sociology of religion. All extend our knowledge about gender and religion. They challenge conventional conceptualizations to varying degrees. Marginal locations, while neither necessary or sufficient, often disrupt taken for granted ideas and help us see things differently, in part because studies that locate subjects away from the centers of organized religion are more likely to also find that the theories and concepts of the discipline do not quite fit. This experience of "not fitting" is the origin of the paradigmatic shift that birthed feminist sociology. In the next section, I explore a type of feminist theorizing that begins in the acknowledgment of the bifurcation of consciousness between the experiences of women and mainstream sociology.

THE FEMINIST THEORY AS A METHOD OF INQUIRY

In 1985, Barrie Thorne and Judith Stacey, in their famous essay, "The Missing Feminist Revolution in Sociology," stated that feminist theory in sociology had been less successful in causing a paradigm shift in the discipline of sociology than it had in history or anthropology. Although acknowledging the many contributions, they argued that, within sociology, feminism has been contained and coopted. In part, they thought this reflected the fragmented nature of the discipline, but they argued it also reflected dominant methodologies and positivist traditions which place a value on knowledge phrased in abstract and universal terms. Stacey and Thorne pointed to the Canadian sociologist Dorothy Smith as someone in sociology who is "reconsidering the relationship between knower and known to develop a method of inquiry that will preserve the presence of the subject as an actor and experiencer" (1985: 309). The promise of

---

[9] This last article points to an emerging body of literature on gay and lesbian experiences with organized religion. I have not included this literature here because it rarely problematizes gender in an explicit way. For examples, see Dillon (1999a) for a discussion of Dignity's confrontation with the heterosexist policies of the Catholic church; Ponticelli (1999) studied Exodus International, a Christian organization dedicated to supporting groups which encourage gays and lesbians to reconstruct their sexual identities as straight. The anthropologist Ellen Lewin's (1998) study of gay and lesbian commitment ceremonies suggests possibilities for studying religious practices of gays and lesbians outside of the institutions.

feminist theory is in its proposal for a method of inquiry that calls us to a different way of doing sociology. In what follows, I present Dorothy Smith and Patricia Hill Collins as proponents of a feminist epistemological shift.

Dorothy Smith: Institutional Ethnography and the Relations of Ruling

Dorothy Smith began publishing her project, the developing "sociology for women" in the mid-1970s. Although sometimes difficult to read, this evolving body of work speaks to an increasing number of second- and third-wave feminist sociologists, women and men.[10] Trained in ethnomethodology and Marxism, Smith critiqued the positivist assumptions of mainstream sociology and advocated for an "interested sociology," a sociology that began from women's experience. In early writings, Smith described her own foundational experience as a graduate student, in which the theories and concepts of sociology constituted a separate cognitive domain from the experience she had as an adult woman, a mother. She did not experience the two different cognitive domains simply as "alternatives" but rather as a "bifurcated consciousness" (1987: 17–43; 45–104).

Smith came to understand her own experiences as a woman and a sociologist in the context of the women's liberation movement. She writes:

> Beginning in women's experience told in women's words was and is a vital political moment in the women's movement. Experience is a method of speaking that is not preappropriated by the discourses of the relations of ruling. This is where women began to speak from as the women's movement of our time came into being. . . . In this political context the category of "women" is peculiarly non-exclusive since it was then and has remained open-ended, such that the boundaries established at any one point are subject to the disruptions of women who enter speaking from a different experience, as well as an experience of difference. (1997: 394)

In recent years, as students have taken up her approach to understand "how things happen" to other groups, Smith has come to call her project a "people's sociology" (1999: 5). Although earlier discussions have tended to frame the contribution of Smith, as well as Collins and others, in terms of "standpoint theory," that term is used in widely varying ways by different authors, and Smith now rejects it for herself.[11] I focus my discussion here on Smith's method of inquiry, institutional ethnography. In conjunction with her students, Smith has continued to develop institutional ethnography as a way of studying structures of power beginning in the location of particular people living their everyday lives (DeVault 1998; Campbell and Manicom 1995). Smith and her students intend that information uncovered through such investigations will be useful for those working for social change.

---

[10] Smith writes of the importance of her continuing dialogs, especially with students, for her efforts to "to make plain just what it is which differentiates this way of doing sociology" (1999: 4).

[11] In her influential book, *The Science Question in Feminism* (1986) Sandra Harding classified three different types of feminist methodologies, and grouped together a number of writers who had used the term "standpoint," including Smith. Within Harding's broad purview, these scholars' positions did indeed have something in common relative to the others Harding surveyed (whom she types "feminist empiricists" and "feminist postmodernists"). Yet their positions remain distinct from one another. See the debate in *Signs* (1997) 22: 341–402.

Institutional ethnography carries out the project of the women's movement. Smith argued for a "sociology for women," beginning with calling for the entry of women into sociology as subjects. This relocates the sociological subject. Smith asks us to begin in the everyday and everynight experience of ordinary women. The everyday world is neither transparent or obvious. The organizing logic of our everyday work lies elsewhere. For Smith, the job of sociologists is to discover how things are put together so that they "happen" to us in the ways that they do.

Smith wants us to start from the margins and look toward the centers of institutional power. In her early work, Smith argued that we should begin our research with "the standpoint of women" (1987). In Smith's usage, this did not mean that all women share one same position. Rather, Smith was saying that analysis begins in the material world of women, rather than with social theories and concepts which are inherently object-fiying. When we use standard concepts we see ourselves and the worlds we study from the outside. Smith rejects the label "standpoint theorist," because, as the above quote suggests, she does not see women as a group occupying a site of epistemic privilege.[12] Instead, she argues that we begin with women's subject location as embodied beings living in the material world, "situating the inquiry in the actualities of people's living, beginning in the experiences of living, and understanding that inquiry and its product are in and of the same actuality" (1992: 90). It is a way of shifting the ground of know-ing: Once one acknowledges that knowledge is socially organized, we can see it as an attribute of individual consciousness (1992: 91). The experience of women is a starting point, but not the ending point. Smith's goal is not to analyze individual women but, rather, to enter into institutions from the position of those who experience them.[13]

Smith's training as a Marxist is apparent in her understanding of social relations. Social relations coordinate activities through the work that people do. Smith is concerned with uncovering the organizational practices through which ordinary people orient themselves to institutions. The social for Smith is the concerting and organizing of activities. While Marx was concerned primarily with the organization of commodity production under capitalism, Smith believes that, at this point, the production of knowledge, ideology, and discourse constitute an essential aspect of what we need to analyze to understand the social relations of ruling. Smith sees language as an organizer of our activities. She has become increasingly interested with how texts mediate between actual practices (and the work that people do) and the discursive. It is often through texts that we enter into an institutional order. Smith reminds us that texts are crucial because power is generated and held in relations which we experience through texts, including the forms we fill out, or others fill out about us, and the cards that we carry (1992: 93). Smith offers a method of inquiry that starts with embodied individuals in the everyday and everynight world, looks at the work that they do, and how texts are present in their lives, mediating between them and the relations of ruling. The sociology that comes out of this meaning of inquiry is in process. Smith uses the metaphor of the map:

> . . . The metaphor of the map directs us to a form of knowledge of the social that shows the relations between various and differentiated local sites of experience without

---

[12] The idea of the standpoint of women as a site of epistemic privilege is clearest in Nancy Hartsock's (1983) feminist revision of historical materialism.
[13] See Scott (1991) for a discussion of the dangers of focusing solely on experience.

subsuming or displacing them. Such a sociology develops from inquiry and not from theorizing: it aims at discoveries enabling us to locate ourselves in the complex relations with others arising from and determining our lives; its capacity for truth is never contained in the text but arises in the map-reader's dialogic of finding and recognizing in the world what the text, itself a product of such an inquiry, tells her she might look for. (1999: 130)

Smith advocates a disruption of how sociologists have understood theory. She looks for a dialogic form of theory, a feminist theory that begins in the experiences of women, and produces an active text, in dialogue with a reader.

Patricia Hill Collins: Black Feminist Thought and Intersectionality

Patricia Hill Collins's project has some basic similarities with Smith. In *Black Feminist Thought* (1991), Hill Collins draws on the voices of black feminist writers and activists to make visible the subjugated knowledges of black women. Collins describes the condition of being "outsiders within" generated by the historical situation of black women's role in retaining and transforming an Afrocentric world view in African-American communities while, at the same time, finding employment as domestic workers in white households. This particular location produced an angle of vision, allowing them to see contradictions in the construction of womanhood, a kind of consciousness that Collins sees produced in many of the setting in which black women in the United States today find themselves. Too often marginal to the movements of white women and black men, the lives of black women point to the intersections of race and gender as well as class.

Also classed as a standpoint theorist (Harding 1986), standpoint means something specific for Collins. It does not refer to the experience of an individual – rather a standpoint is the product of a group's common experience of oppression, and it focuses on the social conditions that produce such experiences. Collins (1991) is one of the founding theorists of what is now being called the "intersectionality paradigm." Standpoint and groups located through intersecting structures of oppression are intimately tied for Collins:

> ... Current attention to the theme of intersectionality situated within assumptions of group-based power relations reveals a growing understanding of the complexity of the processes both of the generating groups and accompanying standpoints. ... What we have now is increasing sophistication about how to discuss group location, not in the singular social class framework proposed by Marx, nor the early feminist frameworks arguing the primacy of gender, but within constructs of multiplicity residing in social structures themselves, and not in individual women. Fluidity does not mean that groups themselves disappear, to be replaced by an accumulation of decontextualized unique women whose complexity erases politics. Instead the fluidity of boundaries operates as a new lens that potentially deepens understanding of how the actual mechanisms of institutional power can change dramatically while continuing to reproduce long standing inequalities of race, gender and class that result in group stability. (1997: 377)

For Collins, both standpoint and intersectionality are ways of talking about group-based oppression and group-based power relations.

In addition to her focus on the standpoint of black women, Collins differs from Smith in that she claims the value of alternative traditions, local knowledges which produce theorizing, often in narrative forms. She calls generations of black women, storytellers, writers, and activists organic intellectuals who offer forms of knowledge outside the circle of sociological insiders, but who have much to offer us, if we would listen to them. While Smith is not sure that knowledge as such can be transformative, and perceives a kind of division of labor between sociologists who reveal the relations of ruling and activists who use that knowledge to produce social change, Collins sees her project of voicing Black Feminist Thought as emancipatory.[14] Collins believes that local knowledges can offer resistance to the dominant knowledge. Her understanding of the importance of local knowledges as tools for resisting the dominant culture is especially useful to sociologists of religion to help us reframe how we think about "religions of the disinherited" or religions of countercultural groups.

Both Smith and Collins write against positivism. What they offer is a different kind of "theory." Rather than a totalizing theory, they offer a method of inquiry. They both offer a vision of sociology that is interested; that is critical. They contend that to be objective is to maintain the relations of ruling.[15] They both understand that writers as well as subjects are located, and that location matters.[16] In the next section, three examples demonstrate this kind of feminist inquiry in the sociology of religion.

BEGINNING IN THE LOCATION OF WOMEN

Beginning in the location of women requires a reorientation in the sociology of religion. It means moving outside the domain of pastors, public religion, formal organizations, denominational creed, and organizations. It suggests more attention to devotional practices, wider cultural discourse, bridging boundaries, and moving between public and private. It suggests more attention to religious practices and to religion outside the institutions. In this section, I discuss three recent works which are particularly rich in their implications for feminist work in the sociology of religion.

Nancy Nason-Clark: Breaking the Silence

Nancy Nason-Clark provides an important example of a scholar-activist whose work starts with the location of women. Nason-Clark's work has focused on examining wife abuse within the context of the Protestant churches in the Maritime Provinces

---

[14] Collins (1997) argues that while Smith's critique of the relations of ruling is powerful, Smith does not attend to the ways that subjugated knowledge provides alternatives.

[15] Sandra Harding's (1986) notion of "strong objectivity" is useful here.

[16] To quote Smith: "The project of inquiry from the standpoint of women is always reflexive. Also, it is always about ourselves as inquirers – not just in our personal selves, but our selves as participants. The metaphor of insider and outsider contains an ambiguity that I should be more watchful of, for I disagree . . . that there is an outside in society. . . . As I have used the metaphor, I want to stress that those outside places are inside. In the sense I'm trying to capture there are no modes of investigation other than those beginning from within. . . . Established sociology has powerful ways of writing the social into the text, which produce society as seen from an Archimedes point. A sociology for women says: "You can't have that wish." There is no other way than beginning from the actual social relations in which we are participants. This fact can be concealed but not avoided" (1992: 94).

of Canada. Issues of violence against women are among the most significant feminist issues of our time with ramifications for the life chances of individual women, and importance for academic debates about how we conceptualize family and formulate our critiques of patriarchal power.

Combining quantitative analysis of surveys and intensive interviews, Nason-Clark has studied battered women, pastors, transition house workers, and church women in evangelical and liberal Protestant churches.

In *The Battered Wife: How Christians Confront Family Violence*, Nason-Clark begins by listening to the voices of abused women. Their faith can be a cultural resource that helps abused women heal. Nason-Clark explores how conservative Christian women face problematic teachings such as the celebration of the intact family, the glorification of suffering, and an emphasis on forgiveness. This can be exacerbated when the faith community is separated from the secular world. Still Nason-Clark reports that evangelical women do not themselves see their faith as a liability. Their Christian community is important to them, and their faith helps them cope (1997).

When Nason-Clark turns to look at the pastors it is from the location of women, asking how is it that the pastors contribute to the relations of ruling. Ninety-eight percent of pastors in the study had experience in counseling women who had marital problems. In cases of repeated physical violence, pastors condemn the violence. In no cases did pastors suggest that women return to the abuser. But pastors are reluctant to see a marriage terminated until all sources of help have been exhausted. They underestimate the extent of violence in their communities and have less knowledge about the impact of male violence on women, tending rather to focus on the harm that is done when a woman leaves the family. Pastors also fail to understand women's economic vulnerability in the family. Nor do they see how women are disadvantaged in the labor market. The clergy tended to see abuse as a spiritual issue related to men's lack of spiritual growth. What distinguishes clergy from other counselors is the importance they place on maintaining the family unit and their excessively optimistic belief that men can stop the violence.

Nason-Clark also reveals the largely unseen work of church women. Although outside of the public domain and largely invisible – even to their own pastors – Nason-Clark finds that these women see the suffering of other women and want to do something about it. They are quick to provide comfort and slow to criticize (2000: 362–3). While church women share the belief that family life is "enshrined with sacred significance," for many this belief fed their distress that church and community offered so little to families in crisis (1997: 130–1). Some of them choose to work with community agencies, despite the tensions between secular and religious cultures.

Nason-Clark's work speaks to several audiences, academic and nonacademic, church people and secular feminists in the battered women's movement. Her project is one that "breaks the silence." To church people, her message is that battering, not divorce, destroys abusive marriages. To the feminists, she argues that abuse, not religion, degrades women.

Cheryl Townsend Gilkes: Black Women in Church and Community

Cheryl Townsend Gilkes's work is exemplified by her recently published collection of essays, *"If it wasn't for the women…": Black Women's Experience and Womanist Culture*

In Church and Community. Gilkes notes in the introduction that, "understanding the importance of women to the institutions of African American life and culture required immersion in the social worlds of black women" (2000: 1). Gilkes's lifelong immersion in the worlds of black women community activists and church women is reflected in how she captures the constraints the women she studied face and their resistance against it in an account that is both celebratory and critical.

Several essays come from her research on gender relations within COGIC (Church of God in Christ). It is worth noting that this is not Gilkes's own denomination. Gilkes's experiences connect her to the women she studies, and her writing moves between locations using fully what she knows from listening to others, and what she knows from her own experiences. In these essays, she explores the relative autonomy of the women, and posits a "dual sex" political system within the black Holiness and Pentecostal churches. Although women could not be ordained, "community mothers" had power and authority. Gilkes notes that white and black women have different experiences in their churches which leads to different understandings of the problems. White women experience exclusion, tokenism, and isolation. Black women share with black men the experience of invisibility in a racialized society, but, in their churches, they are visible, coproducers of the black community.

In a chapter called "Some Mother's Son and Some Father's Daughter: Issues of Gender, Biblical Language and Worship," Gilkes shows how churched and unchurched black women experience the sustaining power of their religious tradition. Gilkes asks, "What is the relationship between the importance of black women to the social construction of black religious knowledge and the ambivalent response of black women to white feminist movements?" (2000: 125). Her analysis of oral tradition and Afro-Christian practices explicates how preaching as a male discourse exists in interdependence with the response to the call. Women's roles as prayer warriors, singers, and givers-of-testimony transform "private troubles" to "public issues" within a covenant community, and establishes their ownership in their churches and traditions.

Several of these essays show African-American women as cultural workers within their own communities. Yet the essays also reveal Gilkes's concerns about the degree to which the historically black churches fail women, by refusing to ordain women and support them, and by failing to address the issue of cultural humiliation. Gilkes calls for an affirmation of life (2000: 194), which values black women. For Gilkes, speaking out of the African-American tradition, sacred centers are power centers organizing an alternative center of power against the relations of ruling. Gilkes is not uncritical of black churches, but she stands within the churches and speaks from the inside out.

Milagros Peña: Border Crossings

The blurring of the boundaries between religious and nonreligious institutions, public and private, sacred and secular, and between grassroots politics and the politics of everyday life that we see in the works of Nason-Clark and Gilkes takes on an added dimension in the work of Milagros Peña (see Peña, Chapter 27, this volume). Focusing on a Woman's Alliance that emerged among Anglos and Latinas on both sides of the border between Mexico and the United States, Peña shows that religious women and lay women found commonalities on women's issues, despite the fact that they were divided by nationality. Working through their differences, women – some of whom had been marginalized in the Latino movement and in the women's movement – mobilized around local issues presented for women in the border context. Peña suggests that the border crisis created fields of opportunity, with a blurring of boundaries occurring on several levels. Peña's work is important here, in part because of her emphasis on starting with local context, but also for its contribution toward our understanding of the global aspects of women's oppressions. Furthermore, her discussion of boundary crossing adds a critical dimension: We need conceptualizations that allow us to explore not just pastors, but congregations, and not just congregations but unbounded movements when that is where the women are.

These three authors follow a research strategy that starts with the experiences of women in a particular location but moves through that to an emergent understanding of institutions of oppression and movements of resistance. They do not impose abstract theories or categories developed outside upon their subjects; the process of inquiry itself is feminist, in part because they write as much *for* their subjects as about them. Their accounts are deep and rich contributions to what we know about the particularity of women's lives and how women's everyday lives intersect with religion.

CONCLUSION

Some of the issues and questions raised here have also been raised by observers of con-temporary religion. For example, there is a sense that the old theories and categories are insufficient in the new work on "lived religion" (Hall 1997). There is a larger con-cern for the collapse of mainline hegemony in American culture. Some who are quite observant about what is going on in the religious scene, however, have not yet thought through fully what the epistemological consequences of the collapse are for the kind of work that we do: We can no longer speak with omniscient neutrality about American religion – if "we" ever could.[17]

Feminists are among those calling for research that begins but does not end in the experiences of the people we study. Dorothy Smith's institutional ethnography is a methodology that helps researchers perform analyses that make connections from em-bodied individuals to work/practices to texts to discourses and the relations of ruling. Patricia Hill Collins draws our attention to the intersectionality of race, class, and gen-der, and shows us the power of the voices of alternative traditions. Feminist theory, as they envision it, reflects a new paradigm in sociology.

Researchers in the sociology of religion have made a substantial shift in the last two decades: Women are no longer absent; gender is no longer ignored. Attending to gender, however, cannot merely be a matter of "add women and stir." Adding women has a wonderfully disruptive potential, especially when looking at women forces us to look in new places and at different things. Adding women raises questions about local practices and about embodiment, emotion, and sexuality. For sociologists of religion,

---

[17] As the essays in Spickard, Landres, and McGuire (2002) demonstrate, reflections on knowledge claims among scholars of religion are not limited to feminists, although feminists are well represented among the authors in the volume.

adding women is a dislocating act. New questions present themselves. Categories are problematized, and they can't so easily be reestablished. Generalizations don't hold. Feminist sociologists show us a world that is gendered, and they show why that matters. To do the feminist project advocated here entails the production of knowledges that are partial and located, and accountable to the open and ongoing discourse that is feminism.

Religion, Political Behavior, and
Public Culture

PART FIVE

Religion, Political Behavior, and
Public Culture

CHAPTER TWENTY-ONE

Religion and Political Behavior

Jeff Manza and Nathan Wright

In the history of social science research on group-based political alignments, religious cleavages have often been shown to be a more powerful predictor of individual voting behavior than class location (e.g., Rose and Urwin 1969; Converse 1974; Lijphart 1979; Dogan 1995; Brooks and Manza 1997). Yet it has received significantly less attention than studies analyzing class politics, and even when acknowledging the existence of religious-based political divides, scholars have often assumed that some other, nonreligious antecedent factor lays behind it. As Demerath and Williams (1990: 434) put it, "While students of voting do cite religious affiliation as a significant variable, they often tend to interpret its effects less in terms of theology and ecclesiastical influence than in terms of ethnic, class, and regional factors lurking beneath the symbolic surface."

Since the late 1970s, however, dramatic religious mobilizations around the world – including a fundamentalist Islamic revolution in Iran, the visibly active role of the Catholic Church in the Solidarity movement in Poland in 1980–1, growing publicity about "liberation theology" movements in Latin America, and, in the United States the rise of politically active conservative Christian organizations such as the Moral Majority – have made it more difficult for scholars to ignore the ways in which religion shapes political action and behavior. And indeed, over the past fifteen years there has been considerable growth in research on (and scholarly controversies about) the association between religious group memberships, doctrinal beliefs and practices, and voting behavior.[1]

This chapter dissects what we have learned from this scholarship about how religion and political behavior are linked. We should note two limitations of our analysis at the outset. First, we consider only one type of political action – voting – and not other types of religious influence on political life, such as participation in social movements, political lobbying, or the impact of religion on public opinion. Second, our analytical focus is limited to the postindustrial democracies of Western Europe and North America, with special attention to the (arguably "exceptional") American case. Lack of space

---

[1] There is, unfortunately, no systematic overview of the growing literature on religion and political behavior. This chapter aims to fill that gap. See Wald (1996) and Leege (1993) for overviews of the research on the American case; a good textbook treatment, again for the United States, can be found in Corbett and Corbett (1999).

precludes a broader consideration of religious impacts on voting behavior in the newer democracies in Eastern Europe, South America, and Asia. This should not be taken to mean that the impact in those latter countries is modest. Quite the contrary: The spread of democratization processes around the world (e.g., Markoff 1996) has frequently been influenced by social movements rooted in churches (not least the civil rights movement in the United States; see Morris 1984; more generally, see Smith 1996a); and in a number of countries a government with direct or strong indirect ties to fundamentalist (or quasi-fundamentalist) religious organizations is in, or has recently been, in office (the list of such countries would include Iran, Turkey, India, and Algeria). These issues are explored more fully elsewhere (Arjomand 1993; Marty and Appleby 1993).

This chapter is in three parts. We begin with a discussion of the diverse ways in which religion may influence political behavior, and how these differences may manifest themselves in different polities. Part two examines, in some detail, the U.S. case, where the most extensive social science research literature has developed, and it provides the case that can most easily be related to all of the analytical elements introduced in part one of the chapter. Part three surveys the comparative evidence from Western Europe, including the factors that strengthen or weaken the religious cleavage across different national contexts.

HOW DOES RELIGION INFLUENCE VOTING BEHAVIOR?

Religion as a Social Cleavage: A General Model

Any enduring and significant social cleavage, whether based on class, race/ethnicity, linguistic preference, region, gender, or religion, will find varying degrees of expression in political conflicts at four distinct levels: (a) social structure; (b) group identity; (c) political organizations and party systems; and (d) public policy outcomes (cf. Coleman 1956; Bartolini and Mair 1990; Manza and Brooks 1999: Chapter 2).

"Social" cleavages are always grounded in the social structure of a given society. In the case of religion, there is of course wide variation in the types of religious divisions found in different countries. In some countries, a single denomination (the Catholic Church in Italy, Ireland, or Belgium, the Anglican Church in Britain, the Lutheran Church in Sweden, and so forth) has the allegiance of most citizens who claim a religious identity. Here the social basis for a cleavage lies in the division between devout or practicing adherents versus secular or nominally affiliated church members. In other countries, however, there is much greater competition between denominations or religious traditions with large memberships (e.g., Germany, the Netherlands, the United States). Religion can, in such societies, provide a basis for social stratification and inequality, in which members of a "dominant" denomination have privileged access to valued positions (e.g., in the long dominance of "WASP" denominations in the United States).

The existence of group divisions at the level of social structure may not matter much for political life unless these are mobilized in some fashion. Actors have to perceive these divisions as meaningful and unequal (Ebersole 1960; Koch 1995). Religious group identities reflect the degree to which religious differences, whether between competing religious denominations or, alternatively, between citizens with and without religious identities, come to be the basis for group consciousness. Here, the question is to what degree do adherents identify with a particular religious tradition, and perceive it to be in conflict with other traditions.

The mechanisms that strengthen or erode religious group conflict have been well charted. Religious movements can activate new or dormant identities and make salient group-based conflicts. High levels of religious homogamy and religious mobility are particularly important for sustaining a sense of group identity (particularly in societies with competitive religious markets), and the decline of either can be expected to produce declining religious conflict in general (Wuthnow 1988: Chapter 5; Kalmijn 1991). Similarly, moves toward ecumenicism and away from explicit denominational competition may reduce group-based identities, although ideological differences between religious liberals and conservatives may be enhanced as a result (Wuthnow 1988: Chapter 12; Wuthnow 1993; Lipset and Raab 1995).

It is through the organizational form of party systems that religious divides in social structure and group identity take on electoral significance. In most early democracies, one or more major parties emerged with the explicit or tacit backing of powerful churches. These parties often came to be called Christian Democratic parties (usually in countries with strong Protestant or mixed Protestant/Catholic traditions, but also in Catholic Italy), while Catholic parties appeared under a variety of names (the Catholic People's Party in Austria and the Netherlands, the Popular Republican Movement in France, and so forth).[2] These religious parties initially sought to mobilize voters on the basis of religious identity, although over time the more successful parties (most notably, the Christian Democratic parties of West Germany and Italy) became "catchall" parties of the right or center-right, with ambitions of appealing to an electoral majority. In other countries, however, the modern party system was secularized – and direct links between parties and churches were cut – but even in some of these countries adherents of particular religious traditions sometimes lined up consistently with one party (with electoral campaigns making more or less explicit attempts to mobilize voters on religious grounds).[3] In the United States, the allegiance of Catholics and Jews with the Democratic Party, and evangelical Protestants with the Republican Party, exemplify this pattern.

Finally, the policy outputs of states provide a crucial feedback mechanism that reinforces the relevance of religious divisions for political life. The historical origins of religious parties can often be traced to "state-church" conflicts in which the growing power of secular states on societies posed a direct threat to church power. More recently, conflicts over public policies, particularly on issues such as education, gender equality, or reproductive rights, have the potential to divide voters on the basis of religious orientation. Such policy conflicts, when they emerge, provide a feedback mechanism by activating latent religious divisions at the group and organizational level.

Types of Religious Cleavages

There are four distinct religious cleavages that have been shown to be associated with voting behavior: (a) church attendance; (b) doctrinal beliefs; (c) denominational groups;

---

[2] For a comprehensive list of postwar religious parties in Europe, see Lane and Ersson (1994: 103).

[3] Examples here would include France, Ireland, and Britain. We discuss this issue later.

and (d) local/contextual aspects of congregational memberships. The first and most basic of these cleavages is between voters who attend religious services and consider religion important in their lives, from those who are not engaged in religion. The most straightforward measure of engagement is attendance at religious services. Church attendance may be important for political preferences for several reasons: (a) it provides reinforcement of religious beliefs and ethical precepts; (b) it may reinforce group identities, especially in ethnically- or linguistically rooted churches; and (c) it connects religious beliefs to the larger world, including politics. This "religiosity" cleavage has been shown to be especially powerful in many countries in Western Europe (Heath et al. 1993), but it has long been understood as significant in the United States as well (e.g., Wright 2001).

The second, and most commonplace, way in which the religious cleavage shows is to examine differences between denominational families, at least in those countries where at least two or more denominations claim the allegiance of substantial proportions of the population. In North America and Western Europe, these divisions are often cast as Protestant versus Catholic, although in some countries divisions among Protestants or with other major religious denominations (notably Jews) may also hold some significance.

A third religious cleavage concerns the impact of religious beliefs held by individuals, as opposed to denominational memberships or identities. Probably the most salient division here is between religious traditionalists, who believe in the literal truth of the Bible, and religious modernizers, who adopt a context-bound interpretation of the teachings of the Bible (Hunter 1983; Smith 1998; but cf. Wright 2001). Traditionalists – once politically engaged – may seek to apply narrowly defined biblical concepts to solve social problems, while modernizers adopt more flexible, context-bound interpretations of the Bible. Divisions based on the content of religious beliefs, including those within religious denominations, have frequently been said to be rising in importance relative to traditional lines of denominational influence.

Finally, a number of analysts have examined the "contextual effects" of local religious communities or individual churches. Individual church leaders provide sources of information and opinions to lay members that may sometimes be at odds with national denominational positions. Local congregations sometimes engage in political projects that draw in members into various forms of political action and experience (e.g., Wuthnow and Evans 2001). Churches can frequently be settings in which friendship networks form, especially in conservative churches, leading to distinct subcultures (Smith 1998). Such networks provide a basis for political discussion and reinforcement of individual beliefs. For all of these reasons, local congregations may have distinct impacts on political behavior (Wald, Owen, and Hill 1988; Gilbert 1993).

The Dynamics of Secularization

At the center of many scholarly debates about religious influences on political behavior has been the question of secularization. Although a number of distinct social processes are often subsumed under the secularization label, the basic assumptions underlying the model of secularization are that one of three processes has occurred (or is occurring) over time: (a) a decline in the importance of religion in the lives of individuals; (b) a decline in the social and political influence of religious organizations; or (c) a decline in engagement in political life by religious organizations (what is sometimes referred to as the "privatization" thesis).[4] These secularization processes imply different things for political behavior. The first suggests individual-level change: As education levels and general societal affluence increase, voters may become less reliant on simple religious heuristics to govern all aspects of their lives, including how they vote (e.g., Dalton 1988, 1990; Inglehart 1990; Dogan 1995). The second and third suggests organizational-level change: As church attendance declines or religious organizations lose members (in absolute or relative terms), the capacity of churches to influence elections and the shape of political debates can be expected to decline (e.g., Wallis and Bruce 1992). Similarly, if churches become less involved in worldly affairs, their capacity to influence the voting behavior of members will likely decline.

The secularization thesis has been widely debated (see, for example, Chapters 5, 8, and 9, this volume), and we cannot take up all of its implications in relation to political behavior here. Evidence of declining levels of religious voting would be consistent with a secularization thesis. Yet correlation is not causation, and we cannot assume that declining religious voting is necessarily the result of the declining religious commitments of individuals, the declining aggregate strength of religious beliefs, or the declining influence of religious organizations, in the absence of other information. For example, changes in party systems (such as the merging of religious and nonreligious parties into new officially secular parties), or the changing shape of national or local issue agendas (such as the declining salience of a particular issue) can sometimes have dramatic and independent impacts on the levels of religious voting independent of secularization processes (Van Kersbergen 1999).

RELIGION AND POLITICS IN THE UNITED STATES: AMERICAN EXCEPTIONALISM?

Viewed from a comparative perspective, the United States has long appeared exceptional in the degree and level of religiosity found among its citizens (Greeley 1991; Tiryakian 1993). Foreign observers – including most famously de Tocqueville and Weber – have long reported evidence of unusually high levels of religiosity in defiance of Enlightenment theories of religious decline. Post–World War II survey data appear to confirm that, when contrasted with other comparable developed capitalist democracies, religiosity among U.S. citizens appears unusually high. Americans routinely claim higher levels of church membership and attendance at religious services, are more likely to believe in God, and to claim that religion is of considerable importance in their lives, than citizens in other postindustrial capitalist democracies (Wald 1996: Chapter 1). They are much more likely to hold fundamentalist beliefs, such as God performing miracles (a belief held by 80 percent of Americans) (Lipset 1996: 61). The evidence also suggests little or no decline in religious affiliation or belief in the post–World War II period, and overall, higher levels of religious participation in the twentieth than in the nineteenth century (cf. Finke and Stark 1992; Lipset 1996: 62). American political leaders of both major parties now routinely declare their devotion to God.

---

[4] For sophisticated overviews of the secularization model, see especially Casanova (1994) and Yamane (1997). The most plausible contemporary defenses of the model would include Chaves (1994), Yamane (1997), and Wallis and Bruce (1992).

The typical European pattern of religious organization – in which a state-sanctioned religious body dominated the religious landscape – failed to materialize in the United States. The absence of a state church has resulted in the flourishing of an unprecedented range of denominations and sects since the beginning of the Republic. The remarkable history of denominational growth and schisms has long interested sociologists of religion (e.g., Liebman, Sutton, and Wuthnow 1988). Alongside periodic moves toward ecumenicism (particularly among the largest and most well-established denominational bodies) has been a long-term process of denominational change that has continually expanded the options for religious practice available to most Americans (Finke and Stark 1992).

Historical Evidence of Electoral Impacts

Religion has long been understood to be an important source of political division in the United States.[5] The "new political history" that developed in the 1960s and 1970s established quantitative evidence of the growth and persistence of religious cleavages in shaping voter alignments throughout the nineteenth century (e.g., Benson 1961; Jensen 1971; Kleppner 1979; Swierenga 1990). "Ethnoreligious" cleavages, as they came to be known in this literature, reflected the intersection of denominational memberships and ethnicity in shaping political behavior. Controversies over the disestablishment of official state churches provided the earliest source of religious political division, beginning virtually at the founding of the Republic (Murrin 1990). Supporters of state churches, especially the Congregationalists, were generally aligned with the Federalist Party, while members of lower status churches challenging the hegemony of the traditional churches were more likely to line up with the Jeffersonian Democratic-Republicans. The antebellum period (1828–60) is generally conceded to have been loosely characterized by the alignment of voters from "liturgical" or "ritualist" religious traditions with the Democratic Party of Andrew Jackson and his heirs, and voters from pietist and evangelical denominations with first the Whig Party and later the Republican Party (Jensen 1971: 62–73; Kleppner 1979; Howe 1990; Swierenga 1990: 151–5).

In the post–Civil War period, party competition in the North and Midwestern sections of the country for white votes appears to have been even more decisively structured by ethnic and religious divides (Kleppner [1979: 196] even goes so far as to describe late-nineteenth-century parties as "political churches.") Up until 1896, the Republican Party received very strong support from Episcopalians, Congregationalists, New School Presbyterians, and Methodists; while the Democrats drew support most heavily from Catholics, and less broadly from Lutherans and Unitarians (Swierenga 1990: 157). In the "system of 1896," Republican domination of the North and Midwest involved strong support from nearly all Protestant denominations, while with rare exceptions the Democrats were limited to the votes of Catholics and the relatively small unionized working class. The post-Reconstruction South, of course, was a very different matter;

---

[5] In *American Commonwealth*, Bryce (1891: 36) claimed, for example, that "Roman Catholics are normally Democrats, because, except in Maryland, which is Democratic anyhow, they are mainly Irish. Congregationalists and Unitarians, being presumably sprung from New England, are apt to be Republicans."

the Democratic monopoly through World War II made religious differences of little consequence in that region.

With the coming of the New Deal, many analysts assumed that the sharp ethnoreligious cleavages in the North would decline in strength as class factors appeared to be increasingly important. But it appears instead that the increase in class divisions during the New Deal largely developed alongside, not in place of, traditional religious cleavages. Roosevelt generally performed better among all electoral groups than Democratic candidate Al Smith did in 1928, leaving mostly unchanged *relative* levels of support from most key religious groups (except for Jews; e.g., Gamm 1986: 45–74). The core of the Democratic coalition continued to be defined by working class Catholic and Jewish voters in the North and Midwest (and white voters of all religions in the one-party South). The greatly weakened Republican coalitions of the 1930s and 1940s, by contrast, continued to receive disproportionate support from Northern white mainline Protestants (Sundquist 1983: Chapter 10; Reichley 1985: 225–9).

The early post–World War II period was one of unusual religious stability but, by the late 1960s and early 1970s, important changes were taking place in nearly every major religious denomination. The mainline Protestant denominations had been experiencing a *relative* membership decline (in which they were losing religious market share) for many decades, and beginning in the late 1960s this decline accelerated. Long associated with the political and economic status quo, these denominations were deeply influenced by the great moral crusades of the period: The Civil Rights Movement (CRM) and the demand for racial justice, protests against the war in Vietnam, and the women's movement. A growing split between liberal Protestant clergy supporting the CRM and other 1960s' movements and a more conservative laity appeared to generate intradenomination (or intrachurch) tensions (see the studies collected in Wuthnow and Evans [2001] for a broad overview of political tensions within mainline Protestant churches). The evangelical Protestant churches also reacted sharply – but very differently – to the social and cultural movements of the period. Resisting most of the trends of the period, many leaders of evangelical churches became involved in organizing or promoting new Christian Right movements and discourses which sought to defend "traditional values" (Bruce 1988; Himmelstein 1983; Smith 1998). Among Catholics, internal reforms associated with the Second Vatican Council in the mid-1960s produced profound transformations within the Church, as have rapidly changing social practices among Catholics (and all Americans) which fundamentally challenge Church teachings on issues such as sex, abortion, and other social issues (Greeley 1985: 55ff). In addition to the changes within the major religious traditions, there also appeared during this period numerous new religious movements of dizzying variety (Wuthnow 1988), large unaffiliated evangelical churches (e.g., Shibley 1996) as well as the rapid growth of more established religious groups outside the mainstream (such as the Mormon Church).

Empirical Research on Recent Trends in Religious Voting

The availability of survey data that go beyond the crude (and largely uninformative) Protestant versus Catholic divide has largely constrained systematic scholarly investigations of religious influence on voting behavior in the United States to the period after 1960 (Manza and Brooks 1999: 102–03). However, this is precisely the period in which the most rapid changes have been hypothesized to have occurred, and not surprisingly a number of empirical questions about these changes have vexed analysts. Four questions have been central in recent debates: (a) What has been the impact of the political mobilization of evangelical Protestant groups since the 1970s? (b) Have Catholic voters become less Democratic, and if so, why? (c) To what extent has a political realignment toward the center occurred among mainline Protestants, and why? (d) How have doctrinal divisions, especially between religious liberals and conservatives and often within denominations, produced changing patterns of political alignment?

Rise of a New Christian Right? Perhaps the most widely debated thesis about religion and politics in both the mass media and among political analysts in recent decades concerns the possibility of a political realignment among conservative Protestant voters. The sudden emergence of the new Christian Right (CR) in the late 1970s as an organizational force in U.S. politics, and the visible role of some early CR groups such as the Moral Majority in the 1980 elections seemed to herald a new type of political conflict in which conservative religious values were becoming increasingly important in the political system. The confluence of Ronald Reagan's 1980 election (and even larger victory in 1984), the 1980 recapture of the Senate by the Republicans for the first time in nearly thirty years, and the intense media attention given to early CR leaders such as Jerry Falwell, Pat Robertson, and others led many observers to draw the conclusion that these events were closely related.

In the relatively brief period since 1980, however, the varying fortunes of the CR at the national level have cast doubt about these hypotheses. The initial social science search for a mass base to the CR in the 1980s unearthed both very modest support for groups such as the Moral Majority and little evidence that the CR mobilized a significant group of voters (see Manza and Brooks [1999: 95–6] for references). Indeed, by the late 1980s, many informed observers were emphasizing the sharp decline of the CR, at least as a force in national politics (e.g., Bruce 1988; Jelen 1991: 135–55).

In the 1990s, the cycle of debates over the CR came full circle around yet again. The rapid growth of the Christian Coalition, a multidenominational organization that grew out of Pat Robertson's failed 1988 presidential bid helped to revive scholarly interest in and respect for the political power of the CR. The Coalition has emphasized state and local politics, working up to the national level by gaining influence with the state-level Republican Party (Rozell and Wilcox 1995). In 1995, the organization claimed some 1.6 million members organized in sixteen hundred chapters across the country. These chapters were said to have distributed some thirty-five million voter guides in the 1994 midterm elections alone (Wald 1996: 233; cf. Regnerus et al. 1999). With the renewed prominence of the CR in politics, a new spate of studies appeared, many advancing arguments or evidence of a recent shift of evangelical voters toward the Republican Party (e.g., Green et al. 1995; Wilcox 1996; Kellstedt et al. 1994: 308). However, the recent organizational decline of the Christian Coalition has again prompted a retreat from scholarly and popular attention to the CR and pessimism about its electoral impact (see, e.g., Green, Guth, and Wilcox 1998; Kohut et al. 2000).[6]

---

[6] A final set of debates about the impact of the CR concerns the mobilization of evangelical voters and its impact on turnout. To the extent that it has been examined, the general conclusion has been that evangelical voters did increase their turnout in 1980 and thereafter (see, for

Analyses of the CR have generally focused on the national level. But the impact of conservative Christian groups may be less visible but have more impact at local or state level. Independent of the trajectory of certain of the more visible national organizations, the CR has remained consistently strong in terms of subcultural institutional infrastructure over the past couple of decades at least. This extensive institutional infrastructure exists as a powerful force for political activism on certain social issues and around local and state elections (Smith 1998). For example, the impact of the CR on mobilizing voters appears to be more significant at the subnational level (Green et al. 1996: 103–16). In these low-turnout elections, the mobilization of even a few hundred additional voters can have a significant impact.

Whither Catholics? The possibility that Catholic voters are shifting away from alignment with the Democratic Party toward a more centrist position is a second issue debated among analysts of religion and U.S. politics. Most social scientists who have studied this question have reported evidence of Catholic dealignment from the Democratic Party (e.g., Reichley 1985: 224–5, 299–300; Petrocik 1987; Kellstedt and Noll 1990; Kenski and Lockwood 1991). Abramson, Aldrich, and Rohde (1998: 156) even characterize the shift among Catholic voters as "precipitous."

Two explanations for the hypothesized shift among Catholic voters have been postulated. The most common explanation has been that it is driven by economic interests: Catholics have become progressively more affluent over time, gaining and even surpassing Protestants on a number of measures of socioeconomic attainment (cf. Greeley 1989: Chapter 7), and are hypothesized as swinging to the right as a consequence. The second explanation hypothesizes that Catholic voters were disproportionately resistant to the increasingly liberal social issue agenda of the Democratic Party since the 1960s.

However, the thesis that Catholic voters have in fact shifted away from the Democrats is somewhat controversial. Greeley (1985, 1989, 1999) has argued that a more careful investigation of the data shows that a lot of the trends emphasized by proponents of the Catholic dealignment thesis are highly exaggerated because they take the 1960s (an unquestioned high point of Catholic support for the Democratic Party, driven in part by the candidacy of Catholic John Kennedy in 1960) as their point of departure. In this view, Catholics were never as closely tied to the Democratic Party as the dealignment imagery implied, and thus have not shifted nearly as much as has been hypothesized. Our own work (Manza and Brooks 1997, 1999) has reached similar conclusions.

Whither Mainline Protestants? "Mainline" or "liberal" Protestant denominations, especially Episcopalians, Congregationalists (after 1957, the United Church of Christ), and Presbyterians, have long been overrepresented among the American political elite and in business, academe, and the military establishment (e.g., Davidson 1994). Reflecting their social and cultural power in American society, the "Protestant establishment," as E. Digby Baltzell (1964) famously characterized them, has thus long been viewed by many social scientists as a solidly Republican constituency in the postwar period. In

example, Bruce 1988: 101–2; Wilcox 1989; Smidt 1989: 2), although the evidence for such claims is often anecdotal or fairly limited and more systematic investigation has found no impact on national elections (e.g., Manza and Brooks 1997).

recent years, however, the stability of the political alignments of mainline Protestants has been questioned. Several analysts have found evidence of a shift of this group away from the Republican Party and toward the political center (e.g., Lopatto 1985; Kellstedt et al. 1994; Manza and Brooks 1997, 2001).

A variety of ways of accounting for these trends has been advanced in the literature on the mainline denominations. One account emphasizes rising levels of social issue liberalism among these groups. The receptivity of many mainline Protestant religious leaders and local congregations to politically liberal messages on such issues, beginning in the 1960s with the Vietnam War and on issues of racial and gender inequality and sexual freedom, suggests one possible explanation for the relative shift away from the Republican Party (cf. Wuthnow and Evans 2001). Second, some analysts have emphasized changes in the demography of the mainline Protestant groups, in which more conservative church members are defecting – or not joining in the first place – in favor of stricter denominations. Left behind is a group of adherents in the mainline churches that is more in tune with the messages of the clergy (e.g., Finke and Stark 1992: Chapter 5). Finally, the relative loss of economic and political power to non-Protestant groups suggests a third possible source for the movement of liberal Protestants away from the Republican Party. A number of scholars have emphasized the relative gains of other religious groups, as we have seen above, that have reduced the power of the established Protestant denominations.

Toward "Culture Wars"? A number of analysts have argued that a religiously rooted set of cultural conflicts have emerged, with religious conservatives of all denominations lined up on one side and religious liberals and seculars on the other (e.g., Wuthnow 1988, 1989, 1993; Hunter 1991; DiMaggio, Evans, and Bryson 1996; Layman 1997). Some highly visible conflicts over issues with clear religious content – abortion, school prayer, the teaching of evolutionary biology, public support for controversial works of art, rising divorce rates and the alleged breakdown of "traditional" family values, gay and lesbian rights, and others – have indeed generated considerable public controversy since the 1960s, and appear to have become increasingly important in shaping voters' political alignments (Brooks 2000). Central to the "culture wars" thesis are two arguments. First, there has been a breakdown of traditional denominational alignments, as *intra*denominational conflict has grown. Second, these conflicts are not only an "elite" phenomenon, but polarization is increasingly reflected in the political consciousness of the mass public. The growing proportion of Americans with no religious identity – doubling from 7 to 15 percent in the 1990s, according to data from the General Social Survey (Hout and Fischer 2002) – also suggests the possibility of increased political divisions between those with versus those without religious identity.

Systematic empirical tests of the culture wars hypothesis have produced decidedly mixed results. Layman (1997) found evidence using the National Election Study that the political impact of doctrinal conservatism has had an increasing effect in that narrow period on partisanship and vote choice, net of other religious, sociodemographic, and political variables. Whether such findings would hold over a longer historical period is unclear. Bolce and De Maio (1999) find that antipathy toward fundamentalists is very high, even among otherwise tolerant segments of the electorate. Brooks (2000) demonstrated that social issues have become increasingly salient in presidential voting, and that general societal-wide liberalization on these issues has significantly benefitted the Democratic Party. In other work, Brooks (1999) shows that family values have become an increasingly important social problem, but that it is primarily religious conservatives who express concern about it.

Other analysts have explicitly challenged the model. DiMaggio, Evans, and Bryson (1996) examined changes in public attitudes toward a wide array of social issues and found little support for the view that any significant polarization has occurred since the 1970s. Davis and Robinson (1996) found that the gap between religious conservatives and liberals is much smaller than often thought, limited to a handful of social issues, and on economic issues religious conservatives are actually somewhat more supportive of governmental action to secure greater equality than religious liberals.

New Evidence Using Relative Measures of Religious Cleavages

The recent investigations of the first author, in collaboration with Clem Brooks, explicitly sought to reconsider these five issues, as well as to develop some overall estimates of the changing impact of religious groups on U.S. party coalitions (Manza and Brooks 1997, 1999, 2001). We briefly summarize this line of research here. Three advances over earlier research on religion and politics defined the methodological contributions of our research. First, analyses of the relationship between social groups and political behavior that fail to employ statistical models that allow for distinctions between trends influencing *all* groups from those influencing only *some* groups neglect important information. Second, research on the social group foundations of political behavior should include analyses of (a) group size and (b) group turnout, alongside group voting patterns. The size of groups and their turnout rates will shape the *impact* of group-based alignments on major party electoral coalitions, a crucial way in which the interaction between religious groups (who seek influence) and political parties (who seek votes) takes place (see Manza and Brooks [1999: Chapter 7] for further discussion). Finally, research on religious cleavages and political behavior in the United States should employ adequate measures of the cleavage itself. Although considerably less common than twenty years ago, some analysts of religion and politics have persisted in failing to take into account the divisions *among* Protestants as well as *between* Protestants, Catholics, Jews, and others.

Employing models embodying these principles, our investigations of the changing contours of religion and political behavior in the United States suggested a number of conclusions, some of which are consistent with the thrust of previous findings, and others that challenge the conventional wisdom:

- The religious cleavage as a whole has declined very modestly since 1960. The decline is due solely to the shift toward the center of one group – liberal Protestants – and thus does not reflect any societal-wide trend toward dealignment.
- Liberal Protestants have moved from being the most Republican religious group in the 1960s, to an essentially centrist position by the 1990s. This transformation has overwhelmingly been driven by their increased liberalism on social issues.
- Conservative Protestants have *not* realigned toward the Republican Party, in large measure because they have always been Republican partisans in the period (since 1960) for which we have adequate measures. Much of the confusion about the political preferences of conservative Protestants reflects a one-time shift toward

the Democratic Party in 1976 (and to a lesser extent in 1980) in response to the candidacy of the born-again Christian, Jimmy Carter.

- Catholic voters have not undergone any significant realignment since the 1950s. The elevated levels of Democratic voting in 1960 and 1964 are not to be found in the 1950s and should properly be understood as reflecting the unusual political context of those elections. While analysts of Catholic dealignment were right to suggest that Catholics were becoming more economically conservative, their Republican shift on economic questions has essentially been offset by increasingly moderate views on social issues.
- Significant changes in the impact of the religious cleavage on the Democratic and Republican parties has occurred. Because of their shrinking size and decreasing loyalty to the Republican Party, mainline Protestants have provided a drastically reduced share of Republican votes in recent elections (declining from 30 percent of all Republican voters in 1960 to just 12 percent in 1992). Conservative Protestants have increased their share of votes within the Republican Party primarily because of the reduction in votes from mainline sources, not because of changing partisanship or increased overall size in the electorate. Voters without any religious preference have grown in both parties from very low percentages to about 7 percent of Republican voters and 14 percent of Democratic voters.

To be sure, these findings hardly settle these issues, and debates can be expected to continue in the future (of particular controversy are findings about the lack of a clear shift among conservative Protestants: see, e.g., Kohut et al. 2000; Layman 2001; we respond to these and other challenges in Brooks and Manza 2002). Furthermore, our investigations – along with those of most other analysts of religion and politics – have primarily focused on presidential elections; it may be that in Congressional elections, or in state and local elections, the impact of religious identities on political behavior will have different effects (cf. Layman 2001). These questions deserve further attention. And of course, future changes in the religious marketplace (a perpetual feature of U.S. religion) and the issue of ideological controversies dividing large religious groups ensure a dynamic environment in which new analyses of old questions will be called for.

A Note on Religion and African-American Voters

To this point, our discussion of religion and politics in the United States has focused almost entirely on the impact of religious identities on white voters. The reason for this is fairly straightforward: The strong alliance of black voters with the Republican Party before the New Deal, and the Democratic Party afterward (an alignment that strengthened significantly in the 1960s and the passage of civil and voting rights legislation) has not been significantly shaped by religious differences among blacks in the same way as among whites. For example, recent surveys find that even African Americans who support a socially conservative agenda are still much more likely to vote Democratic (Wilcox 1992).

Black churches tend to be more embedded in political life than their white counterparts. In national surveys, African Americans consistently report that religion is more important in their daily lives than white respondents, as well as reporting more praying, higher levels of attendance at religious services, and higher rates of church membership.

Church services more often feature political addresses from public officials, and civic political meetings more often feature prayers, hymns, call-and-response-style oratories, and even the passing of offering plates for political contributions, than would be found in comparable white churches and communities (cf. Harris 1999; Pattillo-McCoy 1998; see also McRoberts, Chapter 28, this volume). And African-American religious theology and practice is often characterized by being distinctively concerned with collective political issues. African-American churches are dominated by the key themes of oppression and deliverance, expressed as collective properties that require collective efforts to provide increased opportunities (Lincoln and Mamiya 1990). The powerful and central institutional presence of African-American churches allowed them to be central players in the mobilization of political protests in the Civil Rights Movement of the 1950s and 1960s (Morris 1984). Many African-American churches have made and continue to make explicit efforts to register voters and mobilize them to vote for Democratic candidates (Lincoln and Mamiya 1990; Harris 1994, 1999; Calhoun-Brown 1996).

Given such evidence, however, only small impacts of religion have been found among African-American voters. There is some very modest evidence that religious involvement promotes political participation among African Americans (cf. Harris 1994, 1999). Data from the 1984 Black Election Study indicate that although church attendance is not a strong predictor of voting rates, going to a "political church" strongly influenced the likelihood of voting in a positive direction (Calhoun-Brown 1996). Finally, some analysts have found that both voter turnout and interest in politics are lowest among African Americans with no religious affiliation (Kellstedt et al. 1994).

In short, the existing evidence suggests that the political impact of black churches is strongest in arenas other than voting behavior – for example, on local, community, or neighborhood politics (see McRoberts, Chapter 28, this volume), recruitment to social movements, or as a direct voice through lobbying or other political activities.

RELIGION AND POLITICS IN COMPARATIVE PERSPECTIVE: WESTERN EUROPE

Two peculiarities of the American electoral system and religious landscape potentially make the relationship between religion and political behavior unique: the electoral system and the high degree of pluralism in the religious marketplace. The electoral system, in which legislative candidates compete in single-member districts and in which two political parties have been invariably dominant at the national level for over 130 years, has precluded the emergence of religious parties. In other democratic countries, religious parties have not been so hobbled, and in many cases they have thrived alongside secular parties of the right and left. In the United States, no such party ever developed. The second important difference is that the high level of religious pluralism in the United States opens the possibility of multiple lines of religious cleavage in comparison to polities with one or two main denominational groupings. In this section, we highlight some of these differences from the American model by considering some features of West European party systems.

The comparison between Western Europe and the United States is additionally informative because of the historical origins of the religious cleavage, and significant variation in the religious landscape across Europe. Lipset and Rokkan's (1967) landmark theoretical overview of the sources of social cleavages in democratic societies outlined a complex set of historical processes triggered by two revolutions, a "national" revolution and an "industrial" revolution. The resulting social divisions produced by these twin revolutions were viewed as having produced stable patterns of group-based political conflict, expressed through modern party systems. The most important of these cleavages included those based on class divisions (triggered by the industrial revolution), religion, ethnicity, and language (triggered by the national revolution). The precise articulation and relative magnitude of each of these cleavages varied from country to country, often depending on the sequencing of party formation and democratization (cf. Mann 1993). In some countries, a religious cleavage came to be embedded in the party system, through the formation of political parties with strong ties to dominant religious institutions.

The European religious landscape also varies. Three distinct patterns of religious identity can be found in Western Europe: Countries that are mostly Catholic (e.g., Italy, Ireland, France, Austria, Belgium, Spain); countries that are mostly Protestant (in particular the Scandinavian countries, but also Britain); and countries with more equal proportions of Protestants and Catholics (Germany, the Netherlands, Switzerland). The magnitude and form of the religious cleavages found in different countries can be expected to vary depending on the structure of the religious field (cf. Dalton 1988, 1990). For example, analysts generally find that Catholic countries, religiously divided countries, or countries without a state church, have higher levels of religious division in voting behavior than countries with a state-sanctioned church which claims the allegiance of most citizens.[7] But important exceptions also have been noted: Levels of religious voting in Britain have sometimes been said to be as large as those of class divisions (cf. Miller and Raab 1977; Rogowski 1981), and among the Scandinavian countries (with state churches) religious-based political divisions also can be found (Stephens 1979).

Finally, and again in contrast to the United States, arguments about the importance of secularization processes in the European context have long and repeatedly been asserted. Economic prosperity and rising levels of educational attainment have long been viewed as factors eroding religious cues for voting behavior (see, e.g., Baker, Dalton, and Hildebrandt [1975] on West Germany; Sundberg and Berglund [1984] on the Scandinavian countries; Eisenga, Felling, and Lammers [1994] on the Netherlands; and the various country-specific studies in Franklin, Mackie, and Valen [1992]). Other analysts have argued that the decline in church attendance across many European countries is weakening the salience of religion for voters (see, e.g., Books [1980] on Italy and West Germany; Mendras [1991] on France; and comparatively on a number of countries, Dogan [1995]).

Macro Factors: The Fate of Religious Parties

Most significant religious parties in European polities are located on the center-right of the political spectrum, and are usually known as Christian Democratic parties (for overviews, see Berger 1982; Hanley 1994; Lane and Erson 1994; Gallagher, Laver, and

---

[7] This point can be related to the larger finding in sociology, by now well established, that religious pluralism leads to higher levels of religious practice, belief, and salience than are found under conditions of religious monopoly (Warner 1993; Stark and Finke 2000).

Mair 1995: Chapter 8). The largest of these parties are Catholic in origin, such as those in Italy, Austria, Belgium, Luxembourg, and Switzerland. (The Italian Christian Democratic Party has recently collapsed because of scandal, but governed, or was part of the governing coalition, for most of the postwar period.) The German Christian Democratic Party, which has governed the Federal Republic (West) Germany between World War II and the late 1960s, and again from 1983 until 1998, has been a "biconfessional" party with roots in both Catholic and Protestant traditions. The Christian Democratic Appeal in the Netherlands is another biconfessional party (formed in a merger in the late 1970s between the Catholic People's Party and two smaller Protestant parties). Purely Protestant parties are mostly limited to Scandinavia, where Christian Democratic parties with ties to Protestant churches emerged in the 1950s and 1960s to contest elections in Denmark, Norway, and Sweden (albeit with relatively little success). The only major country in Western Europe without a significant religious party is Britain, and Ireland is a complicated case.[8] In France, a Catholic party in the Fourth Republic (1946–58), the Popular Republican Movement, evolved into the two major conservative parties of the Fifth Republic, the Gaullist, and (to a lesser extent) the Union for French Democracy blocs. Although the direct connection to major religious bodies has largely been broken, there is continuing evidence of a strong association between church attendance and/or religiosity and support for one of the major conservative parties (Heath et al. 1993; Lewis-Beck 1998).

The electoral performance of these parties has traditionally been strong, although declining in most countries in recent years. In those countries where a religious party has been the dominant party on the center-right of the political spectrum, such as in Germany, Italy, Austria, Belgium, Luxembourg, and the Netherlands, vote shares averaged over 30 percent, and in Germany over 45 percent, from the 1950s through the early 1990s (see Gallagher et al. 1995: 194). In all of these countries, secular parties of the right (or sometimes the center, such as in Germany) compete for votes and often become governing coalition partners. The rise of new right-wing parties, and declining rates of church attendance across most European countries (discussed later), have combined to put considerable pressure on religious parties (van Kersbergen 1999). In such an environment, to remain electorally competitive, many of the religious parties have tended to become more secular in their appeals over time, a pattern not unlike that of social democratic parties in these same countries (Przeworski and Sprague 1986). Nonetheless, the persistence and continuing strengths of religious parties across Europe (and their distinctive impact on policy outputs) suggest an important difference with the American model.[9]

---

[8] In overwhelming Catholic Ireland, with very high rates of religiosity, neither of the two major parties (Fine Gael and Fianna Fail) have organized linkages to religion, and both parties are plausibly classified as center-right parties (Gallagher 1985). Yet Fine Gael has affiliated itself with the Christian Democratic parties in the European Parliament and in cross-national bodies. Not coincidentally, the British political system has important parallels to the United States, in that members of Parliament are elected in a first-past-the-post system, which discourages the formation of major third parties (although not to the same degree as in the United States).

[9] In the comparative welfare-state literature, the "conservative" welfare states of continental Europe that have been built or consolidated under governments controlled by religious parties, some unique policy outcomes are visible. Perhaps the most notable are the strong forms of social provision for citizens, especially mothers, outside the labor market. See, for example, Esping-Andersen 1990; Castles 1994.

Individual-Level Factors: Religion and the Alignment of Voters and Parties in Western Europe

The persistence of religious parties in Europe suggests an avenue for political expression of religiosity that is more explicitly connected to the party system than in the United States. At the same time, there is a much wider consensus that secularization processes at the individual level that are weak or nonexistent in the United States have proceeded much farther in Europe (Dobbelaere and Jagodzinski 1995; Jagodzinski and Dobbelaere 1995; Berger 1999). Yet secularization need not imply declining levels of religious voting: New cleavages, such as those between secular and religious voters, may replace older Catholic/Protestant divides; and voters with religious identities may be more likely to act on the basis of those identities even if there are fewer of them. The robustness of the religious cleavage, in those countries where one exists, has frequently been proclaimed (as we noted earlier). So what has been the impact of these factors for individual voting behavior?

The existing literature suggests two paradoxical findings. First, where a religious cleavage has been embedded in the political system, religious identities continue to exert a significant impact on individual voting behavior; at the same time, there has been a general (but not universal) weakening of the religion-vote association in Europe. The most carefully studied case by far is the Netherlands, and we consider some of the evidence from that country first. Dutch society has long been characterized by what have come to be known as "pillars," reflecting stable, lasting, and loyal connections between religion and voting. The four pillars consisted of Catholics, Protestants, and nonconfessionals divided into Labour and Liberal constituents. Each pillar developed its own political organization, with the Catholic and Protestant parties consisting of their followers regardless of their social class, the Liberal party consisting of middle- and upper-class nonconfessionals, and the Labour party consisting of working- and lower-middle-class nonconfessionals (Eisenga et al. 1994). Party loyalty was fierce among all four pillars, particularly among Catholics and Calvinists. From 1922 to the 1960s, Dutch Catholics were considered among the most loyal voting bloc in the world, consistently giving more than 85 percent of their votes to the Catholic party. By 1973, however, Catholics were giving less than half (48 percent) of their votes to the Catholic party, and shortly thereafter the Catholic party merged with the two largest Protestant parties to form the Christian Democratic CDA. This new combined party's first electoral showing in 1977 was a mere 31.9 percent of the overall popular vote in the Netherlands, less than what the Catholic party alone had received in 1963, and it has declined further since then (Eisenga et al. 1994). The breakdown of pillarization has largely been attributed to the forces of modernization and secularization, and these forces are widely believed to have completely eroded what was once the strongest religious voting cleavage in the world (Eisenga et al. 1994; Andeweg 1982; Becker and Vink 1994; Irwin and Dittrich 1984; Miller and Stouthard 1975). The emerging party system has been characterized a number of different ways: As a new left-right political ideological continuum (van der Eijk and Niemoller 1987), as reflecting a postmaterialist cleavage (van Deth and Geurtx 1989), or along new political party lines united by ideological views rather than class and religious makeup (Middendorp 1991).

Yet changes in class structures and secularization processes do not necessarily produce a decline in the actual religious (or class) cleavages. Studies that have focused explicitly on the stability of the religious cleavage have usually found that while attendance at religious services has declined, among those who remain churched levels of religious voting remain stable. Visser (1993) showed with panel data that religious affiliation had a stabilizing impact on individual vote choice in elections in the 1980s. Scheepers et al. (1994) examined the Dutch elections of 1990–1 and found that religion and class still explained a significant amount of the variation in voting. More specifically, religious participation inclined one to vote for a confessional party and decreased the likelihood of voting for a nonreligious party; nonreligious working-class persons were inclined to vote for Labour; and nonreligious middle- or upper-class persons were inclined to vote Liberal. Thus, they conclude the pillar system may have been weakened, but was nowhere near complete dealignment by the time of the early 1990s.

The case of France exhibits some similarities, but also some important differences, with the Dutch case. There is evidence of a persistent relationship between religious service attendance and conservative voting, and this stable cleavage persists despite the fact that there is a growing diversity of political, theological, and social value positions articulated within the Catholic church (e.g., Donegani 1982), and despite the fact that far less than 90 percent of the French who are baptised Catholics are consistently attending religious services and many more of the nonattendees are now showing preferences for left parties. Similarly, Lewis-Beck (1998) has characterized France as a "stalled electorate" because both the religious cleavage and class cleavage have remained roughly the same throughout elections in 1968, 1981, 1988, and 1995, with religiosity remaining the most important predictor of vote choice.

Religious Change and Support for Right-Wing Parties

Finally, we note that a number of analysts have argued that the declining connection between two traditional bases of voter alignments – class and religion – and individual political behavior has opened the door for the resurgence of far-right-wing parties and activism (for overviews, see Ignazi 1997; Karapin 1998). Wust (1993) argues that the rise of the new radical right parties in Germany in the early 1990s is directly attributable to the dealignment of Catholic voters from the Christian Democratic Party (and its Bavarian sister party, the Christian Social Union). As more and more voters became disconnected from the Catholic Church, and when the Church became disconnected from the CDW and CSU, the older patterns of alignment began to dissipate. Veugelers (2000) makes a similar argument for support of the French National Front party (FN) in France in the late 1990s, arguing (like Wust) that support for the FN can be accounted for solely by the dealignment of Catholics with traditional right-wing parties. These issues are likely to generate much further research and scholarly interest in the near future.

CONCLUSION

This chapter has considered the impact of religion on voting behavior in the United States and Western Europe. Religion emerged, alongside class and ethnicity, as central political cleavages at the founding of the modern party system and democratic institutions. The classical secularization model produced a picture of declining religious influences on the vote, but the evidence we have considered in this chapter suggests only modest declines in the association between religion and partisan preference and vote choice. In the United States, most of the change since the 1950s has occurred among mainline Protestants; other major denominational families remain more or less in the same political alignment as before, with the usual election-specific fluctuations (most notably that prompted by born-again Democrat Jimmy Carter's presidential campaigns of 1976 and 1980). In Europe, secularization has proceeded further, and there has been declining support for religious parties in many countries and, in some countries an overall weakening of the religion/vote association. But even here, the amount of change has frequently been overstated or misunderstood. Religious identities and involvements persist in shaping the way voters make political choices, and we expect that this will continue to be the case in the new century.

CHAPTER TWENTY-TWO

Religious Social Movements in the Public Sphere

Organization, Ideology, and Activism

Rhys H. Williams

When Americans want to change something about their society, they often do so by forming, or participating in, a social movement. And when Americans commit their time, money, and energy to some organization outside their immediate families, it is highly probable that it will be to a religious organization. Thus, it is not surprising that religious organizations have been intimately involved with social movements throughout American history; nor is it surprising, given the general religiousness of the American people, that so many social movements have been grounded in religious values and ideas.

These religiously based social movements have ranged across centuries, issues, and the liberal-to-conservative spectrum. Outstanding examples from the nineteenth century include the Abolitionist Movement, the American Protective Association (an anti-immigrant organization), the Women's Christian Temperance Union, and the Anti-Saloon League (anti-alcohol). The twentieth century has witnessed such movements as the Social Gospel Movement, the Civil Rights Movement, the New Christian Right (and its constituent organizations such as the Moral Majority and the Christian Coalition), Operation Rescue (anti-abortion), and Pax Christi (antiwar and nuclear weapons). Religion has been and continues to be a source of people, organizations, and ideas for many attempts at fostering or resisting social change. It can provide the organizational bases, the rhetorical messages, and the motivated adherents that are necessary for social movements to mobilize and be effective.

This chapter will make two arguments. First, as indicated above, I will discuss the ways in which religion and religious communities form natural bases for social movement activism. While this is of course not all that religion does, its affinity for motivating people to try and change the world makes for a natural alignment of religion and social change movements. Second, I will discuss recent developments in American politics and public life that have required social movements to change some of the ways in which they operate. In so doing, religiously based social movements face some challenges now that they did not previously. How they respond to those challenges is

Parts of this essay were delivered as a conference presentation at the Center for the Study of Religion in Public Life, Trinity College, Hartford, Connecticut in April 1999. They subsequently appeared in a monograph published by the Center, and edited by Mark Silk, *Religion and American Politics: The 2000 Election in Context* (2000). The author thanks Mark Silk and the Center for permission to use the material.

shaped by the fact that the movements are reliant on religion, and this in turn shapes the extent to which religious activism continues to matter to our national public life.

I should begin by noting that I will focus in this chapter on social movements that aim to change society at some corporate level – either through influencing legislation, persuading politicians and other institutional elites or pushing other social groups to action. I am less interested in movements that are aimed primarily at *individuals* and want to change them – and to the extent they have any desire to change the world it is only through the actions of changed individuals. This is what is often referred to as a "hearts and minds" or conversionist strategy of social change, in that it relies on the changed attitudes and actions of converts to reshape society.

Limiting my focus in this chapter naturally leaves out a sizeable number of religious movements who are primarily concerned with spreading a religious message and increasing their adherents. Particularly those religious groups often referred to as "New Religious Movements" might fall into this category. The Hare Krishnas, the Divine Light Mission, and the Branch Dravidians might be representative of this type of individualist, conversionist type of movement. They basically eschew the public world, and often encourage a type of withdrawal from public and secular life. The Unification Church of Rev. Sun Yung Moon presents an interesting case that may lie between a conversionist New Religious Movement and a religiously based social movement.

Conversionist religious movements may in fact confront many of the same dynamics and dilemmas that face religiously based movements that try to shape public life, but because the former have a different fundamental purpose they also have some significant differences. My decision is primarily an analytic one, made in order to limit the scope and range of phenomena I discuss. Also, when movements attempt to change aspects of the public sphere, their actions have implications for many people who are not and will never be members. Thus, the interactions between movements and public life take on added meaning and dimensions that are less relevant for movements aiming foremost at private or personal change. While the specific movements I discuss in this chapter are not necessarily "political" in the narrow sense, in that they don't sponsor candidates for elective office, or propose or lobby for legislation, they deliberately engage society at the public level. Some groups, such as Promise Keepers, do both and are interesting precisely because the public-private boundary is such a quandary for them.

RELIGION AS A MOBILIZING FORCE

Every social movement has certain "dilemmas" it needs to solve. Scholars have generally described three: A movement needs to *organize* itself to allow coordinated action and continuity over time; it needs to generate a movement *culture*, including persuasive ideological claims; and it needs to negotiate successfully the social *environment*, including taking advantage of the opportunities available to it (see McAdam et al. 1996 for a general discussion of these features; see Smith 1996a, and Williams 1994 for direct application to religious movements). The first two factors are important mostly because they involve motivating and mobilizing members; I will address them in this section of the chapter. The third feature, negotiating the social environment, involves the interaction between the movement and the larger society and culture, and it is the necessary terrain for movement success. How that environment has changed recently, and the implications for religiously based social movements, is the subject of the second part of the chapter. In somewhat oversimplified terms, I will first discuss religion as a factor in "internal" movement dynamics of motivating and organizing, and then move to consideration of the "external" dynamic between movements and their environments. In the conclusion, I will outline the basic dilemmas contemporary public life presents for religion and social movements.

Religion and Movement Culture

A social movement requires a distinct "movement culture" that will convince people to get moving and keep them committed. People must become convinced that something is wrong with the world and needs fixing, and that they should be active in fixing it. Furthermore, they need a source of support to keep their spirits up during their efforts – both to console them when they fail and to convince them to keep working and not walk away after initial victories. For example, Gamson (1992) discovers that people must attain a cognitive framework for collective action that has three necessary components: Injustice; agency; and identity. Alternatively, Snow and Benford (1988, 1992) describe the need for diagnosis (of the world's ills), prescription (a solution to these problems), and motivation. In other words, people have to believe there is an injustice that can be corrected, be able to identify who perpetrated the injustice, and feel some moral responsibility for addressing the situation.

It is easy to see how religion could provide these rhetorical elements for a movement. Religion is at its essence a cultural system that appraises the moral status of the world in terms of a divine, rather than a worldly, standard. The world as-it-is is not an ultimate value for most religions – they see the world as wanting in important ways, and the appropriate model is godly, rather than of this world. Moreover, religion can give a fairly complete "explanation" as to why the world is the way it is, and how it became that way. This framework provides a moral universe in which concepts such as "injustice" have meaning. Furthermore, because religious beliefs are often central to people's sense of identity, they feel the wrong intensely and are willing to sacrifice to right it. Participants in a religiously based social movement often have their sacred duty and their immortal souls at stake in their actions. So, for example, activists often describe themselves as having "no choice" about their involvement in movement actions, and note that they believe they are following God's will. Thus inspired, many activists will get involved in "high risk" activism that involves civil disobedience and even jail time. Not only does faith give activists the courage to do these things, it often provides a rationale for breaking the law – that is, the necessity for obedience to a higher law makes breaking human laws justified (see Epstein 1991; Williams and Blackburn 1996).[1]

In sum, religious ideas and beliefs can reveal aspects of the world to be unjust or immoral, can provide the identity that people draw on when they are urged to get active on an issue, and can give them a sense of agency because it convinces them that their action matters. And when the movement encounters difficulties and set backs, religion

---

[1] There is no clear connection between strength or intensity of religious belief and involvement in social movement activism. Some strongly held beliefs might even discourage activism, if they convinced adherents that their duty lies elsewhere. However, for those who do believe that their religious duty involves trying to reform the world, those beliefs offer them a powerful justification and motivation for their movement participation.

can provide the comfort people need when they feel defeated, and gives them stories to help convince them to keep on. For example, it was common in the Civil Rights Movements for leaders – who were often clergy – to bolster morale with biblical stories such as the Israelites' deliverance from slavery in Egypt or the trials of Job (Williams and Ward 2000).

As the anthropologist David Kertzer (1988) has argued, all social life gets expressed through ritual and this applies to social movements as well. Ritual helps produce solidarity and emotional connection to others, even if there is not complete agreement on every issue or how they should be addressed. Ritual, whether in the form of rallies, or protest marches, or membership meetings, fuses the cognitive, the affective, and the moral dimensions of action (see Jasper 1998). So, for example, Civil Rights Movement rallies often resembled religious services (e.g., Morris 1984; Robnett 1997; Williams and Ward 2000) complete with a monetary collection. Other large-scale social movements have used gatherings that are reminiscent of the tent revivals used by evangelical religions (e.g., Williams and Alexander 1994). In sum, religious beliefs, symbols, rituals, and stories make sense of the world, give a vision as to how it could be different, and justify and support the spirits of those trying to make that vision a reality. It can form the basis of an effective social movement culture.

Religious Organizations and Movement Activity

Along with the cultural dimensions necessary to prompt and sustain action, religious organizations often play a crucial role when social movements are trying to mount sustained efforts. The 1955–6 boycott of segregated buses in Montgomery, Alabama, was greatly facilitated by the coordination of carpools done through several African-American churches (Morris 1984). In that case, the pastors of several churches were movement leaders (the best known being Martin Luther King, Jr.), but even when clergy are not directly in leadership positions, they often give time during worship services for announcements (Williams and Demerath 1991). This provides a crucial legitimacy for organizing efforts. And perhaps most important, members of religious congregations are familiar with and often skilled at coordinated action – they have experience with volunteering and know what it takes to get people where they are supposed to be when they are supposed to be there. The famed blockades of abortion clinics done by the group Operation Rescue relied on churches as places for people to assemble before going *en mass* to the blockade site (Ginsburg 1993; Williams and Blackburn 1996).

Thus, churches (and synagogues, mosques, sanghas, etc.) possess available meeting places, recognized leadership, fundraising capacities, and connections to many parts of the communities in which they exist. Above all, congregations are groups of people already connected by social networks and used to cooperative activity. Typically people do not "join" social movements as isolated individuals; more often, they get drafted into participating in activities that other people they know are participating in – social networks, not isolates, make up movements. Local religious congregations are exactly that – connections of social networks.

Furthermore, religious congregations are generally fairly homogeneous groups of people. The voluntarism that governs religious participation in American culture means that people "self-select" for the religious associations they are involved in. Racial segregation is a well-known feature, but congregations are also divided by ethnicity, economic class, and locality (sometimes neighborhood). They are, as a rule, fiercely *local* organizations in both resources and orientation. So tapping into congregations can provide access to large numbers of similar, and connected, people.

These organizational resources have helped start a number of social movements, the Civil Rights Movement and the Christian Right are only the most prominent. Both used congregations as the focal point for early movement activity, before more autonomous social movement organizations developed. Churches also play important roles in supporting Pax Christi, the Fellowship of Reconciliation, a number of anti-abortion groups such as Operation Rescue, various environmental causes, and the Witness for Peace groups that have protested U.S. policy in Central America for the past two decades. In addition, congregations are often important players in local controversies – homeless shelters, sex education in local schools, gambling initiatives, and the like (see Demerath and Williams 1992).

Several scholars (e.g., Hart 2001; McRoberts, Chapter 28, this volume; Peña, Chapter 27, this volume; Wood 2002; Chapter 26, this volume), have been studying what is known as "faith-based organizing." Groups such as the Industrial Areas Foundation (IAF) or the Pacific Institute for Community Organization (PICO) are coalitions of organizations, many of which are congregations. They pool their resources, expertise, and personnel and engage in activism (usually concerning local issues of economic or social justice) that deliberately uses their status as religious groups to mobilize participation and to try and persuade established officials. Faith-based organizing is a significant, and if the scholarship is any indication, also a growing phenomenon. It is somewhat different organizationally, however, from the type of role that congregations played in the Civil Rights Movement or the United Farm Workers' efforts, where the congregations helped give birth to movement activities, but then gave way to autonomous and specific social movement organizations (SMOs).

For this reason, Smith's (1996b) study of the Central American Peace movement refers to religious organizations as "movement midwives." In some cases, such as those churches that declared themselves "sanctuaries," congregations organized as such to oppose government policy. But while congregations often play crucial roles in recruiting, advertising, and helping to get a collective action effort started, for the most part they do not become SMOs themselves. This is true at least in part because congregations are multipurpose organizations that serve a variety of social and spiritual needs for their members. Any congregation that turns itself into an advocacy SMO risks losing those other aspects of its existence and alienating substantial parts of its membership (not to mention the possibility that political activity could place the congregation's tax exemption at risk).

The tension between spiritual nurture and social activism is particularly acute in religious groups that employ a "congregational" polity – that is, where there is no denominational structure or bishop to wield religious authority above the congregation. In such settings, clerical leaders usually depend completely on the congregation for their salaries. Any political activity that splits the church could cost the pastor her or his livelihood (along with violating the professional pride in keeping one's church growing and prosperous). Thus, while many anti-abortion groups draw their members from conservative Protestant congregations, and sometimes use church facilities for meetings, the clergy themselves are rarely leaders of such groups. They tend to tolerate rather than lead or encourage such efforts (see Demerath and Williams 1992). Interviews with

activists often reveal a bit of impatience with the tentativeness of clergy on their fa-
vorite issues (Williams and Blackburn 1996). But the organizational consequences show
why spinning off separate SMOs is an advantage.

In contrast, clerical hierarchies can provide important legitimacy and "cover" for activist clergy. Sympathetic bishops can place these clergy in congregations (or nonparish
jobs) where their activism will not be as controversial. This may also have advantages for
the bishop – getting some activist work done without it having to be endorsed directly.
Much of the activism associated with liberal religious groups in the 1960s came from
clergy who were in campus ministries, or jobs in national denominational bureaucracies, and thus insulated from the potential backlash of conservative parishioners (e.g.,
Hadden 1969; McNamara 1969). This dynamic can happen on the conservative side as
well. Some of the most active clergy in the early years of the Moral Majority used their
television and radio programs as the sites of their activism, giving them some distance
from their congregational activities (Frankl 1987).

In sum, religion can be an important source of cultural and organizational resources
for social movements. It brings people together, motivates them through their deeply
held beliefs and identities, and offers a continuity of effort and concern that can last
much longer than many ephemeral single-issue campaigns. While there is, of course,
always some resistance at mixing religion with politics – and religion's importance
as a source of nurturing, comfort, and reconciliation can dim the fires of activism –
the fact that American social movements have so consistently emerged from religious
communities is an empirical fact that cannot be ignored.

THE CHANGING CHARACTER OF AMERICAN POLITICAL LIFE

How, where, against whom, and with what weapons religiously based movements engage society depends on historical circumstances. These circumstances have changed
tremendously in the last half century. Over time, American social movements have
had to change their targets, strategies, and the nature of their constituencies in order
to keep up with these changes. As a general rule, American politics and public life have
become increasingly *nationalized* and *formally organized*. Attempts at influencing it have
had to adjust accordingly.

For much of U.S. history, politics was intensely local. Locally prominent men directed public affairs in various combinations and coalitions (Schudson 1998). Concerns
were local, causes were local, and the impact of political action was usually local (Shain
1994). Then, in the period just before the Civil War, political parties began to take the
basic shape we now recognize, aggregating local and regional interests into national
ones by means of campaign platforms, broad-based coalitions, and electioneering techniques designed to reach mass audiences. Parties began to be professionalized, organizing themselves nationally and carving out a distinct set of tasks that were legitimately
and uniquely theirs.

During this antebellum period, religiously based social movements with national
implications emerged. The major ones concerned slavery, alcohol, and Catholics. These
movements tended to be episodic and ephemeral, and consistently had their issues si-
phoned off by the major parties. It was a pattern that continued into the twentieth
century. By then, new immigration had produced a second wave of nativism; industrialization had led to the crisis in agriculture that spawned populism; and both helped

produce what came to be known as Progressivism. Yet all of the causes above were absorbed into the consolidating institutional structure of the parties and thereby into the federal government.

Part of this emerging societal infrastructure was the development of travel and informational technology that knitted the country together in a way theretofore unknown. Thus the twentieth century saw a truly national politics develop in accord with increasing social and geographic mobility and national economic integration. By the middle of the twentieth century, the political landscape was dominated by two parties, each of which had a solid constituency base, composed of a coalition of different social and economic groups. The "New Deal" coalitions produced several decades of electoral stability, built on such certainties as the "solid South," Catholic Democrats, and an increasing institutional separation of religious organizations and governmental functions.

In the past half century, this situation has changed considerably. The political parties have declined in importance – now essentially acting as fundraising conduits. Dealignment has loosened both sides of the New Deal coalitions. Increasing numbers of Americans identify as "independents," and running on an "antiparty" campaign platform has never been more popular. That people inside the Washington Beltway take their party affiliations so seriously is derided as "partisanship," and further helps distinguish them from "real Americans." In short, although parties still matter enormously in the institutional workings of established government, they have lost their place as the culturally approved way of organizing political attitudes and loyalties.

However, this has not reduced the nationalization of American politics. To the contrary, the weakening of political parties is an indication of the increasing regulation of life by national governmental institutions, and an increasingly national "culture" knit together through entertainment, news, and advertising media. (Although markets may be more sliced along lines of ethnicity, gender, and lifestyle, the slices are increasingly national themselves – as in the case of Hispanic Americans, who are less divided than previously by region and locale.) New technologies have of course abetted these social and political developments; the growth of telecommunications has made the interconnectedness of the national economy more apparent, and facilitated national responses to government policy.

For their part, social movements have increasingly aimed at influencing national politics through federal action, with Washington, DC, becoming center stage. For example, every January the anti-abortion movement stages a huge parade to protest the *Roe v. Wade* Supreme Court decision. But many movements use Washington as their setting even when the original cause of grievances is not there. Thus, the Civil Rights Movement's 1963 March on Washington dramatized and nationalized its cause even as its targets of protest remained in the South. A more recent example is the 1997 Promise Keepers rally in Washington – a rally that was even accompanied by many denials that the movement had a political agenda. But the city is the symbolic heart of the nation, and is the venue par excellence for nationalizing a movement's message (Williams 2001).

Organizing people politically has thus become the job of social movement organizations as much as political parties. But those two forms of organization have significant differences. In its efforts to capture public offices and govern, a political party must create an internal coalition of often heterogeneous groups. This means it must aggregate competing interests and occasionally compromise on often mutually exclusive principles. Parties succeed by balancing interests and creating wide appeal, not through the uncompromising pursuit of a single cause. By contrast, a social movement arises to address a grievance, whether wide-ranging or narrow. Recruiting participants and solidifying their loyalty is a movement's first challenge, and a continuing one (Williams 1994). However, whereas political parties can offer jobs and influence to induce participation, SMOs are by definition challengers that do not have ready access to political spoils. They can promise future benefits, but that is a method of recruitment that generates a loyalty dependent upon observable, tangible victories. To deal with more immediate recruitment needs, SMOs must create solidarity around a cause, a principle, or a collective identity. As a result, social movements are often more vibrant than parties or interest groups (e.g., industry lobbies), but they are also more fragile. Who counts as a "member" is hard to define; a member is harder to win, and harder to keep.

The passions that often attend dedication to a single issue are also conducive to social movement involvement. If material interests are not at stake directly, then moral commitments and a sense of personal identity must keep people motivated to stay involved. Those passions are often difficult to extend over a number of issues. Certainly many people have a number of concerns about the state of society – that is, multiple and (possibly) related grievances. Focusing those concerns on a single issue (or a small set of issues) can provide the intensity necessary for what is essentially volunteer activities outside normal routines of living. Thus, for reasons built into the very nature of the organizational form and purpose, single-issue politics are anathema to political parties and legislative coalitions, but present a comfortable turf for many SMOs.

Stable organization also can offer a rhetorical advantage for a movement. As noted above, SMOs have both rhetorical and organizational needs that must be met to keep adherents mobilized and acting effectively. But if an SMO cannot rely on organizational routines (such as membership dues or periodic fundraising) for gathering resources, the more it will have to escalate its rhetorical appeals in public forums. Furthermore, SMOs have to compete with other movements and with the general din of modern life in order to be heard. The need to stand out as a prophetic moral voice helps explain much of the radicalization of movement rhetoric in public politics, as groups escalate the decibels and severity of their claims in order to attract members or attention.

This dynamic is largely responsible for our recent "culture war." Study after sociological study demonstrates that the American public is not divided into two polarized, warring camps (see DiMaggio et al. 1996; Olson 1997). Public opinion is more diverse, less radical, and not nearly as coherent as the image of a culture war suggests. But movement organizations find that culture wars rhetoric is helpful, perhaps even essential. The rhetoric helps convince us that there is a moral struggle going on in which the sides are clear and the cause imperative. Notice, however, that the language comes not from the center of institutional power but from movement activists – from candidates who run as crusaders, not those who run as organization men with the potential to actually win. Furthermore, to the extent that electoral campaigns are like social movement efforts, the culture wars language is particularly apt, but fades as more institutionalized political routines take over (this analysis is expanded in Williams 1997b).

At the same time that social movements are trying to distinguish themselves from political parties by flaunting their fidelity to a moralized cause, the two types of organizations have at least one common challenge – coordinating political action at a national level often requires bureaucratic and professionalized levels of formal organization far exceeding typical local and grassroots efforts. Organization is hardly new to movement politics. Labor unions have used highly centralized and bureaucratized organizations for decades – a fact that not coincidentally often results in criticisms of them for being more like corrupt political parties than like social movements. But the contemporary social movement scene has a new version of the social movement organization – something scholars call "professional social movement organizations" (PSMOs; Zald and McCarthy 1987). Unlike labor unions, these do not necessarily rely on preexisting constituencies; they often try to build a membership across a number of social categories and groups, but one that is rallied around a particular attitude or commitment. They usually do not offer services or material benefits, but rather focus advocacy on social and political change. They both lobby (a more institutionalized political tactic) and organize protests outside of the standard channels for expressing influence. At the same time, they rely on professional staffs, routinized actions, and organizational hierarchies, thus becoming established players within an issue domain. PSMOs such as the National Organization of Women, the Sierra Club, or the National Right-to-Life Committee are now major players on the political scene.

Admittedly, something seems slightly amiss in the idea of a *professional* social movement. If social movements are challenges to the status quo that rely on passion and volunteer action, how can they be professionalized? If they employ paid professionals who calculate rationally the battles to fight and the tactics to pursue, how can they continue to inspire volunteer adherents to sacrifice for a moral cause? And if a PSMO is headquartered in Washington, DC, and is tackling national issues with a paid staff, how faithfully does it represent the ideas, beliefs, and commitments of local constituencies? The tension between ideology and organization is nowhere more clear than in the form of the PSMO. And yet these abound. How did this new organizational form come about?

In the mid-1970s, scholars began to notice that the social changes of the 1960s had produced a general culture of protest, creating a "social movement industry" of organizational networks, organizing techniques, and, most importantly, experienced activists-organizers who were available to bring their expertise to any social issue deemed worthy (Zald and McCarthy 1987). Professional activists were people with organizing experience in a variety of movements, and their organizing was often done as full-time employment. Focused on the "supply-side" of social movement activity, this analysis assumes that social dissent is relatively consistent and (usually) widespread, and thus that the problem is not the extent of the demand for social change but the resources to achieve it. The resources include organization, money, and members, as well as less tangible items like ideological appeal and symbolic legitimacy. These are the very things that social movement professionals can help supply.

I am not suggesting that professional movement organizers are not motivated by their causes. Most of them believe deeply in what they are doing, do not work for just any cause, and rarely get rich from their efforts. What has become significant is their ability to make their vocational attempts at social change into occupations. There is a well documented spillover effect (Meyer and Whittier 1994) among activists, in that those who gain experience in one movement cause often go on to get involved in other causes, and their knowledge spills over into later efforts. The influence on the women's movement of the large numbers of young women who were first active in the civil rights movement is an excellent example. A technological offshoot of this development is that of activists who specialize in a particular technique needed by SMOs, such as direct mail solicitation or polling, and who sell their services to a variety of organizations or causes. All in all, professional activism, supported by a variety of issues and constituencies and oriented toward a national political scene, has become a major force in U.S. politics in the past thirty years.

This supply-side approach, usually referred to as the "resource mobilization" perspective by sociologists (McCarthy and Zald 1977), recognizes the advantages that formal organization brings to social movements attempting to change society. Formal organization facilitates strategy development, eases communication networks, coordinates fundraising and recruitment, facilitates faster decision making through chains-of-command, and aids in public recognition. Organizations ensure a consistent flow of the resources necessary to pursue public agendas, and when they work well, distribute those resources efficiently even as they regenerate them.

The development of PSMOs has advantages for elected officials as well. They bring predictability to single-issue politics by focusing and channeling ideological claims, giving officials a clear opposition leader to engage, and being available for the type of compromise negotiation that is the mark of pluralist party politics. While many professional activists cannot "deliver votes" the way traditional party leaders could, they nonetheless provide a unified, coherent symbol. Prominent activists act as opinion leaders, or cues, for people who cannot stay up with the intricacies of policy debate and development. And elected officials can use appearances or meetings with recognized leaders of SMOs to send powerful media messages about a politician's sympathies or commitments. Certainly the media are adept at recognizing and interpreting these gestures. Visible, national, professional activists can be important symbolically, whatever the policy reality. In short, PSMOs are useful not only to challengers of the status quo but to the status quo itself.

Of course, it is a form of cooptation when officials use PSMOs in this way. While representatives of a movement are invited "into the game," the game itself is one of insider politics where officialdom has more resources and expertise. This highlights another important difference between established political institutions, such as bureaucracies or parties, and social movements. SMOs do not have the presumption of legitimacy that goes with established government. Their stock in trade is calling issues to public attention, generally in moral terms (Williams and Demerath 1991; Williams 1995). Going into the backrooms of deal-making and compromise cuts them off from their most potent symbolic weapons as well as from their most impassioned constituencies (who are not, after all, established political actors).

Moreover, the organizations themselves have to be maintained. The more nationally oriented, technologically sophisticated, and staff-heavy they are, the more support they need to keep themselves running. And, as in any labor market, the more talented the professionals hired, the more they cost in salaries and other sunk costs. An increasing proportion of the resources raised must thus be channeled into the organization itself. To complicate matters, a social movement is likely to be composed of several SMOs with similar goals and overlapping constituencies. Think of groups such as the Sierra Club, the Audubon Society, the World Wildlife Fund, and the National Federation for Wildlife. All are environmentalist SMOs, but with slightly different issues and foci.

While often allied politically, they also become competitors for resources, tapping the same sources for funds, volunteers, and attention. Energy expended on differentiating themselves from other SMOs is that much less energy available for the main mission. If you cannot easily distinguish the four groups named above, you see the problem in a nutshell.

These tensions for PSMOs are clearly illustrated by the current dilemmas of the Christian Coalition (CC), an SMO founded by the evangelist Pat Robertson and dedicated to the issues of the Christian Right. The CC seems to have fallen between the two stools of galvanizing followers with moral imperatives and being a player in Beltway politics who can broker deals. Perhaps the crucial moment was the 1996 attempt by Ralph Reed to keep the CC in the center of the Republican campaign effort, even as the presidential candidate Robert Dole contemplated backing away from the GOP abortion plank so as not to antagonize moderates. Reed was criticized severely by social conservatives, many of whom were in fact the Coalition's organizational competition within the Right. Shortly thereafter he left the organization to become a pure insider – a paid consultant to Republican politicians. And the Coalition seems to have lost its way – too grass roots to become just another Beltway lobby, too close to the GOP to mobilize a movement. From a historical perspective, this may be another example of a potential third party challenge – by that I mean the Christian Right generally – being absorbed into one of the major parties.

When organizational forms solidify with greater professionalism and bureaucracy, it also tends to produce more rigidity in movements' strategies and tactics. The sit-in, the boycott, the march, the letter-writing campaign – all are available to almost any movement, and in fact are used in a great variety of causes. But a given group is likely to specialize. This hones its abilities, gives it expertise and legitimacy, and provides visibility – witness the United Farm Workers' grape boycott or Operation Rescue's clinic blockade. By the same token, the signature tactic can lead to ossification and impotence, as the powers-that-be learn how to respond effectively (McAdam 1983). At the same time, as movements shift tactics in order to remain effective, they run the risk of leaving their constituencies behind.

The anti-abortion movement, for example, has adopted increasingly radical and violent tactics in the face of its failure to achieve its goal. But different people seem geared for different types of protest. Thus, while there may have been some disaffected National Right-to-Life Committee people who began blockading clinics with Operation Rescue, the bulk of the latter's constituency were not active in more peaceful and legal protests. Randal Terry's own story of founding Operation Rescue indicates he was not involved in the organized lobbying and protest activities of already extant groups (Terry 1988).[2] Similarly, Operation Rescue members have by and large not participated in the recent violence perpetrated by people associated with groups such as the Lambs of God, several of whose members are thought to have murdered abortion providers. Under consistent pressure from the government, Operation Rescue's clinic-blockade tactic has been stymied; and the organization has withered accordingly.

---

[2] Of course, Terry could have deliberately omitted any reference to action in other groups as a way of emphasizing the innovation of Operation Rescue. But his expressed disdain for the strategy of more legal-minded and institutionalized SMOs makes his prior involvement in those groups seem unlikely. Whatever the case, he certainly did not feel the need to legitimate his activism by connecting himself with established anti-abortion SMOs.

In sum, social movement organizations range considerably, from highly organized and bureaucratized operations like the Christian Coalition, to loosely organized, almost haphazard bodies like Promise Keepers, to ephemeral "happenings" and kitchen-table operations with little more than a name, a letterhead, and a website.[3]

But organization matters. Promise Keepers' very disdain for professionalism and formal organization has generally kept the movement from maintaining itself as a national presence that it established with its large rallies from 1995–8. The organization made its rallies free of charge, laid off paid staff, and did not allow a coherent bureaucracy to develop. By systematically refusing to nurture the organizational side of the movement, Promise Keepers has been unable to build on its once considerable momentum. Local groups continue to function, but more as support and prayer groups than as any presence in the public sphere (Williams 2001). It is an open question whether the rank-and-file who participated in stadium rallies would have followed a professionalized leadership into more politicized or institutionally focused action. But that option is clearly not available now, with the national presence in disarray.

DILEMMAS OF IDEOLOGY AND ORGANIZATION

Religiously based social movements and SMOs such as the anti-abortion movement or Promise Keepers are in many ways similar to secular ones. We live in a society in which all organizations tend to take similar forms – driven largely by the regulation of tax laws, accounting practices, and the standard corporate model of governance by boards of directors. Yet religion has distinctive contributions to make, both organizationally and rhetorically. And it presents distinctive challenges as well, both as a basis for organizing and as a motivating force for mobilizing action.

As discussed in the first section of this chapter, religion is a great provider of the rhetoric and symbols that a social movement needs both to attract members and to persuade the public. It is important to recognize, however, that the same religious language cannot necessarily perform both tasks. Ironically, the religious language that best mobilizes church members is often that which is most likely to raise the suspicions of the public at large, while the language most accommodating to public sensibilities is least likely to mobilize the faithful.

Religion offers, as noted, a moral language of good and evil that clearly divides the sides of any given issue into those who are on the side of light versus those who are not – this can produce both passion and perseverance in collective action. Furthermore, this kind of moral and religious language is clearly and easily understood by large portions of the American people as a way of understanding our public life. Not only are Americans generally religious as a people but also religion has a deep public cultural legitimacy. Americans generally think of their society as one that has a responsibility to be moral – in its domestic policy and in its dealings with the world. Our national "civil religious"

---

[3] A promising area for research would be to look at the effect of the Internet on movement activity. While it is certainly a good system for connecting activists across vast areas, I suspect that the individualized nature of participation siphons off some of the ability of groups to generate collective action. Individuals may find comfort and solidarity in chat rooms, but movement groups may well be hamstrung by that dynamic. And the temptation for every webmaster to form his or her own organization may splinter movements beyond effectiveness.

language clearly puts American history and destiny in a divine storyline (Williams and Demerath 1991).

And yet, it is arguable that narrow sectarian language has receded as a public language, particularly as a public political language. Morality and moral language is vitally important, it is the essence of our civil religious understandings. But it must be, at least on the surface, nonsectarian, inclusive, and embracing (note that in President George W. Bush's 2001 inaugural address he mentioned "church," "synagogue," and "mosque"). Indeed, there is some expectation that even a civil religious language of critique – calling the nation to account for its lapses – should be framed in positive and optimistic terms. In that sense, our public religious language has an important debt to the idea of "progress"; that is, that we can overcome any limitations of the past and that the future will be more just and moral than the present. What this means is that even in those situations in which many people do not agree with a movement's stated position on an issue, they will view favorably the religious language in which it is pitched, so long as it is the "right" type of public religious language.

Thus, religiously based social movements must strike a delicate balance in their relations with the media and the general public. To the extent that movements want to reach potential recruits, raise money from sympathetic constituents, and goad people into action, fiery rhetoric full of clearly sectarian language may be the best tool. I am convinced this accounts for much of the popularity of "culture wars" rhetoric (Williams 1997b). But to the extent that movements want to persuade bystanders, lure elected officials to their positions, or participate in institutionalized public processes, they need a civil religious language that maximizes similarities, plays to moderation, and speaks in general abstractions. Overplaying one side of this balance can leave an SMO either without fervent constituents or without greater political influence. The differences in media presentation between the early years of the Moral Majority, and the direction taken by the Christian Coalition under Ralph Reed, illustrate how each direction has potential pitfalls. The sectarian message of the early Moral Majority, particularly one episode when a Baptist minister told an audience that God does not hear the prayers of Jews (Kater 1982), alienated many Americans, and equated the Moral Majority name with intolerance. Despite protests to the contrary, the group had trouble shaking the public impression that it was really a narrow segment of culturally and religiously fundamentalist Protestants. As director of the Christian Coalition, on the other hand, Ralph Reed used to speak generically of "people of faith," potentially opening the door to ecumenism and civil religion.

All SMOs require the media to get the message out, but less formally organized groups need the media more. They have fewer symbols and rituals with which to develop collective identity, fewer networks for recruiting members, and fewer material incentives to offer potential recruits. Lacking regularized organizational and political routines, they must provide moral shocks and dramatic public actions to gain media attention and galvanize sympathizers into action. The coin of their political realm is public exposure and moral indignation.

Media demands for innovation and conflict give these informal – and often more radical – groups a leg up. There is a proliferation of cable talk shows that trade in confrontation and bumper-sticker logic. Moderation is not rewarded in these settings and the drive to garner attention and distinction pushes advocates to stridency and uncompromising moral positions. That this avenue to influence is self-limited by the institutional structures and demands of policy formation – especially at the national level – should be evident. But in a crowded field of competing movement organizations, many PSMOs may feel that they have little choice.

To be sure, more moderate SMOs may benefit from the existence of more radical groups through what sociologists call "flank effects" (see Minkoff 1995). Institutional authorities, faced with some radical factions, become willing to deal with representatives of moderation. For example, by the mid-to-late 1960s, the Student Nonviolent Coordinating Committee made Martin Luther King's Southern Christian Leadership Conference seem moderate to many whites who had been worried about Communists in the SCLC just a few years before. But the flank effect also can work in the other direction, forcing moderate groups to move to the edges. If they must compete for resources from within the same pool of sympathizers, moderate SMOs – especially those with large organizations to support – may be pushed to stretch their rhetoric and stridency in order to prove their fidelity to the cause.

Whatever the benefits of radicalism, it is important to bear in mind that many religious SMOs are not solely focused on political change. James Dobson's "Focus on the Family," or Jerry Falwell's "Old Time Gospel Hour" have been important bases for Christian Right organizing. But that is not all they do. Like ordinary churches, they serve their constituents' religious and family needs as well. One needs to be careful about assuming that average people using an organization's services necessarily align completely with its political messages (or if they do agree, that they are willing to be active in that regard). People have the ability to select among many of the media messages they receive. In some of my own research, I was unable to find "direct effects" of exposure to politicized religious television; that is, those who watched the more political televangelists were not much more likely to be politicized than those who watched more traditional, nonpolitical TV preachers (Will and Williams 1986; see also Frankl 1987). It seemed as though respondents were able to watch such programs largely for their religious content and filter out the politics. Certainly many prominent clergy who have engaged in public politics have had difficulty sustaining their advocacy efforts (Falwell being the best example).

While organizational names, logos, and chains-of-command are meant to provide both the reality and image of unity, that unity should not be assumed (see, for example, the diversity of justifications for involvement in the Civil Rights Movement analyzed by Platt and Fraser 1998). Prominent religious activists use their ideological claims and rhetoric to try to *create* just such unity – they are not merely *expressing* the existing preferences of their constituents. It is obviously in their interest to inflate their membership numbers, but it is also in their interest to exaggerate the unity of that membership. Leaders portray themselves as the servants of their constituents – and there is some truth in that claim – but leaders also must create through their rhetoric some of that unity behind them. Promise Keepers is an obvious example here, where a number of sociological studies show that the rank-and-file participants in the stadium rallies have no common political agenda (see chapters in Williams 2001). Another example would be the Central American Peace Movement of the 1980s. While several groups, such as Witness for Peace and the Fellowship of Reconciliation, shared a common goal of opposing Reagan Administration policies, the grounds of their opposition, and the targets of their actions, were often widely divergent (Smith 1996a). Moreover, SMOs need victories to keep their adherents motivated and the media convinced of their importance. As a result, they will often declare victory on the basis of little evidence, before more sober postelectoral analysis can be done.

Finally, the separation of the public and private spheres has become deeply entrenched in our society. True, many activists with religiously based messages decry that separation and see an irretrievably close relationship between public and private as necessary for a moral society. But, even among evangelical Protestants, that view is not the only perspective available. Evangelicalism has grown in the past two decades, and as it has grown it also has diversified. Many devout Christians are less interested in organizing to change government than in simply keeping government *out* of their lives – in the great American tradition of suspicion of institutions. If they are active at all it is a "defensive" activism that is not easily translated into more ambitious agendas.

In the final analysis, those who put their religious beliefs at the very center of their lives often have reservations about "fellowshipping" with those who do not share their beliefs, whatever their political similarities. To the extent that this reticence coexists with the development of activist religious SMOs, it is yet another sign of the disconnection between the institutions and practices of our political system on one side and the private lives and cultures in which ordinary Americans actually live.

RELIGIOUS SOCIAL MOVEMENTS AND THE PUBLIC SPHERE

In Jose Casanova's (1994) analysis of the "deprivatization" of religion in the contemporary world, he notes that for religion to have an effective public presence it must accept the basic institutional terms of modernity. One of these terms is an institutional differentiation between religion and government. Even in those places where religion dominates the state, such as postrevolutionary Iran, there are concessions made all the time to the practical demands that operating a modern nation-state demands. While no significant religious group in the United States has serious expectations of dominating and controlling the state, the same observation holds about participation in legitimate politics. The price of getting on to the playing field of American politics is a willingness to play by the dominant – and admittedly secular – rules. Religion matters in American politics, but as my discussion of civil religion demonstrated, American public religion is expected to be conciliatory, often generalized and abstract, fundamentally universal (if not always completely inclusive), and at least formally tolerant of pluralism (Williams 1999). Granted, many Americans do not see expressions of Christianity as "sectarian," and to that extent our civil religion is basically Protestant and majoritarian. But many of the same people who are completely comfortable with a Christmas nativity scene on the city hall lawn, or with presidential candidates who claim to be "born again" Christians, still feel it is a basic violation to claim publicly that other religions are false or shouldn't be granted full rights of free exercise. Perhaps those implications just seem a little impolite (a different take on the idea of a "civil" religion) but that uneasiness with sectarian triumphalism is a cultural obstacle for any religiously based social movement that proclaims its faith foundations too vociferously.

While this tension between the sectarian and public religious expression may be thought of as an external dynamic for movements (that is, between a movement and its environment), there is a parallel tension within any religiously based movement. When a social movement is basically a moral crusade, the passion and dedication that it produces among adherents is a great advantage. But how does one "ratchet down" such

passion when a movement needs to make some of the compromise necessary to participate in pluralist politics? If politics is a fundamentally moral endeavor for movement
members, isn't a political compromise actually a moral compromise? How does one
"deal" when the only acceptable moral position is complete victory? Indeed, studies
of religiously based movements repeatedly show the extent to which collective action
stumbles or struggles once the terrain moves from public expression of moral outrage
to crafting public policy (see Demerath and Williams 1992; Williams and Demerath
1991).

So there becomes a tricky balancing act between organizational coordination, political effectiveness, and ideological purity. Organization rigor and political involvement
without sufficient attention to ideological standards appear too much like "politics as
usual" to members and the movement looks more interested in power than in moral
reform to bystander publics. In other words, the movement looks so much like any secular political effort that it loses much of the benefit of its religious resources. However,
overly strident moralist ideology, unconnected to practical considerations or harnessed
to organized cadres of adherents, can produce either absolutist politics or empty and
publicly disregarded rhetoric. In other words, the latter case appears either to be the im-
practical meddlings of preachers into the "real world" about which they are ill-informed
or a religious crusade that is a threat to public pluralism.

This dilemma – between a specific, but often exclusionary, sectarian faith and an
open, pluralistic, but often bland or generic public religion – is a core concern to contemporary society. How does one have a truly "public" sphere if it is built only on the
narrow, partial languages of particular religious faiths? By contrast, how can a society
have a truly inclusive public life if the languages of religious faiths are not allowed in
debates about public policy? Habermas (1987, 1989) has considered these problems at
length and is, in the end, pessimistic about religion's capacity to contribute to "rational
discourse" in public life. Religion's reliance on revealed truth, and its claims to ultimate
and final authority, makes it a cultural system that is incompatible with the needs of an
inclusive, public sphere. Yet Dillon's (1999a) study of pro-change Catholics shows that
not all religion is of a single cloth. Some forms of religious language and thinking are
quite open to reason, to reform, and to negotiating the ways in which society should be
arranged. The ultimacy of religious truth, for these faithful people, does not mandate
any particular social arrangements. Thus, their religion can indeed inform a lively and
vibrant public dialogue within society (see also Hart 2001).

In the end, many religiously based movements succeed in navigating the twin
dilemmas of ideological purity and worldly involvement and efficacy. This is testimony to the dedication and resourcefulness of activists, as well as evidence for the
deep legitimacy religion has in American culture. Religion has a presumption of "dis-
interestedness" and a resonance with the lives and motivations of many people in our
society. Many religiously based social movement efforts turn out to be ephemeral and
unsuccessful, showing some of the challenges that religion faces when trying to influence public life in the contemporary world. By contrast, many of these efforts emerge
from the margins of American society and its political scene – they are the vehicles
of people who often do not have the resources to influence public life in other ways.
Thus, religion is often the best way for disadvantaged populations to make their voices
heard. If for no other reason, religion, organization, ideology, and activism in the public
sphere will be elements of American life indefinitely.

CHAPTER TWENTY-THREE

Mapping the Moral Order

Depicting the Terrain of Religious Conflict and Change

Fred Kniss

INTRODUCTION

The topic of religious conflict and change has been a major theme in the sociology of religion. It has also been one of the most hotly debated. Arguments over concepts like "secularization" or "culture wars" have often generated more heat than light. One of the persistent difficulties in the literature has been the slippery nature of the "stuff" of religious conflict. It is not easy to speak of things like ideas, symbols, or meanings with the same clarity and precision that one might use in analyzing demographic character-istics, for example. In *Meaning and Moral Order*, Robert Wuthnow (1987) offered several programmatic essays charting a way forward in the analysis of culture and religion. As he put it in his conclusion, questions about meaning and moral order "need not remain the domain of subjective analyses or of humanistic exhortations alone. They require careful consideration, including efforts particularly devoted to examining the structure of cultural forms, their relations to the moral order, and the role of social resources in producing and sustaining them" (1987: 348).

Scholars writing about cultural conflicts in the 1980s and 1990s, in an attempt to clarify "the structure of cultural forms," often described the moral order using spatial metaphors. Several authors, for example, engaged in debate about an alleged "great divide" between liberals and conservatives in the U.S. "religious landscape" (e.g., Roof and McKinney 1987; Wuthnow 1988; Olson and McKinney 1997). Most treatments of conflict and change in the moral order posited some sort of unidimensional bipolar distinction around which contesting groups gravitated.

The spatial metaphors seemed promising, but what seemed necessary to me was a more refined mapping of the moral order that would include at least two dimensions. This would allow the placement of competing cultural or religious ideas, paradigms, and systems in relation to each other, clarifying where analysts would be likely to find points of tension or cohesion, distinctions or similarities. Over the course of several projects, I developed a heuristic "map" of the moral order that seemed descriptive of the U.S. context at least, and might be applicable more broadly. Thus, much of the material that follows is a redaction or revision of previously published work (especially Kniss 1997a, 1997b, 1998). Later in the chapter I suggest some ways that this model might be useful for new directions in the sociology of religion.

BIPOLAR CONCEPTIONS OF AMERICAN RELIGION

A number of political observers and social scientists have suggested that post-1950s America has seen a cultural and/or religious polarization that has increased the level of conflict in our public and private lives. Various ways of explaining this divide have been put forward, but most share a unidimensional, bipolar conceptualization of the conflict. For example, explanations of the decline of liberal Protestant denominations have posited cultural polarization between "locals" and "cosmopolitans" (Roof 1978) or between "traditional Christianity" and "scientific humanism" (Hoge and Roozen 1979).

Wuthnow (1988), in his influential work on religious restructuring, suggests that American religion has been restructured into liberal and conservative camps, a divide that increasingly occurs within denominations rather than between them. The effect is that the general level of social conflict is raised. Increased conflict occurs within denominations around liberal/conservative issues, and the restructuring also leads to polarization in the larger culture. This occurs as individuals experience an attenuation of denominational loyalty, transferring their commitment to "para-church" and other special interest groups that are part of the liberal or conservative nexus and crosscut denominational organizations.

Wuthnow (1988) refers primarily to religious liberalism and conservatism, but he views these two camps as also sharing liberal or conservative views on moral, social, and political issues. The ideological affinity within the two across issue domains contributes to the macro-social polarization. Others concur with Wuthnow's claim of a widening "great divide" in American religion, but debate whether this divide occurs primarily within or between denominations (cf. Roof and McKinney 1987; Olson and McKinney 1997).[1]

But it is Hunter (1991, 1994) who has explored the recent polarization in American culture most generally and before a larger public audience. He views the situation more apocalyptically than most other analysts and has helped to bring the notion of a "culture war" into the American public consciousness. Like others, Hunter sees Americans divided into two opposing camps, but the key distinction he draws between the two camps is the issue of cultural or moral authority. The "orthodox" camp adheres to "an external, definable, and transcendent authority" while the "progressive" camp follows "the prevailing assumptions of contemporary life" (Hunter 1991: 44–5). Hunter analyzes this polarization across a range of cultural fields and suggests that it poses a threat to the democratic order. Hirschman (1991), writing from the leftward end of the political spectrum, makes a similar argument about the recent polarization of public discourse, referring to the sides as "reactionary" and "progressive." However, unlike the other analysts noted here, he views the recent polarization as a normal part of the cycle of public political discourse and concerns himself more with the form of the debate than with its content.

A second related set of bipolar distinctions is found in the venerable literature on the tension between individual and community. Marty's (1970) notion of a split between "private" and "public" religion has been highly influential in both the sociology

---

[1] There are others of course who question the restructuring thesis more fundamentally. For example, Ammerman (2000) suggests that many congregations still retain and intentionally construct strong denominational identities.

of religion and the writing of American religious history. Bellah, in much of his writing (alone and with colleagues), has dealt with the polarization between "utilitarian individualism" and "civic republicanism" (e.g., Bellah 1975; Bellah and Hammond 1980; Bellah et al. 1985).

What all of these scholars share is a bipolar conception of the American religious or cultural scene. The most significant problem with this conceptual logic is that it assumes that all or nearly all individuals and groups (or at least those who matter in the public discourse) fall into one of two camps. Occasionally there are passing references to the fact that, of course, there are many groups who do not fit the picture and many individuals who fall somewhere between or outside the poles, but these references are seldom more than passing (e.g., Hunter 1991: 105). Groups that do not fit the proposed bipolar conception are left outside the explanatory model. Methodologically, this makes it difficult to disconfirm hypotheses. Substantively, it leads to three problems: (1) it masks important distinctions within and between the two parties; (2) it exaggerates the level of conflict in society; and (3) it ignores the presence and impact of groups that do not fit the model, groups that may serve as mediators of conflicts or exert countervailing influences in their own right.

In the following section, I propose a multidimensional conception of the cultural battleground that addresses these problems. It takes into account the polarization around the policy issues noted by Wuthnow and others; the authority issue noted by Hunter; and the individual/community tension noted by Marty, Bellah, and others. By proposing a two-dimensional rather than a one-dimensional map, I make space for groups and individuals who are usually ignored in bipolar theories – groups that lie outside the mainstream discourse. This facilitates more nuanced explanations and hypotheses about the dynamic process of religious change and conflict.

A MAP OF THE MORAL ORDER IN THE UNITED STATES

Wuthnow (1987), in trying to develop a more objective approach to cultural analysis, describes an overarching ideological system or "moral order" within which religious and political movements pursue various interests. Wuthnow, of course, is not the only observer to posit such a system. A similar conception is present in many of the works discussed earlier. But in addition to the problems of unidimensionality noted above, most analysts have been rather vague about exactly what makes up the American moral order. In order to more concretely specify its key constituent elements, I propose four paradigms that may be used to characterize different positions within American religious and political ideology.

I do this based on a two-dimensional heuristic scheme. Adding another dimension makes it possible to propose a kind of "ideological map" of the moral order. Such a map still permits the analysis of a dominant or mainstream ideological spectrum, but also permits inclusion of various peripheral positions, and, thus, analysis of the relationship between the periphery and the mainstream. That is, the various configurations of these paradigms will influence ideological conflict both within peripheral ideologies and between them and the mainstream.

The two dimensions represent two central issues in any "moral order." The first is the locus of moral authority, and the second is what constitutes the moral project. The first issue is concerned with the fundamental basis for ethical, aesthetic, or epistemological standards (i.e., the nature of "goodness," "beauty," and "truth"). The second issue addresses the question of where moral action or influence should be targeted. That is, if goodness, beauty, and truth are to be enhanced, what needs to be changed? There is something of a parallel here to Weber's (1925/1978) distinction between *wertrational* (value rationality) and *zweckrational* (instrumental rationality). That is, the issue of moral authority is concerned with the grounds for defining or evaluating ultimate ends, while the question of the moral project is concerned with means to those ends. The former provides the foundation for central values. The latter provides the foundation for particular policies.

Identifying two distinct ideological dimensions can help us to distinguish some key differences between various bipolar theories. That is, the restructuring theories of Wuthnow and others focus on issues related primarily to the second dimension, religious or political moral projects. Hunter, by contrast, deals primarily with tensions over the question of moral authority. Furthermore, the poles on each dimension represent the tension between the individual and the collective that most analysts of American political culture have noted. On the first dimension, the locus of moral authority may reside in the individual's reason or experience or it may reside in the collective tradition. On the second dimension, the moral project may be the maximization of individual utility or it may be the maximization of the (collective) public good. While I am provisionally presenting these two dimensions as dichotomies forming distinct ideal types, the later discussion will indicate that I actually view them as spectra along which a wide variety of ideas may occur. The two dimensions are crosscutting and interact in complex ways.[2]

With respect to the first issue (locus of moral authority), the paradigm of **modernism** holds that the fundamental authority for defining ultimate values (goodness, beauty, and truth) is grounded in an individual's reason as applied to and filtered through individual experience. Reason is located in particular individuals in particular times and places. Thus, there is a denial of traditional transcendent absolute authority. Authority is always subject to rational criticism and legitimation. Ethics are situational, in that determining the good requires the application of reason to particular circumstances. Since modern society is based on reason in the form of scientific technologies and rational forms of social organization, modernists are optimistic about progress and tend to be open to change. Furthermore, insofar as rationality is basic to human nature, human nature is basically "good." There is within modernism, therefore, an inherent trust in human beings resulting in an emphasis on individual freedom and civil liberties. The expressive individualism of recent decades noted (and often decried) by many of the scholars discussed above is a product of modernism as a fundamental paradigm.

Within religion, modernism has been the focus of much conflict during the past century. Modernism legitimized rational criticism of ecclesiastical and biblical authority. Religious modernism holds that (a) religious ideas should be consciously adapted to modern culture, (b) God is immanent in and revealed through human cultural development, and (c) human society is progressively moving toward the realization of the Kingdom of God (Hutchison 1982). Religious conservatives have, of course, opposed

---

[2] Will and Williams (1986) propose a similar typology. However, by making "right versus left" one of the dimensions, they preclude the possibility of anomalous paradigm configurations of the sort I will discuss later.

this view as an attack on "fundamentals" and a challenge to traditional authority (Marsden 1980).

Traditionalism, in contrast to modernism, holds that the definition of ultimate values is grounded in the moral authority of the collective tradition. Rather than focusing on the free individual actor, emphasis is placed on individuals as members of a collectivity, a social group defined by its relation to some higher authority. Authority transcends the particularities of person, place or time. It is absolute and not subject to criticism. The nuclear family, as the smallest, most basic collectivity under a common authority is particularly valued. Practices which are seen to threaten it (e.g., promiscuity, homosexuality, or abortion) are opposed with special tenacity. In religion, traditionalism takes the form of obedience to ecclesiastical and scriptural authority. Ethics are not situational, but absolute. Individual actions are expected to contribute to the social good. Traditionalism stresses submission to the collectivity and restraint on individual appetites. Respect for transcendent authority is paralleled by a respect for transcendent values. The goal of change, then, is not progress toward perfection, but recovery of traditional values. Modern culture is not seen as progress so much as a fall from paradise.

On the second dimension (locus of the moral project), the paradigm of **libertarianism**, like modernism, asserts the primacy of the individual. It holds that the primary moral project is the maximization of individual utility, that is, it applies individualism to questions of economic and political relationships. The ideal economic system is the free market where free individuals acting in their own rational self-interest compete for resources. Economic growth is encouraged as a way of making more goods and services available to everyone. Growth in these terms requires unrestrained individual striving and minimal regulation by the state. Networks formed by the individual pursuit of self-interest in a free market are the bases of the social bond. Hence, only a minimal state is required – one whose function is protection of individual rights but is not concerned with the provision of social services or regulation of the economy.[3] The religious counterpart to libertarianism holds that the primary moral project is the individual's salvation and moral improvement. The problems of the world can be solved "one soul at a time."

As libertarianism is to modernism, so **communalism** is to traditionalism. That is, communalism takes the principle of individual submission to the collective good and applies it to questions of economic and political organization rather than questions of ultimate value. The moral project is the collective good rather than individual utility. A regulated market is valued over an unregulated free market. Egalitarianism is valued over limitless self-interested striving. The state is expected to promote these values by enforcing the redistribution of resources. (Entitlement programs are an example of public policy based upon the paradigm of communalism.) The state is also expected to curtail individual self-interested action when it threatens public goods such as environmental quality, public safety, or public health. Communalism may be applied across generations, as when today's wage earners support Social Security payments to the elderly or when conservation policies are justified as necessary to preserve resources for future generations. In religion, communalism identifies the primary moral project as "building the kingdom of God," establishing an alternative social order rather than

---

[3] Robert Nozick (1974) offers a philosophical justification of this paradigm.

reforming individuals. Religious communalists such as liberation theologians are more likely to talk about "social justice" than about individual "salvation." But communalism is not uniquely characteristic of leftist theologians. Hart (1992), for example, provides an insightful account of how this paradigm operates among mainstream Protestants and Catholics in the United States.

MAPPING U.S. RELIGIOUS GROUPS

So far, I have presented the dominant paradigms as a fairly strict typology with mutually exclusive categories. Empirically, however, these categories occur together in various configurations and interact dynamically. Any group's ideology will need to take a position on both the question of moral authority and the question of the moral project. In American religion, both mainstream and peripheral groups make use of a wide spectrum of ideas and symbols. Some of these ideas and symbols fall neatly into the given categories while others are highly ambiguous. Ideas are never simply given and are rarely stable, but are constantly contested, refined, and adapted, leading to dynamic relationships within and between paradigms.

In thinking about plausible configurations of the paradigms discussed above, one might intuitively expect the individualistic paradigms of modernism and libertarianism to occur together and be opposed to an alliance between the collective paradigms of traditionalism and communalism. In fact, American ideology has been counterintuitive in this respect. Although they may have used different terms, various writers have noted the paradoxical combination of traditionalism and libertarianism in conservative or right-wing American ideology (e.g., Nash 1976; Lipset and Raab 1978; Himmelstein 1983; Platt and Williams 1988). Although many scholars view this paradox as primarily a characteristic of post-1945 American conservatism, de Tocqueville (1831/1969), as far back as the 1830s, noted in *Democracy in America* that traditional religion in the United States had combined with unrestrained self-interest to promote the general welfare. In contrast, the American left has combined modernism with communalism, supporting both the moral autonomy of the individual and the regulation of economic and political activity in defense of the public good. These are, of course, ideal-typical characterizations. They represent two poles on the American ideological spectrum. Clearly, there is a large ambiguous middle position; but there is, nevertheless, a clear contrast between the right and left in its "pure" forms. Recognizing the contrasts between and paradoxes within mainstream American ideological positions is important for understanding specific cases of ideological change or conflict. One can speculate about the reasons for these paradoxical configurations. Perhaps there is a "need" for a balance between individual and collective values. Himmelstein (1983) suggests that, on the right, neither traditionalism nor libertarianism carries much appeal on its own, but each provides a corrective to the unappealing aspects of the other. More recently, writers promoting "communalism" as a school of social thought have made normative arguments about the necessity of balancing individual and collective concerns (e.g., Taylor 1991; Etzioni 1996; Putnam 2000).

Figure 23.1 is a graphic representation of what I call "American mainstream ideological discourse." Here the dimensions defining the paradigms are represented as spectra rather than categories. The x-axis represents the locus of moral authority and the y-axis represents the moral project. Idea systems may theoretically be located at any position

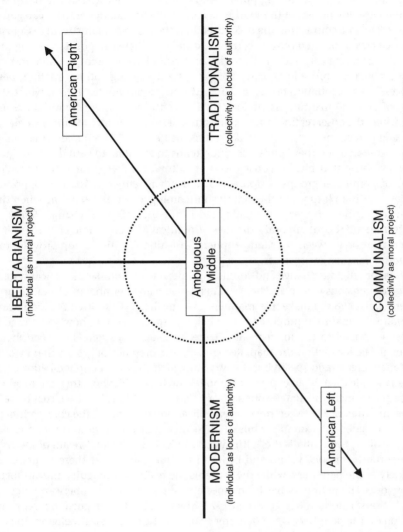

Figure 23.1 American Mainstream Ideological Discourse. Adapted from Kniss (1997a:129).

on the map. Although right-wing purists would tend to be located in the northeast corner and left-wing purists in the southwest corner, the boundaries of these categories are porous. The line connecting the two extremes is the realm of mainstream discourse. There are clear, sharp, often bitterly contested differences between positions along this line, but those located within the mainstream understand the differences. There are routinized vocabularies, procedures, categories, etc., for discussing and negotiating these differences. Most negotiation takes place in the "ambiguous middle." Here is where the majority of political institutions are located. This is the area where compromises are formed, where the observer finds the juxtaposition of seemingly incompatible elements of opposing paradigms as "politics make strange bedfellows." The implementation of policies formulated at either "purist" location tends to gravitate toward this middle.

I argued above that bipolar conceptions of cultural conflict ignored the presence and role of peripheral groups – groups that did not fit either of the two opposing categories. This is an important theoretical shortcoming, especially at a time when the importance of "the periphery" is highlighted in theories of social change. Many of the most influential contemporary theories of political and economic change posit a dialectical relation between core and peripheral institutions. This tension provides the engine for social change processes.

Cultural or religious change and conflict operate within a similar dialectical system of ideological tensions within and between mainstream and peripheral cultural groups. Elsewhere (Kniss 1988), I make this argument in some detail. To shorten the long story, the two-dimensional map proposed above helps to specify exactly how some groups might be peripheral to the mainstream. Figure 23.2 suggests where some peripheral groups might be located on the map. Recognizing the presence of groups that lie outside the mainstream and specifying the ways in which they are peripheral allows the analyst to include them in an explanatory model and to consider how they might affect or be affected by mainstream tensions and/or polarization. Note, however, that there is a significant difference between my conceptualization and some of the core/periphery theories. Consider, for example, Shils's (1975) theory of the cultural center and periphery. For Shils, the center is the "ultimate," "irreducible," "sacred" realm of society's most important symbols, values and beliefs. I am suggesting that these values exist most purely at the periphery, while the center is the realm of ambiguity and competition over ideas.The periphery has been especially fertile ground in American religious history. Various historians (e.g., Gaustad 1973; Moore 1986) have argued that religious innovation on the periphery is the defining characteristic of American religion. In particular, there has been a striking amount of activity in the southeast quadrant of the map. In many of the new religious movements in America over the past two centuries, a millenarian impulse produced a collective moral project, the establishment of a new social order, and stressed the moral authority of the collectivity, even though that authority may have been embodied in a charismatic leader (Bettis and Johannesen 1984; Tuveson 1968). The Mormons are the prime example of such a group.

But other less exotic religious groups are also peripheral to the American cultural mainstream as I have mapped it. Mennonites, Amish, and related groups belong there, as I will discuss in greater detail later. So, too, do many of the African-American Protestant groups, who have combined traditional notions of religious authority with a more progressive social ethic, focusing on transformation of the social order. This was most evident in the central role played by "conservative" African-American religious groups

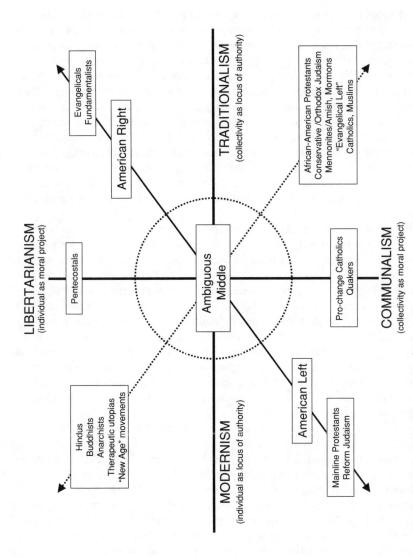

Figure 23.2 Peripheral Locations of Fringe Groups.

LIBERTARIANISM
(individual as moral project)

TRADITIONALISM
(collectivity as locus of authority)

COMMUNALISM
(collectivity as moral project)

MODERNISM
(individual as locus of authority)

Evangelicals
Fundamentalists

American Right

Pentecostals

Ambiguous
Middle

African-American Protestants
Conservative /Orthodox Judaism
Mennonites/Amish, Mormons
"Evangelical Left"
Catholics, Muslims

Pro-change Catholics
Quakers

Hindus
Buddhists
Anarchists
Therapeutic utopias
"New Age" movements

American Left

Mainline Protestants
Reform Judaism

in the civil rights movement. An interesting recent variation on a similar theme is the "new evangelical left." Groups such as the Sojourners in Washington, DC, combine traditional notions of religious/moral authority with collectivist moral projects aimed at both establishing their own alternative utopian social order and reforming the larger secular social order as well. I place the Quakers halfway between the southeast and southwest points on the map. They tend not only to focus on collective moral projects but also place more emphasis on an authoritative "divine spark" within individuals. They stop short of granting complete moral autonomy to individuals, however, since particular manifestations of the divine spark are to be tested and implemented within the context of the collective community. Hamm (1988) documents the Quaker move toward modernist ideas around the turn of the century. Pentecostals, while focusing on individuals as the moral project, hold a similar midway position on the locus of moral authority. They give more credence to individual experience than other conservative Protestants.

American Catholicism and Judaism are especially interesting cases with respect to the scheme I propose. I would argue that they are also best placed in the southeast quadrant with other groups that hold collectivist ideas about both moral authority and moral project. Although individual reason clearly has a prominent role in the development of Catholic and Jewish theology and philosophy, it has also been subject to the authority of tradition and the religious hierarchy. Kurtz (1986) and Burns (1990) document this in their studies of the Catholic controversies over Modernism. However, there is enough diversity within Catholicism, especially post–Vatican II and especially in the U.S. context (cf. Seidler and Meyer 1989), that any attempt to place Catholics in a single location is of necessity a gross generalization. The same is true for Jewish groups. If, as many argue, the history of U.S. Catholicism (and to a lesser extent, Judaism) is one of "Protestantization," it may be that some subgroups (Reform Judaism, for example) now occupy mainstream locations as well.

Dillon (1999a) examines a diverse set of groups that she calls "pro-change Catholics." These include gay and lesbian, pro-choice and pro-women Catholic groups that may seem to belong in the southwest quadrant along with liberal Protestants. But Dillon shows that while these groups apply individual reason in their challenge to the authority of Catholic tradition, they also construct an identity that maintains continuity and solidarity with that tradition, thus recognizing its authority while promoting change within it. In another study recognizing Catholic internal diversity, Burns (1992) shows that, by separating political and economic issues from matters of faith and morals, Catholics are pulled in multiple directions. In my terms, they are pulled toward the southwest where they find allies on issues such as economic justice (a collective moral project), and they are pulled toward the northeast where they find allies on moral issues (that highlight the collective moral authority).

I have said little about the northwest quadrant of the map, largely because few groups tend to locate there. An ideology that is thoroughly individualist will not easily sustain a coherent group identity. To the extent that groups do cohere around an ideology, they tend to move toward the collective end of at least one of the dimensions. So, for example, anarchist ideologies would be located here, but anarchist groups are notoriously short-lived. Some of the highly individualist therapeutic utopias of the 1960s and 1970s also combined individual moral authority with individualist moral projects. Many of these did not survive for long, while others moved rightward in authoritarian directions as they grew and institutionalized. The Church of Scientology is a good example of such an evolution. More recently, "new age" movements and the expansion of Eastern immigrant religions in the United States, especially Hinduism and Buddhism, are repopulating this corner of the map. But many of these groups are also being pulled toward the mainstream. I will discuss this in more detail later.

The presence of so much ideological activity in locations off the mainstream belies the notion that American religion or culture is best described in bipolar terms. It also raises significant questions for the thesis that a "culture war" is underway. The presence of active peripheral ideologies complicates easy coalition building, and mitigates cultural tension within the mainstream by exerting crosscutting pressures. I will say more about this later.

EMPIRICAL AND THEORETICAL APPLICATIONS

Understanding Intragroup Conflict

The "moral order map" provides a useful heuristic for analyzing many of the specific cultural or religious conflicts that interest sociologists, especially those involving "sects" and "cults." These terms usually refer to groups that lie "off the diagonal" on the moral order map. The map helps us to be clearer about just how these groups differ from the mainstream. In my work, I have used the map to analyze ideological conflict among American Mennonites. I argue that Mennonites are a peripheral group because they combine the paradigms of traditionalism and communalism, a configuration that places them outside the mainstream of American ideological discourse. Throughout their history, they have combined an emphasis on transcendent moral and spiritual values, biblical and communal authority, and denial of individual interests in favor of the collectivity (i.e., traditionalism), with a concern for egalitarianism, social justice, pacifism, environmental conservation, mutual aid, and the like (i.e., communalism).

This ideological peripherality has been a source of conflict for Mennonites. Their combination of traditionalism and communalism has been especially uneasy within the context of twentieth-century America. Mennonite individuals and groups who are primarily concerned with traditionalism have often looked to the American right for external supportive links. Those most concerned with communalism, by contrast, have looked to the American left. When these external links come to the fore, various social structural cleavages come into alignment. At particular times in Mennonites' history, the internal cleavage between paradigms has aligned with external cleavages between fundamentalists and modernists in American religion and between the right and the left in American politics. Increased conflict along external cleavages results in the emergence or intensification of internal conflict.

The dotted-line diagonal in Figure 23.2 represents an imaginary line dividing the American right from the left. Note that the right-left division becomes an internal cleavage for Mennonite ideology. It would be expected that, during times of unusual ideological dynamism within the mainstream ("unsettled times" to use the concept suggested by Swidler [1986]), the internal cleavage between traditionalism and communalism would become more salient and thus conflict would be more likely to emerge around these paradigms. The hypothesis would be that if either or both of these paradigms are objects of contention in the mainstream, then the cleavage between them would become sharper within the Mennonite community and the number and intensity of such conflicts would increase. Elsewhere (Kniss 1996), I have presented a comparative historical analysis that finds support for these hypotheses.

Internal conflict within mainstream groups is also affected by their varying position along the main diagonal. The current debates within U.S. Protestant denominations over sexual orientation provide a good example. Within mainline or "liberal" Protestant denominations, the fiercest debates are occurring in those denominations, such as Presbyterians and Methodists, that were formed by earlier mergers of evangelical and liberal wings of the tradition. In these denominations, the argument is rooted in the moral authority dimension, and the two sides of the debate can legitimately draw on differing paradigms within their tradition. The conflicts turn on the question of whether collective canon law should prevail or whether actions should be determined based on individual conscience and local pastoral concerns.

When denominations on the religious right, by contrast, fight about sexual orientation, the terms of the debate are different. Here, the moral authority of the collectivity is taken for granted. The core question is: Which collectivity has the authority to decide policies and procedures regarding sexual orientation? That is, do congregations have the right to make their own decisions on these matters, or can the denomination set policies and hold congregations to them? This basic argument is at the core of the various disagreements that have split the Southern Baptists over the past fifteen years.

Impact of Peripheral Groups on the Mainstream

I have been making the point that bipolar conceptions of cultural conflict lead to ignoring or misunderstanding the experience of sectarian, utopian, or other peripheral groups and movements. But some may argue that this is no great loss – that peripheral groups may be interesting curiosities, but are, after all, peripheral and thus relatively insignificant for understanding large-scale cultural conflicts occurring in the mainstream. However, another implication of the moral order map I propose is that the interaction between groups on and off the diagonal has an impact on both.

My analysis of intra-Mennonite conflict, by focusing on internal events as the dependent variable, highlighted the causal effects of external factors on internal cultural dynamics. But it is a logical implication of the model I propose that peripheral groups like the Mennonites should also have an impact on the larger environment. This kind of argument is much more difficult to make concisely or coherently because the dependent variable, impact on the sociocultural environment, is so diffuse. However, if we focus on specific characteristics of the environment, it is possible to make such an argument.

Probably the best example in the case of Mennonites would be American government policy toward conscientious objectors to war. The rapid succession of wars in the twentieth century and the disastrous experience of Mennonites during the first one led to their increasingly sophisticated dealings with the government (in cooperation with other "peace churches") in developing conscientious objection policies (Kniss 1997a). The successful institution of such policies in U.S. law changed at least this one aspect of the political environment, making conscientious objection to war more respectable and more accessible to many people other than Mennonites. Institutionalizing and expanding the legitimate bases of conscientious objection was one important element of the widespread antiwar activism in the 1960s and 1970s.

Another more recent example, and one that is missed by simple bipolar conceptions of cultural conflict, is the public discourse around abortion and capital punishment. The irony of people's positions on the value of human life has been pointed out by partisans on both sides of the abortion and capital punishment debates. That is, pro-choice parties in the abortion debate accuse pro-lifers of being concerned about saving the life of the fetus, but being unconcerned about the lives of the mothers, or of prisoners on death row, or of victims of American military interventions. Pro-life parties, on the other hand, suggest that pro-choicers are inconsistent in being willing to "kill" innocent unborn children, yet being unwilling to kill convicted murderers and rapists.

However, the seeming paradox in this debate vanishes if we consider it in light of the "moral order map" I propose. That is, the accusations of each party ignore the location of the specific issues with respect to the larger moral questions, since the issue of abortion is primarily an issue of the locus of moral authority, while the issue of capital punishment concerns the moral project.

The point I want to highlight here, however, regards the impact of peripheral groups on the mainstream discourse. A relatively recent development in the public debate is the entrance of Protestant and Catholic groups located "off the diagonal" in the southeast corner of the moral order map who oppose both abortion and capital punishment and refer to themselves as "consistent pro-lifers." They have built alliances with groups on both sides of the culture wars, thus opening space for accommodation and, at least potentially, mitigating tension. For example, there are emerging groups like Common Ground, a Midwestern organization that brings together pro-choice and pro-life activists in cooperative efforts toward lowering rates of unwanted pregnancies and providing services such as improved prenatal care to women who find themselves in that position.

Understanding the New Religious Pluralism

Sociologists of religion have come to understand that religious pluralism in North America constitutes an important form of American exceptionalism, raising important questions about grand theories of secularization and modernization. Over the past two decades, one of the most important debates within the sociology of religion has been over how pluralism has affected religious participation in the United States and elsewhere. Warner (1993) provides a synthetic review of this debate, pointing to the emergence of a "new paradigm" in the sociology of religion that views pluralism as one key source of continued religious vitality in the United States.

In much of this literature, pluralism is treated as a given and the debate focuses on its consequences. Problematizing pluralism, that is, paying attention to the distinctions that constitute pluralism in the United States, may shed some useful light on these ongoing questions. The moral order map I propose would suggest that not all pluralisms are alike. The *kind* of distinctions that are salient in a given social context may have important effects on religious participation. Furthermore, some communities may seem very pluralistic when denominational measures of pluralism are used; but if all the relevant religious groups are clustered in one sector of the moral order map, then it may be incorrect to define that community as "pluralistic."

Research on the religion of new (post-1965) immigrant communities has been a burgeoning subfield in the sociology of religion (Ebaugh, Chapter 17, this volume; Ebaugh and Chafetz 2000b; Warner and Wittner 1998). The new work also draws heavily on theories of religious pluralism, particularly to address questions of religious identity and change. Placing these new (for the United States) religious communities on the moral order map suggests some useful research questions to be explored.[4]

One of the first things we notice when placing new immigrant religious groups on the moral order map is that many of them lie off the main diagonal. Hindu and Buddhist groups cluster in the northwest quadrant where both the locus of moral authority and the moral project are primarily individually based. These communities are an increasingly visible presence, particularly in U.S. cities, populating a sector of the moral order that had previously been quite underpopulated, as I noted earlier.

With regard to moral authority, priests and monks in these traditions are religious virtuosos and exemplars more than authorities or hierarchs directing the religious lives of congregants. Neither is there an authoritative scripture tradition that is the equivalent of the Bible or the Qur'an for Jews, Christians, or Muslims. This was manifested in one of our field sites, a Buddhist temple, when a field researcher observed a conversation between an African-American seeker who had been raised in a Protestant tradition (Nicole) and a temple leader (Qian). Our researcher observed, "It struck me that Qian really seemed to be witnessing to Nicole about the benefits of Buddhism, but whenever Nicole tried to say something like 'So I need to do such and such?' Qian would say, 'This is my experience.' Qian seemed reticent to cast her story in terms of a universal truth" (fieldnotes, 1/31/01, *Religion, Immigration and Civil Society in Chicago Project*).

Similarly, with regard to the moral project, the Hindu and Buddhist temples we are observing focus primarily on individual projects. One storefront Hindu temple promotes nutritional products, selling wheatgrass juice to worshippers and the public. A Buddhist temple offers martial arts classes. Meditation is offered as a solution to a variety of modern problems. We see very little activity around collective social issues compared to the activities of say, a Puerto Rican or Mexican Catholic parish. I noted earlier that communities with thoroughly individualist ideologies are difficult to sustain over time. The Eastern religions that we have observed have overcome this problem by maintaining tight linkages between religion and ethnicity. Where collective concerns are addressed, they tend to be organized around cultural or ethnic identities rather than around religion, per se.

In contrast to the Eastern religious groups, Muslims, currently one of the fastest-growing religious groups in the United States, are clustered in the southeast quadrant where moral authority and the moral project are collective. Moral authority resides in a scriptural tradition that is collectively shared. The moral project, the establishment of the *umma* (the political, social, and religious community of the faithful), is collective as well.

These placements spark a few immediate observations regarding the new groups' relationships to U.S. society. First, we can make predictions about where these groups are likely to find friendly allies in American culture. Note that Hindus and Buddhists

---

[4] The observations I offer here are meant to be suggestive and somewhat speculative, but they are based on early work in a three-year project in which Paul Numrich and I are currently engaged, *Religion, Immigration and Civil Society in Chicago*. The project, supported by The Pew Charitable Trusts, is studying new immigrant religion in the Chicago metropolitan region.

populate the same moral order space as people attracted to the therapeutic utopias of the 1970s and, more recently, "new age" religion. We can empirically observe these relationships developing. Paul Numrich (1996) has identified the phenomenon of "parallel congregations" in Buddhist temples where Euro-American converts often share space with immigrant Buddhists. ISKCON (aka Hare Krishna) is a Hindu-related movement formerly dominated by Euro-Americans, but it now finds itself largely serving an immigrant Indian population and depending on them for institutional survival. At the opposite southeast corner of the map we find Muslims and African-American Protestants sharing space in the moral order. Given this, it is not particularly surprising that African-American converts are such a rapidly growing sector of Islam in the United States. In American cities, this religious affinity also has important effects on the relationship of Arab immigrants to African-American communities, both within the mosques and on "the street."

These juxtapositions raise some interesting questions regarding immigrant identity in a pluralistic U.S. culture. For example, will the dominant culture be more likely to view Muslim immigrants as "black" and Hindu or Buddhist immigrants as "white?" Or, will Muslims' location in a more familiar sector of the moral order lead to an easier legitimation of their religious identity while Hindus and Buddhists remain "exotic?"

Second, we can use the moral order map to make some observations or raise questions about religious change experienced by new immigrant groups. Some observers have suggested that the typical pattern is for immigrant religions to "Americanize," often in the direction of what Warner (1994) has called "de facto congregationalism." For Warner, this refers primarily to structural changes in the organization of immigrant religions. Ironically, perhaps, this form of Americanization may help immigrant groups to resist cultural or religious assimilation. This points to the complexity of concepts like "assimilation" or "Americanization." They are not unidimensional nor are they all-or-nothing propositions. Portes and Rumbaut's (1996) concept of "segmented assimilation" has captured this notion and enriched the study of immigrant change. The moral order map provides a way to speak more concretely about the cultural or religious changes that may or may not follow from structural changes like de facto congregationalism. It also suggests that this process may occur differently for different groups.

For Hindus and Buddhists, movement toward the mainstream could occur in one of two ways. A group could move toward the religious left by adopting communalism, that is, coming to view the moral project as collective. The phenomenon of "engaged Buddhism" in the United States, where Buddhists become actively involved in social concerns would be an example of such a trend. A group might also move toward the religious right by collectivizing moral authority. Kurien (1998) describes this process for two Hindu temples in Los Angeles. In our Chicago-area research, we have observed a similar process in a Hindu temple located in a Republican stronghold in suburban Cook County. By contrast, the inner-city temples in our study are the only ones that have become involved in community political action (even though this is still a relatively rare occurrence). Thus, the direction in which a group moves may be influenced by its context.

But accommodation and Americanization are not inevitable, nor are they unidimensional. Some groups may use religious identity (even "Americanized" congregational forms of it) to resist cultural assimilation. Religion may thus become more important for some immigrants than it was in their country of origin. Again, location within the moral order may have an important influence on whether religion is accommodative or sectarian. On the basis of the moral order map, we might hypothesize that Korean Presbyterians, because of their location on the mainstream diagonal, would be more likely than Korean Buddhists to use religion as an Americanizing cultural resource. Since Buddhism and Hinduism are so closely linked to ethnicity for immigrants, these religions may serve to resist assimilation.

For Muslim immigrants, the question is still more complex. For them, cultural or religious Americanization would involve a move toward modernism (individual as moral authority) in one direction, or libertarianism (individual as moral project) in the other. The observer can find examples of both these alternatives in Muslim immigrant communities. It may be, however, that the pressure toward religious assimilation is not as great for Muslims as it is for Hindus and Buddhists. Note that there are many more American neighbors in the southeast corner of the moral order map where Muslims are located than in the northwest corner where we find Hindus and Buddhists. Muslims can look to numerous other U.S. sectarian religious groups as role models if they wish to use their religion to resist cultural accommodation.

Finally, what impact might the influx and growth of new immigrant religions have on the larger moral order? Here again, a map of the moral order is instructive. If the number of groups located off the mainstream diagonal is increasing, and the groups themselves are growing relative to established groups, then the mainstream diagonal may eventually no longer be the mainstream. The dotted line separating the religious right from the left in Figure 23.2 may become an important realm of discourse in its own right. Phenomena such as the emergent Catholic-Buddhist dialogue may be indicators that this is already happening.[5]

Post–1965 immigration may well be creating a significant shift in the moral order, such that no discourse can claim dominance. Under those conditions, the center's realm of ambiguity may expand. Religious politics may increasingly make strange bedfellows with widespread religious change and innovation the result. By contrast, if interreligious encounters are conflictual rather than dialogical, religious differences may be heightened, and groups may withdraw into their "corners." In this case, religious identity is more likely to become sectarian, sharpening the distinctions between groups. The path that religious change ultimately takes will be shaped by contextual factors that exist outside the moral order as I have mapped it. But the map gives us some basis for understanding change as it occurs, and predicting where the important tensions are likely to appear.

CONCLUSION

In this essay, I have argued that the U.S. religious and cultural terrain, that is, the "moral order," is best depicted in multidimensional terms, rather than the unidimensionality of earlier bipolar conceptions. The map I propose includes most of the bipolar oppositions that others have identified. Creating a two-dimensional space, however, enables a more precise mapping and thus a more nuanced analysis of specific conflicts and

---

[5] One of the most prominent and longest-running of these is the Los Angeles Buddhist-Catholic Dialogue, begun in 1987 (see http://www.kusala.org/bccontent.html).

changes. It permits interesting distinctions to be drawn between different issues and groups, distinctions that are often blurred or ignored by unidimensional schemes. A two-dimensional mapping of the cultural terrain has the further benefit of highlighting the role of peripheral groups and ideologies in the larger moral order. This facilitates a more complete understanding of intragroup conflict and change for groups that occupy different locations on the map; it provides insight on the impact of new, emergent, and peripheral groups on the mainstream; and it suggests questions and hypotheses about the future of religious conflict and change in the United States.

I have been careful in this chapter to limit my applications of the map to the U.S. situation, but it is worthwhile thinking about whether and how it may be applicable more broadly. Certainly, concerns about moral authority and moral project are common to any ideological system. Thus, the map may very well be useful in other settings. However, the sharp distinction between individual and collectivity that forms the poles of the two dimensions may only be applicable in cultures that are rooted in Western Enlightenment traditions. There are important parts of the world, particularly in Africa and Asia, where this distinction may not be very meaningful or important. In these settings it may be necessary to develop other ways of representing the poles of the two dimensions.

By contrast, it is also true that the diffusion of Western cultural assumptions throughout the world is one important consequence of contemporary globalization processes. The individual-collective distinction may be gaining significance even in places where a more holistic Eastern world view is still dominant. Clearly, immigrant Eastern religions in the United States have to deal with the individual-collective distinction, and, at least in some cases, significant religious innovation is the consequence. Likely, similar innovation is occurring in the countries of origin for these religions as global capitalism brings a liberal economic gospel of individualism and the pursuit of self-interest.

These, as they say, are "questions for further research." There is plenty of work still to be done in coming to a clearer understanding of how particular cases of religious change and conflict are related to their larger moral order, how the moral order itself is constituted, and how such cultural systems have an impact on human behavior and social life. We will no doubt continue to debate the specific answers to these more general questions. Our debate will be more productive, however, if we can be as specific and concrete as possible in mapping the terrain we are attempting to traverse.

CHAPTER TWENTY-FOUR

Civil Society and Civil Religion as Mutually Dependent

N. J. Demerath III

In a world teeming with violence, oppression, and depravity, it is little wonder that religion should be seen as a solution. Whether as prayer, theology, or saintly inspiration, religion has been both a first and last hope in confronting social ills. But religion is also involved in more secular responses. As a major contributor to what has been termed "civil society," it can make a social and political difference in two respects. First, at the macro level, religion's various organizations and institutions can play a direct role in the public arena by challenging governmental shortcomings and depredations. Second, at the micro level, religion can foster a sense of "social capital" by giving its lay participants practice in, and encouragement for, participating in wider social and political circles, whether as mere voters or intense activists.

At least this is a theory that has found support in country after country around the globe since the 1980s. To cite just a few examples, the Catholic Church was instrumental in unseating both Brazil's military regime and Poland's Communist state (Glenn 2001); very different Muslim movements have opposed and toppled entrenched governments in Indonesia, and religion has both opposed and been opposed by the state in Iran. Buddhist organizations have been a thorn in the side of political elites in both China and Thailand, and Hindus are demanding changes in the world's largest democracy, India. Certainly U.S. religion offers its own examples of religion in the *polis*.

But even theories with such worldwide support have a tendency to leave loose ends dangling. In what follows, I want to point out a few of these ends and tie them up with a cord fashioned from "civil religion" – a concept that suggests yet another way in which religion is implicated in the political world. Basically, I will argue that there is an inherent ambiguity within the concept of "civil society," that its political hopefulness rests more on ideology than evidence, and that if civil society is to reach the desired ends, it must operate within a cultural climate heavily shaped by civil religion.

CIVIL SOCIETY AND A SOCIETY THAT IS CIVIL

Good theory can be subverted by bad terminology, or in this case, a term that has *two* distinct meanings, both of which have deep scholarly roots in eighteenth-century German and Scottish social thought.

First, the notion of "civil society" introduced earlier goes beyond religion to describe a broad segment or layer of any society's social structure. It refers to that assortment of nonkin, nonwork, mediating institutions, voluntary associations, and social movements separate from the state and government. While it excludes the private world of the family and the working world of the wage earning economy, it includes neighborhood associations, community organizations, trade unions, and religious groups. While it excludes governmental agencies and assemblies, it includes political and social movements that grapple with matters such as the environment, health, sexuality, gender, poverty, or faith itself – unless and until President George W. Bush's "faith-based initiatives" simultaneously make and break the law. Insofar as these initiatives involve government support for faith, they would pose a clear violation of at least the most common reading of the First Amendment that the one thing the government cannot legitimately support is faith itself.

Meanwhile a *second* meaning of "civil society" is a cultural preference for a "civilized" society characterized by civility and the civic virtues, variously defined but generally including such liberal staples as mutual trust, respect, and tolerance as part of a package of good democratic citizenship.

Not surprisingly, these two meanings are often intertwined with each other and with virtually tautological results. Thus, the presence of one seems to guarantee the presence of another almost by definition. It is largely a semantic fluke that persuades us that a civil society of the first sort is a necessary and sufficient condition for a civil society of the second. But that is precisely what the new theory of civil society holds. In both the United States and around the world, this has moved beyond a matter of conjecture to become an article of faith in its own right (cf. Hall 1995).

It is here that I want to introduce some skepticism based on my recent comparative study of religion and politics in some fourteen countries around the globe – including almost all of those mentioned earlier. Without trying to explode the theory altogether, I shall argue that the relationship between the two meanings of civil society is neither necessary nor sufficient.

Civility as a Western Chestnut and Conceit

Few ideas combine longer pedigrees with fonder hopes than that of the civilized society. It is hardly surprising that it should have great appeal among Americans at a time when the United States is described as increasingly divided against itself and the battlefield for a most uncivil "culture war" (e.g., Hunter 1991, 1994; Goggin 1993; Guinness 1993; Gitlin 1995). Putative battles range from inner cities to wilderness fortresses over such fundamental matters as racial discrimination and economic justice, abortion and family values, and the scope of government overall.

This diagnosis has become both a source and a symptom of the illness, and in the confusion it is little wonder that citizens are drawn to simpler nostrums from simpler times. That often unholy alliance of scholarly pundits and media publicists has persuaded many that the country is in desperate need of regaining its moral bearings and recapturing that precious sense of individual trust and institutional integrity on which every successful society depends.

In a variant of the old bad cop/good cop routine, social science has provided both the scare and the solution. In fact, there are problems with each. As for the scare, research has indicated that the so-called American culture war is a hyperbolic misrepresentation of the inevitable cultural skirmishes entailed in what is mostly democracy in action. A true culture war would involve a massive and violent polarization of the public at large with the state itself hanging in the balance. But study after study shows a citizenry huddled in the middle of virtually every contentious issue ranging from race and inequality to abortion and homosexuality (e.g., DiMaggio et al. 1996; Williams 1997a; Mouw and Sobel 2001). There have certainly been inflamed episodes fanned by movement entrepreneurs on the flanks of public opinion; there have even been protracted agonies such as the Civil War of the 1860s and the Civil Rights Movement of the 1960s. But to characterize the current American scene in warlike terms is to make a mockery of those countries around the world where culture wars have become a tragic way of everyday life. These include not only the countries mentioned previously but other violent battlegrounds such as Afghanistan, the Balkans, Egypt, Guatemala, Israel, Northern Ireland, Rwanda, and Sudan.

Of course, one reason why the "scare" of an American culture war is overdone is that the solution of a "civil society" is already in place in the United States and a number of recent scholars have probed its various dimensions. But many have lamented some missing virtues (e.g., Cohen and Arato 1992; Glendon 1995), while others such as Adam Seligman (1992), Robert Putnam (2000), Francis Fukuyama (1995), and S. M. Lipset (1996) have explored problems emanating from America's distinctive value placed on individualism, the special role of American voluntary associations, the unusual American line drawn between the community and the state, and the unique importance attached to American religion. None of these analysts can be accused of playing a starry-eyed Pangloss to a nail-biting Cassandra. All would likely acknowledge problems with both the theory and the reality of American civil society.

References to any civilized society combine the same sense of nostalgia and hope that once characterized earlier accounts of the nature of social order. Indeed, from one vantage point, civil society is simply social order with a handshake and a smile. As one who was involved in the earlier debate over functionalism (e.g., Demerath and Peterson 1967; Demerath 1996), I have an uncomfortable feeling of deja-vu. Many of the same specific issues lurk beneath the current theoretical surface, including questions of consensus versus conflict, stability versus change, culture versus structure, and macro versus micro.

And yet there are also differences. For example, Seligman (1992) quite rightly notes that architects of civility have tended to work from the individual up, assuming an ideal citizen who embodies all the scouting virtues, with trustworthiness above all. But when this model of civil society is identified with the great Emile Durkheim of the turn of the twentieth century, we can almost hear the protests from his Paris grave: "Mon Dieu; this is Herbert Spencer revisited! Individuals take their moral cores from society rather than imparting morality to it." Again, Seligman is aware of the tension; in fact, his central paradox is that, in stressing the individual rather than the collectivity, civil society deemphasizes the very source of the individual's virtues; namely, the moral force of the collectivity itself. But then one might also point out that no collectivity has more legitimacy than one that trumpets the centrality of the individual; the two levels operate in tandem.

Of course, many have lionized America's individualism, including some who have seen it as a mixed blessing gone sour (Bellah et al. 1985; Putnam 2000). But again the discourse leaves a gnawing sense of discomfort. After all, isn't this the same society that is so often chided for its conformity? Isn't there a difference between individua*lism* as a cultural value and individua*tion* as a structural circumstance? Isn't it at least possible that some of our societal uneasiness here is due to the presence of one without the other, that is, individuation without the kind of individualism that makes us comfortable with the result?

Meanwhile, Durkheim (1893/1997) and his French predecessor, Alexis de Tocqueville (1831/1969), would recognize the emphasis on voluntary associations and group affiliations that mediate between the individual and the nation. Both gave special attention to religion, and de Tocqueville to American churches in particular. But this has not been as true of recent civil society theorists. Many have neglected religion altogether even though it is the single largest source of organizations and associations constituting American civil society (Skocpol and Fiorina 1999; Putnam 2000). That is not true of Robert Putnam's compelling moan over "Bowling Alone." Putnam (2000) argues that American democracy, civic virtues and social capital are all rooted in a wide variety of shared activities that are now tragically waning – including organized bowling leagues but also churches, trade unions, and other voluntary associations. The thesis has launched a flotilla of critical responses, many of which argue that there has been a shift more in the *kind* of social participation than in the overall *amount* (e.g., Skocpol and Fiorina 1999; Edwards and Foley 2001; Wilson 2001). A very recent study of religion in Indianapolis, IN, suggests that the social capital engendered by churches has much less significance for participation in the wider community and its politics than Putnam and others have supposed (Farnsley et al. forthcoming)

As Paxton (1999) suggests, it is worth pausing to wonder whether declining associations with their plummeting "social capital" are the cause or the consequence of a loss of civility? As with the related issue of individualism versus individuation, one might also ask if the structural ebbing precedes or follows the cultural shift? Meanwhile, Putnam's concerns cue yet another aspect of Western civil society that is related, namely, its source in ascetic Protestantism.

Virtually every civil historian acknowledges that the "Protestant Ethic" so emphasized by Durkheim's German contemporary, Max Weber (1904–5/1958), was as important to the spirit of political civility as to the spirit of capitalism. The liberal stress on individuals seeking salvation through their own actions accounts for at least some of the "individualisms" among our "habits of the heart" (Bellah et al. 1985).

However, a less-celebrated legacy of Protestantism may be equally important; namely, its emphasis on congregational solidarity. A major secret of Protestantism's early success was that it too provided a cure for its own disease; on the one hand, it promoted the curse of individualism and, on the other hand, it provided the remedy in a new kind of congregational involvement. Loneliness before God can be countered by the support available from one's fellow congregants.

Today the link between Protestant "civil society" and American civility is more complex. It is even arguable that religion's impact has changed from positive to negative as it has taken on a newly uncivil tone. Even though the decline in liberal mainline religion has been partially balanced by an increase in conservative evangelical religion, some see only the former as an authentic staple of civil society and source of social capital (Putnam 2000). But surely it is too simple to plot the rise of incivility and social withdrawal as a function of the decline of liberal and the surge of conservative religion.

At the same time, today's religious right has departed considerably from the agenda of mutual tolerance that has characterized the liberal values at the core of both mainline religion and American democracy.

The term "fundamentalism" was coined in the United States, even though its original biblical meaning has been eclipsed by a broader sense of ideological extremism here and abroad (e.g., Riesebrodt 1993; Marty and Appleby 1995). In some ways, the fundamentalist is now seen as a euphemism for any "fanatic" – or one "who won't change his mind and won't change the subject," according to the variously attributed British witicism. But even in its less extreme form, conservatives have traded an emphasis on individualism for a stress on family values and an enforced traditional morality. Although conservative, evangelical, even fundamentalist religious organizations are undeniably a part of American "civil society," many observers would see them as more responsible for cultural friction than harmony. As some of religion's most prominent forms of civil society have become liabilities rather than assets in the pursuit of older patterns of civility, it is important to remember that civility itself is a matter of cultural taste and is a variable rather than an absolute.

Meanwhile, there is another aspect of America's political tradition whose relation to civil society and civility is more complex than is often supposed. One hears a good deal about democracy as a central tenet of civility. And yet one must define such value-laden terms very carefully. Insofar as democracy entails a spirit of equal rights and responsibilities that goes beyond the voting booth, it involves a sense that what is truly worthwhile in a society is truly accessible. Here conceptions of civil society are sometimes sadly deficient.

Civility often puts a good face on social convention by dictating a hegemonic code that is in the interests of society's winners rather than its losers or indeed those who simply cope. From this standpoint, civility becomes a conceit, and under some circumstances, it can engender sufficient resentment to undermine itself and become a source of actual incivility in response. As civility becomes infected with power, what is seen as appropriate within a dominant class, ethnic, gender, or generational group can become – by virtue of that very perception – alienating to the subdominant.

In fact, both "civility" and "civil society" have different meanings in different countries. In an increasingly globalized (i.e., "Westernized") world, American notions of civility and a civilized society are not without influence, but they are also not without suspicion. If civility can be a high-status conceit *within* the West, it can also be seen as an exported conceit *of* the West.

Meanwhile, the structured layer of "civil society" has also been a common export. But in many countries it has taken on a different emphasis. From Latin America through Eastern Europe and the Middle East, the reference is not so much to an Americanized cultural outcome but to a structural segment of society that is a hopeful means to a variety of ends. The important thing is that "civil society" is distinct from the state and offers an independent voice influencing it.

But here, too, there is a need to make problematic what is often taken for granted. The common assumption is that civil society is the best defense against state oppression and corruption and the best pathway to democratization and all of its manifold blessings. Certainly there are cases feeding such confidence, most notably the collapse of Communism in the Soviet Union and Eastern Europe, including the inspirational saga of Solidarity in Poland where the phrase "civil society" took on special significance.

And yet there are two major difficulties with the scenario. *First*, civil society itself is not always what many might hope. Its myriad associations and organizations often reflect the interests and control of high status elites; alternatively, they may take on the properties of extremist movements with demagogic appeals to short-run emotions at the expense of long-range advantagement – pro-life as well as pro-choice, pro-labor as well as pro-NAFTA. *Second*, the state itself can be a far more positive source of civil outcomes than sometimes modish state-bashing would allow (Gupta 2000). Especially from the standpoint of nonelites and the disadvantaged, government can sometimes be the only realistic source of positive change; it can also serve as a crucial arbiter among conflicting organizations within a civil society that can be far more turbulent than its image would suggest.

So much then for a brief critique of two different versions of "civil society," and the liberal thesis of a causal relationship between civil society in the organizational sense and a civil-ized society overall. Somehow something seems to be missing as an intervening factor. Let us turn to that now in the concept of a "civil religion."

ASSESSING "CIVIL RELIGION"

To those in search of a stable and peaceful social order, "civil society" offers structural hope at the institutional level. However, another source of encouragement is more cultural and more society-wide. It is "civil religion," or any society's most common religious denominator which consecrates its sense of nationhood and pivots around a set of tenets and rituals forged in the fires of a shared history. In the United States, it is a Judeo-Christian heritage invoked by nondenominational public prayers on July 4th, Memorial Day, Thanksgiving, and presidential inaugurations.

Civil religion is another concept with origins in the eighteenth-century European Enlightenment, especially within France, and particularly in the person of Jean Jacques Rousseau (1762). In fact, the very phrase "civil religion" had an ironic ring in such circles. After all, Rousseau and his peers were basically nondeists who looked forward to an age without the religion identified with Christianity and its higher churchly variants. And yet many of these people saw the need for a different sort of "religion" that would compel allegiance to the state through a different sort of faith. In Rousseau's (1762/1960: 305–6) terms:

> But there is a purely civil profession of faith, the articles of which it behooves the Sovereign to fix, not with the precision of religious dogmas, but treating them as a body of social *sentiments* without which no man can be either a good citizen or a faithful subject.

Almost exactly 150 years later, another Frenchman developed the idea further. Toward the end of his great work, *The Elementary Forms of the Religious Life* (1912/1976), that seminal sociologist, Emile Durkheim, took readers by the hand and guided them back to turn-of-century "modern France" following the book's extended excursion among the tribal Arunta in Australia. As part of the concluding chapter – one of the great thirty pages in Western social thought – Durkheim (1912/1976: 427) writes:

> Thus there is something eternal in religion that is destined to outlive the succession of particular symbols in which religious thought has clothed itself. There can be

no society that does not experience the need at regular intervals to maintain and strengthen the collective feelings and ideas that provide its coherence and its distinct individuality. This moral remaking can be achieved only by meetings, assemblies, and congregations in which the individuals, pressing close to one another, reaffirm in common their common sentiments. Such is the origin of ceremonies that . . . are not different in kind from ceremonies that are specifically religious. . . . If today we have some difficulty imagining what the feasts and ceremonies of the future will be, it is because we are going through a phase of moral mediocrity. . . . In short, the former gods are growing old or dying, and others have not been born. It is life itself, and not a dead past, that can produce a living cult. But that state of uncertainty and confused anxiety cannot last forever. A day will come when our society once again will know hours of creative effervescence during which new ideas will again spring forth and new formulas emerge to guide humanity for a time.

Durkheim's concluding prophecy was correct, but chillingly so. World War I was just around the corner – the war to end all wars and the war that took his only son.

Despite the eloquence of both Rousseau and Durkheim, they left us with more of an idea than a concept. The latter finally crystallized in Robert Bellah's classic article (1967). Insofar as there was a basic difference between Rousseau and Durkheim, Bellah sided with the latter. For Bellah, civil religion – at least in the United States – is essentially a bottom-up, emergent phenomenon in the Durkheimian tradition rather than the top-down, imposed doctrine commended earlier by Rousseau (cf. Demerath and Williams 1987). Thus, our civil religion is a kind of religious common denominator that bubbles forth from our long-standing "Judeo-Christian tradition" and underscores the religious significance of the nation as a whole and its government. It is more of a passive cultural legacy than the result of an activist political decision.

But there is another sense in which Bellah departed from *both* Rousseau and Durkheim. Perhaps reflecting his own churchgoing heritage, Bellah focused on church-going religion as the core of America's "civil religion." Both Rousseau and Durkheim had been at pains to introduce a broader concept of the sacred and to note that con-ventional religion *per se* need not constitute the soul of a nation. But Bellah's version was more literal, perhaps even more fundamentalist. And not without reason, given America's strong Judeo-Christian sensibilities – "Judeo" not so much because of the role of the tiny minority of Jews in American life itself but, rather, because Christianity emerged out of Judaism historically, theologically, and ethically.

One of the clearest identifiers of America as a religious society is the way its Chris-tianity is publicly invoked and symbolically brandished. Our most important national holidays such as July 4th and Memorial Day are religiously sanctified. Virtually ev-ery session of the nation's daily legislative business is prefaced by prayer. Both our coins and our politicians proclaim religious mottos. Our national rites of passage – whether weddings, funerals, or presidential inaugurations – are marked with religious observance. And religious solace and supplication accompany every national crisis. In Bellah's (1967) view, all of this forms a rich residue of historical experience that has be-come a binding cultural force. The country is irretrievably religious, both at its roots and in its most luxuriant foliage. Indeed, this is another part of American exceptionalism, since few other societies can boast such a natural melding of religion and nationhood.

But again there are reasons to pause before swallowing an analysis whole hog. It is not clear whether this is an analysis of America's mythology or a contribution to it.

On the one hand, our civil religion may not function quite the way it is depicted. On the other hand, other societies have their own versions of a civil religion, though some stretch the concept and its possibilities rather than merely illustrating it. Let's consider both complications in turn.

AMERICAN CIVIL RELIGION IN DOUBT AND IN DECLINE?

At any given point, almost any society manifests enough cacaphony to give even the most confirmed patriot second-thoughts about whether there is a salvageable chorus sweeter than the sum of its individual voices. In the hurly-burly of the moment, episodes of crime, corruption, and fever-pitched disagreement give ample fodder to the pessimist. Even in the United States, we have had reason to wonder whether a society that has grown so raucously complex could any longer sustain or be sustained by civil religion, and whether its manifestations haven't become vestigial facade rather than a vital sustenance – more icing than cake. Bellah (1975) himself raised the issue of a "broken covenant" in the bitter aftermath of the heightened expectations of the 1960s.

Certainly these symptoms of divisiveness are important. But insofar as any country manages to hang together over the longer run despite its internal differences, it is also worth asking why? In the U.S. case, an answer in terms of civil religion alone has grown steadily more simplistic.

From the very beginning of our nationhood, there has been a paradoxical tension between our heralded civil religion and our no less legendary "separation of church and state." While the former syndrome marks us as highly religious, the latter suggests just the opposite. In fact, foreign observers sometimes see our church-state separation as the basis of a very different version of American exceptionalism – one which singles us out more for secularism than religiosity. Actually, these two seemingly inconsistent syndromes are strangely symbiotic. Each is a guard against the other's excesses, and each provides a countervailing assurance as a boost to the other's legitimacy. That is, we can indulge a symbolic civil religion, precisely because there is a substantive separation of church and state in important matters of government policy; at the same time, our separation is never a total rupture precisely because of the presence of overarching civil religious ceremonials (cf. Williams and Demerath 1991).

Meanwhile, America's civil religion has been pressured by more than its church-state separation. Our ever-expanding pluralism includes increasing groups beyond the conventional religious pale, ranging from cults to the occult, and from new forms of both spiritualism and survivalism to burgeoning numbers of Muslims, Hindus and Buddhists outside the Judeo-Christian tradition. Even within that tradition, some point to growing tensions. Richard Neuhaus (1984) has argued that religion has become conspicuously absent from our "naked public square," and Steven Carter (1993) has termed ours a "culture of disbelief" – although both are really deploring the country's failure to readily accept conservative religion in the national political arena. In fact, many see the rift between religious traditions growing steadily wider. As we have already seen, not all share the diagnosis of a culture war. The problem may be less one of war than of unraveling. Following Robert Wuthnow (1988), it is now common to note that even America's "civil religion" has been bifurcated into liberal and conservative camps. As Wuthnow put it, the two have given priority to different clauses of one of America's great creedal shibboleths: conservatives stressing "one nation under God," and liberals emphasizing "with liberty and justice for all." Of course, this is a major change from Bellah's overarching formulation. Indeed, from this earlier perspective, the detection of two civil religions may signal the absence of any civil religion, insofar as there is no longer a single "sacred canopy" (Berger 1967) for the society as a whole.

However, another reading of present-day America actually cleaves closer to Durkheim and Rousseau, as well as to more recent accounts of civility. As noted earlier, both had a much broader and less theological conception of the sacred. Durkheim's formulation for the France of 1911 and complex societies generally resembled a "religion of the civil" rather than "civil religion" in its sectarian sense. Given the habit of civil society theorists to sharply juxtapose the civil versus the state, and given America's long-standing status as a paragon of the civil society, it is joltingly ironic that one of America's most distinctive characteristics is the extent to which its culture-at-large flows from, instead of competing with, its political norms and institutions.

For a nation that was diverse from the outset and lacked other bases of cultural solidarity and commonality, the Constitution itself has often served as America's civil religious scripture – a statement of political means that soon became elevated to cultural ends. Of course, it is hardly politically correct to talk of consensual norms and values in a society as large and complex as the United States. Still, compared to the other societies before us, it is striking just how rooted our common culture is in our political structures and their enabling documents, laws, and conflict-reducing procedures. In fact, if civility can be operationalized as the extent to which any collectivity conforms to rather than departs from its own values, one reason why the United States might rank high is that its values derive from the implementation procedures themselves. This may be at least as responsible for America's status as a civil exemplar as any of the factors mentioned previously. It is also an interpretation that gains credibility in comparison with other, more conflicted societies elsewhere.

While American civil religion remains alive, if not always well, other countries around the world illustrate different forms of civil religion with sometimes far greater problems. This is not the place for an extensive global survey (cf. Bellah and Hammond 1980; Demerath 2001). But it is worth noting a few important variations on the theme. Northern Ireland offers an especially violent case of a country with two civil religions – one Protestant, one Catholic, both Christian. Many Latin American countries may be moving in the direction of a Catholic-Protestant split, but with a third strand emerging among more indigenous peoples and their traditions. Israel is an especially fractured situation as a nation without a formal constitution or official religious standing, but where civil religious competitors range from orthodox and ultra-orthodox Judaism to secular Zionism, and Islam itself.

In further contrast to the American case, many countries resemble Rousseau's original model in two senses. First, there are some in which civil religion is more of a top-down imposition by a political elite than a bottom-up emergence from the cultural well-springs. This was true of Japan's State Shinto from the 1860s to the 1940s, Turkey's changes under Kemal Attaturk in the 1920s, Indonesia's pan-religious "pancasila" crafted under Sukarno in the 1940s, and the radical shift inflicted on China by Mao Zedong and the Communists after 1949 with its "cultural revolution." Second, the Turkish and Chinese cases alert us to the possibility of a civil religion that is not "religious" at all in the conventional sense. Instead they illustrate what I earlier termed a "religion of the civil" or a broader "civil sacred." Communism in China, Westernism in Turkey, or a national commitment to a welfare state in, say, Sweden all are basically nonreligious but have many of the same hopes as religion for culturally binding a nation and its citizens. In an imperfect world, it goes without saying that these hopes are never perfectly realized over the long run. In some cases, these represent attempts to substitute a new civil sacred for an old and enduring culture that has a way of seeping back and snapping back over time.

In fact, the concept of civil religion raises the important issue of new forms of *nationalism*. It is becoming increasingly clear that the very notion of the nation-state is more an ideal of Enlightenment elitism than a natural reality. From the late eighteenth to the early twentieth century, many nations – including the United States itself – were assembled according to political convenience rather than cultural coherence. As religious, ethnic, and regional communities were cobbled together in a series of strained alliances under the mantle of statehood, politics and statecraft were supposed to provide the required solvent and glue. Using strategies ranging from totalitarianism to civil religion itself, some nations were more effective than others. While the United States offers one of the rare examples of overall success, even it is experiencing internal fractiousness and centrifugality. Many other countries are finding that their centers are not holding at all. For them, the ideal of nationhood has been rendered deeply suspect, if not an outright farce.

CONCLUSION: CIVIL SOCIETY AND CIVIL RELIGION AS MUTUALLY DEPENDENT

Clearly neither that layer of organizations termed "civil society" nor that umbrella of cultural consensus termed a "civil religion" offers a sure path to social civility. Although each works well in theory and even better in ideology, both have major problems in practice. Civil society covers too vast an array of organizational saints and sinners; civil religion is often both too abstract and too fragmented to be both coherent and cohesive.

For the most part, the two conceptual traditions have had very different proponents, who have passed each other in the night. "Civil society" has been an enthusiasm of secular liberals, many of whom are as eager to resist the clutches of an authoritarian religion as a totalitarian state. By contrast, at least since the twentieth century, "civil religion" has reflected the considerable influence of Christian theology.

But rather than regard the two as mutually exclusive, the two are really mutually dependent. The various and sundry associations, movements, and institutions of a civil society require some degree of shared cultural bearings if they are to coordinate successfully on behalf of civility, as that is defined by the culture itself. And insofar as they compete with each other for public priority, those that cleave closest to the civil religion are best able to use it as a source of both legitimacy and cultural power (cf. Demerath and Williams 1992). By contrast, even a widely shared civil religion or sense of the sacred requires effective reinforcement, mobilization, and implementation at the organizational level lest it become mere rhetoric and nostalgia. A civil religion without a coordinated civil society as infrastructure, is likely to ring hollow when the bell to action sounds.

In virtually every recent instance in which a country's civil society has dealt a major blow against perceived oppression and a delinquent state, the uniting factor has been a call to the society's cultural heritage and a civil religion that endures despite its conflict with the political situation of the moment. And in virtually every instance in which cultural nationalism has asserted itself against an imposed nation state, it is the organizations and movements of the civil society that have carried the torch. These converging developments describe to one degree or another the Balkans, Brazil, Poland, Iran, Thailand, Indonesia, Turkey, and even India. They also describe those many episodes in U.S. history when some aspect of the structure of civil society has effectively wielded its interpretation of the culture of civil religion to exert the kind of power necessary to challenge the status quo and make a difference.

Instances in which civil society works in conjunction with civil religion are more potent than they are common. It is true that religion narrowly construed has a narrowing prospect of making a difference in the world of secular affairs. But it is most assuredly not true that religion has become a mere cipher. When its structural and cultural potential are combined, it can still be very powerful indeed.

CHAPTER TWENTY-FIVE

Religion and Violence

Social Processes in Comparative Perspective

John R. Hall

RELIGION AND VIOLENCE: SOCIAL PROCESSES
IN COMPARATIVE PERSPECTIVE

Religion is often held up as a vessel of peace, both inner and social. How, then, to understand its violent currents? Given an uneven trend over the centuries toward cultural
pluralism and freedom, modern theorists optimistically concluded that religion would
either decline in significance or become a pillar of universalistic culture promoting a
veritable community of mankind. Thus, as a flash point for violence, religion scarcely
warranted attention in the metanarratives of modernity. Yet such a reading of historical
development is far too optimistic, as the events of September 11, 2001, all too vividly
demonstrate.

A moment's reflection attests that religion and violence are often woven together in
history's tapestries. Any number of religions have justified violence under certain circumstances, and others have become caught up in its processes. In the ancient world,
Zoroastrianism transformed earlier combat myths into a theology of eternal apocalyptic struggle between good and evil (Cohn 1993: 114), and ancient Judaism forged a
confederacy under conditions of war (Schluchter 1989: 185, 200). Early Christianity
had its martyrs, and the medieval Roman church, its crusades and Inquisition. As for
Islam, the close association between rulership and religion – together with the principle
of *jihad* (or holy war) as a vessel of reformation – infuse politics with enduring potential
for violence.

To be sure, no modern religion promotes violence in its central tenets, and certain
religions – Hinduism, Buddhism, Confucianism – leave little room for violence in either
theology or practice. Moreover, modern social institutions diminish the power of religion by developing legal-rational frameworks legitimated only remotely by religion,
if at all (Schluchter 1989: 235). But these developments cannot undermine the now
incontrovertibly real connection between religion and violence.

Even the violence of modern movements toward the nation-state was interwoven with religious thread, whether in struggles of reformation and counterreformation
(England), or secularization that would eliminate religion (France, the Soviet Union).
Religion also could facilitate colonizing expansion, frequently with violent consequences for the colonized. True, in core regions of the world economy, religiously

framed conflicts became displaced in the nineteenth and twentieth centuries by social struggles that played out along class lines and, in the latter part of the twentieth century, between superpowers. However, these conflicts themselves often had "religious"
overtones. The historian E. P. Thompson showed how religion influenced nineteenth-
century English class formation. And the central struggle of the post–World War II era –
the Cold War – was frequently portrayed by its Western protagonists as a struggle of
Christendom against godless Communism. From formative phases to high modernity,
meta-narratives of universalistic modernization, class struggle, and the geopolitics of
the Cold War obscured these connections between religion and violence. But with the
end of the Cold War and the surge of capitalist globalization in the 1990s, status conflicts supplanted class conflicts, and the potential of religion as a central organizing
basis of violence became increasingly obvious, to both protagonists and scholars, and
now, to the general public.

In short, religion and violence are hardly strangers. Yet neither are episodes in which
they become connected all of a piece. The September 11 terrorist attacks; continuing
struggles between Jews and Palestinians; the Troubles in Northern Ireland; the nationalist conflicts in the Balkans; ethnic wars in Africa; simmering conflict between Pakistan
and India; terrorist actions by extreme right Christian fundamentalists in the United
States; the subway poison gas attack by the Aum Shinrikyô sect in Tokyo; the deaths of
hundreds in a burning church of the Movement for the Restoration of the Ten Com-
mandments of God in Uganda; the persecution of Falun Gong in China – this is but a
cursory list of some of the most dramatic violent events involving religion at the turn
from the modern era's second to its third millennium.

Modern social theory and research have not provided a ready-made basis for understanding these diverse phenomena in large part because connections between religion
and violence have been down played. Major synthetic accounts of religion, it is fair
to say, deemphasize violence. On the other side, until recently, scholars studying violence tended to ignore cultural dimensions altogether (Theda Skocpol on revolutions
is an iconic case). However, there are considerable scholarly resources for exploring the
manifold relationships between violence and religion, and it is now urgently important to map them in ways that encourage further inquiry. I proceed by: (a) surveying
sociological approaches and theories of religion that inform the analysis of violence,
and (b) proposing an exploratory typology that identifies multiple linkages of violence
and religion – on the one hand, within established social orders and, on the other,
in relation to countercultural religious movements. To emphasize the variety of affinities and parallels, I invoke wide-ranging historical and comparative examples. But the
scholarship is extensive, and this survey is hardly comprehensive (for a bibliographical essay, see Candland 1992). My focus is on key theoretical arguments, cases, and
comparisons.

CONFLICT AND VIOLENCE – THEORETICAL CONSIDERATIONS

Four theoretical issues seem important: (a) the analytic stakes of defining violence;
(b) theories of violence *not* centered on religion; (c) theories that treat violence as an
intrinsic aspect of religion; and (d) theorizations of religion, social order, the state, and
violence.

Defining Violence

Defining violence has long been a vexed problem, and it is only exacerbated for a culturally freighted phenomenon such as religion. Conventional definitions center on the use of physical force to cause injury to persons and, sometimes, damage to property. These definitions pose neat objective standards, and they underscore the point that the exercise of force is not always violent. However, they do not hold up very well, either in objective terms, or when cultural issues are considered. After all, any number of intentional practices may result in physical injury, even in the absence of force, and we would be hard put not to think of them as violent. Poison gas and other chemical and biological weapons, for example, have their basis in physical processes, but their use does not involve force per se. And although a woman might seek to avoid physical injury during a rape, and a person might decide not to resist being kidnapped, we ought not conclude that rape and kidnapping are not violent acts. The poison-gas example suggests that force is not an intrinsic feature of violence, while the second two examples suggest that physical injuries are not its only consequences. These difficulties point to a deeper meaning – captured in the third definition of the verb "violate" in *The New World Dictionary* – "to desecrate or profane (something sacred)." Thus, the problem of *symbolic* violence arises, for what is considered sacred and who has a right to control speech concerning it are matters of cultural prescription. For example, people who declaim desecration of religious symbols would not think of owning a work of art that does so, yet this hardly lessens their sense of moral outrage. On a related front, when religious objects themselves are desecrated (as with the destruction of the eight-hundred-year-old Great Buddha statues of Bamiyan in 2001 by Afghanistan's Islamic Taliban government), the act will have a cultural significance exceeding any damage to property.

The twin difficulties of defining violence thus concern (a) the limitations of an understanding keyed to force resulting in physical injury, and (b) the difficulty of acknowledging the symbolic dimension without privileging one or another ethnocentric or hegemonic definition. These challenges have led Mary Jackman (2001: 443) to formulate an expansive but culturally neutral definition. *Violence*, she argues, encompasses "actions that inflict, threaten, or cause injury." Violent *actions*, she continues, may be "corporal, written, or verbal," and the *injuries* may be "corporal, psychological, material, or social." This definition undermines the conventional tendency to assume that violence is always deviant, and it emphasizes that violence takes many forms (ear-piercing, industrial accidents that could be avoided, individual harassment, group repression, as well as assault and murder). It also usefully recognizes that what people view as violence tends to be culturally freighted. In Western eyes, Chinese footbinding is far more likely to be construed as violent than American parents fitting out a child with dental braces.

These considerations are important for tackling the puzzle of religious violence. Jackman's definition does not assume either that physical violence is the only kind of violence, or that visible physical violence occurs in isolation, or even that the targets of violence are necessarily unwitting victims. Even self-inflicted acts can be construed as violent, from relatively minor forms of asceticism to suicide. As reporting in the wake of 9-11 unveils, some people may seek martyrdom.[1] It is also the case that

---

[1] On this point, see, for example, Joseph Lelyveld, "All suicide bombers are not alike," *New York Times Magazine*, October 28, 2001, pp. 48–53, 62, 78–9.

extreme violence may come as an act of escalation in relation to other, less visible violence. In situations where individuals and groups have differential access to tools of violence, less powerful parties sometimes use extreme violence against more powerful (or better positioned) opponents who are themselves engaged in violent acts, just not necessarily ones that involve corporal injury. Put differently, dramatic public violence is sometimes an extreme variant of what James Scott (1985) calls "weapons of the weak."

Two difficulties with Jackman's broad definition, raised by Benjamin Zablocki (personal communication), are that the violence of verbal actions may rest in the eye of the beholder, and that psychological and social injuries are likely to be matters of assertion and contestation. His solution is to treat violent actions as a subset of a larger panoply of antagonistic and aggressive actions.

In their central concerns, Jackman and Zablocki do not seem so far apart. Both emphasize that purely physical violence does not typically happen in isolation from other forms of aggression, and that various parties may lack equal capacities to exercise one or another kind of aggressive action. For the analysis of religion and violence, these considerations require us to locate extreme physical violence within the context of differential capacities of coercion, symbolic violence, and organized social repression. As Georges Sorel (1906/1950) understood, an established social order marshals considerable capacities for the exercise of authority, force, and violence. By contrast, opponents of the established order, Sorel argued, may try to shake the general public out of complacent conformity by violating the norms and laws that keep the peace. Violence, then, is a problem for some, a tool for others.

In matters of religion, there is considerable discussion concerning the character and significance of extreme violence. Mark Juergensmeyer (2000) argues that religious violence sometimes involves symbolic and performative pursuit of a war that cannot be won, in which defeat nevertheless is unthinkable. In a broader context, Brian Jenkins (1975: 1) argued that terrorism is violence for effect. But neither Juergensmeyer nor Jenkins suggests that symbolic violence is devoid of instrumental goals. As both Juergensmeyer and S. N. Eisenstadt (1999: 50) affirm, even purely symbolic violence may legitimate physical violence. And the effects of terrorism are not just symbolic. Rather, terrorist actions can play into larger dynamics in causally substantial ways. For instance, the absolute numbers of deaths in Ku Klux Klan lynchings, was small relative to the black population in the U.S. South, but lynchings gave white racists a potent device of social control (McVeigh 1999). In India, even seemingly spontaneous riots aid and abet a "rational" pogrom against a minority (Basu 1995). Terrorist acts in the Israeli-Palestinian conflict may fail to achieve any direct military objective but to date they have derailed the prospects of peace. And finally, the 9–11 terrorist attacks using planes as weapons targeted particular buildings (the World Trade Center towers, the Pentagon, and, if the fourth plane had reached its target, the White House) as symbols of global capitalism and American geopolitical hegemony, but they killed thousands of innocent people, and provoked an extended military response. Any given act of violence may simultaneously have symbolic and other consequences.

General Theories of Conflict and Violence

In order to better understand the myriad relationships between religion and violence, it is important to try to distinguish between specifically religious violence and violence that may have religious dimensions, but can be better explained in other terms. The general analysis of violence falls within a larger domain of conflict studies, ranging in topic from interpersonal interaction, families, and small groups to large-scale rebellions, revolutions, and wars (Rex 1981). Sometimes violence – for example, a kidnapping – is inflicted on a victim who lacks any social connection to the perpetrator. More often, it is an escalation of conflict which, as Simmel (1908/1995) emphasized, occurs within an ongoing social relationship. Thus, war is a condition in which antagonisms stemming from mutually irreconcilable objective interests come to a head. Building on Simmel, Coser (1956) pointed to the functional consequences: Conflict can enhance in-group solidarity.

Though utilitarian, rational choice, and game theoretic approaches might seem far removed from Simmel and functionalism, Simmel's formal approach readily incorporates structuralist propositions (Hall 1999: 122–7), including utilitarian ones. James Rule (1988: 54) traces the latter approaches back to Hobbes, but notes that rational-action models typically do not explain the exogenous determinants of violence even if they show why people become involved in, or hold back from, violence once it starts. Concerning people's actions, game theory is useful for modeling dynamic processes (for a review, see Bennett 1987). Among many insights, it reveals a central irony: actors pursuing substantively rational strategies may become involved in scenarios with unintended consequences that fail to maximize their objectives. Thus, in religious arenas, a "deviance amplification model" describes a dialectical process that can tip over into unintended violence (Barkun 1997: 256–7). In this and other scenarios, as social psychologists have emphasized, conflict escalation – and sometimes deescalation and resolution – are fueled by cognitive judgments and attributions of conflicting parties toward one another (Stroebe et al. 1988).

James Rule documents a rich history to explanations of civil violence, from Marx's class theory to Vilfredo Pareto's elite-circulation theory, to "irrationalist" theories of crowd behavior – initiated by Tarde and LeBon at the turn of the twentieth century, influenced soon thereafter by currents of psychoanalytic thought, and carried forward during the heyday of modern American sociology both by mass-society theorists and by symbolic interactionists and other theorists of collective behavior. From the 1960s onward, Ted Gurr and other social scientists advanced a theory of "relative deprivation" based on a social psychological thesis that frustration leads to aggression. But as Rule (1988: 223) observes, relative deprivation has proved more resilient as an interpretive precept than as explanatory theory.

The most important recent macro-level analysts of violence are Charles Tilly and other theorists of social movements, and Theda Skocpol (1979) and Jack Goldstone (1991) on revolution. Each explains large-scale violence on the basis of collective action mobilized in relation to shared interests, undertaken by rationally motivated actors who take advantage of strategic opportunities. Skocpol and Goldstone emphasize the structural conditions giving rise to action, while Tilly (1979) gives more attention to contingent conditions and opportunities, and describes forms of collective action such as French protests at the barricades as cultural "repertoires" that may not work as well in other societal contexts. With the "cultural turn," a new wave of analysts has become interested in the role of ideology in mobilization and legitimation of social movements and revolutions. Here, religion is seen as important for its capacity to create a sense of divine destiny and forge solidarity across social cleavages (Goldstone 2001). In geopolitics, religion can be used to sanctify violence and to crystalize and legitimate what Huntington (1996) calls civilizational struggles, dangers of which, he argues, have now displaced the bipolar Cold-War conflict.[2]

General theories of violence suggest two points. First, some religious violence – for example, the bombing of abortion clinics in the United States – may be explicable in the same terms as nonreligious violence (e.g., murder by the Unabomber). Second, religion can amplify violent processes that have their central causes elsewhere. This latter thesis has its uses and its limits. No doubt it applies to the Troubles in Northern Ireland and ethnic conflict in the former Yugoslavia, but it is less useful for explaining the surge of religiously inspired fundamentalist revolutions and terrorist campaigns over the past quarter century. This limitation suggests that although general social theories of violence have begun to acknowledge the significance of religion, they have not centrally addressed religious meanings, and they have not gone far toward theorizing mechanisms involving religion.

The Violence of Religion

Is there, then, some intrinsic relationship between religion and violence? This question has been addressed by René Girard, Walter Burkert, Jonathan Z. Smith, and Georges Bataille, who developed their analyses in parallel during the 1960s. In essence, they took up the longstanding debates among structuralist, phenomenological, and psychoanalytic theories of religion that address the puzzle of sacrifice – the ritualized taking of animal and human life (Hamerton-Kelly 1987; Bataille 1973/1989). These debates connect back to Emile Durkheim's (1912/1976) more general theory that religion involves the practice of a community of believers who affirm both their idealized vision of society and their own social relations through ritual action in relation to positive and negative cults of the sacred. As subsequent analysts have noted, in Durkheim's model, the sacralization of society delineates cultural boundaries of deviance and Otherness that continue to operate in more secularized social formations (Alexander 1988, 1992).

Keeping to the sphere of religion, the sacralization process described by Durkheim is open as to its *contents*, and thus, war and martyrdom potentially can become sacred duties. For instance, in Japanese samurai culture, the Zen Buddhist monk was idealized as a model for warrior asceticism and indifference to death (Bellah 1970b: 90–2, 182; Aho 1981: Chapter 7).

Beyond explaining the sacralization of violence, Durkheim's model of ritual offers a more general template for theorizing the fundamental embeddedness of violence in religion. René Girard's (1977) analysis has been particularly influential, for it can be applied both to sacrifice within a social group, and to a group's violence toward external opponents. Girard theorizes sacrifice as a resolution of the cycle of violence that stems from mimesis – an imitative rivalry centered on desire for the objects that the Other values. A "surrogate victim" who stands in for wider ills, crimes, or malfeasance becomes the object of collective murder. Because the victim lacks effective defenders,

---

[2] Huntington's analysis has been criticized as overly simplified and dualistic; his defense after 9-11 has been to point to Al-Qa'ida as one of competing groups seeking to prevail within Islamic civilization, in its case, precisely to precipitate civilizational struggle. See Nathan Gardels's interview with Huntington, in *Global Viewpoint*, October 22, 2001.

the ritual killing requires no further retribution, and the cycle is brought to an end, while simultaneously achieving a goal of sanctification – establishing the purity of the sacred in its positive aspects, and separating it from sacred evil, and from the profane. The ritual cleansing so widespread in religious ceremony originally takes the form of sacrifice that destroys a representative bearer of evil. In essence, the core ritual practice of religion is a process of scapegoating (Girard 1986).

Although Girard's model of sacrifice concerns mimetic competition within a shared domain, the scapegoating thesis broadens its applicability to individuals or groups that become stand-ins for both wider sins within a culture, as well as external threats. The former instance – within a culture – is exemplified in the ritualized mass-media scapegoating of Jim Jones in the wake of the murders and mass suicide that he and his Peoples Temple followers committed at Jonestown in 1978; Jones bore much sin of his own making, but the scapegoating loaded onto him blame for practices (for example, in politics, public relations, and social control) that were much more widely shared (Hall 1987: 294–311). As for the second possibility, of intercultural conflict, Girard's theory has been invoked in studies of nationalist struggles (Chidester 1991), ethnoreligious violence (Appleby 2000: 78–9), and religious terrorism (Juergensmeyer 2000: 168–9).

Girard meant his theory to apply to archaic religion. In turn, he argued, the crucifix-ion of Jesus exposed the mythic process of scapegoating, and thus transformed human history by making it possible to reflexively critique the violence of scapegoating (Girard 1986: 205; cf. Williams 1975). The hope of Christocentric theories is that subsequent incidents of religious violence amount to historical remnants or resurgences of archaic religion. Yet this quasi-teleological view fails to square with recent critiques of modern-ization theories. As these critiques point out, there have been limits to the processes by which modern universalistic social institutions have displaced ones based on status honor. Thus, the salience of Girard's theory exceeds his theological frame. A theory of ritual offers a powerful basis for interpreting religiously charged violence – from the highly symbolic but nonetheless physical violence of desecrating religious objects and shrines (and sometimes rebuilding on top of them, as the Spaniards did after the *Reconquista* in Andalusia) to "ethnic cleansing" (for debate and case studies centered on Girard, see Juergensmeyer 1992).

Theories that posit an essential or functional relationship between violence and religion are compelling in their parsimony. However, they must be approached with caution. Both Jackman's trans-cultural definition and game-theoretic analyses (e.g., Myerson 1991: 108–12) show that violence will take different forms according to the circumstances of its expression. Put differently, religious violence is embedded in mo-ments of history and structures of culture. Under these circumstances, it seems inap-propriate to embrace a single general theory linking religion and violence. Instead, the task is to theorize the possible institutional relations of religion to society, and explore alternative scenarios under which violence occurs.

Religion, the Social Order, and the State

It was Max Weber who, at the beginning of the twentieth century, most energetically mapped out an alternative to functionalist and essentialist accounts of religion – by centering his analysis on how religion traffics in the ultimate meaning of life. Yet he did not take ultimate meaning as a constant; to the contrary, Weber famously remarked,

"'From what' and 'for what' one wished to be redeemed and, let us not forget, 'could be' redeemed, depended upon one's image of the world" (1919/1946: 280). And despite his emphasis on meaning, Weber rejected idealist reductionism. For meanings to become salient to social action on a wide basis, they would have to become institutionally elaborated by religious virtuosi and other practitioners who operate within particular structures of social organization, and in social relationships with their audiences, typically drawn from some social strata more than others (Weber 1925/1978: Chapter 6). In turn, relatively bounded social strata take on the character of "status groups" that share a sense of honor and solidarity centered on a distinctive style of life – nobilities that justify their positions in relation to lineage and tradition, workers who affirm the dignity of labor, and so on. Religious meaning thus can refine, consolidate, and sacralize status honor, thereby sharpening status-group alliances and boundaries (Weber 1925/1978: 452, 932–3).

In order to theorize violence, it is important to consider relationships between a typical religious community and other religious communities, as well as with any secular or military power that claims political jurisdiction in the territory where the religious community exists. Interestingly, charisma blurs the relationships between religious community and political community. As Guenther Roth has noted, Weber "transferred the concept of the congregation or community ['*Gemeinde*'] from the religious to the political sphere and came to define it as the typical charismatic association" (1975: 151). This conceptual affinity extends to the military organization of patriarchal violence in the "men's house," for which Weber commented, "The communistic warrior is the perfect counterpart to the monk" (1925/1978: 1153).

Weber analyzed relationships between religion and the political by identifying two kinds of domination: Political domination by means of authority and "hierocratic coercion" – a form of "psychic coercion" implemented by "distributing or denying religious benefits" (1925/1978: 45). Thus, at the center of Weber's sociology of domination there are (a) a recognition of continuities between religious and political organization, and (b) a specification of different sources of (and potential conflicts between) religious and political authority. Various possible relations thus obtain between secular powers and religion. When a hierocratic organization affirms a monopoly over religious practice within a given territory (approximating the "church" as an ideal type), it typically seeks to define the limits of political authority, either by subsuming it completely in theocracy (as the Taliban did in Afghanistan in the 1990s), or by legitimating secular rulers. At the other extreme, in caesaropapism, the state asserts legitimacy in nonreligious terms, and on this basis, claims to exercise authority over the exercise of religion (Weber 1925/1978: 1158–211). Paradoxically, each of these resolutions yields a structurally similar situation in which the legitimacy of state power is cloaked in religion, and struggles against the state tend to become framed in sacred terms.

Over the course of modern Western development, there has been a general decline in church monopolies, coupled with the development of religious pluralism and the rise of secular public culture. With secularization (however incomplete), the state has inherited the Durkheimian religious community's function – policing the boundaries that define legitimate religions – while leaving room for pluralism within those boundaries. However, the consolidation of modern religious pluralism within nation-states is precarious, as recent ethnoreligious conflicts, theocratic-national movements, and casaeropapist regulations of religion (especially in Communist states) attest. Moreover, any social order advantages certain social strata and subordinates others, and today, this occurs both within states and in the global spread of the world economy and modernity. The latter are often culturally marked by their Western provenance, and sometimes opposed by actors within alternative civilizational complexes, in particular, Islam (Huntington 1996). Thus, Osama bin Laden's Al-Qa'ida holds as a primary goal ridding Saudi Arabia of both its U.S. military presence and the particular Arab regime which that presence supports. Religions deal in ultimate meanings that bear a claim to exceed merely secular authority. Thus, they remain a potent basis for contesting political legitimacy both within and beyond nation-states, a point underscored by Al-Qa'ida's appeal to Muslims on the street.

Historically and today, religious movements that challenge a given social order sometimes arise on the basis of a shared commitment to ultimate values that links participants across social cleavages in a *déclassé* alliance. More typically, movements originate in social strata that are negatively privileged politically and economically, or socially ascendent but blocked from power.[3] For either negatively privileged or excluded groups, religion represents a special case of status honor that, as Weber comments, is "nourished most easily on the belief that a special 'mission' is entrusted to them.... Their value is thus moved into something beyond themselves, into a 'task' placed before them by God" (1919/1946: 276–7). Religion under Western monotheism, in Weber's account, develops a possibility of "holy war, i.e., a war in the name of god, for the special purpose of avenging a sacrilege." Weber argued that the connection of the holy war to salvation religion is "in general only a formal relation," and "even the formal orthodoxy of all these warrior religionists was often of dubious genuineness" (1925/1978: 473–4).[4]

Not surprisingly, the idea of the holy war that Weber sketched has received considerable scholarly attention. One of the most significant theoretical refinements is James Aho's (1981) distinction between "immanentist-cosmological" versus "transcendent-historical" myths of holy war. In the first, warfare itself is a glorious ritualized *exemplary* activity that ought to symbolize the divine order; the latter myth underwrites a *utilitarian* pursuit of war as a means to fulfill a covenant with a deity. Important as this distinction is, actual instances of warrior ideology sometimes mix the two (Chidester 1991: Chapter 5).

TOWARD A TYPOLOGY OF RELIGION AND VIOLENCE

On the face of it, theories of violence and religion do not yield any obvious grand synthetic model. In this circumstance, the task at hand is to identify alternative situational "cultural logics" by which religious violence manifests. Such an approach makes it

---

[3] Sometimes, a wider *déclassé* alliance is led by a blocked elite. Al-Qa'ida's movement would seem to demonstrate this possibility. Those identified as 9-11 terrorists and key participants in Al-Qa'ida are almost all well educated, and some of them, notably Osama bin Laden, quite wealthy. Despite their relatively privileged social origins, they have demonstrated a capacity to appeal to a much wider audience of Islamic fundamentalists, many of them desperately poor, and living at the margins of the globalizing world economy.

[4] If so, the Taliban – Al-Qa'ida alliance would seem to be an important exception, for theocracy is central to the Taliban regime, and Al-Qa'ida's terrorist training camps have drawn their recruits from *madrassahs*, or Muslim religious schools.

possible to formulate generic ideal-types, while at the same time recognizing the historical circumstances and microcauses of any particular instance of violence (Hall 2000). It also acknowledges that any given religious phenomenon – fundamentalism, for example – may arise in different circumstances, and lead to (or defuse) different kinds of violence.

Given the complex possibilities, the delineation of types of violence associated with religion cannot follow any tidy expository sequence. However, the following discussion may be usefully divided by way of a fundamental distinction between normative *ideological* versus countercultural *utopian* violence (Mannheim 1937). In the first case, religious practices that may be described as violent within one or another definition are legitimated within a given social order, and the violence does not typically become a basis for condemning the religious organization in which it occurs; ideology either explains away violence or treats it as deviant aberration (such ideologically normalized violence occurs in much the same way within deviant religious groups that have their own institutionalized social orders). By contrast, as Mannheim emphasized, utopias should not be regarded as unworkable fantasies but, rather, as projects that are unrealizable only so long as a given established social order is sustained. Compared to phenomena wholly within an institutionalized social order, countercultural utopian movements cannot be so neatly divided between the religious and the nonreligious, for if a given movement proves viable, it brings to the fore questions of ultimate meaning, and is thus religiously tinged (Hall 1978). Thus, as Frederick Engels (1850/1964) already acknowledged in the nineteenth century, revolutionary socialist movements often exhibit sectarian tendencies.

IDEOLOGICALLY NORMALIZED VIOLENCE WITHIN A SOCIAL ORDER

The kinds of violence associated with religion "within" a social order depend to a great extent on the particular social formation and its historical moment. An important contextual factor concerns whether there is a single established religion or religious pluralism.

Violence under Hierocratic Domination

The possibility of routine violence that is part and parcel of a religion's practices has received only scattered attention – most sustained in assessments of accusations concerning religious movements labelled as "cults." However, the issues bear a potentially wider salience. As Weber (1925/1978: 54) observed, a religious organization that claims a monopoly on the control of religious benefits may thereby exert a kind of "psychic coercion." In these terms, two aspects of hierocratic violence may be identified – self-inflicted mortification and violence as a device of social control.

In the first place, people acting under a religious regimen may become willing to engage in self-inflicted violence (ascetic practices of fasting, self-flagellation, and so forth) in order to achieve religious benefits or fulfill religious values. Of course, most devotional acts are nonviolent; they may even benefit the practitioner independent of any ultimate salvation prospects. However, sometimes acts in fulfillment of religious faith are violent. For example, Ronald Knox reports about medieval European Catharists committing suicide by fasting. Possibly, believers wanted to avoid illness or senile decay that might yield death under the control of the alien force of Satan, or it may be that in preparation for death they sought to avoid soiling the body with food after purification (Knox 1950: 97). In contemporary times, parallel issues arise for Christian Scientists who refuse medical treatment for life-threatening but curable illnesses. On an entirely different basis, Buddhist monks engaged in self-immolation during the Vietnam War as testaments for peace. And from all we can glean, the 1997 collective suicide of Heaven's Gate in Rancho Santa Fe, California, was freely chosen by its participants – all adults – who had spent years in perfectionist self-regulation to prepare to enter "the next evolutionary level above human." For them, an apocalyptic narrative of escape animated a pseudo-mystical theology of transcendence through death (Hall, Schuyler, and Trinh 2000: Chapter 5).

The moral stakes of these examples differ dramatically. Any given instance of self-inflicted violence can be regarded as either a testament of ultimate commitment or a demonstration of how far a practitioner has fallen under the sway of psychic coercion. Thus, such practices raise the vexed question of whether individuals are freely exercising choice, or subjected to forces that they are more or less helpless to resist.

The latter trait marks the second aspect of hierocratic violence – its use for social control. Within a given culture, hierocratic control tends to be normalized and naturalized unless it becomes extreme. The standard may be lower for a group considered deviant. Thus, corporal punishment used for "loving correction" of children in the Northeast Kingdom Community in Island Pond, Vermont during the 1980s provoked accusations of child abuse (Hall 1987: 125). More recently, the issue has received broad attention (Bartkowski 1995). Casting a wider warrant, critics of religious social movements have raised charges about deception, psychological manipulation, and control of communal settlement boundaries. The critics argue that such groups control their members to the point where those members lose their will to resist participating. If such social control practices can be shown to eliminate individuals' normal exercise of will, social control becomes tantamount to violence – certainly violation of individuals' rights. A similar issue arises with participants whose commitment to a religious organization begins to erode. If individuals hint at apostasy, they may be subjected to extreme psychological and social pressures to remain within the fold, and they may be physically restrained from leaving it. In turn, controversies about apostasy often have consequences for religious organizations themselves (Bromley 1998a).

Religious organizations have no monopoly on the uses of social control to maintain participants' commitment and solidarity (Hall 1987: 138–9). If social control under religious auspices differs from broader practices, it is because participants seek salvation, and thus may have heightened incentives to submit to hierocratic domination. In doing so, they can undergo "conversion" that normalizes hierocratic violence, rendering themselves accomplices in their own cultural domination. The study of hierocratic domination and violence is thus a vexed agenda in the sociology of religion in part because scholars disagree about the ontological relations between conversion, coercion, faith, and individual identity. In the debates of the past quarter century, cult opponents have often treated psychological coercion as an intrinsic and essential feature of "cults" (Hall, Schuyler, and Trinh 2000: 10). Such a sweeping definitional thesis has not been sustained, however, since it fails to account for the large numbers of people who successfully depart supposedly tyrannical religious movements. Yet the limitations of a strong psychological-coercion thesis should not lead to the conclusion that hierocratic domination never involves coercion. Rather, two agendas ought to be pursued. First, there is a need for more nuanced, situationally detailed, and broadly comparative study of hierocratic domination, since techniques of social control are likely to vary according to the type of religious organization (Hall 1987: 138). Second, to date, the issue of psychological coercion has been addressed most vigorously in the research of religious-movement opponents. Here, culturally biased approaches that differentially focus on hierocratic violence in deviant religions while ignoring it within established religions need to be rectified by a comparative analysis of both (for diverse views on the issues, see Zablocki and Robbins 2001).

Competition between Religions

As Simmel observed, competition is an indirect form of conflict in which both parties seek the same prize (1908/1955: 57). In the absence of churchlike hegemony within a social order, sectarian factions within a religious organization or heterodoxical religious groups may compete for converts, for control over organizational doctrines or resources, and for other advantages – such as state recognition. A systematic causal analysis of religious conflict by Fred Kniss (1997a) shows that, for American Mennonite communities, the outcomes of such conflicts are influenced especially by how defenders respond to challengers, and by third-party intervention. Much competition between religious groups is peaceful, and it unfolds within a larger frame of mutual respect and sometime cooperation. Yet in order to gain advantages, religious groups may be tempted both to increase hierocratic domination over followers (see earlier), and to exceed what competitors regard as fair practices. A sociological catalog of such episodes would be extensive, diverse, and revealing. In the West alone, it would include: factions among fifth-century Christians that sought to prevent opponents from venturing out of their monastic domains (Gregory 1979); skirmishes among rival Protestant groups during the English civil war; Protestant violence toward Catholics in the nineteenth-century United States; probably the 1965 assassination of Malcolm X after he broke with the Black Muslim movement and converted to orthodox Islam; and the gunfire exchanged by rival factions of the Branch Davidian sect, years before the shootout between the Branch Davidians and government agents (Pitts 1995: 376).

Although violence growing out of competition is unusual, when it becomes amplified on a large scale, it can organize broader social boundaries, and thus crystalize nationalist conflicts, anticolonial struggles for independence, or civil war (for instance, in contemporary conflicts between Muslims and Christians in Nigeria). When religious boundaries roughly align with boundaries between nation-states, religious competition may become the grist on which international conflict is ground (as in contemporary tensions between India and Pakistan).

Conversely, broader political events sometimes exacerbate religious competition to the point of violence. Thus, in the first century of the modern era, Zealots assassinated Jews in rival factions deemed insufficiently opposed to Roman rule (Lewy 1974: 80, 84), and in recent years, the Jewish-Palestinian conflict has led to violent actions of both Jewish and Palestinian fundamentalists against moderates in their own nations (Friedland and Hecht 1996). As Eisenstadt (1999: 102) notes, fundamentalist movements often encompass rival organizations. Under such conditions, violence can result from sectarian and schismatic competition for countercultural predominance that occurs in the context of broader counterhegemonic violence (discussed later).

Religion as an Organizing Aspect of State Domination and Colonization

A "colonial" logic consolidates *internal* or *external* territory for a state claiming monopolization of the legitimate use of force. Religion can become a tool of conquest, both through cultural hegemony, and more materially, by settling and organizing populations in a colonized territory. In some cases, as with the Cistercians' medieval expansion into eastern Europe, the religion itself is a colonizing movement. At the extreme, in the Christian crusades, St. Bernard de Clairvaux promoted a fusion between military organization and religious order, arguing that a member of a crusading order "serves his own interest in dying, and Christ's interest in killing!" The Crusades – and especially the Iberian *reconquista* – provided the original template for subsequent European colonization, according to the great nineteenth-century German historian Leopold von Ranke (Partner 1997: 160–1). In the beginning, Roman Catholicism sanctioned state violence, for example with the papal bulls that authorized Henry the Navigator to enslave peoples he encountered on his voyages "to convert and combat the infidel" (Houtart 1997: 2). This pattern continued in the Latin Americas. But with the papal bulls, religion became a subordinate partner. In the spread of the Portuguese and Spanish empires to the Americas, violence was the prerogative of the expansionary state, and conquest was first and foremost a military achievement. For its part, the Roman Catholic Church engaged in forced conversion and organization of indigenous populations through its networks of missions (Rivera 1992).

Even if religion is not directly involved in the exercise of violence to secure and control territory, to the degree that it sacralizes a political regime, it lends legitimacy to that regime and thus functionally supports regime violence. Tacit or explicit religious support of brutal regimes can be significant. The religious justification of slavery in the U.S. South during the nineteenth century is an obvious example, as are religious acquiescence to Hitler's Germany, the United States's prosecution of the Vietnam war, and the Argentine dictatorship in the twentieth century.

UTOPIA, HEGEMONY, AND VIOLENCE

Given that religions sometimes participate in or legitimate state violence, it is not surprising that religion also can be a significant force in counterhegemonic conflict. There are many kinds of utopian religious movements, and the vast majority of groups do not become committed to violence unless they become objects of establishment repression, and for the most part, not even then. However, two countercultural orientations – the mystical and the apocalyptic – have distinctive potentials for grounding violence. Of the two, mysticism recently has underwritten hierocratic violence in the Solar Temple and Heaven's Gate by producing a metaphysical understanding of death as transcendence through suicide (Hall, Schuyler, and Trinh 2000). In other cases, mysticism is invoked in counterhegemonic movements to promote an aura of invincibility, as with the proclamation of participants' immunity from the effects of the colonizers' bullets during the Mau Mau rebellion.

However, the apocalyptic orientation is far more broadly significant. Its temporal structure posits a final battle between the forces of good and the forces of evil – a conflict that leads to the destruction of the existing temporal order and the arrival of a new "timeless" era of "heaven on earth." Ideal typically, there are three significant social orientations toward apocalyptic time. A *post*apocalyptic orientation posits that a pacifistic *otherworldly sect* has somehow "escaped" the apocalypse transpiring in the wider world, typically by decamping to a refuge "beyond" the apocalypse (Hall 1978: 68–79; cf. Lanternari 1960/1963: 314). By contrast, in a *pre*apocalyptic movement, life unfolds in historical time either leading up to or in the throes of apocalyptic struggle. Relatively peaceable *conversionist sects* (especially active within Christianity) have used millennialist motifs to recruit new members before the second coming of Christ. Conversely, preapocalyptic *warring sects* see themselves as agents of apocalyptic history battling to defeat the forces of evil. As I have described this latter type of group,

> the sectarian mission involves a struggle with opposing forces in historical time. A band of true believers, who become certified as charismatic warriors through a process of rebirth, acts alone or in concert with a wider underground network of sympathizers and similar bands. These warriors engage in the moment-to-moment coordination of guerilla-style action in pursuit of strategic, symbolic, and terrorist missions. The members of the sect come out of the quiescent masses to act in historical significance far out of proportion to their actual numbers.... [T]he successful execution of actions related to missions and contingency plans depends on interpersonal trust, the development of high proficiency at various technical and strategic skills, and acts of commitment and bravery which place mission ahead of personal survival. (Hall 1978: 206–7; cf. Wilson 1973: 23)

Such groups invoke a value commitment to what Weber called an "ethic of ultimate ends" – a refusal to sully commitment to a transcendent value by brooking any sort of "political" compromise. This is the essence of the holy war described by Weber (1925/1978: 473–4), and recently identified by Mark Juergensmeyer (2000: Chapter 8) as a central theme of religious terrorism in what he calls "cosmic war."

The missions carried out by militant warring sects are often dramatic, but as the 9–11 attacks make all too evident, it would be a mistake to regard them merely as isolated aberrations. To the contrary, when warring sects arise, it is almost always in the context of wider countercultural ferment, often in relation to social conditions construed within some social strata as constituting a crisis of legitimacy for an existing social order (Lanternari 1960/1963; Wilson 1973; Hall 1978). Yet the cause pursued via apocalyptic war is historically mercurial: At one point it may reflect the assertion of manifest destiny by a rising social stratum, at another, the attempt to salvage honor by a stratum in decline. Whatever the cause, warring sects pursuing violence as the basis for social reconstruction typically are simply the most extreme groups within a broader countercultural milieu. Historically, such groups have ranged in scale from small bands of committed guerrillas to complex, far-flung terrorist organizations and even small armies. Although occasionally the causes embraced by warring sects are centrally religious, more often religious language and organization animate broader nationalist, anticolonial, and revolutionary class movements. As for outcomes, some movements are completely overwhelmed by superior force; others respond to such circumstances with martyrdom and collective suicide. And some movements have far-reaching historical consequences.

Nationalism, Rebellion, and Revolution

Recently, Eisenstadt (1999: 150–2) described modern "Jacobin" political ideologies that seek a total revolutionary transformation of society. Their roots are to be found, Eisenstadt suggests, in earlier monotheistic religions and millenarian movements in conflict with society-at-large. Indeed, there are intimations of a revolutionary impulse to make the world anew to be found in a variety of premodern religious movements, although there are also notable exceptions to Eisenstadt's monotheism thesis, for example, among the numerous syncretic religious sectarian rebellions in ancient China (Lewy 1974: 60–9). Even here, however, the cult of the emperor constituted a *de facto* casaeropapist monotheism (Weber 1925/1978: 1208). In other cases, the monotheistic thesis is more easily established. The ancient Jews reacted to first Persian and later Roman colonization in various sectarian movements, for instance, the revolt of the Maccabees (175–164 B.C.E.), and the struggles of the Zealots (Lewy 1974: 70–86).

W. H. C. Frend, the religious historian, has argued that martyrdom is one continuity that binds the New Testament to the Old. But motifs of martyrdom shifted in their meanings for the early Christians. Under both the old and the new covenant, believers would embrace death rather than forsake their religion. But, whereas Jews regarded their acts as a testament to their faith, after Jesus's crucifixion, some Christians came to believe that their martyrdom might actually *quicken* the coming of the apocalypse that would establish the kingdom of God on earth (Frend 1967; Hall 1987: 296–8). Nor was martyrdom simply an individual act; instead, as Riddle (1931) demonstrated, early Christian martyrdom was collectively organized through techniques of socialization and social control. Much the same techniques as those catalogued by Riddle obtain today in the training of Islamic fundamentalist terrorists.

Because Christians did not treat their religion as limited by ethnicity or nation, monotheistic war escaped the box of tribe and nation. Ronald Knox (1950: 61–3) notes that the Circumcilliones of the fourth century, who practiced martyr-suicide, could be construed as revolutionary Africans opposing domination by Rome. And as Norman Cohn (1961) shows, a direct lineage connects early Christian apocalypticism to the sometimes violent religious movements of the Middle Ages in Europe – from the Crusades to the self-flagellants of Thuringia to the sixteenth-century peasants' movement around Thomas Müntzer. For Frederick Engels (1850/1964), the religious wars of the sixteenth century embodied a revolutionary class consciousness. Others, such as Walzer (1965) and Lewy (1974) reject any reductive class thesis, but nevertheless recognize that religious movements such as the fifteenth-century Bohemian Taborite uprising and Reformation movements such as England's Fifth Monarchy Men were complexly connected with revolutionary transformations of Europe.

In Lewis Namier's pithy formulation, religion is a sixteenth-century word for nationalism. Social scientists may be tempted to try to disentangle European nationalism from religion. However, Eisenstadt (1999: 46) argues that it was the specific *combination* of class and religious intellectuals and their sectarian movements that propelled various European revolutions toward modernity. The Fifth Monarchy Men anticipated the secular Jacobin totalistic urge of the French Revolution to make the world anew, according to a utopian plan. In turn, Karl Marx's theory of revolutionary transformation toward communism consolidated secularized apocalyptic struggle as a dominant motif of the modern era.

Religious Responses to Colonialism

Obviously, not all modern and postmodern revolutionary movements have been secular. Quite to the contrary, religion sometimes animated "archaic" prophetic movements during the nineteenth and twentieth centuries (Hobsbawm 1959). In some cases – such as Tai Ping in China (Boardman 1962; Spence 1996) and Ch'ondogyo (the Religion of the Heavenly Way) in Korea (Weems 1964) – nationalist and anticolonial politics grew out of a this-worldly millenarian religious movement aimed at the rectification of colonialism and economic domination. In the face of such examples, Bryan Wilson nevertheless argues that violent opposition to colonialism typically has had little to do with religion per se, even if religious calls for supernatural aid are sometimes invoked and militant political movements sometimes use religious movements as organizing venues, for example, in the Jamaican Ras Tafarian movement of the 1960s. However, he acknowledges that occasionally resistance becomes organized through prophetic charismatic leadership under fundamentally religious auspices (1973: 68, 222, 228, 234–6, 258).

Both Wilson and Vittorio Lanternari identify a variety of tendencies among what Lanternari called "religions of the oppressed." Faced with military defeat, some anticolonial movements – such as the indigenous American Ghost Dance religion – consolidated a redemptive cultural heritage (occasionally mixed with religious motifs of the colonizers). Others, more firmly under colonial administration, have sought this-worldly redemption – in escape to a promised land (the Ras Tafari movement), or the anticipation of a new era of abundant wealth (Melanesian cargo cults). Elsewhere, mystical and apocalyptic motifs of armed struggle infused messianic movements such as the Joazeiro movement in early-twentieth-century Brazil and the Mau Mau rebellion in sub-Saharan Africa (Lanternari 1960/1963; Wilson 1973). As Michael Adas (1979: 184–5) observes, not just the poorly educated and dispossessed participate; rather, a millenarian leader sometimes transcends differences of social status and mobilizes a specifically anticolonial rebellion.

The significance of religion is highly variable. In the Lord's Resistance Army operating in northern Kenya and the southern Sudan beginning in the 1990s, charismatic warriors seemingly lack any agenda beyond obtaining the spoils of war through brutality. On occasion, however, religion underwrites a broad nationalist movement. For example, in the struggles for India's independence, tensions between Hindu and secular nationalism were never fully resolved (Lewy 1974: 277–323). Today, this religious ambiguity remains a flash point for secular-religious tensions, Hindu-Muslim conflicts (Kakar 1996), and Sikh ethnic mobilization (Juergensmeyer 2000: Chapter 5) – all within India, and conflict between Hindu-dominated India and Muslim Pakistan, itself exacerbated in the wake of 9-11.

Sometimes religion is more than shallow pretext or deep ideology. As Kakar (1996) demonstrates for south India, it can not only manipulate cultural symbols, but also construct communal and personal identities. Moreover, the involvement of Buddhist monks in militant politics in Sri Lanka shows that religions sometimes provide concrete organizational resources and personnel for broader movements that employ violence (Tambiah 1992). And even where such direct connections are absent, religion is a source of potent cultural material for repertoires of collective action. As Esherick (1987) argues for the Boxer rebellion, anti-Christian rituals drew on a *habitus* of rituals and narratives rooted in shamanistic practices widely understood within Chinese peasant society.

Perhaps religious violence is a bridge that traverses modernity. In contrast to Jacobin utopian movements, Eisenstadt regards "national-communal" movements as less fully modern because of their emphasis on putatively primordial ties of solidarity, which yield a reactionary rather than a utopian program (1999: 116). However, communalist nationalist violence has increased after the collapse of the Soviet Empire. The reasons for this development are complex. Juergensmeyer (2000: 227) suggests that a "political form of postmodernism" creates a crisis of "secular nationalism" and uncertainty concerning "what constitutes a valid basis for national identity." In a similar vein, James Aho argues that the postmodern theorization of social constructions as illusory comes head up against fundamentalist quests for certainty in uncertain times. The result is nothing less than the "apocalypse of modernity" (1997).

Countercultural Religious War

Nineteenth- and twentieth-century messianic movements against colonialism usually were overwhelmed militarily. By the latter half of the twentieth century, however, strategic and symbolic violence by so-called religious fundamentalists became a force of substantial significance. Eisenstadt (1999) holds that religious fundamentalism may seem reactionary, but is thoroughly modern not only in its techniques and strategies, but in its assertion of a Jacobin utopian impulse to remake the social world via transformation of the political center. In theoretical terms, both Jacobinist and fundamentalist movements can be located within the broader domain of the apocalyptic utopian conviction that the old order will be transcended through a decisive struggle of the "warring sect" against the putative forces of evil (Hall 1978). Often, warring sectarians participate in and feed back upon a broader movement, which inspires particular groups to take action in fulfillment of utopian doctrines.

The first major harbinger of apocalyptic war as a serious possibility in the contemporary era came in Japan, where the sect Aum Shinrikyô developed an apocalyptic ideology within a quasi-Buddhist framework. Rank-and-file members knew only that by learning Buddhist self-discipline they were preparing to survive an apocalyptic onslaught, but the inner circle of the movement developed chemical weapons as a basis for waging apocalyptic war, and used them in a poison-gas attack on the Tokyo subway system on March 20, 1995 (Hall, Schuyler, and Trinh 2000; Reader 2000). Nor has the West been completely immune from internal movements. In the United States, a militant, racist, right-wing Christian countercultural milieu yielded a number of paramilitary groups, several of which participated in robbery, arson, murder, and armed skirmishes and standoffs with authorities (Aho 1990; Barkun 1997). Also in the United States, moral opposition to abortion diffused a dualistic vision within a wider movement that inspired a small number of individuals to engage in coordinated bombings of abortion clinics and assassinations of abortion providers (Blanchard and Prewitt 1993). Here, as with terrorism more generally, violence had both a symbolic effect and a dampening effect (Joffe 1995). In the wake of 9-11, however, such tactics will delegitimize their perpetrators outside a very narrow counterculture, at least in the near term.

Today, apocalyptic religious war has taken center stage, in a situation presciently described by German social critic Walter Benjamin (1940/1968: 263), when he noted how a historical moment can be shot through with "chips of messianic time." Warring sects active in the Islamic fundamentalist milieu now invoke the long established Islamic repertoire of holy war, or *jihad*. Historically, these struggles have typically been directed at national powers (see, e.g., the analysis by Waterbury 1970). But in the past three decades, Islamic fundamentalism has increasingly become the vehicle of a transnational, pan-Arab, and now even broader mobilization against the West and especially the United States. Its most organized warring sect today, Al-Qa'ida organized by Osama bin Laden, draws together terrorist cells operating in dozens of countries, from the Philippines to the Maghreb, and on to Germany, France, and the United States. Through terrorist action without precedent, they have worked to precipitate a struggle between the modernity initiated by Western Christendom and an alternative, utopian fundamentalist version of Islam.[5]

Conflicts with Countercultural Religious Movements

Warring sects range from small groups engaged in largely symbolic conflict, to violent but ineffectual ones, and on to highly organized armed militaristic cadres that operate effectively on a national or international scale, surviving with support from background sponsoring groups or extensive secondary networks. Sometimes, a strategy of repression is undertaken toward countercultural groups even in the *absence* of any violence, when such groups are defined by moral entrepreneurs of the established order as *outside* the boundaries of societal moral legitimacy. In other cases – rare, but paramount now – the call to war is heeded on both sides of the apocalyptic divide. In either case, when opponents act to counter an apocalyptic sect, this response is invoked by the sectarians to legitimate their apocalyptic ideology among a broader countercultural audience.

Two subtypes mark a continuum of responses to countercultural sects. First, private individuals and groups may take repressive actions against religious movements into their own hands, without state or religious sanction, but as moral entrepreneurs for the established cultural order. Second, there are full-scale public campaigns of religious repression, persecution, or even war, organized either by a hegemonic religion against what is defined as heresy or, in cases where states have assumed de facto authority for legitimation of religion or where a movement threatens state power, by one or more states themselves.

At the ad hoc end of the continuum, distraught family members sometimes forcibly seek to prevent relatives from associating with a particular religion, or they may use violent nonlegitimate force to retrieve a relative from a religious organization. On occasion,

---

[5] For a journalistic report on Osama bin Laden's group prior to the September 11, 2001, terrorist attacks in the United States, see the three-part series in the *New York Times* (January 14, 15, and 16, 2001). As Martin Riesebrodt points out, Islamic fundamentalism shares the typical features of fundamentalism more broadly – patriarchy, gender dualism, and pietism; however, all Islamic religion is hardly fundamentalistic, and thus, Riesebrodt questions the Huntington clash-of-civilizations analysis (lecture, University of California – Davis, Center for History, Society, and Culture, October 18, 2001).

internal family conflicts have led to violence, as when the husband of a nineteenth-century Bishop Hill woman murdered the sect's leader, Eric Janson (Hall 1988). In other cases, ad hoc action becomes more organized. In the "anticult" movements that developed in the United States and Europe in the wake of the countercultural religious ferment that began in the 1960s, family opponents often formed loose alliances, sometimes aided by a broader coalition of "cultural opponents." These anticult countermovements operated within varying national cultural traditions concerning religious freedom, and some groups eschewed violence in favor of conflict mediation. However, the most militant anticult activists facilitated the kidnapping of sect members and forcible "deprogramming," in which sect members were subjected to reeducation until they recanted their sectarian beliefs (Bromley and Richardson 1983; Bromley 1998b).

At the extreme, cultural opponents engage in direct campaigns of intimidation and violence against religious movements. An iconic case concerns the Church of Jesus Christ of the Latter-Day Saints in the United States during the nineteenth century: Not only were Mormons forcibly driven from certain states; in June 1844, an angry mob broke into a jail in Carthage, Illinois, and lynched their leader, Joseph Smith. To only mention another example, Jehovah's Witnesses found themselves subject to similar albeit less extreme intimidations when their patriotism was questioned during World War II (Peters 2000).

At the opposite end of the continuum, public campaigns by established religions and states against religions deemed nonlegitimate are diverse. They range from subjugation of Jews and repression of Christianity in the Roman Empire, to the Church of Rome's campaigns against sectarian heresy and witchcraft in the middle ages (and French King Philip the Fair's pogrom against the Knights Templar), Soviet suppression of religion, and the contemporary campaign of the People's Republic of China against the Falun Gong sect (for one review of contemporary international issues, see Hackett et al. 2000). Most recently, in the initial days after September 11, U.S. President George W. Bush – in a telling but quickly recanted choice of words – called for a "crusade" against Osama bin Laden's Al-Qa'ida movement and terrorism in general (in a similar vein, the military operation was initially named "Infinite Justice").

The comparative research on such developments remains spotty. One line of inquiry traces how deviants or scapegoats become framed as the Other. An important historical study, Norman Cohn's *Europe's Inner Demons* (1975), traces the diffusion of speculations about secret practices of cannibalistic infanticide – anxieties that fueled institutionally sanctioned campaigns of persecution from the Roman Empire through the seventeenth century. Researchers similarly have explored community accusations of witchcraft raised against individuals (e.g., Thomas 1971; Erikson 1966). Such campaigns of repression are subject to Durkheimian functionalist analysis of how social control contains anxiety and enhances dominant group solidarity (Klaits 1985).

Explanatory attention also has been directed to explaining the conditions under which repressive campaigns become unleashed; Behringer (1997), for example, argues that in Bavaria during the late sixteenth century, witchcraft purges came to a head during agricultural crises. In such circumstances, repression might occur even against a powerless religious movement or person, in order to reinforce general norms of cultural conformity. But other countercultural religious movements are harbingers of broad sociocultural change, and as Michael Adas (1979: Chapter 5) argues, efforts at repression can badly backfire, thereby enhancing the legitimacy of a countercultural movement, channeling secondary mobilization of resources and followers to its cause, and undermining the capacity of an established order's organizations to sustain their institutional dominance. This is the substantial risk of the current "war against terrorism": That the coalition's strategy will do nothing to change the conditions that spawn terrorism, and to the contrary, will further alienate and embolden Muslims already of a fundamentalist bent, inspiring further jihad against the West. The result could be a destabilization of states – from the Philippines and Indonesia to Nigeria, and thus, an even further erosion of the established world order.

Violent Countercultural Responses to "Persecution" and Defeat

How do nonlegitimated religious movements respond to perceived repression? One outcome, historically important, has been the success of an insurgent religious movement to the point of either forcing a shift to religious pluralism or even achieving hegemony itself. A second alternative, which occurs when either success or survival in the country of origin seems unlikely, is collective religious migration. From the ancient Jews to medieval heretics, European Protestants coming to North America, nineteenth-century Mormons migrating to Utah, the Peoples Temple abandoning San Francisco for the jungle paradise of Jonestown, Guyana, the formula is similar: A group seeks to escape what its participants deem persecution by finding a region of refuge, a promised land, a Zion in the wilderness.

In the wake of the 1978 murders and mass suicide by Jim Jones's followers at Jonestown, a third long-standing possibility gained renewed attention. Conflict between opponents within an established order and a countercultural religious movement can follow a dialectic of escalation that leads to extreme violence (Hall 1987: Chapters 9–11). As Robbins (1986) argues for Russian Old Believers in the seventeenth century, when a group of true believers finds itself the object of repression by a much more powerful adversary to the point where their survival as a meaningful religious movement is placed in doubt, they may choose collective martyrdom rather than defeat.

Under conditions of modern societal institutionalization (i.e., of the state, religion, and mass media), it is possible to specify a general model of collective martyrdom (Hall, Schuyler, and Trinh 2000). Of course participants in a warring sect already subscribe to a stark ethic that settles for nothing less than victory or martyrdom. But this ethic can also develop within groups under the sway of a less militant, more otherworldly, apocalyptic worldview. In such cases, the apocalyptic character of the group does not in itself explain extreme violence. Rather, violence grows out of escalating social confrontations between, on the one hand, an apocalyptic sectarian movement and, on the other, ideological proponents of an established social order who seek to control "cults" through emergent, loosely institutionalized oppositional alliances, typically crystallized by cultural opponents (especially apostates and distraught relatives of members). Whether the social conflict has violent consequences depends on the degree to which cultural opponents succeed in mobilizing public institutional allies, namely, news reporters and modern governments or their representatives. If opponents credibly threaten or inflict social injury, other conditions being equal, the likelihood increases that there will be a response of violence on the part of movement operatives toward those opponents, followed by a collective suicide that believers take to affirm the collective honor of their sect through its refusal to submit to a more powerful external authority.

Some scholars (e.g., Robbins and Anthony 1995; Robbins 1997) suggest that internal factors – such as an aging or diseased leader – can set a religious movement on a path toward martyrdom. No doubt the Hall-Schuyler-Trinh (2000) model detailed in *Apocalypse Observed* is best treated as a heuristic to be used in comparative analysis. It provides a robust explanation of certain recent cases of violent confrontation – notably Jonestown and the conflagration in which Branch Davidians died near Waco, Texas. But as *Apocalypse Observed* shows, the generic scenario can be altered by situational factors (e.g., cultural meanings of suicide in Japan for Aum Shinrikyô or the permeation of apocalyptic theology with mystical elements in the Solar Temple in Switzerland and France).

Before 9-11, incidents of collective martyrdom mostly seemed isolated and bizarre. Yet even before "everything changed," comparative historical analysis suggested a different view. Collective martyrdom is usually the violent edge of a much broader apocalyptic movement that realigns cultural frameworks of meaning. Authorities may respond to apocalyptic violence by tracking down and neutralizing its perpetrators, and by increasing vigilance against terrorist acts. A policy of preemptive repression may justify state actions against groups deemed potentially dangerous, prior to any concrete acts of violence. But incidents of martyrdom and repressive violence encourage a sense of solidarity among even disparate countercultural movements, and loom large in the public imagination, thus fueling a generalized culture of apocalyptic preoccupation (Wilson 1973: 67–8; Hall, Schuyler, and Trinh 2000). In November 2001, the dénouement of the present apocalyptic moment remains unwritten.

CONCLUSION

Theories that point to sacrifice as primordially embedded in practices of ritual suggest a deep connection between religion and violence, and interpreting violence as sacralized action thus sheds light on the symbolic structures of conflicts. However, this model does not exhaust relationships between religion and violence, nor does it explain the different types of situations in which religion and violence are connected. Sometimes, religion seems epiphenomenal: It is an ideology that gets invoked, or a social cleavage along which other struggles become mapped. Conversely, even when violence occurs completely within the frame of religion, its explanation may lie elsewhere. There is no firewall between religion and other social phenomena, and many social situations that lead to violence – efforts to control people, for instance – occur both inside and outside of religion. Nonetheless, in various strands of historical development, religion is more than symbolic currency, more than epiphenomenon, more than merely a venue of violence; it becomes a vehicle for the expression of deeply and widely held social aspirations – of nationalism, anticolonialism, or civilizational struggle.

Both the varieties of insights produced through different analytic approaches as well as the variety of empirical relations between violence and religion should warn against seeking a single general theory. Nevertheless, and even if some religious violence has a decidedly symbolic cast, the diverse (and often overlapping) kinds of violence seem for the most part occasioned by a rather narrow set of specifiable substantive interests:

- maintenance and expansion of religious commitment (through social control, conversions, competition with other religious organizations, colonial expansion, and repression of deviant movements);
- affirmation of religious beliefs through culturally normative (routine) practices of violence;
- struggles for independence from the regime of an established social order by nationalist, anticolonial, or other countercultural movements; and,
- countercultural martyrdom under conditions of apocalyptic war, "persecution," and/or defeat.

To date, the study of violence and religion has been strikingly uneven. There have been many good case studies, as well as important comparative and general investigations. Yet our understandings of social processes involving religion in violence remain rudimentary. The explanation for this state of scholarship lies, I suspect, in (a) the complex ties between violence and religion; (b) the variety of value-based, theoretical, and methodological approaches to research; and (c) the often liminal and nonrationalized character of religious violence. The study of religion, like history, tends to become located within one or another morally inscribed meta-narrative. Hierocratic domination receives more attention in countercultural religions than established ones. Religious persecution receives more attention when it happens in other countries. And religious wars of independence look quite different depending on who is seeking liberation, and from what. Yet the relationships of religion to processes of violence have become the focus of wide attention at a time when sociologists are well positioned theoretically and methodologically to analyze them. By going beyond conventional moral categorizations of religious phenomena and working to identify relevant analogies between social processes even in disparate cases (Stinchcombe 1978), we can make significant advances in understanding processes that link religious phenomena, conditions that give rise to violence, generic processes by which it is organized, trajectories that tend to lead to escalation, and outcomes. Understanding violence in the context of religion in turn may hold some promise for reducing its likelihood. Thus, studies of recent apocalyptic standoffs and mass suicides (Wagner-Pacifici 2000; Hall, Schuyler, and Trinh 2000; Wessinger 2000) have the potential to sensitize various actors to the potential ramifications of alternative courses of action, both in standoffs themselves, and in more macro-social phenomena that take similar forms.

Specifically addressing such larger-scale, more diffuse, and more enduring conflicts, writing before September 11, 2001, both Scott Appleby and Mark Juergensmeyer assessed the prospects for ending religious violence. But their approaches were different. Appleby wrote that religion can be a transformative force toward peace as well as war (2000; cf. Gopin 2000). He acknowledged that structural economic and social conditions can be the spawning grounds of religiously tinged violence, but promoted religious pluralism, ecumenicism, and dialogue in relation to "the politics of forgiveness" and "conflict transformation," even across cultural divides pitted with mistrust and violence. By contrast, Juergensmeyer (2000: 229–43) described a range of possible outcomes to struggles involving "religious terrorists": Either terrorism is defeated militarily or through repression, or terrorist movements gain sufficient political leverage to force a negotiated settlement. In the longer term, he argued, it would be helpful to disentangle religion from politics, and even, to use religion to provide a moral compass that would defuse conflict.

Of the two, Appleby is more the optimist seeking a realistic basis for hope, Juergensmeyer, the cautiously optimistic realist. The present survey, completed shortly after September 11, 2001, warrants a fusion of the two. Even when violence is "internal" to religion, it is subject to the same forces that operate more widely – competition, social control, rebellion, and revolution. And religiously infused violence is often externally connected to broader social conflicts. Precisely because of religion's capacity to mark the socially sacred, social struggles that become sacralized continue to implicate religion in violence, and in ways that make the violence much more intractable. To sever this connection between religion and violence is an important yet utopian goal that will depend on promoting peace with justice. More modestly, sociological studies of religion should develop reflexive knowledge that can help alter the channels and trajectories of violence, and thus, mitigate its tragic effects. These are both tasks worth our intellectual energies and our social commitment.

PART SIX

Religion and Socioeconomic Inequality

CHAPTER TWENTY-SIX

Religion, Faith-Based Community Organizing, and the Struggle for Justice

Richard L. Wood

On May 2, 2000, three thousand people converged on the State Capitol in Sacramento, California.[1] But this was not the usual frenzy of lobbyists serving the interests of the well-off, using the tools of well-oiled political action committees. Rather, these were working poor, working-class, and lower-middle income people lately referred to as "working families" and they went to Sacramento because they were tired of living on the verge of financial ruin or physical debility. Attendees were demanding adequate health coverage for people left out by current health care arrangements and they were angry about that, at a time when remarkable wealth was being accumulated all around them and California was running a $10 billion budget surplus.

The occasion was an "action" entitled "Healthcare for All Californians: Reweaving the Fabric of American Communities," sponsored by the Pacific Institute for Community Organization (PICO). The day's event drew on recent academic research showing 1.5 million California children formally eligible for subsidized health coverage but still uninsured because of onerous inscription procedures, and a total of 7.3 million Californians uninsured, most relying on community clinics or emergency rooms for their medical care. The same research showed 82 percent of the uninsured to be members of working families, with nearly half headed by a family member working full time for all of 1999.[2]

They packed the hall with a crowd approximately 40 percent Latino, 40 percent white, and 20 percent African American and Hmong. And they were loud: They believed they had to be to turn around a state government that had so far rejected any

---

[1] The author attended the action as a researcher/observer and verified the actual attendance figures through a count of the seating capacity at the Sacramento Community Center Theater plus a large overflow room filled when chairs ran out at the main venue. The large crowd made it impossible to calculate a precise ethnic breakdown of attendees; the figures cited later are approximations done by the author by counting the "apparent ethnicity" of those seated in a representative set of floor sectors.

[2] The key research groups on which PICO leadership relied for their health care campaign were the Health Insurance Policy Program, based out of the Center for Health and Public Policy Studies at UC – Berkeley and the Center for Health Policy Research at UCLA; and the Insure the Uninsured Project based in Santa Monica, California. The data quoted in this political event came from "The State of Health Insurance in California, 1999" report by the UCB/UCLA group (Schauffler and Brown 2000).

solution that might be labeled an "entitlement" to medical care. More than a few lead-ing California politicians and political aides reportedly did double-takes as they entered the largest and most multiracial political gathering in Sacramento in years.

The event began with a reading from the book of Amos, the Hebrew prophet who denounced an earlier time when the wealthy violated Yahweh's covenant by turning their backs on the poor:

> I hate, I despise your feasts
> I take no pleasure in your solemn festivals.
> When you offer me holocausts and grain offerings
> I will not accept them . . .
> Take away from me the noise of your songs;
> I will not listen to the melody of your harps.
> But let justice roll down like waters,
> and righteousness like an overflowing stream.[3]
>   Amos 5:21–4

The event continued with a prayer by a San Francisco pastor, Bill Knezovich:

> Holy God, be here with us. At the beginning of our work, send upon us the spirit of Amos, so that we may go forward knowing that change will only be done by ourselves, advocating for our families and for all those not here with us. Hold before us all those old people forced to choose between food and medicine; all those couples ruined by medical diseases; all our own children whose health is neglected because we cannot afford to pay for medicine. Hold them before us so that we might fight with a righteous anger, as Amos did.

There was much more: Testimony by a woman traumatized by her husband's suicide, he preferred to kill himself rather than ruin his family financially through a long illness. There were reports in English, Spanish, and Hmong from families suffering the gnawing anxiety of living without medical coverage. There were demands that part of California's surplus be used to alleviate the health care crisis, a specific proposal to better fund community health clinics, and talk of a legislative bill to expand the "Healthy Families" medical insurance program in California.

A series of state political figures were then asked to commit themselves to work with PICO on this agenda. Among others, the President Pro-Tempore of the California Senate, John Burton, stepped to the microphone saying, "First of all, I'm overwhelmed at this magnificent turnout." He then committed himself to working with PICO to expand health coverage in California for the working poor.

More followed, but the flavor of the evening is perhaps best captured by two quo-tations. The first was a phrase reiterated by a number of PICO leaders from around the state: "Healthcare now, for all God's people! Alleluia! Amen." The other was invoked repeatedly by PICO leader Cesar Portillo, an immigrant from Mexico. Responding to the political mantra of "No new entitlements" common in American politics today, at

---

[3] The closing lines from Amos also, of course, evoke the American civil rights movement and the legacy of Dr. Martin Luther King, Jr., who used them frequently in his work – most memorably in his "I have a dream" speech at the March on Washington in 1963.

various points in the evening Portillo called out "Se puede?" (Spanish for "Can it be done?"), to which the crowd thundered back, "Sí, se puede!"

Ultimately, through many ups and downs, political wins and political crises, this event reshaped California public policy on health care (see Wood 2002 for a full analysis). Within two months, the state approved $50 million dollars in new funding for the primary care clinics serving poor Californians. More substantial progress came six months later, after sustained pressure from PICO's religiously based leaders from working-class communities around the state: The state expanded access to the "Healthy Families" program, which previously only covered health care for children, to include some 300,000 working parents earning up to double the federal poverty level (about $32,000/year for a family of four). Healthy Families inscription procedures were also eased in an effort to draw in more California children eligible but uninsured.

OVERVIEW

These developments in California are crucial for the health and peace of mind of hundreds of thousands of working families, but are important also as one indicator of a much broader phenomenon: Religion has reemerged in both popular understanding and scholarly analysis as a crucial influence on political dynamics in societies around the world. Much of this attention has focused on either putatively irrational religious influence (e.g., terrorism associated with some strains of Islamic fundamentalism; see Taheri 1987; O'Ballance 1997); religiously based political activity regarding personal moral behavior (e.g., the "Christian Right" in the United States; see Wald 1987; Reed 1996); or the impact of religious cleavages on voting patterns (Manza and Brooks 1999; Marza and Wright, Chapter 21, this volume).

This chapter draws attention to a different facet of religiously based efforts to shape political dynamics: Religiously based advocacy to promote greater economic justice for low-income sectors of society. Such efforts are certainly not new: The Exodus story of the ancient Hebrews' flight from slavery in Egypt has provided the inspiration and cultural pattern for struggles for justice for centuries (Walzer 1965); the early popular struggle against enclosure in England drew vigorously from biblical understandings of justice (Hill 1972); the nineteenth-century American labor movement and struggle against slavery drew crucial support from religion (Voss 1993); and, in the 1950s and 1960s, religious institutions provided the key organizational and recruitment vehicles for the black civil rights movement in the United States (Morris 1984). But three factors justify renewed attention to the religiously based struggle for economic justice. First, we now have greater comparative perspective regarding such efforts due to their recent salience in societies around the world; this makes religiously based movements for justice appear less a case of "American exceptionalism" and more as a common social phenomenon. Second, emerging scholarly work has developed new insight into the internal dynamics of these efforts, how and why they succeed or fail, and why they may be important in shaping democratic life. Third, new systematic data provide the most complete view yet of one influential version of these efforts, the "faith-based organizing model" that has gained prominence in the United States and Great Britain over the last two decades, exemplified in the PICO event described earlier. After first describing the diverse array of religiously rooted struggles for economic justice around the world, this chapter outlines the contours of faith-based organizing in the United

States (from where the only systematic data are available), then discusses recent insights into the importance of faith-based organizing for American democracy. It concludes with a brief discussion of the role of religion in struggles for justice more generally.

FAITH-BASED STRUGGLES FOR JUSTICE AROUND THE WORLD

In Britain, faith-based organizing has taken root in working-class areas of London and other major cities (Farnell 1994; Warren 2000). British faith-based organizing work draws partly on indigenous sources for theological, scriptural, and political inspiration (see, for example, MacLeod 1993, written by an Anglican pastor; and Sacks 1997, written by a British chief rabbi), and partly on sources borrowed from American faith-based organizing.

In Latin America, community organizing based on religious faith continues to occur in the *comunidades eclesiales de base* movement (usually translated "base Christian communities"). This movement developed in the 1960s and 1970s out of the reemphasis on the social dimension of Christianity as Catholic leaders implemented the church reforms of the Second Vatican Council in the context of Latin America's vast social inequality (Marins, Trevisan et al. 1989; Hewitt 1991; Smith 1991). Although a continent-wide movement, it took deepest root in Brazil, Central America, Peru, some parts of Mexico, and Chile prior to the 1973 military coup there. These groups formed initially as Bible study and social reflection groups, partly as a response by Catholic leaders to the challenge presented by proselytism by evangelical groups. But under the influence of pedagogical models for political consciousness-raising (*conscientizâo*) developed by the Brazilian educational theorist Paolo Freire (1970), and under the pressure of rising economic inequality and political repression in many countries, the *comunidades* rapidly became centers of radical social critique and democratic action. Following military governments in the 1960s and 1970s, they contributed both to the redemocratization of much of Latin America in the 1980s and 1990s, and to the rise of guerrilla insurgencies in some countries (Nicaragua, Guatemala, El Salvador, Mexico). Both the concrete experience of these *comunidades* and their theoretical elaboration in the associated "theology of liberation" (Gutiérrez 1973; Sobrino 1978, 1984; Tamez 1982, 1989) have been significant influences on religious movements around the world, including upon faith-based organizing in the United States.

Likewise, evangelical social activism in Latin America has at times been a source of pressure for social justice. Evangelicals have focused primarily on individual moral reform; issues such as alcoholism, marital infidelity, and gang involvement have been more typical concerns in evangelical Latin American networks than have human rights, democratization, or union struggles. But that has not always been the case. Evangelical scholars in Latin America (Pixley and Boff 1989) have written important scriptural, historical, and theological works emphasizing the centrality of prophetic denunciation of social injustice in the biblical tradition. David Stoll (1990) argues convincingly that, even where evangelicals have not focused intentionally on social issues, the unintended political consequences of mass evangelical mobilization may actually foster democratization at least as successfully as the more direct demands for radical reform associated with liberationist Christianity.

In South Africa, the Philippines, and Korea, democratic activists closely linked to Christian churches have elaborated scriptural, theological, and doctrinal positions arguing for deep political reform in those societies as the only appropriate response to the demands of the Christian faith. The best-known of these statements was the "Kairos Document" issued by Protestant and Catholic clergy and lay leaders in South Africa in 1986, arguing that apartheid fundamentally and irrevocably contradicted the central tenets of Christianity, calling the churches to repentance for their collusion in apartheid over the years, and demanding immediate action to end that collusion (Kairos Theologians 1986; Comaroff and Comaroff 1991). In the Philippines, the "theology of struggle" elaborates a position similar to that of liberation theology in Latin America, but reflective of the particular political situation and political culture of that country (Fernandez 1994). In Korea, "Minjung theology" stakes out a similar role for Christianity, advancing an argument for democratization on the basis of "the people" as the subject of history – "subject" here meaning the active historical agent pushing society forward (Kim 1981; Park 1985; Suh 1987; Kwon 1990).

In a similar vein, religious leaders and theologians working within the Christian, Islamic, and Hindu traditions in Indonesia, India, and Sri Lanka have developed extensive statements on the religious vocation in the struggle for social justice in their societies (Yeow, England et al. 1989; Sugden 1997). And various strands of Buddhism have underlain resistance to American involvement in Vietnam, as well as subsequent peace movements in the United States (Nhat Hanh 1967, 1998) and the Tibetan struggle against Chinese occupation (Levenson 1988; Bstan–dzin-rgya and Thupten 1996; Farrar-Halls 1998).

FAITH-BASED COMMUNITY ORGANIZING IN THE UNITED STATES

In the United States, the term "community organizing" typically describes work inspired or influenced by the dean of community organizers in the United States, Saul Alinsky (1969, 1971). Alinsky's work spanned four decades and deeply shaped subsequent grassroots democratic action throughout urban America. The faith-based organizing work described here, also known as "broad-based," "church-based," or "congregation-based" community organizing, incorporates techniques promulgated by Alinsky but transcends his legacy in important ways.

Faith-based organizing roots itself institutionally in urban religious congregations, and culturally in the diverse religious practices and worldviews of participants – their religious culture. Such efforts occur in organizations linked to multiple religious congregations, but autonomous from any single congregation or denomination, and incorporated separately as tax exempt, nonpartisan organizations [typically as 501c(3) organizations under the IRS code].[4]

Faith-based organizing remains rather unknown in academic circles, but today arguably represents the most widespread movement for social justice in America, as documented in a new study (Warren and Wood 2001).[5] With about 133 local or

---

[4] In its goals and ethos, this model is quite distinct from – and should not be confused with – the more familiar model of political mobilization adopted by the Christian Right over the last three decades. See the following accounts of community organizing: Boyte (1989); Greider (1992); and Rogers (1990). Recent scholarly work includes Hart (2001); Warren (2001); and Wood (2002).

[5] Several factors account for the rather anonymous nature of faith-based organizing. First, although they indeed make up a coherent field of similar organizations engaged in similar

metropolitan-area federations linking some thirty-five hundred congregations plus some five hundred public schools, labor union locals, and other institutions (neighborhood associations, social service agencies, community centers, etc.), faith-based organizing can plausibly claim to touch the lives of more than two million members of religious congregations in all the major urban areas and many secondary cities around the United States.[6] These federations operate in thirty-three states and the District of Columbia, with strong concentrations in California, Texas, New York, Illinois, and Florida. Their mean income is $170,500 per year. Almost 90 percent of these organizations are affiliated with one of four major faith-based organizing networks.[7]

Although each federation carries a distinctive organizational emphasis that colors its work and reflects the institutional influence of a particular network, all adopt a similar organizing model. Each federation organizes in a particular city or metropolitan area via interfaith teams of leaders from ten to sixty or more religious congregations – and sometimes public schools, neighborhood associations, or union locals – to do research on a given issue and negotiate with political and economic elites. They gain a place at that negotiating table by mobilizing one thousand to six thousand participants in nonpartisan political actions at which political or corporate officials are asked to commit to specific policies outlined by the federation, or to work with the federation in developing a policy response to a given issue. In this way, the strongest of these metropolitan

practices and organized in an organizational field structured by the four networks, the 130 or so federations go by a diverse set of names so that one might move from one city to another and never know that the same organizing model is at work. Second, a large portion of the national-level publicity has focused on the Industrial Areas Foundation, thus blurring the perception of the wider field. Third, although the IAF or other groups have been mentioned frequently as examples of civic engagement (see Evans and Boyte 1986; Boyte 1989; Greider 1992; Lappe and Dubois 1994), until now relatively little work has focused close analytic attention on faith-based organizing. Fourth, faith-based organizing has largely escaped the attention of national political observers because until recently none of the networks were capable of operating in arenas of political power beyond local or county governments; the Texas Industrial Areas Foundation and the PICO California Project are the clearest examples to date of this new capability, but parallel efforts are underway in other states in all four networks.

[6] These and the following data are from a forthcoming study sponsored by Interfaith Funders and the Catholic Campaign for Human Development, the first important study to gather data on the entire field of faith-based community organizing (Warren and Wood 2001). All figures listed are approximations, projected as follows: The study managed to locate and interview the directors of three-quarters of the organizing federations around the country that we could identify (network-affiliated or independent, with the criteria for inclusion being that they had to practice a form of organizing recognizable as faith-based community organizing and had to have an office and at least one full-time staff member on the payroll at the time of the study). The numbers given in the text are then calculated from the one hundred responding federations, projected to reflect the full universe of 133 federations nationwide, with the projection weighted by network to reflect differential participation. Numbers are rounded off, in order to reflect the projected nature of the data and methodological uncertainties.

[7] The largest and most widely publicized of the networks is the Industrial Areas Foundation (IAF); indeed, in the minds of casual observers faith-based organizing is often synonymous with the IAF, but in fact it incorporates a little more than a third of the more than 133 identified organizations. About 40 percent of the organizations are affiliated with the Pacific Institute for Community Organization or the Gamaliel Network (about a fifth of organizations each). Direct Action, Research, and Training (DART) represents about a tenth of identified federations. The remaining faith-based organizing efforts, a little more than a tenth of the total, are independent federations or members of smaller networks (e.g., Regional Council of Neighborhood Organizations; Organizing, Leadership, and Training Center; Inter-Valley Project).

federations have reshaped government policy on housing, economic development, public schools, policing, working-class wages, recreational programs for youth, medical coverage, and other issues. In some places federations throughout a state or region have jointly influenced state policy on high-profile issues. For example, in the 1990s, the Texas IAF Network led the transformation of Texas public education through the Alliance Schools project – arguably, one of the key innovations that strengthened public schooling in Texas, and for which then-Governor George W. Bush much later claimed credit (Warren 2001). As depicted earlier, in 2000, the PICO California Project was the central force in transforming health care policy in the most populous American state, extending government-sponsored medical coverage to hundreds of thousands of low-income parents.[8] Regional or statewide initiatives have also occurred in New England, Illinois, Louisiana, Minnesota, Florida, Arizona, Colorado, and New Mexico. Taken together, such efforts have arguably produced the most widespread demands for social justice arising from within American civil society in recent years, and the most substantial gains for low-income Americans not arising directly from government policy during the Clinton presidency, with its very mixed legacy of increased social spending, strong economic growth, welfare reform, and economic restructuring.

Also noteworthy is the remarkably cross-racial character of this work. Although the ethnic and racial makeup of these organizations varies considerably across different geographic regions, and although some are rather homogeneous, they are diverse even in their homogeneity: Some organizations are almost exclusively African American; others almost exclusively Latino; and still others almost exclusively European-American. Elsewhere, they are quite multiracial, with some federations strongly biracial and others having memberships evenly split between these same three ethnic groups, with smaller numbers of Filipino, Hmong, Caribbean, and Asian immigrant or Asian American participants. No national data currently exist regarding individual-level participation in faith-based organizing, but the same study (Warren and Wood 2001) assessed the ethnic makeup of the *congregations* who sponsor it: Approximately 33 percent of the congregations are majority African American, 38 percent are majority white/European, and 20 percent are majority Latino (both native and immigrant). The remaining 9 percent are mostly congregations in which no one ethnic group makes up the majority, plus a small number of ethnic Asian, Pacific Islander, Native American, and other groups. Table 26.1 summarizes the race/ethnic and religious makeup of the sponsoring congregations.

As Table 26.2 shows, faith-based organizing also exhibits a fair degree of religious diversity. Nationally, some 35 percent of the congregations engaged in faith-based community organizing are Roman Catholic, 34 percent are members of denominations usually labeled liberal or moderate Protestant (mostly United Methodists, Lutherans, Episcopalians, Presbyterians, and United Church of Christ), 5 percent are affiliated with the historic black church denominations (African Methodist Episcopal, AME-Zion, Christian Methodist Episcopal), 13 percent are Baptist congregations (mostly National Baptists, Primitive Baptists, Missionary Baptist, and independent Baptist – that is, mostly black Baptists), 3 percent are unspecified or nondenominational Christian

---

[8] As of this writing, these health care gains in California are at risk of being lost, because of the budget difficulties resulting from California's vast financial costs in meeting its energy needs in a deregulated utilities market.

Table 26.1. Racial Makeup of Congregations Sponsoring Faith-Based Organizing

Racial/Ethnic Diversity (Majority ethnicity of *congregations*)

38% White/European American
33% African American
20% Hispanic (includes native-born and immigrant)
9% Other(mostly interracial; less than 2% majority Asian,)
    Pacific Islander, Native American)

Table 26.2. Religious Makeup of Congregations Sponsoring Faith-Based Organizing

Religious Diversity (Denomination of *congregations*)

35% Roman Catholic
34% Moderate/liberal Protestant
13% Baptist (mostly National, Missionary, and Primitive Baptists,
    thus mostly African American)
5% Historic black Protestant
3% Traditionalist Protestant
2% Jewish
2% Church of God in Christ (Pentecostal, mostly African-American)
2% Unitarian-Universalist
3% Other Christian
<1% Other non-Christian

congregations, 3 percent are traditionalist Protestants, 2 percent are Unitarian-Universalist congregations, 2 percent are black Pentecostal congregations affiliated with the Church of God in Christ, and a little less than 2 percent are Jewish congregations.

Thus, faith-based organizing is primarily based in Roman Catholic, liberal and moderate Protestant, and African-American religious traditions, with some representation from other faiths. Quite noteworthy is the scarcity of traditionalist or conservative Protestant congregations (including Southern Baptists), who make up nearly a third of religious congregations in the United States today.[9] Congregations from outside the broad Judeo-Christian tradition, including Mormon, Islamic, Buddhist, and Hindu congregations, are present within faith-based organizing, but only minimally.

This particular mix of denominations appears to result from several factors. First, among Christian denominations, they are the denominations most likely to have congregations located in core urban areas, which have faced serious socioeconomic challenges in recent years and are the "home turf" of much faith-based organizing. Second, the Catholic bishops' "Catholic Campaign for Human Development" (formerly CHD)

---

[9] Christians Supporting Community Organizing, an organization based in Boulder, Colorado, is dedicated to trying to increase the involvement of evangelical, Pentecostal, and "Holiness" Christians in the work of faith-based organizing. They have done extensive training with congregations in these traditions, drawing on scriptural, theological, and ethical sources.

has made funding for faith-based organizing a top priority for over twenty-five years; more recently, mainline Protestant and Jewish funding agencies have also funded this field extensively. Third, the African-American, liberal and moderate Protestant, and Catholic (as well as the Jewish and Unitarian) theological, ethical, and scriptural traditions have included this-worldly socioeconomic concerns within their core teachings for many years; this has led these traditions into involvement in social justice issues of many kinds, including faith-based organizing. The relative absence of traditionalist Protestant involvement – despite the extensive presence of these groups in the American religious landscape – appears to result from their stronger emphasis on issues of personal morality and their discomfort within the cultural milieu of faith-based organizing, which they have often experienced as predominantly Catholic/liberal Protestant. Finally, in some cases – most notably that of suburban Southern Baptists – traditionalist Protestant congregations are made up of more affluent members than the typical congregation involved in faith-based organizing, but this is by no means the case for all traditional Protestants.

In addition to the particular efforts represented by faith-based organizing, a wide array of social justice organizing projects in the United States are based in or include linkages to faith communities. Historically, the paradigmatic example of such efforts is the massive movement for the civil rights of African Americans in the 1950s and 1960s, which can only be understood in relation to the institutional strength of the black church in the American South (McAdam 1982; Morris 1984). More contemporary examples include: (a) initiatives around particular social justice issues within a single religious denomination (antiracist work within the Evangelical Lutheran Church in America; the promotion of women's ordination within the Roman Catholic Church (Dillon 1999a); efforts in a variety of denominations to reduce discrimination against gays and lesbians in American society; advocacy by the Catholic bishops in favor of an "option for the poor," "living wage" legislation, and workers' rights (Coleman 1991); (b) secular issue-focused movements with substantial ties to faith communities (affordable housing, immigrant rights groups, peace groups, efforts to protect the environment and/or fight "environmental racism," human rights work, efforts to promote business ethics and corporate accountability, etc.); and (c) substantial efforts by segments of the labor movement to build support in local communities, often through religious congregations (Bronfenbrenner and Juravich 1995; Bronfenbrenner 1998; Rose 2000; Voss and Sherman 2000; see also the AFL-CIO statement at www.aflcio.org/unioncity). Because of the size, scale, resources, and political capacity of the labor movement, the latter outreach efforts may be particularly important. Although this chapter focuses on the specific model of faith-based community organizing discussed earlier, these wider efforts form a crucial part of religious believers' efforts to promote social justice in America.

DEMOCRATIC IMPLICATIONS OF FAITH-BASED COMMUNITY ORGANIZING

The sheer scale and political efficacy of faith-based organizing suggest that it may have important implications for democratic life in the United States in the years ahead. But scale, efficacy, and even democratic intentions do not guarantee that a movement will foster democratic life. Historically, some large-scale, effective, and avowedly democratic movements have fostered democracy (e.g., the women's suffrage and abolitionist movements in the United States; the anti-apartheid movement in South Africa; movements for Irish independence and democracy in Eastern Europe; the FMLN guerrilla insurgency in El Salvador), while others have been obstacles to it or ultimately fostered tyranny (e.g., the Russian Bolshevik movement; some of the anticolonial and national liberation movements in Africa; the movement for Hutu rights in Rwanda; Sendero Luminoso in Peru). Assessing the democratic potential of this movement, then, requires going beyond descriptive work to look more analytically at its possible democratic implications. Six areas of recent scholarly analysis are important in this regard:

First, recent work on how Americans acquire the civic skills that contribute to their political effectiveness suggests that its link to religious congregations may give faith-based organizing greater democratic import. This is because religion diffuses in an egalitarian fashion "democratic skills" such as the ability to write a letter to a political representative, make a public speech, attend a meeting, or plan and lead a meeting (Verba et al. 1995). Although these are essential democratic skills, they are not simply natural attributes of citizens; they are learned abilities and inclinations. Verba and colleagues studied the three kinds of "prepolitical settings" in which people in American society typically learn these skills: The workplace, nonpolitical voluntary organizations, and religious organizations. The first two offer the most abundant learning opportunities, but those opportunities are badly skewed in favor of those who already enjoy the most socioeconomic advantages: Men rather than women; those with the highest salaries, most education, and family wealth rather than those with less of these; and whites rather than African Americans and Hispanics. Only religious organizations offer opportunities for democratic skills-acquisition in egalitarian ways: To women as much as to men; to the socioeconomically disadvantaged as much as to the well off; and to African Americans even more than to white Americans.[10] Faith-based organizing thus taps into a rare institutional arena in which poor, working-, and lower-middle-class families are on relatively equal democratic footing with upper-middle-class and wealthy families.[11]

Second, recent work by political sociologists (Casanova 1994; Wald 1987), political scientists (Leege and Kellstedt 1993), and practitioners (Coleman 1991; Reed 1996) has demonstrated that religion has not in any simple sense succumbed to pressures toward privatization. Rather, religion in the United States and elsewhere has maintained a vital public presence around a variety of issues and in diverse political settings. Faith-based community organizing represents another facet of this public face of religion, but with a twist: Rather than concentrating on the issues of individual morality that have provided the focus of much public religion in the United States in recent years, faith-based organizing focuses on building greater democratic participation and social justice explicitly tied to the economic self-interest and quality of life of those on the lower end of the economic spectrum of American and British society – in keeping

---

[10] Latinos have fewer opportunities for democratic skills acquisition, apparently not because of systematic discrimination in churches but because they are disproportionately Catholic. Despite advances in lay participation and authority in recent years, Catholic churches have apparently not, on average, caught up with Protestant churches in opportunities for such skills acquisition.

[11] This is not to suggest that religious congregations are in any sense fully egalitarian. They are not, in part because some grant implicit or explicit privileges to economic wealth and social status. The point here is that religious congregations are, *on average, relatively more egalitarian* than voluntary organizations or the workplace – at least in terms of offering opportunities for acquiring the civic skills examined by Verba et al. (1995).

with important themes in Catholic, historic black Protestant, and mainline Protestant theology and social teaching. If one accepts, following much democratic thinking from the founding fathers of the United States down to the present, that strong economic polarization contradicts democratic ideals and undermines democratic practices, then this public face of religion in favor of economic justice carries important pro-democratic implications.

Third, scholars of grassroots political culture in the United States have documented the central role of cultural dynamics within social institutions, democratic organizations, and civil society (Bellah et al. 1985, 1991; Demerath and Williams 1992; Lichterman 1996; Eliasoph 1998). More specifically, Stephen Hart (2001) argues that conservative political movements have been much more adept than liberal/progressive movements at doing the "cultural work" to link their priorities to the religious traditions that shape Americans' moral commitments – despite the fact that, as Hart argues, the religious traditions of American life have at least as many resources for supporting progressive political positions as for supporting more conservative ones. Those most committed to the economic well-being of working people have simply failed to do the cultural work to link their agendas to the moral-religious currents flowing in American history. Hart cites faith-based organizing as the best example of progressive organizations doing this cultural work relatively successfully, albeit with important limitations.

Likewise, Wood (1999) examines how the cultural dynamics within democratic movements strengthen or undermine their political outcomes. He argues that – at least within relatively democratic political regimes – those outcomes are strongly conditioned by the organization's ability to simultaneously (a) contest dominant political power, and (b) enter into compromise with political elites. Wood analyzes the efforts of faith-based organizing and other democratic movements to balance these contrasting cultural demands of democratic politics. Simultaneously sustaining both cultural challenges of contestation and compromise represents a difficult task; religious traditions represent one source of the cultural resources and complex worldviews necessary for meeting these challenges. Faith-based organizing has institutionalized the organizational relations between congregations and its own federations in a kind of "structural symbiosis" (Wood 2001) that helps it meet both challenges. In other words, from its relationship with congregations, faith-based organizing draws the complex cultural resources that allow it to make simultaneous sense of both conflict and compromise in its political work; in turn, when done well faith-based organizing gives back to those congregations leaders with better-developed skills and a deeper understanding of the public dimensions of religious faith. Thus, when Father Joseph Justice of Santa Ana, California, said in an interview that organizing had benefitted his parish, and was asked whether he would work with faith-based organizing in the future, he noted:

> I [would] look for certain things. Are the organizers coming in with an agenda or are they looking for what are the needs? PICO certainly was looking for what are the needs here. And they have fulfilled what they said they would do, which is build relationships and develop lay leaders.

Fourth, faith-based organizing may provide some antidote to a key weakness in civil society in the United States in recent decades: The erosion of American society's store of "social capital" (Warren 2001; Wood 2002). Social capital refers to the quantity and quality of ties between individuals, through both personal networks and voluntary associations. Although the concept of social capital continues to be hotly debated, most observers agree that strong social capital allows people to work together more efficiently (for both positive and negative goals). Historically, American society has been particularly rich in social capital, which has provided the basis for political movements and voluntaristic efforts to ameliorate various kinds of social problems. But Robert Putnam (2000) has amassed impressive evidence documenting a significant decline in American social capital over the last four decades; he argues that this erosion of social capital bodes poorly for the future of American democratic life.

Understanding how faith-based organizing may provide an antidote to this erosion requires making a distinction between two kinds of social glue holding people together in society: "Bonding" and "bridging" social capital (Gittell and Vidal 1998; Putnam 2000: 24). Bonding social capital links people *within* communities together, fostering social trust and cohesion among people within a neighborhood, town, religious congregation, racial or ethnic group, and so on. Bridging social capital links people *across* these kinds of communities, fostering social trust and cohesion between people and groups on opposite sides of social divides (black and white; Hispanic and African American and Southeast Asian; Protestant, Catholic, Jew, and Muslim; rival gangs in adjacent neighborhoods). Religion has been an important source of bonding social capital throughout American history but, like other sources of social capital, has not functioned as effectively in building bridging social capital – thus, the common adage that "the most segregated hour in America is Sunday morning." But faith-based organizing in many locations draws people from differing faith traditions, ethnic groups, and economic classes into shared efforts at political change – into social solidarity built on shared democratic endeavor. In this way, it may provide an important source of bridging social capital and (to the extent it helps generate more vibrant religious congregations) it may contribute to rebuilding the store of bonding social capital in low- and middle-income American urban communities.

Fifth, faith-based organizing may compensate for a key structural weakness in American political institutions that appears to have worsened in recent years. Healthy democratic life depends on the flourishing of what scholars call a "public realm" or "public sphere." The public realm is made up of those settings in which people come together and talk about their common future, the problems facing society, and alternative solutions to those problems (Habermas 1989). The public realm can be seen as overlaying three levels of society: (a) Government settings in which officials engage in discerning "public talk"; (b) settings of "political society" – that is, associations linked to but not part of government, such as political parties, the media, labor unions, and employers or professional associations when they transcend narrow self-interest; and (c) settings of "civil society," in which people come together for myriad purposes beyond the control of government or corporate elites (Stepan 1988; Casanova 1994). Democracy can thrive where *both* (a) spaces exist for public deliberation at all these levels; *and* (b) institutions exist to connect public deliberation in civil society with that occurring in political society and government. That is, thriving democracy depends on institutions providing "upward linkages" within the public realm, from grassroots civil society to more elite social sectors. One diagnosis of the ills of contemporary American democracy suggests that, whereas political parties, labor unions, and other associations once provided such linkages, the various levels of the public realm have become fractured from one another: Few connections exist between civil society, political society, and government, and those that do exist are primarily used by political and economic elites to project influence downward. Little pressure for accountability flows upward from civil society (see Wood 2002, drawing on Aldrich 1995; Coleman 1996; Wattenberg 1998).

If one accepts this diagnosis, faith-based organizing becomes particularly important as an example of a "bridging institution" projecting democratic power from civil society upward into the "political" and "government" levels of the public realm.[12] To the extent it does so successfully and democratically – to the extent it "holds officials accountable" to real democratic needs – it compensates for the erosion of other political institutions that once served this function. It also may provide some model for how democratic activists can begin to build greater accountability into the modern political process more broadly.

Finally (sixth), recent studies of social movements have shown the crucial role of sophisticated and creative political strategy in determining whether such movements succeed or fail (Tarrow 1992; Ganz 2000). Numerous recent works describe the politically creative issue work, alliances, and strategies pursued by various sectors of the faith-based organizing movement, including the previously cited work on the PICO California Project and the Texas IAF Network, Gamaliel in the Midwest and independent organizing in African-American churches in Boston. Interfaith Funders (2000) provides a more movement-wide description of strategic initiatives in this field.

Thus, faith-based community organizing offers inspiration and insight to those interested in the struggle for social justice in the contemporary world. This is true in part because of its scale: As one of the largest and most broad-based movements for social justice in American life, it projects democratic influence in most large American cities, many congressional districts, and several politically crucial states. But it is also true for analytic reasons. Faith-based organizing provides one model for how democratic movements can meet some of the fundamental challenges to American democracy that analysts have identified: The widening income gaps between different sectors of American society, plus challenges regarding civic skills acquisition, the public face of religion, cultural dilemmas of progressive activists and democratic organizations, the erosion of social capital in American society, structural dilemmas of U.S. political institutions, and the challenge of strategic innovation for democratic movements.

CAVEAT

In recognizing these strengths of faith-based community organizing, it is important to note that the field has significant shortcomings as well. Some are rooted in its own history and culture as a movement. The potential political influence of the field is undermined by the inability of the various networks to work together (albeit for reasons rooted in negative experiences in the past); these organizations have historically been

---

[12] Despite the similarity of terminology, "bridging institutions" and "bridging social capital" refer to quite different phenomena. The latter refers to network ties between individuals in different social groups. The former refers to an organization-level phenomenon – that is, the existence of organizations and institutions that bridge the gaps across different vertical levels of the public realm, thus linking them into a more coherent and communicative whole.

loathe to collaborate with other democratic efforts (although this has changed in recent years in some parts of the country); some organizers are seen as condescending toward those outside their own organizations; and power and decision making inside some faith-based organizations can be opaque and lacking in internal accountability.

Other shortcomings are rooted in constraints imposed by current American economic and political arrangements. Although better than in many social justice sectors, funding for faith-based organizing is rarely adequate; although it offers professional wages, the field has perennial difficulty attracting sufficient numbers of the multi-talented and dynamic people needed for long-term organizing success; and even the strongest statewide organizing efforts cannot begin to project sufficient power to affect the vast flows of financial capital that determine the life chances of working families in the global economy. Yet, at the margins of those vast flows of global capital, faith-based organizing offers a tool for promoting democratic engagement and improving the quality of life of working families in ways that matter – and matter profoundly for those living without good jobs, health insurance, decent housing, excellent schools, or clean air and water.

THE ROLE OF RELIGION IN THE STRUGGLE FOR JUSTICE

What, then, do we know regarding the contribution of religion to struggles for social justice? Religion can help provide some of the things every social movement needs: People to help lead the movement; material resources such as money, phones, meeting space, and so on; and social capital and organizational structures that facilitate mobilization. Religion represents one among many possible sources for all these. More specific to religion are other factors: Complex cultural resources that can simultaneously undergird both contestation and compromise; symbols, images, and stories that motivate and provide meaning for the struggle (e.g., the Exodus story, the Jewish social prophets, Jesus's confrontations with irresponsible authority, the Jewish mystical tradition of "repairing the world," Islamic understandings of the just community); legitimacy in the eyes of the wider society; and a sense of primary community separate from the struggle that unburdens the organization from needing to provide primary social support for participants. Religion, at least under some circumstances, may be especially adept at providing these.

But Bellah's (1970a) classic statement suggests perhaps the most fundamental contribution of religion to struggles for social justice. He argues that religion, in fostering the spiritual dimension of human life, pulls people out of their embeddedness in the status quo of society, allows them to gain critical distance from it, and helps them to imagine alternatives to current social arrangements. In so doing, religion provides ethical leverage against the taken-for-grantedness that leads people to accept unjust social situations.

CONCLUSION: RELIGION AND SOCIAL JUSTICE

Although many decades ago it appeared to some observers (Lenin 1929; Gramsci 1957/1968) that the struggle for economic justice in the world would be led by vanguard political parties representing the interests of workers – in isolation from religion and perhaps against the opposition of religious institutions – there can be little doubt today that such a vision was always an illusion. People of faith are deeply engaged in the struggle for justice in societies around the world, very often (although by no means always) with the official support of their religious leaders and institutions. One model for such engagement, faith-based community organizing in the United States, has provided the focus of attention for this chapter, because of its scale, political efficacy, and organizational symbiosis with congregation-based forms of religion. But whether one looks to Protestants, Catholics, and Jews engaged in faith-based organizing in working-class neighborhoods of the United States, secular labor leaders reaching out for support from diverse religious congregations throughout the Anglophone world, Hindu untouchables organizing politically in India, liberationist Catholics or reform-minded Pentecostals fighting inequality in Latin America, anticorruption community leaders shaped by the "theology of struggle" in the Philippines, or toward any of a myriad of other examples, religion remains central to struggles for justice throughout the world today. Any effort to turn our societies toward greater fairness for working people – and any scholarly effort to better understand those struggles – must take people's religious commitments seriously indeed.

CHAPTER TWENTY-SEVEN

Latina Empowerment, Border Realities, and Faith-Based Organizations

Milagros Peña

Any discussion of Latinas must begin with some understanding of their experience within the larger context of their communities. To understand Latino/a empowerment in faith-based communities, this chapter begins with a brief overview of the Latino/a religious experience and then outlines Latinas' particular contributions to faith-based community activist organizations. The research literature on Latinos and Latinas and their place in the U.S. religious mosaic parallels non-Latino/a immigration stories when consideration is given to the role of religion and religious institutions within ethnic enclaves. These ethnic studies can be useful because they highlight nuances that some-times are glossed over by sweeping immigration theories. As Jaime Vidal (Dolan and Vidal 1994) found when looking at the Puerto Rican migration story, there were nuances to the Puerto Rican experiences that spilled over into shaping the character of previously established Euro-ethnic faith communities.

One difference was Puerto Rican migrants' insistence on maintaining their culture rather than embracing the expected assimilation with U.S. society: "The insistence of Puerto Ricans on speaking Spanish among themselves and on speaking Spanish at home in order to pass on the language (as a *first* language!) to the next generation was deeply disturbing and even offensive to Americans, who instinctively perceived it as a rejection of the 'melting pot,' a symbolic way of clinging to an alien identity" (Dolan and Vidal 1994: 59). Subverting assimilation and the "melting pot" translated itself into establishing faith communities that insisted on and asserted Puerto Rican ethnic identity in a way that other immigrant communities had not. One could argue that the Puerto Rican story in many ways foreshadowed the present-day expected tolerance for multiculturalism. Of course, Puerto Ricans do not represent the experiences of all Latino/a groups. But as one of a number of ethnic groups with similar stories, we learn from their experiences that even before the current immigration influx, the U.S. religious character was a contested one. Puerto Ricans came to New York "with a culture pervaded by the Catholic ethos – but it was a different kind of Catholic ethos" (Dolan and Vidal 1994: 67; see also Díaz-Stevens's [1993a: 240–76] study of the impact of Puerto Rican migration on the Archdiocese of New York).

These studies show that communities of faith can be, and are often, linked to the struggles of ethnic communities to be accepted in a society that marginalizes them. This is evident, for example, in acts of devotion to La Hermita de la Caridad del Cobre, a patron saint of Cuba. La Hermita is a place of devotion to the Cuban patron saint, an icon in Miami that was taken from Cuba as a symbolic representation of the Cuban dream of return to Cuba. La Hermita is the first place newly arrived Cubans go as an act of thanksgiving for their safe arrival to the United States. It is also a place where Cubans go and express Cubanidad (Cubanness) that for many is central to the Cuban–U.S. experience because dreams deferred become the Cuban-American reality (Garcia 1996). Similarly, La Virgen de Guadalupe is for Mexican Americans both a religious icon and a symbol of a community's struggle, whether embraced in the United Farm Workers' struggle or as a presence in Mexican and Mexican American homes.

In the Latino/a Protestant communities, Latino/a ethnic identity is asserted in the congregational life of the communities. It is also evident within burgeoning organizations in the United States, including Alianza de Ministerios Evangelicos Nacionales (A.M.E.N.), the Hispanic-American Institute, the Hispanic Theological Initiative (HTI), Theologies in the Americas. These organizations and the growing number of theological writings read by both Catholic and Protestant Latinos/as have become the cornerstone of what has been called the Latino resurgence of the 1960s and 1970s in U.S. religion (Díaz-Stevens and Stevens Arroyo 1998). In fact, "Latino Protestants pushed for much the same goals during the resurgence as their Catholic counterparts" (ibid. 169). These goals were cast, as Díaz-Stevens and Stevens Arroyo document, in a historical moment in which religious leaders "announced a mission of restoring and redeveloping Latino religion because it was distinct and nonassimilable to the Euro-American experience" (ibid. 122).

But what is often mentioned as an aside and not told as a central history to the ethnic communities' experiences are the key roles women played in their communities' activism. It is often women scholars who uncover that history. Marina Herrera (1994: 187–8), for example, confirms that "Hispanic women religious were the pioneers in waking up the people of God to all that was happening in the Church" from the beginning of the Latina/o U.S. religious experience. The discussion that follows is part of a growing women's studies literature that seeks to answer questions on the roles Latinas played and continue to play in advancing Latina/o interests, in this case with the support of faith-based organizations. To develop a better understanding of Latinas' roles within their communities and the challenges they pursue within their communities' struggles, I take into account Latino/a culture and the role expectations Latinas have to challenge as women.

CHALLENGING MYTHS: FOUNDATIONS FOR LATINA EMPOWERMENT

Within the Latino community, Latinas are celebrated for their place in the family or home and affirmed for being the mainstays of cultural transmission through their roles as homemakers and in raising children and caring for their families (Segura 1991; Zavella 1987). Such views carry subtle and not so subtle suggestions that their identities and strengths mostly lie in their family responsibilities. Yet Latinas are agents of social change, particularly when they engage in community work. This chapter presents a more accurate picture of the Latina sphere of social influence that encompasses both private and public domains and is expressed in social and community settings as well as in the family and personal life. It argues that in both private and public spheres, religion plays an important role as a place to which Latinas appeal for empowerment.

I develop this account by examining Latina activism in which engagement in pastoral/community work is linked to women's activism, identities, and community roles surrounding a variety of social concerns.

To ignore the broader dimension of Latina religious practice – that is, their place in community or pastoral work – is to fail to recognize the complex ways in which Latinas are active agents of social change, and the variety of roles they play within and outside the Latina/o community. The following discussion, based on my ethnographic research along the U.S.-Mexico border as well as secondary sources, focuses on the important role U.S. Latinas play in both private and public spheres through religiously based community work that often crosses ethnic lines. This activism advances women's interests, allows them to claim a myriad of identities, and at the same time advances the interests of their communities. Through such work, they define themselves in ways that transcend the socially conventional understandings of them as women and as Latinas.

LATINAS, CULTURE, AND THE SUBVERSION OF PASSIVITY

As suggested earlier, Latinas are not a homogenous group and this discussion is not meant to "essentialize" the Latina experience. I highlight how women's empowering processes, rather than only affecting women as individuals, can be linked to communal efforts to challenge socioeconomic realities and cultural inhibitors such as patriarchy. By focusing on the cultural context in which Latinas operate, we can better understand why so many Latina women work with religious groups and other nongovernment organizations (NGOs), to empower themselves within and outside the home. A recent study conducted in two Los Angeles communities found that women's activism grew out of responding to issues that affected their families and that organizing around those issues was nurtured in community networks (Pardo 1998: 228). The activism also became the basis on which they generated broader political involvements. In fact, we learn from Pardo's study that Latinas "use existing gender, ethnic, and community identities to accomplish larger political tasks" (ibid. 228).

In a study of Latina activism in Boston, Carol Hardy-Fanta (1993) found that Latinas spent their organizing efforts going door to door, talking about community concerns with other Latinas over coffee, and making the gender and ethnic connections that proved effective in that community's organizing. In my own research on the border through work I did with the Colonias Development Council in Las Cruces, New Mexico, I observed Latinas take on more active roles in their communities after succeeding in creating community day care centers. From day care centers they moved on to participate in other efforts to force local city and state government to build roads and eradicate sewage problems, particularly because these issues affected the lives of their children.

In community work, Latinas challenge stereotypic notions that portray them as passive and submissive. Latina engagement in the home and in the community contrasts sharply with the passivity/submissiveness paradigms that are often promoted in some Catholic Marian devotions or in religious traditions that promote patriarchy. As one indication, their images of Mary can be described as many Catholics might describe God: As Absolute, Infinite, Omnipresent, Omnipotent, Omniscient, Powerful, Redeeming, and All-Wise (Peña and Frehill 1998). In addition, despite official Catholic teaching against artificial birth control, Latinas admit undergoing sterilization procedures and using artificial birth control, sometimes without the knowledge of their husbands. In several focus group discussions I conducted, women admitted coaxing their husbands to get vasectomies. One woman stated:

> [I]magine, eleven pregnancies with the rhythm method, I surmise that it doesn't work too well, does it? My sisters, I don't know if all of them, but some of them have told me that they went for the "operation," and I know that some of them have not told their husbands. (ibid. 627)

These findings are consistent with American Catholics' attitudes toward birth control and sexuality where there is little support for church teaching (Greeley 1989). Surveys show that even among Hispanic Catholics who both attend Mass and take communion at least once a month – a group that might be considered among the most likely to follow the teaching on contraception – 38 percent of all women of reproductive age were practicing a method not approved by the Vatican (Goldscheider and Mosher 1991).

If we extend to the Latina experience what Patricia Hill Collins (1991) argues about African-American women's empowerment process, understanding women's culture of resistance helps to dispel common myths of Latina passivity/submissiveness. In taking this approach, we are better able to come to a more complex understanding of how Latinas stand against the dominant ideology promulgated in patriarchal societal institutions – those rooted in the Latino community as well as those of the dominant society. We see this particularly clearly when we look at Latinas' resistance to their subordination in marriage. Women question religious leaders who advise them to return to abusive marriages for the sake of preserving the marriage (Peña and Frehill 1998: 13–15). My research also shows that Latinas draw from the strengths of the Latina/o community by participating in local faith-based community groups and organizations. In fact, Latinas often turn to their own culture, and not the dominant one, to find the empowerment they need to confront personal, family, and community crises.

Other scholars offer additional insights on efforts to challenge the passivity/submissiveness paradigm. For example, Oliva M. Espín emphasizes the empowered place middle-aged and elderly Latina women have within the family. She observes that:

> Middle-aged and elderly Hispanic women retain important roles in their families even after their sons and daughters are married. Grandmothers are ever present and highly vocal in family affairs. Older women have much more status and power than their white American counterparts, who at this age may be suffering from depression due to what has been called the "empty-nest syndrome." Many Hispanic women are providers of mental health services in an unofficial way as "curanderas," "espiritistas," or "santeras," for those people who believe in these alternative approaches to health care. (1995: 423)

Thus, research on Latinas points to the importance of considering specific status markers (i.e., age, class, gender, and race), in the cultural context of the Latina, particularly if one dimension of community work bridges popular religious practice and community health practice. That elderly women are held in high esteem in the life of the Latino/a community can be gleaned from the migration narratives of Latinas who, regardless of Latin American country of origin, share a common Spanish colonial cultural heritage. This makes their narratives more similar than distinct when it comes to the social institutions they engage in their daily lives. Challenging the notion of Latina passivity, Díaz-Stevens (1993b) describes a "matriarchal core" in Latino/a Catholicism, in which Latinas play important roles as community leaders in performing popular Catholic rituals. Elderly Latinas have taken on some of the roles of Catholic clergy, calling people to prayer, presiding over Christian gatherings on special occasions such as *Fiestas de Santos, Aniversarios de Difuntos, Velorios, Novenas, Oraciones de Buen Morir, etc.* (ibid. 65). Díaz-Stevens argues that: "Upon a closer examination of how power unfolds, it becomes clear that women exercise a productive function in religion – one that subverts and transforms social values" in these community roles (1993b: 61). The roles Latinas play in performing popular Catholic rituals have had an effect in transforming attitudes regarding Latina leadership within the Latina/o community. Díaz-Stevens (1994: 243) found that two thirds of young Latinos/as (ranging in age from fifteen to twenty-five years) in New York City said that the person they most respected in the community apart from their parents, was an elderly woman in the community known for her piety and her role as the leader of nonecclesiastical religious communal rituals and prayer.

It is not just elderly Latinas, however, who exercise influence within Latina/o communities. Recent studies show patterns of organized community activism led by women in Latino/a communities that cut across age and immigrant generations. As Mary Pardo's work suggests, "ethnic and gender-based traditions" are being "refashioned into strategies for resistance" (1998: 232). Much of this activism can be traced to the Chicana/o and Puerto Rican civil rights demands that began in the 1960s. Paralleling the African-American communities' demands for social justice, Latinos and Latinas took to the streets and challenged the quality of their children's education, work conditions, housing segregation, voting discrimination, and the overall marginalization of Latinos/as within U.S. society. In fact, according to Alma M. Garcia (1989, 1997), the Chicano Movement ("El Movimiento"), offered a context in which Chicanas could critique their traditional gender roles within the romanticized Chicano family. Latinas saw themselves fighting for women's rights while at the same time fighting to end racist oppression against the Latino/a communities. Through that experience, Latinas began to realize that they would have to make their own particular demands within and outside the Latino/a community. This realization led Latinas to form their own protest communities, including their current alliances with and participation in faith-based organizations. This politicization is different to the more subtle forms of cultural resistance evident in the roles Latinas play in Catholic popular rituals. As Gamson has observed, "We know from many studies of social movements how important social networks are for recruiting people and drawing them into political action with their friends. People sometimes act first and only through participating develop the political consciousness that supports the action" (1995: 89).

As noted, during the Chicano movement, Latinas were moved to community activism to protest particular discriminatory acts against them in schools, housing, and public places where they were denied entry. In turn, because Latinas were denied leadership positions within their own social movement organizations, women's marginalization within the Chicano and Puerto Rican movements of the 1960s and 1970s also forced them to confront the sexism within their own ethnic communities. Consequently, Chicanas and other Latinas have formed their own women's organizations to protest both racism and sexism. Crisis events bring Latinas to social movement organizations and it is there that individual level resistance is nurtured into broader collective consciousness. While symbolic forms of resistance are important, it is in collective activism that Latinas have nurtured a more effective political voice. Thus, moving from cultures of resistance to organized protest awakens a different type of consciousness and activism. It is this latter form of collective empowerment that I emphasize here. It includes forming alliances with and becoming politicized in a number of organizations including faith-based organizations.

Lara Medina (1997) notes the historical significance of Las Hermanas, a twenty-five-year-old national organization of mostly Latina Roman Catholics that promotes women's equality within religious institutions and society at large. Medina points out that, as a religious-political organization, Las Hermanas was effectively the first crossover organization that brought the Latina gender and ethnic struggles of the 1960s and 1970s into the religious realm. Between 1971 and 1980, Las Hermanas influenced church politics by promoting women for leadership positions, pushing women's ordination, promoting women's right to choose on the question of abortion, and participated in secular political movements that focused on women's issues. Las Hermanas has also focused specifically on issues affecting grassroots Latinas, including sexuality and domestic abuse. Medina's study of Las Hermanas is among the first to examine issues integral to understanding Latina religious-political organizing. Significant in Medina's work is the link she identifies between group identity, protest strategies, feminist models of leadership, and religious agency.

In broader terms, Carol Hardy-Fanta (1993) offers insight into this gendered process of political mobilization based on her study of Latina/o political mobilization in Boston. She states:

> A key issue within the debate about gender differences is whether there is an essential divide between the public and private dimensions of politics. For Latina women, much more than the men, the boundary between these supposedly distinct spheres of life is blurred or indistinct. With their emphasis on grassroots politics, survival politics, the politics of everyday life, and the development of a political consciousness, Latina women see connections between the problems they face personally and community issues stemming from government policies. (1993: 18–19)

Most notably, Latina activism emerges as Latinas' political consciousness is awakened in their everyday lived experiences. This also explains why Latinas in particular would ally themselves with women's religious groups as they have on the U.S.–Mexico border. They go to women's faith-based organizations for help in confronting, for example, domestic violence or for help with economic problems. In these settings, they meet other women like themselves, participate in programs that empower them, develop skills to confront their own problems, and in the process, often emerge as community activists.

BORDER REALITIES

Latinas on the border are affected by U.S.–Mexico relations, including immigration policies, border politics, and their own continuing ties to families south of the border. Barrera (1979) and Acuña (1988) suggest that these relations are linked to the legacy established in the region when the U.S. border officially crossed into Mexican territory beginning with the Texas War of Independence (1835–6) and the signing of the Treaty of

Guadalupe Hidalgo in 1848. Tensions continue with the influx of "new"[1] immigration, both legal and illegal. Mexicans represent a poor and disenfranchised transnational labor force that is used as a reserve army of labor for the United States. In both low-skill and low-wage occupations Mexicans are exploited, particularly the women who work in the border factories (Ruiz 1987). Border residents complain of intimidation by border patrol agents at checkpoints or when asked for legal documents when leaving food stores. The strains that come with the U.S.–Mexico border reality for people of Mexican descent, especially for women, have created a range of nongovernment organizations that provide social services and strive to raise political consciousness of the social problems faced by border communities.

In response to the social needs in these communities, several Catholic and non-Catholic religious organizations are actively involved in helping Latinas/os mobilize against the violence and economic exploitation occurring along the U.S.–Mexico border. The plight of migrant women along the El Paso/Juárez border, with reports estimating between one hundred and two hundred cases of murdered women in Juárez since 1993, has served as a rallying point for issues relating to violence against women. Church groups responding to this reality have become an important moral and financial support to Latinas and their families. That there is a religious connection in the mobilizing of Latinas should come as no surprise. Pardo's (1998) research shows that several of the founders of Mothers of East Los Angeles (MELA – an organization dedicated to neighborhood improvement) were encouraged by a local Catholic priest. Parish networks proved important to women organizing in East Los Angeles by providing them with space to meet and the mechanism through which they could tap into one another as resources in fixing or cleaning up local parks abandoned by city government. Thus, Latinas' emphasis on grassroots activism and the survival politics of everyday life, suggests expanded possibilities when they can tap their own communities' social networks and those of organizations such as church groups, that lend themselves to grassroots organizing.

Religious groups on the border, many of them influenced by the legacy of the Civil Rights Movement and feminist ideals, have joined Latinas in their struggle for human rights. The surge in the number of NGOs in the border region (61 percent of the NGOs in my border study cluster were established after 1990), and especially of church groups engaged in community work, can only be understood as a product of particular border realities, U.S.–Mexico politics, and the social strains that they produce. For example, for religious groups in El Paso/Juárez, the issue of violence against women highlighted by the murders in Juárez led to an awareness of broader issues concerning border women's struggles and helped the formation of alliances among community groups.

Cubitt and Greenslade (1997) note that the specific focus on violence and economic exploitation is the basis for understanding Mexican women's increasing empowerment in social movement activism. I argue in the following section that this extends to understanding women's mobilization on the border. At the same time, the numbers that have died crossing the U.S.-Mexico border give pause to the notion that social life can be divided into public and private realms. For Latinas, and the non-Latinas on the border

---

[1] Considering that Mexico lost a large percentage of its territory to the United States with the signing of the Treaty of Guadalupe Hidalgo, whether Mexican immigrants entering the United States, or Anglo immigrants entering the Southwest Latino/a homeland should be considered the "new" immigrants is a point of contention.

who support them, violence against migrant women is articulated as not the migrant woman's personal matter, but a matter for all women. As Cubitt and Greenslade (1997: 61) note, treating women's issues as personal matters cripples women's ability to act politically to advance their interests, and in the process undermines all people's capacity to participate in and transform civil society and public policy. In other words, to leave one woman's narrative and the dangers and exploitations she experiences crossing the U.S.–Mexico border at the individual level is to miss the larger communal pattern of these border experiences.

FAITH-BASED COMMUNITY ORGANIZATIONS IN EL PASO-JUÁREZ

Latinas and non-Latinas, linked by their common concern for women in the greater El Paso/Juárez area, have developed a number of mobilization strategies to bring attention to problems facing women in the region. The relational ties among the thirteen NGOs identified in my border research between 1996 and 1999 show a strong link to a mobilization process tied to, or having been sparked by, members of religious organizations. Such patterns reflect how community and faith-based organizations that lend support to NGO activism along the U.S.–Mexico border are embedded in its sociopolitical reality. Ruben Garcia, one of the cofounders of Annunciation House in El Paso, spoke about it and Casa Peregrina, both of which are shelters for predominantly illegal homeless immigrants who come looking for work in El Paso and Juárez. He recalled:

> ... Because of the economic development of the border you have this incredible migration from the interior of Mexico to the border areas. You know the maquiladoras, the famous maquiladoras. The year before Annunciation House came into being, the first maquila opened in Juárez – the RCA plant over at the Bermudez industrial park – and hired the first three thousand maquila workers. Well, twenty-two years later, there's three to four hundred maquiladoras, employing two hundred thousand-plus people.

This mass migration to the region created problems for social service organizations who were quickly overwhelmed by the number of people, many of whom found it difficult to find housing. As the numbers of homeless people increased, church groups responded by forming nonprofit organizations that provided shelter and other services to homeless migrants.

Reflecting on the circumstances under which Annunciation came into existence, Garcia recalled that in 1978 there were no other shelters except for the men's Christian home, there were no transitional living centers, and there were no battered women's shelters. Garcia said that he and a few others made personal commitments to working with the border's poor:

> Little by little, by word of mouth, Annunciation House filled out.... It also so happened that coming into existence in 1978, coincided with the explosion that took place in Central America and the mass of exoduses of people from Guatemala, Nicaragua, El Salvador, Honduras. And so, as these people made their way up to various kinds of borders, El Paso was one of the major crossing points for people. So, we found ourselves doing an immense amount of work with the refugees from Central America, along of course, with the people who have historically crossed over from the interior of Mexico.

This narrative of Annunciation House's history is similar to that of several other NGOs that organized around border issues. And although neither Annunciation House nor Casa Peregrina began as shelters for women, both have come to serve women in various ways. Casa Peregrina (on the Juárez side) eventually became a shelter for women, mostly because the pattern of migration grew to include single women, single mothers with children, as well as families with children.

My interviews with representatives of the women's organizations in the El Paso/Juárez border area highlighted the importance of Annunciation House and Casa Peregrina as part of the grassroots organizational network that Latinas and their families rely on in the region. They become particularly important in moments of crises such as when primary breadwinners lose jobs and find themselves and their families homeless. Many of these organizations are affiliated with a number of Catholic and Protestant church groups who support a wide range of border human rights issues, and many of the individual workers are motivated in terms of living a spirituality committed to the border's poor. As recounted by Garcia,

> Annunciation House was about looking inwardly and saying how can we live our lives with greater meaning, with more purpose.... We approached it from a faith based perspective, as we went through that year [1978], and as we reflected on scripture, we could not get away from the realization of the special relationship that exists between God and oppressed people, God and those who are poor, God and those who are marginalized, excluded, etc.

Similarly, Patricia Monreal Molina of Organización Popular Independiente (OPI) of Juárez, another of the NGOs in this network, noted a connection in the profiles of the people who came to create OPI as people coming to community work out of parish activities. In fact, several of the founders of OPI started organizing via the Base Christian Communities (BCCs) that exist on the edge of Juárez. BCCs emerged in many Catholic communities initially as a response to priest shortages. In Latin America, they are known for allowing the laity to assume broader roles than traditional Catholic parishes. Base community members are encouraged to take greater responsibility for advancing a decentralized and participatory format in community leadership. Their nonhierarchical structure is attractive to women's activism, and it is not surprising that some women activists who join faith-based NGOs (such as Patricia Monreal Molina of OPI) started their activism in BCCs. BCCs have been a force behind a range of movements (Eckstein 1999: 8), and the political reality along the border provides an expanded social context for women's activism. Consequently, when women's faith-based organizations like El Centro Mujeres de la Esperanza of El Paso come along, they find receptive audiences of like-minded lay and religious women to share the group's vision.

BORDER WOMEN'S FAITH-BASED COALITIONS IN EL PASO/JUÁREZ

Founded in 1993, El Centro Mujeres de la Esperanza was among the first truly women's faith-based non-government organizations to emerge in the region. Its members cut across ethnic lines. Ida Berresheim, a Catholic sister and one of the cofounders of El Centro, recalled that the lay and religious women who got involved in El Centro early on worked with refugees and homeless people. After a period of open discussion and evaluation, El Centro's organizers, many of whom were educators and health workers, decided to channel their efforts into programs focused on women's development. As recounted by Sister Ida, after soliciting funds mostly from women's [religious] congregations throughout the United States, they were able to open El Centro. They got to know and form partnerships with the local social service agencies and subsequently developed programs to train women as *promotoras de salud* (promoters of health).

El Centro is one model for women's mobilization in the region. As its mission statement states, El Centro has become a mutual U.S.–Mexican culturally based community of women who work in the El Paso/Ciudad Juárez region. More generally, "As women on the US/Mexico border, they stand in solidarity with women throughout the world who actively seek peace with justice for the earth and for people." Their goal is to work to transform the social structures that oppress or limit women, and they begin by focusing their activism on local projects. For example, El Centro's *Valores y Vida* program focuses on building women's self-esteem and challenging the assumptions of traditional family structures and women's subordinate roles in them. The goal is to provide opportunities for women to discuss alternative family structures where women do not have to be subordinate to men. Other Centro programs are geared to address women's economic marginality – identifying the sources of economic exploitation and developing strategies to combat them. It is by offering programs where women discover alternatives to their subordination and exploitation that organizations like El Centro become empowering organizations for border women.

By challenging the Latino family structure and critiquing other social institutions, namely religious institutions, Latinas/Chicanas/Mexicanas who join these NGOs organize to increase their political mobilization. They promote a nonpatriarchal action-oriented spirituality as part of a social activism that questions existing patriarchal structures affecting their lives. For example, women at El Centro articulate their rejection of church institutions that value keeping families intact without confronting family violence as a social problem, a problem that disproportionately affects women and children. As one woman put it after discounting her priest's advice to return to her husband after a brutal beating, "how can a church, an organization, or society, judge me because of what it teaches us," – expecting women to put up with the violence for the sake of keeping families together.

There is also the questioning of other oppressive social structures that produce economic and political marginalization. One of the characteristics of El Centro is the number of women who come from "colonias," the rural and unincorporated subdivisions of U.S. cities located along the U.S.–Mexico international boundary. Colonias are characterized by substandard housing, inadequate plumbing and sewage disposal systems, and inadequate access to clean water. They are highly concentrated poverty pockets that are physically and legally isolated from neighboring cities. El Centro's programs help these women to transform their everyday lived experiences and their spirituality into local border activism and to maximize efforts through effective networking with other women's NGOs in the region.

Many of the organizations in the cluster I studied are affiliated with religious groups, including Catholic women's congregations, a local Jewish women's organization, and the YWCA. The interviews I conducted with organizers reveal that women's NGOs on the U.S.–Mexico border are linked both by local and transnational concerns for women's rights and human rights. Alliances among and across women's NGOs focused on "being together" around women's issues rather than being divided by nationality.

The research reveals a rich relationship between a number of women's religious groups and the grassroots organizations with which they work.

For example, Sister Kathleen Erickson came to the border because her own background drew her to work in an organization that addressed border women's concerns. As a Sister of Mercy whose religious order made a formal commitment to work with women and children, particularly the poor and marginalized, coming to the border was a calling. That is how Sister Kathleen came to Anthony, New Mexico (a town that is partly in the outskirts of El Paso, Texas, and partly in New Mexico). In 1991, she and several other Sisters of Mercy helped to form what is now known as the Women's Intercultural Center. After several years, a spinoff organization, Mujeres Unidas, was founded to teach women business skills and to provide training that would help them find jobs. It is through these faith-based organizational networks that Latinas' political consciousness has expanded and the resources provided for their successful mobilization (cf. Cohen and Arato 1992).

Among the NGOs in the greater El Paso-Juárez communities, the YWCA and Casa Peregrina serve women by providing transition housing; the Battered Women's Shelter was started with support from the El Paso Jewish Women's Council; La Posada, founded by a group of Catholic Sisters, also provides shelter for women who are victims of domestic violence and for their children; La Mujer Obrera, although not a faith-based NGO but important to the El Paso/Juárez women's NGO network, provides political space for women to organize around labor issues; and other organizations disseminate educational materials on a number of issues important to women. Across the range of NGOs, the goals and objectives center on local activism and while the focus is on women's issues, these are often framed within broader community struggles. It is this local activism that enhances mobilization and empowers the women involved.

Imelda Garcia, a Chicana and cofounder of a spinoff organization of El Centro, emphasized that the basic objectives of her organization were "to give a voice to the community and to work with them, with the community, to better their health and health as not just related to blood pressure and whatever . . . but basically to empower community." Across the river from El Paso, in Juárez, a Mexican Catholic sister saw concerns over women's issues as central to her activism on the border, stating:

> I believe that among the most oppressed people, the most needy are women, especially among the poor, the marginal ones, the mistreated, the humiliated. I feel a great calling to work with women. We are working to recover our dignity, our place in society, families, and churches [translated from Spanish].

Sister María's calling to work with border women reflects the spiritual journey that characterizes many of the women who work in faith-based NGOs. One Dominican sister who works at a faith based NGO in Juárez presented a relatively similar narrative:

> I think I would trace ... my interest to our congregational meetings that we had ... from the seventies on. We made as a congregation a deliberate choice to work for justice and peace and that was really based on what was happening in the church and what was happening, especially in our consciousness of women's position and the injustice through which they are treated in our country and worldwide. We came to El Paso, we crossed over the bridge, saw what was happening in Juárez in the *colonias* there and ... I decided to ask to come here and join Donna [another Dominican sister] who was already in this area to see what we could do together.

These brief excerpts illuminate how religious, class, and ethnic boundaries were crossed in women's border organizing. Spiritual journeys combine with justice concerns and Latina activism to empower border women and their communities. These common goals are part of the tenets of global feminism. As Charlotte Bunch (1993: 251) has exhorted us: "To make global feminist consciousness a powerful force in the world demands that we make the local, global and the global, local. Such a movement... must be centered on a sense of connectedness among women active at the grassroots in various regions."

CONCLUSION

The research drawn on in this chapter speaks to and enriches feminist scholarship in that it shows the potential in global feminist approaches. Community-based activist research shows that "community is created in and through struggles against violence and for social justice and economic security, as well as through casual interactions with people who share some aspects of [their] daily lives" (Naples 1998: 337). This is important, because "as a dynamic process, the social construction of community offers the possibility for redefinition of boundaries, for broadened constituencies, and for seemingly unlikely alliances" (ibid.).

The study of the greater El Paso/Juárez area suggests that the role of women's religious organizations is central to border women's mobilization success. Catholic, Jewish, and YWCA women's groups provide organizational skills, information, and other resources that are integral to Latina centered women's NGOs on the border. Consequently, today, the experiences Latinas have and the work they do alongside non-Latinas in NGOs, creates a forum for the "chispa" – the spark – the passion for a type of women's politics to flower that requires a global view of the women's movement. In the process, Latinas engage with other communities of women and forge new opportunities for creating important alliances. That they are forming alliances with religious groups is part of the larger Latino/a story within the evolving U.S. ethnic and religious mosaic.

Thus, as argued earlier in the chapter, women's activism in the Latina/o community emerges from but is not decoupled from larger community problems – economic exploitation, racism, poverty, and violence. But that the activism evolved into women centered goals speaks to a type of politicization that Latina/o ethnic communities must confront. Women's subordination, marginalization, and exploitation are problems women face both within and outside their ethnic communities. Consequently, what this chapter shows is how "women are politicized and drawn into local political battles in a myriad of ways that reflect a wide diversity of personal and political concerns as well as varying constructions of community and social identities" (Naples 1998: 344). This research highlights why, how, and with whom Latinas came to construct communities of resistance and underscores the potentials for global feminism.

CHAPTER TWENTY-EIGHT

Worldly or Otherworldly?

"Activism" in an Urban Religious District

Omar M. McRoberts

INTRODUCTION

Colloquially, the term "faith-based activism" refers to extroverted forms of social action originating in religious institutions. Churches with food pantries and shelters for battered women, or that build homes and run welfare-to-work programs, or whose leaders organize marches and protests, are considered "activist." It is assumed that religious beliefs and practices are no obstacle for these churches – there is no contradiction between faith and activism. By contrast, churches that do apparently little for nonmembers are called "insular," and it is assumed that these institutions face religious ideological barriers to activity in the secular world. It is tempting to call one group "worldly" and the other "otherworldly," or one "church" and the other "sect" as have so many scholarly observers (Weber 1922/1963; Troeltsch 1931; Iannaccone 1988; Johnson 1963).

Indeed, among those ideas at the heart of the sociology of religion is the distinction between worldly and otherworldly modes of religious presence. Beneath most typologies of religious organizations is the notion that some churches are oriented toward earthly matters, while others completely turn their backs to secular human affairs, seeking solace in the promise of a better world to come. The worldly/otherworldly dichotomy is implicit especially in works attempting to sort African-American churches.

Scholars of black religion have, for instance, divided black churches into "expressive" and "instrumental." Expressive congregations are highly insular religious enclaves whose members avoid all involvement in political and secular social matters. They value emotional catharsis above all else. Instead of confronting in secular terms the societal roots of black suffering, these churches use worship to scrape off the psychic barnacles accumulated "out there" in the world. Church is therefore a way to escape the world, or discard the world, if only temporarily. Commentators usually associate expressive forms with the myriad Pentecostal and other "sect" congregations that occupied (and continue to occupy) countless commercial storefronts in depressed black neighborhoods. By contrast, instrumental congregations are inherently political. The pastors of these typically Baptist and Methodist churches preach politics from the pulpit and run for public office. Here, most religious activities are geared toward "uplifting the race." Instead of escaping the world, these churches plunge headlong into it in order to alter it (Drake 1940; Frazier 1963/1974).

412

Dichotomous typologies such as these are built on the assumption that there is in fact a fundamental distinction between worldliness and otherworldliness. This assumption obstructs social scientific understanding of black religion, and organized religion in general, in at least two important ways. First, it suggests that religious people cannot use ostensibly otherworldly ideas for secular activist purposes. If some theologies are taken to be political opiates (recall that Karl Marx dubbed religion the "opiate of the masses"), others are considered amphetamines for activists. Moreover, both are thought to act unambiguously. That is, no religious tradition can be both worldly *and* otherworldly. No church can change orientations, chameleon-like, to fit the context or issue at hand. The second limiting assumption is that seemingly otherworldly religious practices (such as "shouting" or "getting the holy ghost") do not have practical, even political, implications for the faithful.

Lincoln and Mamiya (1990), who are concerned with the historical development of black religion, and are reluctant to squeeze churches into starkly binary categories, declare that black churches are in fact suspended in perpetual tension not only between "otherworldly and this-worldly," but between "resistance and accommodation," "priestly and prophetic functions," "universalism and particularism," "communal and privatistic," and "charismatic and bureaucratic" (10–16; see also Baer and Singer 1992). At various historical junctures, particular black churches swing toward one pole or another. While the tension model nominally escapes the trap of binary typology and allows us to appreciate some of the complexity and fluidity of black religion, it still describes a "dialectical" process. This assumes that world and otherworld, and other paired categories, are "polar opposites" (Lincoln and Mamiya 1990: 11) in black religious thought and practice. The tension between the two is never resolved, but is experienced in every era by religious actors who struggle to remain true to the transcendent amidst the pressing social, political, and economic exigencies of their time.

Lincoln and Mamiya (1990:12) concede that

> [t]he otherworldly aspect, the transcendence of social and political conditions, can have a this-worldly political correlate which returns to this world by producing an ethical and prophetic critique of the present social order. In some instances, eschatological transcendence can help to critique the present.

Still, no sociological study of black churches directly challenges the idea that worldly and otherworldly ideas and practices are clearly distinct, polar opposites in the first place.

In this chapter, I question the usefulness of the worldly/otherworldly paradigm as a way of thinking about activism, retreatism, and all the combinations thereof, among black religious organizations. I take my conceptual cue from historian Evelyn Brooks Higginbotham (1993), who describes the black church as "a complex body of shifting cultural, ideological, and political significations" whose "multiplicity transcends polarity – thus tending to *blur* the spiritual and secular, the eschatological and political, and the private and public"(16; emphasis added). I concur also with the sociologist Nancy Ammerman (1997a: 213), who states that religious practices in general

> cannot be confined to a realm we call "otherworldly." Like all other either/or dichotomies, that one serves us no better. Those very "otherworldly" experiences are often in clear dialogue with the situations of everyday life.... These are practices that implicate this world in the very midst of providing points of transcendence.

I pose this challenge using ethnographic data collected during a five-year study of religious congregations in an economically depressed Boston neighborhood.

THE SETTING

Four Corners is a .6 square mile, largely poor, predominantly African-American neighborhood containing at least twenty-nine congregations in 1999. Fifteen of these congregations were majority African American. Of these, ten belonged to the Pentecostal-Apostolic constellation of faiths. The remaining five congregations were Jehovah's Witness (three), Baptist (one), and Catholic (one). Nearly all of the churches in Four Corners convene in storefronts. Fifty years ago, when the neighborhood was entirely white and Jewish, these storefronts housed actual stores. The expansion of the black population into the area sparked "white flight," which in turn initiated the downward spiral of systematic economic disinvestment. This process left in its wake a glut of vacant commercial spaces. The result is what I call a "religious district," where religious communities exist in high density not because residents are "overchurched" (Frazier 1963/1974; Myrdal 1944) but because the neighborhood contains an abundance of cheap, vacant commercial spaces on major thoroughfares.

Early in my study of religion in Four Corners, I thought it might be sufficient to classify churches dichotomously and explain why so many fell into the otherworldly, insular, nonactivist category. As I looked more closely, though, it became clear that binary understandings of church work did not capture what most churches in this religious district *thought* they were doing in and for society. Nearly all of the clergy, including those who preached fiercely against "the world," felt their churches needed to leave an indelibly positive imprint *on* the world. As such, these churches could be called not only "worldly" but at least rhetorically "activist." In short, the question for me became not whether, but *how* churches saw themselves as agents for world betterment.

In the following, I discuss two empirical phenomena that proved highly salient in this regard. Both phenomena challenge binary and dialectical modes of thinking by illustrating how religious organizations blur the distinction between world and otherworld so that the latter implies the former. One is the presence of churches that use ideas from stereotypically otherworldly theologies not to shirk, but to justify worldly activities. Second, churches ordinarily use transcendence-oriented practices, such as "shouting" or "getting the holy ghost," not as an existential escape hatch, but to inspire and energize the faithful that they might be powerful agents for change in a twisted, but unavoidable secular world.

Theological Conservatism and Activism

A host of sociological studies have found conservative theology – with its biblical literalism and individualist, conversionist views of salvation – to inhibit ecumenism (Boldon 1985; Myers and Davidson 1984; Kanagy 1992) and social activism (Guest and Lee 1987; Hoge and Faue 1973; Kanagy 1992; Stark and Glock 1965; Hoge et al. 1978: 122). Ethnographic studies of black Pentecostal congregations also reveal a tendency for conservative theology to suppress social activism (Paris 1982; Williams 1974). Meanwhile, studies of ecumenical activist coalitions and recent dispatches from major sponsors of such coalitions report that few, if any, participating churches represent theologically conservative traditions (Davidson 1985; Rogers 1990; Rooney 1995). Scholars have taken this scarcity as further evidence of the "otherworldly" inclinations of theologically conservative people (Davidson 1985; Johnson 1963; Tamney and Johnson 1990; Johnson and Tamney 1986). The implication is that conservative clergy will join or establish efforts that fight only for traditional moral concerns, such as those championed by Christian Right organizations. Otherwise, these clergy will gravitate toward in-church activities that promote retreat from the world and individual spiritual salvation.

Several of the churches in Four Corners challenge the negative association between theological conservatism and "worldliness." Azusa, Holy Road, and Jude Church are all Pentecostal or Apostolic – two very conservative theological traditions – yet engage to various degrees in prophetic, socially transformative activism. These churches do not assume *carte blanche* – like other religious organizations, they still face theological constraints. Even so, they are a testament to the inherent flexibility of conservative religious traditions, and to the blurriness of world/otherworld distinctions in religious practice.

All of the pastors came of age during the Civil Rights/Black Power era and were influenced by the norms of church engagement that crystallized in that era. Also, all of the clergy have done considerable theological work in order to justify their pastoral and prophetic stances. Their ability to do such work supports the view that theology is not a rigid predictor variable but, rather, a cultural resource that believers can use to justify both activism and retreatism (Mock 1992; Roberts 1990; Dudley and Johnson 1991; Wood 1999). Pentecostal theology, in particular, contains elements that may restrict engagement in social activism; but they also contain elements that can facilitate and complement, rather than obstruct, social engagement (Silva 1984; Alexander 1991; Warner 1995).

Saving the "Whole Person." The most powerful enabling element is an understanding of "salvation" that involves the satisfaction of the entire spectrum of human needs, including physical and social, as well as spiritual ones. This understanding is part and parcel of Pentecostal theology, which is distinguished in part by its emphasis on the *tangible*, or "radically embodied" (Cox 1995) presence of God's power in the believer's life, and by its experience-oriented hermeneutic, or method of scriptural interpretation. The theologian Mathew Clark (1989:102) writes that the Pentecostal emphasis on tangibility

> contributes a sense of expectation that truth will not only be held in remembrance, or objectively proclaimed as "pure" doctrine – but that *truth will be realized in the midst of the people*. Liturgy, preaching and missions are all conducted in this expectation – that sins will be forgiven, bodies and psyches will be healed, spirits will be uplifted, relationships will be restored, believers will be endowed with spiritual power, etc. Truth is both personal (i.e., Jesus is the Truth) and empirically realizable, as opposed to merely conceptual.

Simultaneously, the Pentecostal hermeneutic permits the reader of scripture to

> identify with the writer by virtue of common spiritual experience.... [T]he Bible is associated with activity and experience rather than viewed as a textbook of doctrine. Experience after the Biblical pattern takes precedence over confession according to the supposed theological content of Scripture. (ibid. 101)

This understanding of scripture encourages believers to apply biblical insights to the exigencies of daily life.

The pastors in question expressed the idea of radical embodiment in terms of the biblical mandate to serve the "whole person," in all his or her social and spiritual complexity. The following remark, made by Rev. Powell, refers to this mandate. Note his broad scriptural justification for social concern:

> When you look at the Bible – right? – from Genesis to Revelations – there's always been a Christian man who could lead the nation... Christians always got involved with politics. And I think it's really sad when the church say, I'm not gon' get involved with that stuff. That's our problem. We get involved with the spirit too much and not dealing with the *total man*. How do I reach this guy and get him into a job, into a house and into some kind of structure, and let him know he has a reason to live?

This statement reflects an experiential interpretation of the Bible. Such interpretations were also evident when ministers expressed the conviction that Christians are called to fight against sin in all its forms, *especially* social injustice and inequality. A non-experiential reading of the Bible might have excluded social injustice from the catalogue of fightable sins, despite the fact that the faithful claimed to encounter injustice daily.

The clergy's application of "whole person" theology supports the findings of previous studies, which show that theological conservatives tend to justify their views and activities in strictly religious terms (Tamney and Johnson 1990). It also contributes to scholarly evidence that charismatic/evangelical religion, with its heavy reliance on the Holy Spirit and biblical insight, can be used as a "fuel" for liberatory struggle and community development work as well as priestly, personal functions.

Community Building and Conversionism. Even those religious ideas sometimes used to shut out "the world" can also become fuel for worldly engagement. Some Pentecostals have tended to build exclusive, priestly communities that stand at high tension with the social and cultural environment – even if individual members are allowed to support social change work outside of the church. The clerics in question have extended this community ethic to help build communities of clergy and laypersons committed to social transformation. Rev. Rivers was a founding member of a city-wide, ecumenical antiviolence coalition. Pastor Calvin has convened several regional conferences of black women clergy concerned with violence and drug abuse. Rev. Powell has begun organizing "small churches" like his own, that want to balance organizational growth with demonstrations of social concern. For each minister, the idea of the highly committed community serves as a kind of mediator between Pentecostal practice and social activism.

This connection became clear during discussions about the effectiveness of structural and individual-level strategies for social change. All of the pastors agreed that both societal and personal transformations were necessary to improve life in poor inner city neighborhoods. They also favored the development of independent activist structures to meet the social, political, and economic needs of black people. This sentiment did not conflict in any way with the pastors' commitment to Pentecostal practice. In fact, their advocacy of do-for-self social and political empowerment tended to jibe with statements stressing the traditional conversionist values of "reborn social identity, personal dignity, and newfound community" (Baer and Singer 1992: 172). The unifying theme, however, was the value of the highly committed community, within which moral consistency, trust, and equality would provide a basis for unity against a perceived adversary – whether that adversary be global capitalism, racist members of the U.S. Congress, or cities that ignore the needs of poor urban neighborhoods. In no case, however, was the perceived enemy "the world" in its entirety.

Religious and Ideological Constraints on Activism. Although conservative theology provides the "fuel" for their activism, the clergy are constrained by elements of the same theology, sometimes in combination with nonreligious ideological tendencies. They avoid forms of activism that might make them sublimate their faith or compromise the spiritual integrity of their churches. Like their priestly, personalistic counterparts, these pastors are still committed to the spiritual person as much as the social, political, and economic person. In fact, they use the "whole person" concept as a kind of measuring stick to evaluate and compare local social programs before supporting them. Each expressed strong preferences for church-based efforts designed to propagate Christian moral standards as well as generate life opportunities for disprivileged people. Efforts lacking a religious foundation, they felt, would ultimately leave people in the "same position" despite temporary physical, social, or economic amelioration.

Sometimes the constrictive elements of conservative theology interact with wholly separate ideas regarding the nature of worldly politics to produce wariness of certain kinds of activism. Pastors Calvin and Powell, for instance, have told me about the conspiratorial, if not genocidal, motives of whites and agents of the state. Although they are committed to activism in general, both have avoided collaborative efforts that might make them vulnerable to these actors, thereby severely diluting the only institution in black society committed to serving the whole person: the church.

Pastor Calvin believes that black-on-black violence is perpetuated in part by white conspiracy. She argues, for instance, that the white-controlled media has helped "immobilize" black people with respect to youth violence. By assaulting the black public with regular images of black youth murdering each other, the media leads blacks to "hate the kids," and to don an attitude of helplessness. She also believes that black youth are getting guns from the white-dominated law enforcement community, for blacks neither import nor manufacture military grade assault weapons.

Her suspicion of white motives surfaced again only when she explained her refusal to join a Boston-based organization of clergy concerned with youth violence. The organization was spurred by an instance of the "street" coming into the "church": In 1992, gang violence erupted at a black Baptist church during a funeral for a youth murdered in a drive-by shooting. In response to this incident, which included a shootout and multiple stabbings, a handful of black clergy gathered to devise a plan of action. Calvin has avoided the group because she does not trust the motives of the white clergy who have since rallied around it. She believes the organization is now a lavish expression of "white guilt," designed to further *distract* black churches from the real work in the street.

Pastor Powell is suspicious of white politicians and other agents of the state. He is therefore wary of public programs, such as Charitable Choice, that contract churches to administer social services to poor people. In one conversation, Powell worried that, despite the neighborhood revitalization efforts of churches such as Azusa and Highlands, the neighborhood still appeared too "disorganized" to attract public money for community development. He suspected that white people from Community Development Corporations (CDCs) in adjacent neighborhoods, who attended community organizing meetings at both churches, were reporting to City Hall and telling officials "that Four Corners isn't ready." He feared that the city would ultimately "give the neighborhood" to one of the powerful CDCs in nearby locales.

Later I asked if he had heard about the Charitable Choice clause. Powell grew visibly disturbed at the mere mention of that particular piece of legislation:

> We [churches] should try to get *away* from the secular world's money. Because they want to come control what you do. The Feds are trying to *control* the churches. We used to be an institution that nobody touched, but preachers like PTL [Praise The Lord television ministries], Swaggert – the Feds want to crack down on them. The Feds are 'round about, giving churches money through organizations so they can take control. They will come and say what you can't teach and preach.

On another occasion I met Rev. Powell at his apartment, which is located just above the church. He told me he was trying to purchase the entire building so that the church could open a youth education complex there. He complained about the paucity of money available for churches to do this work. I asked if he had approached any public agencies for funding. "I can't sell out to politicians," he replied in a cynical conflation of politicians with agencies. "They'll try to put something in the neighborhood, and I'll have to support it even if it's bad for the neighborhood. Then I have to be the one who goes to the people to tell them."

The words of Pastors Calvin and Powell indicate that there are ideological constraints to certain forms of activism other than those embedded in theological conservatism. To be certain, both clergy seek to protect the integrity of the black church; their high esteem for the church partly reflects their conservative belief in Christianity's exclusive possession of Truth. That is, they believe Jesus' statement, "I am the way and the truth and the life. No one comes to the Father except through me"(John 14:6), and they believe that their religious doctrines and practices constitute the surest path "through" Jesus. Still, their objections to certain forms of activism do not come from the same cognitive place as the "trickle down" philosophy discussed previously. Calvin and Powell are not protecting their churches from the corrupting influence of "the world" in its entirety. They are protecting their churches from the perceived malintentions of white people and agents of the state. This protectiveness in turn betrays a latent conspiracy theory that partly attributes black suffering to the malicious actions of hostile outsiders.[1]

RELIGIOUS RITUAL AND "TRICKLE DOWN" SPIRITUAL ACTIVISM

Many black churches in Four Corners could be called "priestly" – that is, they are organizationally geared entirely toward the spiritual and social needs of members. This could imply that they are otherworldly and have little or no impact on the wider society. One might conclude that these churches operate as alternative social worlds, as isolated

---

[1] For more on conspiracy theories in African-American public opinion, see Waters (1997) and Cohen (1999).

"sanctuaries" (Roozen et al. 1988), within which individuals diligently pursue their own salvation while enjoying a modicum of respect and social status (Paris 1982; Williams 1974). That conclusion would not be invalid. It would, nevertheless, be grossly out of sync with what the churches themselves believe they are doing with worship and fellowship.

Priestliness, like theological conservatism, may turn people's thoughts toward an otherworld, but not simply or solely for the purpose of personal transcendence. Some of the churches use ritual interaction inside church walls to equip members to function in, and perhaps transform, social worlds *beyond* the church. Like parents who attempt to make a mark on the world by raising well-adjusted children, these churches try to change the world by injecting socially and spiritually well-adjusted individuals into it.

This strategy was particularly evident in the eight churches of southern migrants. The clergy in these churches do not condemn all direct attempts at social transformation. Social transformation is considered necessary to meet widespread needs and right large-scale injustices. Nor do these clergy eschew *individual* activism in the secular world: Most encourage congregants to vote, at least. Yet they believe that unjust systems are the bitter fruits of a societal spiritual crisis: A crisis that must be resolved through spiritual means, one prodigal soul at a time. Churches, therefore, should avoid prophetic varieties of struggle, such as political mobilization, protest, and large-scale social service provision, lest they forget the privileged role of the church: to be an incubator of saved souls and sound psyches, ready to *face* the world. Churches are thought to catalyze social change by creating communities that instill in individuals the virtues of equanimity, confidence, and determination. Once empowered with these qualities, individuals are not only able to handle the trials and indignities of life in the northern city, but are better able to resist and challenge oppressive systems.

In these churches it was not unusual for preachers to make pronouncements such as this: "The same God in Jesus is in you . . . 'I gave man power over all the earth. Nothing shall hurt you. I gave you the power to speak to beast, the sun and moon.'" This affirmation, delivered by Pastor Pride (of the Remembrance church), is not otherworldly – it aims, in fact, to connect the believer with divine forces that might enable him or her to function *in* the world with a sense of power and agency. This is an implied meaning of Pride's church motto: "Where everybody is somebody . . . "

At Pastor Pride's church and other charismatic migrant religious communities[2] in Four Corners, affirmations of power are internalized, experienced firsthand, during periods of "ritual antistructure" (Turner 1977; Ammerman 1997a). According to the anthropologist Victor Turner, certain aspects of ritual are designed to thrust participants into a liminal state "betwixt and between" conventional roles and statuses in the social structure. Once roles and statuses are dissolved, a "communitas" emerges, characterized by shared feelings "of lowliness and sacredness, of homogeneity and comradeship" (1977: 96). Turner recognized the socially subversive potential of communitas when he wrote:

> My view is briefly that from the perspectival viewpoint of those concerned with the maintenance of "structure," all sustained manifestations of communitas must

---

[2] Seven of the eight migrant churches are charismatic. The remaining one, a Church of Christ, eschews glossalalia and other charismatic signs.

appear as dangerous and anarchical, and have to be hedged around with prescriptions, prohibitions, and conditions. (ibid. 109)

Turner's communitas is a glimpse of radical equality – a vision that can be carried into the world of structures, statuses, and hierarchies to effect social transformation. Scholars of black religion have followed suit, noting the communitas-generating, hierarchy-subverting qualities of ecstatic worship (Sanders 1996; Alexander 1991; Kostarelos 1995).

Ritual antistructure begins with the descent of the Holy Ghost, which manifests in glossalalia, ecstatic shouting, and dancing. At such times it appears that the entire structure of the service, with all its assigned roles, has irreparably broken down. Men and women alike weep and "fall out" under the Holy Ghost. Church leaders become nearly indistinguishable from common congregants in the emotional outpouring. After this liminal period, while individuals are still drying tears and riding out the last shudders of the Spirit, congregations often sing in unison a slow hymn of thanks, as if to solidify the communitas generated during the liminal period. During these parts of religious services, the "cosmic power" referred to earlier reveals itself to believers as more than a feel-good rhetorical device; that power actually descends into the room and *demonstrates* its ability to level social distinctions. Charismatic churches use this ritual leveling not to separate members from the world, but to affirm their ability to operate in the world.

Pastors of the migrant churches in this study agree that people "built up" in the church community are uniquely suited to push for social transformation outside the church. Pastor Winspeare sums up the attitude this way: "If the people in the church are being built up spiritually they must be spiritually fed, spiritually built up in order to go into the community to be able to feed the people that need to be fed." He calls this a "trickle down" approach to social transformation, since spiritual power metaphorically comes from "above." Pastor Pride shares the "trickle down" perspective. In one sermon she used the example of Jesse Jackson to illustrate the connection between in-church socialization and social change. According to Pride, Jackson delivered a speech in Boston in which he likened his childhood experiences to those of today's youth-at-risk. He allegedly credited his positive attitude, acquired in the nurturing social world of the church, for his ability to escape the "ghetto," pursue advanced education, and struggle for social justice. Pride implied that the *church community*, through its spiritual ministrations, had saved Jackson so that he could engage in socially transformative work.

DISCUSSION

The foregoing discussion illustrates why theological conservatism, usually associated with "otherworldliness," need not always lead to an avoidance of secular affairs. The faithful are not forced to choose between theological commitments and desires for social change, as if the two were mutually exclusive, or "polar opposites." Religious agents, particularly clergy, take their theology as is, and sift and knead it to support their extroverted, socially transformative imperatives. Put differently, these clergy work comfortably *within* the theological traditions they have inherited, strategically mining the religion for supportive tenets and traditions.

To be sure, religious ideas and ideological leanings limit the pastors to certain kinds of activism and collaboration. Religious ideas at once open up certain avenues of action, and suggest boundaries for that action. But this does not betray a tension, contradiction, or opposition between otherworldly ideas and worldly practices. It indicates simply that religious traditions contain ideas that speak to the moral and ethical limits of activism. In this sense, "sacred" and "secular" activisms are more similar than different. For instance, contemporary secular social movement organizations have debated internally over the propriety of sabotage, civil disobedience, and armed struggle. All of these debates are saturated with moral and ideological considerations. In short, *all* activism is enabled and limited by ideas. The point though, is that religious agents, like secular ones, play the pivotal role in determining the implications of ideas for action.

I also have shown how an expressive religious practice, namely "getting the holy ghost" can be directed toward instrumental purposes in the secular world. Rather than using worship to escape the world, churches attempt to change the world by "orient[ing] worship toward redeeming the worlds in which members live" (Davidson and Koch 1998: 299). In other words, otherworldly practice often *is* worldly practice. One exists not in spite of the other, but for the sake of the other.

These illustrations are not to deny that there are churches that choose one over the other in homiletics and/or doctrine. Numerous black religious groups reject aspects of the world or otherworld (such as the Nation of Islam, which rejects the concept of a personal life after death). But these beliefs should not be considered predictive or indicative of any church's impact on secular politics and society. When our analyses do so, they implicitly accept the distinction between world and otherworld. They become oblivious to the impact of otherworldly religious ideas and practices on worldly affairs because they begin by assuming that world and otherworld really are opposites. As a result, the worldly/otherworldly paradigm not only obscures dichotomy-busting religious activities, but lets social scientists avoid explaining how ostensibly "otherworldly" churches come to view themselves as agents of "worldly" social change.

The dichotomous paradigm can also lead scholars hastily and falsely to attribute instances of retreatism to the "otherworldly" ideologies of particular religious groups. The temptation to do so will be particularly high as government, under the aegis of Charitable Choice and the Office of Faith-Based and Community Initiatives, increasingly funds church-spawned social service agencies. In an analysis of a nationally representative survey of 1,236 religious congregations in the United States, Chaves (1999: 841) found that "64 percent of predominantly African American congregations expressed a willingness to apply for government funds compared with only 28 percent of those from predominantly white congregations."

Which churches make up that hefty minority – 36 percent – of black churches that would *refuse* to accept government funds? Kneejerk speculation would probably associate these resistors with the most theologically conservative black churches, since these are considered the most "otherworldly." Future studies may find that Pentecostals and other highly conservative groups do indeed refuse government funds more frequently than black Baptists, Methodists, and other "mainliners." If this is true, though, it need not be because of the otherworldliness of theologically conservative bodies. Some of the resistors, I suspect, would look something like Pastors Powell and Calvin: interested in prophetic, worldly activism, yet wary of white and state interference in black church affairs. Studies situated within world/otherworld frameworks risk overlooking, or underanalyzing, such richly significant cases.

Social scientific research should be open to the *simultaneity* of world and otherworld in black religious thought and practice, and in all of organized religion. Promising in this regard are some recent studies that show how the religious ideas and practices generally associated with black church culture can fuel worldly engagement (Pattillo-McCoy 1998; Harris 1999; McRoberts 1999). By thinking about religion as a cultural resource instead of a set of polar oppositions, these studies point in the right direction. They take beliefs and practices seriously, but do not assume that these effect actions in a linear causal fashion. This perspective reveals how institutions creatively combine worldly and otherworldly, instrumental, and expressive elements to form unique modes of religious presence. Only when sensitive to simultaneity will social scientists appreciate fully the dizzying diversity of institutions that make up the deceptively euphemistic "Black Church."

References

Abramson, Paul R., John H. Aldrich, and David W. Rhode. 1998. *Change and Continuity in the 1996 Elections*. Washington, DC: Congressional Quarterly Press.

Abusharaf, Rogaia Mustafa. 1998. "Structural Adaptations in an Immigrant Muslim Congregation in New York." In R. Stephen Warner and Judith G. Wittner, eds., *Gatherings in Diaspora: Religious Communities and the New Immigration* (pp. 235–64). Philadelphia: Temple University Press.

Acock, Alan. 1984. "Parents and Their Children: The Study of Inter-Generation Influence." *Sociology and Social Research* 68: 151–71.

Acock, Alan, and Vern Bengtson. 1978. "On the Relative Influence of Mothers and Fathers: A Covariance Analysis of Political and Religious Socialization." *Journal of Marriage and the Family* 40: 519–30.

Acuña, Rodolfo. 1988. *Occupied America: A History of Chicanos*. 3rd ed. New York: Harper Collins.

Adas, Michael. 1979. *Prophets of Rebellion: Millenarian Protest Movements against the European Colonial Order*. Chapel Hill: University of North Carolina Press.

Aho, James A. 1981. *Religious Mythology and the Art of War*. Westport, CT: Greenwood Press.

_____. 1990. *The Politics of Righteousness: Idaho Christian Patriotism*. Seattle: University of Washington Press.

_____. 1997. "The Apocalypse of Modernity." In Thomas Robbins and Susan Palmer, eds., *Millennium, Messiahs, and Mayhem* (pp. 61–72). New York: Routledge.

Akerlof, George A. 1997. "Social Distance and Social Decisions." *Econometrica* 65: 1005–27.

Alba, Richard D., and Victor Nee. 1997. "Rethinking Assimilation Theory for a New Era of Immigration." *International Migration Review* 31: 826–874.

Aldrich, John A. 1995. *Why Parties? The Origin and Transformation of Political Parties in America*. Chicago: University of Chicago Press.

Aldridge, A. 2000. *Religion in the Contemporary World: A Sociological Introduction*. Cambridge, UK: Polity Press.

Alexander, Bobby C. 1991. "Correcting Misinterpretations of Turner's Theory: An African American Pentecostal Illustration." *Journal for the Scientific Study of Religion* 30: 26–44.

Alexander, Jeffrey C., ed. 1988. *Durkheimian Sociology: Cultural Studies*. New York: Cambridge University Press.

_____. 1992. "Citizen and Enemy as Symbolic Classification." In Michele Lamont and Marcel Fournier, eds., *Cultivating Differences* (pp. 289–308). Chicago: University of Chicago Press.

Alexander, June Granatir. 1987. *The Immigrant Church and Community: Pittsburgh's Slovak Catholics and Lutherans, 1880–1915*. Pittsburgh, PA: University of Pittsburgh Press.

Alinsky, Saul. 1969. *Reveille for Radicals*. New York: Vintage Books.

_____. 1971. *Rules for Radicals: A Practical Primer for Realistic Radicals*. New York: Random House.

Allport, Gordon, and J. M. Ross. 1967. "Personal Religious Orientation and Prejudice." *Journal of Personality and Social Psychology* 5: 432–43.

Almond, Philip C. 1988. *The British Discovery of Buddhism*. Cambridge: Cambridge University Press.

Ammerman, Nancy T. 1987. *Bible Believers: Fundamentalists in the Modern World*. New Brunswick, NJ: Rutgers University Press.
_____. 1994. "Telling Congregational Stories." *Review of Religious Research* 36.
_____. 1997a. *Congregation and Community*. New Brunswick: Rutgers University Press.
_____. 1997b. "Golden Rule Christianity." In David Hall, ed., *Lived Religion in America* (pp. 196–216). Princeton, NJ: Princeton University Press.
_____. 2000 (March). "New Life for Denominationalism." *Christian Century*.
Ammerman, Nancy T., and Wade Clark Roof, eds. 1995. *Work, Family, and Religion in Contemporary Society*. New York: Routledge.
Anderson, Benedict. 1991. *Imagined Communities*. London: Verso.
Anderson, Elijah. 1992. *Streetwise: Race, Class, and Change in an Urban Community*. Chicago: University of Chicago Press.
_____. 1999. *Code of the Street: Decency, Violence, and the Moral Life of the Inner City*. New York: Norton.
Andeweg, Rudy B. 1982. *Dutch Voters Adrift: On Explanations of Electoral Change (1963–1977)*. Unpublished Ph.D. Dissertation, University of Leiden.
Anzuldua, Gloria. 1987. *Borderlands: La Frontera*. San Francisco: Aunt Lute Books.
Appleby, R. Scott. 2000. *The Ambivalence of the Sacred: Religion, Violence, and Reconciliation*. Lanham, MD: Rowan & Littlefield.
Arjomand, Said, ed.. 1993. *The Political Dimensions of Religion*. Albany: State University of New York Press.
Armstrong, Elizabeth H. 1937/1967. *The Crisis of Quebec, 1914–18*. New York: AMS Press.
Asad, Talal. 1993. *Genealogies of Religion: Discipline and Reasons of Power in Christianity and Islam*. Baltimore, MD: Johns Hopkins University Press.
Ashford, Shena, and Noel Timms. 1992. *What Europe Thinks: A Study of European Values*. Aldershot, UK: Dartmouth.
Atchley, Robert. 1997. "Everyday Mysticism: Spiritual Development in Later Adulthood." *Journal of Adult Development* 4: 123–34.
Atkinson, Robert. 1998. *The Life Story Interview*. Newbury Park, CA: Sage.
Babbie, Earl. 1992. *Practicing Social Research*. 6th ed. Belmont, CA: Wadsworth.
_____. 1997. *The Practice of Social Research*. San Francisco: Wadsworth.
Bäckström, A., and Bromander, J. 1995 *Kyrkobyggnaden och det offentliga rummet*. Uppsala: Svenska Kyrkans Utredningar. [Contains an English summary.]
Bacon, L. 1832. The Christian Doctrine of Stewardship in Respect to Poverty. Unpublished sermon preached at the request of the Young Men's Benevolent Society, of New Haven, Conneticut by Leonard Bacon, Pastor of the First Church in New Haven. New Haven, CT.
Badr, Hoda. 2000. "The Al-Noor Mosque: Strength through Unity." In Helen Rose Ebaugh and Janet Chafetz, eds., *Religion and the New Immigrants: Continuities and Adaptations in Immigrant Congregations* (pp. 193–227). Walnut Creek, CA: AltaMira Press.
Baer, Hans. 1993. "The Limited Empowerment of Women in Black Spiritual Churches: An Alternative Vehicle to Religious Leadership." *Sociology of Religion* 54: 65–82.
Baer, Hans A., and Merrill Singer. 1992. *African-American Religion in the Twentieth Century*. Knoxville: University of Tennessee Press.
Bagwell, Laurie Simon, and B. Douglas Bernheim. 1996. "Veblen Effects in a Theory of Conspicuous Consumption." *American Economic Review* 86: 349–73.
Bainbridge, William Sims, and Rodney Stark. 1981. "The Consciousness Reformation Reconsidered." *Journal for the Scientific Study of Religion* 20: 1–16.
Baird, Robert. 1844/1969. *Religion in America; or, An Account of the Origin, Progress, Relation to the State, and Present Condition of the Evangelical Churches in the United States*. New York: Arno Press.
Baker, K. L., Russell J. Dalton, and K. Hildebrandt. 1975. *Political Affiliations: Transition in the Bases of German Partisanship*. University of Essex: European Consortium for Political Research.
Baltzell, E. Digby. 1964. *The Protestant Establishment*. New York: Random House.
Barker, Eileen. 1984. *The Making of a Moonie: Choice or Brainwashing?* Oxford: Blackwell.
Barkun, Michael. 1997. "Millenarians and Violence: The Case of the Christian Identity Movement." In Thomas Robbins and Susan Palmer, eds., *Millennium, Messiahs, and Mayhem* (pp. 247–60). New York: Routledge.

Barrera, Mario. 1979. *Race and Class in the Southwest: A Theory of Racial Inequality*. South Bend, IN: Notre Dame Press.

Barrett, David B. 1982. *World Christian Encyclopedia*. Oxford: Oxford University Press.

Bartkowski, John. 2000. "Breaking Walls, Raising Fences: Masculinity, Intimacy, and Accountability among the Promise Keepers." *Sociology of Religion* 61: 33–53.

Bartkowski, John P. 1995. "Spare the rod…, or spare the child?" *Review of Religious Research* 37: 97–116.

Bartolini, Stefano, and Peter Mair. 1990. *Identity, Competition and Electoral Availability*. New York: Cambridge University Press.

Basch, Linda, Nina Glick-Schiller, and Cristina Szanton Blanc. 1994. *Nations Unbound: Transnational Projects, Postcolonial Predicaments, and Deterritorialized Nation-States*. Langhorne, PA: Gordon and Breach.

Bass, Dorothy C. 1994. "Congregations and the Bearing of Traditions." In James P. Wind and James W. Lewis, eds., *American Congregations* (pp.169–91). Chicago: University of Chicago Press.

Basu, Amrita. 1995. "Why Local Riots are not Simply Local: Collective Violence and the State in Bijnor, India, 1988–1993." *Theory and Society* 24: 35–78.

Bataille, Georges. 1973/1989. *Theory of Religion*. New York: Zone Books.

Bauberot, Jean, ed. 1994. *Religions et laïcité dan l'Europe des douze*. Paris: Syros.

Bauman, Zygmunt. 1996. "From Pilgrim to Tourist – or a Short History of Identity." In S. Hall and P. DuGay, eds., *Questions of Cultural Identity* (pp. 18–36). Thousand Oaks, CA: Sage.

Baumgardner, Jennifer, and Amy Richards. 2000. *Manifesta: Young Women, Feminism and The Future*. New York: Farrar, Straus, and Giroux.

Becker, E. 1973. *The Denial of Death*. New York: Free Press.

Becker, Howard. 1932. *Systematic Sociology*. New York: Wiley.

Becker, J. W., and Vink, R. 1994. *Secularization in the Netherlands; 1966–1991*. Rijswijk: Sociaal en Cultureel Planbureau.

Becker, Penny E. 1997. "'What is Right? What is Caring?' Moral Logics in Local Religious Life." In Penny E. Becker and Nancy Eiesland, eds., *Contemporary American Religion: An Ethnographic Reader* (pp. 121–46). Walnut Creek, CA: AltaMira/Sage.

———. 1998. "Making Inclusive Communities: Congregations and the 'Problem' of Race." *Social Problems* 45: 451–472.

———. 1999. *Congregations in Conflict: Cultural Models of Local Religious Life*. New York: Cambridge University Press.

———. 2000. "Boundaries and Silences in Post-Feminist Sociology." *Sociology of Religion* 61: 399–408.

———. Forthcoming. *Religion and Family in a Changing Society: Understanding the Transformation of Linked Institutions*. Princeton, NJ: Princeton University Press.

Becker, Penny E., and Nancy L. Eiesland, eds. 1997. *Contemporary American Religion: An Ethnographic Reader*. Walnut Creek, CA: AltaMira/Sage.

Becker, W., et al. 1990. *Zur Geschichte der Christlich-Demokratischen Bewegung in Europa*. Melle: E. Knoth.

Beckford, James. 1989. *Religion and Advanced Industrial Society*. London: Unwin-Hyman.

Behringer, Wolfgang. 1997. *Witchcraft Persecutions in Bavaria: Popular Magic, Religious Zealotry and Reason of State in Early Modern Europe*. Cambridge: Cambridge University Press.

Bell, Catharine. 1992. *Ritual Theory, Ritual Practice*. New York: Oxford.

———. 1997. *Ritual: Perspectives and Dimensions*. New York: Oxford.

Bell, Wendell. 1958. "Social Choice, Life Styles, and Suburban Residence." In William Dobriner, ed., *The Suburban Community* (pp. 225–47). New York: Putnam.

Bellah Robert N. 1967. "Civil Religion in America." *Daedalus* 96: 1–21.

———. 1970a. *Beyond Belief: Essays on Religion in a Post-traditional World*. New York: Harper & Row.

———. 1970b. *Tokagawa Religion*. Boston: Beacon Press.

———. 1975. *The Broken Covenant: American Civil Religion in Time of Trial*. New York: Seabury Press.

———. 1976. "New Religious Consciousness and the Crisis of Modernity." In Chacles Glock and Robert Bellah, eds., *The New Religious Consciousness* (pp. 332–52). Berkeley: University of California Press.

Bellah, Robert N., and Phillip E. Hammond. 1980. *Varieties of Civil Religion*. New York: Harper & Row.

Bellah, Robert N., Richard Madsen, William M. Sullivan, Ann Swidler, and Steven M. Tipton. 1985. *Habits of the Heart: Individualism and Commitment in American Life*. New York: Harper & Row.

Bellah, Robert N., Richard Madsen, William M. Sullivan, Ann Swidler, and Steven Tipton. 1991. *The Good Society*. New York: Knopf.

Bengtson, Vern L. 1975. "Generation and Family Effects in Value Socialization." *American Sociological Review* 40: 358–71.

Bengtson, Vern L., and K. D. Black. 1973. "Intergenerational Relations and Continuities in Socialization." In Paul Baltes and Warner K. Schaie, eds., *Life Span Developmental Psychology: Personality and Socialization* (pp. 207–34). New York. Academic Press.

Bengtson, Vern L., and Joseph A. Kuypers. 1971. "Generational Difference and the Developmental Stake." *Aging and Human Development* 2: 249–60.

Bengtson, Vern L., and Lillian Troll. 1978. "Youth and Their Parents: Feedback and Intergenerational Influence in Socialization." In Richard M. Lerner and Graham B. Spanier, eds., *Child Influences on Marital and Family Interaction: A Life-Span Perspective* (pp. 215–40). New York: Academic Press.

Walter Benjamin. 1940/1968. *Illuminations*. New York: Harcourt, Brace and World.

Bennett, P. G. 1987. *Analysing Conflict and its Resolution*. Oxford: Clarendon Press.

Ben-Sasson, Haim Hillel. 1971. "History." *Encyclopedia Judaica*. Jerusalem: Keter.

Benson, Lee. 1961. *The Concept of Jacksonian Democracy: New York as a Test Case*. Princeton, NJ: Princeton University Press.

Berger, Helen. 1998. *A Community of Witches: Contemporary Neopaganism and Witchcraft in the United States*. Columbia: University of South Carolina Press.

Berger, Peter. 1954. "The Sociological Study of Sectarianism." *Social Research* 21: 467–87.

_____. 1967. *The Sacred Canopy*. Garden City, NY: Anchor Books.

_____. 1974. "Some Second Thoughts on Substantive versus Functional Definitions of Religion." *Journal for the Scientific Study of Religion* 13: 125–33.

_____. 1992. *A Far Glory: The Quest for Faith in an Age of Credulity*. New York: Free Press.

_____. 1997 (October). "Epistemological modesty: An interview with Peter Berger." *Christian Century* 11: 972–75, 978.

_____. 1999. "The Desecularization of the World: A Global Overview." In Peter Berger, ed., *The Desecularization of the World: Resurgent Religion and World Politics* (pp. 1–18). Grand Rapids, MI: Eerdmans.

Berger, Peter, and Thomas Luckmann. 1966. *The Social Construction of Reality: A Treatise in the Sociology of Knowledge*. Garden City, NY: Doubleday Anchor.

Berger, Suzanne, ed. 1982. *Religion in West European Politics*. London: Cass.

Bernheim, B. Douglas. 1994. "A Theory of Conformity." *Journal of Political Economy* 102: 841–77.

Bettis, Joseph, and S. K. Johannesen, eds. 1984. *The Return of the Millennium*. Barrytown, NY: New Era Books.

Beyer, Peter. 1994. *Religion and Globalization*. London: Sage.

_____. 1998. "The Modern Emergence of Religions and a Global Social System for Religion." *International Sociology* 13: 151–72.

_____. 1999. *The Modern Construction of Religions in the Context of World Society: A Contested Category in Light of Modern Chinese History*. Paper presented to the second conference on Chinese and Comparative Historiography and Historical Culture, Wolfenbüttel, Germany.

_____. 2001. "What Counts as Religion in Global Society? From Practice to Theory." In P. Beyer, ed. *Globalisierung und Religion: Ausgewählte Aufsätze aus der Englischen Literatur* (pp. 125–50). Würzburg: Ergon Verlag.

Bianchi, Eugene. 1987. *Aging as a Spiritual Journey*. 2nd. ed. New York: Crossroad.

Bishop, George. 1992. *The Greater Cincinnati Survey*. Cincinnati: University of Cincinnati Institute for Policy Research.

_____. 1999. "Trends: Americans' Belief in God." *Public Opinion Quarterly* 63: 421–34.

Blanchard, Dallas A., and Terry J. Prewitt. 1993. *Religious Violence and Abortion: The Gideon Project*. Gainesville: University Press of Florida.

Blau, Joseph L., ed. 1950. *Cornerstones of Religious Freedom in America*. Boston: Beacon Press.

Blau, J. R., K. C. Land, and K. Redding. 1992. "The Expansion of Religious Affiliation." *Social Science Research* 21: 329–52.

Bloch, Jon. 1997. "Countercultural Spiritualists' Perceptions of the Goddess." *Sociology of Religion* 58: 181–190.

Boardman, Eugene P. 1962. "Millenary Aspects of the Taiping Rebellion (1851–64)." In Sylvia Thrupp, ed., *Comparative Studies in Society and History* (pp. 70–9), supplement II. The Hague: Monton.

Bock, Geoffrey E. 1976. *The Jewish Schooling of American Jews: A Study of Non-cognitive Educational Effects*. Unpublished Ph.D. dissertation, Harvard University, Cambridge, MA.

Bodnar, John E. 1985. *The Transplanted: A History of Immigrants in Urban America*. Bloomington: Indiana University Press.

Bolce, Louis, and Gerald De Maio. 1999. "Religious Outlook, Culture War Politics, and Antipathy Toward Christian Fundamentalists." *Public Opinion Quarterly* 63: 29–61.

Boldon, Dean A. 1985. "Organizational Characteristics of Ecumenically Active Denominations." *Sociological Analysis* 46: 261–73.

Books, John W. 1980. "Class and Religious Voting in Three European Nations: Political Changes in the 1960s." *Social Science Journal* 17: 69–87.

Bornewasser, A., L. Scholten, I. Schöffer, et al. 1969. *De Confessionelen. Onstaan en Ontwikkeling van de Christelijke Partijen*. Utrecht: Ambo.

Bossy, John. 1985. *Christianity in the West 1400–1700*. New York: Oxford University Press.

Bourdieu, Pierre. 1987. "What Makes a Social Class? On the Theoretical and Practical Existence of Groups." *Berkeley Journal of Sociology* 32: 1–32.

———. 1990. *In Other Words: Essays Towards a Reflexive Sociology*. Stanford, CA: Stanford University Press.

Bourdieu, Pierre, and Loïc J. D. Wacquant. 1992. *An Invitation to Reflexive Sociology*. Chicago: University of Chicago.

Boulard, F., and G. Le Bras. 1947. *Carte Religieuse de la France Rurale*. Paris: Aux Cahiers du Clergé Rural.

Boulard, F., and J. Rémy. 1968. *Pratique Religieuse Urbaine et Régions Culturelles*, Paris: Economie et Humanisme/ Editions Ouvrières.

Boyte, Harry C. 1989. *Commonwealth: A Return to Citizen Politics*. New York: Free Press.

Braam, A. W., P. van den Eeden, M. J. Prince, A. T. F. Beekman, S.-L. Kivelae, B. A. Lawlor, A. Birkhofer, R. Fuhrer, A. Lobo, H. Magnusson, A. H. Mann, I. Meller, M. Roelands, I. Skoog, C. Turrina, and J. R. Copeland, 2001. "Religion as a Cross-cultural Determinant of Depression in Elderly Europeans: Results from the EURODEP Collaboration." *Psychological Medicine* 31: 803–14.

Brasher, Brenda. 1998. *Godly Women: Fundamentalism and Female Power*. New Brunswick, NJ: Rutgers University Press.

Braude, Ann. 1997. "Women's History Is American Religious History." In Thomas A. Tweed, ed., *Retelling U.S. Religious History* (pp. 87–107). Berkeley: University of California Press.

Breault, K. D. 1989a. "New Evidence on Religious Pluralism, Urbanism, and Religious Participation." *American Sociological Review* 54: 1048–53.

———. 1989b. "A Re-examination of the Relationship between Religious Diversity and Religious Adherence: Reply to Finke and Stark." *American Sociological Review* 54: 1056–9.

Brenner, Leon O. 1961. *Hostility and Jewish Group Identification*. Unpublished Ph.D. dissertation, Boston University.

Brodkin, Karen. 1998. *How Jews Became White Folks and What That Says about Race in America*. New Brunswick, NJ: Rutgers University Press.

Bronfenbrenner, Kate. 1998. *Organizing to Win: New Research on Union Strategies*. Ithaca, NY: ILR Press.

Bronfenbrenner, Kate, and T. Juravich. 1995. *Union Organizing in the Public Sector: An Analysis of State and Local Elections*. Ithaca, NY: ILR Press.

Bromley, David G. 1998a. "The Social Construction of Contested Exit Roles: Defectors, Whistle-blowers, and Apostates." In David Bromley, ed., *The Politics of Religious Apostasy* (pp. 19–48). Westport, CT: Praeger.

———. 1998b. "Transformative Movements and Quasi-Religious Corporations: The Case of Amway." In N. J. Demerath, III, Peter D. Hall, Terrence Schmitt, and Rhys Williams, eds., *Sacred*

Companies: Organizational Aspects of Religion and Religious Aspects of Organizations (pp. 349–63). New York: Oxford University Press.

Bromley, David, and Phillip Hammond. 1987. *The Future of New Religious Movements*. Macon, GA: Mercer University Press.

Bromley, David G., and James T. Richardson, eds. 1983. *The Brainwashing/Deprogramming Controversy*. New York: Mellen Press.

Brooks, Clem. 1999. *Public Concern with Family Decline in the United States: Trends, Social Sources, and the Emergence of a New Political Cleavage*. Unpublished Manuscript, Department of Sociology, Indiana University.

———. 2000. "Civil Rights Liberalism and the Suppression of a Republican Political Realignment in the United States, 1972 to 1992." *American Sociological Review* 65: 483–505.

Brooks, Clem, and Jeff Manza. 1997. "Social Cleavages and Political Alignments: U.S. Presidential Elections, 1960–1992," *American Sociological Review* 62: 937–46.

———. 2002. "A Great Divide?" Religion and Electoral Politics in the United States, 1972–2000. Unpublished Manuscript, Department of Sociology, Indiana University.

Brown, C. 2001. *The Death of Christian Britain*. London: Routledge.

Brown, Karen McCarthy. 1991. *Mama Lola: A Vodou Priestess in Brooklyn*. Berkeley: University of California Press.

Brown, Richard Harvey. 1993. "Cultural Representation and Ideological Domination." *Social Forces* 71: 657–76.

Brown, Steven. 2000. "The 'Musilanguage' Model of Music Evolution." In Nils Wallin, Bjorn Merker, and Steven Brown, eds., *The Origins of Music* (pp. 271–91). Cambridge: MIT Press.

Brown, Steven, Björn Merker, and Nils J. Wallin. 2000. "An Introduction to Evolutionary Musicology." In Nils Wallin, Bjorn Merker, and Steven Brown, eds., *The Origins of Music* (pp. 3–21). Cambridge, MA: MIT Press.

Bruce, Steve. 1988. *The Rise and Fall of the Christian Right*. New York: Oxford University Press.

———. 1992. "Pluralism and religious vitality." In Steve Bruce, ed., *Religion and Modernization: Sociologists and Historians Debate the Secularization Thesis* (pp. 170–94). Oxford: Clarendon Press.

———. 1996. *Religion in the Modern World*. Oxford: Oxford University Press.

———. 1997. "The Pervasive World-View: Religion in Pre-Modern Britain." *British Journal of Sociology* 48: 667–80.

———. 1999. *Choice and Religion: A Critique of Rational Choice Theory*. Oxford: Oxford University Press.

Brunner, Edmund deS. 1927. *Village Communities*. New York: George H. Doran Company.

Bryce, James. 1891. *The American Commonwealth*. Volume 2. Toronto: Copp, Clark.

Bstan-'dzin-rgya, Mtsho, and J. Thupten 1996. *The Power of Compassion: A Collection of Lectures by His Holiness the XIV Dalai Lama*. Trans. Geshe Thupten Jinpa. New Delhi: Indus.

Bunch, Charlotte. 1993. "Prospects for Global Feminism." In Allison M. Jaggar and Paula S. Rothenberg, eds., *Feminist Frameworks* (pp. 249–52). 3rd ed. New York: McGraw-Hill.

Burawoy, Michael. 1991. *Ethnography Unbound: Power and Resistance in the Modern Metropolis*. Berkeley: University of California Press.

Burman, Rickie. 1986. "'She Looketh Well to the Ways of Her Household': The Changing Role of Jewish Women in Religious Life, 1880–1930." In Gail Malmgreen, ed., *Religion in the Lives of English Women, 1760–1930* (pp. 234–59). Bloomington: Indiana University Press.

Burns, Gene. 1990. "The Politics of Ideology: The Papal Struggle with Liberalism." *American Journal of Sociology* 95: 1123–52.

———. 1992. *The Frontiers of Catholicism: The Politics of Ideology in a Liberal World*. Berkeley: University of California Press.

Butler, Judith P. 1990. *Gender Trouble*. New York: Routledge.

Butts, R. Freeman, and Lawrence A. Cremin. 1958. *A History of Education in American Culture*. New York: Henry Holt and Company.

Calhoun, Craig. 1991. "Indirect Relationships and Imagined Communities: Large-scale Social Integration and the Transformation of Everyday Life." In Pierre Bourdieu and James S. Coleman, eds., *Social Theory for a Changing Society* (pp. 95–121). New York: Russell Sage.

Calhoun-Brown, Allison. 1996. "African American Churches and Political Mobilization: The Psychological Impact of Organizational Resources." *Journal of Politics* 58: 935–53.

Campbell, Marie, and Ann Manicom. 1995. *Knowledge, Experience, and Ruling Relations: Studies in the Social Organization of Knowledge*. Toronto: University of Toronto Press.

Candland, Christopher. 1992. *The Spirit of Violence: An Interdisciplinary Bibliography of Violence and Religion*. New York: Guggenheim Foundation.

Caplow, Theodore. 1998. "The Case of the Phantom Episcopalians." *American Sociological Review* 63: 112–13.

Carroll, Glenn, and Michael T. Hannan. 2000. *The Demography of Organizations*. Princeton, NJ: Princeton University Press.

Carroll, Michael. 1996. "Stark Realities: And the Androcentric/Eurocentric Bias in the Sociology of Religion." *Sociology of Religion* 57: 225–40.

Carter, Stephen L. 1993. *The Culture of Disbelief*. New York: Basic Books.

Casanova, Jose. 1994. *Public Religions in the Modern World*. Chicago: University of Chicago Press.

————. 2001. "Religion, the New Millennium and Globalization." *Sociology of Religion* 62: 415–41.

Castles, Francis G. 1994. "On Religion and Public Policy: Does Catholicism Make a Difference?" *European Journal of Political Research* 25: 19–40.

Cerulo, Karen A. 1997. "Identity Construction: New Issues, New Directions." *Annual Review of Sociology* 23: 385–409.

Cerulo, Karen A., J. M. Ruane, and M. Chayko. 1992. "Technological Ties that Bind: Media Generated Primary Groups." *Communication Research* 19: 109–29.

Chai, Karen. 1998. "Competing for the Second Generation: English-language Ministry in a Korean Protestant Church." In R. Stephen Warner and Judith G. Wittner, eds., *Gatherings in Diaspora: Religious Communities and the New Immigration* (pp. 295–331). Philadelphia: Temple University Press.

Chan, Sucheng. 1990. "European and Asian Immigration into the United States in Comparative Perspective, 1820s to 1920s." In *Immigration Reconsidered: History, Sociology, and Politics*. Ed. Yans-McLaughlin. New York: Oxford University Press.

Chang, Patricia M. Y. 1997. "Female Clergy in the Contemporary Protestant Church: A Current Assessment." *Journal for the Scientific Study of Religion* 36: 565–73.

————. 2001. "The Effecs of Organizational Variation in The Employment Relationship on Gender Discrimination in Denominational Labor Markets." In H. Z. Lopata and K. D. Henson, eds., *Unusual Occupations* (pp. 213–40). Stamford, CT: JAI Press.

Charlton, Joy. 1997. "Clergywomen of the Pioneer Generation: A Longitudinal Study." *Journal for the Scientific Study of Religion* 36: 599–613.

Chaves, Mark. 1989. "Secularization and Religious Revival: Evidence from U.S. Church Attendance Rates, 1972–1986." *Journal for the Scientific Study of Religion* 28: 464–77.

————. 1991. "Family Structure and Protestant Attendance: The Sociological Basis of Cohort and Age Effects." *Journal for the Scientific Study of Religion* 30: 501–14.

————. 1994. "Secularization as Declining Religious Authority." *Social Forces* 72: 749–74.

————. 1997. *Ordaining Women: Culture and Conflict in Religious Organizations*. Cambridge, MA: Harvard University Press.

————. 1999. "Religious Congregations and Welfare Reform: Who Will Take Advantage of 'Charitable Choice'?" *American Sociological Review* 64: 836–46.

Chaves Mark, and David McCann. 1992. "Regulation, Pluralism, and Religious Market Structure: Explaining Religion's Vitality." *Rationality and Society* 4: 272–90.

Chaves, Mark, and James C. Cavendish. 1994. "More Evidence on U.S. Catholic Church Attendance." *Journal for the Scientific Study of Religion* 33: 376–81.

Chaves, Mark, and Philip E. Gorski. 2001. "Religious Pluralism and Religious Participation." *Annual Review of Sociology* 27: 261–81.

Chidester, David. 1991. *Shots in the Streets: Violence and Religion in South Africa*. Boston: Beacon Press.

————. 1996. *Savage Systems: Colonialism and Comparative Religion in Southern Africa*. Charlottesville: University of Virginia.

Chiswick, Barry R., and Teresa A. Sullivan. 1995. "The New Immigrants." In Russell Farley, ed., *State of the Union: America in the 1990's /Social Trends* (pp. 211–70). Volume 2. New York: Russell Sage Foundation.

Chong, Kelly H. 1998. "What It Means to Be Christian: The Role of Religion in the Construction of Ethnic Identity and Boundary Among Second-Generation Korean Americans." *Sociology of Religion* 59: 259–86.

Christiano, Kevin. 2000. "Religion and Family in Modern American Culture." In Sharon Houseknecht and Jerry Pankhurst, eds., *Family, Religion, and Social Change in Diverse Societies* (pp. 43–78). New York: Oxford University Press.

Christiano, Kevin J. 1991. "The Church and the New Immigrants." In Helen Rose Ebaugh, ed., *Vatican II and U.S. Catholicism: Twenty-five Years Later*. Greenwich: JAI Press.

Clark, Mathew S. 1989. *What is Distinctive about Pentecostal Theology?* Pretoria: University of South Africa Press.

Cnaan, Ram A. 1997. *Social and Community Involvement of Religious Congregations Housed in Historic Religious Properties: Findings From a Six-City Study*. Philadelphia: University of Pennsylvania.

———. 1999. *The Newer Deal: Social Work and Religion in Partnership*. New York: Columbia University Press.

Cohen, Asher, and Bernard Susser. 2000. *Israel and the Politics of Jewish Identity*. Baltimore, MD: Johns Hopkins University Press.

Cohen, Cathy. 1999. *Boundaries of Blackness: AIDS and the Breakdown of Black Politics*. Chicago: University of Chicago Press.

Cohen, J. 1988. *Statistical power analysis for the behavioral sciences*. 2nd ed. Hillsdale, NJ: Erlbaum.

Cohen, Jean L., and Andrew Arato. 1992. *Civil Society and Political Theory*. Cambridge, MA: MIT Press.

Cohen, Steven M. 1983. *American Modernity and Jewish Identity*. New York: Tavistock.

———. 1988. *American Assimilation or Jewish Revival?* Bloomington: Indiana University Press.

———. 1991. *Content or Continuity? Alternative Bases for Commitment: The 1989 National Survey of American Jews*. New York: American Jewish Committee.

———. 1997. *Religious Stability and Ethnic Decline: Emerging Patterns of Jewish Identity in the United States*. Jerusalem: Hebrew University Melton Center for Jewish Education in the Diaspora.

Cohen, Steven M., and Arnold M. Eisen. 1998. *The Jew Within: Self, Family and Community in America*. Bloomington: Indiana University Press.

Cohen, Steven M., and Gabriel Horenczyk. 1999. *National Variations in Jewish Identity: Implications for Jewish Education*. Albany: State University of New York Press.

Cohen, Steven M., and Charles Liebman. 1987. *The Quality of American Jewish Life-Two Views*. New York: American Jewish Committee.

Cohen, S., and T. A. Wills. 1985. "Stress, Social Support, and the Buffering Hypothesis." *Psychological Bulletin* 98: 310–57.

Cohn, Norman. 1961. *Pursuit of the Millennium*. New York: Oxford University Press.

———. 1975. *Europe's Inner Demons*. New York: Basic.

———. 1993. *Cosmos, Chaos and the World to Come*. New Haven, CT: Yale University Press.

Coleman, James S. 1956. "Social Cleavage and Religious Conflict." *Journal of Social Issues* 12: 44–56.

Coleman, John A. 1991. *One Hundred Years of Catholic Social Thought: Celebration and Challenge*. Maryknoll, NY: Orbis.

Coleman, J. J. 1996. *Party Decline in America: Policy, Politics, and the Fiscal State*. Princeton, NJ: Princeton University Press.

Coleman, S. 2001. *The Globalization of Charismatic Christianity: Spreading the Gospel of Prosperity*. Cambridge: Cambridge University Press.

Collins, Patricia Hill. 1991. *Black Feminist Thought: Knowledge, Consciousness, and the Politics of Empowerment*. New York: Routledge.

———. 1992. "Dorothy Smith's Challenge to Sociological Theory." *Sociological Theory* 10: 73–80.

———. 1997. "Comment on Hekman's 'Truth and Method: Feminist Standpoint Theory Revisited': Where's the Power." *Signs* 22: 375–81.

Collins, Randall. 1992. "Women and the Production of Status Cultures." In Michele Lamont and Marcel Fournier, eds., *Cultivating Differences: Symbolic Boundaries and the Making of Inequality* (pp. 213–31). Chicago: University of Chicago Press.

———. 1993. "Emotional Energy as the Common Denominator of Rational Action." *Rationality and Society* 5: 203–30.

_____. 1998. *The Sociology of Philosophies: A Global Theory of Intellectual Change*. Cambridge, MA: Harvard University Press.

Comaroff, Jean. 1985. *Body of Power, Spirit of Resistance*. Chicago: University of Chicago Press.

Comaroff, John, and Jean L. Comaroff 1991. *Of Revelation and Revolution*. Chicago: University of Chicago Press.

Comstock, G. W., and J. A. Tonascia. 1977. "Education and Mortality in Washington County, Maryland." *Journal of Health and Social Behavior* 18: 54–61.

Comte, Auguste. 1830–1842/1969. *Cours de Philosophie Positive*. Brussels: Culture et Civilisation.

Converse, Philip E. 1974. "Some Priority Variables in Comparative Electoral Research." In Richard Rose, ed., *Electoral Behavior: A Comparative Handbook* (pp. 727–45). New York: Free Press.

Conzen, Kathleen Neils. 1991. "Mainstreams and Side Channels: The Localization of Immigrant Cultures." *Journal of American Ethnic History* Fall: 5–20.

Cook, David. 2000. "Iglesia Cristiana Evangelica: Arriving in the Pipeline." In Helen Ebaugh and J. S. Chafetz, eds. *Religion and the New Immigrants: Continuities and Adaptations in Immigrant Congregations* (pp. 171–92). Walnut Creek, CA: AltaMira Press.

Coontz, Stephanie. 1992. *The Way We Never Were: The American Family and the Nostalgia Trap*. New York: Basic Books.

Corbett, Michael, and Julia M. Corbett. 1999. *Politics and Religion in the United States*. New York: Garland.

Corten, A. 1997. "The Growth of the Literature of Afro-American, Latin American, and African Pentecostalism." *Journal of Contemporary Religion* 12: 311–24.

Cornwall, Marie. 1989. "The Determinants of Religious Behavior: A Theoretical Model and Empirical Test." *Social Forces* 68: 572–92.

Coser, Lewis. 1956. *The Functions of Social Conflict*. New York: Free Press.

Coser, Rose Laub. 1991. In *Defense of Modernity: Role Complexity and Individual Autonomy*. Stanford: Stanford University Press.

Coulton, G. G. 1938. *Medieval Panorama*. Cambridge: Cambridge University Press.

Cox, Harvey. 1995. *Fire From Heaven*. New York: Addison-Wesley.

Crapanzano, Vincent. 1981. "Rite of Return: Circumcision in Morocco." In Werner Muensterberger and L. Bryce Boyer, eds., *The Psychoanalytic Study of Society* (pp. 15–36). New York: International Universities Press.

Cubitt, Tessa, and Helen Greenslade. 1997. "Public and Private Spheres." In Elizabeth Dore, ed., *Gender Politics in Latin America: Debates in Theory and Practice* (pp. 52–64). New York: Monthly Review Press.

Culbertson, F. M. 1997. "Depression and Gender: An International Review." *American Psychologist* 52: 25–31.

Cushman, Philip. 1995. *Constructing the Self, Constructing America*. Reading, MA: Addison-Wesley.

Czikszentmihalyi, Mihaly. 1990. *Flow: The Psychology of Optimal Experience*. New York: Harper & Row.

Dalmia, Vasudha, and Heinrich von Stietencron, eds. 1995. *Reinventing Hinduism: The Construction of Religious Traditions and National Identity*. New Delhi: Sage.

Dalton, Russell J. 1988. *Citizen Politics in Western Democracies: Public Opinion and Political Parties in the United States, Great Britain, West Germany, and France*. Chatham, NJ: Chatham House Publishers.

_____. 1990. "Religion and Party Alignment." In Risto Sankiaho et al., eds., *People and their Polities* (pp. 66–88). Helsinki: Finnish Political Science Association.

D'Antonio, William. 1980. "Family and Religion: Exploring a Changing Relationship." *Journal for the Scientific Study of Religion* 19: 89–104.

Darnell, Alfred, and Darren E. Sherkat. 1997. "The Impact of Fundamentalism on Educational Attainment." *American Sociological Review* 62: 306–15.

Dashefsky, Arnold. 1972. "And the Search Goes On: The Meaning of Religio-ethnic Identity and Identification." *Sociological Analysis* 33: 239–45.

Dashefsky, Arnold, and Alyson Bacon. 1994. "The Meaning of Jewish Continuity in the North American Community: A Preliminary Empirical Assessment." *Agenda* 4: 22–8.

Dashefsky, Arnold, and Howard M. Shapiro. 1993/1974. *Ethnic Identification Among American Jews*. Lanham, MD: University Press of America.

Davidman, Lynn. 1990. "Accommodation and Resistance: A Comparison of Two Contemporary Orthodox Jewish Groups." *Sociological Analysis* 51: 35–51.

_____. 1991. *Tradition in a Rootless World: Women Turn to Orthodox Judaism.* Berkeley: University of California Press.

_____. 1994. "I Come Away Stronger: The Religious Impact of a Loosely Structured Jewish Feminist Group." In Robert Wuthnow, ed., *"I Come Away Stronger": How Small Groups are Shaping American Religion* (pp. 322–44). Grand Rapids, MI: William B. Eerdmans.

Davidman, Lynn, and Shelly Tenenbaum. 1994. "Toward a Feminist Sociology of American Jews." In Lynn Davidman and Shelly Tenebaum, eds., *Feminist Perspectives on Jewish Studies* (pp. 140–68). New Haven, CT: Yale University Press.

Davidson, James. 1994. "Religion Among America's Elite: Persistence and Change in the Protestant Establishment." *Sociology of Religion* 55: 419–40.

Davidson, James D., and Jerome R. Koch. 1998. "Beyond Mutual and Public Benefits." In N. J. Demerath, III, Peter Dobkin Hall, Terry Schmitt, and Rhys H. Williams, eds., *Sacred Companies: Organizational Aspects of Religion and Religious Aspects of Organizations* (pp. 292–306). New York: Oxford University Press.

Davidson, Powell D. 1985. *Mobilizing Social Movement Organizations.* Storrs, CT: Society for the Scientific Study of Religion.

Davie, Grace. 1994. *Religion in Britain Since 1945: Believing Without Belonging.* Oxford: Blackwell.

_____. 1999. "Europe: The Exception that Proves the Rule?" In Peter Berger, ed., *The Desecularization of the World. Resurgent Religion and World Politics* (pp. 65–83). Grand Rapids MI: Eerdmans.

_____. 2000. "The Sociology of Religion in Britain: A Hybrid Case." *Swiss Journal of Sociology* 26: 196–218.

Davis, James Allan, Tom W. Smith, and Peter V. Marsden. 1998. *General Social Surveys, 1972–1998: Cumulative Codebook.* Principal Investigator, James A. Davis; Director and Co-Principal Investigator, Tom W. Smith. Chicago: National Opinion Research Center.

Davis, Nancy J., and Robert V. Robinson. 1996. "Are the Rumors of War Exaggerated? Religious Orthodoxy and Moral Progressivism in America." *American Journal of Sociology* 102: 756–87.

de Tocqueville, Alexis. 1831/1969. *Democracy in America.* Volumes 1 and 2. Trans. George Lawrence. Ed. J. P. Mayer. Garden City, NY: Anchor Books.

De Vaus, David, and Ian McAllister. 1987. "Gender Differences in Religion." *American Sociological Review* 52: 472–81.

Deacon, Terrence. 1997. *The Symbolic Species: The Co-evolution of Language and the Brain.* New York: Norton.

Delumeau, Jean. 1977. *Catholicism Between Luther and Voltaire.* London: Burnes and Oates.

Demerath, N. J. 1965. *Social Class in American Protestantism.* Chicago: Rand-McNally.

_____. 1967. "Son of Sow's Ear." *Journal for the Scientific Study of Religion* 6: 275–77.

_____. 1996. "Who Now Debates Functionalism? From System, Change and Conflict to Culture, Choice and Praxis," *Sociological Forum* (June) 2: 333–45.

_____. 2001. *Crossing the Gods: World Religions and Worldly Politics.* Piscataway, NJ: Rutgers University Press.

Demerath, N. J., and Richard A. Peterson, eds. 1967. *System, Change and Conflict.* New York: Free Press.

Demerath, N. J., and Rhys Williams. 1990. "Religion and Power in the American Experience." In Thomas Robbins and Dick Anthony, eds., *In Gods We Trust: New Patterns of Religious Pluralism in America* (pp. 427–48). 2nd rev. ed. New Brunswick, NJ: Transaction Publishers.

_____. 1992. *A Bridging of Faiths.* Princeton, NJ: Princeton University Press.

Demmitt, Kevin P. 1992. "Loosening the Ties That Bind – The Accommodation of Dual-Earner Families in a Conservative Protestant Church." *Review of Religious Research* 34: 3–19.

Denny, Frederick. 1987. *Islam and the Muslim Community.* San Francisco: Harper & Row.

Despland, Michel. 1979. *La Religion en Occident: Evolution des Idées ed du Vécu.* Montreal: Fides.

Detwiler-Breidenbach, A. 2000. "Language, Gender and Context in an Immigrant Ministry: New Spaces for the Pastor's Wife." *Sociology of Religion* 61: 455–9.

DeVault, Marjorie. 1998. *Liberating Method: Feminism and Social Research.* Philadelphia: Temple University Press.

Díaz-Stevens, Ana María. 1993a. *Oxcart Catholicism on Fifth Avenue: The Impact of the Puerto Rican Migration upon the Archdiocese of New York*. South Bend, IN: Notre Dame University Press.

———. 1993b. "The Saving Grace: The Matriarchal Core of Latino Catholicism." *Latino Studies Journal* 4: 60–78.

———. 1994. "Latinas and the Church." In Jay P. Dolan and Allan Figuerosa Deck, eds., *Hispanic Catholic Culture in the U.S.: Issues and Concerns* (pp. 240–76). South Bend, IN: University of Notre Dame Press.

Díaz-Stevens, Ana María, and Anthony M. Stevens-Arroyo. 1998. *Recognizing the Latino Resurgence in U.S. Religion: The Emmaus Paradigm*. Boulder, CO: Westview Press.

Dillon, Michele. 1995. "Religion and Culture in Tension: The Abortion Discourses of the U.S. Catholic Bishops and the Southern Baptist Convention." *Religion and American Culture: A Journal of Interpretation* 5: 159–80.

———. 1999a. *Catholic Identity: Balancing Reason, Faith, and Power*. New York: Cambridge University Press.

———. 1999b. "The Authority of the Holy Revisited: Habermas, Religion, and Emancipatory Possibilities." *Sociological Theory* 17: 290–306.

———. 2001. "Pierre Bourdieu, Religion, and Cultural Production." *Cultural Studies: An Annual Review.* 1: 411–29.

Dillon, Michele, and Paul Wink. In press. "American Religion, Generativity, and the Therapeutic Culture." In Ed de St. Aubin, Dan McAdams, and T. Kim, eds., *The Generative Society*. Washington, DC: American Psychological Association Press.

DiMaggio, Paul J. 1988. "Interest and Agency in Institutional Theory." In Lynne Zucker, ed., *Institutional Patterns and Organizations: Culture and Environment* (pp. 3–22). Cambridge, MA: Ballinger Publishing Co.

———. 1991. "Constructing an Organizational Field as a Professional Project: U.S. Art Museums, 1920–1940." In Walter Powell and Paul DiMaggio, eds., *The New Institutionalism in Organizational Analysis* (pp. 267–92). Chicago: University of Chicago Press.

———. 1994. "Introduction." *Poetics* 22: L263–7.

———. 1997. "Culture and Cognition." *Annual Review of Sociology* 23: 263–87.

DiMaggio, Paul, John Evans, and Bethany Bryson. 1996. "Have Americans' Social Attitudes Become More Polarized?" *American Journal of Sociology* 102: 690–755.

Dissanayake, Ellen. 2000. "Antecedents of the Temporal Arts in Early Mother-Infant Interaction." In Nils Wallin, Bjorn Merker, and Steven Brown, eds., *The Origins of Music* (pp. 387–404). Cambridge, MA: MIT Press.

Dobbelaere, Karel. 1981. *Secularization: A Multi-Dimensional Approach*. Beverly Hills, CA: Sage.

———. 1987. "Some Trends in European Sociology of Religion: The Secularization Debate." *Sociological Analysis* 48: 107–37.

———. 1997. *Towards an Integrated Perspective of the Processes Related to the Descriptive Concept of Secularization: A Position Paper*. Paper read at the Annual Meeting of the Society for the Scientific Study of Religion, San Diego, CA.

Dobbelaere, Karel, and Wolfgang Jagodzinski. 1995. "Religious Cognitions and Beliefs." In Jan Van Deth and Elinor Scarbrough, eds., *The Impact of Values* (pp. 197–217). New York: Oxford University Press.

Dobriner, William, ed. 1958. *The Suburban Community*. New York: Putnam.

Dodson, Jualynne. 1996. "Women's Ministries in the African Methodist Episcopal Tradition." In Catherine Wessinger, ed., *Religious Institutions and Women's Leadership: New Roles Inside the Mainstream* (pp. 124–38). Columbia: University of South Carolina Press.

———. 2002. *Engendering Church*. Boulder, CO: Rowman and Littlefield.

Dodson, Jualynne, and Cheryl Gilkes. 1995. "There is Nothing Like Church Food." *Journal of the American Academy of Religion* 63: 519–38.

Dogan, Mattei. 1995. "Erosion of Class Voting and Religious Voting in Western Europe." *International Social Science Journal* 47: 525–38.

Dolan, Jay P. 1975. *The Immigrant Church: New York's Irish and German Catholics, 1815–1865*. Baltimore, MD: Johns Hopkins University Press.

———. 1985. *The American Catholic Experience: A History from Colonial Times to the Present*. Garden City, NY: Doubleday.

Dolan, Jay P., and Jaime Vidal. 1994. *Puerto Rican and Cuban Catholics in the U.S., 1900–1965*. Notre Dame, IN: University of Notre Dame Press.

Donegani, J. M. 1982. "The Political Cultures of French Catholicism." *West European Politics* 5: 73–86.

Douglas, Mary. 1966. *Purity and Danger: An Analysis of the Concepts of Pollution and Taboo*. London: Routledge & Kegan Paul.

———. 1983. "The Effects of Modernization on Religious Change." In Mary Douglas and Steven Tipton, eds., *Religion and America* (pp. 25–43). Boston: Beacon.

———. 1986. *How Institutions Think*. Syracuse: Syracuse University Press.

Drake, Clair. 1940. *Churches and Voluntary Associations in the Chicago Negro Community*. Chicago: Works Projects Administration District 3.

Dudley, Carl S., and Sally Johnson. 1991. "Congregational Self-images for Social Ministry." In Carl S. Dudley, Jackson W. Carroll, and Powell Wind, ed., *Carriers of Faith: Lessons From Congregational Studies*. Louisville, KY: Westminister-John Knox Press.

Duffy, Eamon. 1992. *Stripping of the Altars*. New Haven, CT: Yale University Press.

Dufour, Lynn. 2000. "Sifting Through Tradition: The Creation of Jewish Feminist Identities." *Journal for the Scientific Study of Religion* 39: 90–106.

Durkheim, Emile. 1893/1997. *The Division of Labor in Society*. New York: Free Press.

———. 1897/1951. *Suicide: A Study in Sociology*. Glencoe, IL: Free Press.

———. 1912/1976. *The Elementary Forms of the Religious Life*. London: Allen & Unwin.

Ebaugh, Helen Rose. 1993. "The Growth and Decline of Catholic Religious Orders of Women Worldwide: The Impact of Women's Opportunity Structures." *Journal for the Scientific Study of Religion* 32: 68–75.

Ebaugh, Helen Rose, and Janet Chafetz. 1999. "Agents for Cultural Reproduction and Structural Change: The Ironic Role of Women in Immigrant Institutions." *Social Forces* 78: 585–612.

Ebaugh, Helen Rose, and Janet Saltzman Chafetz. 2000a. *Religion and the New Immigrants: Continuities and Adaptations in Immigrant Congregations*. Walnut Creek, CA: AltaMira Press.

———. 2000b. "Structural Adaptations in Immigrant Congregations." *Sociology of Religion* 61: 135–53.

———. 2000c. "Dilemmas of Language in Immigrant Congregations: The Tie that Binds or the Tower of Babel?" *Review of Religious Research* 41: 432–52.

Ebaugh, Helen Rose, and Paula Pipes. 2001. "Immigrant Congregations as Social Services Providers: Are they Saftey Nets for Welfare Reform?" In Paula Nesbitt, ed., *Religion and Social Policy for the 21st Century* (pp. 95–110). Walnut Creek, CA: AltaMira Press.

Ebersole, Luke. 1960. "Religion and Politics." *Annals of the American Academy of Social and Political Sciences* 332: 101–11.

Echikson, William. 1990. *Lighting the Night: Revolution in Eastern Europe*. New York: William Morrow.

Eck, Diana. 1997. *On Common Ground: World Religions in America*. New York: Columbia University Press.

Eckstein, Susan. 1999. *Globalization and Mobilization: Civil Society Resistance to the New World Order*. Paper presented at the annual meeting of the American Sociological Association, Chicago.

Edwards, Bob, and Michael W. Foley. 2001. "Much Ado About Social Capital." *Contemporary Sociology* 30: 227–30.

Eiesland, Nancy L. 2000. *A Particular Place: Urban Restructuring and Religious Ecology in a Southern Exurb*. New Brunswick, NJ: Rutgers University Press.

Eisenga, Rob, Albert Felling, and Jan Lammers. 1994. "Religious Affiliation, Income Stratification, and Political Party Preference in the Netherlands, 1964 to 1992." *Netherlands Journal of Social Sciences* 30: 107–27.

Eisenstadt, S. N. 1970. In Philip Gillon, "What is a Jew?" *Jerusalem Post* (February 2), p. 7.

———. 1992. *Jewish Civilization – The Jewish Historical Experience in a Comparative Perspective*: Albany: State University of New York Press.

———. 1999. *Fundamentalism, Sectarianism, and Revolution: The Jacobin Dimension of Modernity*. Cambridge: Cambridge University Press.

Eister, A. W. 1967. "Toward a Radical Critique of Church-Sect Typologizing." *Journal for the Scientific Study of Religion* 6: 85–90.

Elazar, Daniel J. 1999. "Jewish Religious, Ethnic and National Identities: Convergence and Conflicts." In Steven M. Cohen, ed., *National Variations in Jewish Identity* (pp. 35–52). Albany: State University of New York Press.

Elazar, Daniel J., and Rela Mintz Geffen. 2000. *The Conservative Movement in Judaism: Dilemmas and Opportunities*. New York: State University of New York Press.

Elias, M., and J. Blanten. 1987. "Dimensions of Ethnic Identity in Israeli Jewish Families Living in the United States." *Psychological Reports* 60: 366–87.

Eliasoph, Nina. 1998. *Avoiding Politics: How Americans Produce Apathy in Everyday Life*. New York: Cambridge University Press.

Eller, Cynthia. 1993. *Living in the Lap of the Goddess: The Feminist Spirituality Movement in America*. New York: Crossroad.

Ellis, John Tracy. 1962. *Documents of American Catholic History*. 2nd ed. Milwaukee: Bruce.

Ellison, Christopher, and Jeffrey Levin. 1998. "The Religion-Health Connection: Evidence, Theory, and Future Directions." *Health Education and Behavior* 25: 700–20.

Ellison, Christopher, and Darren Sherkat. 1995. "The Semi-Involuntary Institution Revisited: Regional Variations in Church Participation Among Black Americans." *Social Forces* 73: 1415–37.

Ellwood, Robert S. 1997. *The Fifties Spiritual Marketplace: American Religion in a Decade of Conflict*. New Brunswick, NJ: Rutgers University Press.

El-Or, Tamar. 1992. *Educated and Ignorant: On Ultra-Orthodox Women and Their World*. Tel Aviv: Am Oved Publishers.

Elster, Jon. 1983. *Sour Grapes: Studies in the Subversion of Rationality*. Cambridge: Cambridge University Press.

Emirbayer, Mustafa, and Ann Mische. 1998. "What is Agency?" *American Journal of Sociology* 103: 962–1023.

Engelman, U. Z. 1928. "Intermarriage Among Jews in Switzerland." *American Journal of Sociology* 34: 516–23.

Engels, Frederick. 1850/1964. "The Peasant War in Germany." In Reinhold Niebuhr, ed., *Karl Marx and Frederick Engels on Religion* (pp. 97–118). New York: Schocken.

Epstein, Barbara. 1991. *Political Process and Cultural Revolution*. Berkeley: University of California Press.

Erikson, Erik H. 1963. *Childhood and Society*. 2nd ed. New York: Norton.

———. 1964. *Insight and Responsibility*. New York: Norton.

———. 1968. "The Development of Ritualization." In Donald R. Cutler, ed., *The Religious Situation* (pp. 711–33). Boston: Beacon Press.

Erikson, Erik H., Joan Erikson, and Helen Kivnick. 1986. *Vital Involvement in Old Age*. New York: Norton.

Erikson, Kai. 1966. *Wayward Puritans*. New York: Wiley.

Erickson, Victoria. 1993. *Where Silence Speaks: Feminism Social Theory and Religion*. Minneapolis: Fortress.

Esherick, Joseph W. 1987. *The Origins of the Boxer Uprising*. Berkeley: University of California Press.

Espín, Oliva M. 1995. "Cultural and Historical Influences on Sexuality in Hispanic/Latin Women: Implications for Psychotherapy." In Mary L. Andersen and Patricia Hill Collins, eds., *Race, Class, and Gender* (pp. 423–8). Belmont, CA: Wadsworth.

Esping-Andersen, Gosta. 1990. *The Three Worlds of Welfare Capitalism*. Princeton, NJ: Princeton University Press.

Etzioni, Amitai. 1996. *The New Golden Rule: Community and Morality in a Democratic Society*. New York: Basic Books.

Etzioni-Halvey, Eva. 2000. *The Divided People*. Kefar Sava, Israel: Aryeh Nit Publications.

Evans, Sara M., and Harry C. Boyte. 1986. *Free Spaces: The Sources of Democratic Change in America*. New York: Harper & Row.

Ewick, Patricia, and Susan S. Silbey. 1995. "Subversive Stories and Hegemonic Tales: Toward a Sociology of Narrative." *Law and Society Review* 29: 197–226.

Farber, Roberta Rosenberg, and Chaim I. Waxman, eds. 1999. *Jews in America: A Contemporary Reader*. Waltham, MA: Brandeis University Press.

Farnell, R. 1994. *Broad-Based Organising: An Evaluation for the Church Urban Fund*. Coventry, UK: Coventry University Center for Local Economic Development.

Farnsley, Arthur E., N. J. Demerath, Etan Diamond, Mary Mapes, and Elfriede Wedam. Forthcoming. *Sacred Circles and Public Squares: The Multi-Centering of Religion in Indianapolis and the Nation.* Bloomington: Indiana University Press.

Farrar-Halls, Gill. 1998. *The World of the Dalai Lama: An Inside Look at His Life, His People, and His Vision.* London: Thorsons.

Fenton, John Y. 1988. *Transplanting Religious Traditions: Asian Indians in America.* New York: Praeger.

Fernandez, Eleazar S. 1994. *Toward a Theology of Struggle.* Maryknoll, NY: Orbis Books.

Ferraro, Kenneth, and Jessica Kelley Moore. 2000. "Religious Consolation Among Men and Women: Do Health Problems Spur Seeking?" *Journal for the Scientific Study of Religion* 39: 220–34.

Fields, Karen. 1985. *Revival and Rebellion in Colonial Central Africa: Revisions to the Theory of Indirect Rule.* Princeton, NJ: Princeton University Press.

Fields, Rick. 1992. *How the Swans Came to the Lake: A Narrative History of Buddhism in America.* Boston: Shambhala.

Fine, Gary Alan. 1987. *With the Boys.* Chicago: University of Chicago Press.

Finke, Roger. 1992 "An Unsecular America." In Steve Bruce, ed., *Religion and Modernization: Sociologists and Historians Debate the Secularization Thesis,* (pp. 145–69). Oxford: Clarendon Press.

Finke, Roger, and Rodney Stark. 1988. "Religious Economies and Sacred Canopies: Religious Mobilization in American Cities, 1906." *American Sociological Review* 53: 41–9.

———. 1992. *The Churching of America, 1776–1990: Winners and Losers in Our Religious Economy.* New Brunswick, NJ: Rutgers University Press.

———. 1998. "Religious Choice and Competition," *American Sociological Review* 63: 761–6.

Finke, Roger, Avery M. Guest, and Rodney Stark. 1996. "Pluralism and Religious Participation: New York, 1855–1865." *American Sociological Review* 61: 203–18.

Finlay, Barbara. 1996. "Do Men and Women have Different Goals for the Ministry? Evidence from Seminarians." *Sociology of Religion* 57: 311–18.

Finney, C. G. 1979. *Reflections on Revival.* Minneapolis: Bethany Fellowship.

Fishburn, Janet. 1991. *Confronting the Idolatry of Family: A New Vision of the Household of God.* Nashville, TN: Abingdon Press.

Fishman, Sylvia Barack. 2000. *Jewish Life and American Culture.* Albany: State University of New York Press.

Fiske, Susan T., and Shelley E. Taylor. 1991. *Social Cognition.* 2nd ed. New York: McGraw-Hill.

Fitzgerald, Timothy. 1997. "A Critique of 'Religion' as a Cross-Cultural Category." *Method & Theory in the Study of Religion* 9: 91–110.

Fix, Michael, and Jefferey S. Passel. 1994. *Immigration and Immigrants: Setting the Record Straight.* Washington, DC: The Urban Institute.

Flores, Richard R. 1994. "Para el Niño Dios: Sociability and Commemorative Sentiment in Popular Religious Practice." In Anthony M. Stevens Arroyo and Ana Maria Diaz-Stevens, eds., *An Enduring Flame.* New York: Bildner Center for Western Hemispheric Studies.

Foltz, Tanice. 2000. "Thriving, Not Simply Surviving: Goddess Spirituality and Women's Recovery from Alcoholism." In Wendy Griffin, ed., *Daughters of the Goddess: Studies in Healing, Identity, and Empowerment* (pp. 119–35). Walnut Creek, CA: AltaMira Press.

Fortner, B. V., and R. A. Neimeyer. 1999. "Death Anxiety in Older Adults: A Quantitative Review." *Death Studies* 23: 387–411.

Fowler, James. 1981. *Stages of Faith.* New York: Harper & Row.

Francis, Leslie, and Carolyn Wilcox. 1998. "Religiosity and Femininity: Do Women Really Hold a More Positive Attitude." *Journal for the Scientific Study of Religion* 37: 462–9.

Frank, Blanche. 1975. *The American Orthodox Jewish Housewife: A Generation Study in Ethnic Survival.* Unpublished Ph.D. dissertation, City University of New York.

Frank, Robert H. 1993. "The Strategic Role of Emotions: Reconciling Over and Undersocialized Accounts of Behavior." *Rationality and Society* 5: 160–84.

Frankl, Rozelle. 1987. *Televangelism.* Carbondale: Southern Illinois University Press.

Franklin, Mark, Thomas Mackie, and Henry Valen, eds. 1992. *Electoral Change.* New York: Cambridge University Press.

Frazier, E. Franklin. 1963/1974. *The Negro Church in America.* New York: Schocken Books.

Freedman, Samuel G. 2000. *Jew vs. Jew: The Struggle for the Soul of American Jewry.* New York: Simon and Schuster.

Freeman, Walter. 2000. "A Neurobiological Role of Music in Social Bonding." In Nils Wallin, Björn Merker, and Steven Brown, eds., *The Origins of Music* (pp. 411–22). Cambridge, MA: MIT Press.

Freire, Paolo. 1970. *Pedagogy of the Oppressed*. New York: Herder and Herder.

Frend, W. H. C. 1967. *Martyrdom and Persecution in the Early Church*. Garden City, NY: Doubleday.

Freston, P. 2001. *Evangelicals and Politics in Asia, Africa and Latin America*. Cambridge: Cambridge University Press.

Freud, Sigmund. 1928/1985. *Civilization, Society, and Religion*. London: Pelican.

Friedland, Roger, and Robert Alford. 1991. "Bringing Society Back In: Symbols, Practices, and Institutional Contradictions." In Walter Powell and Paul DiMaggio, eds., *The New Institutionalism in Organizational Analysis* (pp. 232–66). Chicago: University of Chicago Press.

Friedland, Roger, and Richard Hecht. 1996. *To Rule Jerusalem*. Cambridge: Cambridge University Press.

Frimer, Aryeh A., and Dov I. Frimer. 1998. "Women's Prayer Services – Theory and Practice." *Tradition* 32: 5–118.

Fukuyama, Francis. 1995. *Trust: The Social Virtues and the Creation of Prosperity*. New York: Free Press.

Furstenberg, Frank. 1999. "Family Change and Family Diversity." In Neil Smelser and Jeffrey Alexander, eds., *Diversity and its Discontents: Cultural Conflict and Common Ground in Contemporary American Society* (pp. 147–66). Princeton, NJ: Princeton University Press.

Gallagher, Michael. 1985. *Political Parties in the Republic of Ireland*. Manchester: Manchester University Press.

Gallagher, Michael, Michael Laver, and Peter Mair. 1995. *Representative Government in Modern Europe*. New York: McGraw-Hill.

Gallup, George, Jr., and D. Michael Lindsay. 1999. *Surveying the Religious Landscape: Trends in U.S. Beliefs*. Harrisburg, PA: Morehouse.

Gamm, Gerald. 1986. *The Making of the New Deal Democrats*. Chicago: University of Chicago Press.

Gamson, William A. 1992. *Talking politics*. New York: Cambridge University Press.

_____. 1995. "Constructing Social Protest." In Hank Johnston and Bert Klandermans, eds., *Social Movements and Culture* (pp. 85–106). Minneapolis: University of Minnesota Press.

Ganz, Marshall. 2000. "Resources and Resourcefulness: Strategic Capacity in the Unionization of California Agriculture, 1959–1966." *American Journal of Sociology* 105: 1003–63.

Garcia, Alma M., ed. 1989. "The Development of Chicana Feminist Discourse, 1970–1980." *Gender and Society* 3: 217–38.

_____. 1997. *Chicana Feminist Thought*. New York: Routledge.

Garcia, María Cristina. 1996. *Havana USA: Cuban Exiles and Cuban Americans in South Florida, 1959–1994*. Berkeley: University of California Press.

Garfinkel, Harold. 1967. *Studies in Ethnomethodology*. Englewood Cliffs, NJ: Prentice Hall.

Gartner, J. 1996. "Religious Commitment, Mental Health, and Prosocial Behavior: A Review of the Empirical Literature." In E. Shafranske, ed., *Religion and the Clinical Practice of Psychology* (pp. 187–214). Washington, DC: American Psychological Association.

Gaustad, Edwin Scott. 1973. *Dissent in American Religion*. Chicago: University of Chicago Press.

Geertz, Clifford. 1973. *The Interpretation of Cultures*. New York: Basic Books.

Geismar, L. 1954. "A Scale for the Measurement of Ethnic Identification." *Jewish Social Studies* 16: 33–60.

Genia, Vicky. 1997. "The Spiritual Experience Index." *Review of Religious Research* 38: 344–61.

George, Linda, David Larson, Harold Koenig, and Michael McCullough. 2000. "Spirituality and Health: What We Know, What We Need to Know." *Journal of Social and Clinical Psychology* 19: 102–16.

George, Sheba. 1998. "Caroling with the Keralities: The Negotiation of Gendered Space in an Indian Immigrant Church." In R. Stephen Warner and Judith G. Wittner, eds., *Gatherings in Diaspora: Religious Communities and the New Immigration* (pp. 265–294). Philadelphia: Temple University Press.

Gerami, Shahin, and Melodye Lehnerer. 2001. "Women's Agency and Household Diplomacy: Negotiating Fundamentalism." *Gender and Society* 15: 556–73.

Giddens, Anthony. 1971. *Capitalism and Modern Social Theory*. Cambridge, UK: Cambridge University Press.

———. 1991. *Modernity and Self-Identity: Self and Society in the Late Modern Age*. Stanford, CA: Stanford University Press.

Gieryn, Thomas N. 1999. *Cultural boundaries of science: Credibility on the line*. Chicago: University of Chicago Press.

Gilbert, Christopher P. 1993. *The Impact of Churches on Political Behavior: An Empirical Study*. Westport, CT: Greenwood Publishers.

Gilkes, Cheryl Townsend. 1996. "'Go Tell Mary and Martha': The Spirituals, Biblical Options for Women, and Cultural Tensions in the African American Religious Experience." *Social Compass* 43: 563–81.

———. 1998. "Plenty Good Room: Adaptation in a Changing Black Church." *Annals of the American Academy of Political and Social Science* 558: 101–21.

———. 2000. "*If It Wasn't for the Women...*": Black Women's Experience and Womanist Culture in Church and Community. Maryknoll, NY: Orbis Books.

Gill, Anthony J. 1998. *Rendering Unto Caesar: The Roman Catholic Church and the State in Latin America*. Chicago: University of Chicago Press.

———. 1999. "The Struggle to be Soul Provider: Catholic Responses to Protestant Growth in Latin America." In Christian Smith and Joshua Prokopy, eds., *Latin American Religion in Motion* (pp. 17–42). New York: Routledge Press.

Ginsburg, Faye. 1993. "Saving America's Souls: Operation Rescue's Crusade Against Abortion." In Martin Marty and Scott Appleby, eds., *Fundamentalisms and the State* (pp. 557–88). Chicago: University of Chicago Press.

———. 1998. *Contested Lives: The Abortion Debate in an American Community*. Berkeley: University of California Press.

Girard, René. 1977. *Violence and the Sacred*. Baltimore, MD: Johns Hopkins University Press.

———. 1986. *The Scapegoat*. Baltimore, MD: Johns Hopkins University Press.

Gitlin, Todd. 1995. *The Twilight of Common Dreams*. New York: Metropolitan Books.

Gittell, Ross, and Avis Vidal. 1998. *Community Organizing: Building Social Capital as a Development Strategy*. Thousand Oaks, CA: Sage.

Glass, Jennifer, Vern L. Bengtson, and Charlotte Chorn Dunham. 1986. "Attitude Similarity in Three-Generation Families: Socialization, Status Inheritance, or Reciprocal Influence?" *American Sociological Review* 51: 685–98.

Glazer, Nathan. 1957/1989. *American Judaism*. 2nd rev. ed. Chicago: University of Chicago Press.

Glazer, Nathan, and Daniel P. Moynihan. 1963. *Beyond the Melting Pot*. Cambridge, MA: MIT Press and Harvard University Press.

Glendon, Mary Ann, ed. 1995. *Seedbeds of Virtue: Sources of Competence, Character, and Citizenship in American Society*. Lanham, MD: Madison Books.

Glenn, John K. 2001. *Framing Democracy: Civil Society and Civic Movements in Eastern Europe*. Stanford, CA: Stanford University Press.

Glick-Schiller, Nina. 1999. "Transmigrants and Nation-States: Something Old and Something New in the U. S. Immigrant Experience." In C. Hirshman, P. Kasinitz, and J. DeWind, eds., *The Handbook of International Migration: The American Experience* (pp. 94–119). New York: Russell Sage Foundation.

Glock, Charles. 1993. "The Churches and Social Change in Twentieth-Century America." *The Annals of the American Academy of Political and Social Science* 527: 67–83.

Glock, Charles Y., and Rodney Stark. 1965. *Religion and Society in Transition*. Chicago: Rand McNally.

Godin, H. and Daniel, Y. 1943. *La France, Pays de Mission*. Paris: Cerf.

Goette, Robert D. 1993. "The Transformation of a First Generation Church into a Bilingual Second Generation Church." In H.Y. Kwon and S. Kim, eds., *The Emerging Generation of Korean-Americans*. Kyung Hu University Press.

Goffman, Erving. 1959. *Presentation of Self in Everyday Life*. New York: Doubleday.

———. 1967. *Interaction Ritual: Essays on Face-to-Face Behavior*. New York: Doubleday.

Goggin, Malcolm L., ed. 1993. *Understanding the New Politics of Abortion*. Los Angeles: Sage Publications.

Goldbourt, U., S. Yaari, and J. H. Medalie. 1993. "Factors Predictive of Long-term Coronary Heart Disease Mortality Among 10,059 Male Israeli Civil Servants and Municipal Employees." *Cardiology* 82: 100–121.

Goldman, Ari L. 1991 "Religion Notes." *New York Times*, 15 June, p. A10.

Goldman, Marion S. 2000. *Passionate Journeys: Why Successful Women Joined a Cult.* Ann Arbor: University of Michigan Press.

Goldman, Marion S., and Lynne Isaacson. 1999. "Enduring Affiliation and Gender Doctrine for Shiloh Sisters and Rajneesh Sannyasins." *Journal for the Scientific Study of Religion* 38: 411–22.

Goldman, N., S. Korenman, and R. Weinstein. 1995. "Marital status and health among elderly." *Social Science and Medicine* 40: 1717–30.

Goldring, Luin. 1996. "Blurring Borders: Constructing Transnational Community in the Process of U.S.-Mexico Migration." *Research in Community Sociology* 6: 69–104.

Goldscheider, Calvin. 1986. *The American Jewish Community: Social Science Research and Policy Implications.* Atlanta: Scholars Press.

Goldscheider, Calvin, and William D. Mosher. 1991. "Patterns of Contraceptive Use in the United States: The Importance of Religious Factors." *Studies in Family Planning* 22: 102–15.

Goldstein, Alice. 1994. "Grounds for Cautious Optimism: A Response to Lipset's Remarks." *Contemporary Jewry* 15: 182–6.

Goldstein, Sidney. 1996. *Jews on the Move: Implications for Jewish Identity.* Albany: State University of New York Press.

Goldstein, Sidney, and Calvin Goldscheider. 1968. *Jewish Americans: Three Generations in a Jewish Community.* Englewood Cliffs, NJ: Prentice Hall.

Goldstein, Sidney and Alice Goldstein. 1996. *Jews on the Move: Implications for Jewish Identity.* New York: State University of New York Press.

Goldstone, Jack. 1991. *Revolution and Rebellion in the Early Modern World.* Berkeley: University of California Press.

———. 2001. "Toward a Fourth Generation of Revolutionary Theory." *Annual Review of Political Science* 4: 139–187.

Goode, E. 1967a. "Some Critical Observations on the Church-Sect Dimension." *Journal for the Scientific Study of Religion* 6: 69–84.

———. 1967b. "Further Reflections on the Church-Sect Dimension." *Journal for the Scientific Study of Religion* 6: 270–5.

Gopin, Marc. 2000. *Between Eden and Armageddon.* Oxford: Oxford University Press.

Gordon, Milton M. 1964. *Assimilation in American Life.* New York: Oxford University Press.

Gorski, Philip. 2000. "Historicizing the Secularization Debate: Church, State and Society in Late Medieval and Early Modern Europe, ca. 1300 to 1700." *American Sociological Review* 65: 138–167.

Gorski, Philip, and F. Wilson. 1998. "The Problem of Unbelief in the Nineteenth Century: Religious Pluralism and Religious Vitality in the Netherlands, 1800–1996." Paper presented to the annual meeting of the Social Science History Association. Chicago, IL.

Gove, Walter. 1994. "Why We Do What We Do: A Biopsychosocial Theory of Human Motivation." *Social Forces* 73: 363–94.

Gramsci, Antonio. 1957/1968. *The Modern Prince, and Other Writings.* New York: International Publishers.

Granovetter, Mark. 1973. "The Strength of Weak Ties." *American Journal of Sociology* 78: 1360–80.

Greeley, Andrew M. 1985. *American Catholics Since the Council: An Unauthorized Report.* Chicago: Thomas More.

———. 1989. *Religious Change in America.* Cambridge, MA: Harvard University Press.

———. 1991. "American Exceptionalism: The Religious Phenomenon." Pages 94–115 in Byron E. Shafer, ed., *Is America Different?* New York: Oxford University Press.

———. 1996. "The New American Paradigm: A Modest Critique." Paper presented at the German Sociological Association annual meeting, Köln.

Greeley, Andrew M., and Michael Hout. 1988. "Musical Chairs: Patterns of Denominational Change in the United States, 1947–1986." *Sociology and Social Research* 72: 75–86.

———. 1999. "Americans' Increasing Belief in Life After Death." *American Sociological Review* 64: 813–35

Green, John C., James L. Guth, and Clyde Wilcox. 1998. "Less Than Conquerors: the Christian Right in State Republican Parties." In Anne Costain and Andrew McFarland, eds., *Social Movements and American Political Institutions* (pp. 117–35). Lanham, MD: Rowman and Littlefield.

Green, John C., James L. Guth, Corwin E. Smidt, and Lyman A. Kellstedt. 1995. "Evangelical Realignment: The Political Power of the Christian Right." *Christian Century* 112: 676–79.

———. 1996. *Religion and the Culture Wars: Dispatches from the Front.* Lanham, MD: Rowman and Littlefield.

Green, Victor. 1975. *For God and country: The Rise of Polish and Lithuanian Ethnic Consciousness in America, 1860–1910.* Madison: State Historical Society of Wisconsin.

Greenberg, Blu. 1981. *On Women and Judaism: A View from Tradition.* Philadelphia: The Jewish Publication Society of America.

Greenwood, Royston, and C. R. Hinings. 1996. "Understanding Radical Organizational Change: Bringing Together the Old and the New Institutionalism." *Academy of Management Review* 21: 1022–45.

Gregory, Timothy E. 1979. *Vox Populi: Popular Opinion and Violence in the Religious Controversies of the Fifth Century A.D.* Columbus: Ohio State University Press.

Greider, William. 1992. *Who Will Tell the People? The Betrayal of American Democracy.* New York: Simon & Schuster.

Griffin, C. S. 1960. *Their Brothers' Keepers: Moral Stewardship in the United States, 1800–1865.* New Brunswick, NJ: Rutgers University Press.

———. 1999. "The Abolitionists and the Benevolent Societies, 1831–1861." In J. R. McKivigan, ed., *History of the American Abolitionist Movement: A Bibliography of Scholarly Articles* (pp. 101–22). Indianapolis: Garland.

Griffith, R. Marie. 1997. *God's Daughters: Evangelical Women and the Power of Submission.* Berkeley: University of California Press.

——— ed. 2000. *Daughters of the Goddess.* Walnut Creek, CA: AltaMira Press.

Guest, Avery, and Barrett A. Lee. 1987. "Metropolitan Residential Environments and Church Organizational Activities." *Sociological Analysis* 47: 335–54.

Guinness, Oz. 1993. *The American Hour.* New York: Free Press.

Gupta, Dipankar. 2000. *Culture, Space and the Nation State.* Delhi: Sage Publishers.

Gutierrez, David. 1997. "Transnationalism and Ethnic Americans: A Case Study in Recent History." Paper presented, Immigrants, Civic Culture, and Modes of Political Incorporation: A Contemporary and Historical Comparison, Santa Fe, NM.

Gutiérrez, Gustavo. 1973. *A Theology of Liberation: History, Politics, and Salvation.* Maryknoll: NY: Orbis Books.

Habermas, Jurgen. 1984. *The Theory of Communicative Action: Reason and the Rationalization of Society.* Volume 1. Boston: Beacon Press.

———. 1987. *The Theory of Communicative Action: Lifeworld and System.* Volume 2. Boston: Beacon Press.

———. 1989. *The Structural Transformation of the Public Sphere.* London: Polity.

Hackett, Rosalind, Mark Silk, and Dennis Hoover, eds. 2000. *Religious Persecution as a U.S. Policy Issue.* Hartford, CT: Center for the Study of Religion in Public Life, Trinity College.

Hadaway, C. Kirk, and Penny Long Marler. 1997a. "The Measurement and Meaning of Religious Involvement in Great Britain." Paper presented at the annual meeting of the International Society for the Sociology of Religion, Toulouse, France.

———. 1997b. "Do Canadians Over-report Church Membership and Attendance? A Case Study of Religion in a Canadian County." Paper presented at the annual meeting of the Association for the Sociology of Religion, Toronto, Canada.

Hadaway, C. Kirk, Penny Long Marler, and Mark Chaves. 1993. "What the Polls Don't Show: A Closer Look at U.S. Church Attendance." *American Sociological Review* 58: 741–52.

———. 1998. "Overreporting Church Attendance in America: Evidence that Demands the Same Verdict." *American Sociological Review* 63: 122–30.

Haddad, Yvonne Yazbeck, and Adair T. Lummis. 1987. *Islamic Values in the United States: A Comparative Study.* New York: Oxford University Press.

Hadden, Jeffrey K. 1969. *The Gathering Storm in the Churches.* Garden City, NY: Doubleday.

———. 1987. "Toward Desacralizing Secularization Theory." *Social Forces* 65: 587–611.

Hagestad, Gunhild O. 1982. "Parent and Child: Generations in the Family." In T. M. Field, A. Huston, H. C. Quay, and G. E. Finley, eds. *Review of Human Development* (pp. 485–99). New York: Wiley.

Hall, David D., ed. 1997. *Lived Religion in America.* Princeton, NJ: Princeton University Press.

Hall, John A., ed., 1995. *Civil Society: Theory, History, Comparison*. Cambridge, UK: Cambridge University Press.

Hall, John R. 1978. *The Ways Out: Utopian Communal Groups in an Age of Babylon*. London: Routledge and Kegan Paul.

———. 1987. *Gone From the Promised Land: Jonestown in American Cultural History*. New Brunswick, NJ: Transaction Books.

———. 1988. "Jonestown and Bishop Hill: Continuities and Disjunctures in Religious Conflict." *Communal Studies* 8: 77–89.

———. 1999. *Cultures of Inquiry: From Epistemology to Discourse in Sociohistorical Inquiry*. Cambridge: Cambridge University Press.

———. 2000. "Cultural Meanings and Cultural Structures in Historical Explanation." *History and Theory* 39: 331–47.

Hall, John R., Philip D. Schuyler, and Sylvaine Trinh. 2000. *Apocalypse Observed: Religious Movements and Violence in North America, Europe, and Japan*. London: Routledge.

Hall, Peter D. 1999. "Vital Signs: Organizational Population Trends and Civic Engagement in New Haven, Connecticut, 1850–1998." In Theda Skocpol and Morris P. Fiorina, eds., *Civic Engagement in American Democracy* (pp. 211–48). Washington, DC, and New York: Brookings Institution Press and Russell Sage Foundation.

Hall, Stuart. 1996. "Introduction: Who Needs Identity?" In S. Hall and P. DuGay, eds. *Questions of Cultural Identity* (pp. 1–17). Thousand Oaks, CA: Sage.

Hamberg, Eva M., and Thorleif Pettersson. 1994. "The Religious Market: Denominational Competition and Religious Participation in Contemporary Sweden." *Journal for the Scientific Study of Religion* 33: 205–16.

———. 1997. "Short-term Changes in Religious Supply and Church Attendance in Contemporary Sweden." *Research on the Social Scientific Study of Religion* 8: 35–51.

Hamerton-Kelly, Robert G., ed. 1987. *Violent Origins: Walter Burkert, René Girard, and Jonathan V. Smith on Ritual Killing and Cultural Formation*. Stanford, CA: Stanford University Press.

Hamm, Thomas D. 1988. *The Transformation of American Quakerism: Orthodox Friends, 1800–1907*. Bloomington: Indiana University Press.

Hammond, Phillip E. 1988. "Religion and the Persistence of Identity." *Journal for the Scientific Study of Religion* 27: 1–11.

Hanley D., ed. 1994. *Christian Democracy in Europe: A Comparative Perspective*. New York: St. Martin's Press.

Hanson, Sharon. 1997. "The Secularization Thesis: Talking at Cross Purposes." *Journal of Contemporary Religion* 12: 159–79.

Harding, Sandra. 1986. *The Science Question in Feminism*. Ithaca, NY: Cornell University Press.

Hardy-Fanta, Carol. 1993. *Latina Politics, Latino Politics: Gender, Culture, and Political Participation in Boston*. Philadelphia: Temple University Press.

Harlow, Robert, and Nancy Cantor. 1996. "Still Participating After all these Years: A Study of Life Task Participation in Later Life." *Journal of Personality and Social Psychology* 71: 1235–49.

Harris, Frederick. 1999. *Something Within: Religion in African-American Political Activism*. New York: Oxford University Press.

Harris, Fredrick C. 1994. "Something Within: Religion as a Mobilizer of African-American Political Activism." *Journal of Politics* 56: 42–68.

Harrison, Michael, and Bernard Lazerwitz. 1982. "Do Denominations Matter?" *American Journal of Sociology* 88: 356–77.

Harrison, P. M. 1959. *Authority and Power in the Free Church Tradition*. Princeton, NJ: Princeton University Press.

Harrison, Peter. 1990. *"Religion" and the Religions in the English Enlightenment*. Cambridge, UK: Cambridge University Press.

Hart, Stephen. 1992. *What Does the Lord Require?* New York: Oxford University Press.

———. 2001. *Cultural Dilemmas of Progressive Politics: Styles of Engagement among Grassroots Activists*. Chicago: University of Chicago Press.

Hartman, Moshe, and Harriet Hartman. 1996. *Gender Equality and American Jews*. Albany: State University of New York Press.

Hartsock, Nancy. 1983. "The Feminist Standpoint: Developing the Ground for a Specifically Feminist Historical Materialism." In Sandra Harding and Merrill Hintikka, eds., *Discovering*

Reality: Feminist Perspectives on Epistemology, Metaphysics, Methodology, and the Philosophy of Science (pp. 283–310). Dordrecht: Reidel.

Heath, Anthony, Bridget Taylor, and Gabor Toka. 1993. "Religion, Morality, and Politics." In Roger Jowell, Lindsay Brooki, and Lizanne Dowds, eds. *International Social Attitudes: The Tenth BSA Report* (pp. 49–80). Aldershot, UK: Dartmouth.

Heckathorn, Douglas D. 1993. "Collective Action and Group Heterogeneity: Voluntary Provision Versus Selective Incentives." *American Sociological Review* 58: 329–50.

Heelas, Paul. 1996. *The New Age: Religion, Culture and Society in the Age of Posmodernity*. Oxford: Blackwell.

Heelas, P., and Woodhead, L. eds. 2000. *Religion in Modern Times: An Interpretive Anthology*. Oxford: Blackwell.

Heilman, Samuel C. 1996. *Portrait of American Jews: The Last Half of the 20th Century*. Seattle: University of Washington Press.

Heilman, Samuel C., and Steven M. Cohen. 1989. *Cosmopolitans & Parochials: Modern Orthodox Jews in America*. Chicago: The University of Chicago Press.

Heirich, Max. 1977. "Change of Heart: A Test of Some Widely Held Theories About Religious Conversion." *American Journal of Sociology* 83: 653–80.

Hepner, Randal L. 1998. "The House that Rasta Built: Church-building Among New York Rastafari." In R. Stephen Warner and Judith G. Wittner, eds., *Gatherings in Diaspora: Religious Communities and the New Immigration* (pp. 197–234). Philadelphia: Temple University Press.

Herberg, Will. 1960. *Protestant-Catholic-Jew: An Essay in American Religious Sociology*. Garden City, NY: Doubleday.

Herman, Simon N. 1970a. *Jewish Identity: A Social Psychological Perspective*. Beverly Hills, CA: Sage Publications.

———. 1970b. *Israelis and Jews: The Continuity of an Identity*. Random House: New York.

Herrera, Marina. 1994. "The Context and Development of Hispanic Ecclesial Leadership." In Jay P. Dolan and Allan Figuerosa Deck, S. J., eds., *Hispanic Catholic Culture in the U.S.: Issues and Concerns* (pp. 166–205). Notre Dame, IN: University of Notre Dame Press.

Herrnstein, Richard, and Charles Murray. 1994. *The Bell Curve: Intelligence and Class Structure in American Life*. New York: The Free Press.

Hertz, Debora. 1998. "Emancipation Through Intermarriage? Wealthy Jewish Salon Women in Old Berlin." In Judith R. Baskin, ed., *Jewish Women in Historical Perspective*, 2nd ed. (pp. 193–207). Detroit: Wayne State University Press.

Hertzberg, Arthur. 1971. "Jewish Identity." *Encyclopedia Judaica*. Jerusalem: Keter.

Hervieu-Léger, Daniele. 1993. "Present-Day Emotional Renewals: The End of Secularization or the End of Religion?" In W. H. Swatos, Jr., ed., *A Future for Religion* (pp. 129–48). Newbury Park, CA: Sage.

———. 2000. *Religion as a Chain of Memory*. New Brunswick, NJ: Rutgers University Press.

Hervieu-Léger, D. and Willaime, J.-P. 2001. *Sociologies et Religion: Approches Classiques*. Paris: Presses Universitaires de France.

Herzog, Hanna. 2000. "The Status of Women in Israel: A Fifty-Year Perspective." In Stuart A. Cohen and Milton Shain, eds., *Israel: Culture, Religion and Society, 1948–1998* (pp. 53–74). Cape Town: Jewish Publications.

Hewitt, John P. 1989. *Dilemmas of the American Self*. Philadelphia: Temple University Press.

Hewitt, William E. 1991. *Base Christian Communities and Social Change in Brazil*. Lincoln: University of Nebraska Press.

Heyer-Gray, Zoey. 2000. "Gender and Religious Work." *Sociology of Religion* 61: 467–71.

Higginbotham, Evelyn Brooks. 1993. *Righteous Discontent: The Women's Movement in the Black Baptist Church, 1880–1920*. Cambridge, MA: Harvard University Press.

Hill, Christopher. 1972. *The World Turned Upside Down: Radical Ideas During the English Revolution*. New York: Viking.

Himmelfarb, Harold. 1982. "Research on American Jewish Identity and Identification: Progress, Pitfalls, and Prospects." In Marshall Sklare, ed., *Understanding American Jewry* (pp. 56–95). New Brunswick, NJ: Transaction.

Himmelstein, Jerome L. 1983. "The New Right." In Robert C. Liebman and Robert Wuthnow, eds. *The New Christian Right* (pp. 133–48). New York: Aldine.

Hirschman, Albert O. 1970. *Exit, Voice, and Loyality.* Cambridge, MA: Harvard University Press.

———. 1991. *The Rhetoric of Reaction: Perversity, Futility, Jeopardy.* Cambridge, MA: Harvard University Press.

Hirschman, Charles, Philip Kasinitz, and Josh DeWind, eds. 1999. *The Handbook of International Migration: The American Experience.* New York: Russell Sage Foundation.

Hobsbawm, Eric J. 1959. *Primitive Rebels.* New York: Norton.

Hochschild, Alie. 1997. *The Time Bind.* New York: Henry Holt.

Hofferth, Sandra L., and John F. Sandberg. 2001. "Changes in American Children's Time, 1981–1997." In Timothy Owens and S. Hofferth, eds., *Children at the Millennium: Where Have We Come From, Where Are We Going? Advances in Life Course Research.* New York: Elsevier Science.

Hoffman, John, and Alan Miller. 1998. "Denominational Influences on Socially Divisive Issues." *Journal for the Scientific Study of Religion* 37: 528–46.

Hoge, Dean. 2000. "Jewish Identity and Catholic Identity: Findings and Analogies." Paper presented at the annual meeting of the Religious Research Association, Houston, TX.

Hoge, Dean R., and David A. Roozen. 1979. "Some Sociological Conclusions About Church Trends." In Dean R. Hoge and David A. Roozen, eds., *Understanding Church Growth and Decline: 1950–1978* (pp. 315–34). New York: Pilgrim Press.

Hoge, Dean R., and Jeffrey L. Faue. 1973. "Sources of Conflict Over Priorities of the Protestant Church." *Social Forces* 52: 178–94.

Hoge, Dean R., Benton Johnson, and Donald A. Luidens. 1994. *Vanishing Boundaries: The Religion of Mainline Protestant Baby Boomers.* Louisville, KY: Westminster/John Knox.

Hoge, Dean R., Everett L. Perry, and Gerald L. Klever. 1978. "Theology as a Source of Disagreement about Protestant Church Goals and Priorities." *Review of Religious Research* 19: 116–38.

Holahan, Carole, and Robert Sears. 1995. *The Gifted Group in Later Maturity.* Stanford, CA: Stanford University Press.

Holifield, E. Brooks. 1994. "Towards a History of American Congregations." In James P. Wind and James W. Lewis, eds., *American Congregations, Volume 2: New Perspectives in the Study of Congregations* (pp. 23–53). Chicago: University of Chicago Press

Hollenbach, David. 1989. "The Common Good Revisited." *Theological Studies* 50: 71–94.

Höllinger, Franz. 1996. *Volksreligion und Herrschaftskirche. Die Würzeln religiösen Verhaltens in westlichen Gesellschaften.* Opladen: Leske und Budrich.

Hoover, Stewart M. 1997. "Media and the Construction of the Religious Public Sphere." In Stewart M. Hoover and K. Lundby, eds., *Rethinking Media, Religion and Culture* (pp. 283–97). Thousand Oaks, CA: Sage.

Horowitz, Bethamie. 1998. *Connections and Journeys: Shifting Identities Among American Jews.* Working paper.

———. 1999. *Indicators of Jewish Identity: Developing a Conceptual Framework for Understanding American Jewry.* Discussion Paper Prepared for the Mandel Foundation.

———. 2000. *Connections and Journeys: Assessing Critical Opportunities for Enhancing Jewish Identity.* New York: UJA-Federation.

Horowitz, Irving L. 1998. "Minimalism or Maximalism: Jewish Survival at the Millennium." In Ernest Krausz and Gitta Tulea, eds., *Jewish Survival: The Identity Problem at the Close of the Twentieth Century* (pp. 1–18). New Brunswick, NJ: Transaction.

Hout, Michael, and Claude S. Fischer. 2002. "Why More Americans Have No Religious Preference: Politics and Generations." *American Sociological Review* 67: 165–90.

Hout, Michael, and Andrew Greeley. 1987. "The Center Doesn't Hold: Church Attendance in the United States 1940–1984." *American Sociological Review* 52: 325–45.

———. 1998. "What Church Officials' Reports Don't Show: Another Look at Church Attendance Data." *American Sociological Review* 63: 113–19.

Hout, Michael, Andrew Greeley, and Melissa J. Wilde. 2001. "The Demographic Imperative in Religious Change in the United States." *American Journal of Sociology* 107: 468–500.

Houtart, François. 1997. "The Cult of Violence in the Name of Religion: A Panorama." In Wim Beuken and Karl-Josef Kuschel, eds., *Religion as a Source of Violence?* (pp. 1–9). Maryknoll, NY: Orbis.

Howard, G. S., S. E. Maxwell, and K. J. Fleming. 2000. "The Proof of the Pudding: An Illustration of The Relative Strengths of Null-hypothesis, Meta-analysis, and Bayesian Analysis." *Psychological Methods* 5: 315–32.

Howe, Daniel W. 1990. "Religion and Politics in the Antebellum North." In Mark Noll, ed., *Religion and American Politics* (pp. 121–45). New York: Oxford University Press.

Howell, Julia Day. 1998. "Gender Role Experimentation in New Religious Movements: Clarification of the Brahma Kumari Case." *Journal for the Scientific Study of Religion* 37: 453–61.

Hudnut-Buemler, James. 1994. *Looking for God in the Suburbs: The Religion of the American Dream and its Critics, 1945–1965*. New Brunswick, NJ: Rutgers University Press.

Hummer, R. A., R. G. Rogers, C. B. Nam, and Christopher Ellison. 1999. "Religious Involvement and U.S. Adult Mortality." *Demography* 36: 273–85.

Hunsberger, Bruce E. 1985. "Parent-University Student Agreement on Religious and Nonreligious Issues." *Journal for the Scientific Study of Religion* 24: 314–20.

Hunsberger, Bruce E., and L. B. Brown. 1984. "Religious Socialization, Apostasy, and the Impact of Family Background." *Journal for the Scientific Study of Religion* 23: 239–51.

Hunter, James D. 1983. *American Evangelicalism: Conservative Religion and the Quandary of Modernity*. New Brunswick, NJ: Rutgers University Press.

———. 1987. *Evangelicalism: The Coming Generation*. Chicago: University of Chicago Press.

———. 1991. *Culture Wars: The Struggle to Define America*. New York: Basic Books.

———. 1994. *Before the Shooting Begins: Searching for Democracy in America's Culture War*. New York: Free Press.

Huntington, Samuel P. 1996. *The Clash of Civilizations and the Remaking of World Order*. New York: Simon and Schuster.

Hurh, Won Moo, and Kwang Chung Kim. 1984. *Korean Immigrants in America: A Structural Analysis of Ethnic Confinement and Adhesive Adaptation*. Cranbury, NJ: Associated University Press.

Hutchison, William R. 1982. *The Modernist Impulse in American Protestantism*. Oxford: Oxford University Press.

Huynh, Thuan. 2000. "Center for Vietnamese Buddhism: Recreating Home." In Helen Rose Ebaugh and Janet S. Chafetz, eds., *Religion and the New Immigrants: Continuities and Adaptations in Immigrant Congregations* (pp. 45–66). Walnut Creek, CA: AltaMira Press.

Iannaccone, Laurence. 1988. "A Formal Model of Church and Sect." *American Journal of Sociology* 94(S): S241.

———. 1990. "Religious Practice: A Human Capital Approach." *Journal for the Scientific Study of Religion* 29: 297–314.

———. 1992a. "Religious Markets and the Economics of Religion." *Social Compass* 39: 123–32.

———. 1992b. "Sacrifice and Stigma: Reducing Freeriding in Cults, Communes, and Other Collectives." *Journal of Political Economy* 100: 271–91.

———. 1994. "Why Strict Churches are Strong." *American Journal of Sociology* 99: 1180–211.

Idler, Ellen, and V. S. Kasl. 1997. "Religion Among Disabled and Nondisabled Persons. I: Cross-sectional Patterns in Health Practices, Social Activities, and Well-being." *Journal of Gerontology: Social Sciences* 52B: S294–S305.

Ignazi, Piero. 1997. "New Challenges: Postmaterialism and the Extreme Right." In M. Rhodes, P. Heywood, and V. Wright, eds., *Developments in European Politics* (pp. 200–319). Houndmills, UK: Macmillan.

Inglehart, Ronald. 1990. *Culture Shift in Advanced Industrial Society*. Princeton, NJ: Princeton University Press.

———. 1997. *Modernization and Postmodernization*. Princeton, NJ: Princeton University Press.

Inglehart, Ronald, and Wayne E. Baker. 2000. "Modernization, Cultural Change, and the Persistence of Traditional Values." *American Sociological Review* 65: 19–51.

Interfaith Funders. 2000. *Annual Report 2000 from Interfaith Funders*. Jericho, NY: Interfaith Funders.

Irwin, Galen A., and Dittrich, Karl. 1984. "And the Walls Came Tumbling Down: Party Dealignment in the Netherlands." In R. J. Dalton, S. C. Flanagan, and P. A. Beck, eds., *Electoral Change in Advanced Industrial Democracies, Realignment of Dealignment* (pp. 267–297). Princeton: Princeton University Press.

Isaac, Glynn. 1978. "The Food Sharing Behavior of Proto-Human Hominids." *Scientific American* 238: 90–108.

Isambert, F., and J. P. Terrenoire. 1980. *Atlas de la Pratique Religieuse des Catholiques en France.* Paris: FNSP-CNRS.

Jackman, Mary R. 2001. "License to kill: violence and legitimacy in expropriative social relations." In John T. Jost and Brenda Major, eds., *The Psychology of Legitimacy: Emerging Perspectives on Ideology, Justice, and Intergroup Relations* (pp. 437–67). New York: Cambridge University Press.

Jacobs, Janet L. 1995. "The Violated Self and the Search for Religious Meaning." In *Sex, Lies, and Sanctity: Religion and Deviance in Contemporary North America* (pp. 237–50). Greenwich, CT: JAI Press.

———. 1996. "Women, Ritual, and Secrecy: The Creation of Crypto-Jewish Culture. *Journal for the Scientific Study of Religion* 35: 97–108.

———. 2000. "The Spiritual Self-In-Relation: Empathy and the Construction of Spirituality Among Modern Descendants of the Spanish Crypto-Jews." *Journal for the Scientific Study of Religion* 39: 53–63.

Jacob, Simon, and Pallavi Thakur. 2000. "Jyothi Hindu Temple: One Religion, Many Practices." In Helen Rose Ebaugh and Janet S. Chafetz, eds., *Religion and the New Immigrants: Continuities and Adaptations in Immigrant Congregations* (pp. 229–42). Walnut Creek, CA: AltaMira Press.

Jagodzinski, Wolfgang, and Karel Dobbelaere. 1995. "Secularization and Church Religiosity." In Jan Van Deth and Elinor Scarbrough, eds., *The Impact of Values* (pp. 76–199). New York: Oxford University Press.

James, William. 1902/1961. *The Varieties of Religious Experience.* New York: Macmillan.

Janoff-Bulman, R., and G. Marshall. 1982. "Mortality, Well-being, and Control: A Study of a Population of Institutionalized Aged." *Personality and Social Psychology Bulletin* 8: 691–8.

Jasper, James. 1998."The Emotions of Protest: Affective and Reactive Emotions in and Around Social Movements." *Sociological Forum* 13: 397–424.

Jelen, Ted. G. 1991. *The Political Mobilization of Religious Beliefs.* New York: Praeger.

Jenkins, Brian. 1975. *International Terrorism: A New Mode of Conflict.* Los Angeles: Crescent Publications.

Jensen, Lionel M. 1997. *Manufacturing Confucianism: Chinese Traditions and Universal Civilization.* Durham, NC: Duke University Press.

Jensen, Richard. 1971. *The Winning of the Midwest: Social and Political Conflict, 1888–1896.* Chicago: University of Chicago Press.

Jepperson, Ronald L., and Ann Swidler. 1994. "What Properties of Culture Should We Measure?" *Poetics* 22: 359–71.

Joffe, Carole. 1995. *Doctors of Conscience.* Boston: Beacon.

Johnson, Allan G. 1992. *Human Arrangements: An Introduction to Sociology.* 3rd ed. Fort Worth, TX: Harcourt Brace Jovanovich.

Johnson, Benton. 1957. "A Critical Appraisal of the Church-Sect Typology." *American Sociological Review* 22: 88–92.

———. 1963. "On Church and Sect." *American Sociological Review* 28: 539–49.

Johnson, Carson D. 1995. "Supply-side and Demand-side Revivalism? Evaluating the Social Influences on New York State Evangelism in the 1830s." *Social Science History* 19: 1–30.

———. 1997. "Formal Education vs. Religious Belief." *Journal for the Scientific Study of Religion* 36: 231–46.

Johnson, Robert Allan. 1980. *Religious Assortative Marriage in the United States.* New York: Academic Press.

Johnson, Stephen D., and Joseph Tamney, eds. 1986. *The Political Role of Religion in the United States.* Boulder, CO: Westview.

Jones, Kenneth W. 1976. *Arya Dharm: Hindu Consciousness in 19th-Century Punjab.* Berkeley: University of California.

Jones, Maldwyn Allen. 1992. *American Immigration.* Chicago: University of Chicago Press.

Joselit, Jenna Weissman. 1994. *The Wonders of America: Reinventing Jewish Culture 1880–1950.* New York: Hill and Wang.

Juergensmeyer, Mark, ed. 1992. *Violence and the Sacred in the Modern World.* London: Frank Cass.

———. 2000, ed. *Terror in the Mind of God: The Global Rise of Religious Violence.* Berkeley: University of California Press.

Jung, Carl, G. 1964. *Man and His Symbols.* New York: Laurel.

Kairos Theologians. 1986. *The Kairos Document: Challenge to the Church – A Theological Comment on the Political Crisis in South Africa*. Grand Rapids, MI: Eerdmans.

Kakar, Sudhir. 1996. *The Colors of Violence: Cultural Identities, Religion, and Conflict*. Chicago: University of Chicago Press.

Kalmijn, Matthijs. 1991. "Shifting Boundaries: Trends in Religious and Educational Homogamy." *American Sociological Review* 56: 786–800.

Kanagy, Conrad. 1992. "Social Action, Evangelism, and Ecumenism: The Impact of Theological, and Church Structural Variables." *Review of Religious Research* 34: 34–51.

Kaplan, Marian. 1982. "Tradition and Transition: The Acculturation, Assimilation, and Integration of Jews in Imperial Germany-A Gender Analysis." In *Leo Baeck Institute Year Book* (pp. 3–35). London: Leo Baeck Institute.

Kapur, Rajiv. 1986. *Sikh Separatism: The Politics of Faith*. London: Allen & Unwin.

Karapin, Roger. 1998. "Radical-right and Neo-fascist Political Parties in Western Europe." *Comparative Politics* 30: 212–34.

Karlenzig, B. 1998. "Peter Berger." In W. Swatos, ed. *Encyclopedia of Religion and Society* (pp. 52–54). Walnut Creek, CA: AltaMira Press.

Kashima, Tetsuden. 1977. *Buddhism in America: The Social Organization of an Ethnic Religious Institution*. Westport, CT: Greenwood Press.

Kater, J. L. 1982. *Christians on the Right*. New York: Seabury Press.

Katz, Jacob. 1961. *Tradition and Crisis: Jewish Society at the End of the Middle Ages*. New York: Schocken Press.

Katzenstein, Mary. 1995. "Discursive Politics and Feminist Activism in the Catholic Church." In Myra Marx Ferree and Patricia Yancey Martin, eds., *Feminist Organizations: Harvest of the New Women's Movement* (pp. 35–52). Philadelphia: Temple University Press.

_____. 1998. *Faithful and Fearless: Moving Feminist Protest Inside the Church and the Military*. Princeton, NJ: Princeton University Press.

Kaufman, Debra. 1991. *Rachel's Daughters: Newly Orthodox Jewish Women*. New Brunswick, NJ: Rutgers University Press.

Kellstedt, Lyman A., and Mark. A. Noll. 1990. "Religion, Voting for President, and Party Identification, 1948–1984." In Mark A. Noll, ed., *Religion and American Politics: From the Colonial Period to the 1980s* (pp. 355–79). New York: Oxford University Press.

Kellstedt, Lyman A., John C. Green, James L. Guth, and Corwin E. Smidt. 1994. "Religious Voting Blocs in the 1992 Election: Year of the Evangelical?" *Sociology of Religion* 55: 307–26.

Kennedy, James, Robert Davis, and Bruce Taylor. 1998. "Changes in Spirituality Well-Being Among Victims of Sexual Assault." *Journal for the Scientific Study of Religion* 37: 322–8.

Kennedy, Robert. 1973. *The Irish: A Demographic Analysis*. Berkeley: University of California Press.

Kenski, Henry C., and William Lockwood. 1991. "Catholic Voting Behavior in 1988: A Critical Swing Vote." In James L. Guth and John C. Green, eds., *The Bible and the Ballot Box* (pp. 173–8). Boulder, CO: Westview Press.

Kertzer, David I. 1988. *Ritual, Politics, and Power*. New Haven, CT: Yale University Press.

Keysar, Ariela, and Barry Kosmin. 1995. "The Impact of Religious Identification on Differences in Educational Attainment Among American Women in 1990." *Journal for the Scientific Study of Religion* 34: 49–62.

Keysar, Ariela, Barry A. Kosmin, and Jeffrey Scheckner. 2000. *The Next Generation: Jewish Children and Adolescents*. Albany: State University of New York Press.

Kim, Andrew E. 2000. "Korean Religious Culture and its Affinity to Christianity: The Rise of Protestant Christianity in South Korea." *Sociology of Religion* 61: 117–33.

Kim, Au Ra. 1996. *Women Struggling for a New Life: The Role of Religion in the Cultural Passage from Korea to America*. Albany: State University of New York Press.

Kim, Illsoo. 1981. *The New Urban Immigrants: The Korean Community in New York*. Princeton, NJ: Princeton University Press.

Kim, Jung Ha. 1996. "The Labor of Compassion: Voices of "Churched" Korean American Women." *Amerasia Journal* 22: 93–105.

Kim, Yong Bok. 1981. *Minjung Theology: People as the Subjects of History*. Singapore: Commission on Theological Concerns, Christian Conference of Asia.

Kivisto, Peter A. 1992. "Religion and the New Immigrants." In William H. Swatos, ed., *A Future for Religion? New Paradigms for Social Analysis* (pp. 92–108). Newbury Park, CA: Sage.

Klaits, Joseph. 1985. *Servants of Satan.* Bloomington: Indiana University Press.

Klandermans, Bert, Hanspieter Kriesi, and Sydney Tarrow, eds. 1988. *From Structure to Action: Comparing Social Movements Research Across Cultures.* International Social Movement Research, Vol. 1. Greenwich, CT: JAI Press.

Klassen, Pamela. 2001. *Blessed Events: Religion and Home Birth in America.* Princeton, NJ: Princeton University Press.

Kleppner, Paul. 1979. *The Third Electoral System: 1853–1892.* Chapel Hill: University of North Carolina Press.

Kniss, Fred. 1988. "Toward a Theory of Ideological Change: The Case of the Radical Reformation." *Sociological Analysis* 49: 29–38.

———. 1996. "Ideas and Symbols as Resources in Intrareligious Conflict: The Case of American Mennonites." *Sociology of Religion* 57: 7–23.

———. 1997a. *Disquiet in the Land: Cultural Conflict in American Mennonite Communities.* New Brunswick, NJ: Rutgers University Press.

———. 1997b. "Culture Wars(?): Remapping the Battleground." In Rhys H. Williams, ed., *Cultural Wars in American Politics: Critical Reviews of a Popular Myth* (pp. 259–80). New York: Aldine de Gruyter.

———. 1998. "Listening to the Disenfranchised: Toward a Multiparty Conception of American Religion." In Douglas Jacobsen and William Vance Trollinger, Jr., eds., *Re-Forming the Center: American Protestantism, 1900 to the Present* (pp. 72–90). Grand Rapids, MI: Eerdmans.

Knox, Ronald A. 1950. *Enthusiasm, a Chapter in the History of Religion.* Oxford: Clarendon Press.

Koch, Jeffrey W. 1995. *Social Reference Groups and Political Life.* Lanham, MD: University Press of America.

Koenig, Harold, Judith Hays, David Larson, Linda George, H. J. Cohen, Michael McCullough, Keith Meador, and Dan Blazer. 1999. "Does Religious Attendance Prolong Survival? A Six-year Follow-up Study of 3, 968 Older Adults." *Journal of Gerontology: Medical Sciences* 54A: M370–M376.

Koenig, Harold, David Larson, Judith Hays, Michael McCullough, Linda George, P. S. Branch, Keith Meador, and M. Kuchibhatla. 1998. "Religion and Survival of 1, 010 Male Veterans Hospitalized with Medical Illness." *Journal of Religion and Health* 37: 15–29.

Koenig, Harold, Michael McCullough, and David Larson. 2001. *Handbook of Religion and Health.* New York: Oxford University Press.

Kohut, Andrew, John C. Green, Scott Keeter, and Robert C. Toth. 2000. *The Diminishing Divide: Religion's Changing Role in American Politics.* Washington, DC: Brookings Institute Press.

Konieczny, Mary Ellen, and Mark Chaves. 2000. "Resources, Race, and Female-Headed Congregations in the United States." *Journal for the Scientific Study of Religion* 39: 261–71.

Kornblum, William. 1991. *Sociology in a Changing World.* 2nd ed. Fort Worth, TX: Holt, Rinehart, and Winston.

Kosmin, Barry A. 1991. *The National Survey of Religious Identification: 1989–90* [MRDF]. New York: The Graduate School and University Center of the City University of New York.

Kosmin, Barry A., and Seymour P. Lachman. 1993. *One Nation Under God: Religion in Contemporary American Society.* New York: Harmony Books.

Kosmin, Barry A., S. Goldstein, J. Waksberg, N. Lerer, A. Keysar, and J. Scheckner. 1991. *Highlights of the CJF 1990 National Jewish Populations Survey.* New York: Council of Jewish Federations.

Kosselleck, Reinhart. 1988. *Critique and Crisis: Enlightenment and the Pathogenesis of Modern Society.* Cambridge, MA: MIT Press.

Kostarelos, Frances. 1995. *Feeling the Spirit: Faith and Hope in an Evangelical Black Storefront Church.* Columbia: University of South Carolina Press.

Kotre, John. 1984. *Outliving the Self.* New York: Norton.

Kramarow, E., H. Lentzer, R. Rooks, J. Weeks, and S. Saydah. 1999. *Health and Aging Chartbook: Health, United States, 1999.* Hyattsville, MD: National Center for Health Statistics.

Krueger, J. 2001. "Null Hypothesis Significance Testing: On the Survival of a Flawed Method." *American Psychologist* 56: 16–26.

Kuhn, Manford H., and Thomas S. McPartland. 1954. "An Empirical Investigation of Self-Attitudes." *American Sociological Review* 19: 68–76.

Kurien, Prema. 1998. "Becoming American by Becoming Hindu: Indian Americans Take Their Place at the Multicultural Table." In R. Stephen Warner and Judith G. Wittner, eds., *Gatherings in Diaspora: Religious Communities and the New Immigration* (pp. 37–70). Philadelphia: Temple University Press.

Kurtz, Lester R. 1986. *The Politics of Heresy: The Modernist Crisis in Roman Catholicism.* Berkeley: University of California Press.

Kwon, Huong Chu, Helen Rose Ebaugh, and Jacqueline M. Hagan. 1997. "The Structure and Function of Cell Group Ministry in a Korean Christian Church." *Journal for the Scientific Study of Religion* 36: 247–56.

Kwon, Jin-Kwan. 1990. *The Emergence of Minjung as the Subject of History: A Christian Political Ethic in the Perspective of Minjung Theology.* Unpublished Ph.D. dissertation, Drew University.

Kwon, Victoria Hyonchu. 1997. *Entrepreneurship and Religion: Korean Immigrants in Houston, Texas.* New York: Garland.

Laguerre, Michael S. 1998. *Diasporic Citizenship.* New York: St. Martin's Press.

Lakoff, George. 1996. *Moral Politics: What Conservatives Know that Liberals Don't.* Chicago: University of Chicago Press.

Lambert, F. 1990. "'Pedlar in Divinity': George Whitefield and the Great Awakening 1737–1745." *Journal of American History* 77: 812–37.

Lambert, Malcolm. 1992. *Medieval Heresy: Popular Movements from the Gregorian Reform to the Reformation.* 2nd ed. Oxford: Basil Blackwell.

Lamont, Michele. 1992. *Money, Morals, and Manners: The Culture of the French and the American Upper-Middle Class.* Chicago: University of Chicago Press.

Lamont, Michele, and Marcel Fournier, eds. 1992. *Cultivating Differences: Symbolic Boundaries and the Making of Inequality.* Chicago: University of Chicago Press.

Lane, Jan-Erik, and Svante O. Ersson. 1994. *Politics and Society in Western Europe.* 3rd ed. Newbury Park, CA: Sage.

Lanternari, Vittorio. 1960/1963. *The Religions of the Oppressed.* New York: Knopf.

Lappe, Frances Moore, and Paul M. DuBois. 1994. *The Quickening of America: Rebuilding our Nation, Remaking our Lives.* San Francisco: Jossey-Bass.

Lawler, Edward J., Cecilia Ridgeway, and Barry Markovsky. 1993. "Structural Social Psychology and the Micro-Macro Problem." *Sociological Theory* 11: 268–90.

Lawson, Ronald. 1999. "When Immigrants Take Over: The Impact of Immigrant Growth on American Seventh'day Adventism's Trajectory from Sect to Denomination." *Journal for the Scientific Study of Religion* 38: 83–102.

Layman, Geoffrey. 1997. "Religion and Political Behavior in the United States: The Impact of Beliefs, Affiliations, and Commitment From 1980 to 1994." *Public Opinion Quarterly* 61: 288–316.

———. 2001. *The Great Divide: Religion and Cultural Conflict in American Party Politics.* New York: Columbia University Press.

Lazerwitz, Bernard. 1973. "Religious Identification and its Ethnic Correlates: A Multivariate Model." *Social Forces* 52: 204–20.

———. 1995a. "Denominational Retention and Switching among American Jews." *Journal for the Scientific Study of Religion* 34: 499–506.

———. 1995b. "Jewish-Christian Marriages and Conversions, 1971 and 1990." *Sociology of Religion* 56: 433–43.

Lazerwitz, Bernard, J. Alan Winter, Arnold Dashefsky, and Ephraim Tabory. 1998. *Jewish Choices: American Jewish Denominationalism.* Albany, NY: State University of New York Press.

Lechner, Frank. 1991. "The Case Against Secularization: A Rebuttal." *Social Forces* 69: 1103–19.

———. 1996. "Secularization in the Netherlands?" *Journal for the Scientific Study of Religion* 35: 252–64.

———. 1998. "Talcott Parsons." In William Swatos, ed., *Encyclopedia of Religion and Society* (pp. 352–5). Walnut Creek, CA: AltaMira Press.

Leege, David C. 1993. "Religion and Politics in Theoretical Perspective." In David C. Leege and Lyman A. Kellstedt, eds., *Rediscovering the Religious Factor in American Politics* (pp. 3–25). Armonk, NY: M.E. Sharpe.

Leege, David C., and Lyman A. Kellstedt. 1993. *Rediscovering the Religious Factor in American Politics.* Armonk, NY: M.E. Sharpe.

Lehman, Edward. 1993. *Gender and Work: The Case of the Clergy*. Albany, NY: State University of New York Press.

Lenin, V. I. 1929. *What Is to Be Done? Burning Questions of Our Movement*. New York: International Publishers.

Lenski, Gerhard. 1961. *The Religious Factor*. New York: Doubleday

León, Luis D. 1998. "Born again in east Los Angeles: The congregation as border space." In R. Stephen Warner and Judith G. Wittner, eds., *Gatherings in Diaspora: Religious Communities and the New Immigration* (pp. 163–196). Philadelphia: Temple Univeristy Press.

Levenson, Claude B. 1988. *The Dalai Lama: A Biography*. London: Unwin Hyman.

Levin, Jeffrey S. 1994. "Religion and Health: Is There an Association, is it Valid, and is it Causal?" *Social Science and Medicine* 38: 1475–82.

Levin, Jeffrey S., and Linda Chatters. 1998. "Research on Religion and Mental Health: An Overview of Empirical Findings and Empirical Issues". In Harold Koenig, ed., *Handbook of Religion and Mental Health* (pp. 33–50). San Diego: Academic Press.

Levitt, Peggy. 1998. "Local-Level Global Religion: U.S.-Dominican Migration." *Journal for the Scientific Study of Religion* 37: 74–89.

_____. 2000. "Comparative Perspectives on Transnational Religious Life." Paper presented at the annual meeting of the Society for the Scientific Study of Religion, Houston, TX.

Lewin, Ellen. 1996. "Confessions of a Reformed Grant Hustler." In E. Lewin and W. Leap, eds., *Out in the Field: Reflections of Lesbian and Gay Anthropologists* (pp. 111–27). Urbana: University of Illinois Press.

Lewin, Kurt. 1948. *Resolving Social Conflicts*. New York: Harper.

Lewis-Beck, Michael. 1998. "Class, Religion, and the French Voter: A 'Stalled' Electorate?" *French Politics and Society* 16: 43–51.

Lewy, Guenter. 1974. *Religion and Revolution*. New York: Oxford University Press.

Lichterman, Paul. 1996. *The Search for Political Community: American Activists Reinventing Commitment*. New York: Cambridge University Press.

Lieberson, Stanley. 1985. *Making it Count: The Improvement of Social Research and Theory*. Berkeley: University of California Press.

Liebman, Charles. 2000. "Changing Jewish Identity in Israel and the United States." In Stuart Cohen and Milton Chain, eds. *Israel: Culture, Religion and Society, 1948–1998* (pp. 23–37). Cape Town: University of Capetown Caplan Centre for Jewish Studies and Research.

_____. 2001. *A Research Agenda for American Jews*. Ramat Gan, Israel: The Argov Center for the Study of Israel and the Jewish People.

Liebman, Charles, and Steven M. Cohen. 1990. *Two Worlds of Judaism: The Israeli and American Experiences*. New Haven, CT: Yale University Press.

Liebman, Robert C., John R. Sutton, and Robert Wuthnow. 1988. "Exploring the Social Sources of Denominationalism: Schisms in American Protestant Denominations, 1890–1980." *American Sociological Review* 53: 343–52.

Lifton, Robert Jay. 1993. *The Protean Self: Human Resilience in an Age of Fragmentation*. New York: Basic Books.

Lijphart, Arend. 1979. "Religious vs. Linguistic vs. Class Voting." *American Political Science Review* 73: 442–58.

Lin, Irene. 1996. "Journey to the Far West: Chinese Buddhism in America." *Amerasia Journal* 22: 106–32.

Lincoln, C. Eric, and Lawrence H. Mamiya. 1990. *The Black Church in the African American Experience*. Durham, NC: Duke University Press.

Lindbeck, George. 1984. *The Nature of Doctrine*. Philadelphia, PA: Westminster.

Lipset, Seymour Martin. 1996. *American Exceptionalism: A Double-Edged Sword*. New York: Norton.

Lipset, Seymour Martin, and Earl Raab. 1978. *The Politics of Unreason: Right-wing Extremism in America, 1790–1977*. Chicago: University of Chicago Press.

_____. 1995. *Jews and the New American Scene*. Cambridge, MA: Harvard University Press.

Lipset, Seymour Martin, and Stein Rokkan. 1967. "Cleavage Structures, Party Systems, and Voter Alignments: An Introduction." In Seymour M. Lipset and Stein Rokkan, eds., *Party Systems and Voter Alignments* (pp. 1–64). New York: Free Press.

London, P., K. I. Carr, A. Reach, N. L. Frank, and I. Minkin. 1988. *Personal Identity Inventory: Jewish Identity Form*. Cambridge, MA: Harvard Graduate School of Education.

Lopatto, Paul. 1985. *Religion and the Presidential Election*. New York: Praeger.

LoPrinzi, C. L., Laurie, J. A., Wieand, H. S., Krook, J. E., Novotny, P. J., Kugler, J. W., et al. 1994. "Prospective Evaluation of Prognostic Variables from Patient-completed Questionnaires." *Journal of Clinical Oncology* 12: 601–7.

Löwith, K. 1982. *Max Weber and Karl Marx*. London: Allen & Unwin.

Luckmann, Thomas. 1963. *Das Problem der Religion in der Modernen Gesellschaft*. Freiburg: Verlag Rombach.

———. 1967. *The Invisible Religion: The Problem of Religion in Modern Society*. New York: Macmillan.

———. 1991. "The New and the Old in Religion." In Pierre Bourdieu and James S. Coleman, eds., *Social Theory for a Changing Society* (pp. 167–82). Boulder, CO: Westview Press.

Luhman, Reid. 1992. *The Sociological Outlook: A Text with Readings*. San Diego: Collegiate Press.

Luhmann, Niklas. 2000. *Die Religion der Gesellschaft*. Frankfurt: Suhrkamp.

Luker, Kristin. 1984. *Abortion and the Politics of Motherhood*. Berkeley: University of California Press.

Lukes, Steve 1973. *Emile Durkheim: His Life and his Work*. London: Allen Lane.

Lundgren, Eva. 1998. "The Hand that Strikes and Comforts: Gender Construction and the Tension Between Body and Symbol." In R. Emerson Dobash and Russell P. Dobash, eds., *Rethinking Violence Against Women* (pp. 169–98). Thousand Oaks, CA: Sage Publications.

MacIntyre, Alasdair. 1984. *After Virtue: A Study in Moral Theory*. 2nd ed. Notre Dame, IN: University of Notre Dame Press.

MacLeod, Jay. 1993. *Community Organising: A Practical and Theological Appraisal*. London: Christian Action.

Maffesoli, Michel. 1995. *The Time of Tribes*. Beverly Hills: Sage.

Maffy-Kipp, L. F. 1997. "Eastward ho! American Religion from the Perspective of the Pacific Rim." In Thomas Tweed, ed., *Retelling U.S. Religious History* (pp. 127–48). Berkeley: University of California Press.

Mann, Michael. 1993. *The Sources of Social Power*. Volume 2. New York: Cambridge University Press.

Mannheim, Karl. 1937. *Ideology and Utopia*. New York: Harcourt, Brace, and World.

Manning, Christel. 1997. "Women in a Divided Church: Liberal and Conservative Catholic Women Negotiate Changing Gender Roles." *Sociology of Religion* 58: 375–90.

———. 1999. *God Gave Us the Right: Conservative Catholic, Evangelical Protestant, and Orthodox Jewish Women Grapple with Feminism*. New Brunswick, NJ: Rutgers University Press.

Mansbridge, Jane. 1995. "What is the Feminist Movement?" In Myra Marx Ferree and Patricia Yancey Martin, eds., *Feminist Organizations: Harvest of the New Women's Movement* (pp. 27–34). Philadelphia: Temple University Press.

Manville, Julie. 1997. "The Gendered Organization of an Australian Anglican Parish." *Sociology of Religion* 58: 25–38.

Manza, Jeff, and Clem Brooks. 1997. "The Religious Factor in U.S. Presidential Elections, 1960–1992." *American Journal of Sociology* 103: 38–81.

———. 1999. *Social Cleavages and Political Change*. New York: Oxford University Press.

———. 2001. "The Declining Political Fortunes of Mainline Protestants." In Robert Wuthnow and John Evans, eds., The *Quiet Hand of God* (pp. 159–180). Berkeley: University of California Press.

Marcum, John P. 1999. "Measuring Church Attendance: A Further Look." *Review of Religious Research* 41: 121–9.

Marins, Jose, T. M. Trevisan, et al. 1989. *The Church from the Roots: Basic Ecclesial Communities*. London: CAFOD.

Markoff, John. 1996. *Waves of Democracy*. Thousand Oaks, CA: Pine Forge Press.

Marler, Penny Long. 1995. "Lost in the Fifties: The Changing Family and the Nostalgic Church." In Nancy Ammerman and Wade Clark Roof, eds., *Work, Family, and Religion in Contemporary Society* (pp. 23–60). New York: Routledge.

Marler, Penny Long, and C. Kirk Hadaway. 1999. "Testing the Attendance Gap in a Conservative Church." *Sociology of Religion* 60: 175–86.

Marsden, George M. 1980. *Fundamentalism and American Culture: The Shaping of Twentieth-century Evangelicalism, 1870–1925*. Oxford: Oxford University Press.

Marsh, Charles. 1997. *God's Long Summer: Stories of Faith and Civil Rights*. Princeton: Princeton University Press.

Martin, David. 1978. *A General Theory of Secularization*. Oxford: Blackwell.

———. 1990. *Tongues of Fire: The Explosion of Protestantism in Latin America*. Oxford: Basil Blackwell.

———. 1999. "Christian Foundations, Sociological Fundamentals." In Leslie J. Francis, ed., *Sociology, Theology and the Curriculum* (pp. 1–49). New York: Cassell.

———. 2002. *Global Pentecostalism: The World Their Parish*. Oxford: Blackwell.

Marty, Martin E. 1970. *Righteous Empire: The Protestant Experience in America*. New York: Harper & Row.

Marty, Martin E., and R. Scott Appleby, eds. 1993. *Fundamentalisms and the State: Remaking Polities, Economies, and Militance*. Chicago: University of Chicago Press.

———. 1995. *Fundamentalisms Comprehended*. Chicago: Chicago University Press.

Marx, Karl. 1844/1964. *Karl Marx: Early Writings*. Trans. T. B. Bottomore. New York: McGraw-Hill.

Marx, Karl, and Friedrich Engels. 1878/1964. *On Religion*. New York: Schocken Books.

Maslow, Abraham. 1962. *Toward a Psychology of Being*. Princeton: Van Nostrand.

Massey, Douglas. 2002. "A Brief History of Human Society: The Origin and Role of Emotion in Social Life." *American Sociological Review* 67: 1–29.

Mauss, Marcel. 1935/1973 "Techniques of the Body." *Economy and Society* 2: 70–88.

May, Elaine Tyler. 1999. *Homeward Bound: American Families in the Cold War Era*. New York: Basic Books.

Mayer, Egon. 1985. *Love and Tradition: Marriage Between Jews and Christians*. New York: Plenum.

McAdam, Doug. 1982. *Political Process and the Development of Black Insurgency 1930–1970*. Chicago: University of Chicago Press.

———. 1983. "Tactical Innovation and the Pace of Insurgency." *American Sociological Review* 48: 735–54.

McAdam, Doug, John D. McCarthy, and Mayer N. Zald, eds. 1996. *Comparative Perspectives on Social Movements: Political Opportunities, Mobilizing Structures, and Cultural Framing*. New York: Cambridge University Press.

McCann, Joseph F. 1993. *Church and Organization: A Sociological and Theological Enquiry*. Scranton, PA: University of Scranton Press.

McCarthy, John D., and Mayer N. Zald. 1977. "Resource Mobilization and Social Movements: A Partial Theory." *American Journal of Sociology* 82: 1212–41.

McCullough, Michael. 2001. "Religious Involvement and Mortality: Answers and More Questions." In Thomas Plante and Allen Sherman, eds., *Faith and Health* (pp. 53–74). New York: Guilford.

McCullough, Michael, William Hoyt, and David Larson. 2001. "Small, Robust, and Important: Reply to Sloan and Bagiella." *Health Psychology* 20: 228–9.

McCullough, Michael, William Hoyt, David Larson, Harold Koenig, and Carl Thoresen. 2000. "Religious Involvement and Mortality: A Meta-Analytic Review." *Health Psychology* 19: 211–22.

McCullough, Michael, and David Larson. 1998. "Future Directions in Research." In Harold Koenig, eds., *Handbook of Religion and Mental Health* (pp. 95–107). San Diego: Academic Press.

McCutcheon, Allan L. 1988. "Denominations and Religious Intermarriage: Trends Among White Americans in the Twentieth Century." *Review of Religious Research* 29: 213–27.

McDannell, Colleen. 1986. *The Christian Home in Victorian America, 1840–1900*. Bloomington: Indiana University Press.

———. 1995. *Material Christianity*. New Haven, CT: Yale University Press.

McFadden, Susan. 1996. "Religion, Spirituality, and Aging." In J. Birren & W. Schaie, eds., *Handbook of the Psychology of Aging* (pp. 41–52). San Diego: Academic Press.

McGuire, Meredith B., and James Spickard. 1998. "Feeding Religiosity: Food Preparation and Eating as Religious Practice." Paper presented at the annual meeting of the Society for the Scientific Study of Religion, Montreal, Canada.

McLeod, Hugh. 1995. *European Religion in the Age of the Great Cities, 1830–1930*. New York and London: Routledge.

———. 1996. *Religion and Society in England, 1850–1914*. New York: St. Martin's.

McLeod, W. H. 1989. *The Sikhs: History, Religion, and Society*. New York: Columbia University Press.

McNamara, Patrick N. 1969. "Priests, Protests, and Poverty." *Social Science Quarterly* 10: 143–59.

_____. 1992. *Conscience First, Tradition Second: A Study of Young American Catholics*. Albany: State University of New York Press.

McNeill, William H. 1995. *Keeping Together in Time: Dance and Drill in Human History*. Cambridge, MA: Harvard University Press.

McPherson, J. M., and Lynn Smith-Lovin. 1987. "Homophily in Voluntary Organizations." *American Sociological Review* 52: 370–9.

McRoberts, Omar M. 1999. "Understanding the 'New' Black Pentecostal Activism: Lessons from Boston Ecumenical Ministries." *Sociology of Religion* 60: 47–70.

McVeigh, Rory. 1999. "Structural Incentives for Conservative Mobilization: Power Devaluation and the Rise of the Ku Klux Klan, 1915–1925." *Social Forces* 77: 1461–96.

Mead, George Herbert. 1934. *Mind, Self and Society*. Chicago: University of Chicago Press.

Mead, Sidney E. 1963. *The Lively Experiment*. New York: Harper and Row [1976 Reprint].

Medding, P. Y., G. A. Tobin, S. B. Fishman, and M. Rimor. 1992. *Jewish Identity in Conversionary and Mixed Marriages*. New York: American Jewish Committee.

Medina, Lara. 1997. "Las Hermanas: Chicana/Latina Religious Activism, 1971–1996." Paper presented at the annual meeting of the Society for the Scientific Study of Religion, San Diego.

Mendras, Henri. 1991. *Social Change in Modern France: Towards a Cultural Anthropology of the Fifth Republic*. Cambridge: Cambridge University Press.

Mensch, Barbara S., and Denise B. Kendel. 1988. "Underreporting of Substance Use in a National Longitudinal Youth Cohort: Individual and Interviewer Effects." *Public Opinion Quarterly* 52: 100–24.

Mercer, Calvin, and Thomas Durham. 1999. "Religious Mysticism and Gender Orientation." *Journal for the Scientific Study of Religion* 38: 175–82.

Meyer, David S., and Nancy Whittier. 1994. "Social Movement Spillover." *Social Problems* 41: 277–98.

Meyer, John W., and B. Rowan. 1977. "Institutionalized Organizations: Formal Structure as Myth and Ceremony." *American Journal of Sociology* 83: 340–63.

Meyer, John W., and W. Richard Scott, eds. 1992. *Organizational Environments: Ritual and Rationality*. Beverly Hills, CA: Sage.

Meyer, Katherine, Helen Rizzo, and Yousef Ali. 1998. "Islam and the Extension of Citizenship Rights to Women in Kuwait." *Journal for the Scientific Study of Religion* 37: 131–44.

Meyerowitz, Joanne, ed. 1994. *Not June Cleaver: Women and Gender in Post-War America, 1945–1960*. Philadelphia: Temple University Press.

Middendorp, Cees P. 1991. *Ideology in Dutch Politics: The Democratic System Reconsidered 1970–1995*. Assen/Maastricht: Van Gorcum.

Miller, Alan, and John Hoffman. 1995. "Risk and Religion: An Explanation of Gender Differences in Religiosity." *Journal for the Scientific Study of Religion* 34: 63–75.

Miller, Alan, and Rodney Stark. 2002. "Gender and Religiousness." *American Journal of Sociology* 107: 1399–423.

Miller, E. Willard, and Ruby M. Miller. 1996. *United States Immigration: A Reference Handbook*. Santa Barbara: ABC-CLIO.

Miller, Warren E., and G. Raab. 1977. "The Religious Alignment at English Elections between 1918 and 1970." *Political Studies* 25: 227–51.

Miller, Warren E., and P. C. Stouthard. 1975. "Confessional Attachment and Electoral Behavior in the Netherlands." *European Journal of Political Research* 3: 219–58.

Mills, C. Wright. 1940. "Situated Actions and Vocabularies of Motive." *American Sociological Review* 5: 904–13.

Min, Pyong Gap. 1992. "The Structure and Social Functions of Korean Immigrant Churches in the United States." *International Migration Review* 26: 1370–94.

Minkoff, Debra. 1995. *Organizing for Equality: The Evolution of Women's and Racial-Ethnic Organizations in America, 1955–1985*. New Brunswick, NJ: Rutgers University Press.

Minow, Martha. 1997. *Not Only for Myself*. New York: The New Press.

Moaddel, Mansoor 1998. "Religion and Women: Islamic Modernism versus Fundamentalism." *Journal for the Scientific Study of Religion* 37: 108–30.

Mock, Alan. 1992. "Congregational Religious Styles and Orientations to Society: Exploring Our Linear Assumptions." *Review of Religious Research* 34: 20–33.

Mohl, Raymond A., and Neil Betten. 1981. "The Immigrant Church in Gary, Indiana: Religious Adjustment and Cultural Defense." *Ethnicity* 8: 1–17.

Moniére, Denis. 1981. *Ideologies in Quebec: The Historical Development.* Toronto: University of Toronto Press.

Moore, R. Laurence. 1986. *Religious Outsiders and the Making of Americans.* New York: Oxford University Press.

———. 1994. *Selling God: American Religion in the Marketplace of Culture.* New York: Oxford University Press.

Morawska, Ewa T. 1989. "Labor Migrations of Poles in the Atlantic World Economy, 1880–1914." *Comparative Study of Society and History* 31: 237–70.

Morris, Aldon D. 1984. *The Origins of the Civil Rights Movement: Black Communities Organizing for Change.* New York: Free Press.

Morris, Colin. 1993. "Christian Civilization (1050–1400)." In John McManners, ed., *The Oxford History of Christianity* (pp. 205–42). Oxford: Oxford University Press.

Mosher, William D., and Christine A. Bachrach. 1996. "Understanding U. S. Fertility: Continuity and Change in the National Survey of Family Growth, 1988–1995." *Family Planning Perspectives* 28: 4–12.

Mouw, Ted, and Michael E. Sobel. 2001. "Culture Wars and Opinion Polarization: The Case of Abortion." *American Journal of Sociology* 106: 913–43.

Mowrer, Ernest R. 1958. "The Family in Suburbia." In William Dobriner, ed., *The Suburban Community* (pp. 147–64). New York: Putnam.

Mullen, B., P. Muellerleile, and B. Bryant. 2001. "Cumulative Meta-analysis: A Consideration of Indicators of Sufficiency and Stability." *Personality and Social Psychology Bulletin* 27: 1450–62.

Mullins, Mark R. 1987. "The Life-cycle of Ethnic Churches in Sociological Perspective." *Japanese Journal of Religious Studies* 14: 321–34.

Murphy, P. E., J. W. Ciarrocchi, R. L. Piedmont, S. Cheston, M. Peyrot, and G. Fitchett. 2000. "The Relation of Religious Belief and Practices, Depression, and Hopelessness in Persons with Clinical Depression." *Journal of Consulting and Clinical Psychology* 68: 1102–6.

Murray, Alexander. 1972. "Piety and Impiety in Thirteenth-Century Italy." *Studies in Church History* 8: 83–106.

Murrin, John M. 1990. "Religion and Politics in America from the First Settlements to the Civil War." In Mark Noll, ed., *Religion and American Politics* (pp. 19–43). New York: Oxford University Press.

Myers, Phyllis G., and Powell Davidson. 1984. "Who Participates in Ecumenical Activity?" *Review of Religious Research* 25: 185–203.

Myers, Scott. 1996. "Families and the Inheritance of Religiosity." *American Sociological Review* 61: 858–66.

Myerson, Roger B. 1991. *Game Theory: Analysis of Conflict.* Cambridge, MA: Harvard University Press.

Myrdal, Gunnar. 1944. *An American Dilemma.* New York: Harper and Brothers.

Nagengast, C., and M. Kearney. 1990. "Mixtec Ethnicity: Social Identity, Political Consciousness, and Political Activism." *Latin American Research Review* 25: 61–91.

Naples, Nancy A. 1998. "Women's Community Activism: Exploring the Dynamics of Politicization and Diversity." In Nancy A. Naples, ed., *Community Activism and Feminist Politics: Organizing Across Race, Class, and Gender* (pp. 327–49). New York: Routledge Press.

Nash, Dennison, and Peter Berger. 1962. "The Child, the Family and the 'Religious Revival' in Suburbia." *Journal for the Scientific Study of Religion* 2: 85–93.

Nash, George H. 1976. *The Conservative Intellectual Movement in America Since 1945.* New York: Basic Books.

Nash, Laura. 1994. "The Evangelical CEO." *Across the Board* 26–33.

Nason Clark, Nancy. 1997. *The Battered Wife: How Christians Confront Family Violence.* Louisville, KY: Westminster/John Knox Press.

———. 2000. "Making the Sacred Safe: Woman Abuse and Communities of Faith." *Sociology of Religion* 61: 349–68.

Neitz, Mary Jo. 1987. *Charisma and Community.* New Brunswick, NJ: Transaction Press.

———. 1990. "In Goddess We Trust." In Tom Robbins and Dick Anthony, eds., *In Gods We Trust* (pp. 354–72). New Brunswick, NJ: Transaction Press.

———. 1993. "Inequality and Difference: Feminist Research in the Sociology of Religion." In William H. Swatos, ed., *The Future for Religion: New Paradigms for Social Analysis* (pp. 165–84). Newbury Park, CA: Sage Publications.

———. 2000. "Queering the Dragonfest: Changing Sexualities in a Post-Patriarchal Religion." *Sociology of Religion* 61: 369–91.

———. 2002. "Walking Between the Worlds: Permeable Boundaries, Ambiguous Identities." In James Spickard, J. Shawn Landres, and Meredith McGuire, eds., *Personal Knowledge and Beyond: Reshaping the Ethnography of Religion* (pp. 33–46). New York: New York University Press.

Neitz, Mary Jo, and Peter Mueser. 1997. "The Problem with Economic Man: A Critique of Rational Choice Theory in the Sociology of Religion." In Larry Young, ed., *Rational Choice Theory and Religion* (pp. 105–18). New York: Routledge.

Neitz, Mary Jo, and James V. Spickard. 1990. "Steps Toward a Sociology of Religious Experience." *Sociological Analysis* 51: 15–33.

Nelsen, Hart M. 1981. "Religious Conformity in an Age of Disbelief: Contextual Effects of Time, Denomination, and Family Processes upon Church Decline and Apostasy." *American Sociological Review* 46: 632–40.

Nelsen, Hart M., and R. H. Potvin. 1981. "Gender and Regional Differences in the Religiosity of Protestant Adolescents." *Review of Religious Research* 22: 278–85.

Nelson, Timothy J. 1997. "He Made a Way Out of No Way: Religious Experience in an African-American Congregation." *Review of Religious Research* 39: 5–26.

Nesbitt, Paula. 1997. *Feminization of the Clergy in America*. New York: Oxford University Press.

Nettle, Bruno. 2000. "An Ethnomusicologist Contemplates Universals in Musical Sound and Musical Culture." In Nils Wallin, Bjorn Merker, and Steven Brown, eds., *The Origins of Music* (pp. 463–72). Cambridge, MA: MIT Press.

Neuhaus, Richard. 1984. *The Naked Public Square: Religion and Democracy in America*. Grand Rapids, MI: Eerdmans.

Newcomb, Theodore. 1943. *Personality and Social Change: Attitude Formation in a Student Community*. New York. Holt.

Nhat Hanh, T. 1967. *Vietnam: Lotus in a Sea of Fire*. New York: Hill & Wang.

———. 1998. *Interbeing: Fourteen Guidelines for Engaged Buddhism*. Berkeley: Parallax Press.

Nichols, Johanna. 1998. "The Origin and Dispersal of Languages: Linguistic Evidence." In Nina J. Jablonski and Leslie C. Aiello, eds., *The Origin and Diversification of Language* (pp. 127–70). San Francisco: Memoirs of the California Academy of Sciences, Number 24.

Niebuhr, H. Richard. 1929. *The Social Sources of Denominationalism*. New York: Henry Holt.

———. 1963. *The Responsible Self: An Essay in Christian Moral Philosophy*. New York: Harper & Row.

Nolen-Hoeksema, S., J. Larson, and C. Grayson. 1999. "Explaining the Gender Difference in Depressive Symptoms." *Journal of Personality and Social Psychology* 77: 1061–72.

Nord, D. P. 1995. "Religious Reading and Readers in Antebellum America." *Journal of the Early Republic* 15: 241–72.

Nozick, Robert. 1974. *Anarchy, State and Utopia*. New York: Basic Books.

Numrich, Paul David. 1996. *Old Wisdom in the New World: Americanization in Two Immigrant Theravada Buddhist Temples*. Knoxville: University of Tennessee Press.

———. 2000. "The Numbers Questions: Thoughts Prepared for Pew's Religion and the New Immigrant Research Initiative." Unpublished Essay.

O'Ballance, Edgar. 1997. *Islamic Fundamentalist Terrorism, 1979–95: The Iranian Connection*. Basingstoke, UK: Macmillan.

Obelkevich, James. 1979. *Religion and the People, 800–1700*. Chapel Hill: University of North Carolina Press.

Olson, Daniel V.A. 1997. "Dimensions of Cultural Tension Among the American Public." In Rhys H. Williams, ed., *Cultural Wars in American Politics* (pp. 237–57). Hawthorne, NY: Aldine.

———. 1998. "Comment: Religious Pluralism in Contemporary U.S. Counties." *American Sociological Review* 63: 759–61.

———. 1999. "Religious Pluralism and U.S. Church Membership: A Reassessment." *Sociology of Religion* 60: 149–73.

Olson Daniel V.A., and C. Kirk Hadaway. 2000. "Religious Pluralism and Affiliation Among Canadian Counties and Cities." *Journal for the Scientific Study of Religion* 38: 490–508.

Olson, Daniel V.A., and William McKinney. 1997. "United Methodist Leaders: Diversity and Moral Authority." In William B. Lawrence, Dennis Campbell, Russell Richey, eds., *The People(s) Called Methodist: Forms and Reforms of Their Life* (pp. 109–26). Nashville, TN: Abingdon Press.

Olson, Laura, Sue Crawford, and James Guth. 2000. "Changing Issue Agendas of Women Clergy." *Journal for the Scientific Study of Religion* 39: 140–53.

Oman, Doug, and D. Reed. 1998. "Religion and Mortality Among the Community-dwelling Elderly." *American Journal of Public Health* 88: 1469–75.

Ong, Aiwha, and Donald Nonini, eds. 1997. *Ungrounded Empires: The Cultural Politics of Modern Chinese Transnationalism.* New York: Routledge.

Orsi, Robert. 1985. *The Madonna of 115th Street: Faith and Community in Italian Harlem, 1880–1950.* New Haven, CT: Yale University Press.

———. 1996. *Thank You, St. Jude: Women's Devotion to the Patron Saint of Hopeless Causes.* New Haven, CT: Yale University Press.

———. 1997. "Everyday Miracles: The Study of Lived Religion." In David D. Hall, ed., *Lived Religion in America: Toward a History of Practice* (pp. 3–21). Princeton: Princeton University Press.

———. 1999. *Gods of the City: Religion and the American Urban Landscape.* Bloomington: Indiana University Press.

O'Toole, Roger. 1984. *Religion: Classic Sociological Approaches.* Toronto: McGraw-Hill Ryerson.

———. 2000. "Classics in the Sociology of Religion: An Ambiguous Legacy." In Richard Fenn, ed., *The Blackwell Companion to the Sociology of Religion* (pp. 133–60). Oxford: Blackwell.

Ozorak, Elizabeth Weiss. 1996. "The Power, but not the Glory: How Women Empower Themselves Through Religion." *Journal for the Scientific Study of Religion* 35: 17–29.

Pace, E., and R. Guolo. 1998. *I fondamentalismo.* Roma-Bari: Editori Laterza.

Palmer, Susan. 1993. "Women's 'Cocoon Work' in New Religious Movements: Sexual Experimentation and Feminine Rites of Passage." *Journal for the Scientific Study of Religion* 32: 343–55.

Papaioannou, George. 1994. "The History of the Greek Orthodox Cathedral of the Annunciation." In James P. Wind and James W. Lewis, eds., *American Congregations* (pp. 520–71). Volume 1. Chicago: University of Chicago Press.

Pardo, Mary S. 1998. *Mexican American Women Activists: Identity and Resistance in Two Los Angeles Communities.* Philadelphia: Temple University Press.

Pargament, Kenneth. 1997. *The Psychology of Religion and Coping.* New York: Guilford.

Pargament, Kenneth, Harold Koenig, N. Taraweshwar, and J. Hahn. 2001. "Religious Struggle as a Predictor of Mortality Among Medically Ill Patients: A Two-year Longitudinal Study." *Archives of Internal Medicine* 161: 1881–5.

Paris, Arthur E. 1982. *Black Pentecostalism.* Amherst: University of Massachusetts Press.

Park, Daniel K. 1985. *An Evangelical Evaluation of Minjung Theology in Korea.* Unpublished M.A. thesis, Fuller Theological Seminary, Los Angeles, CA.

Park, Robert E. 1950. *Race and Culture.* Glencoe, IL: Free Press.

Parry, Hugh, and Helen Crossley. 1950. "Validity of Responses to Survey Questions." *Public Opinion Quarterly* 14: 61–80.

Parsons, Talcott. 1963. "Christianity and Modern Industrial Society." In Edward A. Tiryakian, ed., *Sociological Theory, Values and Sociocultural Change* (pp. 33–70). New York: The Free Press.

Partner, Peter. 1997. *God of Battles: Holy Wars of Christianity and Islam.* New York: HarperCollins.

Pattillo-McCoy, Mary. 1998. "Church Culture as a Strategy of Action in the Black Community." *American Sociological Review* 63: 767–84.

Paxton, Pamela. 1999. "Is Social Capital Declining in the United States." *American Journal of Sociology* 105: 88–127.

Payne, I. R., A. E. Bergin, K. A. Bielema, and P. H. Jenkins. 1991. "Review of Religion and Mental Health: Prevention and the Enhancement of Psychosocial Functioning." *Prevention in Human Services* 9: 11–40.

Peña, Milagros, and Lisa M. Frehill. 1998. "Latina Religious Practice: Analyzing Cultural Dimensions in Measures of Religiosity." *Journal for the Scientific Study of Religion* 37: 620–35.

Perl Paul, and Daniel V.A. Olson. 2000. "Religious Market Share and Intensity of Church Involvement in Five Denominations." *Journal for the Scientific Study of Religion* 39: 12–31.

Perlmann, Joel, and Roger Waldinger. 1999. "Immigrants, Past and Present: A Reconsideration." In Charles Hirschman, P. Kasinitz, and J. DeWind, eds., *The Handbook of International Migration: The American Experience* (pp. 223–38). New York: Russell Sage Foundation.

Peters, Shawn. 2000. *Judging Jehovah's Witnesses*. Lawrence: University Press of Kansas.

Peterson, Bill, and Eva Klohnen. 1995. "Realization of Generativity in Two Samples of Women at Midlife." *Psychology and Aging* 10: 20–9.

Petrocik, John. 1987. "Realignment: New Party Coalitions and the Nationalization of the South." *Journal of Politics* 49: 347–75.

Pettersson, Thorleif, and Eva Hamberg. 1997. "Denominational Pluralism and Church Membership in Contemporary Sweden: A Longitudinal Study of the Period, 1974–1995." *Journal of Empirical Theology* 10: 61–78.

Philipson, David. 1967. *The Reform Movement in Judaism*. New York: Ktav Publishing House.

Phillips, B. A. 1997. *Re-examining Intermarriage*. Boston and New York: Wilstein Institute and American Jewish Committee.

———. 1991. "Sociological Analysis of Jewish Identity." In David M. Gordis and Yoav Ben-Horin, eds. *Jewish Identity in America*. Los Angeles: University of Judaism.

Phillips, R. 1998. "Religious Market Share and Mormon Church Activity." *Sociology of Religion* 59: 117–30.

Pickering, W., ed. 1975. *Durkheim on Religion*. London: Routledge.

Pitts, William L., Jr. 1995. "Davidians and Branch Davidians: 1929–1987." In Stuart A. Wright, ed., *Armageddon in Waco* (pp. 20–42). Chicago: University of Chicago Press.

Pixley, Jorge V., and Clodovis Boff. 1989. *The Bible, the Church, and the Poor*. Maryknoll, NY: Orbis Books.

Platt, Gerald M., and Michael Fraser. 1998. "Race and Gender Discourse Strategies: Creating Solidarity and Framing the Civil Rights Movement. *Social Problems* 45: 160–79.

Platt, Gerald M., and Rhys H. Williams. 1988. "Religion, Ideology and Electoral Politics." *Society* 25: 38–45.

Ponticelli, Christy. 1999. "Crafting Stories of Sexual Identity Reconstruction." *Social Psychology Quarterly* 62: 157–72.

Popkin, Eric. 1999. "Guatemalan Mayan Migration to Los Angeles: Constructing Transnational Linkages in the Context of the Settlement Process." *Ethnic and Racial Studies* 22: 267–89.

Porter, Jack N. 1998. *The Sociology of Jewry: A Curriculum Guide*. 2nd ed. Washington, DC: American Sociological Association.

Portes, Alejandro. 1996. "Transnational Communities: Their Emergence and Significance in the Contemporary World-system." In R. P. Korzeniewicz and W. C. Smith, eds., *Latin America in the World Economy*. Westport, CT: Greenwood Press.

———. 2000. "The Hidden Abode: Sociology as Analysis of the Unexpected." *American Sociological Review* 65: 1–18.

Portes, Alejandro, and Rubén G. Rumbaut. 1996. *Immigrant America: A Portrait*. 2nd ed. Berkeley: University of California Press.

Powell, Milton B., ed. 1967. *The Voluntary Church: Religious Life, 1740–1860, Seen Through the Eyes of European Visitors*. New York: Macmillan.

Powell, Walter W., and Paul J. DiMaggio, eds. 1991. *The New Institutionalism in Organizational Analysis*. Chicago: University of Chicago Press.

Pozzetta, George, ed. 1991. *Ethnicity, Ethnic Identity, and Language Maintenance*. New York: Garland Publishers.

Prelinger, C., ed. 1992. *Gender, Spirituality and Commitment in American Mainline Denominations*. New York: Oxford University Press.

Prell, Riv-Ellen. 2001. "A Response to Charles Liebman." Paper presented at the Annual Meeting of the Association for Jewish Studies and the Association for the Social Scientific Study of Jewry, Boston, Massachusetts.

Prentice, Deborah A., and Dale Miller. 1992. "When Small Effects are Impressive." *Psychological Bulletin* 112: 160–4.

Presser, Stanley, and Linda Stinson. 1998. "Data Collection Mode and Social Desirability Bias in Self-Reported Religious Attendance." *American Sociological Review* 63: 134–45.

Presser, Stanley, and Michael Traugott. 1992. "Little White Lies and Social Science Models." *Public Opinion Quarterly* 56: 77–86.

Primer, B. 1979. *Protestants and American Business Methods*. Ann Arbor: UMI Research Press.

Princeton Religion Research Center. 1978. *The Unchurched American*. Princeton, NJ: The Gallup Organization.

Pritt, Ann. 1998. "Spiritual Correlates of Reported Sexual Abuse among Mormon Women." *Journal for the Scientific Study of Religion* 37: 273–85.

Przeworski, Adam, and John Sprague. 1986. *Paper Stones: A History of Electoral Socialism*. Chicago: University of Chicago Press.

Putnam, Robert. 2000. *Bowling Alone*. New York: Simon and Schuster.

Quicke, A., and Quicke, L. 1992. *Hidden Agendas: The Politics of Religious Broadcasting in Britain 1987–91*. Virginia Beach, VA: Dominion Kings Grant Publications.

Radcliffe-Brown, A. R. 1922/1964. *The Andaman Islanders*. Glencoe, IL: The Free Press.

Rahman, Momin. 2000. *Sexuality and Democracy: Identities and Strategies in Lesbian and Gay Politics*. Edinburgh: Edinburgh University Press.

Rappaport, Roy A. 1999. *Ritual and Religion in the Making of Humanity*. Cambridge, UK: Cambridge University Press.

Read, Jen'nan Ghazal, and John Bartkowski. 2000. "To Veil or not to Veil? A Case Study of Identity Negotiation among Muslim Women in Austin, Texas." *Gender and Society* 14: 395–417.

Reader, Ian. 2000. *Religious Violence in Contemporary Japan: The Case of Aum Shinrikyô*. Honolulu: University of Hawaii Press.

Reed, Andrew. 1835. *A Narrative of the Visit to the American Churches*. London: Jackson and Walford.

Reed, Ralph. 1996. *Active Faith: How Christians are Changing the Soul of American Politics*. New York: Free Press.

Regnerus, Mark, David Sikkink, and Chrisitian Smith. 1999. "Voting with the Christian Right: Contextual and Individual Patterns of Electoral Influence." *Social Forces* 81: 1375–403.

Reichley, James A. 1985. *Religion in American Public Life*. Washington, DC: The Brookings Institution.

Rex, John. 1981. *Social Conflict*. London: Longman.

Reynolds, D., and F. Nelson. 1981. "Personality, Life Situation, and its Life Expectancy." *Suicide and Life-Threatening Behavior* 11: 99–110.

Richardson, Herbert. 1967. *Toward an American Theology*. New York: Harper & Row.

Richman, Bruce. 2000. "How Music Fixed 'Nonsense' into Significant Formulas: On Rhythm, Repetition, and Meaning." In Nils Wallin, Bjorn Merker, and Steven Brown, eds., *The Origins of Music* (pp. 301–12). Cambridge, MA: MIT Press.

Ricoeur, Paul. 1981. *Hermeneutics and the Human Sciences*. Ed. and trans. John B. Thompson. Cambridge: Cambridge University Press.

Riddle, Donald W. 1931. *The Martyrs: A Study in Social Control*. Chicago: University of Chicago Press.

Rieff, Philip. 1966. *The Triumph of the Therapeutic: Uses of Faith After Freud*. New York: Harper.

Riesebrodt, Martin. 1993. *Pious Passion: The Emergence of Fundamentalism in the United States and Iran*. Berkeley: University of California Press.

Rivera, Luis N. 1992. *A Violent Evangelism: The Political and Religious Conquest of the Americas*. Louisville, KY: Westminster/John Knox Press.

Robbins, Mandy, Leslie Francis, and C. J. F. Routledge. 1997. "The Personality Characteristics of Anglican Stipendiary Parochial Clergy: Gender Differences Revisited." *Personality and Individual Differences* 23: 199–204.

Robbins, Mandy, Leslie Francis, John Haley, and William Kay. 2001. "The Personality Characteristics of Methodist Ministers: Feminine Men and Masculine Women." *Journal for the Scientific Study of Religion* 40: 123–8.

Robbins, Thomas. 1986. "Religious Mass Suicide Before Jonestown: The Russian Old Believers." *Sociological Analysis* 47: 1–20.

———. 1988. *Cults, Converts, and Charisma: The Sociology of New Religious Movements*. Beverly Hills, CA: Sage.

———. 1997. "Religious Movements and Violence: A Friendly Critique of the Interpretive Approach." *Novio Religio* 1: 17–33.

Robbins, Thomas, and Dick Anthony. 1995. "Sects and Violence: Factors Affecting the Volatility of Marginal Religious Movements." In Stuart A. Wright, ed., *Armageddon in Mount Carmel* (pp. 236–59). Chicago: The University of Chicago Press.

Roberts, Michael K. 1990. "Nazarenes and Social Ministry: A Holiness Tradition." In Powell Davidson, C. Lincoln Johnson, and Alan K. Mock, eds., *Faith and Social Ministry: Ten Christian Perspectives* (pp. 157–8). Chicago: Loyola University Press.

Robnett, Belinda. 1997. *How Long, How Long?: African-American Women in the Struggle for Civil Rights*. New York: Oxford University Press.

Rochford, E. Burke. 1985. *Hare Krishna in America*. New Brunswick, NJ: Rutgers University Press.

Rogers, Mary Beth. 1990. *Cold Anger*. Denton, TX: University of North Texas Press.

Rogowski, Ronald. 1981. "Research Note: Social Class and Partisanship in European Electorates: A Re-Assessment." *World Politics* 33: 639–49.

Ronsvalle, John, and Sylvia Ronsvalle. 1996. *Behind the Stained Glass Windows: Money Dynamics in the Church*. Grand Rapids, MI: Baker Books.

Roof, Wade Clark. 1978. *Community and Commitment: Religious Plausibility in a Liberal Protestant Church*. New York: Elsevier.

_____.1993. *A Generation of Seekers: The Spiritual Journeys of the Baby Boom Generation*. San Francisco: Harper & Row.

_____. 1999a. *Spiritual Marketplace: Baby Boomers and the Remaking of American Religion*. Princeton, NJ: Princeton University Press.

_____. 1999b. "Religious Studies and Sociology." *Contemporary Sociology* 28: 522–24.

Roof, Wade Clark, and William McKinney. 1987. *American Mainline Religion*. New Brunswick, NJ: Rutgers University Press.

Rooney, Jim. 1995. *Organizing the South Bronx*. Albany NY: State University of New York Press.

Roozen, David A., William McKinney, and Jackson W., Carroll. 1988. *Varieties of Religious Presence*. New York: Pilgrim Press.

Rose, Arnold M., and Caroline B. Rose, eds. 1965. *Minority Problems*. New York: Harper & Row.

Rose, Fred. 2000. *Coalitions Across the Class Divide : Lessons from the Labor, Peace, and Environmental Movements*. Ithaca, NY: Cornell University Press.

Rose, Richard, and Derek Urwin. 1969. "Social Cohesion, Political Parties, and Strains in Regimes." *Comparative Political Studies* 2: 7–67.

Rose, Susan. 1990. *Keeping Them Out of the Hands of Satan*. New York: Routledge.

Rosenthal, E. 1963. "Studies in Jewish Intermarriage in the U.S." *American Jewish Yearbook* 64: 3–53.

Rosenthal, R. 1979. "The "File Drawer Problem" and Tolerance for Null Results." *Psychological Bulletin* 86: 638–41.

_____. 1990. "How are we Doing in Soft Psychology?" *American Psychologist* 45: 775–7.

_____. 1991. "Effect Sizes: Pearson's Correlation, its Display via the BESD, and Alternative Indices." *American Psychologist* 46: 1086–7.

Roshwald, Mordecai. 1970. "Who is a Jew in Israel?" *Jewish Journal of Sociology* 12: 233–66.

Rossi, Alice S., ed. 2001. *Caring and Doing for Others: Social Responsibility in the Domains of Family, Work, and Community*. Chicago: University of Chcago Press.

Rossi, Alice S., and Peter H. Rossi. 1990. *Of Human Bonding: Parent-Child Relations Across the Life Course*. New York: Aldine de Gruyter.

Roth, Guenther. 1975. "Socio-historical Model and Developmental Theory: Charismatic Community, Charisma of Reason, and the Counterculture." *American Sociological Review* 40: 148–57.

Rouse, Roger. 1992. "Making Sense of Settlement: Class Transformation, Cultural Struggle, and Transnationalism among Mexican Migrants in the U.S." In N. Glick-Schiller, L. Basch, and C. Blanc-Szanton, eds., *Toward a Transnational Perspective on Migration: Race, Class, Ethnicity and Nationalism Reconsidered*. New York: Annals of the New York Academy of Sciences.

Rousseau, Jean Jacques. 1762/1960. *The Social Contract*. New York: Oxford University Press.

Rozell, Mark J., and Clyde Wilcox. 1995. *God at the Grass Roots: The Christian Right in the 1994 Elections*. Lanham, MD: Rowman and Littlefield.

Ruiz, Vicki L. 1987. "By the Day or the Week: Mexicana Domestic Workers in El Paso." In Vicki L. Ruiz and Susan Tiano, eds., *Women on the U.S.- Mexico Border: Responses to Change* (pp. 61–76). Boston: Allen & Unwin.

Rule, James. 1988. *Theories of Civil Violence*. Berkeley: University of California Press.

Rustomji, Yezdi. 2000. "The Zoroastrian Center: An Ancient Faith in Diaspora." In Helen Rose Ebaugh and Janet S. Chafetz, eds., *Religion and the New Immigrants: Continuities and Adaptations in Immigrant Congregations* (pp. 243–54). Walnut Creek CA: AltaMira Press.

Sacks, Jonathan. 1997. *Faith in the Future: The Ecology of Hope and the Restoration of Family, Community, and Faith*. Macon, GA: Mercer University Press.

Saint-Simon, Henri. 1969. *Le Nouveau Christianisme et les Écrits sur la Religion*. Ed. H. Desroche. Paris: Éditions de Seuil.

Samet, Moshe. 1985. "Who is a Jew? (1958–1977)." *The Jerusalem Quarterly* 36: 88–108.

———. 1986. "Who is a Jew? (1978–1985.)" *The Jerusalem Quarterly* 37: 109–39.

Sanders, Cheryl J. 1996. *Saints in Exile: The Holiness-Pentecostal Experience in African American Religion and Culture*. New York: Oxford University Press.

Sandomirsky, Sharon, and John Wilson. 1990. "Processes of Disaffiliation: Religious Mobility Among Men and Women." *Social Forces* 68: 1211–29.

Sarna, Jonathan D., and Karla Goldman. 1994. "From Synagogue-Community to Citadel of Reform: The history of K.K. Bene Israel (Rockdale Temple) in Cincinnati, Ohio." In James P. Wind and James W. Lewis, eds., *American Congregations*. Vol. 1 (pp. 159–220). Chicago: University of Chicago Press.

Sartre, Jean-Paul. 1948. *Anti-Semite and Jew*. New York: Schocken.

Saz, P., and M. E. Dewey. 2001. "Depression, Depressive Symptoms and Mortality in Persons Aged 65 and Over Living in the Community: A Systematic Review of The Literature." *International Journal of Geriatric Psychiatry* 16: 622–30.

Schaff, Philip. 1855/1961. *America: A Sketch of Its Political, Social, and Religious Character*. Cambridge MA: Harvard University Press.

Schantz, M. 1997. "Religious Tracts, Evangelical Reform, and the Market Revolution in Antebellum America." *Journal of The Early Republic* 17: 425–66.

Schauffler, H. H., and E. R. Brown. 2000. *The State of Health Insurance in California, 1999*. Berkeley: University of California Press.

Scheepers, Peer, Jan Lammers, and Jan Peters. 1994. "Religious and Class Voting in the Netherlands 1990–1991: A Review of Recent Contributions Tested." *Netherlands' Journal of Social Sciences* 30: 5–24.

Schiller, Anne. 1997. *Small Sacrifices: Religious Change and Cultural Identity Among the Ngaju of Indonesia*. New York: Oxford University Press.

Schluchter, Wolfgang. 1989. *Rationalism, Religion, and Domination*. Berkeley: University of California Press.

Schnittker, J. 2001. "When is Faith Enough? The Effects of Religious Involvement on Depression." *Journal for the Scientific Study of Religion* 40: 393–411.

Schoenfeld, Stuart. 1998. "On Theory and Methods in the Study of Jewish Identity." In Ernest Krausz and Gitta Tulea, eds. *Jewish Survival: The Identity Problem at the Close of the Twentieth Century* (pp. 107–19). New Brunswick NJ: Transaction.

Schudson, Michael. 1998. *The Good Citizen: A History of American Civic Life*. New York: Free Press.

Schwartz, Jim, and Sarit Amir. 2001. *Jewish Identity and Intermarriage – Towards a Definition*. New York: United Jewish Communities Research Department.

Schwartz, J., and J. Scheckner. 1999. "Jewish Population in the United States, 1998." *American Jewish Yearbook* 99: 209–31.

Schweid, Eliezer. 1999. "Judaism in Israeli Culture." In Dan Urian and Efraim Karsh, eds. *In Search of Identity: Jewish Aspects in Israeli Culture* (pp. 9–28). London: Frank Cass.

Scott, James C. 1985. *Weapons of the Weak: Everyday Forms of Peasant Resistance*. New Haven CT: Yale University Press.

Scott, Joan Wallach. 1991. "The Evidence of Experience." *Critical Inquiry* 17: 773–97.

Scott, Marvin B., and Stanford Lyman. 1968. "Accounts." *American Sociological Review* 33: 46–62.

Scott, W. Richard. 1987. *Organizations: Rational, Natural and Open Systems*. Englewood Cliffs, NJ: Prentice Hall.

———. 1995. *Institutions and Organizations*. Beverly Hills, CA: Sage.

Scott, W. Richard, and John W. Meyer. 1991. "The Organization of Societal Sectors: Propositions and Early Evidence." In Walter W. Powell and Paul J. DiMaggio, eds., *The New Institutionalism in Organizational Analysis* (pp. 108–40). Chicago: University of Chicago Press.

Seeman, T., G. Kaplan, L. Knudsen, R. Cohen, and J. Guralnik. 1987. "Social Network Ties and Mortality Among the Elderly in the Alameda County Study." *American Journal of Epidemiology* 126: 714–23.

Segalman, Ralph. 1967. "Jewish Identity Scales: A Report." *Jewish Social Studies* 29: 92–111.

Segura, Denise A. 1991. "Ambivalence or Continuity?: Motherhood and Employment among Chicanas and Mexican Immigrant Women Workers." *Aztlan* 20: 119–50.

Seidler, John, and Katherine Meyer. 1989. *Conflict and Change in the Catholic Church*. New Brunswick, NJ: Rutgers University Press.

Seligman, Adam B. 1992. *The Idea of Civil Society*. New York: Free Press.

Sen, Amartya. 1973. "Behavior and the Concept of Preference." *Economica* 40: 241–59.

———. 1993. "Internal Consistency of Choice." *Econometrica* 61: 495–521.

Sered, Susan. 2000. *What Makes Women Sick? Maternity, Modesty, and Militarism in Israeli Society*. Waltham MA: Brandeis University Press.

Sewell, William H. Jr. 1992. "A Theory of Structure: Duality, Agency, and Transformation." *American Journal of Sociology* 98: 1–29.

Shain, Barry Alan. 1994. *The Myth of American Individualism: The Protestant Origins of American Political Thought*. Princeton: Princeton University Press.

Shand, Jack. 1990. "A Forty-Year Follow Up of the Religious Beliefs and Attitudes of a Sample of Amherst College Grads." *Research in the Social Scientific Study of Religion* 2: 117–36.

Shaw, Stephen J. 1994. "An Oak among Churches: St. Boniface Parish, Chicago, 1864–1990." In James P. Wind and James W. Lewis, eds., *American Congregations*. Volume 2 (pp. 349–95). Chicago: University of Chicago Press.

Sherkat, Darren E. 1991a. "Leaving the Faith: Testing Sociological Theories of Religious Switching Using Survival Models." *Social Science Research* 20: 171–87.

———. 1991b. *Religious Socialization and the Family: An Examination of Religious Influence in the Family over the Life Course*. Unpublished Ph.D. Dissertation. Department of Sociology. Duke University.

———. 1997. "Embedding Religious Choices: Integrating Preferences and Social Constraints into Rational Choice Theories of Religious Behavior." In Lawrence A. Young, ed., *Rational Choice Theory and Religion: Summary and Assessment* (pp. 65–86). New York: Routledge.

———. 1998. "Counterculture or Continuity? Examining Competing Influences on Baby Boomers' Religious Orientations and Participation." *Social Forces* 76: 1087–1115.

———. 2001. "Tracking the Restructuring of American Religion." *Social Forces* 79: 1459–93.

Sherkat, Darren E., and T. Jean Blocker. 1997. "Explaining the Political and Personal Consequences of Protest." *Social Forces*. 75: 1049–76.

Sherkat, Darren E., and Shannon A. Cunningham. 1998. "Extending the Semi-Involuntary Institution: Social Constraints and Regional Differences in Private Religious Consumption Among African Americans." *Journal for the Scientific Study of Religion* 37: 383–96.

Sherkat, Darren, and Alfred Darnell. 1999. "The Effect of Parents' Fundamentalism on Children's Educational Attainment: Examining Differences by Gender and Children's Fundamentalism." *Journal for the Scientific Study of Religion* 38: 23–36.

Sherkat, Darren, and Christopher Ellison. 1999. "Recent Developments and Current Controversies in the Sociology of Religion." *Annual Review of Sociology* 25: 363–94.

Sherkat, Darren E., and John Wilson. 1995. "Preferences, Constraints, and Choices in Religious Markets: An Examination of Religious Switching and Apostasy." *Social Forces* 73: 993–1026.

Sheskin, Ira. 2001. *How Jewish Communities Differ: Variations in the Findings of Local Jewish Demographic Studies*. New York: City University of New York, North America Jewish Data Bank.

Shibley, Mark A. 1996. *Resurgent Evangelicalism in the United States: Mapping Cultural Change Since 1970*. Columbia: University of South Carolina Press.

Shils, Edward. 1975. *Center and Periphery: Essays in Macro-Sociology*. Chicago: University of Chicago Press.

Shin, Eui Hang, and Hyung Park. 1988. "An Analysis of Causes of Schisms in Ethnic Churches: The Case of Korean-American Churches." *Sociological Analysis* 49: 234–48.

Shiner, Larry. 1967. "The Concept of Secularization in Empirical Research." *Journal for the Scientific Study of Religion* 6: 207–20.

Shotter, John. 1984. *Social Accountability and Selfhood*. New York: Blackwell.

Shupe, Anson, William Stacey, and Susan Darnell, eds. 2000. *Bad Pastors*. New York: New York University Press.

Sigel, Roberta S. 1989. "Conclusion: Adult Political Learning – A Lifelong Process." In Roberta S. Sigel, ed., *Political Learning in Adulthood: A Sourcebook of Theory and Research* (pp. 458–72). Chicago. University of Chicago Press.

Sikkink, David. 1999. " 'I Just Say I'm a Christian': Symbolic Boundaries and Identity Formation Among Church-Going Protestants." In D. Jacobsen, J. Trollinger, and William Vance, eds., *Re-Forming the Center: American Protestantism 1960 to the Present* (pp. 49–71). Grand Rapids, MI: Eerdmans.

Silva, Cynthia. 1984. *Pentecostalism as Oppositional Culture.* Unpublished undergraduate thesis, Harvard University.

Silver, Brian D., Barbara A. Anderson, and Paul R. Abramson. 1986. "Who Overreports Voting?" *American Political Science Review* 80: 613–24.

Simmel, Georg. 1908/1955. *Conflict and the Web of Group-Affiliations.* New York: Free Press.

Simpson, George E., and J. Milton Yinger. 1972. *Racial and Cultural Minorities: An Analysis of Prejudice and Discrimination.* New York: Harper & Row.

Sinnott, Jan. 1994. "Development and Yearning: Cognitive Aspects of Spiritual Development." *Journal of Adult Development* 1: 91–9.

Sklare, Marshall. 1971. *America's Jews.* New York: Random House.

Sklare, Marshall, and Joseph Greenblum. 1979/1967. *Jewish Identity on the Suburban Frontier: A Study of Group Survival in the Open Society.* 2nd ed. Chicago: University of Chicago Press.

Skocpol, Theda. 1979. *States and Social Revolutions.* New York: Cambridge University Press.

Skocpol, Theda, and Morris Fiorina, eds. 1999. *Civic Engagement in American Democracy.* Washington DC: Brookings Institute.

Skolnick, Arlene. 1991. *Embattled Paradise: The American Family in an Age of Uncertainty.* New York: Basic Books.

Sloan, R. P., and E. Bagiella. 2001. "Religion and Health." *Health Psychology* 20: 228.

Smelser, Neil J. 1994. "The Sociological Perspective on the Economy." In Neil J. Smelser and Richard Swedberg, eds., *The Handbook of Economic Sociology* (pp. 3–26). Princeton, NJ: Princeton University Press.

———. 1995. "Economic Rationality as a Religious System." In R. Wuthnour, ed., *Rethinking Materialism: Perspectives on the Spiritual Dimension of Economic Behavior* (pp. 73–92). Grand Rapids, MI: Eerdmans.

Smelser, Neil J., and Richard Swedberg, eds. 1994. *The Handbook of Economic Sociology.* Princeton, NJ: Princeton University Press.

Smidt, Corwin. 1989. "Contemporary Evangelical Political Involvement: An Overview." In Corwin Smidt, ed., *Contemporary Evangelical Political Involvement.* Lanham, MD: University Presses of America.

Smith, Christian. 1991. *The Emergence of Liberation Theology: Radical Religion and Social Movement Theory.* Chicago: University of Chicago Press.

———, ed. 1996a. *Disruptive Religion: The Force of Faith in Social-Movement Activism.* New York: Routledge.

———. 1996b. *Resisting Reagan: The U.S. Central America Peace Movement.* Chicago: University of Chicago Press.

Smith, Christian, with Michael Emerson, Sally Gallagher, Paul Kennedy, and David Sikkink. 1998. *American Evangelicalism: Embattled and Thriving.* Chicago: University of Chicago Press.

Smith, Dorothy. 1987. *The Everyday World as Problematic.* Boston: Northeastern University Press.

———. 1992. "Sociology from Women's Experience: A Reaffirmation." *Sociological Theory* 10: 88–98.

———. 1997. "Comment on Hekman's Truth and Method: Feminist Standpoint Theory Revisited." *Signs* 22: 392–398.

———. 1999. *Writing the Social.* Toronto: University of Toronto Press.

Smith, M. P. 1994. "Can you Imagine? Transnational Migration and the Globalization of Grassroots Politics." *Social Text* 39: 15–33.

Smith, Timothy B., Michael McCullough, and J. Poll. 2002. "A Meta-analytic Review of the Religiousness-Depression Association: Evidence for Main Effects and Stress-buffering Effects." Manuscript submitted for publication.

Smith, Timothy L. 1978. "Religion and Ethnicity in America." *American Historical Review* 83: 1155–85.

_____. 1980. *Revivalism and Reform: American Protestantism on the Eve of the Civil War.* Baltimore, MD: Johns Hopkins University Press.

Smith, Tom W. 1990. "Classifying Protestant Denominations." *Review of Religious Research* 31: 225–45.

Smith, Wilfred C. 1978. *The Meaning and End of Religion.* San Francisco: Harper.

Snow, David A., and Robert D. Benford. 1988. "Ideology, Frame Resonance and Participant Mobilization." *International Social Movement Research* 1: 197–217.

_____. 1992. "Master Frames and Cycles of Protest." In Aldon Morris and Carole Mueller, eds., *Frontiers in Social Movement Theory* (pp. 133–55). New Haven, CT: Yale University Press.

Snow, David A., E. Burke Rochford, Steven K. Worden, and Robert D. Benford. 1986. "Frame Alignment Processes, Micromobilization, and Movement Participation." *American Sociological Review* 51: 464–81.

Sobrino, Jon. 1978. *Christology at the Crossroads: A Latin American Approach.* Maryknoll, NY: Orbis Books.

_____. 1984. *The True Church and the Poor.* Maryknoll, NY: Orbis Books.

Soeffner, Hans-Georg. 1997. *The Order of Rituals: The Interpretation of Everyday Life.* New Brunswick, NJ: Transaction.

Somers, Margaret R. 1994. "The Narrative Constitution of Identity: A Relational and Network Approach." *Theory and Society* 23: 605–49.

Sommerville, C. John. 1992. *The Secularization of Early Modern England.* New York: Oxford University Press.

Sorel, Georges. 1906/1950. *Reflections on Violence.* New York: Free Press.

Spence, Jonathan D. 1996. *God's Chinese Son: The Taiping Heavenly Kingdom of Hong Xiuquan.* New York: Norton.

Spickard, James V., J. Shawn Landres, and Meredith McGuire, eds. 2002. *Personal Knowledge and Beyond: Reshaping the Ethnography of Religion.* New York: New York University Press.

Spivak, Gayetri. 1988. *In Other Worlds: Essays in Cultural Politics.* New York: Methuen.

Stacey, Judith, and Susan E. Gerrard. 1990. "We Are Not Doormats: The Influence of Feminism on Contemporary Evangelicalism in the United States." In Faye Ginsburg and Anna Tsing, eds., *Uncertain Terms: Negotiating Gender in American Culture* (pp. 98–117). Boston: Beacon Press.

Stacey, Judith, and Barrie Thorne. 1985. "The Missing Feminist Revolution in Sociology." *Social Problems* 32: 301–16.

Stack, Steve, Ira Wasserman, and Augustine Kposowa. 1994. "The Effects of Religion and Feminism on Suicide Ideology: Analysis of National Survey Data." *Journal for the Scientific Study of Religion* 33: 110–21.

Stark, Rodney. 1985. "From Church-Sect to Religious Economies." In Phillip E. Hammond, ed., *The Sacred in a Post-Secular Age* (pp. 139–49). Berkeley: University of California Press.

_____. 1992. "Do Catholic Societies Really Exist?" *Rationality and Society* 4: 261–271.

_____. 1996. *The Rise of Christianity: A Sociologist Reconsiders History.* Princeton, NJ: Princeton University Press.

_____. 2000. "Physiology and Faith: Addressing the 'Universal' Gender Difference in Religious Commitment." Paper presented at the annual meeting of the Religious Research Association, Houston, Texas.

Stark, Rodney, and William Sims Bainbridge. 1980. "Networks of Faith: Interpersonal Bonds and Recruitment to Cults and Sects." *American Journal of Sociology* 85: 1376–85.

_____. 1985. *The Future of Religion: Secularization, Revival, and Cult Formation.* Berkeley: University of California Press.

_____. 1987. *A Theory of Religion.* New Brunswick, NJ: Rutgers University Press.

Stark, Rodney, and Roger Finke. 2000. *Acts of Faith: Exploring the Human Side of Religion.* Berkeley: University of California Press.

Stark, Rodney, and Laurence Iannaccone. 1994. "A Supply-Side Reinterpretation of the Secularization of Europe." *Journal for the Scientific Study of Religion* 33: 230–52.

Stark Rodney, Roger Finke, and Laurence Iannaccone. 1995. "Pluralism and Piety: England and Wales, 1851." *Journal for the Scientific Study of Religion* 36: 431–44.

Stark, Rodney, Laurence Iannaccone, and Roger Finke. 1996. "Religion, Science and Rationality," *American Economic Review* (Papers and Proceedings): 433–437.

Stark, Rodney, and James McCann. 1993. "Market Forces and Catholic Commitment: Exploring the New Paradigm." *Journal for the Scientific Study of Religion* 32: 111–24.

Steensland, Brian, Jerry Z. Park, Mark D. Regnerus, Lynn D. Robinson, W. Bradford Wilcox, and Robert D. Woodberry. 2000. "The Measure of American Religion: Toward Improving the State of the Art." *Social Forces* 79: 291–318.

Stepan, Alfred C. 1988. *Rethinking Military Politics: Brazil and the Southern Cone*. Princeton, NJ: Princeton University Press.

Stephens, John D. 1979. "Religion and Politics in Three Northwest European Democracies." *Comparative Social Research* 2: 129–57.

Stern, Barry. 2001. "Jewish Identity Research and the Social Psychology of Ethnic Identity." Paper presented at University of Connecticut Faculty Forum in Judaic Studies.

Stigler, George G., and Gary S. Becker. 1977. "De Gustibus Non Est Disputandum." *American Economic Review* 67: 76–90.

Stinchcombe, Arthur L. 1968. *Constructing Social Theories*. Chicago: Rand McNally.

———. 1978. *Theoretical Methods in Social History*. New York: Academic Press.

Stokes, Kenneth. 1990. "Faith Development in the Adult Life Cycle." *Journal of Religious Gerontology* 7:167–84.

Stoll, David. 1990. *Is Latin America Turning Protestant?: The Politics of Evangelical Growth*. Berkeley: University of California Press.

Stolzenberg, Ross M., Mary Blair-Loy, and Linda J. Waite. 1995. "Religious Participation Over the Early Life Course: Age and Family Life Cycle Effects on Church Membership." *American Sociological Review* 60: 84–103.

Strauss, Alena Janet. 1979. *Social Psychological Determinants of Jewish Identification Among Canadians in Their Twenties*. Unpublished Master's Thesis, University of Toronto.

Strauss, Anselm L., and Juliet M. Corbin. 1998. *Basics of Qualitative Research: Techniques and Procedures for Developing Grounded Theory*. Newbury Park, CA: Sage.

Strawbridge, William, R. D. Cohen, S. J. Shema, and G. A. Kaplan. 1997. "Frequent Attendance at Religious Services and Mortality Over 28 Years." *American Journal of Public Health* 87: 957–61.

Strawbridge, William, R. D. Cohen, and S. J. Shema. 2000. "Comparative Strength of Association Between Religious Attendance and Survival." *International Journal of Psychiatry in Medicine* 30: 299–308.

Stroebe, Wolfgang, Arie W. Kruhlanski, Daniel Bar-Tal, and Miles Hewstone, eds. 1988. *The Social Psychology of Intergroup Conflict*. Berlin: Springer-Verlag.

Sugden, Chris. 1997. *Seeking the Asian Face of Jesus*. Oxford: Regnum.

Suh, Changwon J. 1987. *A Formulation of Minjung Theology Toward a Socio-historical Theology of Asia*. Unpublished Ph.D. dissertation, Union Theological Seminary, New York.

Sullins, D. Paul. 1993. "Switching Close to Home: Volatility or Coherence in Protestant Affiliation Patterns." *Social Forces* 72: 399–419.

Sullivan, Kathleen. 1998. "Immigrant Religion and the Challenge of the Second Generation: Religion as the Anti-dote to 'Amoral' U.S. Society." Paper delivered at the annual meetings of the Society for the Scientific Study of Religion, Montreal, Canada.

———. 2000a. "Iglesia de Dios: An Extended Family." In Helen Rose Ebaugh and Janet S. Chafetz, eds., *Religion and the New Immigrants: Continuities and Adaptations in Immigrant Congregations* (pp. 141–51). Walnut Creek, CA: AltaMira Press.

———. 2000b. "St. Catherine's Catholic Church: One Church, Parallel Congregations." In Helen Rose Ebaugh and Janet S. Chafetz, eds., *Religion and the New Immigrants: Continuities and Adaptations in Immigrant Congregations* (pp. 125–40). Walnut Creek, CA: AltaMira Press.

Sundquist, James. 1983. *Dynamics of the Party System*. Rev. ed. Washington, DC: Brookings Institute.

Sundberg, Jan, and Sten Berglund. 1984. "Representative Democracy in Crisis? Reflections on Scandinavian Party Systems." Congres Mondial de Science Politique.

Susser, Bernard, and Charles S. Liebman. 1999. *Choosing Survival: Strategies for a Jewish Future*. New York: Oxford University Press.

Suziedelis, A., and R. H. Potvin. 1981. "Sex Differences in Factors Affecting Religiousness Among Catholic Adolescents." *Journal for the Scientific Study of Religion* 20: 38–51.

Swartz, David. 1998. *Culture and Power: The Sociology of Pierre Bourdieu*. Chicago: University of Chicago Press.

Swatos, William H., and Kevin Christiano. 1999. "Secularization Theory: The Course of a Concept." *Sociology of Religion* 60: 209–28.

Swatos, William, Peter Kivisto, and P. Gustafson. 1998. "Max Weber" In William Swatos, ed., *Encyclopedia of Religion and Society* (pp. 547–52). Walnut Creek, CA: AltaMira Press.

Swidler, Ann. 1986. "Culture in Action: Symbols and Strategies." *American Sociological Review* 51: 273–86.

Swierenga, Robert P. 1990. "Ethnoreligious Political Behavior in the Mid-Nineteenth Century: Voting, Values, Cultures." In Mark A. Noll, ed., *Religion and American Politics* (pp. 146–71). New York: Oxford University Press.

Tabory, Ephraim. 1983. "Reform and Conservative Judaism in Israel: A Social and Religious Profile." *American Jewish Yearbook* 83: 41–61.

———. 1984. "Rights and Rites: Women's Roles in Liberal Religious Movements in Israel." *Sex Roles* 11:155–62.

———. 1998. *Reform Judaism in Israel: Progress and Prospects*. New York: The Institute on American Jewish-Israel Relations; and Ramat Gan: The Argov Center of Bar Ilan University.

———. 2003a. "The Israel Reform and Conservative Movements and the Market for Liberal Judaism." In Uzi Rebhun and Chaim I. Waxman, eds., *Jews in Israel*. Hanover, NH: University Press of New England/Brandeis University Press.

———. 2003b. "'A Nation that Dwells Alone': Judaism as an Integrating and Divisive Factor in Israeli Society." In L. Eisenberg, N. Caplan, N. Sokoloff and M. Abu Nimer, eds. *Traditions and Transitions in Israel Studies*. Volume Six. Albany, NY: State University of New York Press.

Tabory, Ephraim, and Sharon Erez. 2003. "Circumscribed Circumcision: The Motivations and Identities of Israeli Parents Who Do Not Circumcise Their Sons." In Elizabeth Mark, ed., *My Covenant in Your Flesh*. Hanover, NH: University Press of New England/Brandeis University Press.

Tabory, Joseph. 2001. "The Benedictions of Self-Identity and the Changing Status of Women and of Orthodoxy." *Kenishta 1:* 107–38.

Taheri, Amir. 1987. *Holy Terror: Inside the World of Islamic Terrorism*. Bethesda, MD: Adler & Adler.

Takayama, K. P. 1974. "Administrative Structures and Political Processes in Protestant Denominations." *Publius* 4: 5–37.

———. 1979. "Formal Polity and Power Distribution in American Protestant Denominations." *Sociological Quarterly* 20: 321–32.

Tambiah, Stanley Jeyaraja. 1992. *Buddhism Betrayed?: Religion, Politics, and Violence in Sri Lanka*. Chicago: University of Chicago Press.

Tamez, Elsa. 1982. *Bible of the Oppressed*. Maryknoll, NY: Orbis Books.

———. 1989. *Through Her Eyes: Women's Theology from Latin America*. Maryknoll, NY: Orbis Books.

Tamney, Joseph B., and Stephen D. Johnson. 1990. "Religious Diversity and Ecumenical Social Action." *Review of Religious Research* 32: 1.

Tarrow, Sidney. 1992. *Power in Movement: Social Movements, Collective Action, and Politics*. Cambridge: Cambridge University Press.

Taylor, Robert J. 1988. "Structural Determinants of Religious Participation Among Black Americans." *Review of Religious Research* 30: 114–25.

Taylor, Charles. 1989. *Sources of the Self: The Making of the Modern Identity*. Cambridge, MA: Harvard University Press.

———. 1991. *The Ethics of Authenticity*. Cambridge, MA: Harvard University Press.

Tenenbaum, Shelly. 2000. "Good or Bad for the Jews? Moving Beyond the Continuity Debate." *Contemporary Jewry* 21: 91–7.

Terry, Randall. 1988. *Operation Rescue*. Springdale, PA: Whitaker House.

Teske, Nathan. 1997. *Political Activists in America: The Identity Construction Model of Political Participation*. New York: Cambridge University Press.

Thio, Alex. 1992. *Sociology: An Introduction*. 3rd ed. New York: Harper Collins.

Thomas, John L. 1956. *The American Catholic Family*. Englewood Cliffs, NJ: Prentice-Hall.

Thomas, Keith. 1971. *Religion and the Decline of Magic*. New York: Scribner's.

Thomas, William I., and Florian Znaniecki. 1918. *The Polish Peasant in Europe and America*. Chicago: University of Chicago Press.

Thomas, Darwin L., and Marie Cornwall. 1990. "Religion and Family in the 1980's: Discovery and Development." *Journal of Marriage and the Family* 52: 983–92.

Thumma, Scott. 1991. "Negotiating a Religious Identity." *Sociological Analysis* 52: 333–47.

Tilly, Charles. 1979. "Repertoires of Contention in America and Britain, 1750–1830." In Mayer Zald and John D. McCarthy, eds., *The Dynamics of Social Movements* (pp. 126–55). Cambridge: Winthrop.

Tiryakian, Edward. 1993. "American Religious Exceptionalism: A Reconsideration." *Annals of the American Academy of Political and Social Science* 527: 40–54.

Tomasi, Silvano M. 1975. *Piety and Power: The Role of the Italian American Parishes in the New York Metropolitan Area, 1880–1930*. Staten Island, NY: Center for Migration Studies.

Tornstam, Lars. 1999. "Late-Life Transcendence: A New Developmental Perspective on Aging." In L. Eugene Thomas and Susan Eisenhandler, eds., *Religion, Belief, and Spirituality in Late Life* (pp. 178–202). New York: Springer.

Torrance, Robert M. 1994. *The Spiritual Quest: Transcendence in Myth, Religion, and Science*. Berkeley: University of California Press.

Traugott, Michael, and John P. Katosh. 1979. "Response Validity in Surveys of Voting Behavior." *Public Opinion Quarterly* 43: 359–77.

Treas, Judith. 1999. "Diversity in American Families." In Phyllis Moen, D. Dempster-McClain, and H. Walker, eds., *A Nation Divided: Diversity, Inequality, and Community in American Society* (pp. 245–59). Ithaca, NY: Cornell University Press.

Trinh, T. Minh-ha. 1988. *Woman, Native, Other: Writing Postcoloniality and Feminism*. Bloomington: University of Indiana Press.

Troeltsch, Ernest. 1931. *Social Teachings of the Christian Churches*. Volumes 1 and 2. New York: Harper and Brothers.

———. 1981. *The Social Teachings of the Christian Church*. Chicago: University of Chicago Press.

Tschannen, Olivier. 1991. "The Secularization Paradigm: A Systematization." *Journal for the Scientific Study of Religion* 30: 395–415.

———. 1992. *Les Théories de la Sécularisation*. Geneva: Droz.

Turner, Victor. 1977. *The Ritual Process*. Ithaca, NY: Cornell University Press.

Tuveson, Ernest Lee. 1968. *Redeemer Nation: The Idea of America's Millennial Role*. Chicago: University of Chicago Press.

Tweed, Thomas A. 1997. *Our Lady of the Exile: Diasporic Religion at a Cuban Catholic Shrine in Miami*. New York: Oxford University Press.

Twenge, J., and S. Nolen-Hoeksema. 2001. *Age, Gender, Race, SES, and Birth Cohort Differences on the Children's Depression Inventory: A Meta-analysis*. Manuscript submitted for publication.

Tzuriel, D., and M. M. Klein. 1977. "Ego Identity: Effects of Ethnocentrism, Ethnic Identification and Cognitive Complexity in Israeli, Oriental, and Western Ethnic Groups." *Psychological Reports* 40: 1099–110.

Van der Eijk, Cees, and K. Niemoller. 1987. "Electoral Alignments in the Netherlands." *Electoral Studies* 6: 17–30.

Van Deth, Jan, and Peter A. Geurtx. 1989. "Value Orientation, Left-Right Placement, and Voting." *European Journal of Political Research* 17: 17–34.

Van Gennep, Arnold. 1908/1960. *The Rites of Passage*. Chicago: University of Chicago Press.

Van Kersbergen, Kees. 1999. "Contemporary Christian Democracy and the Demise of the Politics of Mediation." In Herbert Kitschelt et al., eds., *Continuity and Change in Contemporary Capitalism* (pp. 346–70). New York: Cambridge University Press.

Verba, Sidney, Kay Schlozman, and Henry Brady. 1995. *Voice and Equality: Civic Voluntarism in American Politics*. Cambridge, MA: Harvard University Press.

Veugelers, John W.P. 2000. "Right-Wing Extremism in Contemporary France: A 'Silent Revolution'?" *Sociological Quarterly* 41: 19–40.

Visser, Margaret. 1992. *Rituals of Dinner: The Origins, Evolution, Eccentricities, and Meaning of Table Manners*. New York: Penguin.

Visser, Max. 1993. "Group Identifications and Voting Behavior: The Dutch Case." *Politics and the Individual* 3: 57–73.

Voas, David, Daniel V. A. Olson, and Alasdair Crockett. 2002. "Religious Pluralism and Participation: Why Previous Research is Wrong." *American Sociological Review* 67: 212–30.

Voss, Kim. 1993. *The Making of American Exceptionalism: The Knights of Labor and Class Formation in the Nineteenth Century*. Ithaca, NY: Cornell University Press.

Voss, Kim, and R. Sherman. 2000. "Breaking the Iron Law of Oligarchy: Union Revitalization in the American Labor Movement." *American Journal of Sociology* 106: 303–49.

Voyé, Liliane, and Billiet, J., eds. 1999. *Sociology and Religions: An Ambiguous Relationship*. Leuven: Leuven University Press.

Voyé, Liliane, and Karel Dobbelaere. 1994. "Roman Catholicism: Universalism at Stake." In Roberto Cipriani, ed., *Religions Sans Frontières?* (pp. 83–113). Roma: Dipartimento per L'Informazione e Editoria.

Wagner-Pacifici, Robin. 2000. *Theorizing the Standoff*. Cambridge: Cambridge University Press.

Wald, Kenneth. 1987. *Religion and Politics in the United States*. New York: St. Martin's Press.

———. 1996. *Religion and Politics in the United States*. 3rd ed. Washington, DC: Congressional Quarterly Press.

Wald, Kenneth, Dennis Owen, and Samuel Hill. 1988. "Churches as Political Communities." *American Political Science Review* 82: 531–48.

Wall, Sally N., Irene Hanson Frieze, Anuska Ferligoj, and Eva Jarosova. 1999. "Gender Role and Religion as Predictors of Attitudes toward Abortion in Croatia, Slovenia, the Czech Republic, and the United States." *Journal of Cross-Cultural Psychology* 30: 443–65.

Wallace, Anthony F.C. 1966. *Religion: An Anthropological View*. New York: Random House.

Wallace, Ruth. 1975. "Bringing Women In: Marginality in the Churches." *Sociological Analysis* 36: 291–303.

———. 1992. *They Call Her Pastor*. Albany, NY: State University of New York Press.

———. 1997. "The Mosaic of Research on Religion: Where Are the Women?" *Journal for the Scientific Study of Religion* 36: 1–12.

———. 2000. "Women and Religion: The Transformation of Leadership Roles." *Journal for the Scientific Study of Religion* 39: 497–508.

Wallin, Nils L., Björn Merker, and Steven Brown, eds. 2000. *The Origins of Music*. Cambridge, MA: MIT Press.

Wallis, Roy, and Steve Bruce. 1992. "Secularization: The Orthodox Model." In Steve Bruce, ed., *Religion and Modernization* (pp. 8–30). New York: Oxford University Press.

Walter, T., and Davie, Grace. 1998. "The Religiosity of Women in the Modern West." *British Journal of Sociology* 49: 640–60.

Walzer, Michael. 1965. *The Revolution of the Saints: A Study in the Origins of Radical Politics*. Cambridge, MA: Harvard University Press.

Warner, R. Stephen. 1993. "Work in Progress Toward a New Paradigm for the Sociological Study of Religion in the United States." *American Journal of Sociology* 98: 1044–93.

———. 1994. "The Place of the Congregation in the American Religious Configuration." In James P. Wind and James W. Lewis, eds., *American Congregations*. Volume 2 (pp. 54–99). Chicago: University of Chicago Press.

———. 1995. "The Metropolitan Community Churches and the Gay Agenda: The Power of Pentecostalism and Essentialism." *Religion and the Social Order* 5: 81–108.

———. 1997. "Religion, Boundaries, and Borders." *Sociology of Religion* 58: 217–39.

———. 1998. "Introduction: Immigration and Religious Communities in the United States." In R. Stephen Warner and Judith G. Wittner, eds. *Gatherings in Diaspora: Religious Communities and the New Immigration* (pp. 3–36). Philadelphia: Temple University Press.

Warner, R. Stephen, and Judith G. Wittner, eds. 1998. *Gatherings in Diaspora: Religious Communities and the New Immigration*. Philadelphia: Temple University Press.

Warner, W. Lloyd. 1962a. *The Family of God*. New Haven, CT: Yale University Press.

———. 1962b. *American Life*. Chicago: University of Chicago Press.

Warren, Mark. 2000. "Can Religious Communities Revitalize the British Inner City?" Paper presented at the Association for the Sociology of Religion, Washington, DC.

Warren, Mark. 2001. *Dry Bones Rattling*. Princeton, NJ: Princeton University Press.

Warren, Mark, and Richard L. Wood. 2001. *Faith-Based Community Organizing: The State of the Field*. Jericho, NY: Interfaith Funders.

Waterbury, John. 1970. *The Commander of the Faithful*. New York: Columbia University Press.

Waters, Anita M. 1997. "Conspiracy Theories as Ethnosociologies: Explanation and Intention in African American Political Culture." *Journal of Black Studies* 28: 112–25.

Wattenberg, Martin P. 1998. *The Decline of American Political Parties, 1952–1996*. Cambridge, MA: Harvard University Press.

Waugh, Earle H. 1994. "Reducing the Distance: A Muslim Congregation in the Canadian North." In James P. Wind and James W. Lewis, eds. *American Congregations*. Volume 1. Chicago: University of Chicago Press.

Waxman, Chaim. 2001. *Jewish Baby Boomers*. Albany: State University of New York Press.

Weber, Max. 1904–05/1958 *The Protestant Ethic and the Spirit of Capitalism*. Translated by Talcott Parsons. New York: Scribner.

_____. 1919/1946. *From Max Weber: Essays in Sociology*. Edited by H. H. Gerth and C. Wright Mills. New York: Oxford University Press.

_____. 1922/1993. *The Sociology of Religion*. Boston: Beacon Press.

_____. 1925/1978. *Economy and Society: An Outline of Interpretive Sociology*. Edited and translated by Guenther Roth and Claus Wittich. Berkeley: University of California Press.

_____. 1927. *General Economic History*. New York: Free Press.

Wedam, Elfriede. 1997. "Splitting Interests or Common Causes: Styles of Moral Reasoning in Opposing Abortion." In Penny Edgell Becker and Nancy Eiesland, eds., *Contemporary American Religion: An Ethnographic Reader* (pp. 147–68). Newbury Park, CA: Alta Mira/Sage.

Weems, Benjamin B. 1964. *Reform, Rebellion, and the Heavenly Way*. Tucson: University of Arizona Press.

Wellmeier, Nancy J. 1998. "Santa Eulalia's People in Exile: Maya Religion, Culture and Identity in Los Angeles." In R. Stephen Warner and Judith G. Wittner, eds., *Gatherings in Diaspora: Religious Communities and the New Immigration* (pp. 97–122). Philadelphia: Temple University Press.

Wentz, Richard E. 1999. "The Hidden Discipline of Religious Studies." *Chronicle of Higher Education* 46 (October 1): A72.

Wertheimer, Jack, ed. 2000. *Jews in the Center: Conservative Synagogues and Their Members*. New Brunswick: Rutgers University Press.

Wessinger, Catherine. 1993. *Women's Leadership in Marginal Religions: Explorations Outside the Mainstream*. Urbana: University of Illinois Press.

_____. 1996. *Religious Institutions and Women's Leadership, New Roles Inside the Mainstream*. Columbia: University of South Carolina Press.

_____. 2000. *How the Millennium Comes Violently*. New York: Seven Bridges Press.

Westoff, Charles F., and Elise F. Jones. 1979. "The End of 'Catholic Fertility.'" *Demography* 16: 209–17.

Wilcox, Clyde. 1989. "The New Christian Right and the Mobilization of the Evangelicals." In Ted Jelen, ed., *Religion and Political Behavior in the United States* (pp. 139–56). New York: Praeger.

_____. 1992. *God's Warriors*. Baltimore, MD: Johns Hopkins University Press.

_____. 1996. *Onward Christian Soldiers? The Christian Right in American Politics*. Boulder, CO: Westview Press.

Wilcox, W. Bradford. 1998. "Conservative Protestant Childrearing: Authoritarian or Authoritative?" *American Sociological Review* 63: 796–809.

Will, Jeffry, and Rhys Williams. 1986. "Political Ideology and Political Action in the New Christian Right." *Sociological Analysis* 47: 160–8.

Willaime, J.-P. 1995. *Sociologie des Religions*. Paris: Presses Universitaires de France.

_____. 1999. "French Language Sociology of Religion in Europe Since the Second World War." *Swiss Journal of Sociology* 25: 343–71.

Williams, Melvin D. 1974. *Community in a Black Pentecostal Church*. Prospect Heights, IL: Waveland Press.

Williams, Raymond Brady. 1988. *Religions of Immigrants from India and Pakistan: New Threads in the American Tapestry*. New York: Cambridge University Press.

Williams, Rhys H. 1994. "Movement Dynamics and Social Change: Transforming Fundamentalist Ideology and Organization." In Martin Martin and R. Scott Appleby, eds., *Accounting for Fundamentalisms: The Dynamic Character of Movements* (pp. 785–833). Chicago: University of Chicago Press.

_____. 1995. "Constructing the Public Good: Social Movements and Cultural Resources." *Social Problems* 42: 124–44.

_____. 1996. "Religion as Political Resource: Culture or Ideology?" *Journal for the Scientific Study of Religion* 35: 368–78.

_____, ed. 1997a. *Cultural Wars in American Politics: Critical Reviews of a Popular Myth*. Hawthorne, NY: Aldine de Gruyter.

_____. 1997b."Afterword: Culture Wars, Social Movements and Institutional Politics." In Rhys H. Williams, ed., *Cultural Wars in American Politics* (pp. 283–95). Hawthorne, NY: Aldine de Gruyter.

_____. 1999."Public Religion and Hegemony: Contesting the Language of the Common Good." In William Swatos and James Wellman, eds., *The Power of Religious Publics: Staking Claims in American Society* (pp. 169–86). Westport, CT: Praeger.

_____. ed. 2001. *Promise Keepers and the New Masculinity: Private Lives and Public Morality.* Lanham, MD: Lexington Books.

_____. 2002. "From the 'Beloved Community to 'Family Values': Religious Language, Symbolic Repertoires, and Democratic Culture." In David Meyer, B. Robnett, and Nancy Whittier, eds., *Social Movements: Identity, Culture, and the State* (pp. 247–65). New York: Oxford University Press.

Williams, Rhys H., and Susan M. Alexander. 1994. "Religious Rhetoric in American Populism: Civil Religion as Movement Discourse." *Journal for the Scientific Study of Religion* 33: 1–15.

Williams, Rhys H., and Jeffery Neal Blackburn. 1996. "Many are Called but Few Obey: Ideological Commitment and Activism in Operation Rescue." In Christian Smith, ed., *Disruptive Religion: The Force of Faith in Social Movement Activism* (pp. 167–85). New York: Routledge.

Williams, Rhys H., and N.J. Demerath III. 1991. "Religion and Political Process in an American City." *American Sociological Review* 56: 417–31.

Williams, Rhys H., and Kathryn B. Ward. 2000. "Religion and the Civil Rights Movement: Constructing Priestly and Prophetic Mobilizing Ideologies." Paper presented at the annual meeting of the American Sociological Association, Washington, DC.

Williams, Sam K. 1975. *Jesus' Death as a Saving Event: The Background and Origin of a Concept.* Harvard Dissertations in Religion, Number 2. Cambridge, MA: Harvard Theological Review.

Willits, Fern K., and Donald M. Crider. 1989. "Church Attendance and Traditional Religious Beliefs in Adolescence and Young Adulthood: A Panel Study." *Review of Religious Research* 31: 68–81.

Wilson, Bryan. 1959. "An Analysis of Sect Development." *American Sociological Review* 24: 3–15.

_____. 1969. *Religion in Secular Society: A Sociological Comment.* Harmondsworth, UK: Penguin.

_____. 1973. *Magic and the Millennium: A Sociological Study of Religious Movements of Protest Among Tribal and Third-World Peoples.* New York: Harper & Row.

_____. 1982. *Religion in Sociological Perspective.* Oxford: Oxford University Press.

Wilson, John. 2001. "Dr. Putnam's Social Lubricant." *Contemporary Sociology* 30: 225–27.

Wilson, John, and Darren E. Sherkat. 1994. "Returning to the Fold." *Journal for the Scientific Study of Religion* 33: 148–61.

Wilson, John, and Marc Musick. 1997. "Who Cares? Toward an Integrated Theory of Volunteer Work." *American Sociological Review* 62: 694–713.

Winch, Robert F. 1962. *Identification and its Familial Determinants.* Indianapolis: Bobbs-Merrill.

Wind, James P., and James W. Lewis, eds. 1994. *American Congregations.* Volumes 1 and 2. Chicago: University of Chicago Press.

Wink, Paul, and Michele Dillon. 2001. "Religious Involvement and Health Outcomes in Late Adulthood." In Thomas Plante and Allen Sherman, eds., *Faith and Health* (pp. 75–106). New York: Guilford.

_____. 2002. "Spiritual Development Across the Adult Life Course." *Journal of Adult Development* 9: 79–94.

_____. In press. "Religiousness, Spirituality, and Psychosocial Functioning in Late Adulthood." *Psychology and Aging.*

Wink, Paul, and Harrison Gough. 1990. "New Narcissism Scales for the California Psychological Inventory and MMPI." *Journal of Personality Assessment* 54: 446–62.

Wink, Paul, and Ravenna Helson. 1997. "Practical and Transcendent Wisdom: Their Nature and Some Longitudinal Findings." *Journal of Adult Development* 4: 1–15.

Winter, G. 1967. *The Emergent American Society: Large Scale Organization.* New Haven, CT: Yale University Press.

Wirth, Louis. 1928. *The Ghetto.* Chicago: University of Illinois Press.

Wittag, Monique. 1981/1993."One is Not Born a Woman." In H. Abelove, M.A. Barale and D. Halperin, eds., *The Lesbian and Gay Studies Reader* (pp. 103–10). New York: Routledge.

Wittberg, Patricia. 1994. *The Rise and Fall of Catholic Religious Orders: A Social Movement Perspective.* Albany, NY: State University of New York Press.

Wolpe, David J. 1995. *Why Be Jewish?* New York: Henry Holt.

Wood, Richard L. 1999. "Religious Culture and Political Action." *Sociological Theory* 17: 307–32.

———. 2001. "Does Religion Matter? Projecting Democratic Power into the Public Arena," In Corwin Smidt, ed. *Religion and Social Capital*. Washington, DC: Georgetown University Press.

———. 2002. *Faith in Action: Religion, Race, and Democratic Organizing in America*. Chicago: University of Chicago Press.

Woodberry, Robert D. 1998. "When Surveys Lie and People Tell the Truth: How Surveys Oversample Church Attenders." *American Sociological Review* 63: 119–22.

Woodberry, Robert D., and Christian S. Smith. 1998. "Fundamentalism et al: Conservative Protestants in America. *Annual Review of Sociology* 24: 25–56.

Wright, Nathan. 2001. "Attendance Matters: Religion and Attitudes Towards Homosexuality." Unpublished paper, Department of Sociology, Northwestern University.

Wulff, David M. 1997. *Psychology of Religion: Classic and Contemporary*. New York: Wiley.

Wust, Andreas M. 1993. "Right-Wing Extremism in Germany." *Migration World Magazine* 21: 27–31.

Wuthnow, Robert. 1976. "Recent Patterns of Secularization: A Problem of Generations?" *American Sociological Review* 41: 850–67.

———. 1985. "Science and the Sacred." In Phillip E. Hammond, ed., *The Sacred in a Secular Age* (pp. 187–203). Berkeley: University of California Press.

———. 1987. *Meaning and Moral Order: Explorations in Cultural Analysis*. Berkeley: University of California Press.

———. 1988. *The Restructuring of American Religion: Society and Faith Since World War II*. Princeton, NJ: Princeton University Press.

———. 1989. *The Struggle for America's Soul: Evangelicals, Liberals, and Secularism*. Grand Rapids, MI: Eerdmans.

———. 1991. *Acts of Compassion: Caring for Others and Helping Ourselves*. Princeton, NJ: Princeton University Press.

———. 1993. *The Future of Christianity*. New York: Oxford University Press.

———. 1994. *Sharing the Journey*. New York: Free Press.

———. 1998. *After Heaven: Spirituality in America Since the 1950s*. Princeton, NJ: Princeton University Press.

———. 1999. *Growing Up Religious: Christians and Jews and Their Journeys of Faith*. Boston: Beacon Press.

Wuthnow, Robert, and John Evans, eds. 2001. *The Quiet Hand of God: The Public Role of Mainline Protestants*. Berkeley: University of California Press.

Wuthnow, Robert, and Glen Mellinger 1978. "The Religiosity of College Students: Stability and Change over Years at University." *Journal for the Scientific Study of Religion* 17:159–64.

Wyman, Mark. 1993. *Round-trip to America*. Ithaca, NY: Cornell University Press.

Yamane, David. 1997. "Secularization on Trial: In Defense of a Neo-Secularization Paradigm." *Journal for the Scientific Study of Religion* 36: 109–22.

Yang, Fenggang. 1999. *Chinese Christians in America: Conversion, Assimilation, and Adhesive Identities*. University Park: Penn State University Press.

———. 2000a. "Chinese Gospel Church: The Sinicization of Christianity." In Helen Rose Ebaugh and Janet S. Chafetz, eds., *Religion and the New Immigrants: Continuities and Adaptations in Immigrant Congregations* (pp. 89–107): Walnut Creek, CA: AltaMira Press.

———. 2000b. "The Hsi-Nan Chinese Buddhist Temple: Seeking to Americanize." In Helen Rose Ebaugh and Janet S. Chafetz, eds., *Religion and the New Immigrants: Continuities and Adaptations in Immigrant Congregations* (pp. 67–87): Walnut Creek, CA: AltaMira Press.

Yang, Fenggang, and Helen Rose Ebaugh. 2001. "Religion and Ethnicity: The Impact of Majority/Minority Status in the Home and Host Countries." *Journal for the Scientific Study of Religion* 40: 367–78.

Yeow, Choo Lak, J. C. England, et al. 1989. *Doing Theology with People's Symbols & Images*. Singapore: Atesea.

Yinger, J. Milton. 1970. *The Scientific Study of Religion*. New York: Macmillan.

———. 1946. *Religion in the Struggle for Power: A Study in the Sociology of Religion*. Durham, NC: Duke University Press.

Yishai, Yael. 1997. *Between the Flag and the Banner: Women in Israeli Politics*. Albany: State University of New York Press.

Young, Katharine. 1989. "Narrative Embodiments: Enclaves of the Self in the Realm of Medicine." In J. Shotter and Kenneth Gergen, eds., *Texts of Identity* (pp. 152–65). London: Sage.

Young, Lawrence, ed. 1997. *Rational Choice Theory and Religion : Summary and Assessment*. New York: Routledge.

Zablocki, Benjamin. 1980. *Alienation and Charisma: A Study of Contemporary American Communes*. New York: Free Press.

Zablocki, Benjamin, and Thomas Robbins, eds. 2001. *Misunderstanding Cults: Searching for Objectivity in a Controversial Field*. Toronto: University of Toronto Press.

Zak, I. 1973. "Dimensions of Jewish-American Identity." *Psychological Reports* 33: 891–900.

Zald, Mayer N. 2000. "Ideologically Structured Action: An Enlarged Agenda for Social Movement Research." *Mobilization* 5: 1–16.

Zald, Mayer N., and John D. McCarthy. 1987. *Social Movements in an Organizational Society: Collected Essays*. New Brunswick, NJ: Transaction.

Zaleski, P.A., and Charles Zech. 1995. "The Effect of Religious Market Competition on Church Giving." *Review of Social Economics* 53: 350–67.

Zavella, Patricia. 1987. *Women's Work and Chicano Families: Cannery Workers of the Santa Clara Valley*. Ithaca, NY: Cornell University Press.

Zhou, Min, and Carl L. Bankston III. 1998. *Growing Up American: How Vietnamese Children Adapt to Life in the United States*. New York: Russell Sage Foundation.

Zikmund, Barbara, Adair Lummis, and Patricia Chang. 1998. *Clergy Women: An Uphill Calling*. Louisville, KY: Westminster John Knox.

Zohar, Zvi, and Avi Sagi. 1994. *Conversion to Judaism and the Meaning of Jewish Identity*. Jerusalem: The Bialik Institute and the Shalom Hartman Institute.

Zuckerman, Phillip. 1997. "Gender Regulation as a Source of Religious Schism." *Sociology of Religion* 58: 353–74.

Index

Minow, Martha: and identity, 212
Mische, Ann: and agency, 212
Moaddel, Mansoor, 283
mobilization: as sensitizing concept, 22
modernization theory, 9, 18, 19, 71, 97; and individual moral authority, 334–5, 336, 343. *See also* secularization
moral order: religious groups analyzed in terms of, 336–41; and religious pluralism, 343–6; as multidimensional, 346–7
Moral Majority, 304
morality: and ideology, 13
Mormons. *See* Church of Jesus Christ of the Latter-Day Saints
movement: as sensitizing concept, 22; culture, 316, 317–18
Moynihan, Daniel P., 258
Mullins, Mark, 229
Murphy, P. E., 192
Myers, Scott: and parental influence on religious choices, 155

Nam, C. B.: and impact of religion on health, 195–6
Namier, Lewis, 373
narrative: in construction of identity, 213–15, 217–22
Nason-Clark, Nancy, 289–90
nationalism, 13; role of rhythmic ritual in, 42–3; religion as factor in, 48; and civil religion, 357
Native Americans: spirituality of differentiated from religion, 52
Neitz, Mary Jo, 12–13, 98, 285; on conversion and charismatic Catholics, 208–9, 221
neoinstitutional theory, 123; and study of congregations, 23; role of culture in, 129–30; weaknesses of application to religion, 130–3
neopagan cults: shock value of, 154. *See also* Wicca
Nettl, Bruno, 35
Neuhaus, Richard, 355
new paradigm. *See* rational choice theory
New Age: as religious movement, 57
Niebuhr, H. Richard: and church-sect typology, 125, 126
normative issues: in sociology of religion, 26–7
normativity, 26–7; compared with empirical questions, 7

Numrich, Paul, 227, 228; and American Buddhists, 345

Olson, Laura, 280
Operation Rescue, 318, 325
ordination: of women. *See* clergy: women as
Orsi, Robert, 144, 228, 261, 274
Orthodox Jews: impact of feminism on, 250–1. *See also* Jewish identity: denominations

Pacific Institute for Community Organization (PICO), 385–7, 391
Palmer, Susan, 282
Pardo, Mary, 402, 404, 406
Pareto, Vilfredo, 363
Park, Robert E., 258
parochial education, 161
Parsons, Talcott: contributions of to sociology of religion, 66
patriarchy: in evangelical ideology, 166–7, 169–71, 172; Latinas' subversion of, 309
Pattillo-McCoy, Mary: and social movements, 221
Pax Christi, 319
Paxton, Pamela, 351
Pentecostalism, 10, 14, 94, 340; as transnational phenomenon, 71, 72. *See also* fundamentalism
Pentecostals, Black: image of as otherworldly, 412; and activism, 414–22
Peña, Milagros, 13, 283, 291–2
Pettersson, Thorleif, 69
Philippines: faith-based social justice organizing in, 389
Phillips, Bruce A., 245
pluralism: in new paradigm, 98–9; in religious economy model, 100–1, 104–6, 113; in sociopolitical conflict model, 116–17; and legitimation of alternative family schema, 166; as result of schisms, 126; in moral order, 343–6; as challenge to civil religion, 355
polarization: as undermining democracy, 395
politics, 9, 14, 297–8, 313–14: boundary between religion and, 51; and politicized religion, 55–6, 59–60; religion and voting behavior, 298–301; U. S. religion and, 301–9; western European religion and, 309–13
Portes, Alejandro: on assimilation, 345
Portillo, Cesar, 386